KU-215-168

Using Microsoft® Office 2000

Ed Bott

QUE®

A Division of Macmillan Computer Publishing, USA
201 W. 103rd Street
Indianapolis, Indiana 46290

Contents at a Glance

Using Microsoft® Office 2000

Copyright© 1999 by Que Corporation

All rights reserved. No part of this book shall be reproduced, stored in a retrieval system, or transmitted by any means, electronic, mechanical, photocopying, recording, or otherwise, without written permission from the publisher. No patent liability is assumed with respect to the use of the information contained herein. Although every precaution has been taken in the preparation of this book, the publisher and author assume no responsibility for errors or omissions. Neither is any liability assumed for damages resulting from the use of the information contained herein.

International Standard Book Number: 0-7897-1843-X

Library of Congress Catalog Card Number: 98-86860

Printed in the United States of America

First Printing: May 1999

01 00 99 4 3 2 1

Trademarks

All terms mentioned in this book that are known to be trademarks or service marks have been appropriately capitalized. Que Corporation cannot attest to the accuracy of this information. Use of a term in this book should not be regarded as affecting the validity of any trademark or service mark.

Screen reproductions in this book were created using Collage Plus from Inner Media, Inc., Hollis, NH.

Executive Editor
Jim Minatel

Acquisitions Editor
Jill Byus

Senior Development Editor
Rick Kughen

Development Editor
Susan Hobbs

Managing Editor
Thomas F. Hayes

Project Editor
Lori A. Lyons

Copy Editor
Chuck Hutchinson

Technical Editors
Vince Averello
Mitch Milan
Verley & Nelson

Indexer
Angie Bess

Proofreader
Tricia Sterling

Layout Technicians
Darin Crone
Wil Cruz

Graphic Conversion
Benjamin Hart

Contents

About the Author

Ed Bott is a best-selling author and award-winning computer journalist with more than 12 years' experience in the personal computer industry. As senior contributing editor of *PC Computing* magazine, he is responsible for the magazine's extensive coverage of Windows 95/98, Windows NT, Windows 2000, and Microsoft Office. From 1991 until 1993, he was editor of *PC Computing*, and for three years before that he was managing editor of *PC World* magazine. Ed has written eight books for Que Publishing, including *Special Edition Using Windows 98*, and at least one book on every version of Microsoft Office.

Ed is a two-time winner of the Computer Press Award, most recently for *PC Computing*'s annual *Windows SuperGuide*, a collection of tips, tricks, and advice for users of Windows 95, Windows 98, and Windows NT. For their work on the sixth annual edition of the *Windows SuperGuide*, published in 1997, Ed and coauthor Woody Leonhard earned the prestigious Jesse H. Neal Award, sometimes referred to as "the Pulitzer Prize of the business press." Ed lives in Scottsdale, Arizona, with his wife, Judy, and two incredibly smart and affectionate cats, Katy and Bianca.

About the Contributor

Debbie Walkowski has worked in the computer industry since 1981, selling, teaching, designing, and writing. These days she specializes in writing computer trade books and providing writing services to corporations such as Microsoft Corporation, Digital Equipment Corporation, and AT&T Wireless Services. Debbie has a degree in scientific and technical communication and has authored and coauthored 14 books on popular computer software, including Microsoft Excel, Microsoft PowerPoint, Microsoft Office, Microsoft Works for DOS and Works for Windows, Microsoft Project, Visio, Quicken, WordPerfect, and Lotus 1-2-3.

Dedication

To Judy

Acknowledgments

This is a big book, about a big collection of software. So, it should come as no surprise that it took a big team of professionals to bring everything together. Dozens of people—editors, designers, proofreaders, technical reviewers, production specialists, and executives—had a hand in the making of this book. It's impossible to thank them all personally, but I would like to mention a few whose efforts were truly noteworthy.

Executive editor Jim Minatel was instrumental in helping build a solid framework for this book and to define what makes this series of books so special. Acquisitions editor Jill Byus made sure that all the pieces arrived in the right place, at the right time. Development editor Rick Kughen asked all the right questions to make sure every definition made sense and every set of instructions worked correctly. Thanks for working nights and weekends, Rick.

Thank you also to Susan Hobbs, development editor, and Vince Averello, technical editor. Lori Lyons, project editor, and Tricia Sterling, proofreading shepherd, were instrumental in helping to ensure that all pieces of this book fit together when we were ready to ship it to the printer.

I'd also like to thank Debbie Walkowski, who wrote the excellent section on Microsoft Publisher 2000.

I owe a heartfelt thanks to the people who've helped me learn about Word, Excel, PowerPoint, Outlook, and the rest of Office over the past decade, including the editors and readers of *PC Computing* magazine and many folks at Microsoft. Special thanks to Microsoft's Chris Peters, who first showed me Word for Windows and whose leadership made Office what it is today.

Tell Us What You Think!

As the reader of this book, *you* are our most important critic and commentator. We value your opinion and want to know what we're doing right, what we could do better, what areas you would like to see us publish in, and any other words of wisdom you're willing to pass our way.

As the Executive Editor for the General Desktop Applications team at Macmillan Computer Publishing, I welcome your comments. You can fax, email, or write me directly to let me know what you did or didn't like about this book—as well as what we can do to make our books stronger.

Please note that I cannot help you with technical problems related to the topic of this book, and that due to the high volume of mail I receive, I might not be able to reply to every message.

When you write, please be sure to include this book's title and author as well as your name and phone or fax number. I will carefully review your comments and share them with the author and editors who worked on the book.

Fax: 317-581-4666

Email: `office_que@mcp.com`

Mail: Executive Editor
General Desktop Applications
Macmillan Computer Publishing
201 West 103rd Street
Indianapolis, IN 46290 USA

INTRODUCTION

I'VE BEEN WORKING WITH THE INDIVIDUAL programs that make up Microsoft Office for more than a decade now. In a dark corner of a cluttered storage room, in a box labeled "Old Software," I still keep the floppy disks that contain the first versions of Microsoft Excel (vintage 1988) and Word for Windows (1989). Of course, the antique 286 and 386 PCs that ran that old software are long gone.

A few years ago, Microsoft decided to bundle up its most popular programs in a single package called Microsoft Office, and roughly every two years they deliver a new version. Word, Excel, and the other programs that make up the most recent edition, Office 2000, are light-years ahead of their humble ancestors. The Pentium-class computers they run on are hundreds of times more powerful, too, and they let you connect with the rest of the world via the World Wide Web—a technological marvel that didn't exist when this decade began.

The individual programs that make up Office today have changed dramatically throughout the past decade, but one thing has remained the same: Hardly a week goes by that I don't learn something new. In the course of writing this book, for example, I discovered several new Office features that I now use every day, as well as a few old but still useful capabilities, buried under layers of dialog boxes and barely mentioned in the official documentation and Help files.

Of course, struggling with a PC is probably not part of your job description. No one pays you to install software, or to learn how to use it, or to poke through dialog boxes and pull-down menus so that you can edit or print a document or worksheet that was due yesterday. So, what should you do with this huge, feature-packed, powerful, and occasionally intimidating collection of Windows programs called Microsoft Office 2000? Well, this book is a great place to start.

About This Book

As I wrote this book, I made a few assumptions about you, the reader. I'm guessing you're not afraid of computers; in fact, you probably use a PC at work every day and have another computer at home, for work and play. I know you're busy, so you want answers and no-nonsense explanations about how you can make this software do what it's supposed to do. I'm sure you don't want to read long-winded explanations of the inner workings of technology; instead, you want step-by-step instructions with as little jargon as possible.

And I'm absolutely certain you're no dummy.

With the help of some skilled editors and designers at Macmillan Computer Publishing, I've organized this book so that you can quickly find the answers you're looking for. Each section covers an essential Office topic, and every chapter stands on its own—if there's important information in another chapter, you'll find a cross-reference to that part of the book so that you can quickly jump there.

One of the most compelling reasons to use Office is the common interface that all Office programs share. When you learn how to perform a task in Word, for example, the same technique should work in Excel or PowerPoint. Part I, "Getting Started with Office 2000," introduces the Office interface, including menus, toolbars, keyboard shortcuts, common dialog boxes, and customization techniques. This section also details the many new ways that Office 2000 enables you to create and publish Web pages.

Without question, the two most popular Office applications are Word and Excel. Both are all-purpose software marvels that let you tackle any project involving words or numbers. Use Word to create a wide range of document types: simple letters and memos, résumés, complex reports, Web pages, even newsletters and other sophisticated desktop-publishing projects. If your working days revolve around numbers, you'll appreciate Excel's capability to perform sophisticated calculations—turning budgets, forecasts, and sales results into easy-to-follow tables and charts.

Part II, "Using Word 2000," covers basic and advanced Word tasks, including creating and formatting documents, mixing text and graphics, and printing. Skip straight to Chapter 15, "Letters, Labels, and Envelopes," for details on how to customize Word's built-in letter templates with your own personal information, and then merge a list of addresses with a form letter or a stack of envelopes. To turn any Word document into a Web page with a few clicks, look at the step-by-step instructions in Chapter 16, "Creating Web Pages with Word."

Part III, "Using Excel 2000," covers the full range of tasks for designing, formatting, and printing worksheets and workbooks. To quickly get up to speed on formulas and functions, turn to Chapter 18, "Building Smarter Worksheets with Formulas and Functions." After you master the basics, you can create more complex calculations using the techniques outlined in Chapter 23, "Analyzing Data and Sharing Workbooks." To turn any set of numbers into a compelling visual display, follow the instructions in Chapter 22, "Creating and Editing Charts."

Does your job description require that you deliver presentations to other people? If you ever have to sell anything—products, services, or ideas—you'll welcome PowerPoint's tools for creating dazzling electronic slide shows. Part IV, "Using PowerPoint 2000," offers everything you need to get started, including instructions on how to add graphics and multimedia, and how to convert your presentations into attention-getting Web pages.

And then there's Outlook, the all-in-one scheduler, contact manager, and email client that debuted with the initial release of Office 97. Unfortunately, the first version, Outlook 97, also included a broad assortment of bugs and an interface so cryptic that even Office experts had trouble with simple tasks.

In 1998, Microsoft completed a sweeping new version of Outlook that fixed many of the problems associated with that first release. The new version, Outlook 2000, builds on the improvements in Outlook 98, especially in its less complicated setup options. Turn to Part V, "Using Outlook 2000," for details on the Outlook interface, as well as step-by-step instructions for setting up email accounts, sending and receiving messages, and organizing personal information.

Finally, there's Publisher, the newest addition to the Office family. It's not as smoothly integrated as the rest of the programs that make up Office, but it's unmatched for sheer ease of use. Part VI, "Using Publisher 2000," describes how to use Publisher to quickly produce simple business and personal documents, from newsletters to holiday greeting cards.

If your copy of Office doesn't include some of the features you see on these pages, skip straight to Appendix A, "Adding, Removing, and Updating Office Components." Here you'll find details on how to add new features and keep your copy of Office completely up to date. And if you want to explore Visual Basic for Applications, the powerful programming language at the heart of all Office applications, check out Appendix B, "Using Macros to Automate Tasks."

Conventions Used in This Book

Commands, directions, and explanations in this book are presented in the clearest format possible. The following items are some of the features that will make this book easier for you to use:

- *Menu and dialog box commands and options.* You can easily find the onscreen menu and dialog box commands by looking for bold text like you see in this direction: Open the **File** menu and click **Save**.
- *Hotkeys for commands.* The underlined keys onscreen that activate commands and options are also underlined in the book as shown in the previous example.
- *Combination and shortcut keystrokes.* Text that directs you to hold down several keys simultaneously is connected with a plus sign (+), such as Ctrl+P.
- *Graphical icons with the commands they execute.* Look for icons like this in text and steps. These indicate buttons onscreen that you can click to accomplish the procedure.
- *Cross references.* If there's a related topic that is prerequisite to the section or steps you are reading, or a topic that builds further on what you are reading, you'll find the cross reference to it after the steps or at the end of the section like this:

SEE ALSO

➤ *To learn how to save an Office document as a Web page, see page 57*

- *Glossary terms.* For all the terms that appear in the glossary, you'll find the first appearance of that term in the text in *italic* along with its definition.
- *Sidenotes.* Information related to the task at hand, or "inside" information from the author, is offset in sidebars so as not to interfere with the task at hand and to make it easy to find this valuable information. Each sidebar has a short title to help you quickly identify the information you'll find there. You'll find the same kind of information in these that you might find in notes, tips, or warnings in other books, but here the titles should be more informative.

Your screen may look slightly different from some of the examples in this book. This is practically inevitable, and it simply reflects the result of various options you may have selected during installation; it also may reflect differences in hardware setup. Despite these cosmetic differences, all the features of Office should work as described.

PART I

Getting Started with Office 2000

CHAPTER

1

Introducing Microsoft Office 2000

Get a quick overview of what's new in Office 2000

Discover the differences between Office editions

Learn which Office programs are best for everyday tasks

Examine the smaller Office programs

Find fonts, templates, and other goodies on the Office CD-ROM

What's New in Office 2000?

Upgrading from Office 4 or 95?

If you skipped over Office 97 completely, you have a lot of catching up to do. The basic techniques you use to work with Word, Excel, and PowerPoint have changed dramatically since earlier versions of Office, and Outlook didn't exist in Office 4 or Office 95. To get a quick overview of all the things you can do with these Office 2000 programs, I recommend you skim through the table of contents first.

If you've just upgraded to Office 2000, you're probably wondering what's changed. At first glance, the differences aren't that obvious. If you open Word or Excel, for example, the toolbar buttons and menus look almost identical to their Office 97 equivalents. You'll have no problem opening documents, worksheets, and presentations you created using Office 97, either, because the Office 2000 file formats are identical to those in Office 97.

There are some noteworthy improvements in Office 2000. To see the most dramatic of these changes, click the **Open** button on the Standard toolbar in any Office program; you see the Open dialog box shown in Figure 1.1. This dialog box (like the nearly identical Save As dialog box that appears when you save a file) is different from anything you've seen in earlier versions of Office—or other Windows programs, for that matter.

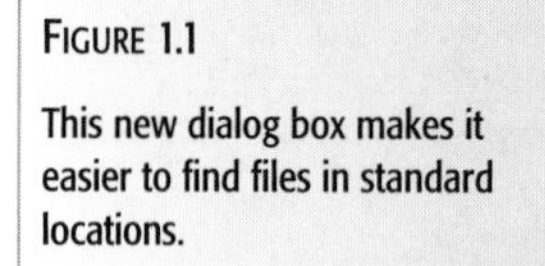

FIGURE 1.1

This new dialog box makes it easier to find files in standard locations.

These new dialog boxes include a *Places Bar* with five shortcuts to common locations where you're likely to store files. Instead of clicking through layers of folders to find files you've opened previously, the Places Bar puts you a click away from your most-used folders.

SEE ALSO

To learn how to use the new Open and Save As dialog boxes, see page 31

Other changes in Office 2000 are similarly designed to make programs more usable. When you open two or more data files at the same time, for example, each file gets its own button on the Windows taskbar; there's only one copy of Word or Excel open, but the individual buttons make it easier for you to quickly switch from one document or workbook to the other. Every Office program uses a new Clipboard toolbar that enables you to copy up to 12 items at a time and paste them all with one click.

Some of the changes in Office 2000 designed to make the programs more usable can actually make Office more confusing to work with. For example, when you first install Office 2000 many of the choices on each pull-down menu are hidden; as you work with each program, Office monitors the features you use and changes the lineup on each pull-down menu. If you like these shorter, less cluttered menus, you don't need to change a thing; if you want to see the long version of every menu, it's easy to disable this feature and restore the full menus and toolbars.

SEE ALSO

➤ *For instructions on how to make menus and toolbars work the way you want them to work, see page 92*

And then there's the Office Assistant, Microsoft's cheerful cartoon character that dispenses advice with an attitude (and sound effects). In Office 2000, there's a new lineup of Assistant characters, including Links the Cat, shown in Figure 1.2.

Use the My Documents folder

The standard location for Office files you create is a special folder called My Documents, which gets its own icon on the Places Bar. If you currently store your files in a different folder, you can customize Windows so that clicking the My Documents icon opens that folder instead. I explain exactly how to do that in Chapter 2, "How Office Works."

No short menus here

Throughout this book, when I show examples of menus, I generally show the long versions of the menus. If you use the shorter, personalized menus, your screen may look a little different, but the basic functioning of Office is exactly the same.

FIGURE 1.2

Links the Cat is one of several new Office Assistant characters.

SEE ALSO

➤ *To learn how to change the behavior of the Office Assistant (or disable it completely), see page 78*

Advice without the attitude

In Office 97, you had to use the Office Assistant to ask for help in plain English. In Office 2000, you can get help without talking to a cartoon character; just type your question in the Answer Wizard box in any standard Help window.

In Office 2000, the Windows Help system is completely new. With its browser-style Back and Forward buttons and a text-based Answer Wizard pane, the new Help interface makes it easier to find information, especially when you're not sure what you're looking for.

SEE ALSO

➤ *For instructions on how to use the new Office Help system, see page 71*

You don't need a Web site to use Web pages

Turning Office documents into Web pages is a great way to share files with other people via email, especially when they don't use Office. You can save Word documents, Excel charts and worksheets, and even PowerPoint presentations in HTML format, then send them as email attachments. All the recipient has to do is open the attached file in any up-to-date Web browser to see the file exactly as you created it.

Office 2000 also makes it easier to create Web pages. When you create or open a Word document, Excel workbook, or PowerPoint presentation and pull down the **File** menu, you see a new choice: **Save as Web Page**. Documents you save this way look almost exactly the same in your browser as they do in the program you used to create the page. Saving documents to a Web server is no longer a nightmare, either. One of the shortcut icons on the Places Bar in the Save As dialog box lets you create "Web folders," which are special shortcuts to Web servers on the Internet or on your company's *intranet*. Using Web folders literally makes posting a page to a Web server as easy as saving a file to your local hard disk.

SEE ALSO

➤ *For full details on how to turn Office 2000 documents into Web pages, see page 75*

Which Edition of Microsoft Office Are You Using?

Microsoft sells at least five separate collections of software under the Office 2000 name. Each version includes three common programs—Word, Excel, and Outlook—plus other software tailored to the needs of different types of users. You can find version information on the Office CD and on the packaging (box, manuals, and so forth): Look for a banner underneath the product logo.

Even if you don't have the CD at hand, you can still see which Office version is installed on a given PC. Open the **Start** menu, choose **Settings**, and click **Control Panel**. Open the **Add/Remove Programs** option and inspect the list of installed software, as in Figure 1.3. The entry for Microsoft Office includes its full name.

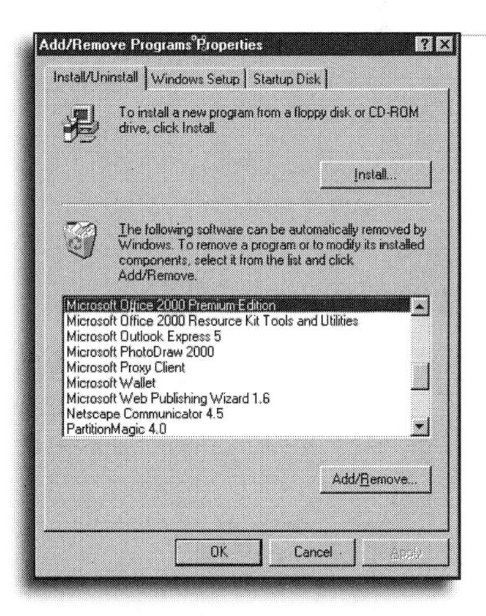

FIGURE 1.3
Use this dialog box to determine which edition of Office is installed on your computer.

The following sections outline the differences in each Office edition.

SEE ALSO

➤ *To set up Office 2000, see page 692*
➤ *To learn about installing patches and updates, see page 701*

Standard Edition

The Standard edition of Office includes Word, Excel, PowerPoint, and Outlook, plus Internet Explorer 5.0. The CD also includes a liberal assortment of utility software, additional *templates*, sound and graphics files, and clip art.

This book covers all Office editions

Although this book emphasizes the applications found in the Standard edition of Office 2000, you'll find it useful even if you've installed a different edition. The three programs that are included in every edition—Word, Excel, and Outlook—look and act exactly the same. You'll find no difference in the Office interface or in the techniques you use to work with files and folders.

Small Business Edition

The Small Business edition, intended primarily for owners and managers of small businesses, is different from the Standard edition in two important respects: Instead of PowerPoint, it includes Publisher 2000, which enables you to create postcards, brochures, and other business-oriented pieces. It also includes Microsoft Small Business Tools, a set of Excel add-ons that lets you exchange data with popular accounting software and generate financial reports. This version of Office is often bundled with new computers, and it's an excellent package even if you don't own a business.

Professional Edition

Most commonly found in corporate settings, the Professional edition includes all the programs in the Small Business edition, plus Access 2000, a database manager.

Premium Edition

This package includes all the programs in the Professional edition, plus two more applications that help you create and manage Web sites. FrontPage 2000 is the latest upgrade to an award-winning program that has been around for several years, although never as a part of Office. It enables you to build sophisticated Web pages that are far more complex than those you can create with Word; it also lets Web site managers maintain links between pages within a site. PhotoDraw 2000 is a brand-new program that enables you to create drawings and automatically resize and reformat scanned photos for use in Web pages. (It also includes a library of more than 20,000 images.)

Developer Edition

As the name implies, the Developer edition is for programmers who want to build custom programs based on Office applications. It includes all the software found in the Professional edition, plus an assortment of development tools, controls, and reference materials intended for use by corporate developers.

Upgrading and Installing Office

Office 2000 uses a brand-new setup program called the Microsoft Windows Installer. The new program handles most of the details of upgrading automatically, as soon as you insert the Office 2000 CD into your computer. If your system supports the Windows AutoPlay feature, the Windows Installer runs automatically when you insert the Office 2000 CD-ROM. If it doesn't start on its own, you can open an Explorer window and double-click the Setup icon to get started.

The new installer isn't just for Office

Although this new setup program comes with Office 2000, it's actually an upgrade to Windows. It will also be available in Windows 2000 and future upgrades to Windows 98; additional programs from Microsoft and other software developers will use this technology as well.

When you upgrade over an existing version of Office, the Installer program removes unnecessary files from the previous version while preserving any personal preferences and option settings. If you have the disk space and you need access to Office 95 or Office 97 for compatibility reasons, you can choose to install Office 2000 in its own folder and preserve the old version.

SEE ALSO

➤ *For more details on installing Office 2000 if you currently use Office 95 or 97, see page 696*

Using the Windows Installer lets Office 2000 keep track of files, Registry keys, and other resources for each component. This capability lets Office 2000 repair some kinds of problems automatically; if you accidentally delete a crucial file that you need to run Word, for example, the Installer will notice the change the next time you try to use Word and will ask you to insert the Office CD-ROM so that it can replace the file.

The new Installer includes one potentially confusing new feature. When you install Office 2000, some features (or even entire programs) will appear on menus, although they're not actually installed. The first time you try to use one of these "advertised" features, such as a file converter for an obscure format, the Installer asks you to insert the Office CD-ROM so that it can complete the installation. On corporate networks, an administrator can configure Office 2000 so that it installs from a shared folder on a server; in this type of environment, you'll see a brief dialog box when the Windows Installer adds new features, but you won't need access to a CD.

Notebook users, beware!

If you use Office 2000 on a notebook, make sure the features you need are available before you leave on a business trip. If your portable computer includes a CD-ROM, it's a good idea to carry the Office 2000 CD with you for at least the first few weeks after you install the program, to make sure you can add missing features when you need them.

When you run the Office Setup program again after initially installing Office, it launches in *maintenance mode*. At this point, you can choose one of three options:

- **Repair Office** restores your installation to its original state using the settings you specified during the original installation.
- **Add or Remove Features** displays the Update Features dialog box (Figure 1.4), which lets you change the selection of installed programs and features, including utility programs.
- Choose **Remove Office** to remove all traces of Office 2000 from the computer.

FIGURE 1.4

Use this dialog box to add or remove Office features and applications.

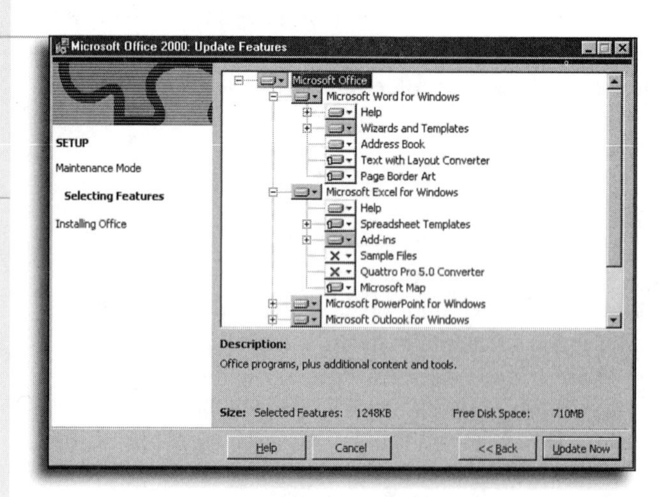

Your data files are safe

When you uninstall Office 2000 (or any of its components), the setup program does not remove data files you've created.

If an Office application stops working properly, click the **Help** menu and choose the **Detect & Repair** option. This feature launches the Installer program and automatically checks and repairs registry entries, replaces damaged system files, and rebuilds program shortcuts.

About the Office Applications

The Standard edition of Office 2000 includes the following four large applications:

- Word 2000 is a word processor that enables you to compose and edit letters, memos, reports, Web pages, and other documents. Its sophisticated formatting options enable you to work with long and complex projects. Use its advanced features to create tables, arrange text in newspaper-style columns, and merge addresses and other types of data into Word documents to create custom letters. To learn more about the features and capabilities of Word 2000, see Part II, "Using Word 2000."
- Excel 2000 enables you to organize words and numbers into rows and columns, and then use formulas to sort, manipulate, and analyze it all. Use colors, fonts, borders, and other formatting options to arrange the results into easy-to-understand reports. Excel's Chart Wizard turns any set of numbers into a visual display so that you can quickly visualize trends and relationships. For more information about the features and capabilities of Excel 2000, see Part III, "Using Excel 2000."
- PowerPoint 2000 enables you to create colorful slide shows to publish onscreen, on paper, or across the Internet. Create formal presentations, complete with sound, video, and other multimedia content, for delivery in front of large audiences, or use PowerPoint's outlining capabilities to quickly create meeting agendas and other tools for informal gatherings. For details on how you can use the features and capabilities of PowerPoint 2000, see Part IV, "Using PowerPoint 2000."
- Outlook 2000 is an all-purpose information manager that handles two primary functions. It enables you to send, receive, and organize email; it also includes folders that let you organize all sorts of personal information, including schedules, phone numbers, addresses, and to-do lists. The first version of this program, Outlook 97, was deservedly criticized as buggy and slow, and its setup dialog boxes even

baffled email experts. In early 1998, Microsoft released a major upgrade called Outlook 98, streamlining most dialog boxes and adding a completely new startup screen called Outlook Today. All those changes, and more, are in Outlook 2000. For detailed instructions on how to set up email accounts, manage your contacts and calendar, and coordinate meetings and tasks with coworkers, see Part V, "Using Outlook 2000."

In addition, every Office package, except the Standard Edition, includes Publisher 2000. This easy-to-use page layout package enables you to create newsletters, flyers, greeting cards, business cards, and other common publications for business and personal use. I explain how to get started with Publisher 2000 in Part VI.

All about version numbers

Every current Office program has a year tacked onto the end of its name: Word 2000, for example. Each program also includes a *version number*. You'll rarely see these numbers, but the details can be important when you exchange data files with other users, or if you need to poke around in the Windows Registry. All Office 2000 programs share a single version number, 9.0. All programs in Office 97 were designated as version 8.0, and the applications in Office for Windows 95 were designated as version 7.0. Before that, version numbers for Office applications were inconsistent; Word for Windows jumped from version 2 to version 6, for example, skipping over intervening numbers. Fortunately, all Office applications can detect files created in previous versions and convert them to newer formats automatically; you can also create files in Office 2000 and save them in formats compatible with previous Office versions.

Using the Office Applets

You'll use the major Office applications for most jobs, but Office includes some interesting and useful smaller programs as well.

Microsoft Graph, for example, enables you to enter a few numbers and quickly turn them into a chart. Equation Editor is a specialized tool that enables students and mathematicians to create simple or complex equations for use in technical documents.

Which charting program should you use?

Office 2000 includes a simple charting program in Microsoft Graph, but Excel offers many more options to help you display numbers in a visual format. Use Graph for basic charts in which you can quickly enter the numbers and you don't plan to reuse the results. Choose Excel if your data is already stored in a worksheet or if you want to create a richly formatted chart that you can easily edit and reuse later.

Office also includes a simple program called Organization Chart. Use it to create basic diagrams that show the reporting relationships in a department or company, or to show the connections between different divisions of a company. One of the basic PowerPoint slide designs includes a placeholder that inserts a blank organizational chart, as in Figure 1.5.

All three of the previously mentioned programs are designed to create editable *objects* in data files created by other Office applications. After installing any of these utilities, you can add a graph, an organizational chart, or an equation to a document or presentation by pulling down the **Insert** menu and choosing **Object**.

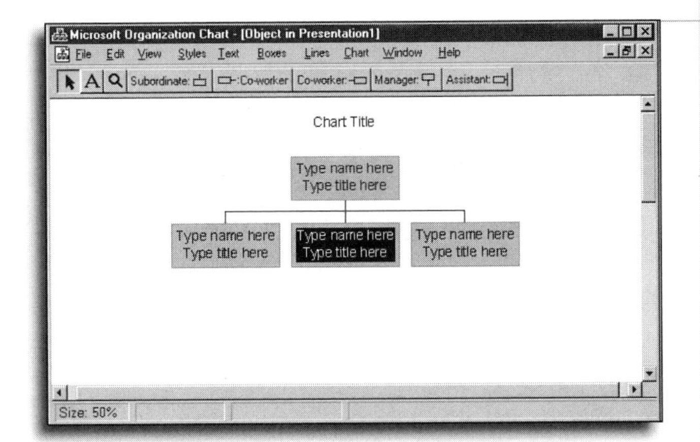

FIGURE 1.5
Use this tool to create simple organizational charts for use in presentations and documents.

SEE ALSO
➤ *To learn how to save different types of data in one file, see page 143*

Adding Images from the Clip Art Gallery

Simple graphics can effectively emphasize a point in a document or presentation. The Office 2000 CD-ROM includes an enormous selection of illustrations, sound clips, photographs, and videos you can use to spice up otherwise dull data. To keep it all organized, Office includes an accessory called the Clip Gallery, shown in Figure 1.6.

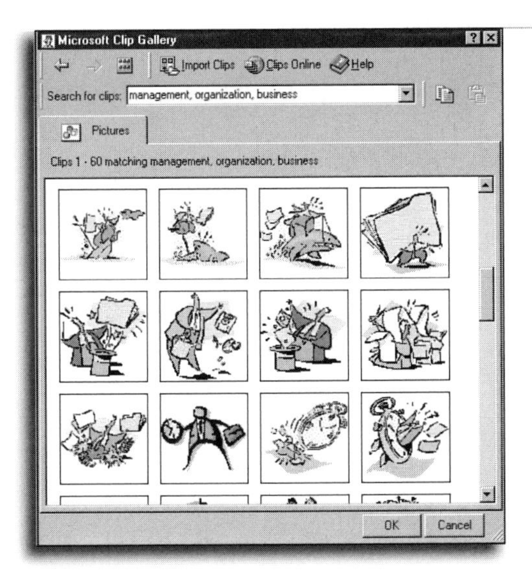

FIGURE 1.6
The Clip Gallery lets you search by keyword for just the right illustration or multimedia file.

SEE ALSO

➤ *For information on adding clip art to Office documents, including Web pages and presentations, see page 131*

Scanning and Editing Photographs

If you have a scanner connected to your computer, you can use it to insert photos directly into documents and presentations. Microsoft Photo Editor, an optional component in Office 2000, enables you to crop and resize images, adjust their color and brightness, or apply artistic effects to create interesting backgrounds. (If you use the Premium edition of Office 2000, you can choose a much more powerful graphics program called PhotoDraw 2000, which enables you to retouch and manipulate scanned images and graphics files using tools that are much more powerful than those in Photo Editor.)

SEE ALSO

➤ *For information on adding scanned images to Office files, see page 130*

Like the other accessories, Photo Editor allows you to create objects within documents. But unlike those other applets, it is a full-featured program that you can use on its own. You'll find a shortcut to Photo Editor in the Office Tools group on the **Programs** menu.

CHAPTER

2

How Office Works

- Use menus to accomplish common tasks
- Master 10 time-saving keyboard shortcuts
- Use the Standard and Formatting toolbars
- Learn the best place to store documents
- Open and save documents
- Find any Office file, anywhere
- Find out how to fix typos, on-the-fly, in any Office program

An Overview of the Office Interface

The three programs that form the core of Office 2000—Word, Excel, and PowerPoint—were once individual packages, with different menus, options, and toolbars. Over time, as Office has progressed through different versions, these separate programs have become more and more alike. In Office 2000, the three senior Office programs (and the newest additions, Outlook and Publisher) share not only a common look but also a great many common program files. The *toolbars* and menus in all Office programs, for example, are actually stored in the same program file: that means all the button icons and commands look exactly alike throughout Office.

If you dig deep enough into Office 2000, you'll find places where the programs are maddeningly dissimilar. But for the most part, the common Office interface is consistent enough to help you achieve an important goal: When you learn how one Office program works, you're well on your way to mastering all of them.

Figure 2.1 shows the common features you'll find in all Office programs.

Be sure you've closed Office before shutting down

Always close all Office programs and shut down Windows properly before you turn off your PC. If you simply shut off the power to your computer while you have data files open, you risk losing data. To shut down properly, click the **Start** button, choose **Shut Down**, select one of the options from the Shut Down Windows dialog box, and then click **OK**.

Starting Up and Shutting Down

Although the installation program for Office 2000 lets you install all programs at once, you'll typically work with programs one at a time. You can find *shortcuts* for each Office program on the Start menu. To start any Office program, open the **Start** menu, choose **Programs**, and click the program shortcut.

SEE ALSO

➤ *To learn how to work with the* Office Shortcut Bar, *see page 108*

Finally, you can create shortcuts that launch Office applications and place them on the *Quick Launch bar* or on the desktop. On most Windows systems, you'll also see the Quick Launch bar on the taskbar, just to the right of the Start button. If you look back at Figure 2.1, you'll see I've added shortcuts for all the Office programs to the Quick Launch bar.

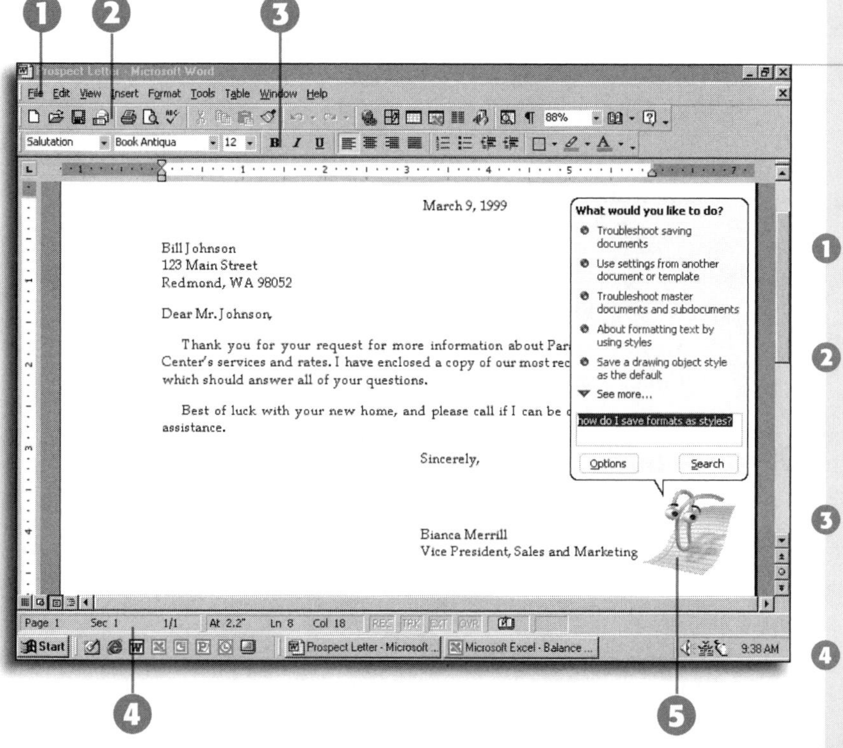

FIGURE 2.1

Office programs share a common interface, with nearly identical toolbars, menus, and other interface elements.

1. The main *menu bar* offers the same top-level choices for all Office applications.
2. Use the *Standard toolbar* to perform the most common Office functions, including opening and saving files, printing, and getting help.
3. The *Formatting toolbar* is visible by default in all applications: use it to change the appearance of the current document.
4. The *status bar* displays important information about the current document.
5. The *Office Assistant* is the main source of help information.

Creating Program Shortcuts for the Quick Launch Bar or Desktop

1. Right-click on any empty area of the desktop and choose **New** from the shortcut menu. Select the **Shortcut** option. The Create Shortcut Wizard appears.
2. Click the **Browse** button and open the Program Files folder, then the Microsoft Office folder, and finally the Office folder.
3. Select a program icon (such as Winword, Excel, Powerpnt, Outlook, or Mspub) from the list of available icons, and then click **Open**. (Note that the names here are the names of the program files themselves; because they all use eight characters or less, they don't necessarily match the program name you expect.)

Use this technique for any file

Although the examples I suggest here use the Office Standard Edition programs, you can create shortcuts to any program or even a data file. If you use Office Premium Edition, for example, add FrontPage to your Quick Launch bar.

Creating custom shortcuts

When you launch Word, Excel, or PowerPoint using a shortcut, several things happen by default: You start with a blank document, for example, and any macro named AutoExec runs automatically. You can control these default behaviors by using *startup switches* after the command line.Add `/m` after `Winword.exe`, for example, to open Word without running any startup macros. In Excel, use the `/r` switch followed by a filename to open the specified workbook in read-only mode. To see all startup options available for a particular program, click in the Office Assistant window and search using the phrase `startup switches`.

4. If you want to add a filename or any *startup switches* to the shortcut, click in the box labeled **Command line**, position the *insertion point* at the end of the line, and type the additional information.
5. Click **Next**. Edit the default name for the shortcut, if you want. If you've used switches to create a special-purpose shortcut, give it a descriptive name like `Word without macros`. Click **Finish**.
6. To copy the shortcut from the desktop to the Quick Launch bar, drag the icon onto any empty space in the Quick Launch bar, and release it.

Opening Documents Directly

When you open a folder window or browse files with the Windows Explorer, you see data files (such as Word documents, Excel workbooks, and so on) you've created using Office programs. When you open these data files, Windows automatically opens the associated program. If the program is already open, Windows switches to that window and opens the data file. To open multiple data files at one time, hold down the Ctrl key while you select individual files; then right-click and choose **Open** from the shortcut menu.

Caution: Don't open files from a floppy disk

Although you can open any Office data file from a floppy disk, I strongly recommend that you avoid this practice. Not only are floppy disk drives painfully slow, but the disks themselves are typically limited in capacity to 1.44MB. You can easily run out of room on a floppy disk, at which point you'll have to deal with annoying error messages and possible data loss. To edit a data file stored on a floppy disk, first copy the data file to a folder on a local hard drive and open that copy. After you've finished working with the file, copy it back to the floppy disk.

SEE ALSO

➤ *For information on opening and saving files, see pages 103 and 105*

Using Shortcuts to Open or Create Documents

The Setup program for Office 2000 automatically adds two icons to the top of the Start menu. Click the **New Office Document** icon to create a new file based on a template. When you select an option from the New Office Document dialog box, the associated Office program opens automatically. Use the **Open Office Document** icon, also found at the top of the **Start** menu, to select data files created by any Office application.

Using Office Menus

Every feature and function in every Office application is available through one or more menus. Use the comprehensive main menu or right-click for context-sensitive shortcut menus.

How Toolbars and Menus Work

When you first install Office 2000 and begin using the pull-down menus, be prepared for a period of adjustment. In previous versions of Office—and, in fact, in virtually every Windows program—the contents of these menus are fixed. When you click any item on the menu bar in an Office 2000 program, however, you'll see only some of the choices normally available on that menu. In theory, these *personalized menus* are supposed to make you more productive by showing you only the menu choices you use regularly. If you're experienced with Office menus, however, you might find the new menu system more confusing because choices disappear and reappear, seemingly at random.

What does this mean for you? If you've just started Excel 2000 for the first time, you might want to install the AutoSave add-in, which automatically saves your worksheets at regular intervals while you work. When you click the **Tools** menu, however, you see the short version shown on the left in Figure 2.2, and the **Add-Ins** menu is nowhere to be found. If you wait a few seconds, the full menu appears, as shown at the right of the figure.

Your menus will vary

Throughout this book, I've shown menus and toolbars in their long version, with the Standard and Formatting toolbars one over the other instead of side by side. If you've left the personalized menus option enabled, your default menus will look slightly different from the ones in this book; in fact, they'll look slightly different from the menus you used yesterday! But all the features are still there.

Other menus are shorter, too

With personalized menus turned on, the cascading menus that appear to the right of some menu choices are shorter also. Use the same techniques described here to switch from short menus to long ones.

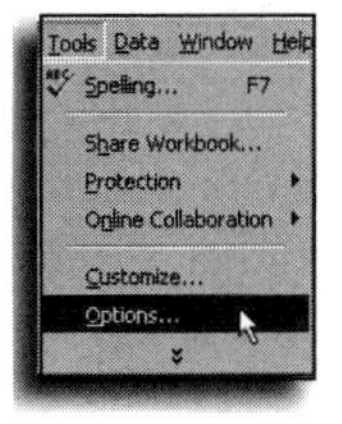

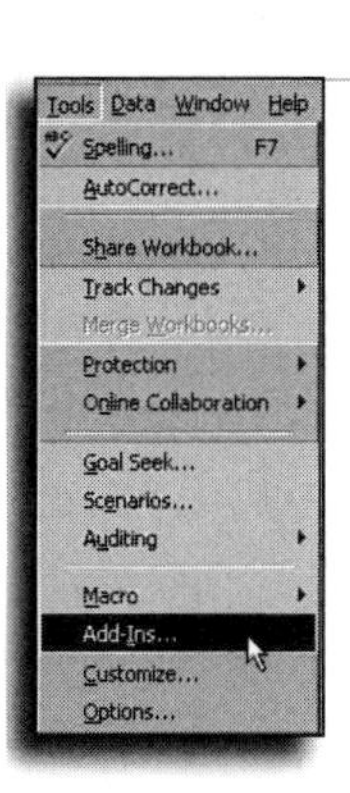

FIGURE 2.2

The default short version of this Excel menu (left) includes only 7 choices, compared to 15 in the long version (right).

Some menu choices are gray for a reason

Don't confuse the grayed-out choices on a menu with those that are hidden. As in all Windows programs, a grayed-out menu choice means that option is currently not available; for example, the Paste menu is grayed out when there's nothing on the Clipboard. Office programs use 3D effects to display the difference between visible and hidden menu choices.

Don't even try to figure out the rules

Office uses incredibly complex algorithms to determine how menu choices move on and off the short menus. In general, though, the more you use a menu item, the longer it stays around. If you work on a complex PowerPoint presentation for several weeks, for example, and you regularly use the **Action Buttons** choice on the **Slide Show** menu, that option will remain visible for much longer than if you simply clicked it one day as an experiment.

There are short versions of toolbars, as well. If you leave Office at its default settings, for example, the Standard and Formatting toolbars appear side by side on the same row, and only some of the buttons are visible. (I'll show you how to change these settings shortly.) Click the double-headed arrow (sometimes called a "chevron") at the far right of each toolbar to drop down a list of the missing buttons.

When you first install Office 2000, every program uses the default short menus. As you work with each program, Office monitors which menu choices and toolbar buttons you use, personalizing the short list to show you those you've used most recently. When you click the **Add-Ins** option on Excel's **Tools** menu, for example, Excel assumes you might want to use it again, and the next time you choose the **Tools** menu it will include that option.

Each time you use a hidden menu item or toolbar button, it moves up to the list of visible entries. In the case of toolbars, Office may have to hide a button that's currently visible to make room for the button you just used. Office never changes the order of items on toolbars and menus (although you can customize the menus yourself to do so); when an Office program promotes a menu choice or makes a toolbar button visible, it appears in the exact same position as when you display full menus.

If the menu option you want isn't on the short menu, you can force the full menus to appear by using any of the following three techniques:

- Click the double-arrow character at the bottom of the short menu.
- Leave the short menu open for more than three seconds without making a selection.
- Double-click a specific menu item; the first click displays the short menu, and the second expands it to the full menu.

SEE ALSO

I explain how you can turn off personalized menus and change toolbar settings on page 92

Pull-Down Menus

Word, Excel, PowerPoint, and Publisher include nearly identical arrangements of 9 *pull-down menus* (10, in Publisher) that you can use to accomplish nearly any task. Each menu on the *menu bar* is identified by a single word, and they are all arranged in a neat row, just below the title bar. Eight of the top-level menu choices are identical in each program. (Because Outlook organizes data rather than letting you create and edit files, its menus are completely different.)

Because each program handles a different kind of data, the exact contents of each menu vary from program to program, but you can expect to find similar entries under each. When you want to save your work, for example, you always use the **File** menu. And each program has one unique top-level menu choice that's reserved for it alone. (Publisher has two additional top-level menus.) Some (but not all) menu choices include images that match the toolbar button available for that command.

The main menu bar is completely customizable—you can remove or rearrange any menu and add new commands or top-level choices to the menu bar. You can add, remove, or reorder choices under each menu as well.

SEE ALSO

➤ *To learn more about customizing toolbars and menus, see page 92*

Table 2.1 offers a brief summary of the common options available under each menu choice.

Use the Shift key with menus

Here's a trick even some Office experts don't know. When you hold down the Shift key and click a pull-down menu, the choices change in subtle ways. In Word, for example, Shift+clicking the **File** menu changes the **Close** and **Save** options to **Close All** and **Save All**, respectively. This little trick comes in handy if you're working with a large number of Word files and you want to save them all without switching to each one in turn.

TABLE 2.1 **Top-Level Menu Choices**

Menu Name	Typical Options Available
File	Save your work; find files you've saved previously; send work to the printer.
Edit	Move, copy, and delete text or objects; search for words and phrases.
View	Look at the current document in a different way—zoom in for a close-up, for example, or organize as an outline. Also lets you show or hide toolbars, rulers, headers, footers, and so on.

continues...

Publisher's a little different...

Because Publisher allows you to work with only one publication at a time, you won't find a **Window** choice on its main menu bar. The first six menu choices are the same as in other Office programs, as is the **Help** menu at the far right. Despite the name, Publisher's **Table** menu is unlike Word's, and its **Arrange** and **Mail Merge** menus are unique as well.

TABLE 2.1 Continued

Menu Name	Typical Options Available
Insert	Add special information (like today's date or page number) to the current document; or add objects, such as a picture, a graph, or a hyperlink to a Web page.
Format	Change the typeface, text alignment, colors and shading, and more, for selected text, numbers, and parts of the current document.
Tools	Perform specialized tasks like spell-checking; change program options, such as the place where your data files are automatically stored.
Table/Data/Slide Show	The only "uncommon" menu choices; lets you insert and edit Word tables, Excel lists, and PowerPoint slides, respectively.
Window	Switch from one open document window to another, or rearrange open document windows.
Help	Access the Office Assistant, browse installed help files, or jump to Microsoft's Web site to find answers to technical questions.

Swapping right and left mouse buttons

When I refer to the right mouse button, I'm referring to the *secondary mouse button*–the one that *isn't* the main button. You'll find the same assumption in online help and other Microsoft documentation. If you're left-handed, you may prefer to configure the mouse so that the right button is your primary one, in which case you'll have to swap the directions mentally when reading this book. To switch mouse buttons, open the **Mouse** option in Control Panel. The exact steps to change this option vary depending on your operating system and mouse driver; on a system running Windows 98 with an IntelliMouse, for example, you click the **Basics** tab and select options from the **Button Selection** group.

Shortcut Menus

Throughout Office (and, in fact, throughout Windows), selecting or pointing to an object and clicking the right mouse button usually pops up a *context-sensitive* shortcut menu. Unlike pull-down menus, which include the full range of program features, these menus include only choices that are appropriate for the object to which you are pointing. Figure 2.3, for example, shows typical shortcut menus from Word and Excel.

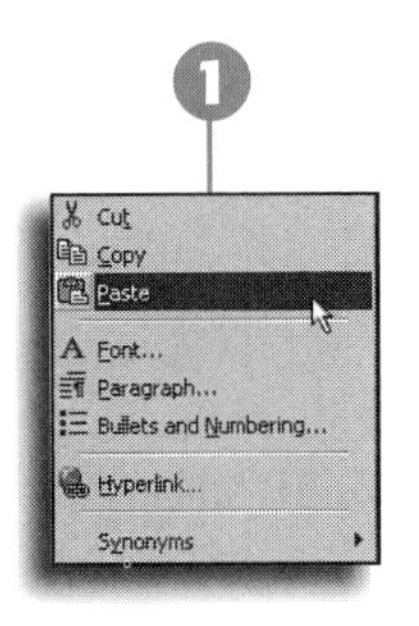

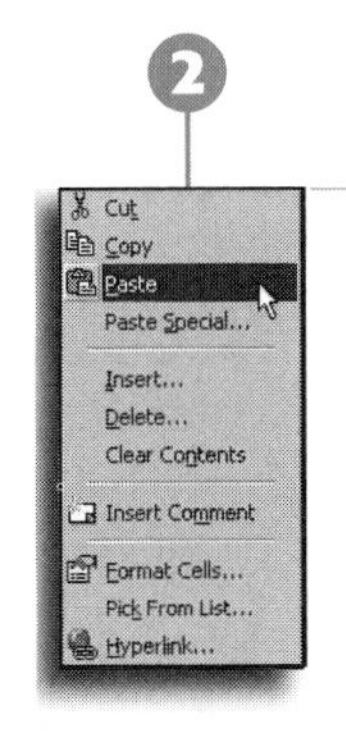

FIGURE 2.3

Click the right mouse button to pop up a context-sensitive shortcut menu. The exact choices available depend on the object under the mouse pointer.

1. Typical Word shortcut menu
2. Typical Excel shortcut menu

Bypassing Menus Using Keyboard Shortcuts

Using pull-down menus can sometimes get in the way of productivity. When you're working on a lengthy file, for example, saving your work regularly is smart; by doing so, you minimize the risk of data loss from a power failure or system crash. To use the pull-down menus, you have to take your hand off the keyboard, grab the mouse, pull down the **File** menu, click **Save**, and then resume typing. A faster approach is to press Ctrl+S, which accomplishes the same task in one motion.

Each Office program contains literally hundreds of *keyboard shortcuts*. No one expects you to memorize them all, but you can increase your productivity by learning the keyboard shortcuts for the tasks you perform most often.

Here are some essential facts about keyboard shortcuts:

- Using a shortcut key combination has the exact same effect as choosing the menu option with which it's associated.
- Many pull-down menus list available keyboard shortcuts; look on the **Edit** menu to see examples.
- Word is the only Office application that enables you to customize keyboard shortcuts easily.
- To see a comprehensive list of keyboard shortcuts for any Office program, use the Office Assistant to search for the Keyboard Shortcuts help topic.

Want to learn more shortcuts?

If you want to see keyboard shortcuts for a particular Office program, turn on the option that displays these shortcuts in ScreenTips. Pull down the **Tools** menu, select **Customize**, click the **Options** tab, and check the box labeled **Show shortcut keys in ScreenTips**. The shortcuts will now appear when you hover your mouse over toolbar buttons.

Outlook doesn't follow the standards

Office applications are remarkably consistent in their use of keyboard shortcuts, with one notable exception: Outlook 2000 is the black sheep, with many, many non-standard keyboard shortcuts guaranteed to drive you crazy. Throughout every other Office application, for example, you use Ctrl+F to display the Find and Replace dialog box; in Outlook, however, that key combination forwards an item via email. To find text in the open Outlook item, you press F4 instead, which works as the Repeat key everywhere else in Office.

F4: The amazing Repeat key

This one is my absolute favorite keyboard shortcut, but even some Office experts don't know about it. Use the F4 key when you want to do the same thing repeatedly, without having to return to menus. For example, if you're inserting several rows at different spots in an Excel worksheet, click in the first location, pull down the **Insert** menu, and choose **Rows**. Then click in the next location, press F4, and do the same with each additional location. The Repeat key works when applying styles, formatting text, and countless other actions.

SEE ALSO

➤ *To learn more about customizing keyboard shortcuts, see page 99*

The 10 shortcuts listed in Table 2.2 are worth knowing because they handle common tasks identically in all the Office applications—and, in most cases, throughout Windows. Several of these shortcuts are easy to remember because the commands (**Save**, **New**, **Bold**) start with the same letter as the shortcut keys (Ctrl+S, Ctrl+N, Ctrl+B).

TABLE 2.2 Top Ten Keyboard Shortcuts

Press This Key Combination	To Perform This Action
Alt+F4 or Ctrl+F4	Close a program window or close a document window, respectively
Ctrl+C/Ctrl+X/Ctrl+V	Copy/cut/paste the selected text or object
Ctrl+Z/Ctrl+Y	Undo/redo the most recent action
Ctrl+B	Make the selected text or object bold
Ctrl+I	Make the selected text or object italic
Ctrl+S	Save the current document
Ctrl+N	Start a new document/worksheet/presentation using default formats
F4	Repeat the previous action
Ctrl+F	Find some text in the current document
Ctrl+A	Select all of the current document/worksheet/presentation

Working with Office Toolbars

Office *toolbars* give you one-button access to commonly used features. The Office programs share more than a dozen built-in toolbars, two of which are visible by default under the menu bar. No matter which program you're working with, these toolbars look and work exactly the same. You can change the ready-made toolbars to suit your style or create new ones personalized for the way you work.

In previous versions of Office, toolbars contained only buttons. In Office 2000, they can include icon-style buttons, text buttons, drop-down lists, and menus, in any combination. To display pop-up help, let the mouse pointer hover over any button for a second or two until a *ScreenTip* appears. The ScreenTip gives you a short description of the function performed by the button.

SEE ALSO

➤ *To learn how to customize your toolbar buttons, see page 92*

Toolbars, AKA Command Bars

If you want to find information about toolbars in the Office Help files, here's a secret: Look for references to *Command Bars*, the official (but rarely used) name for this feature.

Using the Standard Toolbar

The *Standard toolbar* includes single-click shortcuts for the most common Office tasks. The collection of buttons on this toolbar is not identical for each Office program. Some buttons, like those that open and save files, are universal, but the Standard toolbar also includes buttons that perform application-specific tasks. For example, Word has an Insert Table option, Excel includes an AutoSum button, and PowerPoint offers a New Slide button.

Table 2.3 lists the common buttons included on the Standard toolbar for Word, Excel, and PowerPoint.

Instant email

The Mail Recipient button can be a real time-saver when you're working with Word and you want to quickly compose an email message. Clicking this button leaves the current document in place, adding a new toolbar that includes the Address and Subject bars and a Send button. The effect is the same as if you had opened a New Message form in Outlook. When you click this button in Excel or PowerPoint, Office gives you the choice of using the current worksheet or slide as the body of the message or sending the entire file as an attachment.

TABLE 2.3 The Standard Toolbar

Button	Button Name	What It Does
	New	Creates a new file
	Open	Opens or finds a saved file
	Save	Saves the current file
	Mail Recipient	Converts the current file to an email message
	Print	Sends the current document to the printer
	Spelling	Checks the current document for spelling errors; in Word, checks grammar as well
	Cut	Removes the current selection and places it on the Clipboard

continues...

TABLE 2.3 Continued

Button	Button Name	What It Does
	Copy	Copies the current selection to the Clipboard
	Paste	Inserts the Clipboard's contents at the current insertion point, replacing any selected text or objects
	Format Painter	Copies formatting from the selected text or object to the text or object you click
	Undo	Reverses last command or deletes last text entry
	Redo	Reverses the action of the last Undo command
	Insert Hyperlink	Inserts or edits a hyperlink to another file, a named location in the current document, or a Web page
	Help	Shows or hides the Office Assistant, or opens Windows Help

Move the toolbar

When you first install Office 2000, the Standard and Formatting toolbars are on the same row, and some buttons are hidden. The first thing I do after installing Office 2000 on a new computer is to put these two toolbars back where they belong, one over the other. Pull down the **Tools** menu, choose **Customize**, click the **Options** tab, and clear the box labeled **Standard and Formatting toolbars share one row**.

Using the Formatting Toolbar

The second common toolbar appears directly alongside or below the Standard toolbar in all three of the principal Office programs. Besides the Font and Font Size controls (both of which are drop-down lists), you will find only a handful of common buttons on the *Formatting toolbar*, as Table 2.4 shows. Most of the additional buttons handle attributes that are unique to each program's default data type: number formatting options for Excel, for example, style lists for Word, and animation effects for PowerPoint.

TABLE 2.4 **The Formatting Toolbar**

Button	Button Name	What It Does
B	Bold	Adds or removes bold formatting from selected text or numbers
I	Italic	Adds or removes italic formatting from selected text or numbers
U	Underline	Adds or removes underlining from selected text or numbers
	Align Left	Aligns selection to left, with ragged right edge
	Center	Centers selection
	Align Right	Aligns selection to right, with ragged left edge

Customize those toolbars!

You can add all sorts of extra buttons to the Formatting toolbar–custom underlines, strikethrough characters, and shortcuts to grow or shrink the size of text. Flip ahead to Chapter 6 "Customizing Office," for step-by-step instructions.

Hiding, Displaying, and Repositioning Other Toolbars

Each Office program lets you access an assortment of other toolbars, most of them designed for specialized jobs such as drawing, charting, editing pictures, or reviewing changes made by coworkers. When you first start Office, all but the Standard and Formatting toolbars are hidden.

Some toolbars appear automatically. Word's Outlining toolbar, for example, appears whenever you switch into Outline view (at which point you can choose to hide it). You can also choose a position for each toolbar: Some toolbars work best when they float over the program window, whereas others dock to an edge of the window. Figure 2.4 shows an assortment of docked and floating toolbars.

Show only the needed toolbars

In theory, you can display every one of the additional toolbars simultaneously, but each new toolbar uses up precious space that you need to see the current document, worksheet, or presentation. Instead, showing additional toolbars only when you need them is best.

- Right-click on any visible toolbar or the main menu bar to display the list of available toolbars.
- To show or hide a toolbar, click its name in the list. A check mark to the left of the toolbar means it is currently visible.
- To "dock" a toolbar in a new position, point to the *menu handle* (the double vertical lines at the left edge of the toolbar) and drag the toolbar to the top, bottom, or either side of the program window, where it will snap into place.

- To let a toolbar float, grab the menu handle and drag it into the program window.
- To move a floating toolbar, grab its title bar. To close a floating toolbar, click the **Close** button at the right edge of its title bar.

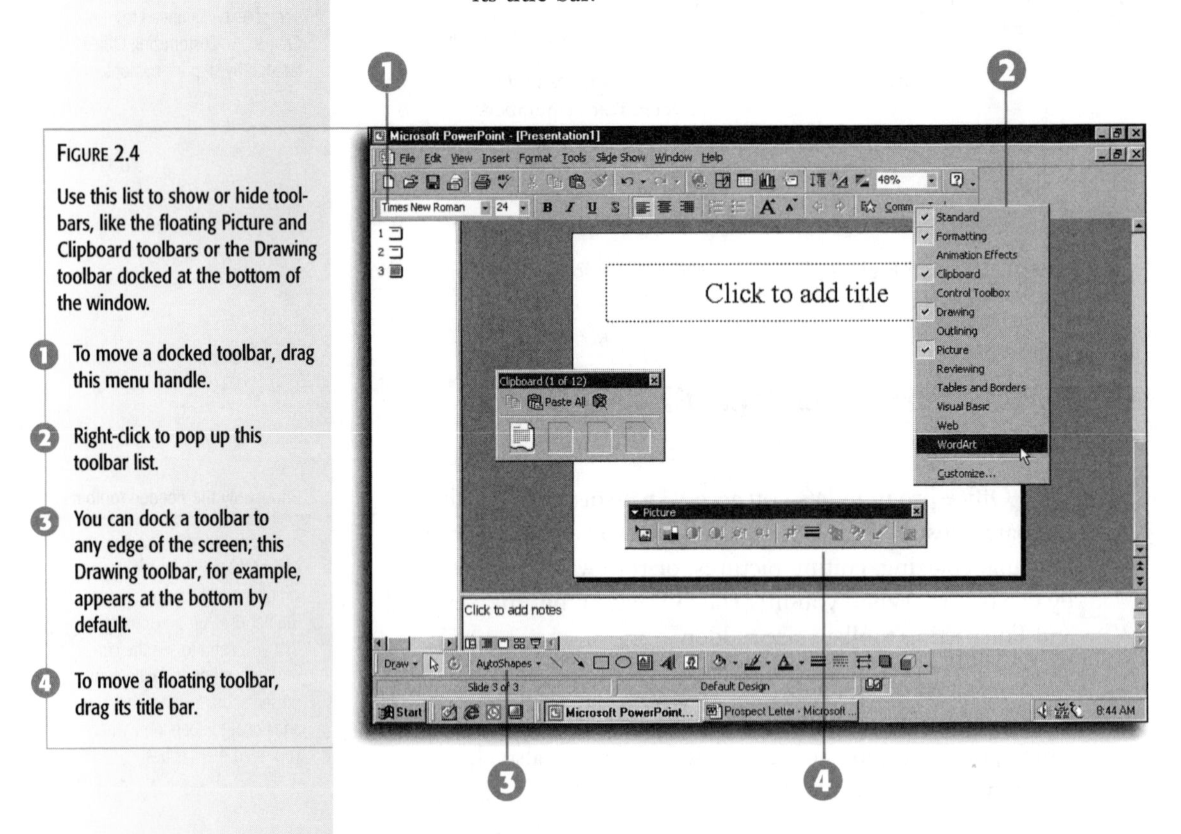

FIGURE 2.4

Use this list to show or hide toolbars, like the floating Picture and Clipboard toolbars or the Drawing toolbar docked at the bottom of the window.

1. To move a docked toolbar, drag this menu handle.
2. Right-click to pop up this toolbar list.
3. You can dock a toolbar to any edge of the screen; this Drawing toolbar, for example, appears at the bottom by default.
4. To move a floating toolbar, drag its title bar.

Organizing Your Documents

Office 2000 expects that you'll store almost all your working files in one place: the My Documents folder. Instead of scattering files across your hard disk and on far-flung network servers, use this default location for all your personal data files; in theory, at least, having one standard location makes it easier for you to find files later, when you need them.

Using the My Documents folder is a good idea. You'll be much more productive if you keep your files in a single, well-organized place. If you would rather store each program's files in a separate location, it's relatively easy to configure your system that way.

SEE ALSO

For instructions on how to specify a default data folder for each Office program, see page 105

By default, every Office program displays the contents of the My Documents folder whenever you open or save a file. It's easy to return to that location, or to find other files you've worked with recently, thanks to the common Open and Save As dialog boxes that are brand-new in Office 2000. Unlike previous versions of Office, which required you to navigate through hierarchies of folders to find a folder, these new dialog boxes include five icons along the left side that let you quickly open the folders where you're most likely to store files you work with daily.

One of the most noticeable changes in Office 2000 is in these common dialog boxes. When you pull down the **File** menu and choose **Open**, you see the dialog box shown in Figure 2.5. (The Save As dialog box is nearly identical.) The column of five icons at the left, called the *Places Bar*, can help you keep files flawlessly organized.

- Click the **History** icon to open the Recent folder, which contains shortcuts to the 20 files and folders you've worked with most recently in each program.
- Click the **My Documents** icon to open your personal data folder for the user currently logged on. As I'll explain shortly, the exact location of this folder depends on your Windows version and how you've configured your system.
- Click the **Desktop** icon to open or save files on the Windows desktop.
- Click the **Favorites** icon to display the contents of Internet Explorer's Favorites menu.
- Click the **Web Folders** icon to save or open files on a Web server.

Toolbar buttons disappear unexpectedly

As you resize a program window that contains toolbars, Office selectively hides buttons to avoid having the right side of the toolbar scroll out the right side of the window. The Office Assistant button is always visible, but other buttons begin disappearing from right to left as the window becomes narrower. Look for faint >> characters (sometimes called *chevrons*) at the right side of the toolbar to indicate that some buttons are hidden. You need to enlarge the window to see the hidden toolbar buttons. To restore the full display of buttons, resize the window.

Windows and the My Documents folder

If you're using Office 2000 with Windows 98, the My Documents folder is an integral part of Windows. It has its own icon on the Windows desktop, and you can right-click to change the folder that opens when you double-click this icon.

Organize the My Documents folder

You can add as many subfolders as you like within the My Documents folder; even if you use many subfolders to organize work–by date or by project, for example–using the My Documents folder as your home folder ensures that you'll always start in the right place.

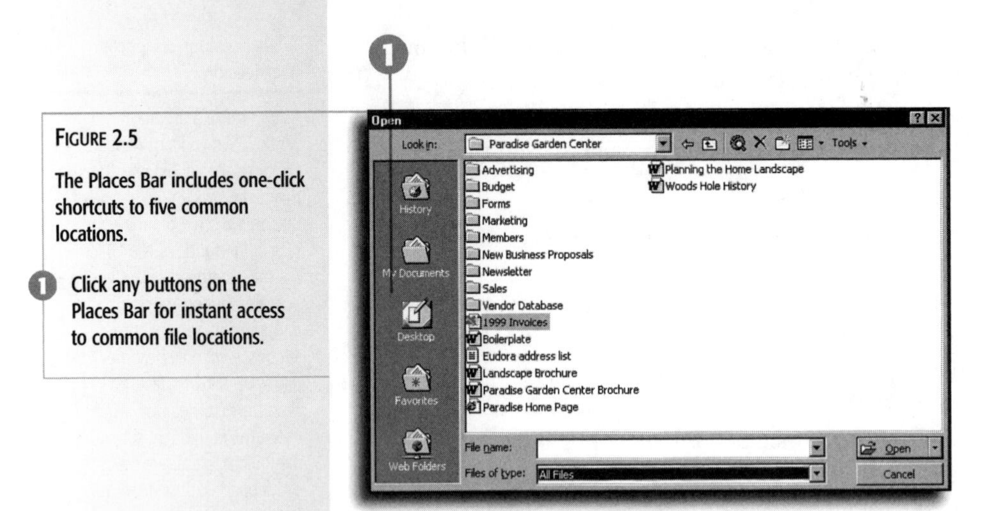

FIGURE 2.5

The Places Bar includes one-click shortcuts to five common locations.

1 Click any buttons on the Places Bar for instant access to common file locations.

Office filters this list for you

Because the History folder contains shortcuts for every Office file type, this folder can get crowded. To reduce clutter, when you click this icon from within an Office program, you'll see only shortcuts for the program you're using.

Use the desktop as a holding area

In general, it's not a good idea to use the desktop for storing large numbers of files. However, this location is handy for temporarily storing one or two files, or when you know you're going to move a file to a location on your company's network and you want to be able to find it in a hurry.

SEE ALSO

- *For more details on how Office lets you work with Web pages, see page 63*
- *The only way to change the icons on the Places Bar is by editing the Windows Registry; you'll find full details in* Special Edition Using Microsoft Office 2000, *Chapter 3, "Office File Management for Experts."*

The exact location of the My Documents folder varies, depending on which Windows version you have installed:

- If you're the only user of a system running Windows 95 or Windows 98 and you haven't set up user profiles, the My Documents folder appears in the root of the system drive, usually C:\My Documents.
- On a system running Windows 95 or Windows 98 with user profiles enabled, the My Documents folder appears in your local profile folder, typically C:\Windows\Profiles\ <*username*>\My Documents.
- On a system running Windows NT 4.0 or earlier, the My Documents shortcut opens the Personal folder in your local profile, typically C:\Winnt\Profiles\<*username*>\Personal.

SEE ALSO

- *To specify an alternate startup location for each Office application, see page 100*

Working with Office Files

All the Office applications use identical techniques to open and save files. To use the common Open dialog box, pull down the **File** menu and choose **Open** (or press Ctrl+O). To save a document, open the **File** menu and then choose **Save** or **Save As** (or press Ctrl+S).

Creating a New File

When you're working in an Office program, the quickest way to create a new file is to click the **New** button (or press Ctrl+N). This technique creates a new Word document, Excel workbook, PowerPoint presentation, or Publisher publication using the default settings; in Outlook, this shortcut creates a new item of the type defined in the current folder. In all programs except Outlook, opening the **File** menu and choosing **New** opens the New dialog box and lets you choose a template.

To create a new Office file without first starting a program, click the **New Office Document** button at the top of the **Start** menu. Then choose one of the templates from the tabbed dialog box shown in Figure 2.6.

Office includes a number of additional templates that are not included in the standard installation. If you choose one of these templates, Office will attempt to install the new files automatically, prompting you for the Office CD-ROM if necessary.

SEE ALSO

➤ *For more information on adding templates, see page 691*

Saving a Document

When you're ready to save a file, you have three choices:

- Pull down the **File** menu and choose **Save**.
- Press Ctrl+S.
- Click the **Save** button on the Standard toolbar .

If the current document, workbook, presentation, or publication

How user profiles work

In all versions of Windows, user profiles allow different people to log in to the same machine under separate usernames, usually with a password. When you enable user profiles, Windows creates separate data directories for each user—with separate My Documents and Application Data folders, among many others. If you use Windows NT, user profiles are required; to see whether a Windows 98 system has user profiles, open the **Users** option in Control Panel.

Finding the My Documents folder

If you've installed Windows 98, you can find a shortcut to the My Documents folder on the Windows desktop. Right-click on that shortcut to change the default location of the My Documents folder. Windows NT users may find that Office applications open by default in a folder called Personal, stored with other files associated with their user profile. Although the name of this folder is different, its function is the same as My Documents.

Files, documents—what's the difference?

Throughout Office, you'll find the terms *file* and *document* used interchangeably in Help files and dialog boxes. That's no problem when you're working with Word, where the default file type is a document. However, it can cause confusion in Excel and PowerPoint, where the default file types are workbooks and presentations, respectively. In this chapter, I've used the term *document* as a general way to refer to the default file type for any Office program.

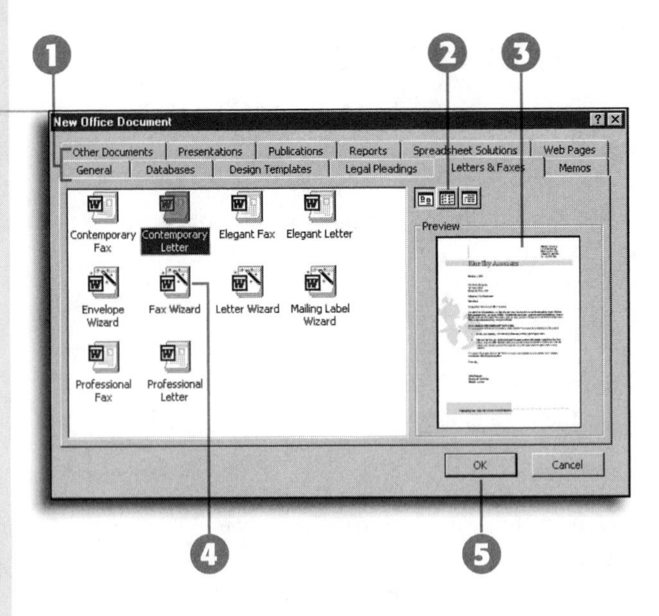

FIGURE 2.6

Use this all-in-one dialog box to create a new document, workbook, or presentation based on a ready-made template.

1. Templates are organized into categories for you. Click on one of these tabs to see which templates are available.
2. Click one of these buttons to switch the display to large or small icons, or a detailed list.
3. The Preview window shows you a thumbnail sketch of the document you've selected (not all templates have thumbnails).
4. Select an icon. Wizard-based templates walk you through the process of creating a new document.
5. Click **OK** to create the new file, and open the program (Word, in this case) that you'll use to work with it.

already has a name, any of these actions replaces the existing copy, using the current filename, options, and location. If this is the first time you've saved the file, you'll see the Save As dialog box. If the file already has a name and you want to save it under a new name, open the **File** menu and click **Save As**.

Although you can simply enter a filename and press Enter, checking the location, file format, and options is always a good idea when you're saving a file.

Checking Options and Saving a Document

1. Enter the name you want to use in the box labeled **File name**.
2. Click the **Places Bar** to choose one of the standard storage locations, or use the drop-down list labeled **Save in** to specify the drive (or network server) and folder where you want to store the file.
3. Choose a file format from the drop-down list labeled **Save as type**. Normally, Office programs suggest the default format for the program you're using; you should choose another type only if you plan to open the file using another program or share it with someone who doesn't use Office 2000.

New folders, on demand

Click the **Create New Folder** button to create a folder inside the current folder without having to close the dialog box.

4. To adjust optional settings that can protect a Word document or Excel workbook, click the **Tools** button, and then choose **General Options**.
5. Click the **Save** button to save the file and close the dialog box.

SEE ALSO

➤ *For an exhaustive discussion of Office file formats, see* Special Edition Using Microsoft Office 2000, *Chapter 3, "Office File Management for Experts."*

Naming Documents

What's in a (legal) filename? Office programs have to follow the same filenaming rules as other Windows applications, which means you must heed these rules when assigning a name to a document:

- A filename can use any of the letters from A to Z and numbers from 0 to 9.
- A filename can be as short as one character. Windows limits filenames to a total length of 260 characters, including the extension and the full DOS-style path. For practical purposes, you should never use filenames longer than about 40 characters.
- Every filename can also have an *extension*, usually three characters in length. The extension is whatever appears after the last period in a filename. As I explain a bit later in this chapter, Office programs create extensions automatically, and Windows hides registered extensions from view unless you set the Windows Explorer option that displays them.
- The following special characters are allowed in a filename: $ % ë - _ @ ~ ` ! ( ) ^ # & + , ; =.
- You can use spaces, brackets ([ ]), curly braces ({ }), single quotation marks, apostrophes, and parentheses as parts of the name.
- You *cannot* use a slash (/), backslash (\), colon (:), asterisk (*), question mark (?), quotation mark ("), or angle brackets (< >) as part of a filename.

Essential information about file formats

The Typical Office setup includes a limited number of converters that allow you to open and save documents created using other programs. If you choose a converter that wasn't installed initially, Office will install the new files automatically. You can find extensive information about importing and converting files in the Help topics "Troubleshoot Converting File Formats" and "How to Import Files from Another Office Program."

- You *can* use periods within a filename. Windows treats the last period in the name as the dividing line between the filename and its extension.

Options That Let You Protect Files

Whenever you save a file in Word or Excel, the dialog box includes a **Tools** button; click to display a menu that includes a choice for **General Options**. That menu in turn displays another dialog box (see Figure 2.7).

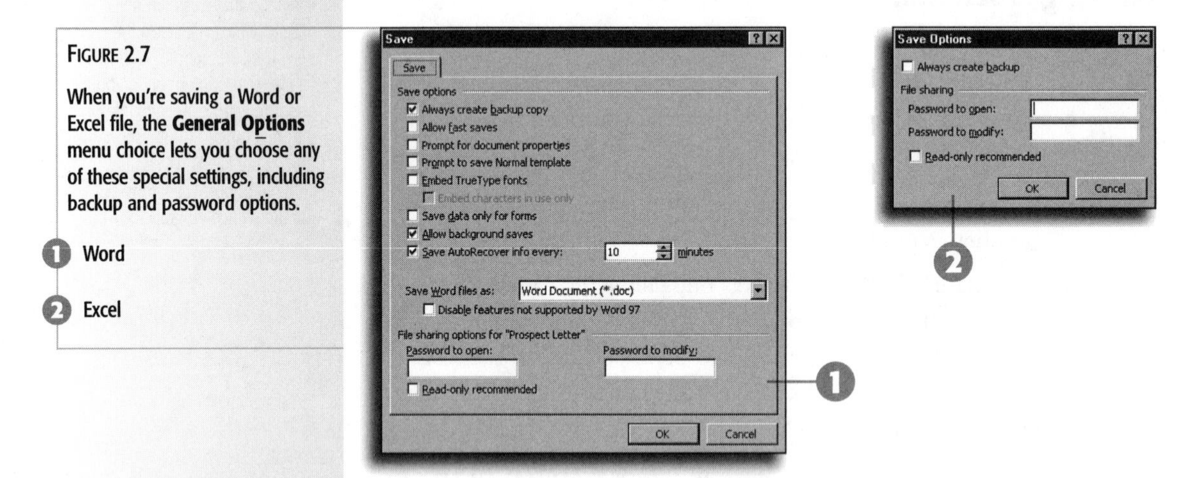

FIGURE 2.7

When you're saving a Word or Excel file, the **General Options** menu choice lets you choose any of these special settings, including backup and password options.

1 Word

2 Excel

Restoring a backup document

When you choose to create automatic backup copies of your Word or Excel files, Office creates the backup copy in the same folder as the document itself. To restore that copy, pull down the **File** menu and choose **Open**; in the **Files of type** box, choose **All Files**, and then browse through the folder and search for a document called Backup of *filename*. Open this file and save it under a new name to restore the original version.

These options let you protect your files in four useful ways:

- If you worry that saving might accidentally overwrite information in an earlier version of a document or worksheet, use the option labeled **Always create backup copy** to save the original version every time you edit a file.
- Use the **Save AutoRecover info** option to tell Word to save a copy of your work at regular intervals. If the power fails or your computer crashes, you can use these specially formatted backup copies to restore the file you were working on at the time. (PowerPoint offers the *AutoRecover* option, but not from the Save As dialog box; to activate it, pull down the **Tools** menu, choose **Options**, click the **Save** tab, and check the appropriate box. Excel does not support AutoRecover.)

- Use the Password options in the **File sharing** section to lock your Word document or Excel worksheet so that other users can open or modify it only when they enter the password you specify. PowerPoint does not offer password protection.
- To discourage users (including yourself) from editing the original document, check the box labeled **Read-only recommended**. When you set this option, Word and Excel prevent you from saving changes using the existing filename. This technique is useful when you have a template document (such as a budget worksheet) that you regularly use as the base for other files.

SEE ALSO

➤ *Don't check that option labeled **Allow fast saves**! I explain why not on page 105*

Caution: Passwords are forever

If you forget the password you've assigned to a document or worksheet, you can kiss your data good-bye. You will find no tools that allow you to recover a password, short of trying every possible combination of letters and numbers–a task that could take hundreds of years. If your data is important, write down the password and put it in a safe place.

Working with File Extensions

If you've used older versions of Office, you're probably used to adding a period and a three-letter *file extension* at the end of each file you create: .doc for Word documents, .xls at the end of Excel workbooks, and so on. That extension in turn identifies the *file type*. When you open a document icon in a folder window or in the Windows Explorer, Windows looks in the list of registered file types to see which program is associated with that file type; it then automatically starts that program and loads the document you selected.

When opening and saving files, you can choose from a drop-down list of available file types. In the Open dialog box, this action filters the list so that you see only files of a specific type. In the Save As dialog box, Office 2000 programs automatically add the file extension that matches the file type you choose. When you select Word document, for example, Word automatically adds a period and the `doc` extension. Windows hides these extensions by default in Explorer windows.

Changing a file extension

When saving a file, you can always choose to use a different extension, or no extension at all. To force a program to use the exact name and extension you specify, enter the full name, including extension, between quotation marks. Note that if you change the extension, you may be unable to open the file from an Explorer window; also, if you choose an unregistered file extension, the file will not appear in the Open dialog box unless you choose **All Files** from the drop-down list of file types.

Caution: Drag and drop with care

You can open any file by dragging it from an Explorer window into an Office document window, but the effect may not be what you expect. When you drop a Word document icon into a window that already contains an open document, Word inserts the contents of the new document at the spot where you released the mouse button. To open the document in its own window instead, drag it onto Word's title bar and then release the mouse button.

Case doesn't count

Windows filenames are not case sensitive, so don't worry about upper- and lowercase letters when entering a filename.

Or click the Views button...

When you click the **Views** button, you cycle from one view to the next, using all four views. Each time you click, the view changes.

Opening a Saved Document

If you've already opened the Office program you want to use, you can easily open a file. To do so, pull down the **File** menu and choose **Open**; then pick the name of the file from the list in the Open dialog box. However, you don't need to open an Office program to open an Office file. Click the **Start** button and choose **Open Office Document** to see a dialog box that opens in the My Documents folder and shows Office files of all types—Word documents, Excel workbooks, and PowerPoint presentations.

Most of the time, you open files by browsing through folders until you find the right one and then clicking the name of the file you want to open. You can also enter the full name of a file, including its path, by typing backslashes to separate the folder names from one another, as in C:\Data\Sales Forecasts\1999\September\Eastern Region Consolidated Report.

Browsing the List of Files

The Open and Save As dialog boxes let you view files as a simple list or as a list with details; you can also choose to preview each file's contents or properties. To switch between the four available views, click the drop-down arrow to the right of the **Views** button at the top of the dialog box and choose one of these four options:

- **List** uses small icons to display as many files as possible in the box.
- **Details** displays size, file type, and other information; click any heading to sort the list by that category.
- **Properties** displays summary information about the selected document in the right half of the dialog box.
- **Preview** displays a thumbnail version of the document in the right half of the dialog box as you move from file to file in the list.

You can also manage files in Open and Save As dialog boxes: Just select the filename and right-click. The shortcut menus here work the same as in the Windows Explorer: You can view the file's name, size, and other properties, and you can move, copy, delete, or rename a file using this menu.

Opening More Than One File at Once

All three main Office programs let you open more than one file at a time. Start by opening the **File** menu, and then choose **Open**. In the Open dialog box, hold down the Ctrl key and click to select multiple filenames; then click **Open**. Each document appears in its own window, just as if you had opened each file individually.

Adding Details About Your Documents

Your computer's operating system (Windows 95, Windows 98, or Windows NT) keeps track of some details about each file stored there: its size, when it was created, and when you last modified it, for example. Office allows you to store extra details about documents, workbooks, and presentations, including the author's name and comments, or keywords you can use to search for documents later. To add or view these details for the current file, open the **File** menu and choose **Properties**. You then see a dialog box like the one in Figure 2.8.

For some simple documents, you may choose not to save *Summary information* because a descriptive filename can tell you everything you need to know about the document. For more complicated documents, though, the extra information found here—including keywords and categories—can help you search for a data file months or years after you last worked with it. The **Comments** box enables you to add free-form notes about a given document.

No properties for Publisher

Unlike other Office programs, Publisher's **File** menu doesn't include a **Properties** option, and if you choose the Properties view in the Open dialog box, you'll see an error message. Curiously, however, right-clicking a Publisher file in the Windows Explorer does allow you to view and edit its title and other Office properties.

Students and journalists, take note

Use the Statistics tab on the Properties dialog box for a Word document to quickly count pages, paragraphs, words, and characters. You must check this dialog box from within Word, however, to get a truly accurate count. If you right-click on the file icon and choose Properties, the Statistics tab shows you the information as it appeared the last time you checked the properties from within Word, and these values may be hopelessly wrong.

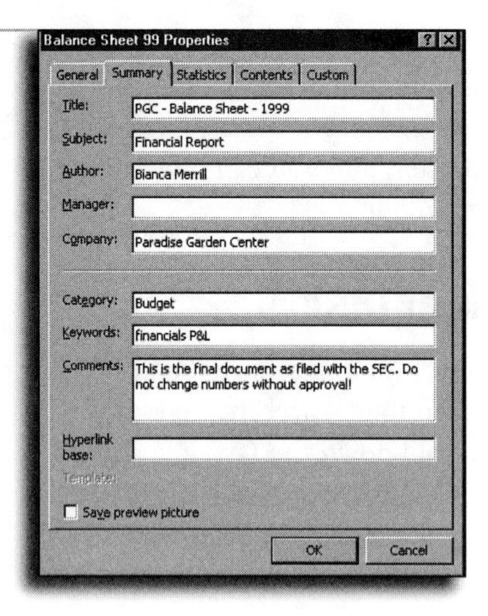

FIGURE 2.8

What's inside that file? The Properties dialog box lets you add keywords and comments to your documents, presentations, and worksheets.

Manage properties from Windows

Right-click any Office document in an Explorer window and choose **Properties** to view all summary information about that file. If you're using Windows 98 or Windows NT 4.0, you can edit that information directly, without opening the file. If you're using Windows 95, you can view selected document properties but must open the document with its associated program to change those properties.

To see and edit the Summary information for a document, open the **File** menu and choose **Properties**. The four tabs to the right of the **General** tab display information about the file itself, its contents, statistics (such as the number of words in a Word document or the number of slides in a presentation), and even custom fields you can create to track your own information. These dialog boxes work exactly the same in every Office program.

SEE ALSO

➤ *To configure the three main Office programs to prompt you to enter Summary information every time you save a file, see page 100*

Switching Between Open Documents

When you open an Office 2000 program, it gets its own button on the Windows taskbar, just as you'd expect. But when you open a second document in the same program, you'll notice that each new document also gets its own taskbar button. You haven't opened a separate new copy of your program; that's just the Office interface designers trying to make it easier for you to work with multiple documents. This is a big change from Office 97—and it means you can switch between document windows by clicking on taskbar buttons, the same way you switch between programs.

Using Microsoft's IntelliMouse with Office 2000

Microsoft's *IntelliMouse* (and compatible competitors such as Logitech's MouseMan+) includes something you won't find in traditional pointing devices: a thumbwheel perched between the two buttons. This wheel is also a button, and it works with all the Office programs and with Internet Explorer to let you move more easily through documents:

- Turn the wheel to scroll through documents and worksheets (or skip from one PowerPoint slide to the next) without having to click repeatedly on the scrollbars.
- Hold down the Ctrl key as you turn the wheel to zoom in and out of a document.
- Hold down the wheel button and move the mouse in any direction to scroll in that direction automatically. Click the wheel button to toggle this *AutoScroll* capability off and on.

Where to find an IntelliMouse

Some versions of Office 2000 include an IntelliMouse in the box. Many PC makers bundle the new-style mouse with new computers. You can also replace your current mouse with an IntelliMouse if you want to take advantage of the wheel features. Check with your favorite computer dealer for pricing and availability.

Finding Files You've Created

If you work with many documents or store files in many locations, you can easily lose track of the work you've done. Office includes several tools that make finding your files easier, whether you created them yesterday or last year.

The Find dialog box is versatile

You can use these search capabilities to track down a single file or create complex searches that find large groups of related documents. For example, you might look on a shared network file server to see all the worksheets anyone in your department updated in the past week. Or, if you're trying to clean out space on your hard drive, you can search for all Word documents that were created more than six months ago or PowerPoint presentations that are larger than 100KB in size. You can save these searches and reuse them later.

Opening a File You've Worked with Recently

Want to pick up today where you left off yesterday? Start any Office program and look at the bottom of the **File** menu. There, you can find entries for the four files you've worked with most recently. This menu works on the first-in, first-out principle—the newest document you work with replaces the oldest one on the list. To open any file from the **Recently Used Files** list, just click its entry. By default, the **Recently Used Files** list includes four entries. You can increase that number to as many as nine.

SEE ALSO

➤ *For more information on increasing the number of Recently Used Files tracked by Office, see page 100*

Tracking Down a Misplaced File

When you first pull down the **File** menu and choose **Open**, you see a list of all the document files stored in the current folder. What happens if the file you're looking for isn't in that list? If you can remember a few scraps of information about the file—part of the name, a date, or even a word or phrase you remember using in the document—you can ask Office to look for the file in one or more folders.

To begin your search, click the **Tools** menu in the Open dialog Box, then choose **Find** to display the dialog box shown in Figure 2.9. Tell Office what you're looking for by defining criteria in this dialog box.

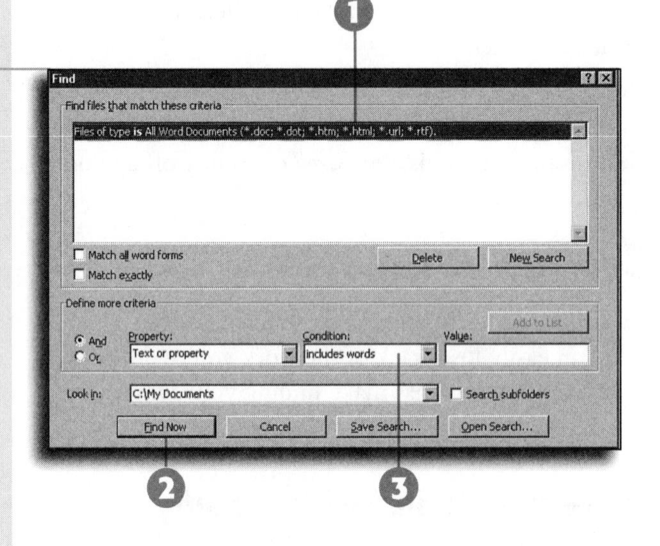

FIGURE 2.9

The Find dialog box lets you build a sophisticated search by adding multiple criteria, one at a time.

1 Each search criterion you enter appears here automatically; you can delete individual items or clear all criteria to start over.

2 Click here to begin searching.

3 Choose a **Property**, a **Condition**, and a **Value**, and then click here to add the entry to the list; repeat until the list is complete.

More help is available

For more details on how to use the Find feature, search for the Help topic "Use Conditions and Values in the Find Dialog Box."

Finding One or More Files

1. In the **Define more criteria** section, use the drop-down lists to begin building your search. If you know part of the name you used in the missing file, for example, choose **File name** from the **Property** list, **includes** from the **Condition list**, and type a word or even a few letters in the **Value** box.
2. Click the **Add to List** button. The criterion you defined appears in the list above.

3. To add another condition, first choose the **And** or **Or** option, and then repeat steps 1 and 2.
4. Choose from the **Look in** list to specify the drive or folder where you want to look. By default, this is set to the folder where you began searching. Check the **Search Subfolders** button to expand the search.
5. To begin searching, click the button labeled **Find Now** (or press Enter). The status bar at the bottom of the dialog box displays a progress report during the search and then shows a list of all the matching files Office found.

Try these search techniques

If you can't remember any of the file's name, or if you want to narrow the search further, use the criterion **Text or property includes *phrase***. Enter a unique word or phrase that you think may be in the document. If you know when you last saved the document, try the **Last modified** property and choose an option from the list—**yesterday**, **last week**, and so on—or enter a specific date or range of dates.

AutoCorrect, AutoFormat, and Other Common Features

Some (but not all) of the Office programs share one more set of common features. As you type, the programs follow along behind you, automatically correcting spelling mistakes, applying the correct formatting, and offering to finish words or sentences after you've typed the first few letters. Invariably, these features have names that begin with *Auto*, and sorting out what each one does can be confusing.

I'll discuss each of these features in more detail in the parts devoted to the specific programs in which they're used. The following sections provide a brief overview of the most common tasks that Office can help you accomplish automatically.

AutoCorrect: Fix Typos On-the-Fly

AutoCorrect fixes common spelling or typing errors, quickly and quietly. When you type `teh`, for example, Office assumes that you meant to type `the` and changes the text for you as soon as you press the Spacebar or a punctuation key, such as a period or comma.

By default, the AutoCorrect list includes more than 500 entries. See Figure 2.10 for examples of some of the ready-made entries. Note that the tabs in this dialog box differ for the Office applications. If you regularly misspell a specific word in a specific way, you can add your own entries to the list. The feature is also useful for creating shortcuts for common words and phrases you type regularly, like your company name. When I type `mcp`, for example, AutoCorrect automatically replaces that shorthand entry with `Macmillan Computer Publishing`. You can also replace a shortcut phrase with a graphic such as a company logo. AutoCorrect works in all Office programs except Outlook, and when you add or edit an AutoCorrect entry in one program, it's available in all other Office programs that use this feature.

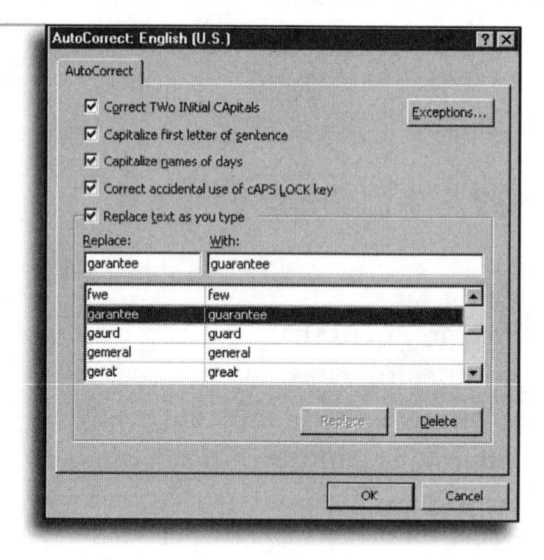

FIGURE 2.10

This scrolling list includes more than 500 common typos that Office can automatically correct.

Adding an AutoCorrect Entry

1. Select the correctly spelled text and/or graphics you want to reuse.
2. Open the **Tools** menu and click **AutoCorrect**. In the resulting dialog box, note that the selected text appears in the box labeled **With**.
3. Type a shortcut name or the commonly misspelled version of the word in the text box labeled **Replace**. The name you enter can be up to 31 characters long but cannot include spaces; making the entry as short as possible makes it easier to use. Do not use a real word or common abbreviation.
4. Word (but not Excel or PowerPoint) lets you also include formatting, such as font and alignment information, with the AutoCorrect entry. Choose the **Formatted text** option only if you want the entry to use the current formatting in every document (This feature is available only if you have selected

text in the document. If you have simply opened the AutoCorrect dialog box and manually entered a new selection, the **Formatted Text** option is disabled).

5. Click **Add** to save the new entry in your AutoCorrect list. Click **OK** to close the AutoCorrect dialog box.

Another way to create an AutoCorrect entry is to type it directly in the AutoCorrect dialog box. Type the shortcut (or misspelled word) in the **Replace** box on the left, type the replacement text in the **With** box on the right, and then click **Add**. This method is a fast and easy way to create a group of AutoCorrect entries at one time; however, this option does not allow you to save formatting.

To delete an AutoCorrect entry, open the AutoCorrect dialog box, choose an entry from the scrolling list, and then click the **Delete** button.

Why isn't AutoCorrect working?

Maybe it's turned off. Open the **Tools** menu, choose **AutoCorrect**, and make sure that a check mark appears in the box labeled **Replace text as you type**.

AutoComplete: Save Keystrokes When Entering Common Words

What's the difference between AutoCorrect and AutoComplete? AutoCorrect replaces your text automatically as soon as you press the Spacebar or a punctuation key. AutoComplete, on the other hand, works only when you specifically request it by pressing Enter or F3. Word and Excel have different ideas of what AutoComplete is supposed to do, PowerPoint and Publisher don't offer this feature at all, and Outlook has something called AutoCreate, which is completely different. (If that's not confusing enough, you can find Word's version of AutoComplete on the **AutoText** tab in the AutoCorrect dialog box!)

I'll discuss AutoComplete in greater detail in the parts on Word and Excel.

SEE ALSO

➤ *For more details on Word's version of this feature, see page 203*

➤ *To learn how Excel uses AutoComplete, see page 347*

AutoFormat: Office 2000's Instant Design Expert

Think of AutoFormat as the "Make It Look Good" button. AutoFormat (available in Excel and Word only) analyzes your document and tries to make sense out of it by identifying and formatting headings, lists, body text, and other elements. Unfortunately, the results, more often than not, are disappointing.

When you use AutoFormat in Word, the program works its way through your document from top to bottom, replacing straight quotes with smart quotes, taking out extra spaces and unnecessary paragraph marks, creating bulleted lists, and so on. It also applies styles to the different sections of the document.

Excel, on the other hand, tries to turn a selected region of your current worksheet into neat rows and columns, using lines, colors, fonts, and other design elements to set off headings and totals and generally make it visually appealing. With Excel, unlike Word, you get a choice of different looks that you can apply to your worksheet.

SEE ALSO

- *To learn how to use AutoFormat with Word, see page 245*
- *For information about using AutoFormat with Excel, see page 403*

CHAPTER

3

Office and the Web

Make Office work right with any browser

Save and edit Web pages

Set up Web Folders for instant access to Web servers

Control how and where Office saves Web pages

How Office and Your Web Browser Work Together

If you used previous versions of Office to create and save Web pages, you're intimately familiar with the hassles and headaches that come with trying to translate your work into *HTML* format. In Office 2000, creating Web pages is much, much easier. After you create a Word document, Excel workbook, or PowerPoint presentation, pull down the **File** menu and choose **Save as Web Page**. When you do, Office saves your file in HTML format so that you can view it in a browser, such as Microsoft Internet Explorer or Netscape Navigator. It also preserves the original Office formatting information in the same file, so when you want to edit the file again, you can double-click its icon and get to work.

It's easy to take this capability for granted, because it all works so effortlessly. In fact, the Web features in Office 2000 are truly revolutionary. If you use an older version of Office—or, for that matter, a current version of just about any other software you can name—you have to convert your files into HTML format. That conversion process is a one-way ticket; if you open the converted Web page in Office, it looks different, and some of the information is gone for good.

In Office 2000, by contrast, when you create a Word document, an Excel workbook, or a PowerPoint presentation and save it as a Web page, virtually all your formatting—and, more importantly, all your data—can survive the "round trip" from your Office program to the browser and back again. If you open the Web page in a browser, it looks remarkably close to the document or workbook you created; when you open the file for editing, you see the original file you created, with every piece intact. The transition from Office to the Web and back is practically invisible, and best of all, you don't have to know anything about HTML. If you want to become an HTML expert, pick up a copy of *Using HTML 4*, also published by Que.

When creating Office documents for the Web, you must pay attention to three important issues:

- Which browser will your intended audience use to view the pages? Some features of Office are incompatible with some browsers, as you learn later in this chapter.
- What happens to graphics and multimedia files? Office documents can include pictures and drawing objects right in the file; HTML pages, on the other hand, contain only text. When you save a file as a Web page, Office has to strip the graphics into separate files and create links to them.
- Finally, how do you open the file for editing after you've saved it as a Web page?

In this chapter, you learn how to configure Office so that it works well with any browser. In Chapter 4, "Creating and Publishing Web Pages," you learn how to create and publish your own Web pages. You can also find information on how to use each Office program with the Web in the sections that are specific to those programs.

SEE ALSO

- *For details on how to save any Office file as a Web page, see page 57*
- *To learn how to use Word to create or edit Web pages, see page 319*
- *If you want to put Excel charts or workbooks on a Web page, see page 461*
- *To save your PowerPoint presentations as Web pages so that anyone can view them in a browser, see page 535*

What about Publisher and Outlook?

You'll notice I didn't mention Publisher or Outlook in this section. As an email client, Outlook naturally works with the Internet; but with the single exception of publishing your calendar to a Web page, it isn't really appropriate for creating content for the Web. And as for Publisher, well...let's just say it's not up to the standards of the rest of Office. Some of Publisher's Wizards do a wonderful job of creating Web pages; but when you want to save the publication in HTML format so that you can use it on the Web, you have to go through a one-way conversion. Publisher doesn't allow you to open a Web page after you've converted it.

Using Office with Internet Explorer 4.0 and 5.0

If you save an Office 2000 document as a Web page and open that page in Internet Explorer 4.01 or later, the result looks almost exactly like the file you created in the original application. Figure 3.1, for example, shows an Excel workbook that was saved as a Web page and opened in Internet Explorer 5 (IE5 is included with Office 2000).

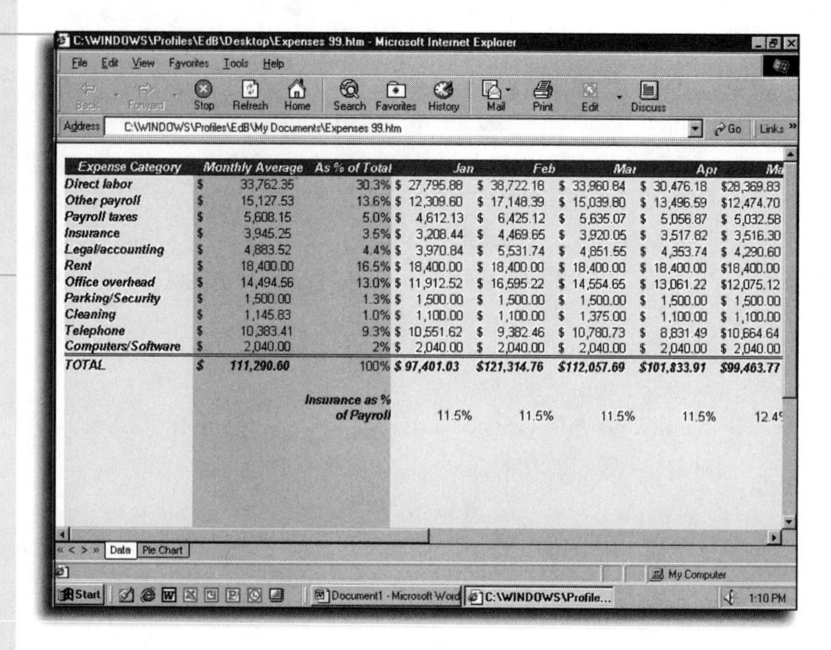

Expense Category	Monthly Average	As % of Total	Jan	Feb	Mar	Apr	Ma
Direct labor	$ 33,762.35	30.3%	$ 27,795.88	$ 38,722.18	$ 33,960.84	$ 30,476.18	$28,369.83
Other payroll	$ 15,127.53	13.6%	$ 12,309.60	$ 17,148.39	$ 15,039.80	$ 13,496.59	$12,474.70
Payroll taxes	$ 5,608.15	5.0%	$ 4,612.13	$ 6,425.12	$ 5,635.07	$ 5,056.87	$ 5,032.58
Insurance	$ 3,945.25	3.5%	$ 3,208.44	$ 4,469.65	$ 3,920.05	$ 3,517.82	$ 3,516.30
Legal/accounting	$ 4,883.52	4.4%	$ 3,970.84	$ 5,531.74	$ 4,851.55	$ 4,353.74	$ 4,290.60
Rent	$ 18,400.00	16.5%	$ 18,400.00	$ 18,400.00	$ 18,400.00	$ 18,400.00	$18,400.00
Office overhead	$ 14,494.56	13.0%	$ 11,912.52	$ 16,595.22	$ 14,554.65	$ 13,061.22	$12,075.12
Parking/Security	$ 1,500.00	1.3%	$ 1,500.00	$ 1,500.00	$ 1,500.00	$ 1,500.00	$ 1,500.00
Cleaning	$ 1,145.83	1.0%	$ 1,100.00	$ 1,100.00	$ 1,375.00	$ 1,100.00	$ 1,100.00
Telephone	$ 10,383.41	9.3%	$ 10,551.62	$ 9,382.46	$ 10,780.73	$ 8,831.49	$10,664.64
Computers/Software	$ 2,040.00	2%	$ 2,040.00	$ 2,040.00	$ 2,040.00	$ 2,040.00	$ 2,040.00
TOTAL	$ 111,290.60	100%	$ 97,401.03	$121,314.76	$112,057.69	$101,833.91	$99,463.77
		Insurance as % of Payroll	11.5%	11.5%	11.5%	11.5%	12.4

FIGURE 3.1

When you save an Excel workbook as a Web page and view it in Internet Explorer 5, it looks remarkably like the original. Click the tabs at the bottom, for example, to see different sheets.

Some types of data don't appear

A few unusual data types don't display properly in a Web browser. If you use workbook scenarios, for example, they're not visible in the Web-format version of the workbook. That information is still present, however, if you reopen the page in Excel.

The workbook shown in Figure 3.1 doesn't look exactly the same as it does in Excel, but it's remarkably close. The columns don't line up perfectly, as they do in Excel, and the sheet tabs at the bottom of the workbook look different. Still, anyone who opens this page can view all the data on every sheet in your workbook.

If you work in an environment where everyone uses Internet Explorer 4.01 or later, you needn't do anything special to your office configuration. If you save a document as a Web page and store it in a shared folder, anyone who opens it will see the page as you designed it.

Configuring Office for Use with Other Browsers

If some people in your Office use other browsers, including Internet Explorer 3.*x* or any version of Netscape Navigator, you'll need to exercise greater care when you save Office documents as Web pages. Office applications take advantage of many advanced HTML features. Two features in particular may cause your document to look different when viewed in browsers other than Internet Explorer 4.01 or later:

- *Cascading style sheets*—Allow Office to define fonts, colors, margins, and other formatting properties as part of the HTML layout. When you save an Office document as a Web page, Office adds this style sheet automatically. If you then open the page in a browser that doesn't know how to interpret this information, the browser will display the page using its default fonts and layout properties. In general, all the data will appear on the page, but it probably won't look pretty, and it may not line up properly, either. Internet Explorer 3.x works properly with cascading style sheets, but Netscape Navigator 3.x does not.
- *Extensible Markup Language (XML)*—Adds tags that look like standard HTML, but instead of describing how to display data, they describe the data itself. For example, XML tags tell the browser which Office program created the page. Most advanced Office features rely on XML; if a browser doesn't understand XML, it ignores this information and displays the data as best it can. Internet Explorer 3.x and Netscape Navigator 3.x and 4.x do not understand XML.

If you regularly create and share Web documents with people who use browsers other than Internet Explorer 5.0, you can configure some Office programs so that they automatically produce pages that look good for everyone. You'll need to do this for each Office program you use.

In Word, pull down the **Tools** menu and choose **Options**. Click the **General** tab, then click the **Web Options** button. On the **General** tab of the Web Options dialog box (see Figure 3.2), adjust the setting in the **Browser** box so that it reads **Microsoft Internet Explorer 4.0 and Netscape Navigator 4.0**. To turn off cascading styles sheets so that even older browsers can read pages you save, remove the check mark from the **Rely on CSS for font formatting** check box.

X marks the version

Why do I refer to browser versions using an *x*, as in Netscape Navigator 4.*x*? More so than any other type of software, browsers are updated frequently to fix bugs and add features. Netscape, for example, updated version 4 of its Navigator browser several times; depending on whether you've downloaded the latest version, you might be using version 4.03, 4.05, or 4.08. When I refer to Navigator 4.*x*, that means the information applies to all versions that begin with 4, regardless of the numbers after the decimal point.

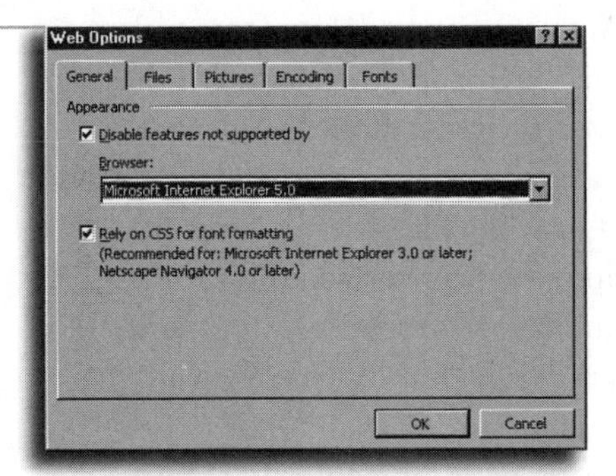

FIGURE 3.2

Set this option to make Office-generated Web pages more compatible with other browsers.

PowerPoint offers similar options, in a roundabout way. After you choose the **Save as Web Page** option, click the **Publish** button and adjust options in the **Browser support** area of the Publish as Web Page dialog box. Excel doesn't offer any compatibility options.

When you choose to disable some Office features this way, the appearance of your document may change. Word gives you a warning about features and formatting you will lose, in a dialog box like the one shown in Figure 3.3. Click the **Tell Me More** button to read a Help topic that explains in detail what each change means.

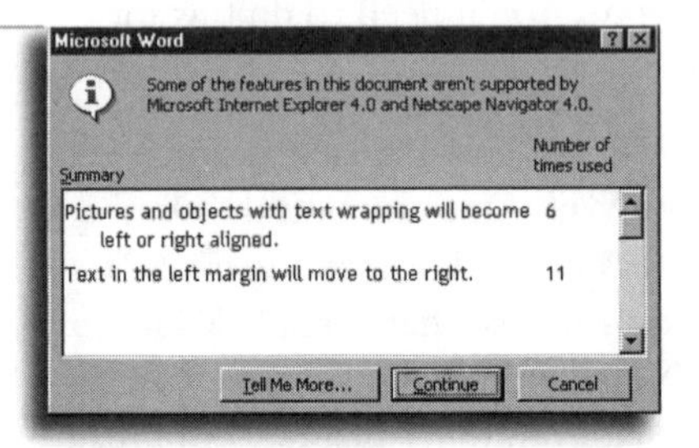

FIGURE 3.3

If you adjust Word's compatibility options when saving a Web page, you may see this dialog box.

Check your results!

If you receive any compatibility warnings, open the file in a browser and see what it looks like. You may need to reopen the page and adjust the position of some graphics and headlines, for example.

Moving Between HTML and Office Formats

When you save any Office file as a Web page, the program saves it as a new file type. If you use Word, for example, it changes the document type from Word Document (with a .doc extension) to a Microsoft HTML Document 4.0 type (with a .htm extension). When you double-click this icon, it automatically opens the page in your Web browser. What if you want to edit the file? You have two choices:

- Right-click the file's icon and choose **Edit** from the shortcut menu. This action opens the file using the program that you used to create it.
- If the file is open in Internet Explorer 5, click the **Edit** button to immediately begin editing it using the default editing program. In most cases, this will be Microsoft Word; if you've installed the Premium Edition of Office, you may be able to use Microsoft FrontPage for this task.

...or set different options on each file

You can also set Web options on a file-by-file basis. If you normally share files with people who use only Internet Explorer 4.01, you might want your default settings to include all Web features. On the rare occasions when you save a file to go on a Web server that Netscape Navigator users will access, set Web options just for that file: Pull down the **File** menu, choose **Save as Web Page**, click the **Tools** button, and choose **Web Options** from the menu. This dialog box is exactly the same as the one you use to set defaults, but its settings affect only the current file.

Use Word to edit all Web pages

To set Word as your default Web editor, open Internet Explorer. With any Web page open, pull down the **Tools** menu in the browser, then choose **Internet Options**. Click the **Programs** tab and choose **Microsoft Office** from the **HTML Editor** drop-down list. (On some systems, this option may appear as **Microsoft Word for Windows**.)

Skip the wizard

If you installed the Web Publishing Wizard with a previous version of Office or Internet Explorer, it's probably still in your system. You can use it to save pages to a Web site, but you don't need to with Office 2000. Web Folders are a much easier alternative.

Working with Web Folders

When you choose the **Save as Web Page** option in any Office program, you can choose to save the file (and all its associated files, including graphics) to a folder on your computer or on a network server. You can also publish the page to a *Web server*, either on your company's *intranet* or on the World Wide Web. In previous Office versions, you had to save your files first, then use the *Web Publishing Wizard* to publish them to a Web server. In Office 2000, you can save and open files directly from Web servers; the secret is defining shortcuts, called *Web Folders*. As the name implies, these shortcuts look and act like folders on your computer, but they actually connect you directly to the Web server.

To choose a Web server as the destination, click the **Web Folders** icon in the Places Bar. This displays a list of all the Web Folders you've already set up; double-click any icon to browse files and folders stored there. If this is the first time you're saving a file to a particular server, you must run through a brief setup routine first.

Adding a Web Server to the Web Folders List

1. In the Open or Save As dialog box, click the **New Folder** button.
2. In the Add Web Folder Wizard (see Figure 3.4), enter the *URL* of the Web server where you want to be able to save files. You can either type this information directly in the **Type the location to add** box (**http://www.example.com**) or use your Web browser to locate the Web page you want to add. To let Office fill in the blank for you, click the **Browse** button to open your Web browser, then navigate to the location where you want to save files; return to the wizard and the address appears automatically.

Set up Web Folders anytime

You don't need to use the Save As dialog box to set up a Web Folder. Office 2000 adds a **Web Folders** icon in the Windows Explorer. Open any Explorer window and click the **Address** drop-down list to choose this icon; or double-click the **My Computer** icon on the Windows Desktop. In either case, you can double-click the **Add Web Folder** button to start the wizard.

FIGURE 3.4

Use this wizard to set up a Web server so you can save files directly from Office programs.

3. Click the **Next** button. The wizard connects to the URL you specified and verifies that the location exists and will allow you to publish pages. If you see an error message, check your typing, or call the server administrator and ask for assistance.
4. In the final step of the wizard, enter a friendly name for the server and click **Finish**.

Intranet addresses are different

You're used to specifying `http://www.something.com` as the location of pages on the World Wide Web. If your office uses an intranet, the address will probably be simpler. At my office, for example, there are three servers, each named after one of the Marx Brothers. So I save Web pages to `http://harpo/public`.

Controlling How Office Saves Web Pages

Each Office program includes a variety of options for customizing what happens when you save Web pages. The most important option deals with graphics and other linked files.

By definition, Web pages are plain text files; they cannot contain graphics or multimedia content. So what happens when you create a Word document, Excel workbook, or PowerPoint presentation, add a graphic object, and then save it as a Web page? In that event, Office goes through a two-step process:

- First, the program converts the picture (or other object) to a separate file. If you used the Office drawing tools to create a flowchart, for example, saving as a Web page creates a copy of the drawing in *GIF* format (a standard image format used on the Internet).
- Next, the program creates a link to the file and adds it to the HTML text in the main page.

If your document contains any embedded graphics or other objects, Word, Excel, and PowerPoint all handle these extra files in the same way, by creating a folder with a name similar to the file you created, then storing the graphics (and other items) in that folder.

Let's say you create a Word document called Annual Report, then save it as a Web page in your My Documents folder. When you look in that folder, you'll see a file called Annual Report.htm, along with a folder called Annual Report_files. Inside that folder, you'll find all the graphics from the original page, translated (if necessary) into GIF or *JPEG* format. You'll also find a few other files that Office uses to manage links and to make the page look right in your browser.

Word, Excel, and PowerPoint let you change this behavior so that all files—the main page, graphics, and all supporting files alike—go into a single folder. This option is useful if you want to completely avoid the risk of separating the main page from the supporting files. Pull down the **Tools** menu, then choose **Options**. On the **General** tab, click the **Web Options** button. Click the **Files** tab to display the dialog box shown in Figure 3.5.

Move the page and folder together

What happens if you move a Web page and its associated graphics? As long as you move the file and the folder full of supporting files together, everything works just fine. Office creates *relative links* in the Web pages it creates, meaning that the links refer only to the subfolder name, not their full location. Just move the file and folder together, without renaming either one, and everything will work perfectly.

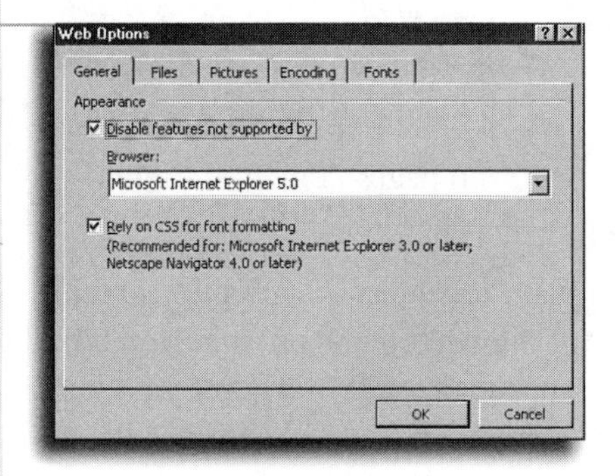

FIGURE 3.5

Use these options to control how Office saves supporting files (such as graphics) in Web pages.

This dialog box includes several options. Here's what each one does:

- To save all files in a single folder, clear the check mark from the **Organize supporting files in a folder** check box.
- To save files using short names, clear the check mark from the **Use long file names whenever possible** check box. Use this option only if you have to—for example, when you plan to post the Web page on a server that doesn't correctly process long filenames.
- The **Update links on save** option automatically refreshes data from linked pages when you save the page. Under most circumstances, you should leave this box checked; otherwise, you risk publishing a page that contains incorrect data.

Create a new folder

If you use this "all in one folder" option, get in the habit of creating a new folder for each page you create. Otherwise, you'll end up with a confusing mess of supporting files, and if you save two pages to the same folder, you'll make it more difficult to manage everything.

Believe it or not, Office programs do an excellent job of maintaining all these files. If you open a Web page you created in Word, for example, the program notices if you remove a graphic from the page, and it removes the matching graphic file from the folder full of supporting files.

Don't reuse that folder!

Publisher warns you if you're trying to save a Web site to a folder that already contains a Web site. If you disregard the warning, your new Index.html page will overwrite the old one, and you'll lose the original Web site. If you want to keep both sites, choose a new folder name.

Publisher stores Web pages differently from all Office programs. When you choose the **Create Web Site from Current Publication** or **Save as Web Page** option from the **File** menu, Publisher automatically suggests saving the Web page and all its files in a folder called Publish, in the same folder as your publication. (You can specify a new folder name if you prefer.) When you click **OK**, Publisher saves the main document using the name Index.html, with all other supporting files in the same folder.

CHAPTER

4

Creating and Publishing Web Pages

Choose the right program for creating Web pages

Save any Office document as a Web page

Print your Outlook calendar and view it in a browser window

Create and edit hyperlinks in any Office file

Turn Excel data into interactive Web pages

Choosing the Right Office Program for Web Pages

All Office programs allow you to create a file and save it as a Web page. But that doesn't mean you can just open any Office program and end up with exactly the Web page you want. Each program has particular strengths, weaknesses, and quirks. Where should you start? That depends on the specific task you're trying to accomplish.

- For general-purpose Web pages, including a basic personal home page, Word is your best choice. You can start with a Web template or build a page from scratch.

SEE ALSO

➤ *For specifics on how to create and edit Web pages in Word, see page 319*

- If the content you want to put in Web format translates easily into a series of single screens, consider using PowerPoint—even if you have no desire to ever stand in front of an audience and deliver your message. PowerPoint is an excellent tool for creating easy-to-read Web pages, each of which fits on a single screen with a navigation frame on the left.

SEE ALSO

➤ *To save your PowerPoint presentations as Web pages so that anyone can view them in a browser, see page 535*

PowerPoint gets you started

Check out PowerPoint's AutoContent Wizard for a handful of ready-made templates that are ideal for use on the Web. The Corporate home page template includes the basic screens for setting up a small company site, for example.

- Use Excel for publishing data that's already in a workbook or chart. You can save an entire workbook or select a range of data or a chart to publish as an individual page. Excel is a terrible choice for working with other text and graphics on the same page, however. If you want to use data or a chart from Excel in a Web page with other content, create the page in Word instead, then paste the Excel data into the page.

SEE ALSO

➤ *For more details on working with Excel charts, see page 461*

- Outlook does a super job on one specific task: turning a calendar into a Web page. I provide full details at the end of the next section.
- Publisher is a good choice for building "canned" Web sites using its templates. If you prefer to start from scratch, however, you'll probably find Word much easier to use.

Saving an Office Document As a Web Page

You don't have to take any special steps to create a Web page; Office can save virtually any Word document, Excel workbook, or PowerPoint presentation as a file that can be viewed in a Web browser. If the data in your file extends outside the visible window, anyone viewing the page can use the browser's scrollbars to move right or down.

In general, the process of saving a Web page works the same in Word, PowerPoint, and Excel. (These steps do not apply to Publisher or Outlook, however.)

Creating a Web Page with Office

1. Create a document, workbook, or presentation as usual. Add graphics and apply all formatting you want to appear in the Web page. If you want to publish only a portion of an Excel workbook or worksheet, you can save time by selecting the correct sheet and range at this point. If you want to save only part of a Word document as a Web page, save the document under a new name and delete the sections you don't want to include.
2. If you're not certain your document will look good in a Web browser, pull down the **File** menu and choose **Web Page Preview**. This optional step saves a temporary copy of your file in HTML format, opens your Web browser, and loads the page. Return to the Office program to make any necessary changes and preview again, or close the browser window and proceed to the next step.

Heavy-duty Web work? Choose "None of the above"

If your job includes lots of Web-related work, or if you have to manage a Web site rather than just produce pages for it, get a copy of FrontPage 2000. FrontPage was designed from the ground up as a Web editor, and it includes features that full-time Web designers and site administrators truly appreciate, especially if they need to add scripts or edit HTML tags manually. FrontPage is available as a standalone package or as part of the Office 2000, Premium Edition.

Save that document first!

Before you save a file as a Web page, be sure to save it in the standard format of the program you created it with before you choose **Save as Web Page**. If you have any problems with your Web page, this step lets you start over with the original document without losing any changes you made in the current session.

Don't forget other browsers

Of course, previewing your Web page only tells you whether it will look good in the browser you use. If your intended audience includes people who use other browsers, such as Netscape Navigator or an older version of Internet Explorer, consider enlisting a coworker to help test your page. Save the Web page as usual, and ask your coworker to view the page in his or her browser, then report to you if anything looks out of the ordinary.

3. Pull down the **File** menu and choose **Save as Web Page**. You see the Save As dialog box with several extra options that aren't visible when you save in the program's standard format. In PowerPoint and Excel, for example, this dialog box includes a **Publish** button, which lets you specify which portions of the worksheet or which slides you want to save. Figure 4.1 shows the Excel version of this dialog box.

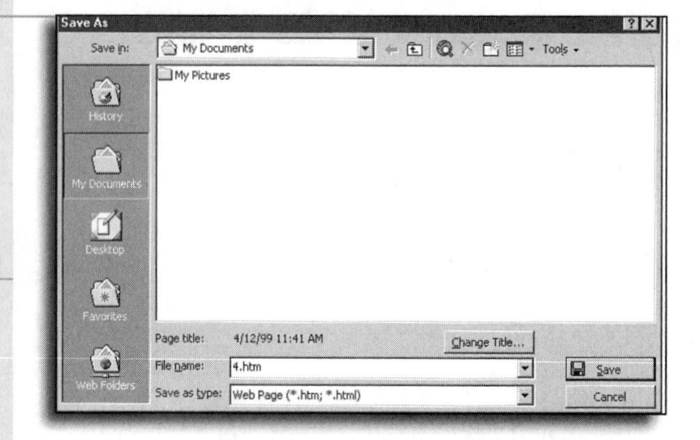

FIGURE 4.1

When you save an Office document as a Web page, you get some extra options. In Excel, for example, you can choose a range or a chart instead of saving the entire workbook.

4. Give your Web page a title, which will appear in the title bar of the Web browser whenever the page is opened. Just above the **File name** box, the Office program displays the name of the current title. Click the **Change Title** button to edit this text.

Let the title tell the story

Don't confuse the title of the Web page with the name of your file. The filename is what you enter to store the page on a hard disk or a server; typically, your audience will open the Web page by clicking a link on another page, so the name of the page doesn't matter. They will see the title in the browser's title bar, on the other hand. If someone viewing this page wants to save it as a Favorite or find it in their History list, this is the entry they'll see, so it's important that you choose a title that describes the current page well.

SEE ALSO

> *Office programs use the Title field in the Properties dialog box as the Web page title; for more details on document properties, see page 37*

5. Choose any of the following Web options, depending on the file type and program you started with.
   - When saving an Excel workbook, an option just below the file list lets you choose **Entire Workbook** or **Selection**. If you selected a range before you opened the Save As dialog box, that range is shown here; otherwise, the **Selection** option lets you choose just the current worksheet. Click the **Publish** button to choose other options from the dialog box shown in Figure 4.2.

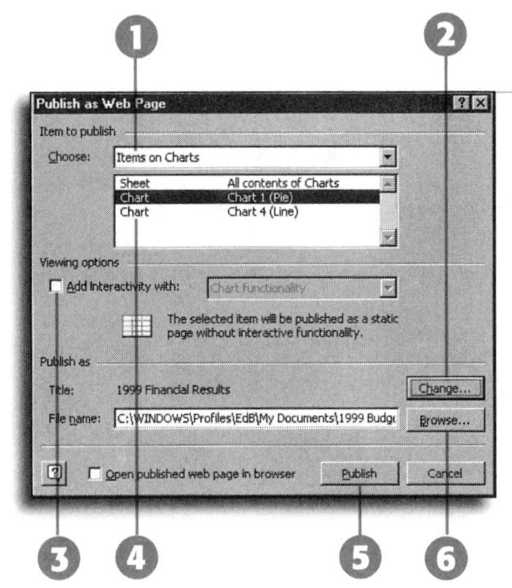

FIGURE 4.2

Excel gives you these options for saving a workbook as a Web page.

1. Choose from this drop-down list to specify which items to publish.
2. Change the page title or filename.
3. Make the Web page interactive for other Office 2000 users. (Read more details later in this chapter.)
4. Choose individual items from this list; if you pick Range of Cells from the list above, this area changes to a box in which you can select one or more ranges of data.
5. Click here to save the Web page.
6. Check here to open the page in your browser as soon as you finish saving it.

- When saving a PowerPoint presentation, click the **Publish** button to choose additional options from the dialog box shown in Figure 4.3.
- In all programs, click the **Tools** button and choose **Web Options** to display a dialog box containing advanced options.

6. Choose a filename and location (on a hard disk or on a Web server). To specify a Web server, click the **Web Folders** icon in the Save As dialog box, or click the **Browse** button in the Publish dialog box.
7. Click **Save** to store your file in Web format in the specified location. If you opened the Publish dialog box in Excel or PowerPoint, click the **Publish** button instead.

SEE ALSO

➤ *For a full description of how Office programs save Web pages and supporting files, see page 53*

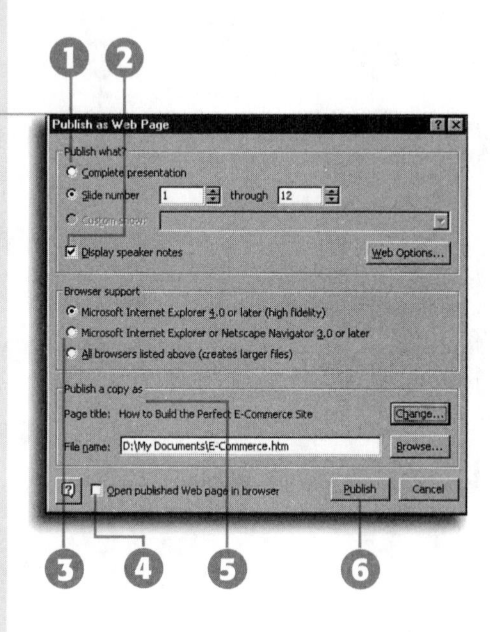

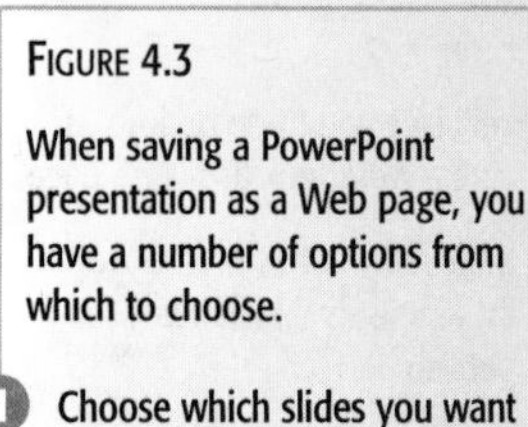

FIGURE 4.3

When saving a PowerPoint presentation as a Web page, you have a number of options from which to choose.

1. Choose which slides you want to publish–all, or a consecutive range.
2. Clear this check box to leave your speaker notes off the page.
3. Choose **Browser support** options (see Chapter 3 for more details).
4. Check here to open the page in your browser as soon as you finish saving it.
5. Change the page title or filename.
6. Click here to save the Web page.

After you save your file as a Web page, what happens to the original document, workbook, or presentation? Absolutely nothing. It stays right where it was originally. That's good news if you want to throw away your Web page and start over, but it's a potential source of great confusion, because you may end up with two files in the same folder with similar names. You'll have to be careful to open the right one when you make changes in the future. If you don't pay attention, you could use Word to open the document version and make some changes on Tuesday, then open the Web page version on Wednesday and make a different set of changes. The next time you open either document, you'll find half your previous changes missing, and you can't easily consolidate the two.

To head off this potential problem before it arises, follow this advice:

- If you're completely satisfied with the look of your new Web page and that file will always be available to you (for example, if you've saved it on your own hard drive), delete the original document file and use the new Web page file for any future changes. (See the next section for details).

- If the Web page you published was a one-shot deal—for example, if you posted a few slides from your favorite presentation on your company's intranet—keep the original file in a safe place—and use it for any changes. Keep your original document, workbook, or presentation in a separate folder from the one that holds the Web page, if possible; in any case, be sure to use different names for the two files.
- If you've saved the entire file in Web format on a server that is sometimes not available, keep a local copy of the Web page version of the file and delete the other version. (The icon for the file in Web page format uses the Internet Explorer document icon shown in Figure 4.4.)

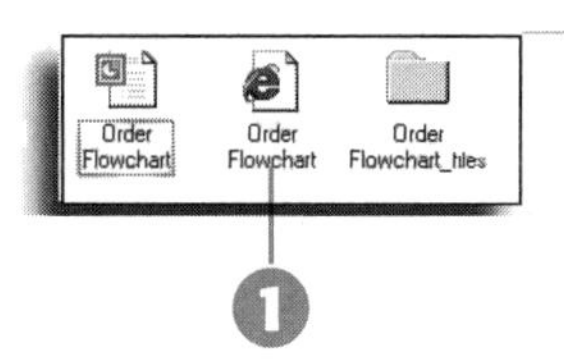

FIGURE 4.4
After saving a file as a Web page, you'll have two versions of the same file—be careful which one you open for editing.

1 Web page format

Publishing Your Outlook Calendar As a Web Page

Outlook lets you produce only one kind of Web page, but it's a good one. You can turn your Calendar into an HTML page, complete with hyperlinks that jump to more detailed information along the side of the page.

SEE ALSO

For more details about how to work with your Outlook Calendar, see page 606

Publishing an Outlook Calendar As a Web Page

1. Open Outlook and click the **Calendar** icon on the Outlook Bar to display the contents of your Calendar folder.
2. Pull down the **File** menu and choose **Save as Web Page**. You see the Save as Web Page dialog box shown in Figure 4.5.

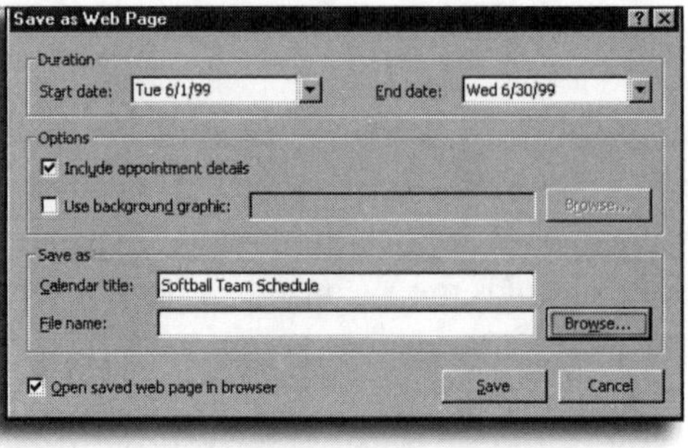

FIGURE 4.5

Outlook lets you turn your calendar into a gorgeous HTML page, suitable for posting on the Web.

Create custom calendars

You don't have to save your own calendar as a Web page. If you belong to a group or committee, you can also keep a separate Outlook Calendar and save it for use on the Web. From Outlook, pull down the **File** menu and choose **New**, and then **Folder**. Give the folder a name, such as Softball Team Schedule, and choose **Appointment Items** from the **Folder contains** list. Enter events and meetings for the group in this folder, and then save.

Where are the supporting files?

Outlook uses the filename you enter to create a folder that contains supporting files for your calendar as well as the Calendar file itself. If you want to move the Calendar Web page, be sure to move this entire folder.

3. Enter the **Start date** and **End date** you want to use for the Web calendar.
4. If you want the calendar to show only the titles of appointments and events, clear the **Include appointment details** check box; leave this box checked if you want anyone viewing the page to see times and notes in a column on the right.
5. Check the **Use background graphic** box and choose a graphic file, if you want.
6. Give the calendar a title—the information you enter here will appear on the page.
7. Enter the name you want to use for the calendar file in the **File name** box. By default, Outlook saves this file in you're My Documents folder; click the **Browse** button to choose a different location, if necessary.
8. Leave the **Open saved web page in browser check** box checked, then click **Save** to finish and see your Web page. It should look something like the one in Figure 4.6.

Note that you can't save your Calendar Web page to a Web server directly. Instead, save it and its supporting files to a location on your hard drive, then open an Explorer window, open any server icon in your Web Folders location, and drag the calendar file and its folder full of supporting files into the server's window.

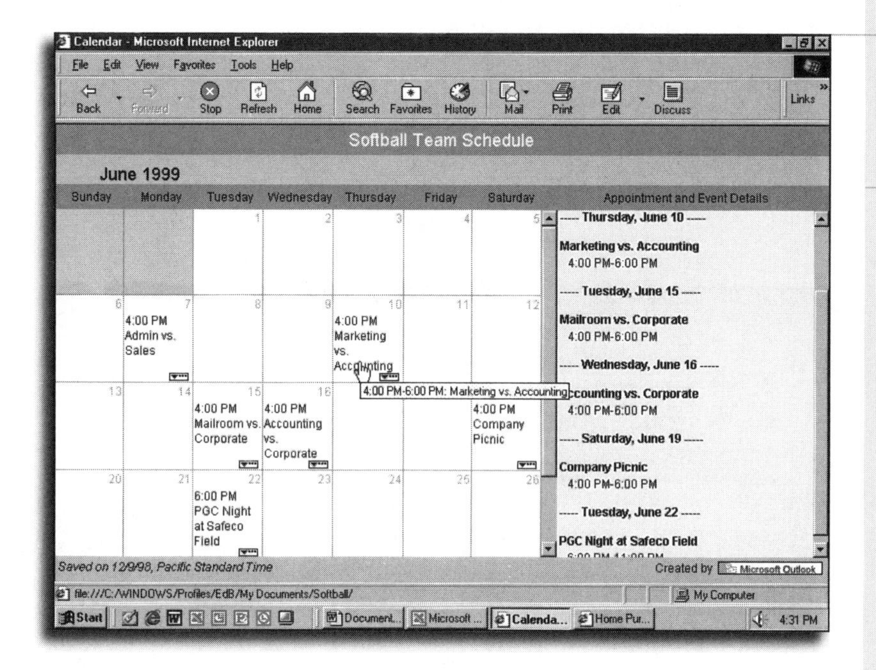

FIGURE 4.6
Saving an Outlook Calendar as a Web page produces this kind of impressive output.

Opening and Editing Web Pages

When you open a Web page in Internet Explorer, you can click the **Edit** button on the browser window to open it so that you can make changes. It doesn't matter how that page got into your browser:

- If the document was originally created in an Office program, it opens in that Office program.
- If the document was not created in an Office program, it opens using your default Web editor (Word, for example).
- If you have several Web editors available—such as FrontPage, Word, and Notepad—click the arrow to the right of the **Edit** button on the browser window to choose which one you want to use.

When you use hyperlinks to move back and forth between Web pages and Office documents, the results might surprise you at first, because the toolbars and menus you see will occasionally include both those from Internet Explorer and those from the

Office program. For example, on a corporate intranet, a Web page may contain hyperlinks to Word documents stored on the same server. Figure 4.7 shows what a Word document file looks like when you click a hyperlink to open it in a Web browser.

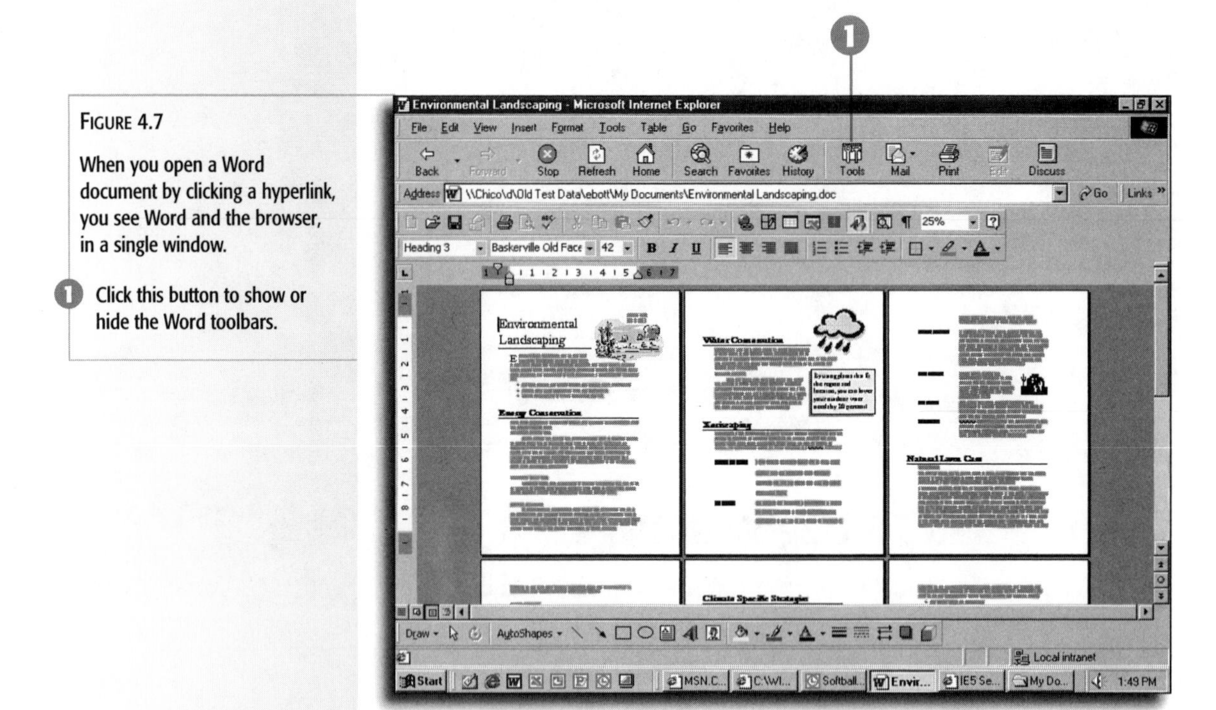

FIGURE 4.7

When you open a Word document by clicking a hyperlink, you see Word and the browser, in a single window.

1. Click this button to show or hide the Word toolbars.

You can't always save your work

You can click the **Edit** button to open any Web page in Word or another Web-editing program, but that doesn't mean you can save the results to the original location. If you visit a restricted page on your corporate intranet—your company benefits page, for example—then click the **Edit** button, you can change the page all you want; but because you don't have permission to save files, you can't replace that page. When this happens to you, save your work to your local hard disk instead.

Scroll through the document using the same techniques you use in Word if all you want to do is read the document. You can also edit the document in this window. Use the pull-down menus to access Word commands; click the **Tools** button on the browser window to show or hide Word's toolbars.

Working with Hyperlinks

When you're creating a Web page, you'll almost certainly want to create *hyperlinks* to other locations. In fact, Office lets you use hyperlinks in any kind of document, even if you don't save it in Web page format. Hyperlinks in Office documents have special text formatting, including underlining, just like those in Web pages; they also work much the same way. When you add a hyperlink, you specify that clicking that link will let the user jump straight to one of the following destinations:

- To another Web page—This is possible no matter whether the page is stored on a hard disk, on your company intranet, or on the World Wide Web.
- To another Office file—a Word document or Excel workbook, for example. If your company keeps its benefits manual on the intranet in Word format, the Web designer can add a link to that document right on the site's home page.
- To a location within the same Office document—A table of contents on the first page of a Word document or the first sheet of an Excel workbook might contain hyperlinks that let the reader jump to other pages or sheets in the same file.
- To an email address—On your company's benefits page, the insurance coordinator might include a link with his or her email address; when you click an email hyperlink, your default email program (usually Outlook) opens a blank message form with the address already filled in.

Every Office hyperlink has three parts:

- The "hot" part of the page, such as a graphic or a word in text.
- The link information, such as a Web page location, a filename, or an email address.
- ScreenTip text that pops up when the user lets the mouse pointer rest over the hyperlink.

To add a hyperlink in Word, Excel, or PowerPoint, follow this procedure (Publisher uses a simpler version of this dialog box, which has fewer options, and Outlook forces you to type in the hyperlink manually).

Selecting first is the easiest way

You must make a selection before you can create a hyperlink in PowerPoint; in Word and Excel, this step is optional. If you don't select any text in Word, or if you select a blank cell in Excel, the program creates a new hyperlink using the text you enter in the **Text to display** box.

Adding a Hyperlink to an Office Document or Web Page

1. Select the text or graphic that you want to use as the "hot" part of your document.
2. Click the **Insert Hyperlink** button on the Standard toolbar (you can also press Ctrl+K or choose **Hyperlink** from the **Insert** menu). In all three programs, you see the dialog box shown in Figure 4.8.

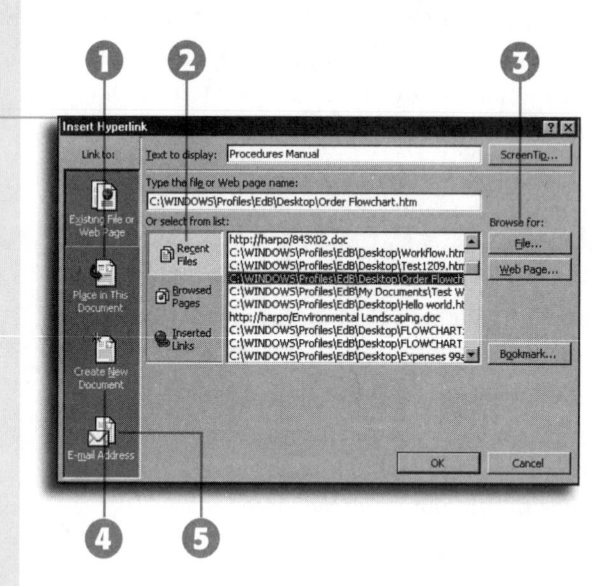

FIGURE 4.8

To create or edit hyperlinks in Word, Excel, or PowerPoint, don't type a name here; point and click instead.

1. Click here to choose from named ranges in Excel, slide titles in PowerPoint, or bookmarks and headings in Word.
2. Click one of these icons to select from a list of files, pages, or links you've used recently.
3. Click either of these buttons to open an Explorer window and browse for files or Web pages. Select the file icon or load the Web page, then return to this dialog box.
4. Click here to create a link that launches a new document using a template you select.
5. Click here to enter an email address and subject line to use as a hyperlink.

3. If you selected text before opening this dialog box, the text appears in the **Text to display** box; if you chose an object (such as a picture or a range of Excel data), this box is grayed out. If necessary, add or edit text here.
4. Click in the **Type the file or Web page name** box. Don't be fooled by this wording: You don't have to type a name here; in fact, it's much easier to point and click, using the techniques described in Figure 4.8.
5. Click the **ScreenTip** button to add custom text that appears over the hyperlink, such as "Click here to send email to your insurance coordinator."

To edit a hyperlink after you create it, point to the underlined text or the "hot" object and right-click, then choose **Hyperlink** from the shortcut menu. The choices you see here let you select the hyperlink, copy it, or remove the hyperlink completely (while leaving the text or graphic to which it was attached). Choose **Edit Hyperlink** from this menu, and you reopen the same dialog box used to create hyperlinks, so you can change any part of the link, or remove it completely.

Working with hyperlinks in a document can be frustrating, because you can't select text using the same techniques you normally use. As soon as you click a hyperlink in Word or Excel (or in PowerPoint when running a slide show) you jump to the location specified in the hyperlink. To select part or all of the text that describes a hyperlink in Word, click to position the insertion point on either side of the link, then hold down the Shift key and use the arrow keys to select the link text. In Excel, click in a cell on either side of the one that contains the link, then use the arrow keys to select the cell containing the link and click in the Formula bar to edit the text.

Stop Word's automatic hyperlinks

When you enter anything in a Word document that looks like a hyperlink, such as a Web address, Word instantly turns it into a hyperlink using the AutoFormat As You Type feature. If you're producing a document strictly for printed output and you don't want Word to add these hyperlinks, turn off this capability. Pull down the **Tools** menu, choose **AutoCorrect**, and click the **AutoFormat As You Type** tab. In the **Replace as you type** section, clear the check mark from the **Internet and network paths with hyperlinks** check box.

SEE ALSO

➤ *For more details on how to select and edit the contents of cells in a worksheet, see page 338*

Using Interactive Office Components in Web Pages

When you publish data from an Excel workbook to a Web page, you have an extra choice not available in any other program. If you click the **Publish** button, then check the **Add interactivity with** box, you can turn the page from a static display of data into one that other Office users can work with directly in the browser window.

When you check the **Add interactivity with** box, Excel creates a page that includes a *Web component*. Depending on the type of data you select, you can allow the viewer to manipulate the data in a spreadsheet component, a PivotTable component, or a chart component, just as they would if they were running Excel itself.

Web components are strictly for IE4 and IE5

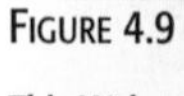

If you expect that some persons will use Internet Explorer 3.x or any version of Netscape Navigator to open a Web page you create in Excel, do not use Web components to add interactivity. Only Internet Explorer 4.01 or later will correctly display the pages you create using these components.

They can enter and edit data, move or copy cells, change formulas, and adjust column widths, for example, and then see the impact of those changes in spreadsheets, charts, or PivotTables.

Figure 4.9 shows the results when I selected a range of data on an Excel worksheet used to calculate mortgage payments. If I were in the business of selling mortgages, I might allow my customers to access this site, then enter information about their budget and finances to see how much house they can afford.

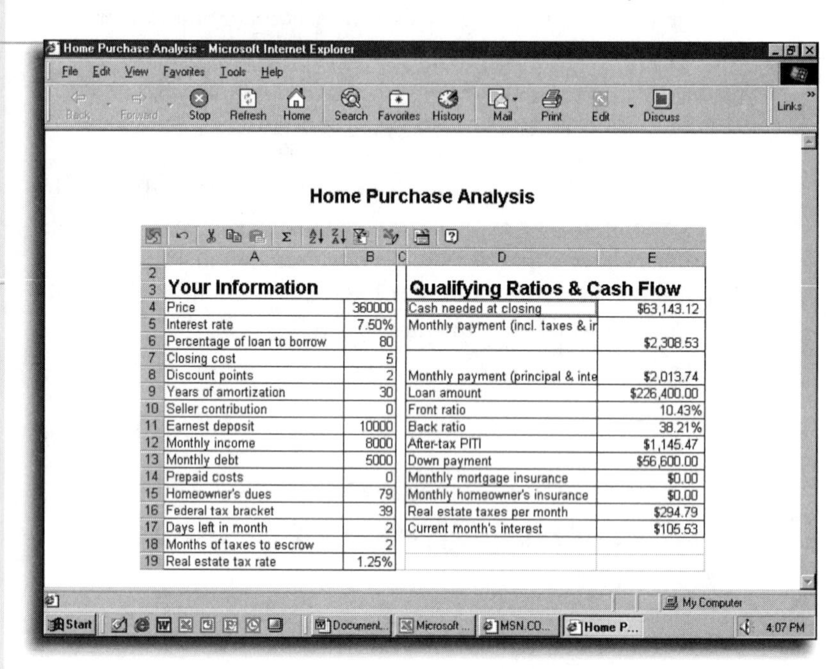

FIGURE 4.9

This Web page includes a spreadsheet component that lets another Office user interact with the data. Similar components are available for charts and PivotTable reports.

When you encounter a page that contains a Web component, you can simply enter data. Use the buttons to perform common actions like sorting data. To change the properties of the data range—for example, to change the font formatting so that the data looks better in your browser window, select one or more cells, then right-click and choose **Property Toolbox**. This technique gives you access to many settings, using the dialog box shown in Figure 4.10.

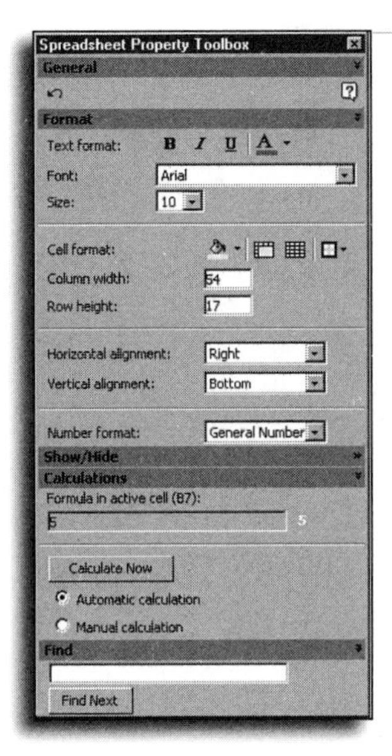

FIGURE 4.10
Want to change the look of data in a Web page that contains Web components? Right-click and use this dialog box.

SEE ALSO

➤ *For more details on how to create PivotTable reports, see page 435*

➤ *To read about how to create and edit Excel charts, see page 444*

Getting Help

Get answers from the Office Assistant

Change the way the Office Assistant works

Point and click for instant pop-up Help

Find Help on the Internet

Let wizards do the work for you

Getting Answers from the Office Assistant

Office 2000 includes a comprehensive Help system designed to deliver everything from quick definitions to tutorials to step-by-step instructions for working through complicated procedures. Whatever your problem, wherever you're stuck or baffled, Help is always available. In some cases, Help is practically psychic, delivering the exact answers you need; in other cases, you find it frustratingly incomplete or just plain wrong.

Although you can use a variety of Help tools, the primary interface for your questions is an animated character called the Office Assistant.

If you've recently switched from Office 95 to Office 2000, you may be familiar with the Answer Wizard, which allows you to pull down the **Help** menu, type a question using your own words (like "How do I create a table"), and get immediate answers. The Office Assistant, which was introduced in Office 97, takes the same idea and adds a distinct personality. By default, this little animated character takes up a modest amount of space in the lower-right corner of your screen. If it's not visible, you can make it appear by clicking the **Office Assistant** button on the Standard toolbar of any Office application. The default character is Clippit, an animated paperclip.

Stupid Assistant tricks

Want to see the full range of tricks each Assistant can perform? Switch to a new character; then right-click on the Office Assistant and choose **Animate!** from the shortcut menu. The character launches into one of its animated routines, selected at random. Keep clicking this menu choice, and eventually you see every trick in that character's repertoire.

Microsoft's interface designers built a surprising number of animated behaviors into the Office Assistant. For example, watch how Clippit's eyes shift to follow the mouse pointer or the insertion point as you type or move around in a dialog box. When you save a document, send an email message, or use a wizard, the paper clip becomes even more animated—eyes bugging out, eyebrows flying every which way, body twisting into impossible shapes, all accompanied by sound effects. This concept sounds silly, but the idea is to get your attention, and it succeeds.

To ask for help, click the Office Assistant, and then click in the box labeled **What would you like to do?** Type a question or a few keywords that describe your problem, and then click the **Search** button or press Enter. Your results appear immediately, as in the example in Figure 5.1.

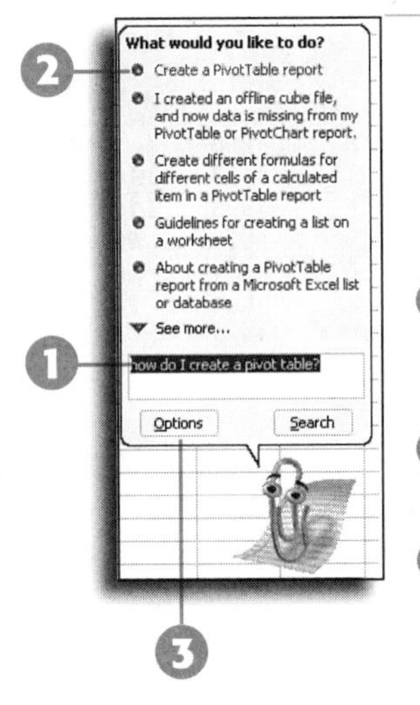

FIGURE 5.1

Enter a question or phrase, and the Office Assistant produces a list of suggested help topics. Each topic is a hyperlink; click to read its full details.

1. Type a phrase or question here, then click the **Search** button or press Enter.
2. Click here to read the selected topic.
3. Click here to adjust the Assistant's behavior or choose a new character.

When you enter a question, the Office Assistant pops up a list of topics that it thinks are related to what you're trying to do. In fact, if you perform a sequence of actions, such as centering and bold-facing a headline in a Word document, and then click the Office Assistant, you see a list of related topics before you even ask a question. When you use keywords the Assistant understands, it generally does a good job of suggesting topics.

Each topic in the Office Assistant's list is a hyperlink. Click the topic to open a window containing the full text of that topic. When you do, you notice that the program window changes size, and the Help window attaches itself to the side of the screen, as in Figure 5.2. When you close the Help window, your program window automatically returns to its previous size and position.

Just start typing

You don't need to erase the text inside the box; because it's already highlighted, it disappears as soon as you begin typing. You can type anything in the box: a word, a phrase, or a whole sentence. If you don't get the results you hoped for, try rephrasing your question.

Watch your spelling!

Punctuation and capitalization don't count. Spelling, on the other hand, does count. If you misspell a word, the Assistant simply responds `I don't know what you mean. Please rephrase your question`. Fix the typo and try again.

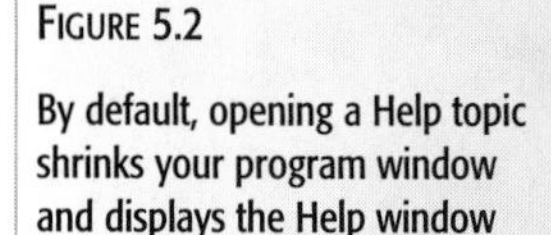

FIGURE 5.2

By default, opening a Help topic shrinks your program window and displays the Help window alongside.

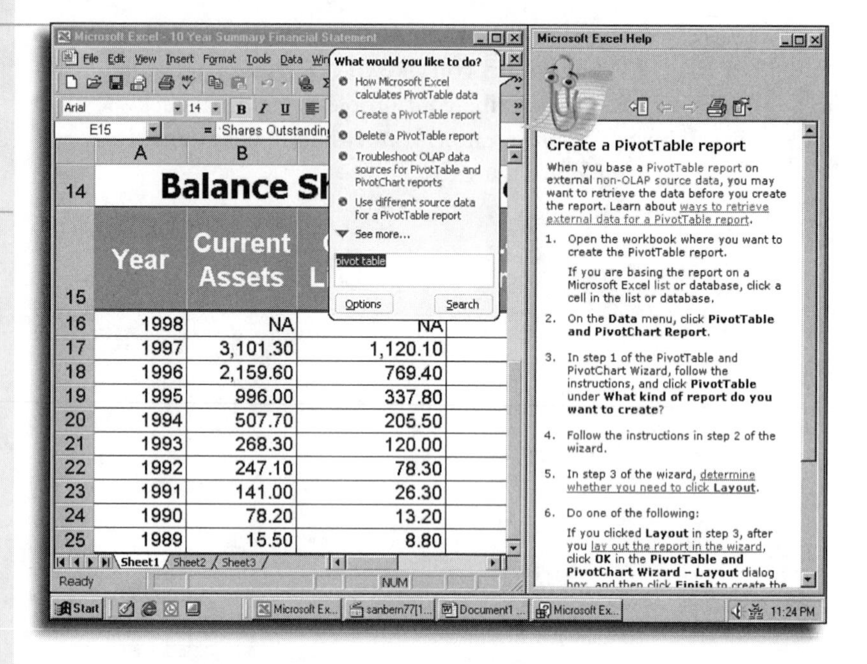

In theory, rearranging your program window in this way lets you continue working with your document while keeping the instructions in the Help window visible at all times. In practice, I find this constant rearranging of windows downright annoying, especially on a machine with a slow CPU or limited memory. If you'd like the Help window to pop up in a constant position over your program window, follow these steps:

Repositioning the Help Window

1. Display any Help topic. Note that the Help window appears docked to the side of the screen, and the program window changes size to make room for it.
2. Click the title bar of the Help window and drag it into the center of the screen.
3. Resize the Help window to the dimensions you prefer, and move it to the position you prefer. Be careful not to drag the Help window too close to the side of the screen, or you redock it!
4. Click the **Close** (X) button in the top-right corner of the Help window. Your program window returns to its previous size and shape.

The next time you open a Help topic, it appears in the center of the screen, in a window matching the size and position of the one you saved.

The Office Assistant sticks around

In Office 97, the Office Assistant vanished whenever you opened a Help topic. In Office 2000, the Assistant and its list of topics remain visible. If the topic you read first doesn't contain the answers you were looking for, click another one, and keep clicking until you turn up the right topic.

Reading a Help Topic

Each Office Help topic typically includes some or all of the following elements: explanatory text, step-by-step instructions, graphics, and buttons or hyperlinks that lead to additional information. Some key topics include full-blown graphical displays, complete with hyperlinks that lead to additional detailed explanations. When I can't remember the names of each part of a Word table, for example, I use the Help screen shown in Figure 5.3 to get a quick refresher course on the topic.

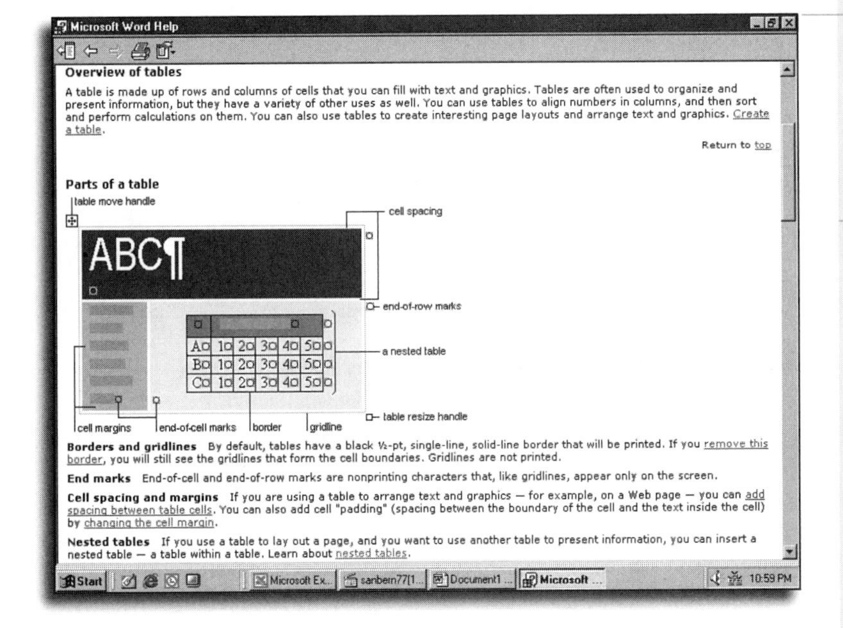

FIGURE 5.3

This Help screen includes a well-rounded introduction to the topic of Word tables. Hyperlinks allow you to jump to related topics for more information.

A word or phrase highlighted in blue indicates a hyperlink; click the link to display a definition of the term in a pop-up window. Underlined hyperlinks jump to related Help topics. You occasionally see hyperlinks attached to pictures of toolbar buttons as well.

Jump buttons (small buttons marked with an arrow or other symbol) let you click to quickly open a related Help screen or a Windows dialog box.

Figure 5.4 includes examples of both types of interactive elements: a hyperlink that explains the potentially confusing term *end-of-cell mark*, and a jump button labeled **Show me**, which takes you directly to the dialog box it describes.

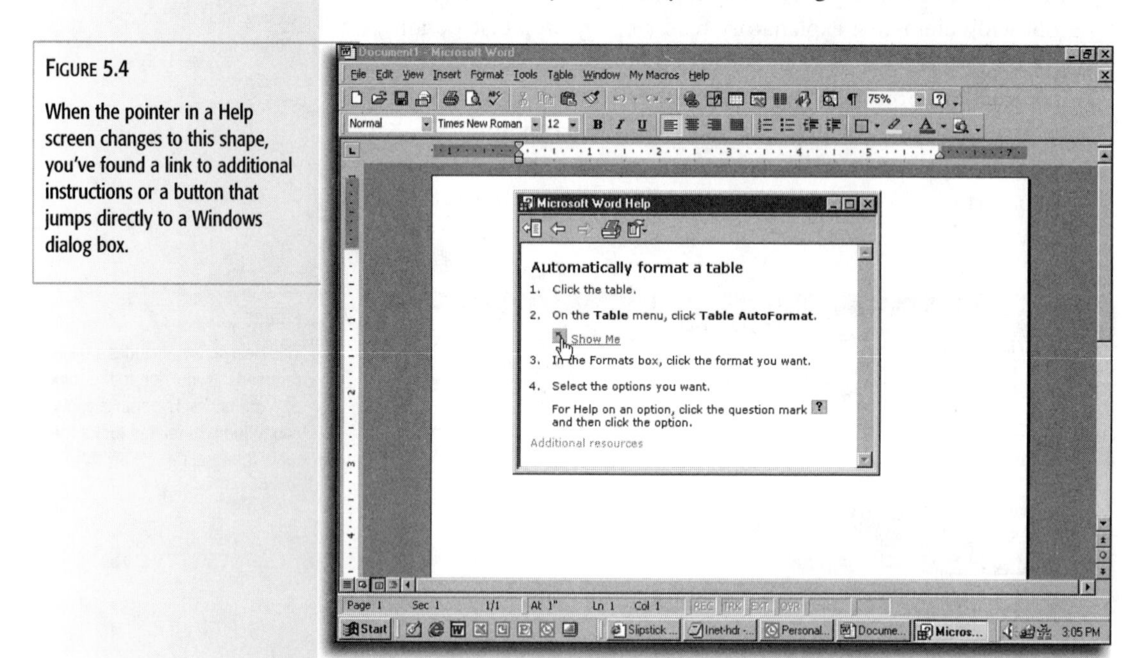

FIGURE 5.4

When the pointer in a Help screen changes to this shape, you've found a link to additional instructions or a button that jumps directly to a Windows dialog box.

Using the Assistant for Warnings and Tips

When you leave the Office Assistant onscreen while you work, it intercepts warning messages that Windows would normally display in standard dialog boxes. If you try to save a file using a name that already exists, for example, the Office Assistant displays a confirmation dialog box. As the example in Figure 5.5 shows, these warning messages are much more vivid than their standard Windows equivalents.

FIGURE 5.5

If the Office Assistant is visible, it takes over the display of warning messages like this one.

When you allow the Office Assistant to watch you work, it occasionally offers unsolicited help. If you've begun a particularly difficult task, for example, such as creating a PivotTable in Excel, the Assistant offers to display relevant Help screens. The Assistant is also programmed to recognize when you're struggling with a menu or feature, or when you're tackling a task that can be accomplished in an easier or quicker way. In either case, you see a bright yellow light bulb just above the Office Assistant.

Click the light bulb, and the tip box pops open; when the Office Assistant is in its usual spot in the lower-right corner of the screen, this window pops out to the left. Some tips (like the one shown in Figure 5.6) are particularly useful because they include a button that lets you actually perform the technique the tip suggests. The Office Assistant keeps track of the tips you've seen already, so you shouldn't have to look at the same tip more than once.

Yes, the Assistant moves

As you work, the Assistant moves out of the way automatically to avoid interfering with your work. In some cases, it disappears from the screen (temporarily) when you perform a task that requires the full screen.

FIGURE 5.6

Some tips include buttons that open dialog boxes or perform actions directly.

Changing the Way the Assistant Works

Some people find the Office Assistant irresistible; others can't stand the cartoon characters' antics. I find Clippit amusing most of the time, but when he starts to bug me, I simply right-click and choose **Hide** from its shortcut menu. You can modify the Assistant's behavior in a variety of ways. I routinely turn off sounds, for example, and disable its capability to display warning messages. If you don't like Clippit, you can choose from a gallery of other characters. Finally, if you really despise the idea of animated help, you can disable the Office Assistant completely.

Changing Office Assistant Options

To adjust the Assistant's options, click the Office Assistant window and then click the **Options** button. Click the **Options** tab, if necessary, to display the dialog box shown in Figure 5.7.

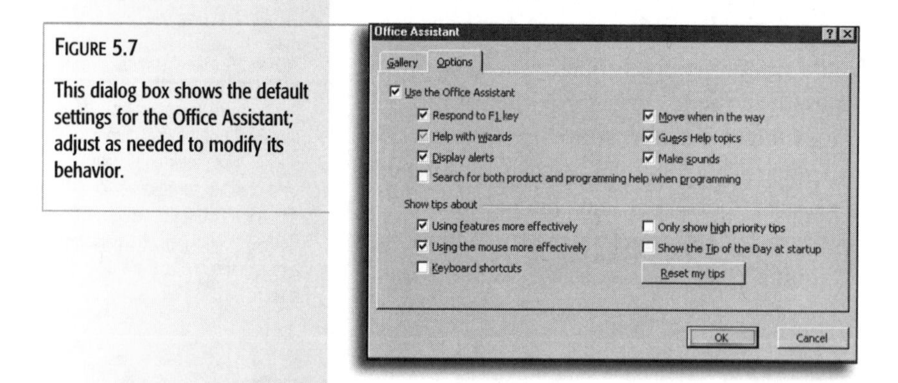

FIGURE 5.7

This dialog box shows the default settings for the Office Assistant; adjust as needed to modify its behavior.

Table 5.1 describes the effect of each option for the Office Assistant.

TABLE 5.1 Office Assistant Options

Option	Default Setting	Effect
	Assistant capabilities	
Use the Office Assistant	On	Clear this check box to hide the Office Assistant and use only standard Windows Help.
Respond to F1 key	On	Clear this check box to display standard Windows Help instead of the Office Assistant when you press F1.
Help with wizards	On	When this box is checked, the Assistant automatically offers to help with most wizards.
Display alerts	On	By default, the Assistant takes over display of warning messages and confirmation dialog boxes; clear the check box to use standard Windows messages instead.
Move when in the way	On	Check this box, and the Assistant moves out of the way when you type or click.
Guess Help topics	On	When you clear this check box, the Assistant suggests Help topics only in response to questions you enter.
Make sounds	On	Clear this check box to shut down the Assistant's sound effects.
Search for both product and programming help when programming	Off	Check this box if you want the Assistant to help with Visual Basic for Applications.
	Show tips about	
Using features more effectively	On	Clear this check box to reduce the number of tips the Assistant offers.

continues...

TABLE 5.1 **Continued**

Option	Default Setting	Effect
	Show tips about	
Using the mouse more effectively	On	Clear this check box to suppress mouse-related tips.
Keyboard shortcuts	Off	When this box is checked, the Assistant suggests keyboard equivalents to common mouse actions.
	Other tip options	
Only show high priority tips	Off	Check this box to minimize the number of tips the Assistant suggests.
Show the Tip of the Day at startup	Off	Check this box to display a new tip every time you start an Office program.
Reset my tips	N/A	Normally, the Assistant displays each tip only once; click this button to start fresh and let the Assistant show you tips you've already viewed.

Picking a Different Assistant

Additional Assistants are available

Microsoft made several new Assistant characters available on its Web site for Office 97 users. Those characters won't work with Office 2000, but it's likely that Microsoft will eventually produce new Assistant characters that are compatible. To search for new characters, open any Office program, choose **Help**, and click **Office on the Web** to jump to Microsoft's Web page. Use the Search feature to look for new Office Assistant characters.

Don't like the paper clip? Then choose another Assistant. The gallery of Office Assistants includes nine characters in all, each with its own distinct personality. You can find a clone of Albert Einstein, for example, or a clanking robot named F1. Dog lovers can choose the tail-thumping Rocky, while cat enthusiasts can select the considerably more animated Links.

Although the characters may look frivolous, Microsoft spent a fortune in "social interface" research to produce a broad cross-section of characters so that most users will find at least one that is appealing.

Changing the Office Assistant Character

1. Right-click the Assistant window, and click **Choose Assistant** from the shortcut menu. You see the dialog box shown in Figure 5.8.

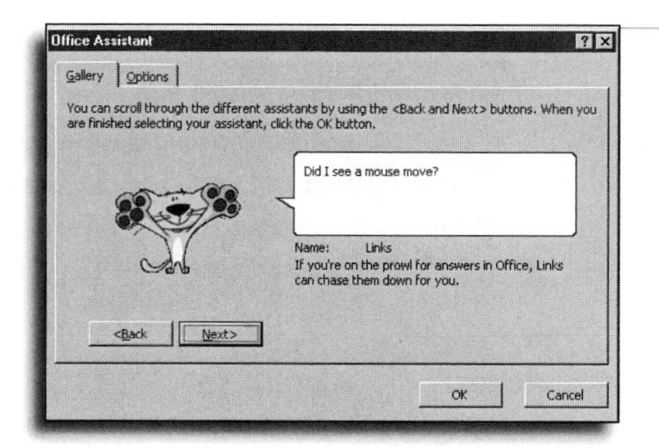

FIGURE 5.8
Take your choice of nine Assistants from this dialog box. Each one introduces itself and offers a quick animation sample.

2. Use the **Back** and **Next** buttons to run through all the characters.
3. When the character you want to use appears on the **Gallery** tab, click **OK.** (You may have to insert the Office CD-ROM to install the appropriate files.)

You can change Office Assistants anytime, without affecting the documents you're working with or changing the type of help you get from Office. When you change the Office Assistant, your change applies to all Office programs.

Where are the other Assistants?

The Typical Office setup includes only the Clippit character. To install one Assistant at a time, have the Office 2000 CD handy when you choose a new character. To install all Assistant characters at one time, you need to rerun the Office 2000 Setup program. You can find the Office Assistant characters under the **Office Tools** option.

Making the Office Assistant Disappear

If you would prefer to work without the Office Assistant, that's your privilege. To remove the Assistant temporarily, just close it by right-clicking the Assistant character and choosing **Hide** from the shortcut menu. If the Assistant is hidden when you close an Office program, it won't appear when you start that program the next time. In fact, if you hide the Office Assistant several times without using it to search for help, it will ask you if you want to stop using it.

To stop using the Office Assistant completely and rely on the standard Windows Help interface, right-click the Office Assistant and choose **Options**. Click the **Options** tab, clear the check box labeled **Use the Office Assistant**, and click **OK**.

Removing the Office Assistant permanently is possible, although it takes some extra effort. Make sure you have the Office CD-ROM handy before you attempt this procedure.

Restoring the Office Assistant

To re-enable the Office Assistant, run the Office 2000 Setup program again and change the status of one or more Office Assistant characters to **Run from My Computer**.

Permanently Removing the Office Assistant

1. Close all Office programs.
2. Click the **Start** button and choose **Settings**, then click **Control Panel** and run the **Add/Remove Programs** option.
3. Click the Install/Uninstall tab and select **Microsoft Office 2000**, and then click the **Add/Remove** button.
4. In the Microsoft Office 2000 Setup dialog box, click **Add or Remove Features**.
5. Click the plus sign to the left of the **Office Tools** entry to expand that list, and then click the icon to the left of the **Office Assistant** entry and choose **Not Available**.
6. Click **Update Now** to remove all installed Office Assistant characters.

Getting Help Without Using the Office Assistant

In Office 2000 applications, you can always use the standard Windows Help system without involving the Office Assistant. Both user interfaces lead to the exact same set of explanations, which are contained in Windows Help topics.

The Windows Help engine organizes information in book style, using a two-paned dialog box. The navigation pane at left contains three tabs—**Contents**, **Answer Wizard**, and **Index**—while the contents pane at the right displays the currently selected topic. To make the navigation pane visible, click the **Show** button at the left side of the toolbar window while reading any Help topic. When these three tabs are visible, the left button changes shape and function—click it to **Hide** the Help tabs and view only the current topic.

Searching the Table of Contents

When you want to explore a full set of features systematically for an Office application, use the **Contents** tab. This dialog box organizes all the Help topics for that program into a hierarchy of topics, arranged in alphabetical order. The Help file's authors determine the organization of the Contents dialog box; if they've done a good job, scanning the list of top-level topics should give you a broad overview of all the program's major features.

When you first open the **Contents** pane, you see only the top-level topics, with a closed-book icon to the left of each one. To learn about a feature or capability, double-click a topic; as the example in Figure 5.9 shows, each category includes individual topics that provide more detailed information. Click each topic to display it in the pane to the right.

Drag to resize the panes

Click the dividing line between the **Contents** tab and the topic window to adjust the size of each pane. Use scrollbars along the bottom and right side of the **Contents** pane to read items that won't fit in the window.

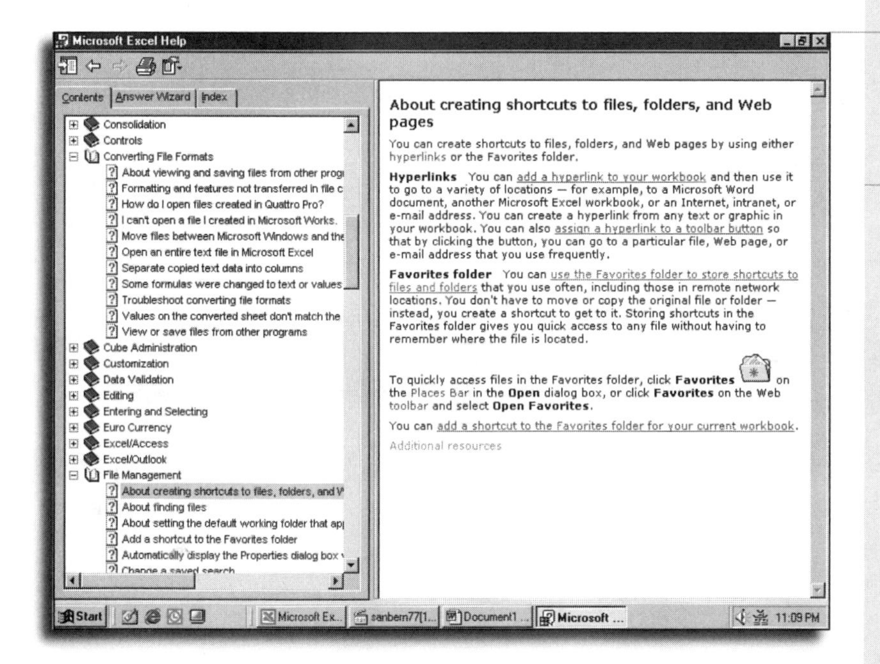

FIGURE 5.9

Use the **Contents** tab to explore the features of an Office program in detail.

Using the Index of Individual Help Topics

When you open the standard Windows Help interface and click the **Index** tab, you get a completely different view of the topics in that program's Help file. This list, analogous to the index in the back of a book like this one, is organized in alphabetical order using keywords linked to the title and text of each topic. As long as the Help file's indexer chose to include the keyword you're looking for, you should be able to find a specific section or page and jump straight to it.

To find one or more Help topics, click on the **Index** tab. You see a display like the one in Figure 5.10.

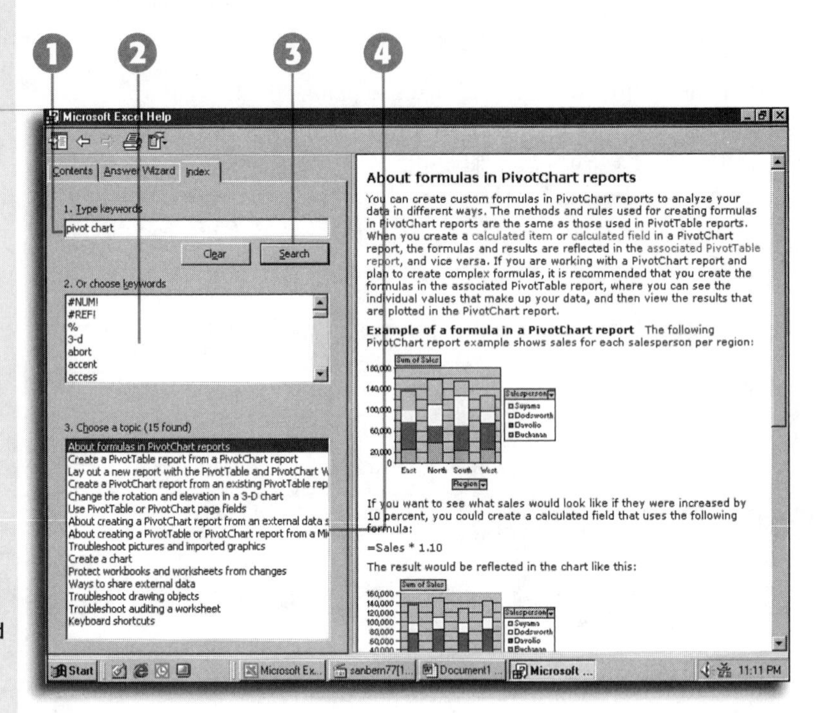

FIGURE 5.10

The Help index works like the index in the back of this book. Choose one or more keywords from the alphabetical list to display topics containing those words.

1. Enter the first few letters of the keyword you're searching for to ump to that entry in the list of topics...
2. ...or scroll through the list until you find the right entry.
3. After you've selected an entry, click this button to display the help topic. Use a second or third keyword to narrow your search even further.
4. Click each entry in the results list to read the topics in the pane to the right.

If you enter multiple keywords in the box at the top of the **Index** pane, then click **Search**, Help displays only topics that contain all the words you entered.

The Answer Wizard is more flexible

Using the Answer Wizard offers one significant advantage over the Office Assistant. While the Office Assistant is limited to nine topics, the Answer Wizard can display up to 20 topics. If you're having trouble finding the right topic, the Answer Wizard will give you a better shot at finding the answer you're looking for.

Using the Answer Wizard

The **Answer Wizard** tab in the middle of the navigation pane duplicates the function of the Office Assistant, without the personality. Just as you can with the Office Assistant, enter a question or a set of keywords in the box labeled **What would you like to do?** And then click **Search**. The search results appear in the box labeled **Select topic to display**. Click any topic in this list to view it in the contents pane to the right.

Printing Help Screens for Quick Reference

For most situations, your best bet is to use online help. It's quick, it stays on the screen while you work, and you can easily follow links to other topics or definitions within the help screen.

Sometimes, though, printing out a help screen is helpful; this technique is useful when you want to follow a complex series of steps without continually switching between the program window and the Help topic. Click the **Print** button at the top of the Help window to display the Print dialog box. If you've selected a heading in the Contents pane, you'll see the Print Topics dialog box first; click **Print the selected topic** to print only the topic that's visible in the contents pane, or click **Print the selected heading and all subtopics** to send all topics in that heading to the printer.

Better yet, make your own Help file

Instead of building up a huge stack of printouts of useful Help topics, use the Windows Clipboard to copy information from Help topics and paste it into a Word document. Create a shortcut to your custom Help document and place it on the Windows desktop, where you can consult it whenever you need a helping hand.

Getting Help with the Office Interface

Sometimes you don't need detailed explanations or step-by-step instructions. All you really need is quick information about what a button, check box, or menu choice does. Office includes two helpful features that offer this information on demand.

ScreenTips

When you're not certain what a toolbar button does, move the mouse pointer over the button and let it rest for a second or so. Eventually, a tiny label called a ScreenTip pops up. After the first ScreenTip is visible, you can run the mouse pointer rapidly across the toolbar to identify each button.

ScreenTips aren't just for buttons, though; they're particularly welcome when they pop up over confusing interface controls. For example, I have trouble remembering the exact function of each slider on Word's ruler. Which one handles hanging indents, and which one is just for the first line? With Office 2000, I don't need to guess because each element on the ruler gets its own ScreenTip, as you can see in Figure 5.11. Likewise, you can use ScreenTips in Word or PowerPoint to identify the tiny **View** buttons at the lower-left edge of the document or presentation window.

ScreenTip = ToolTip (and more)

In Office 95, Microsoft referred to the pop-up labels over toolbar buttons as *ToolTips*. Although you may still see a few references to this old name in Office 2000's online help, the new name, *ScreenTips*, accurately reflects the wider use of these helpful labels.

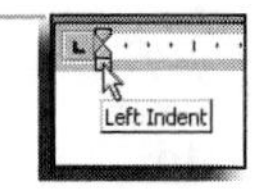

FIGURE 5.11

ScreenTips are available throughout Office. Let the mouse pointer sit over Word's ruler, for example, to see what each sliding control does.

What's This?

Right-clicking in Windows generally produces a shortcut menu, and sometimes it pops up a menu with a single choice: **What's this?** (You'll find this choice most often when you right-click over a command button or option in a dialog box.) Click the **What's this?** label for a brief description of the object underneath.

You can display the same Help text when you click the question mark icon in the title bar of some dialog boxes (as in the example shown in Figure 5.12). When you click this button, the pointer changes shape, adding a question mark alongside the regular arrow. Click any part of the dialog box to see a pop-up message that describes what that button or option does.

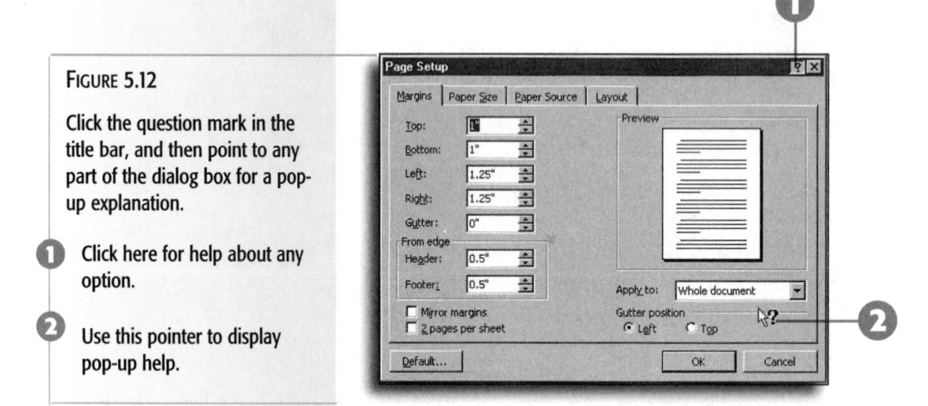

FIGURE 5.12

Click the question mark in the title bar, and then point to any part of the dialog box for a pop-up explanation.

1. Click here for help about any option.
2. Use this pointer to display pop-up help.

"What's This?" help is available throughout Office. Pull down the **Help** menu for any Office program, and you find a **What's This?** menu choice. (Or press Shift+F1, the keyboard shortcut for this command.) When the pointer turns to the question-mark-with-arrow combination, point to any part of the screen (buttons on the toolbar, text in a document, cells in a worksheet, and so on). If the program's designers included a description of the interface element you're pointing to, it will pop up.

This Help feature typically offers a more detailed explanation than you get with a ScreenTip, but you don't have to deal with the Office Assistant or wade through a complicated Help screen to access it. If you press Shift+F1 and point to Word's ruler, for example, you see the text box shown in Figure 5.13.

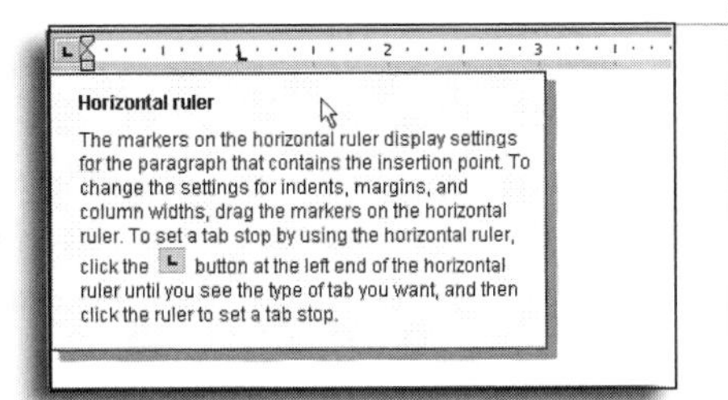

FIGURE 5.13
When you use **What's This?** help and point to a portion of the screen, you see an instant explanation like this one.

Special Help for WordPerfect and 1-2-3 Users

If you're a recent convert to Office from the MS-DOS versions of WordPerfect and Lotus 1-2-3, your fingers probably jump to certain keystroke combinations without even consulting your brain first. Using those old familiar keystrokes can be frustrating when you first begin using Word and Excel, because function keys and menus work in completely different ways. To ease the transition, pull down the **Help** menu in Word or Excel, and select **WordPerfect Help** or **Lotus 1-2-3 Help**.

Both Help screens tell you which menus to select or which keys to press to achieve what you're trying to do. (See Figure 5.14 for an example of Help for WordPerfect users.)

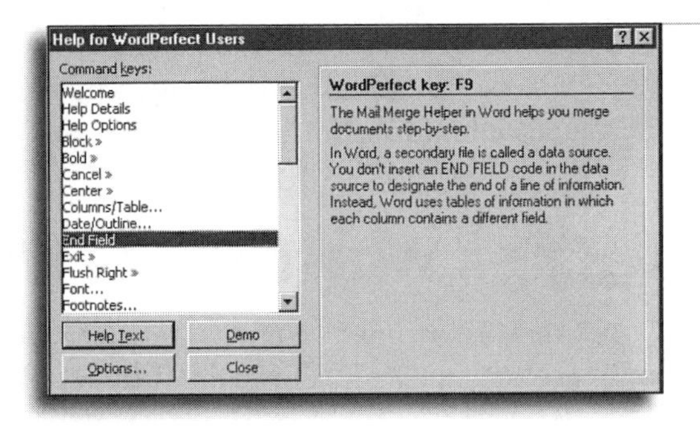

FIGURE 5.14
Special Help options ease your transition to Office from WordPerfect or 1-2-3. Use the **Demo** buttons to see how Word and Excel perform the selected task.

WordPerfect users get an extra helper, which lets them use some WordPerfect keystrokes in Word.

Even more help for WordPerfect users

Longtime WordPerfect users who switch to Word sometimes feel lost when they can't find an easy way to reveal formatting codes. To see most formatting information at a glance, pull down the **Help** menu and then click **What's This?** Now point to any part of the document, and you see paragraph and font formatting information in a pop-up window. To turn off the **What's This?** pointer, click any toolbar button or press Esc.

Enabling Extra Help for WordPerfect Users

1. Choose **Help** and then choose **WordPerfect Help**.
2. Click the **Options** button.
3. Select **Navigation keys for WordPerfect users** from the dialog box. This option changes the function of the Home, End, Page Up, Page Down, and arrow keys. When you enable this option, you can press Home and then the Up arrow to go to the top of the document, just as you would in WordPerfect.

Finding Help on the Internet

The Help files in Office 2000 were created around the same time as the software itself, and that can cause problems. When Microsoft discovers bugs in the original software, those defects are not documented in the original Help files, and if the program designers made last minute changes to menus or dialog boxes, the Help files may not reflect those changes. The Office Assistant cannot know about any patches to the original software, nor can it point you to information about problems and solutions discovered as a result of users' calls to Microsoft's technical support department.

If you've found an Office feature that doesn't work the way it should, the best place to turn for up-to-date support information is the World Wide Web. If you have access to the Internet, pull down the **Help** menu from any of the Office programs and choose **Office on the Web**. This shortcut takes you directly to Microsoft's Office Update page, where you'll find links to updated information about Office programs, features, and bugs.

Letting a Wizard Do the Work

Some of the most helpful features in Office aren't on the **Help** menu at all. Throughout this book, you'll find frequent descriptions of various wizards. Unlike help topics, which tell you how to accomplish a task, wizards actually do some or all of the work for you. Wizards typically include a series of step-by-step dialog boxes that walk you through a complex process. PowerPoint, for example, includes AutoContent Wizards that help you put together presentations for specific objectives, such as setting a meeting agenda.

Some wizards appear only when you specifically choose them from a menu, whereas others appear automatically in response to your actions. Figure 5.15 shows how the Office Assistant offers to let you use a wizard whenever it notices that you've started a letter (by typing `Dear Mr. Merrill`, in this example).

FIGURE 5.15
When the Office Assistant notices you've begun writing a letter, it offers to start the Letter Wizard.

SEE ALSO

For more details on how to use the Letter Wizard effectively, see page 303

Most of the time, a wizard is just an option, and you can work without the wizard's help if you choose. But I generally recommend using these helpers when they're available. Using a wizard is typically as easy as filling in the blanks on a series of forms, and the results are guaranteed to be exactly what you want. Excel's Chart Wizard, for example, organizes every chart option into four dialog boxes. You can see the wizard for yourself in Figure 5.16.

Watch for wizards

Every Office program uses wizards to take some of the drudgery or confusion out of common tasks. I'll point out the most useful ones and explain how to use them in the appropriate chapters.

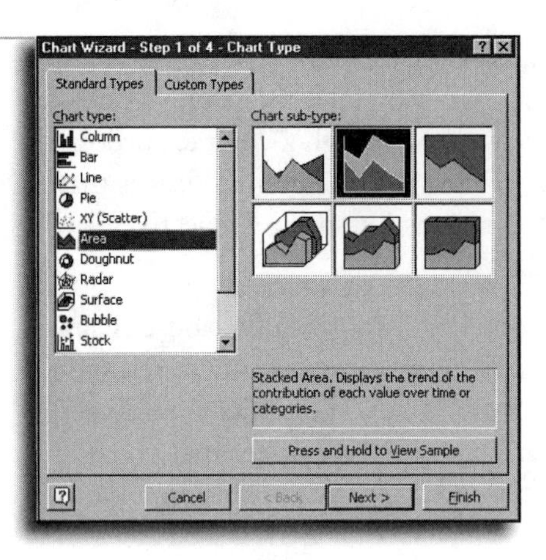

FIGURE 5.16

The four dialog boxes in Excel's Chart Wizard eliminate much of the drudgery and detail work from the process of creating a chart.

CHAPTER 6

Customizing Office

- Take control of Office menus and toolbars
- Make your own keyboard shortcuts in Word
- Scroll and zoom with the IntelliMouse
- Change the way you open and save files
- Turn down the volume on Office sound effects
- Work with the Office Shortcut Bar

Customizing Toolbars and Menus

You can't change Publisher's toolbars

As the newest member in the Office family, Publisher still has some growing up to do. One noteworthy difference between it and the other programs is that you can't customize its toolbars. You can hide or show the Standard and Formatting toolbars, but that's it.

Everyone knows a camel is a horse designed by committee. Well, some committee at Microsoft went to a lot of trouble to select which items go on each Office menu, and which buttons go on which toolbars. If you're like me, those designed-by-committee Office toolbars don't match the way you *really* work. In my case, the Standard and Formatting toolbars contain a handful of buttons I never use; for example, I can't remember the last time I clicked the Cut, Copy, and Paste buttons, because the keyboard shortcuts and right-click menus are so much easier. On the other hand, several commands I use regularly didn't earn a place on the default toolbars—like the Save All button, which I use whenever I work with three or four files at once, or the Find command, which I use everyday.

That same committee also designed Office 2000 so that menu items and toolbar buttons appear and disappear depending on how often you use them. If you like the less cluttered look of the personalized menus and you don't mind occasionally searching for a command that's temporarily hidden, leave these settings alone. If, like me, you prefer to work with the full menus, change this setting right now to preserve your sanity.

How to reset a toolbar

There *is* such a thing as too much customizing. If you've experimented with custom toolbars and menus and you're not happy with the results, start over. Click the arrow at the right of the toolbar, click **Add or Remove Buttons**, and then choose the **Reset Toolbar** option from the bottom of the list. Using this method restores the selected toolbar buttons and menus to their default arrangements.

I recommend that you spend a week or two keeping track of the commands you use regularly and those you never use. Then, when you're ready, change the toolbars to eliminate commands you never use and buttons that will make you more productive. You can give each Office program a complete makeover: Take buttons off any toolbar, add new ones, rearrange the buttons and commands, and even reposition each toolbar on the screen.

Figure 6.1 shows what Word looked like after I reworked the Standard and Formatting toolbars. I cleared away a handful of buttons from each toolbar (including Cut, Copy, and Paste) and added a few others (Save All and Find), and the whole process took only a few seconds. (Although I've focused on Word for the examples in this chapter, the process works exactly the same with other Office programs, except Publisher.)

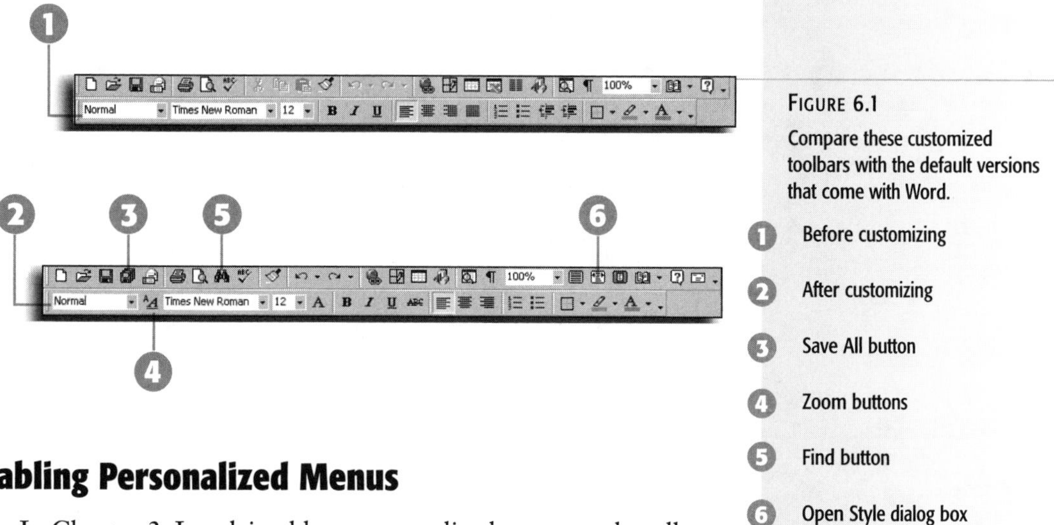

FIGURE 6.1
Compare these customized toolbars with the default versions that come with Word.

1. Before customizing
2. After customizing
3. Save All button
4. Zoom buttons
5. Find button
6. Open Style dialog box

Disabling Personalized Menus

In Chapter 2, I explained how personalized menus and toolbars work. If you find the constant "Now you see it, now you don't" shifting of menus and toolbars more confusing than helpful, you can disable this option. When you do so, the long versions of all menus appear automatically, just as in previous versions of Office. I also recommend that you stack the Standard and Formatting toolbars over each other, as in Office 97, rather than allowing them to share a single row.

Turning Off Personalized Menus

1. Pull down the **Tools** menu and choose **Customize**.
2. In the Customize dialog box, click the **Options** tab, and clear the check mark from the box labeled **Menus show recently used commands first**, as shown in Figure 6.2.
3. If you prefer to display the two default toolbars on separate rows, as in Office 97, clear the check mark from the box labeled **Standard and Formatting toolbars share one row**.
4. Set other toolbar options, if you want, and then click the **Close** button to save your changes.

Personalized menus work throughout Office

When you turn off personalized menus in one Office program, your change affects all other programs. If you make this change in Word, for example, you'll find that it changes your Excel and PowerPoint menus as well, without any extra work on your part. The option that lets you stack the Standard and Formatting toolbars over each other is different for each program, however.

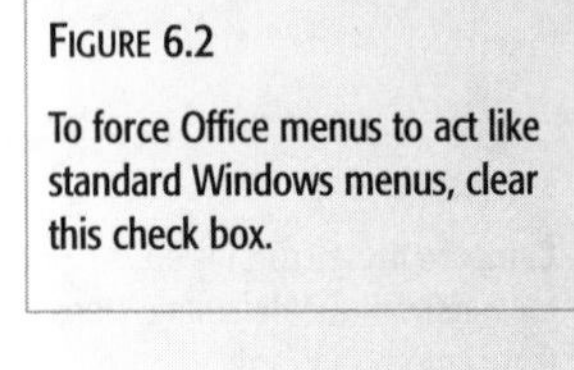

FIGURE 6.2

To force Office menus to act like standard Windows menus, clear this check box.

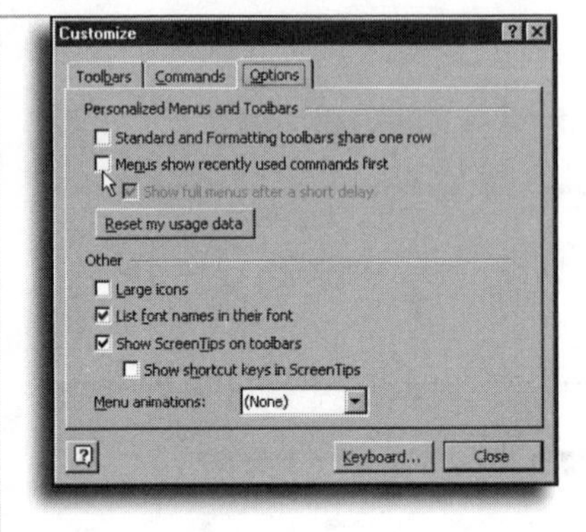

Reset your resolution

To adjust your screen resolution, click the **Start** button, choose **Settings**, open **Control Panel**, and open the **Display** option. You can find sliders for screen area and color palettes on the **Settings** tab. (The exact labels vary, depending on your operating system and video driver.)

Adding a Button to a Toolbar

The Standard and Formatting toolbars are designed to fill the width of the screen if you're running Windows at 640 × 480 *resolution*. If you position each toolbar on its own row and you've configured your system to use a higher resolution, as most people do, you have plenty of room to add more buttons to these basic toolbars. You can add any command button, menu item, or *macro* to any toolbar.

Every customizable toolbar contains an assortment of default buttons, some of which are hidden when you first start Office. You can add or remove any of these buttons by clicking entries in an easy-to-access list; the full contents of this list remain the same, regardless of whether buttons are visible or hidden. If the button or menu you want to add isn't in this list, use the Customize dialog box to choose from a list of every available command, sorted by categories.

Adding a Toolbar Button

1. Make sure the toolbar you want to customize is visible. Then click the drop-down arrow at the right of the toolbar and click **Add or Remove Buttons** to display a list like the one in Figure 6.3.
2. Check marks to the left of each entry in the list indicate whether the button is visible; if the button you want to add is not checked, click its entry in the list.

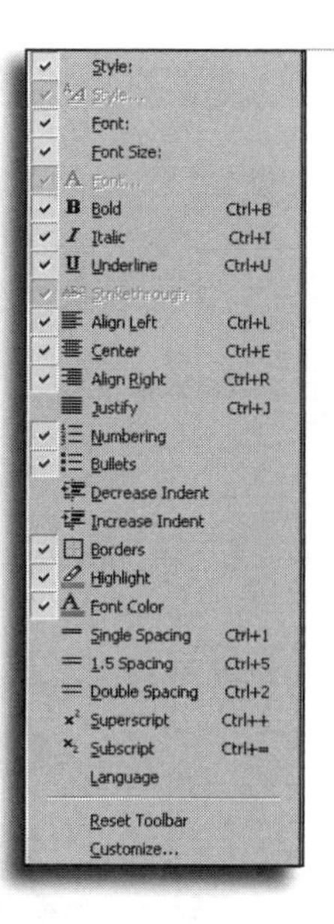

FIGURE 6.3

Check marks to the left of each entry indicate that a button on this toolbar is normally visible. Click to show or hide each button.

3. If the button you want to add is not on this list, choose **Customize** from the bottom of the menu. Then, in the Customize dialog box, click the **Commands** tab to display a list of categories and commands like the one shown in Figure 6.4.
4. Click on an entry in the **Categories** list; then browse through the choices in the **Commands** list to find the command you want to add.
5. Hold down the left mouse button and drag the command entry from the **Commands** list onto the toolbar.
6. Watch as the pointer passes over the toolbar; release the left mouse button when you see a thick black bar in the right location.
7. Repeat steps 4 through 6 to add more buttons to any visible toolbar.
8. Click the **Close** button to save your changes and close the Customize dialog box.

What does that command do?

If you're not sure what a button or command does, click on its entry in the **Commands** list, and then click the **Description** button to see pop-up help.

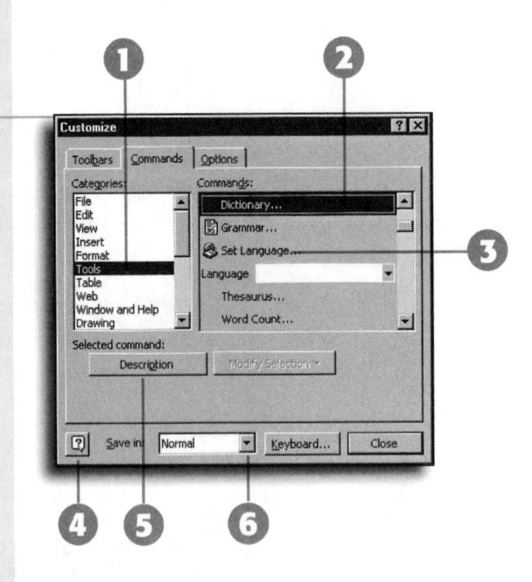

FIGURE 6.4

Drag any command from this box and drop it onto a toolbar or menu to customize your workspace.

1. Scroll to the bottom of this list to see menus and other special choices.
2. Some commands include images; others have only text labels.
3. The ellipsis (...) means this button opens a dialog box.
4. Click here to get help from the Office Assistant.
5. Click here to see a pop-up description of the selected command.
6. Word lets you specify a template and customize the keyboard; these choices are not available in other Office programs.

Build your own toolbars

Special jobs deserve special tools. If you have a group of Office tasks that you use with a particular type of document, such as a corporate report that has to be formatted just so, consider putting buttons for all those tasks on a custom toolbar. Open the Customize dialog box, click the **Toolbars** tab, and click the **New** button. Give the toolbar a name; then add buttons or menu options to it just as you would work with a built-in toolbar. Then, you can choose to show the toolbar only when you are working with that specific document type.

Deleting and Rearranging Toolbar Buttons

If you use a button so rarely that it's more of a distraction than a helper, take it off the toolbar. This technique can be useful if you want to reduce clutter; it can also help make room if you want to add other buttons to a particular toolbar. While you're customizing the toolbar in this fashion, take advantage of the opportunity to rearrange other buttons so that they're easier to find and use.

Removing and Rearranging Toolbar Buttons

1. If the toolbar or menu you want to customize is not visible, right-click on any toolbar or the main menu bar and select its entry in the list of available toolbars.
2. To delete any button, hold down the Alt key, point to the button, and drag it off the toolbar. When you see an x in the lower-right corner of the mouse pointer, release the mouse button.
3. To rearrange buttons, hold down the Alt key as you click and drag each button to a new position. You can rearrange buttons on the same toolbar or move buttons to a different toolbar. When you see a thick black bar between buttons, that indicates it's okay to drop the button.

4. To add a thin separator between two buttons, aim your mouse pointer at the button to the right of the place where you want the space to appear; then hold down the Alt key and drag the button to the right (if the thick I-beam appears, you've gone too far). To remove the separator line, hold down the Alt key and drag to the left.

Save your customizations!

If you've extensively customized toolbars and menus, you can save these and other changes using a tool called the Office Profile Wizard. This utility isn't included with the Office CDs; instead, you have to download it from Microsoft's Office Update Web site. From the **Help** menu, choose **Office on the Web**, and then follow the links to the Office 2000 Resource Kit.

Changing the Text or Icon on a Toolbar Button

To change a toolbar icon or label, open the Customize dialog box and right-click the button (in the toolbar) you want to change. You then see a shortcut menu like the one in Figure 6.5.

Click in the **Name** box to edit the name of the button or menu item. For buttons that use only an image, the text you enter will appear as part of the ScreenTip. To change the button back to its default image, name, and other settings, right-click and choose **Reset**.

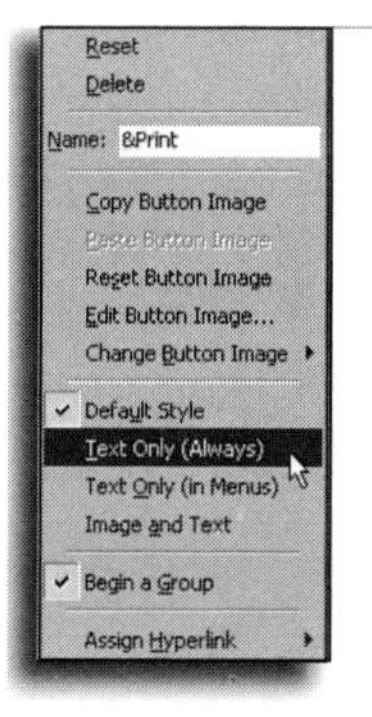

FIGURE 6.5

The four choices near the bottom of this menu let you select whether to show text, icons, or both.

Customizing a Pull-Down Menu

All Office programs, including Outlook, allow you to rearrange pull-down menus, which are simply special forms of Office toolbars. You can change the order of top-level menu choices or of items on pull-down menus. You can also delete or rename existing menu choices, and you can add command buttons or other choices to any menu.

Or use shortcut menus

If the Customize dialog box is open, you can add or remove a separator line between buttons by right-clicking the button to the right of the place you want the separator line to appear. Then check or uncheck the **Begin a Group** item to add or remove the separator line.

Customizing a Pull-Down Menu

1. Right-click on the menu bar and choose **Customize**.
2. To remove a command from a menu, click the menu, select the command, and drag it off the menu bar. When you see an X on the mouse pointer, release the mouse button.
3. To add a menu command, select an entry from the **Categories** list and then select the entry you want to add from the **Commands** list.
4. Drag the command onto the top-level menu where you want to add it. The menu scrolls down automatically, as shown in Figure 6.6.
5. The thick line shows you where the new menu choice will appear. Release the mouse button to add the new menu choice.

Adding a shortcut key to your new command

Add an ampersand (&) before any character in the **Name** box to make it an underlined hotkey in pull-down menus. For example, the Print button shown in Figure 6.5 is named `&Print`, meaning that the "P" appears as an underlined hotkey in the **File** menu.

Mix menus and toolbars

Although you wouldn't know it to look at it, the main menu bar in every Office program is actually a toolbar, which happens to contain only menus. You can use the techniques I describe here to add buttons to the main menu bar, just as you can add menus to any toolbar.

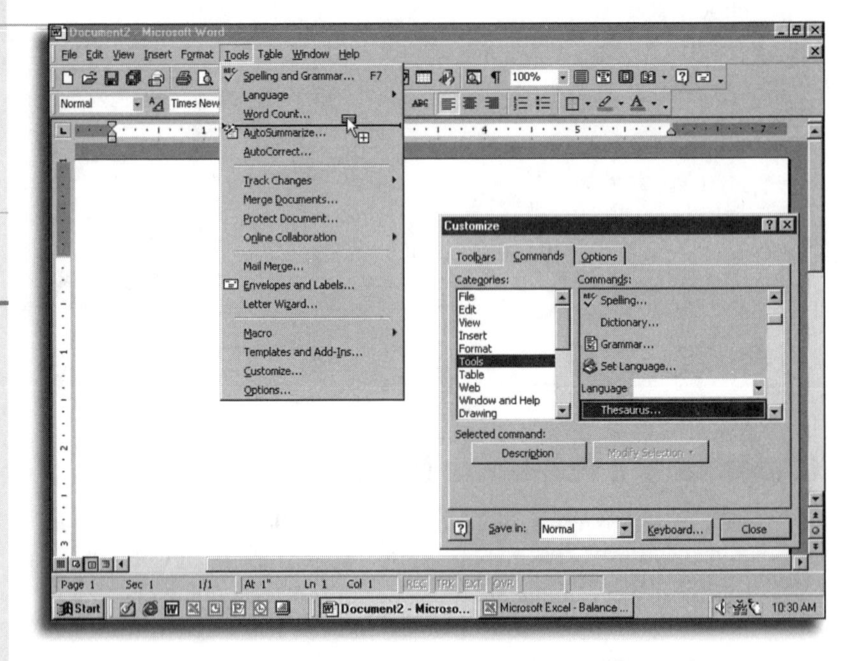

FIGURE 6.6

To add a Thesaurus command to Word's Tools menu, drag it from the Customize dialog box and drop it here.

Using Office to edit toolbar icons

Office doesn't officially include an icon editing program, but if you have the desire and the artistic talent, you can work with its toolbar customizing capabilities to create icons that you can use anywhere in Office or in Windows. Open the Customize dialog box, right-click any icon in the toolbar (not the Customize dialog box), and choose **Edit Button Image** to open the Button Editor. After you've created the icon you want to use, close the Button Editor and select **Copy Button Image** to place the icon on the Windows Clipboard.

Customizing a Shortcut Menu

Word and PowerPoint also allow you to add, remove, or reorder options on right-click shortcut menus. Place a check mark next to **Shortcut Menus** in the **Toolbars** list to make all these menus available for customization. Because I frequently use the **Paste Special** command in Word, for example, I've added that command to all shortcut menus that normally contain only **Cut**, **Copy**, and **Paste** choices. The techniques for customizing a shortcut menu are the same as those you use to customize options on the main menu bar.

Creating, Editing, and Using Keyboard Shortcuts

Using keyboard shortcuts is a powerful way to increase your productivity, especially if you're a touch typist. Office includes a wide selection of built-in keyboard shortcuts, but only Word lets you create new shortcuts of your own or adjust existing shortcuts.

Removing annoying keyboard functions

I use this feature to remove one of Word's most annoying features. Normally, pressing the Ins key toggles between Insert mode (where everything you type pushes existing text to the right) and Overtype mode (which erases characters to the right as you type). Every time I tapped the Ins key by accident, Word inadvertently wiped out my work until I noticed the mistake. But it doesn't happen anymore, because I used the techniques described here to remove the Overtype function from the Ins key and replace it with Ctrl+Alt+Ins, which I certainly won't press by accident.

Creating a Custom Keyboard Shortcut in Word

1. Open the **Tools** menu and choose **Customize**.
2. Click the **Keyboard** button to open the Customize Keyboard dialog box (see Figure 6.7).
3. In the **Categories** list, select **All Commands**.
4. Scroll through the **Commands** list and select the command you want to associate with a new keyboard shortcut.
5. Click in the **Press new shortcut key** field and hold down the key combination you want to use as your new keyboard shortcut. If you make a mistake, press the Backspace key and start over.
6. Click **Assign** and then click **Close** to accept your new keyboard shortcut.

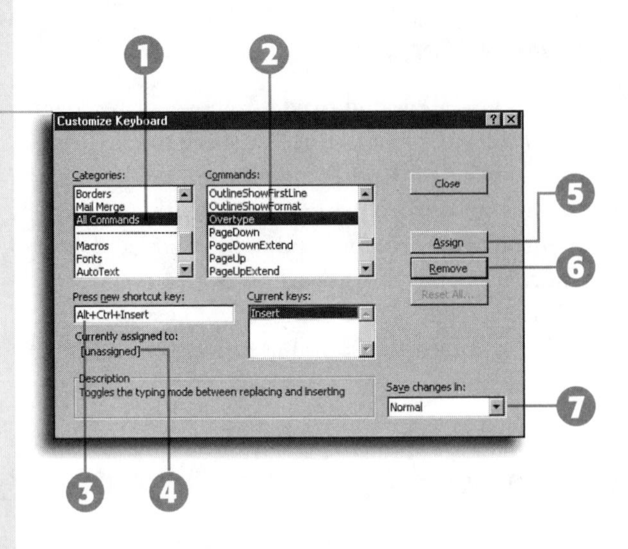

FIGURE 6.7

Use this dialog box to create your own custom keyboard shortcuts–but only in Word.

1. Choose a category from this list...
2. ...then choose a command here.
3. Click in this box and press a key combination.
4. These labels offer a brief description of the command you selected and show the command currently assigned to the key combination you entered.
5. Click to assign the key combination to the selected command.
6. Select an assigned key combination and click here to remove the assignment.
7. Choose a template; save changes in Normal to make keyboard shortcuts available in all documents.

Removing a Word Keyboard Shortcut

1. Open the **Tools** menu and choose **Customize**.
2. Click the **Keyboard** button to open the Customize Keyboard dialog box (refer to Figure 6.7).
3. In the **Categories** list, select **All Commands**.
4. Scroll through the **Commands** list and select the command you want to change or remove.
5. In the **Current keys** list, select the entry for the command you want to remove.
6. Click the **Remove** button.
7. Click the **Close** button.

Customizing Office Applications

Literally hundreds of customization options are available for each Office program. Some, like Excel's calculation options, are tailored to the data formats of a specific program. Others are esoteric or unusual settings that won't apply to most users. However, you can find a handful of options that are widely applicable and available in multiple Office programs.

The following sections list some of these common customization options.

Entering Your Name and Initials

When you first set up Office 2000, a dialog box prompts you to enter your name, initials, and company name. Office programs use this information in a variety of places; for example, when you create a new file and then pull down the **File** menu and choose **Properties**, the **Author** box on the **Summary** tab shows this name by default. Office also uses this information when you insert *comments* in a data file. All three programs tag comments with the name of the person who inserted them; Word also uses your initials to mark each comment in the text.

When you change user information in one program, Office records the changes in other programs as well. To change the user information at any time, open Word, Excel, or PowerPoint, pull down the **Tools** menu, and choose **Options**.

If you started with Word, click the **User Information** tab, as shown in Figure 6.8, and fill in the boxes labeled **Name** and **Initials**. If you want Word to add your return address automatically to letters and envelopes, fill in the box labeled **Mailing address** as well.

On the PowerPoint Options dialog box, click the **General** tab and fill in the boxes labeled **Name** and **Initials**. Excel users should click the **General** tab and fill in the box labeled **User name**.

Publisher includes the most extensive personalization options of all, with the capability to store different addresses, phone and fax numbers, and even logos for business, organization, and personal use. Pull down the **Edit** menu and choose **Personal Information** to see and adjust these options.

Word lets you assign keys to nearly anything

Built-in keyboard shortcuts typically apply only to commands, such as Cut, Copy, and Paste. Word's powerful customization capabilities let you go much further, however; you can assign keyboard shortcuts to styles, macros, symbols and special characters from other alphabets, individual files (but only if they're already open in the current session of Word), fonts, and AutoText entries. Explore the **Categories** list to see all your options. Used sparingly, this feature can increase your productivity dramatically.

Whose name is on your PC?

When you purchase a new computer that includes Office 2000, the PC maker often installs the software using default settings. Unless you change this information, every file you create lists `Authorized Gateway Customer` (or an equally generic name) as the author, and that label appears in comments and in the Properties dialog box for each Office document you create.

Excel doesn't let you change initials

If you want to change user information, avoid using Excel because its Options dialog box doesn't let you edit the default initials. Changing the username in Excel also changes the name that Word uses for comments, but it doesn't change the initials Word uses to tag comments.

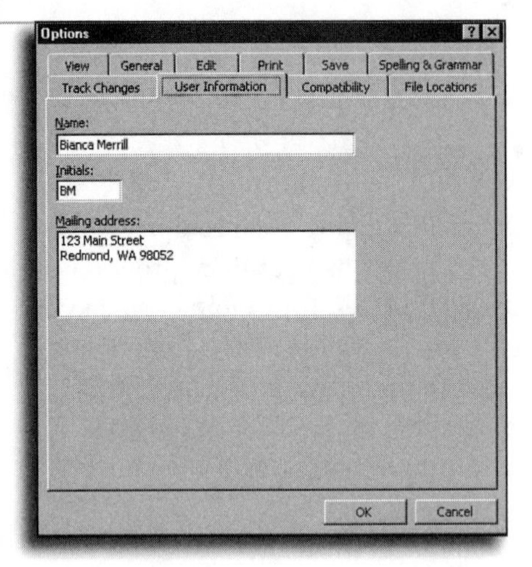

FIGURE 6.8

All Office applications insert the name you enter here in the **Name** field for new data files.

Changing the Appearance of a Program Window

The Options dialog box for every Office program includes a View tab that lets you change the appearance of document windows. Although most options are specific to each program, some let you hide parts of the window so that you see slightly more data in each. Pull down the **Tools** menu, choose **Options**, and click the **View** tab to adjust any of the options shown in Table 6.1.

TABLE 6.1 **Office View Options**

Option	Application	How to Change
Show or hide the status bar	Excel, Word, PowerPoint	Check the box labeled **Status bar**.
Show or hide scrollbars	Excel, Word	Check the boxes labeled **Horizontal scroll bar** and **Vertical scroll bar**.
Show or hide the vertical ruler	Word, PowerPoint	Check the box labeled **Vertical ruler**.

Opening Files

By default, Office displays the contents of the My Documents folder whenever you choose **Open** from the **File** menu. You can change this default location; in fact, you can specify a different starting folder for Word, PowerPoint, Excel, and Publisher, although the exact procedure is different for each program.

Changing the Default Document Folder in Word

1. Pull down the **Tools** menu, choose **Options**, and click the **File Locations** tab.
2. In the **File types** list, select the **Documents** option.
3. Click the **Modify** button; then use the Modify Location dialog box to browse through drives and folders. Select the correct folder and click **OK**.
4. Click **OK** to close the Options dialog box and save your change.

SEE ALSO

For more details about the best way to organize your documents, see page 28

Follow the same basic procedure for Publisher, Excel, and PowerPoint, with the following exceptions. In Publisher, click the **General** tab, select the entries for Publications or Pictures, and then click the **Modify** button. In Excel, click the **General** tab. In PowerPoint, click the **Save** tab, click the box labeled **Default file location**, and then enter the full name of the folder you want to specify as the new default. Include the full pathname—drive letter, colon, slashes, and all—as illustrated in Figure 6.9. Unfortunately, neither Excel nor PowerPoint lets you browse through drives and folders to find the one you want, so you need to know the full directory path before you can change the default file location.

All three programs also let you adjust another option that can make it easier for you to open files you've worked with recently. Normally, at the bottom of every **File** menu, you see a list of the four files you opened most recently. To change this setting, pull down the **Tools** menu, choose **Options**, and click the **General** tab; check the box labeled **Recently used file list** and pick a number between 1 and 9.

Or move the My Documents folder

Windows 98 lets you change the folder to which the My Documents icon refers. If you prefer to store your files in a folder called C:\Data, right-click on the My Documents icon on the desktop (or in Windows Explorer) and choose **Properties**, and then enter that folder name in the **Target** box. Now, whenever you click on the My Documents icon in the Places Bar in any Office program, you'll go straight to your Data folder.

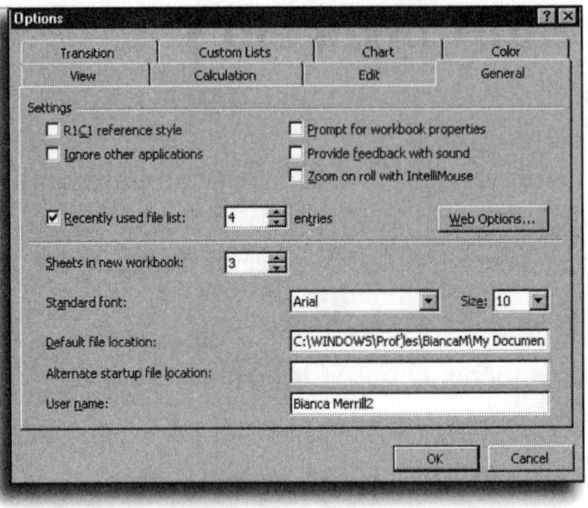

FIGURE 6.9

To change the default starting folder in Excel, enter the full name, including the path, in this dialog box.

Editing Options

The mouse is your most effective tool when editing text in documents, worksheets, presentations, and mail messages. All Office applications allow you to select words, sentences, or other chunks of text and then drag them to a new location. In tables and worksheets, you can also drag cells, rows, and columns from one place to another.

Two other editing options are worth checking, however. In Word, PowerPoint, Publisher, and Outlook, dragging the mouse pointer over any portion of a word selects the entire word; that can be frustrating if you intended to select only a few characters. Likewise, Word and PowerPoint use a feature called *Smart Cut and Paste* to adjust spacing around words and sentences automatically when you move them. If you don't like either one of these options, you can turn off the behavior. Table 6.2 displays these three common editing options.

TABLE 6.2 Office Editing Options

Feature	Application	How to Change
Enable or disable drag-and-drop editing	Excel, Word, PowerPoint, Publisher	Click the **Edit** tab; then check the box labeled **Allow cell drag and drop** (Excel) or **Drag-and-Drop text editing** (Word and PowerPoint).

Understanding Excel's alternate startup file location

On the **General** tab of the Options dialog box, Excel lets you specify an **Alternate startup file location**. Each time you start Excel, it checks a folder called Xlstart for workbook and template files it should load automatically; this feature is typically used to run macros and install Excel add-ins automatically. If you specify a folder name here, Excel loads any workbooks stored in this folder. Don't confuse this setting with the default document folder. Under normal circumstances, you should leave this box blank.

Disabling drag-and-drop text editing

If you prefer to move or copy text using only the Clipboard or keyboard shortcuts, you can disable drag-and-drop text editing. To disable this feature, simply choose the **Tools** menu, select **Options**, click the **Edit** tab, and remove the check mark from the **Drag-and-drop text editing** box. (In Excel, clear the check mark from the box labeled **Allow cell drag and drop**.) Most users should leave this option at its default setting.

Feature	Application	How to Change
Automatically select entire word	Word, PowerPoint, Publisher	Click the **Edit** tab and check the box labeled **When selecting, automatically select entire word**.
Automatically select entire word	Outlook	Click the **Other** tab and click the **Advanced Options** button, then check the box labeled **When selecting text, automatically select entire word**.
Smart cut and paste	Word, PowerPoint	Click the **Edit** tab and check the box labeled **Use smart cut and paste**.

Saving Files

Although you can set options for individual files every time you save them under a new name, all Office programs let you adjust a handful of options that apply to every file. Four of these settings are particularly useful (see Table 6.3):

- You can order any Office program to pop up the Properties dialog box every time you save a file; if you regularly use this information to find documents you or your coworkers have created, this option is indispensable.
- Word and PowerPoint offer a feature called Fast Save. On a "clean" installation of Office 2000, this feature is turned on in PowerPoint and off in Word; if you upgraded to Office 2000 over a previous version of Office, this setting may or may not be checked.
- Word and PowerPoint include options to save the current document automatically at regular intervals as you work. Turn on this AutoRecover option to avoid losing data in the event of a system crash or power failure.
- Finally, all three main Office programs let you specify a default format to use when saving documents. Adjust these options if your company uses a variety of word processors or spreadsheet programs and you've standardized on a common format other than the Office 2000 defaults.

Turn off Fast Save!

Fast Save sounds like a wonderful idea, but its effects can be damaging to your privacy. As the name implies, this feature speeds up saving documents and presentations. How? By leaving text and other objects you've deleted in a file instead of cleaning up deleted material and compressing the file. Anyone who knows how to peek at the binary contents of a file can see material you thought you deleted; that capability can have disastrous side effects if someone inadvertently reads an early draft of a confidential memo or budget presentation. On a modern PC, you save only a few seconds at most using this feature, and the risks aren't worth it. I strongly recommend turning Fast Save off at all times.

TABLE 6.3 Office File-Saving Options

Feature	Application	How to Change
Prompt for document properties	Excel, Word, PowerPoint	Excel: Click the **General** tab and check the box labeled **Prompt for workbook properties**.
		Word: Click the **Save** tab and check the box labeled **Prompt for document properties**.
		PowerPoint: Click the **Save** tab and check the box labeled **Prompt for file properties**.
Allow or prevent fast saves	Word, PowerPoint	Click the **Save** tab and check the box labeled **Allow fast saves**.
Set AutoRecover interval	Word, PowerPoint	Click the **Save** tab and check the box labeled **Save AutoRecover info every *nn* minutes**; choose a number between 1 and 120 (10 is default).
Default Save As format	Excel, Word, PowerPoint	Excel: Click the **Transition** tab and choose from the drop-down list labeled **Save Excel files as**.
		Word: Click the **Save** tab and choose from the drop-down list labeled **Save Word files as**.
		PowerPoint: Click the **Save** tab and choose from the drop-down list labeled **Save PowerPoint files as**.

Spelling

All Office programs include spell-checking capabilities. Word and PowerPoint (and, to a lesser extent, Outlook) allow you to adjust spelling options for all documents. For example, both Word and PowerPoint check spelling as you type, adding a wavy red line under potentially misspelled words; you can turn this feature on or off at will.

To adjust spelling options, pull down the **Tools** menu and choose **Options**. In Word, click the **Spelling and Grammar** tab; in PowerPoint, click the **Spelling and Style** tab; in Outlook, click the **Spelling** tab. You can adjust any of the settings shown in Table 6.4.

TABLE 6.4 Office Spelling Options

Feature	Application	How to Change
Check spelling as you type	Word, PowerPoint	Check the box labeled **Check spelling as you type**.
Hide spelling errors in current document	Word, PowerPoint	Check the box labeled **Hide spelling errors in this document**.
Ignore words in all caps or words with numbers when checking spelling	Word, PowerPoint, Outlook	Check the boxes labeled **Ignore words in UPPERCASE** and **Ignore words with numbers**.
Always suggest corrections when checking spelling	Word, PowerPoint, Outlook	Check the box labeled **Always suggest corrections** (Word and PowerPoint), or **Always suggest replacements for misspelled words** (Outlook).

SEE ALSO

➤ *To learn how to use Word to check your spelling, see page 197*

Sound and Animation

Office 2000 includes an option to play sound effects when you perform common tasks, such as changing views, creating a new item, or deleting text. You can also choose to replace the standard mouse pointer with animated versions that give you instant feedback when you print, repaginate, save, sort, or use the AutoFormat feature. Office sounds and animated pointers work in all programs.

Outlook and Excel spelling options

In Excel, you have to hunt for spell-checking options. When you choose **Spelling** from the **Tools** menu, note the options available on the dialog box. Unlike Word and PowerPoint, Excel cannot check spelling automatically as you type (although Excel does include AutoCorrect features, which are explained in Chapter 2, "How Office Works"). Likewise, Outlook doesn't flag misspelled words for you (unless you use Word as your email editor), but it can check spelling in every new message you create. Click the **Spelling** tab on the Options dialog box and check the box labeled **Always check spelling before sending**.

Word, Excel, and PowerPoint also include animated effects for actions such as background saving and adding or deleting worksheet rows. The primary purpose of these effects is to slow down the graphic display so that you can actually see Excel delete a column, or watch Word's Find and Replace dialog box zoom up from the **Select Browse Object** button in the lower-right corner of the window.

Changing sound schemes

To install Office sounds, you need to go to Microsoft's Office Update Web site. If you turn on sound options, the Office Assistant will prompt you to visit that Web site and download the necessary files. Installing this option creates new sound events in Windows. To adjust the sounds associated with these events, open the **Sounds** option in **Control Panel** and then scroll through the list of events until you see the group labeled **Microsoft Office**.

Adjusting the sound options in one program affects all Office programs. To turn sound effects on or off, pull down the **Tools** menu, choose **Options**, click the **General** tab, and check the box labeled **Provide feedback with sound**.

Only Word allows you to enable or disable animated mouse pointers. Click the **General** tab in the Options dialog box and then check the box labeled **Provide feedback with animation**. Excel users can click the **Edit** tab and check the box labeled **Provide feedback with animation**; however, this option affects only the way Excel displays editing changes and does not suppress animated pointers.

Organizing Your Desktop with the Office Shortcut Bar

Where is the Office Shortcut Bar?

When you install Office 2000 as an upgrade over an earlier version of Office, the Setup program installs the Office Shortcut Bar only if it was also installed in the previous version. Some personal computer makers automatically add the Office Shortcut Bar on new PCs that include Office 2000. If you don't see the Office Shortcut Bar on your system, click its shortcut in the Office Tools group on the Programs menu to install it automatically.

In Windows 95, Windows 98, and Windows NT 4.0, you use the Start menu and taskbar to launch programs and switch between windows. Microsoft Office includes its own control center that lets you perform many of the same tasks. It's called the *Office Shortcut Bar*, and you can use it in place of or in conjunction with the Start menu and Quick Launch bar.

The Office Shortcut Bar looks a little like an Office toolbar, but it serves a slightly different function. Its built-in buttons let you create new documents or open existing ones, add information to Outlook, and start any Office program. You can also add icons for other programs and folders to the Office Shortcut Bar, and you can create new toolbars as well, practically eliminating the need to use the Start menu.

Opening and Closing the Office Shortcut Bar

When you install the Office Shortcut Bar, it automatically gets its own shortcut in the Startup group, which is located on your Programs menu. If you leave this shortcut in the Startup group, Windows loads the Office Shortcut Bar automatically whenever you start your computer.

To close the Office Shortcut Bar, right-click on the four-color square in the top-left corner. From the shortcut menu that appears, select **Exit**. When you choose this option, Office asks whether you want to start the Office Shortcut Bar the next time you start Windows. Click **Yes** to leave the shortcut in your Startup folder; click **No** to remove the shortcut and stop using the Office Shortcut Bar automatically.

To start the Office Shortcut Bar, open a folder window or use the Windows Explorer. You can find the program shortcut in the Program Files\Microsoft Office folder.

Using the Shortcut Bar

Initially, only one toolbar is visible on the Office Shortcut Bar. This toolbar includes a title (`Office`) and 10 buttons, which let you start an Office program, switch between running programs, create a new Office document or open an existing one, and create Outlook items, such as contacts, tasks, and email messages.

To see what each button does, let the mouse pointer hover over the button until a ScreenTip appears. Click the button once to open the program, folder, or task associated with that button.

Program buttons can switch windows

Normally, clicking the button for an Office program launches the program in a new window. If the program is already running, however, clicking the button switches to the open window instead of opening a second copy of the program.

Customizing the Office Shortcut Bar

You can add, remove, rearrange, and rename buttons on the Office toolbar. You can also add any of five additional prebuilt toolbars to the Office Shortcut Bar. If you want, you can even create new toolbars from scratch. Probably the simplest and most productive customization is to add program icons to the Office toolbar.

Adding Buttons to the Office Shortcut Bar

1. Right-click on the Office Shortcut Bar and choose **Customize** from the shortcut menu.
2. Click the **Buttons** tab to display the dialog box shown in Figure 6.10.

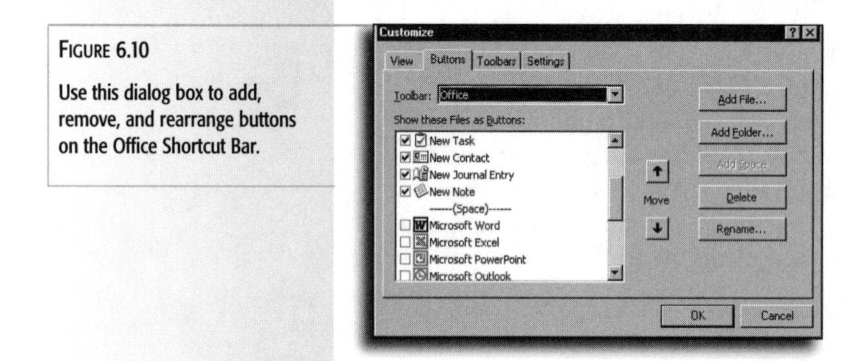

FIGURE 6.10

Use this dialog box to add, remove, and rearrange buttons on the Office Shortcut Bar.

3. Scroll through the list of available buttons and check the box to the left of each one to add it to the Office toolbar. In the example here, I've added buttons for Word, Excel, PowerPoint, and Outlook.
4. Click the **Add File** or **Add Folder** buttons to add an individual file or folder to the toolbar.
5. Clear the check mark next to any item to remove its button from the toolbar. Select an item and click **Delete** only if you want to remove its entry permanently from the list of available buttons.
6. To change the order of buttons on the toolbar, select an entry in the list and click the up and down arrow buttons.
7. Click **OK** to save your changes and close the Customize dialog box.

Including the Office toolbar, there are five built-in toolbars available for use with the Office Shortcut Bar. Right-click and choose any of the following options from the **Toolbars** tab to add one or more of these toolbars:

Folder Name	Contents
Favorites	Adds all shortcuts from Favorites folder; difficult to use because all shortcuts have the same icon.
Programs	Adds buttons for all program shortcuts and groups in the Programs menu; can be unwieldy if you have many programs installed.
Accessories	Adds buttons for all program shortcuts in Accessories folder; useful way to get to Notepad, Calculator, and so on.
Desktop	Adds a button for every object on the Windows desktop; updates automatically when you add new items to desktop.

Each folder you add to the Office Shortcut Bar gets its own button and title. To switch to a different toolbar, click the toolbar's button; Office slides toolbars up or down to make the one you selected visible.

Positioning the Office Shortcut Bar on the Screen

By default, the Office Shortcut Bar docks along the right edge of your screen. You can arrange it differently, if you like. You can tuck the Shortcut Bar at the top of the screen, for example, where it uses smaller icons and fits neatly into the title bar of any maximized window. Another alternative is to use the big buttons and line them up along any edge of the screen. You can even let the shortcut bar "float" in a box that you can move around on the screen.

To adjust View options, right-click on the Office Shortcut Bar and choose **Customize**. Click the **View** tab to display the dialog box shown in Figure 6.11.

Options in this dialog box let you keep the Shortcut Bar on top of all other windows, if you prefer, or hide it when it's not in use; move the mouse pointer to the edge of the screen to reveal the Shortcut Bar if you've hidden it using this trick. You can also hide or show ScreenTips, turn sound effects on and off, and change the colors in the title bar.

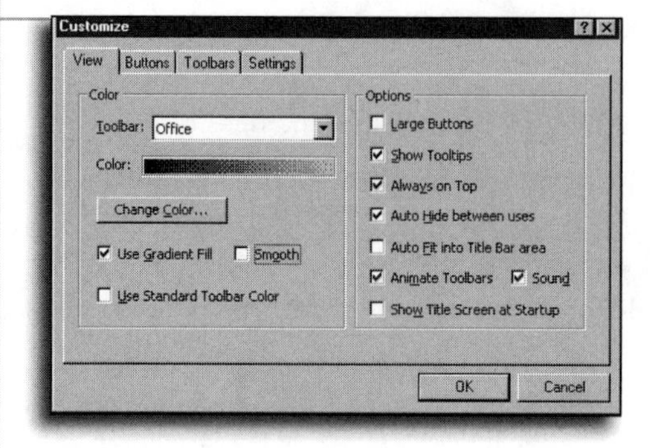

FIGURE 6.11

Options in this dialog box control the size and position of the Office Shortcut Bar.

Protecting Your System from Viruses

Don't let virus paranoia destroy ya

You should take reasonable precautions to avoid macro viruses, but you should also know that almost all virus scares are precisely that–scares, with little or no foundation in reality. You're far more likely to receive an infected file from a coworker, a friend, or a network server than by downloading documents from the Internet. Similarly, you are far more likely to lose data due to a dumb mistake or a hardware problem than to a macro virus.

Every Office data file is capable of containing macros—programs written in Visual Basic for Applications. By writing your own macros or using those created by a professional in your company, you can automate tasks and eliminate some drudgery from your daily work.

But macros have a dark side as well. When you open a data file that contains a macro virus, the effects can range from annoying to disastrous. Because macros can delete files or corrupt information on your hard disk, you should always be careful not to let them run unless you're certain you know what they do.

Office 2000 includes two features that let you intercept macros before they run and disable those that comes from sources you don't trust. To check these settings in each Office program, pull down the **Tools** menu, click **Macros**, and choose **Security**. The dialog box shown in Figure 6.12 appears.

Want more information on macros?

For an exhaustive explanation of how macro security works and how you can use it, pick up a copy of *Special Edition Using Microsoft Office 2000,* and read Chapter 53, "Using Macros to Automate Office Tasks."

The Low setting allows all macros to run, regardless of where they came from; using this setting is simply foolish. With security set to the High level (the default in Word), only macros that contain a digital signature from a trusted source will run. If macro developers at your company use this type of security, you can choose this option to remain safe. Using the default Medium level (the default for all Office programs except Word), you'll see a dialog box when you open a document that contains macros, and if you're not certain that the macros are safe you can disable them.

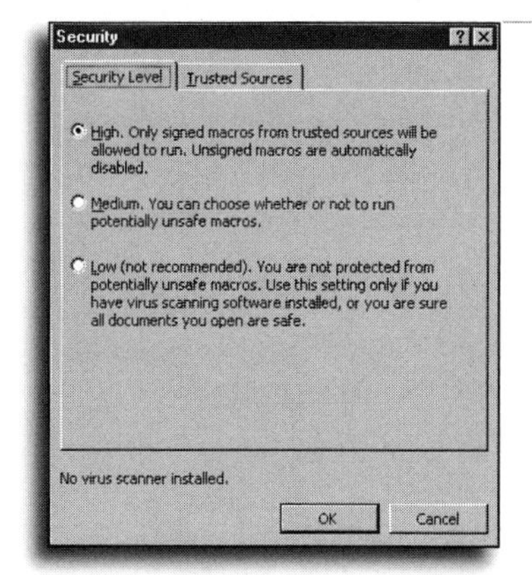

FIGURE 6.12

Office programs use these security settings to protect you from macro viruses.

Working with Graphics

- Draw flowcharts and shapes using Office drawing tools
- Add attention-getting backgrounds to graphic objects
- Mix text and graphics
- Use WordArt to create your own logo
- Add pictures to any document
- Find free images in the Clip Gallery

Using Office Drawing Tools and AutoShapes

If you think you need a separate program to create impressive graphics in your Office documents, think again. Then click the **Drawing** button on the Standard toolbar in Word or Excel. In PowerPoint, the Drawing toolbar is normally visible; if it's hidden, right-click any visible toolbar or the main menu bar and check **Drawing** from the list of toolbars. In Publisher, if the Drawing toolbar is hidden, pull down the **Insert** menu and choose **Picture**, then select **New Drawing**.

By default, the Drawing toolbar docks to the bottom of the screen, and it packs a surprising amount of graphics power into a small space. Best of all, you don't need to be a professional artist to use these tools effectively.

No Drawing toolbar in Outlook

Outlook doesn't include a Drawing toolbar, but you can use these tools in Word, Excel, or PowerPoint, then click the **E-mail** button to send the drawing as an HTML message in Outlook.

Using the tools on the Drawing toolbar, you can accomplish any of the following tasks quickly and easily:

- Draw geometric shapes, such as squares, circles, and ovals, and drag them to the exact size you need. Office calls these graphic objects *AutoShapes*.
- Add lines and arrows to call attention to text or other objects; in PowerPoint and Excel (but not Word), you can use special lines called *connectors*, which automatically snap into place to connect AutoShapes.
- Add text to any AutoShape or insert *text boxes*, so you can drag a block of text anywhere within a document, worksheet, or slide.
- Align, resize, and group AutoShapes, so you can treat them as a single object.
- Add colors, shadows, and backgrounds to create images with impact.

Figure 7.1 shows an example of how you can combine AutoShapes, text, and even some clip art to produce a graphic image that turns a complex process into an easy-to-follow flowchart.

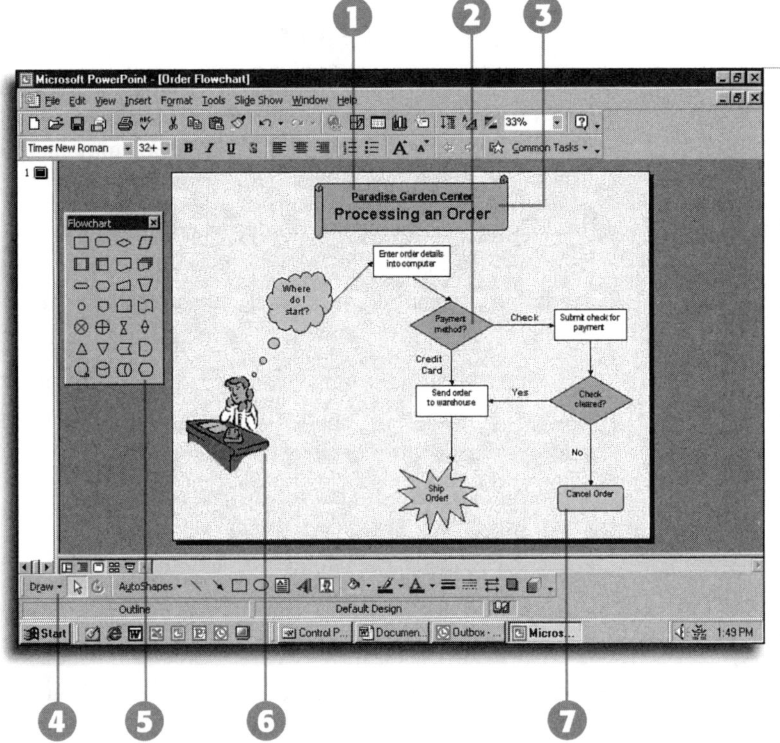

FIGURE 7.1

Click, drag, and type to quickly create easy-to-follow flowcharts from basic AutoShapes.

1. Choose fancy AutoShapes, like this banner...
2. ...or use simple geometric shapes, such as these standard flowcharting shapes.
3. Mix and match formatting for text within an AutoShape.
4. Use the tools on the Drawing toolbar to work with AutoShapes and other drawing objects.
5. To avoid having to constantly click menus, "tear off" individual menus like this one and let them float in the document window.
6. Combine clip art and AutoShapes for a humorous or dramatic effect.
7. Add background colors to help individual AutoShapes stand out.

Drawing Objects and Selecting Shapes

The drawing tools available throughout Office include 130 AutoShapes and a common Drawing toolbar. As the name implies, AutoShapes start with the basic definition of a shape—a square, for example, or an eight-pointed star. Use sizing handles on each AutoShape to resize and stretch an AutoShape in any direction.

Creating a Drawing with AutoShapes

1. If necessary, click the **Drawing** button to display the Drawing toolbar.
2. Click the **AutoShapes** option on the Drawing toolbar; if this toolbar is docked at the bottom of the window (its default setting), the menu pops up, rather than down. Choose one of the following options to display a cascading menu of shapes:

Tear-off toolbars

Many of the cascading menus on the Drawing toolbar actually "tear off" to form new toolbars. For example, if you plan to create a flowchart, click the **AutoShapes** menu to pop up the list of available categories, then click **Flowchart** to display a cascading menu with 28 shapes on it. Click the bar at the top of this menu and drag it into the document window; when you do, you see a new floating toolbar with all the Flowchart shapes on it. The **Borders**, **Font Color**, and **Fill Color** menus (also found on the Formatting toolbar) work the same way.

AutoShape shortcuts

Four buttons on the Drawing toolbar let you add the most common AutoShapes with hardly any effort. Click the **Line**, **Arrow**, **Rectangle**, or **Oval** buttons to add the no-frills version of these shapes to your document. Hold down the Shift key while dragging to draw straight lines or perfect circles and squares.

Callouts are great on charts

If you're preparing an Excel chart that shows an important point–such as a sudden drop in sales in one region–use a *callout* to point to that portion of the chart, then enter text in the callout box.

- **Lines** let you connect other shapes or sketch free-form shapes. This category includes simple arrows.
- **Basic Shapes** range from simple squares, circles, and triangles to whimsical selections such as a happy face, a heart, and a lightning bolt.
- **Block Arrows** represent a bolder way to connect shapes. All 28 options in this category allow you to specify a background color, unlike the arrows in the Lines category.
- **Flowchart** symbols contain standard symbols for portraying activities in a sequential process. A diamond, for example, represents a decision point.
- **Stars and Banners** are useful for flyers, ads, and certificates.
- **Callouts** are cartoon-style balloons in a variety of shapes, useful for attaching captions or explanatory text to objects such as images or text.
- **Connectors** are available only in Excel, PowerPoint, and Publisher; these shapes are like lines, except they include the intelligence to snap to defined positions on the sides or corners of other AutoShapes, and they have the capability to reroute themselves if you move the shapes to which they're attached.
- **Action Buttons** are available only in PowerPoint. These are custom shapes designed to help you navigate through Web-based presentations.

SEE ALSO

➤ *For a full explanation of how to use Action Buttons, see page 530*

3. Click the button for any shape, then drag the cross-shaped mouse pointer to define the area in which you want the AutoShape to appear. Some shapes, such as the FreeForm line tool, may require that you click multiple points to complete the process.

4. Click and drag the square *sizing handles* to change the size of the AutoShape. Hold down the Shift key while dragging to maintain the same proportions while resizing; this step is crucial if you want to avoid turning a square into a rectangle or a circle into an oval when dragging.
5. Click and drag the yellow *adjustment handles* to change the appearance of complex shapes, such as the point of an arrow or the center of a banner. (See Figure 7.2 for an example; not all AutoShapes include these handles.)

Use the ScreenTips

Can't figure out what an AutoShape is? Let the mouse pointer hover over any of the AutoShape buttons until a ScreenTip displays the name of the selected button.

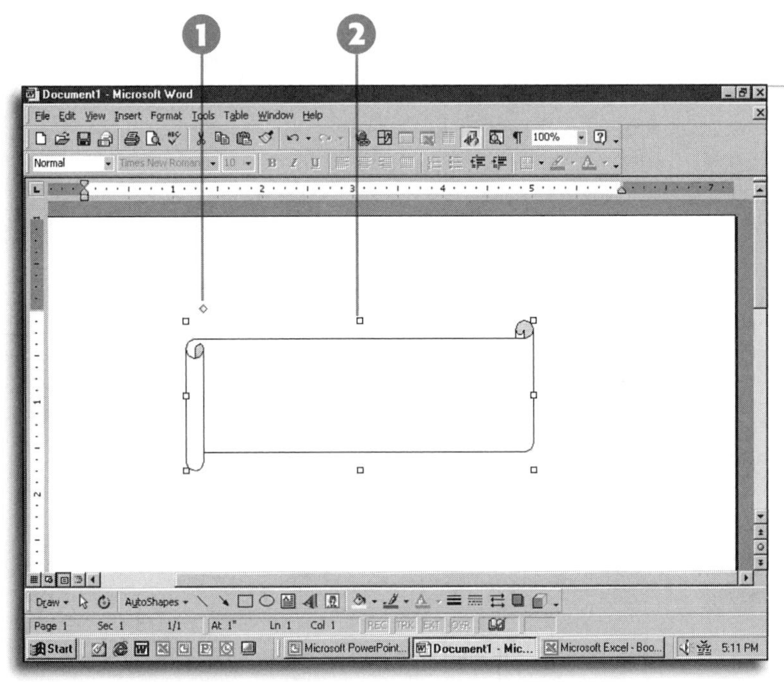

FIGURE 7.2
The diamond-shaped adjustment handle lets you change the shape and position of the scroll in this AutoShape.

1. Adjustment handle
2. Sizing handle

Working with AutoShapes

After you add an AutoShape to a document, slide, or worksheet, you can make all sorts of changes to it: move it, resize it, change the background color, or change the font formatting, for example. Before you can do anything, however, you have to select it, and that's not as easy as it sounds.

Shift AutoShapes whenever you like

Did you choose the wrong AutoShape? No problem. Just click to select the AutoShape; then click the **Draw** menu on the Drawing toolbar. Choose **Change AutoShape** and make a different selection from the cascading menus. The new AutoShape appears in the exact position of the existing one; if the original AutoShape contained text, the new shape incorporates the text as well.

"Lasso" all the shapes

If you want to select all the shapes in a given area–for example, if you want to change the border style or font formatting for all boxes in a flowchart–click the **Select Objects** arrow on the Drawing toolbar and draw a rectangle around the entire region that contains the shapes. When you release the mouse button, you'll see that you've selected all the AutoShapes within it, just as surely as if you'd tossed a lasso around them.

Snap to it!

Word, Excel, PowerPoint, and Publisher all include an invisible grid on the drawing layer. As you move objects around, they "snap" to the grid and, in some cases, to other shapes. To turn this behavior on or off in Excel, PowerPoint, or Publisher, click the **Draw** menu and choose **Snap**. Click the **To Grid** and **To Shape** buttons to toggle "snapping" on or off. In Word, click the **Draw** menu and choose **Grid**, then check or uncheck the two "snap" boxes.

To select an AutoShape, move the mouse pointer in its general vicinity until you see it change to a four-pointed arrow. To select multiple AutoShapes at the same time, select the first one, then hold down the Shift key and repeat the process for each additional shape.

To move an AutoShape, just drag it from one position to another. If you select several shapes, you can drag them all at once.

To copy an AutoShape, you can use the Windows Clipboard, but it's much easier to use the mouse. Just select the shape you want to copy, then hold down the Ctrl key as you drag it to a new location. This technique is great if you're creating a diagram that contains several of the same shapes: Add one shape, drag it to the right size, format it using colors and fonts, and then Ctrl+drag as many copies as you need.

SEE ALSO

➤ *For more details on how to use the Windows Clipboard, see page 134*

To delete an AutoShape, select it and press the Delete key.

To rotate an AutoShape 90 degrees, click the **Draw** menu, choose **Rotate or Flip**, and choose either **Rotate Right** or **Rotate Left**. To rotate a shape a little at a time, click the **Free Rotate** button, then point to any of the sizing handles and drag left or right. To flip a shape, choose **Flip Horizontal** or **Flip Vertical** from the **Draw** menu.

Using Lines, Arrows, and Connectors

Drawing straight line arrows works much the same as other AutoShapes. After you draw the line, however, you can spruce it up dramatically. Click to select the line, then click the **Line Style** button on the Drawing toolbar to adjust the thickness of the line. Use the **Dash Style** button to change a solid line to a dashed or dotted line, and click the **Arrow Style** button to select different options on the Drawing toolbar.

For times when you don't want to draw a straight line, you have three choices in the **Lines** group on the **AutoShapes** menu:

- **Curve** starts by drawing a straight line, but each time you click the mouse button, the line anchors and curves in the direction you go next. Double-click or press Esc to quit drawing. It takes practice, but you can draw interesting, graceful arcs with this tool.
- **Freeform** works like the Curve tool, except that it produces only straight lines that anchor and allow you to go in a new direction each time you click.
- **Scribble** turns the mouse pointer into a pencil and lets you draw in any direction for as long as you hold down the mouse button. If you're a sketch artist, this is your tool.

Excel, PowerPoint, and Publisher include an option not available in Word documents. If you choose the **Connectors** option from the **AutoShapes** menu, you can add lines that snap into place on the sides or corners of shapes and stay there as you move the shapes around. If you use connectors in a flowchart for example, then rearrange the objects in the chart, the connectors move as well; if you move the connected shapes so that the connector is no longer attached to the best points, click the **Draw** button and choose **Reroute Connectors** to have Office move the connectors automatically.

Pick an exact size

Do you want your shape to be an exact size? If you're using text boxes and AutoShapes to draw a picture of a business reply card in Word, for example, you might want its outside dimensions to be exactly six inches by four inches. Start by drawing a rectangle that's approximately the right dimensions, then right-click the shape, choose **Format AutoShape** from the shortcut menu, and click the **Size** tab. Options in this dialog box let you specify a precise size for the shape.

To Connect Two AutoShapes

1. In Excel or PowerPoint, draw the shapes you want to connect.
2. On the Drawing toolbar, click the **AutoShapes** menu and choose **Connectors**. Pick the type of connector you want to use. Your mouse pointer turns into a crosshair.
3. Move the mouse pointer over the first shape you want to connect. The pointer turns into a square with lines radiating from each side, and the predefined connection points on the shape show up as blue dots on the perimeter of the shape. In some cases, as you move around the shape, different connection points become visible. Click the point where you want the connection to start.
4. Aim the mouse pointer at the second shape you want to connect. A dashed line indicates the direction of the connection.

Working around Word's lines

Why Word's drawing tools lack connectors isn't obvious, but it's a fact just the same. Using lines to connect shapes in Word is such a pain, that I recommend you build flowcharts in a PowerPoint slide so that you can use connectors. When you've got everything looking the way you want it, copy the drawing to the Clipboard and paste it into your Word document.

Find the desired connector point on the second shape and click to complete the connection.

Red means a solid connection

When you select a connector line that's attached to two shapes, the connection points on either end are bright red. To change a connection, click the red connection point and drag. As you drag, the point glows green; when you make a connection, it turns red again.

Changing Colors, Backgrounds, and Borders

Office includes a set of common tools you can use to change the background of nearly any kind of graphic object, including AutoShapes, Excel charts, and PowerPoint slides. You can add a solid fill color, use a *gradient fill* that consists of two colors, or pick a picture or texture to use as the background.

In the example that follows, I explain how to work this magic on an AutoShape, but you can pop up the same dialog box in PowerPoint. The placeholders on a PowerPoint slide that hold text, titles, and other objects are actually just AutoShapes. Select the placeholder containing a bulleted list, for example, then right-click the thick line surrounding it and choose **Format Placeholder**—lo and behold, you see the Format AutoShape dialog box.

Changing the Background of a Graphic Object

1. Right-click the graphic object or slide placeholder whose background you want to change and choose **Format AutoShape** from the shortcut menu.
2. In the Format Object dialog box (see Figure 7.3), click the **Colors and Lines** tab. Use the **Color** drop-down list in the **Fill** area to choose the background color you want to use. If you want the background to be invisible, so you can see right through it to any text or objects behind it, choose **No Fill**.
3. If you want to be able to see objects behind the shape, check the **Semitransparent** box. A semitransparent shape makes the objects underneath fuzzy; if the color you chose is light, you may be able to read text or see pictures underneath.
4. Use the options in the **Line** section to change the color, style, and thickness of the border around the object. If you

Thick border or thin?

If an AutoShape contains text, it has a thick border. If it doesn't contain text, it has a thin border with sizing handles. In either case, just right-click the border to pop up the shortcut menu.

want no border, click the **Color** drop-down list and choose **No Line**.

5. Click **OK** to close the dialog box and accept the changes.

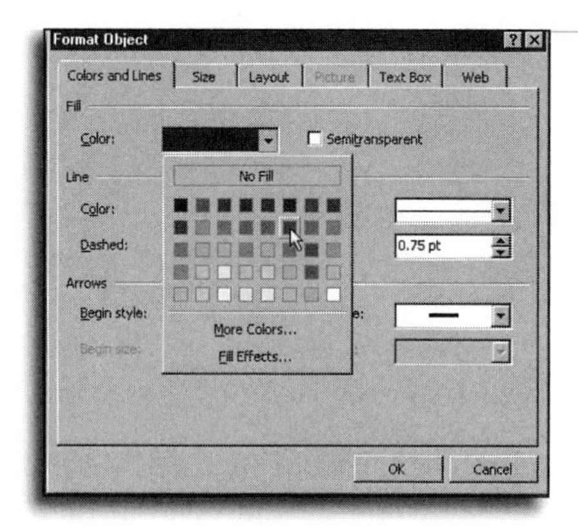

FIGURE 7.3
Use the Colors and Lines dialog box to change the background color and border style for any object.

To go way beyond plain background colors, click the **Color** drop-down list and choose **Fill Effects** from the bottom of the list. The Fill Effects dialog box gives you four choices:

- Use the options on the **Gradient** tab to add an interesting background, including two-color gradients like those found in PowerPoint slides.

SEE ALSO

For an explanation of how you can use gradients on the background of a PowerPoint slide, see page 505

- **Pattern** options let you add dots, lines, or stripes to a chart or a chart object. You can specify the foreground and background colors.
- Click the **Texture** tab to choose from a wide assortment of background art that gives your chart the look you often see on Web pages. Figure 7.4 shows some of the 24 textures included with Office 2000.

Subtlety is the best policy

When selecting textures, keep your overall goal in mind. A wood-grain texture may look interesting, but is it really appropriate in a corporate presentation? The subtler textures, such as recycled paper and parchment, are effective ways to tone down the shock of a harsh white background without drawing too much attention to the texture itself.

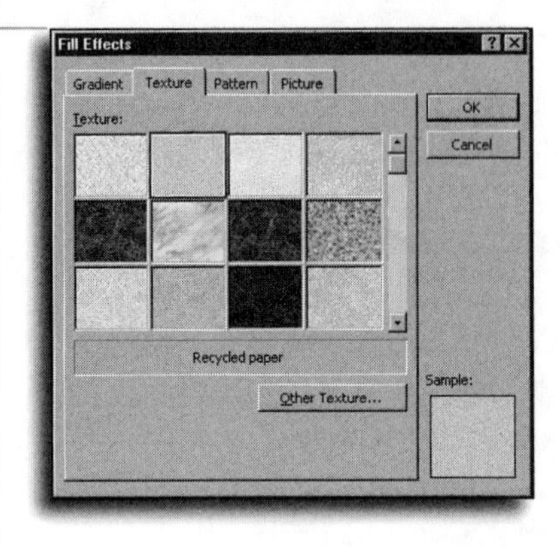

FIGURE 7.4

Pick one of these textures to give an object's background some extra dimension. The name of the texture appears in the bottom of this dialog box.

Save your defaults

If you want to use one set of formatting—backgrounds, lines, fonts, and all—on all AutoShapes you create, right-click an AutoShape that contains the formatting you want to use as the model. From the shortcut menus, choose **Set AutoShape Defaults**.

- To use an image file as your chart's background, switch to the **Picture** tab and click the **Select Picture** button. Browse through folders until you find the image you want, then click **OK**. You may need to adjust fonts and colors for chart titles and other text when you use a photo as a background.

Mixing Text and Graphics

Many AutoShapes work well with text—to identify the steps in a flowchart, for example, or the decision points in a decision matrix. To add text to an AutoShape in Word, right-click the AutoShape and choose **Add Text** from the shortcut menu, then begin typing at the insertion point. In PowerPoint or Excel, just click to select the AutoShape and then begin typing.

You can't add text to a line

Word lets you add and edit text within most AutoShapes but not lines or free-form shapes. If you choose one of these objects, the **Add Text** menu is not available.

When you create an AutoShape with text in Word, the text box includes a paragraph mark. You can apply both paragraph and character formatting to the text in the AutoShape. In Excel, PowerPoint, and Publisher, you can apply font formatting to the entire AutoShape or to selected text within the shape. In all three applications, you can cut, copy, and paste text just as if it were in a document.

Although the Drawing toolbar includes a **Text Box** button, there's nothing special about it—this shortcut adds a rectangle that's ready for you to start typing text. In fact, the term *text box* is a bit misleading. In Word, PowerPoint, and Publisher, you can paste anything into a text box, including graphics. (In Excel, however, a text box can only contain text.)

You can think of a text box as a mini-document with its own separate existence. If you want to call special attention to a block of text in a report, for example, use a trick that magazine publishers use all the time: Put a pull quote in a text box. These quotes use large type, usually bold, to make a provocative or attention-getting quote stand out.

Figure 7.5 shows a good example of a pull quote. Making it look good takes a few little tricks.

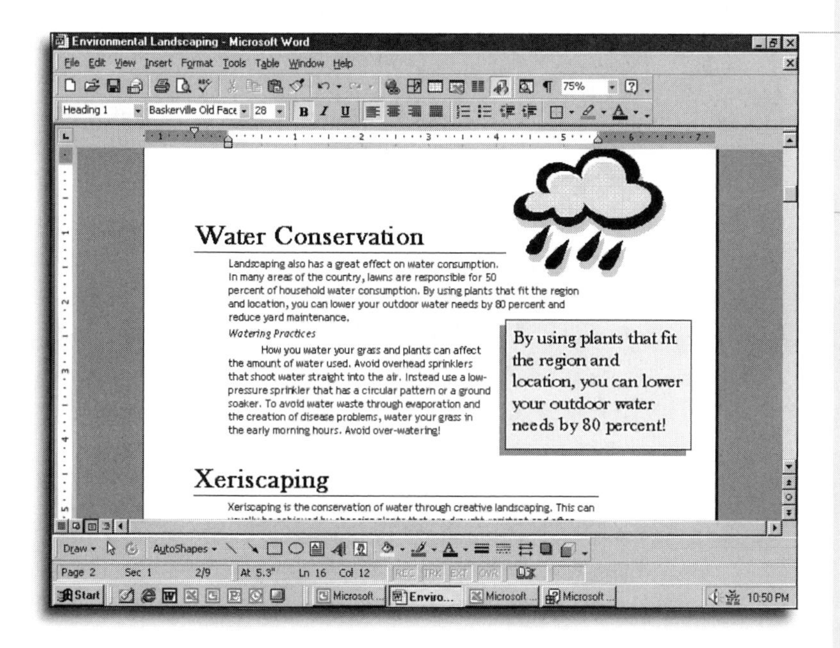

FIGURE 7.5
This pull quote is nothing more than some text in a box, but making it look good takes a few extra steps.

Adding a Pull Quote to a Word Document

1. Click the **Text Box** button on the Drawing toolbar and drag to create a text box in the right size and position.
2. Select the quote in your document, then press Ctrl+C to copy it to the Clipboard.
3. Click in the text box and press Ctrl+V to paste the copied text.

Don't select text first!

If you select text in a Word document and click the **Text Box** button, the selected text disappears from your document and moves into the text box. That's a great shortcut if you intended it, but it's a rude shock if you simply wanted a blank box. Click the **Undo** button and remove the selection to start over.

4. Select the entire block of text, right-click, and choose **Font** from the shortcut menu. Pick a font, size, style, color, and other attributes. In this case, note that I chose the same fonts as the headline on the page, and I made the type large enough to stand out from the body type. Adjust the size of the box if necessary.
5. Right-click the border of the AutoShape and choose **Format AutoShape**. On the **Colors and Lines** tab, pick a background color and border style using the techniques I described earlier in this chapter. Don't close the dialog box just yet.
6. The pull quote looks great, except for one problem: It covers up the text underneath! Click the **Layout** tab and click the **Square** box in the **Wrapping style** section, as I've done in Figure 7.6. Now click OK, and watch as the document text adjusts to wrap around the box.

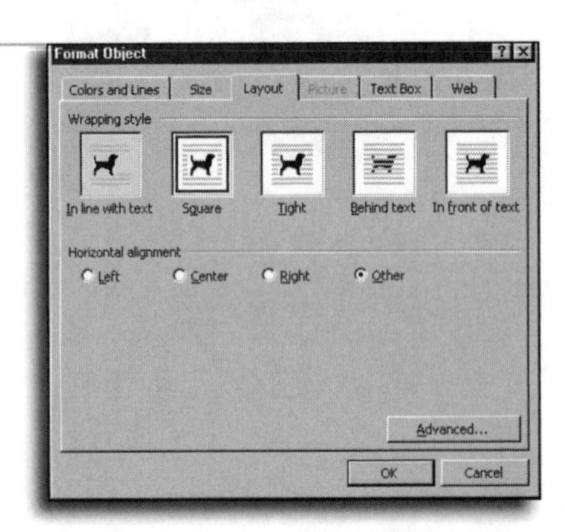

FIGURE 7.6

Use this dialog box to control how text wraps around a picture or other object. Click the question mark in the title bar and then click any option for helpful instructions.

For more on type wrapping...

You can choose exactly how you want text to wrap around any graphic object or AutoShape in Word. Within a report, for example, you can place graphics directly within a long block of text, or insert a graphic between columns and maintain the column format. For an exhaustive discussion of all your options, however, you need an expert-level book like *Special Edition Using Word 2000*, also published by Que.

7. For one last artistic touch, select the text box and click the **Shadow** button on the Drawing toolbar. Using this option creates the illusion that the text box is floating above the page and casting a shadow on the paper below. In this example, I chose a shadow to the lower-left to match the

direction of the falling rain.

Grouping and Aligning Graphic Objects

Graphic objects, including AutoShapes and pictures, don't sit on the same plane as text in a Word document or cells in an Excel worksheet.

Instead, they exist in a separate *drawing layer*. If you include multiple graphic objects in a document, each one sits in its own layer, just as if they were printed on transparent plastic sheets. The contents of your document or worksheet are on their own layer as well. As a result, you can position each object within the drawing layer independently, from front to back. When you're satisfied with the order and arrangement, you can group objects together so that they move as one.

How did I line up all the elements on the flowchart at the beginning of this chapter? I sure didn't do it with the naked eye. Instead, I used alignment tools on the Drawing toolbar. It's easy, as long as you think ahead.

The first step is to select the AutoShapes you want to align. If your flowchart includes a group of three objects, for example, and you want them centered one over the other, select all three, then click the **Draw** menu, choose **Align or Distribute**, and click **Align Center**. You can align other shapes vertically, along the left or right edge, or horizontally, along the top, bottom, or middle.

Two other menu choices let you space objects evenly from one another. After selecting the objects, click **Draw**, choose **Align or Distribute**, and select **Distribute Horizontally** or **Distribute Vertically**.

You can also change the order of objects, so one is in front of another. By default, when you create or position a graphic element so that it overlaps another graphic element, the new element appears on top of the old one. To change the front-to-back ordering, right-click the graphic element you want to move, then choose **Order**.

PowerPoint is different

In this explanation, I refer only to Word and Excel. PowerPoint is slightly different, because it doesn't contain a text layer. Instead, you enter all text–titles, bullet points, footers, and so on–in text boxes called placeholders. You can treat these text objects just like graphics, changing their size, order, alignment, background colors, and other formats. The only thing you can do with the slide itself is change its background.

Nudge, nudge (wink, wink)

You don't need to use the mouse to move AutoShapes on a page. Instead, select the object and use the arrow keys to move it in any direction. When you do so, the object moves in fairly large jumps on the grid. To nudge the selected object or objects a little at a time, hold down the Ctrl key and tap the arrow keys.

- Choose **Bring to Front** if you want the selected graphic to appear at the top of the stack.
- Choose **Bring Forward** or **Send Backward** to move the object up or down one level in the stack.
- In Word only, you can move an object so that it's on top of the document itself (**Bring in Front of Text**), or place it behind the text layer (**Send Behind Text**).

After you format, connect, align, and distribute all your AutoShapes, take one last crucial step: Group them all into a single graphic object. This step helps prevent the chance that you'll accidentally move or resize one of the shapes in the group and mess up your careful design. Select all the elements you want to group, and then click the **Draw** menu and choose **Group**.

Did you forget one?

Whenever I create a drawing from a large number of AutoShapes, it's a good bet I'll leave at least one out when I go to group them. After selecting multiple items, I suggest you drag the entire collection left and right just a little; that lets you see which pieces you might have missed.

After you group a collection of AutoShapes and other drawing objects, you can no longer edit the individual elements independently. (You can, however, change the text in a text box within a group.) If you need to make a revision, click the **Draw** menu and choose **Ungroup**, make your changes, then click the **Draw** menu again and choose **Regroup**.

Using WordArt for Logos

Don't let the name fool you

Despite the name, WordArt isn't just for Word. It works throughout Office.

Reusing WordArt

You can't save a WordArt drawing as a separate file, but you can create and save your WordArt logo in a blank document. When you're satisfied with the way it looks, copy it to the Windows Clipboard and paste it into the document where you want to use it. Open the saved document whenever you want to reuse your logo.

WordArt is an extremely simple program that takes a few words and lets you stretch, bend, distort, and colorize them into a work of art. The effect can be hideously ugly, if you're not careful; if you keep good taste in mind, however, it's a useful tool for creating logos and headlines.

Creating a Work of WordArt

1. Select the text you want to use for your logo or headline, then click the **WordArt** button on the Drawing toolbar. (It isn't necessary to enter text first, but it's quicker.)
2. Choose a style from the WordArt dialog box shown in Figure 7.7 and click OK. (Feel free to experiment—you'll have a chance to change this design later if you're not satisfied with the results.)

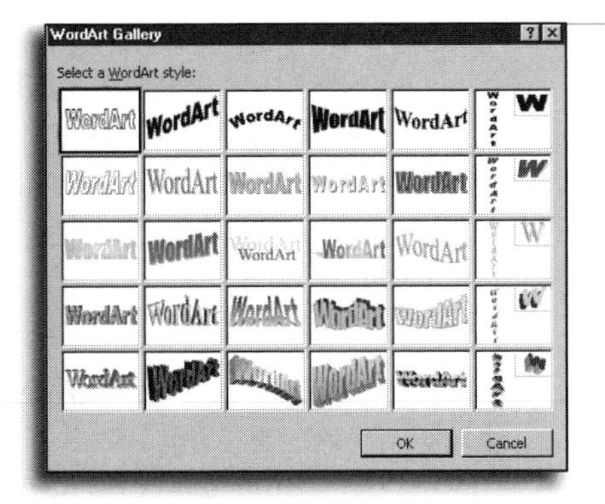

FIGURE 7.7
Choose a WordArt style from this dialog box. These choices actually produce custom AutoShapes.

3. In the next dialog box, you'll see the text you selected before you started. If you didn't select text, enter whatever you want to use as your logo.
4. Pick a font and size, and then click **OK**.
5. Inspect the results. If you're not satisfied, use the buttons on the WordArt toolbar to adjust your work.

The results appear in your document as an AutoShape. (See

Keep it simple

When creating a WordArt object, stick with TrueType fonts, and start with a simple font. Decorative fonts generally make bad WordArt.

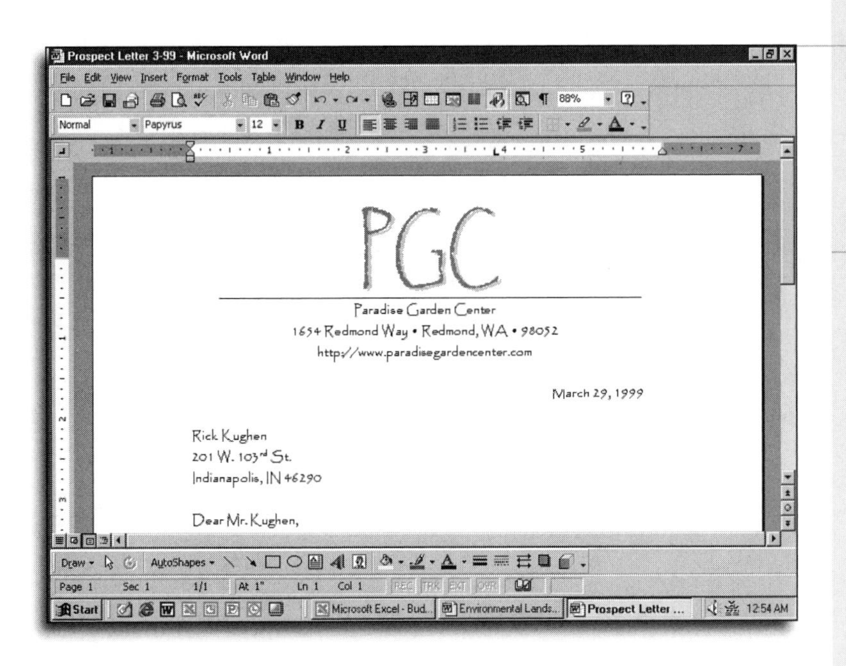

FIGURE 7.8
Creating this logo with WordArt took only a few clicks. I used the Papyrus typeface and added the address information to make a compelling letterhead.

Figure 7.8 for an example I created with just three letters and four clicks.) Drag any of the sizing handles to change its appearance, or click the **Free Rotate** button on the Drawing toolbar to slant the WordArt object up or down.

Compatible graphics formats

Office recognizes and imports the following common graphics file formats: *Windows Metafile* (WMF) and *Enhanced Metafile* (EMF), *JPEG File Interchange Format* (JPG and JPEG), *Windows Bitmap* (BMP), and *Graphics Interchange Format* (GIF) files. If you have an image in another file format, such as those created by professional drawing and drafting programs like AutoCAD, you may be able to import it directly into Office if you first install the correct graphics filter. For a detailed list of compatible file formats, open Word and search for the Help topic "Graphics file types Word can use."

Adding Pictures to Your Documents

To add a picture or a graphic image to any Word document, Excel worksheet, PowerPoint slide, or Publisher publication, position the insertion point at the spot where you want the picture to appear, pull down the **Insert** menu, and then choose **Picture**.

Choices on this menu include the following:

- **Clip Art**—This selection opens the Microsoft Clip Gallery application. Your options include hundreds of drawings and a smaller number of high-quality scanned photos.
- **From File**—Import a file saved in any of several graphics formats. The Web is a good source of high-quality images.
- **From Scanner or Camera**—If you've installed a scanner, you can convert photographs, documents, magazine pages, and other hard copy to editable images. Office 2000 includes a scanner add-in that lets you scan directly into Office without having to use an external image editing program.

Use the corners

Dragging the sizing handles on the top, bottom, or sides of a picture will stretch and distort the image. To maintain the aspect ratio of the picture so that it looks normal, use the sizing handles in any of the corners instead.

When you insert a picture into a document it appears full size. If the picture file is six inches wide, that's what you'll see in your document. To resize the picture, select it and maneuver the sizing handles.

All new in Office 2000

If you were turned off by the Clip Gallery in previous Office versions, try it again. The version in Office 2000 is remarkably easy to use and well worth experimenting with. The images are better, too.

Working with the Clip Gallery

Flip to the back of any computer magazine and you'll find enormous collections of clip media for sale at bargain prices.

Most commercially available collections, unfortunately, are stuffed onto CD-ROMs in separate files, and it's nearly impossible to find the image you're looking for. The Microsoft Clip Gallery, a utility included with Office 2000, actually makes it easy to browse through hundreds or thousands of clips to find the one that's just right for your document.

The Clip Gallery is a fully indexed graphics database that lets you search for images in a wide variety of ways. To open the Clip Gallery, pull down the **Insert** menu, choose **Picture**, and select **Clip Art**. The opening screen lets you browse through thumbnail sketches of the images in your collection, organized by category. Drill down through categories until you find the right image, or enter a keyword in the **Search for clips** box to narrow the selection, as shown in Figure 7.9 (the clip art available to you might be different depending on which of the Office applications you've installed—particularly if you've installed Publisher).

When you find an image you like, right-click and choose **Insert** to pop the image into place. The Gallery window stays open, so you can use it again. If you click an image, you see a collection of four buttons that let you insert it into your document, preview it in a larger window, add it to your list of favorite clips, or search for similar clips.

Want more images?

Click the **Clips Online** button to connect to Microsoft's Web site and search for even more clip art, sounds, and videos.

Watch out for copyright violations

"Borrowing" an image from any Web page is easy. When you see a graphic image you want to save and reuse, right-click and choose **Save Picture As** from Internet Explorer's shortcut menu. Be aware, however, that many images are copyrighted material, and you legally cannot reuse them without the permission of the copyright owner. Pay particular attention to copyrights when your document is intended for the Web or for distribution to a wide audience. One of the chief advantages of most clip art collections (including the images in the Clip Gallery included with Office 2000) is that you're free to reuse them without additional payments or permissions.

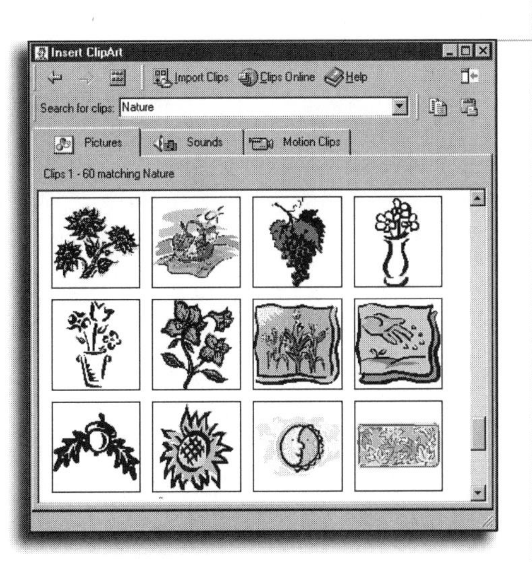

FIGURE 7.9

Enter a keyword to search through the Clip Gallery collection for images that match a concept.

CHAPTER

8

Sharing Data Between Documents

- Use the Clipboard to share data between documents
- Collect and copy multiple objects
- Drag and drop with the right mouse button for maximum control
- Copy formats from one place to another
- Link files and let Office keep each one up-to-date
- Save two or more types of data in one file
- Use Office binders to manage large files

Cutting and Pasting Data

Words are words. Numbers are numbers. A picture is a picture. And thanks to the *Windows Clipboard*, you can effortlessly copy words, numbers, and graphics from one document to another, regardless of which Office program created the file, without tedious retyping. To cut, copy, and paste data using the Clipboard, you can take your choice of techniques: Click toolbar buttons, right-click menus, or use keyboard shortcuts. Special paste options let you control the exact appearance of the data when it lands in its new destination.

The Clipboard is one of the most powerful common features in Windows, and Office 2000 extends its capabilities dramatically. Normally, Windows stores only one object at a time on the Clipboard; each time you cut or copy a new object, it clears the previous contents from the Clipboard. When you cut or copy information from an Office 2000 application, however, Office retains up to 12 objects at a time. That feature lets you collect several pieces of text, worksheet ranges, or other objects and paste one or all of them in a new location.

When the *Clipboard toolbar* is hidden, the Clipboard works just as it does elsewhere in Windows. To add an object to the Clipboard, start by selecting something—a block of text in a Word document or a PowerPoint slide, for example, or a range in an Excel worksheet—then right-click and choose **Cut** or **Copy** from the shortcut menu.

When you place a chunk of data on the Clipboard, it remains in memory. To reuse the object you stored on the Clipboard most recently, move the *insertion point* to the spot where you want to insert the data—in the same document, in a different document window, or in a completely different program—right-click, and then choose **Paste**. This action inserts the last item you cut or copied into the current document at the insertion point.

Office only

The Office 2000 Clipboard enhancements are available only within Office programs. The Windows Clipboard has room for only one item at a time. If you cut or copy data from other programs, including Windows accessories like Notepad or Calculator, the information you copy appears on the Office Clipboard and you can paste it into Office programs; however, only the most recent item you cut or paste from Office appears on the Windows Clipboard. You can't paste data from the Office Clipboard into a non-Office program.

Why Clipboard commands are sometimes grayed out

Before you can use the **Cut** and **Copy** commands, you first have to make a selection. If you position the insertion point within a block of text in Word or PowerPoint, the **Cut** and **Copy** buttons on the Standard toolbar are grayed out and unavailable, as are the matching menu commands. Similarly, the **Paste** button and menu commands are unavailable until you place something on the Clipboard.

What's New in Office 2000

If you cut or copy an object to the Clipboard, then immediately paste it somewhere else, the Office Clipboard acts just like the Windows Clipboard. As soon as you copy a second item, however, the Clipboard toolbar, shown in Figure 8.1, appears.

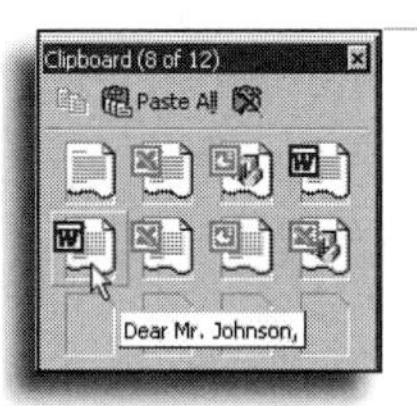

FIGURE 8.1
Office 2000 programs let you store up to 12 items on the Clipboard. The icon tells which program it came from, and a ScreenTip identifies the contents.

As you continue to cut or copy text, graphics, and objects, the Clipboard keeps track of the entire collection. You can use this collection as a convenient way to distribute boilerplate text or graphics through a document. To insert any one of the items on the Clipboard, click to position the insertion point at the spot where you want the Clipboard data to appear, then click the appropriate icon on the Clipboard toolbar.

Essential shortcuts

In most Windows programs (including all the Office programs), you can press Ctrl+C to copy the current selection to the Clipboard. If you never use any other keyboard shortcuts, you should memorize this one and its companions: Ctrl+X to cut and Ctrl+V to paste.

Clipboard Limitations

You should be aware of three significant limitations when using the Clipboard. First, remember that as far as Windows is concerned, the Clipboard holds only one clipping at a time. When you cut or copy data, it replaces the current contents of the Clipboard. If you use Windows-standard keyboard shortcuts or toolbar buttons to move Clipboard data from one place to another, those shortcuts will work only with the object you cut or copied most recently.

Second, Office stores multiple Clipboard objects in memory only. If you place two or more objects on the Office Clipboard, those objects will be available only as long as an Office program is open. If you close all Office programs, only the most recently cut or copied object will remain on the Clipboard.

Now you see it, now you don't

Working with the Clipboard toolbar can tax your patience. Sometimes it appears when you don't want it; other times it remains stubbornly hidden. If you click the Close button on the Clipboard toolbar three times without using any of its buttons, the toolbar remains hidden until you choose to display it again. To make the toolbar visible at any time, press Ctrl+C twice in a row, or right-click on any toolbar or the main menu bar and choose Clipboard from the list of available toolbars.

Undo lets you recover from data disasters

If you lose crucial data, don't forget that you can get it back by using the Undo feature in all Office programs. Press Ctrl+Z or click the **Undo** button to reverse the changes you've made in the current document, worksheet, or presentation. When the deleted data reappears, select it and copy it to the Clipboard; then press Ctrl+Y or click the Redo button to restore the changes you made. Paste the recovered data into the current file or a new document to use it.

Finally, Excel users should be aware of a quirk in the way that program handles the Clipboard. With virtually all Windows applications, whatever you copy to the Clipboard stays available until you replace it with other data or shut down the computer. Excel, however, uses the Clipboard differently.

- When you *copy* Excel data to the Clipboard, the border around the selection moves, and you see a prompt in the status bar at the bottom of the worksheet window. The data on the Clipboard remains available for pasting in multiple locations until you click in another cell or press Esc. When the status bar message disappears, Excel no longer allows you to paste the contents of the Clipboard using Windows-standard techniques.
- When you *cut* Excel data to the Clipboard, you see the same moving border and status bar message. You can paste the data into multiple locations in another program, such as Word, but when you paste it into another location in a worksheet, Excel removes the selection and clears the contents of the Clipboard. At that point, the Paste button and keyboard shortcut no longer respond as they normally do; the only way to reuse the cut data is to use the corresponding button on the Clipboard toolbar.

When should you drag and drop?

Drag-and-drop editing is the fastest, easiest way to move words and numbers around on the same screen, but it takes practice and considerable manual dexterity when you're trying to move data between two separate document or program windows. When you want to share data between different windows, use the keyboard shortcuts or **Copy**, **Cut**, **Paste**, and **Paste Special** menu options instead.

Dragging and Dropping Data

For simple moves, such as rearranging a few sentences in a Word document or moving a block of cells from one place to another on an Excel worksheet, it's often easiest to just drag the text or numbers from one spot and drop them in the new location. When you use this technique with Office programs, you bypass the Clipboard completely.

All Office programs allow you to use either of two variations on the basic drag-and-drop technique. If you hold down the left mouse button while dragging text or other data from one location, you move the data; when you drop it in its new location, the data in the original location disappears.

To copy text or objects (even entire documents) from one place to another without deleting the original data, hold down the Ctrl key while you drag. When you do so, you see a small plus sign at the bottom of the mouse pointer to indicate that you're about to copy the selection. The original data remains in place.

You can also hold down the right mouse button while dragging data in any Office program. This technique typically pops up a shortcut menu that lets you choose what you want to do with the data. In an Excel worksheet, for example, you can copy or move values and formats instead of formulas; in all Office programs, you can right-drag to create links and hyperlinks.

Dragging Text or Objects from One Place to Another

1. Select the block of text or object (such as a chart or graphic) that you want to move or copy.
2. Hold down the right mouse button and drag the selection to its new location.
3. Release the mouse button. You then see a shortcut menu like the one in Figure 8.2. (The exact choices depend on the type of data you've selected.)
4. Choose an action from the menu.

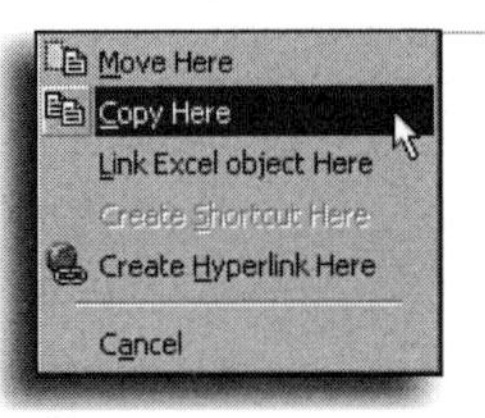

FIGURE 8.2
When you hold down the right mouse button while dragging a selection, Office programs offer you a menu of choices when you release the button. Choose a simple copy to leave the original text undisturbed.

Collecting and Copying Multiple Items

Use the **Paste All** button to insert all items on the Clipboard at the insertion point. This is a powerful way to gather and summarize items in a file. For example, you can collect paragraphs of text from several memos and paste them into a new document that summarizes all of them. Or you might gather related data from different Excel worksheets and paste it into a new sheet to consolidate results.

Mix and match data—carefully

You can gather any mix of items on the Clipboard, including text from a Word document or a PowerPoint outline, ranges in Excel worksheets, charts, and graphics. However, you can't paste all those data types into every kind of Office document. When you're collecting and copying information, your best bet is to stick with a single data type.

What happens when the Clipboard is full?

After you've filled all 12 slots on the Clipboard toolbar, cutting or copying another item triggers a warning from the Office Assistant that you're about to remove the oldest item on the Clipboard and add the one you just cut or copied. Click **OK** to add the new data to the Clipboard; click **Cancel** to retain the current Clipboard contents.

Collecting and Copying Multiple Items

1. If the Clipboard toolbar is not visible, display it. Pull down the **View** menu, choose **Toolbars**, and select **Clipboard** from the list.
2. If there are any items on the Clipboard, click the **Clear Clipboard** button to remove them.
3. Add the first item to the Clipboard using any standard technique, including the Cut and Copy buttons and keyboard shortcuts.
4. Cut or copy more items to the Clipboard using the same technique. You can add up to 12 items to the Clipboard.
5. Position the insertion point at the spot where you want to add the copied material. Click the **Paste All** button to add the entire contents of the Office Clipboard.

Here are a few rules to keep in mind when you use the **Paste All** button on the Clipboard toolbar:

- Pasting multiple items is an all-or-nothing proposition; you cannot select a subset of items and paste them in a single operation.
- You cannot control the format of pasted items when you use this technique. Each item appears in the default Paste format.
- When you paste multiple items, they appear in the current document, presentation, or worksheet just as if you had pressed the Enter key between items. You cannot control the position of each item within the document.
- The Clipboard toolbar is not available in Slide Sorter view in PowerPoint.

Controlling the Format of Data When You Paste

Copying data from one location to another in the same document is a straightforward process. But what happens when you use the Clipboard to copy a range from an Excel worksheet and paste it into a Word document?

If you simply use the **Copy** and **Paste** commands, your worksheet range ends up as a Word table, formatted more or less like the original Excel range. But what if you want to copy the text into your document? Or what if you want to keep the original worksheet formulas?

To control exactly what happens when you paste data, pull down the **Edit** menu and choose **Paste Special**. When you copy an Excel range to the Clipboard and choose this command in your Word document, for example, you see a dialog box like the one in Figure 8.3.

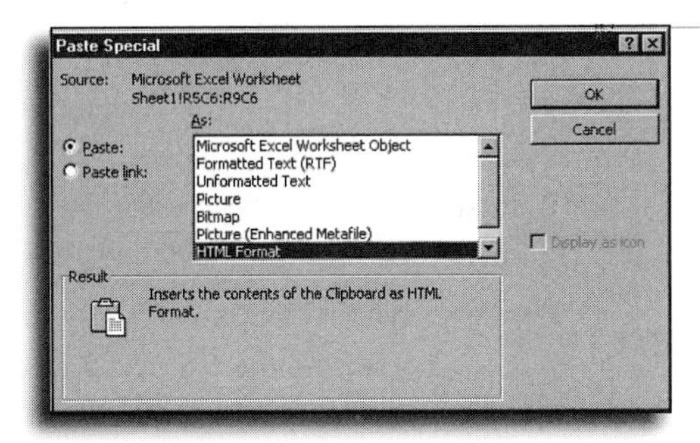

FIGURE 8.3
Use the **Paste Special** command to specify exactly how Windows translates your data from one program to another.

In the Paste Special dialog box, you can choose one of the following special formats:

- **HTML format**—When you copy and paste formatted text between Office programs, this is the standard. *HTML format* is ideal for capturing character formats, font information, tables, and other formatting.

SEE ALSO

➤ *For an explanation of how Office uses HTML, see page 46*

- **Formatted Text (RTF)**—This option is typically available when you paste data into Word documents or PowerPoint presentations. RTF stands for *Rich Text Format*, which matches fonts, colors, shading, and column widths. When you copy an Excel range into a Word document using this format, you lose column headings and formulas, but you retain most of the original look.

When in doubt, choose HTML or RTF

If you're pasting data from a non-Office application (such as a Web page you're viewing in Internet Explorer) and you want to preserve formatting information, select **HTML format**. If that option isn't available, use the **Formatted Text (RTF)** option in the Paste Special dialog box. Rich Text Format preserves the maximum amount of formatting, even when the underlying document format is different.

What is Unicode?

Unicode is an international standard for encoding characters from any language. Unlike ASCII text, which is restricted to the Latin alphabet used in English and other Western European languages, Unicode supports characters, punctuation, technical symbols, dingbats, and other characters from virtually every language on Earth. To learn more about Unicode, visit `http://www.unicode.org`.

- **Unformatted Text** or **Text** or **Unicode Text**—Letters and numbers appear in your document window just as if you had typed them directly. Formatting and formulas are lost, and the text picks up the formatting of the paragraph, slide, or worksheet range into which you insert it.
- **Picture** or **Picture (Enhanced Metafile)**—An image of the selection appears in the document window. If you use this format to paste text or a worksheet range into a Word document or a PowerPoint presentation, the pasted data appears in a text box, and you can edit its contents. Text pasted into Excel using this format is not editable.
- **Bitmap** or **Device Independent Bitmap**—An image of the selection appears in the document window. You can move or crop a pasted bitmap, but you cannot edit it. Whenever possible, use the Picture format instead of this one; Picture format uses less memory and looks better.
- ***[Object type]*** **Object**—When you paste data as an embedded object, it retains the formatting of the original data type. Double-click on the embedded object (a Microsoft Excel Worksheet Object, for example) to edit the data in place. I'll discuss objects in more detail later in this chapter.
- **Hyperlink** or **Attach Hyperlink** or **Word Hyperlink**—Some of these options are visible only when you choose the **Paste link** option in the Paste Special dialog box. This option creates a clickable link that jumps to the original location (a slide in a PowerPoint presentation, for example).

Copying Formats

You can quickly copy character formatting and named styles from place to place, regardless of which program you're using. You'll find the **Format Painter** button on the Standard toolbar in Word, Excel, and PowerPoint. Use it to copy font information, text and number formats, colors, spacing, and other attributes for nearly any object.

Using the Format Painter

1. Select the text or object whose formatting you want to copy. If you position the insertion point within a Word document without selecting any text, the Format Painter picks up and paragraph formats.
2. Click the **Format Painter** button on the Standard toolbar. The mouse pointer changes to a small animated paintbrush that resembles the drawing on the button.
3. Click in the new location to copy formats to a single word, paragraph, cell, or bullet point. Use the paintbrush to "sweep" the new format across a group of objects or a block of text.
4. If you double-clicked the **Format Painter** button to copy formats to multiple locations, press Esc (or click the **Format Painter** button again) to restore the normal mouse pointer.

Format Painter limitations

You can use the Format Painter button to copy formats between different documents created by the same program, but it doesn't work between programs. To copy formatting from a Word document to a PowerPoint presentation, you have to use the Clipboard. After you've copied formatted text or an object into the second program, you can then use the Format Painter to share that formatting with other text or objects.

Paint more than once

Double-click on the **Format Painter** button to lock it in place; this way, you can "paint" formats to multiple locations in the same document. If you click the button once, the painter is good for one swipe only.

Clearing the Clipboard

To clear all cut or copied objects from the Clipboard, click the **Clear Clipboard** button on the Clipboard toolbar.

Careful with that Clipboard!

When you clear the Clipboard, there's no way to bring back its contents. The Undo button doesn't have any effect—data that was on the Clipboard is gone for good.

Using Links to Keep Data Up-to-Date

Some documents are under nearly constant revision. As the deadline for annual budgets approaches at my company, for example, the business manager updates her Excel worksheet every day and then circulates the relevant portions to five department managers with a cover memo summarizing the previous day's changes. She could simply copy the worksheet data and paste it into a new set of memos each day, but that would mean repeating the tedious cut-and-paste process five times every morning. There's a much more efficient alternative.

Instead of just copying the worksheet data and pasting it into her document, she creates a *link* to the data in the Excel worksheet and pastes it into the Word document. Each time she opens the document, Word checks the current version of the worksheet. If the data in the worksheet has changed, those changes appear automatically in the Word document, too. She opens the budget memo for each manager, adds a few comments, and sends the file to the appropriate manager.

Use these steps for any link

Although this example focuses on the common scenario of pasting a worksheet range into a Word document, the same techniques apply regardless of the type of data you're linking.

How to Link Two or More Office Documents

To create a link between a document and a worksheet, start by copying data to the Windows Clipboard; then use the **Paste Special** command to paste the data and information about the linked file.

Linking Worksheet Data to a Document

You can link in several formats

Although it's common to *embed* a linked Excel object in a Word document or PowerPoint presentation, you can also link an object using HTML format. Changes you make to the source data appear in the document that contains the link, regardless of the format you choose.

1. In your Excel worksheet, select the range you want to copy.
2. Right-click the selection and choose **Copy** from the shortcut menu.
3. Switch to Word and position the insertion point at the place where you want to add the worksheet data.
4. Pull down the **Edit** menu and choose **Paste Special**.
5. In the Paste Special dialog box, choose the **Paste link** option.
6. Select **Microsoft Excel Worksheet Object** from the list labeled **As** and then click **OK**. After a few seconds, you'll see the copied range in your document, as in the example in Figure 8.4. Although it resembles a Word table, it's actually stored in Excel format.

Using links over a network

Links are especially useful when you're working with shared documents on a corporate network. When you store a shared file in a network folder, anyone with access rights to that folder can update the file. When you create a link to that file in another document, Word automatically updates the linked data with the most recent version, regardless of who updated it. Two users cannot simultaneously work with a linked Word document, however.

How to Change a Link

Office programs track links between files by using hidden formulas within a document, worksheet, or presentation. When you rename the source file or move it to a different drive or folder, you can break the link between it and another file. In that case, the information in the file that contains the link doesn't update properly when you update the source document. To fix the problem, you can delete the linked data and insert a fresh copy, or edit the link information.

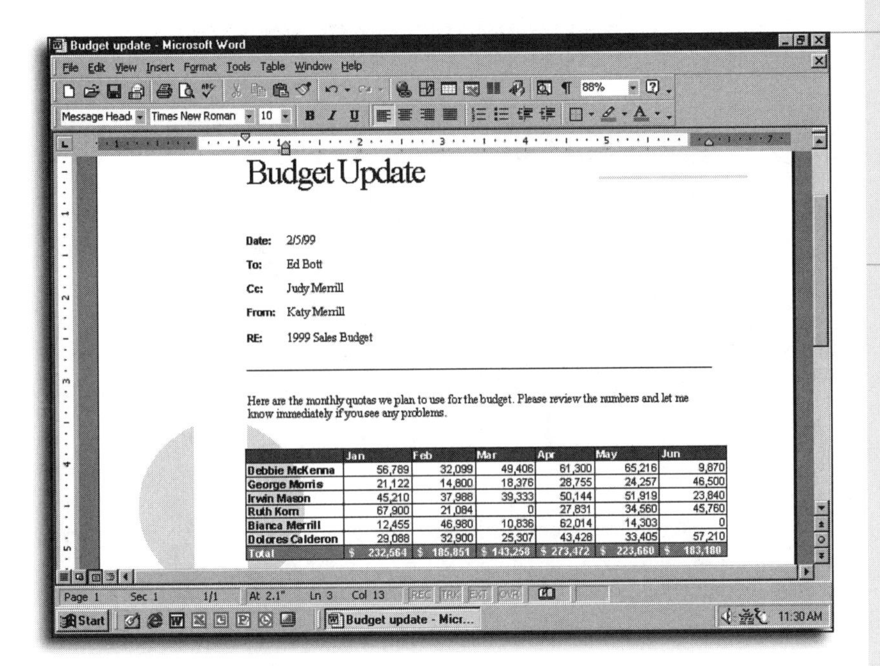

Budget Update

Date: 2/5/99
To: Ed Bott
Cc: Judy Merrill
From: Katy Merrill
RE: 1999 Sales Budget

Here are the monthly quotas we plan to use for the budget. Please review the numbers and let me know immediately if you see any problems.

	Jan	Feb	Mar	Apr	May	Jun
Debbie McKenna	56,789	32,099	49,406	61,300	65,216	9,870
George Morris	21,122	14,800	18,376	28,755	24,257	46,500
Irwin Mason	45,210	37,988	39,333	50,144	51,919	23,840
Ruth Korn	67,900	21,084	0	27,831	34,560	45,760
Bianca Merrill	12,455	46,980	10,836	62,014	14,303	0
Dolores Calderon	29,088	32,900	25,307	43,428	33,405	57,210
Total	$ 232,564	$ 185,851	$ 143,258	$ 273,472	$ 223,660	$ 183,180

FIGURE 8.4

At a glance, you can't tell that the table in this Word memo is linked to an Excel worksheet. However, if the worksheet numbers change, the data in this memo changes, too.

To change a link after you've set it up, pull down the **Edit** menu and choose **Links**. (The command is available in all Office programs, but only if the current document, workbook, or presentation contains linked data.) You then see a dialog box like the one in Figure 8.5.

Saving Different Types of Data in One File

Links between files can be fragile, especially when you send one of the files away from your computer or your network. If the source file is unavailable—because someone deleted it or moved it, or because the recipient of the file doesn't have access to the network folder where it's stored—your carefully constructed link doesn't work anymore. The numbers are still visible in the document that contains the link, but updates to the source file don't appear properly.

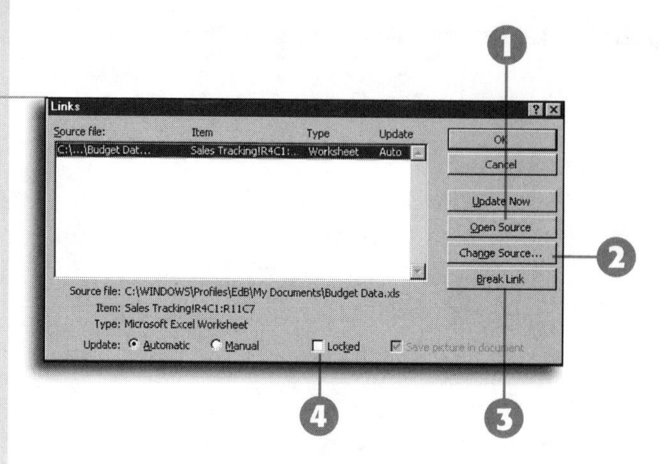

FIGURE 8.5

Use this dialog box to update links between files or to change the source of linked information in a document.

1. To edit the linked file (a worksheet, in this example), click here.
2. If the name or location of the linked file has changed, click here to change the link information.
3. To remove a link, click here. (This option is not available when you link two Excel workbooks.)
4. To prevent updates to your document temporarily, check this box.

In these circumstances, links are inappropriate. Say, for example, that you want to insert live data from your most recent sales-tracking worksheet (created in Excel) into a lengthy report (created using Word). If you attach two separate, linked files to an email message, you have no guarantee that the recipient will copy the two files to the right folders. If the two files are separated, the links no longer work.

Fortunately, there's an alternative that lets you store two or more different types of data within the same document. *Embed* the Excel worksheet in your Word report. Embedding one type of data in a file alongside another type of data lets you preserve the ability to edit the original data, while guaranteeing that the information is up-to-date at all times.

How Embedding and Linking Differ

When you create a link to a file, you paste a picture of the source data into the file that contains the link; the data itself remains in the source file. When you *embed* a worksheet range in your Word document, on the other hand, you save the data in Excel format and then store it within the Word document. The result is a single file that contains all your data.

When you open a Word document that contains an embedded worksheet, it still looks as if you've pasted the worksheet data onto the page. Double-clicking on the worksheet lets you edit the worksheet data using Excel; you can view and change all the values, formulas, and formats of the original worksheet. When you save the Word document, it also saves changes to the embedded Excel data.

Creating a New Object

Just as you can copy or link data, the secret of successfully embedding data into another file is to use the Windows Clipboard. (Although the sample procedure here uses Word and Excel, you could just as easily embed an Excel chart in a PowerPoint presentation.)

Embedding Excel Data in a Word File

1. Open the Excel worksheet and select the range you want to embed.
2. Right-click the selection and choose **Copy** from Excel's shortcut menu.
3. Switch to Word and position the insertion point at the place in the current document where you want to insert the worksheet range. (If you want, you can create a new document or open another document at this point.)
4. Pull down the **Edit** menu and choose **Paste Special**.
5. Choose **Microsoft Excel Worksheet Object** from the list. Do not click the **Paste link** option.
6. Click **OK** to embed the worksheet in your document.

When you embed an Excel range into a Word document, the data looks as though it's stored in a Word table, but it behaves differently. For example, when you click the embedded object, the status bar shows this message: `Double-click to Edit Microsoft Excel Worksheet.`

Changing the Data in an Embedded Worksheet

1. Double-click the embedded data (in this case, the Excel range).

Data types you can link and embed

You can mix and match data from all three major Office applications. Within any file created by Word, Excel, or PowerPoint, you can embed a Word document or picture, an Excel worksheet or chart, or a PowerPoint presentation or slide. You cannot link or embed Outlook data in other Office document types, nor can you link or embed Office data into Outlook items. You can, however, insert an Outlook item as an icon in any Office file, and you can attach Office document icons to Outlook items.

Be careful with shortcut menus

When you want to embed data or paste a link into Word or PowerPoint, you must use the pull-down menus because the right-click shortcut menus do not include the **Paste Special** option. Excel users have it a little easier, because that program's shortcut menus include this handy choice.

Embedding a fresh new object

Typically, Windows applications that support object linking and embedding offer a way to insert any kind of *object* into a document. In Office, you find this feature when you pull down the **Insert** menu and choose **Object**. The list of choices lets you choose any type of object that is registered with Windows, including audio and video clips, bitmap images, and objects created with Office applets, such as Organization Chart.

The embedded data remains in place and the name of the Word document remains in the title bar, but Excel's toolbars and menus replace Word menus and toolbars. You also see a thick gray border (complete with row and column headings) around the embedded data, as in Figure 8.6.

2. Edit the data as you want, using the Excel menus and toolbars.
3. After you've finished working with the embedded range, click on any spot in the main Word document to restore the Word toolbars and menus and resume editing.

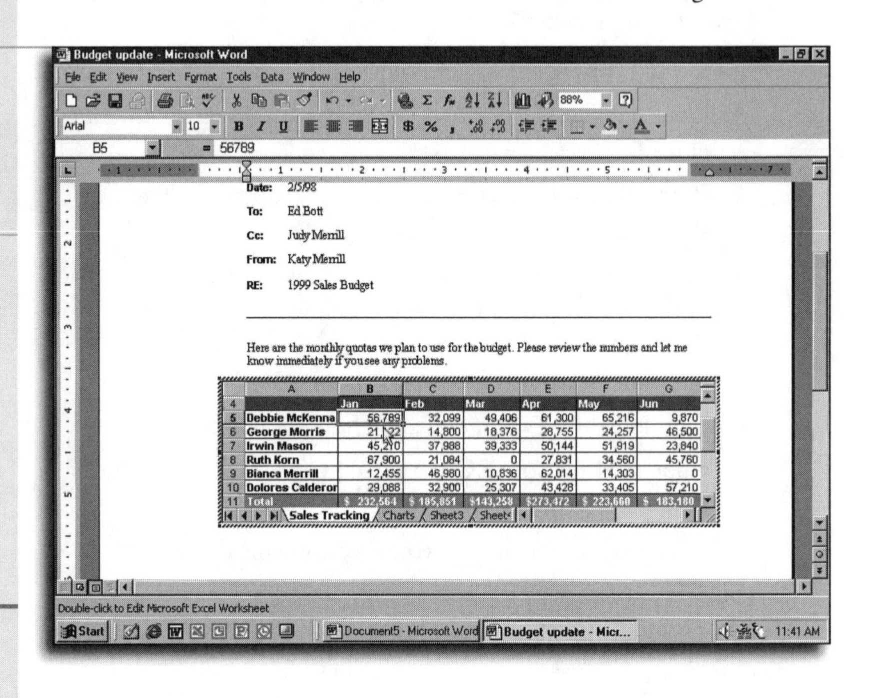

FIGURE 8.6

The title bar is from Word, but the toolbars and menus belong to Excel; that's typical when working with embedded data.

Moving and resizing embedded objects

You can move and resize embedded objects within a document, and you can adjust a wide range of other properties as well. For example, you can add or remove borders and colors from objects. To move an object, point to the object and use the four-headed arrow to drag it. Use resizing handles on all four sides and corners to change its shape. To see other properties you can change, point to the object, right-click, and choose **Format Object** from the shortcut menu.

SEE ALSO

➤ *For in-depth discussions of what you can and can't do with linked and embedded objects in the most popular Office programs, pick up a copy of* Special Edition Using Word 2000 *or* Special Edition Using Excel 2000, *both published by Que Corporation.*

Managing Large Projects with Office Binders

A *binder* is a special type of document file specifically designed to store multiple Office documents. To work with binders, you use an Office application called Binder. When you drop a file into a binder, you tell Office to treat it as one section of a single, larger file. You can store as many Office files as you want within a binder. The name of the binder file serves the same function as the label on the spine of a three-ring binder; to work with the individual pieces, you have to look inside.

SEE ALSO

➤ *For instructions on how to install the Binder program, see page 691*

Binders offer some time-saving advantages when you work with large projects that include multiple documents. If any of the following issues are of concern to you, consider using binders; if not, you can safely skip this section.

- You can perform a task such as spell-checking on a group of documents at once, instead of starting and stopping the same job separately for each file.
- You can share styles among several files, even if they were created by different applications.
- You can print the entire group of files at once, with consecutive page numbers—all by clicking one button.

When you save a binder, you create a single file on your disk. If you look in a folder window or in the Windows Explorer, you see its type listed as Microsoft Office Binder (the MS-DOS filename ends with the .OBD extension). This file holds all the other files (Word documents, Excel worksheets and charts, and PowerPoint presentations) contained within your binder. Figure 8.7 shows an example of an Office binder.

Should you use binders?

Microsoft introduced the Binder program years ago in Office 95, and since then it's hardly changed a bit. In fact, when you install Office 2000 on a new system, you have to go out of your way to add the Binder program—it's not part of the default installation. A small number of Office users find this omnibus file format indispensable, but for most people it's simply not necessary.

Outlook and binders don't work together

You can't store any kind of Outlook item in a binder, nor can you store Web pages in a binder. However, you can create or add files created in Microsoft Project to a binder file.

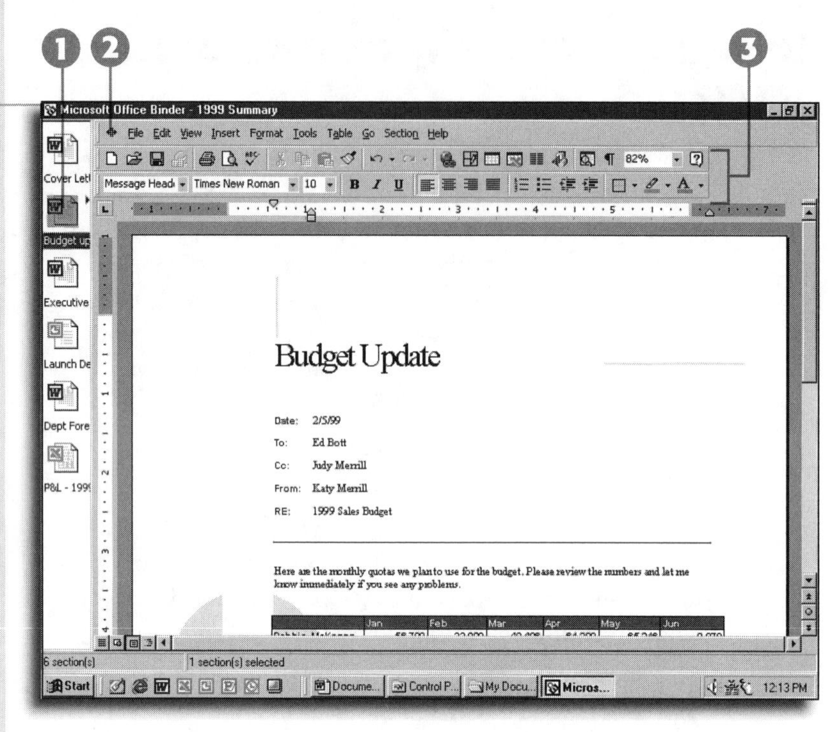

FIGURE 8.7

In an Office binder, each section has its own icon and filename. The commands on the **File** menu apply to the entire binder. The commands on the **Section** menu apply only to the document in that section.

1. The *binder pane* shows all the files contained in this binder. This binder includes Word, Excel, and PowerPoint files. To add new files, drag them from a folder window into this pane.
2. Click the **Show/Hide Left Pane** button to hide the binder pane, letting you see just the file you're working on at the moment. Click again to make the pane visible.
3. When you click a binder file's icon, Office opens the application that the file uses. The toolbars, menus, and rulers here tell you you're working with Word in the Binder window.

To create a new binder and begin filling it with sections, click the **New Office Document** button on the **Start** menu or the Office Shortcut Bar. Click the **General** tab, select the icon for a Blank Binder, and click **OK**. Drag and drop files from any Explorer window to add them to a binder, or use the **Section** menu to create a new section from scratch.

No icon? Run Setup

If you don't see the Blank Binder icon in the list of available Office templates, you need to run Setup and install the Microsoft Binder program.

Rearranging Sections in a Binder

The order of sections in a binder can be crucial for tasks such as page numbering. As you would expect, you can rearrange sections by simply dragging and dropping icons in the left pane. You can also use the **Section** menu (found only when you're working within a binder) to rename, rearrange, or hide a section.

To move a section, click its icon in the left pane until you see a small document icon appear over the mouse pointer. Drag the icon up or down within the left pane of the binder. A small arrow along the right edge of the pane indicates where the document will land when you release your mouse button.

To delete files in a binder, select the file's icon, right-click, and choose **Delete** from the shortcut menu.

No safety net

Be careful when you're deleting files from a binder. No Recycle Bin is available here, and the Binder doesn't have an Undo button, either. When you delete a section, it's gone for good.

Printing Binders

Complex reports and proposals might be assembled from many Word documents and Excel workbooks. This is especially true when several workers share responsibility for individual pieces. There's no easy way to print a collection of separate files in one smooth operation, and the hardest part of the job is numbering pages correctly. I've seen otherwise sensible people surrender completely, collating all the pieces by hand, writing in the page numbers with a ball-point pen, and making photocopies of the complete package.

Binders allow a far more elegant solution, however. Assemble that same group of documents in an Office binder, add headers and footers to keep track of page numbers and sections, and choose which sections you want to print. Office keeps page numbers in the right sequence and in a consistent position throughout the job.

Printing Multiple Office Files in a Binder

1. Open the binder file, pull down the **File** menu, and choose **Print Binder**. You see the dialog box shown in Figure 8.8.
2. To select specific sections you want to print, hold down the Ctrl key as you click icons in the left pane. Skip this step if you want to print all sections in the binder.
3. In the options labeled **Print what**, tell Office whether you want to print **All visible sections** or only the **Section(s) selected in left pane**.
4. In the area labeled **Numbering**, choose **Consecutive** to have Office number each page in sequence, regardless of which section it's in. Choose **Restart each section** to number individual sections as though they were self-contained files.

5. Click the **Preview** button to see all the pages in each section, complete with page numbers, headers, and footers, exactly as they will be printed. The binder switches to the print preview window for the application that created the documents in each section.
6. Choose the number of copies to print, and click **OK** to send the job to the printer.

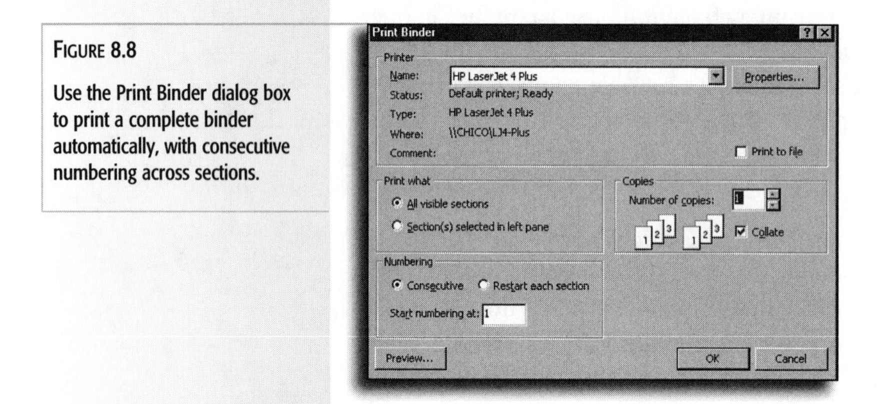

FIGURE 8.8

Use the Print Binder dialog box to print a complete binder automatically, with consecutive numbering across sections.

PART

II

Using Word 2000

CHAPTER

9

Getting Started with Word

Build Word documents from scratch

Use templates to jump-start a document

Convert files from other formats

Prevent document disasters

Change your view to edit more easily

Zoom in for a closer view and zoom out for the big picture

Creating a New Document

Do you know what kind of document you want to create? As I explain later in this chapter, Word includes a slew of ready-made templates that can get you started with letters, reports, Web pages, fax cover sheets, and other common document types. If you simply want to start putting words on the page, without concern for formatting, you can start with the equivalent of a blank sheet of paper.

When you start Word by clicking its shortcut on the **Programs** menu, it automatically creates a new, blank document with the generic name Document1. At that point, just start typing. You can also choose to create a new document based on a wizard or template, if the right one is available.

Document1 disappears if you don't use it

When you open Word, it starts with a new, blank document called Document1. If you immediately open a saved document without using the blank document, the blank document goes away quietly.

To create a new blank document at any time, use one of the following three techniques:

- Click the **New** button.
- Press Ctrl+N.
- Pull down the **File** menu and choose **New**. Select **Blank Document** from the **General** tab and click **OK**.

When you use any of these techniques, the new document you create looks like a blank sheet of paper. Although no text appears on the page, your new document is actually based on the Normal document template, which is contained in a file called Normal.dot.

Can't find Normal.dot?

If Normal.dot isn't in either of the locations specified here, you can find it easily enough: Just click the Start button, choose **Find**, and then click **Files or Folders**. Enter the word `Normal` in the **Named** box, and specify that you want to search all local hard drives.

Word automatically creates the Normal document template using default settings the first time you run Word. Unless you've specified a new location for your Windows system files or user templates, you can find Normal.dot in the C:\Windows\ Application Data\Microsoft\Templates folder. (If you've enabled user profiles on your machine, each user will have a separate copy of Normal.dot stored as part of their profile; if you're not sure where your copy is located, click **Start** and use the **Find** option.)

If you've customized Word's default toolbars, menus, or styles at all, make a backup copy of Normal.dot and keep it in a safe place! If you want to remove your customizations and restore the default Normal document template, close Word and rename Normal.dot, using a name like Old-norm.dot. The next time you start Word, it will generate a new Normal document template file using standard settings.

The Normal document template is a tremendously important part of Word. Settings stored here define the basic look of every new document you create. Table 9.1 lists the basic settings for Normal.dot.

Why is your text at 10 points?

In Word 97, the default point size for text was 10 points. In Word 2000, this value is slightly larger, at 12 points. (Maybe Microsoft's programmers are getting older.) If you upgrade to Office 2000 over an existing copy of Office, Word will keep the old setting. If you install a fresh new copy of Office 2000, Word will use the new default size.

TABLE 9.1 Document Options Saved in the Normal Document Template

Document Option	Default Setting
Default margins	1 inch at top and bottom of page, 1.25 inches on each side
Default paper size and orientation	In the United States, Word uses 8.5×11 (Letter) paper in portrait orientation
Default font and font size	12-point Times New Roman
Styles	More than 90 built-in paragraph and character styles for specifying the look of text, lists, headings, and so on
Customization	Layouts for default menu bar, Standard and Formatting toolbars, plus 14 more toolbars and all shortcut menus

You can change any or all of the Normal document settings. You might prefer different margins, or you might want to use 12-point Garamond as the default font for all new documents you create.

Changing Settings for New Documents

1. Click the **New** button to open a new document based on the Normal document template.
2. Pull down the **File** menu and choose **Page Setup**. Make any adjustments to margins, paper size and orientation, paper source, and layout.

3. Click the **Default** button to save these changes, and click **Yes** when Word displays a dialog box warning that you're about to change the default settings. Click **OK** to close the Page Setup dialog box.
4. Pull down the **Format** menu and choose **Font**. Change font, font size, and other options, if you want.
5. Click the **Default** button (see Figure 9.1) to save font changes; then click **OK** to close the Font dialog box.
6. Change any built-in styles, if you want. Customize toolbars or menus, and add any macros or AutoText entries as necessary.
7. When you close Word, it saves the changes to the Normal document template. (You don't need to save the new document you created.) The next time you create a new document based on this template, it will use your custom options.

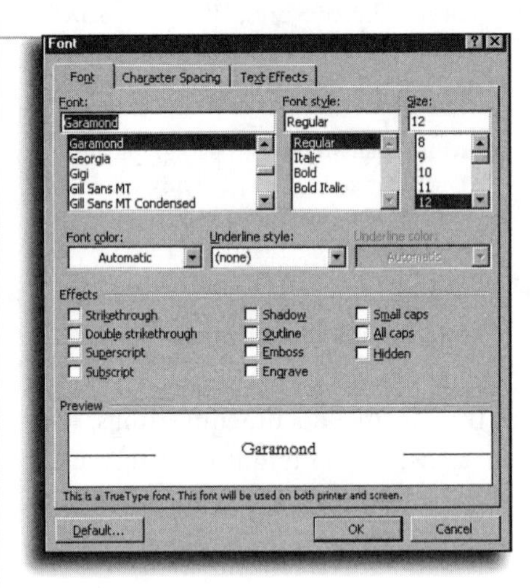

FIGURE 9.1

Click the **Default** button to use the selected font and size whenever you open a new document.

SEE ALSO

➤ *For an overview of your formatting options, see page 220*

➤ *To learn how to save your favorite formats as named styles, see page 255*

When you open a new document based on the Normal document template, just start typing. The thin flashing line that appears at the top of the page is called the *insertion point*, and it marks the spot where your letters and numbers will appear when you start typing. After your document contains text, you can click in a new place to move the insertion point. The insertion point remains in the same place regardless of where you aim the mouse pointer; to move the insertion point, you must click in a new location where you can enter text.

SEE ALSO

➤ *For a detailed description of Word 2000's new Click and Type option, see page 182*

Save all documents at one time

To force Word to save all open documents immediately, including the Normal document template, hold down the Shift key as you pull down the **File** menu and then choose **Save All**. This alternative pull-down menu also gives you a **Close All** option, which closes every open document window but leaves Word open. (Word will prompt you to save any changes first.)

Creating New Documents with Templates and Wizards

For an impressive overview of the kinds of documents you can produce with Word, look through its collection of ready-made *templates*. Start Word, click **File**, **New**, and browse the different tabs on the New dialog box. You'll find a diverse collection of professionally designed starter documents, including memos, letters, fax cover sheets, Web pages, brochures, directories, and press releases. For graduate students, a thesis template is even included. Word also includes a total of 10 wizards that walk you through the process of creating personalized faxes, letters, Web pages, newsletters, and other documents.

Great ideas, free!

I strongly recommend that you look at as many of these templates as possible, even if you think you'll never use that type of document. The sample text typically includes tips on how you can use Word more effectively. Because the documents themselves were designed by skilled graphic artists, they're a great source of ideas you can use to make your own documents more interesting and readable. As sample documents, they help illustrate some of Word's more advanced features.

Some of these ready-made Word templates are immediately useful as a starting point for your own documents. The Professional Fax cover sheet template shown in Figure 9.2, for example, lets you quickly replace the sample text and graphics with your own data.

Other Word templates demonstrate design principles and let you see how you can use Word features to create interesting documents. The Directory template shown in Figure 9.3, for example, offers a concise tutorial in using the Wingdings font to create interesting headings; it also shows how sections and columns look on the printed page.

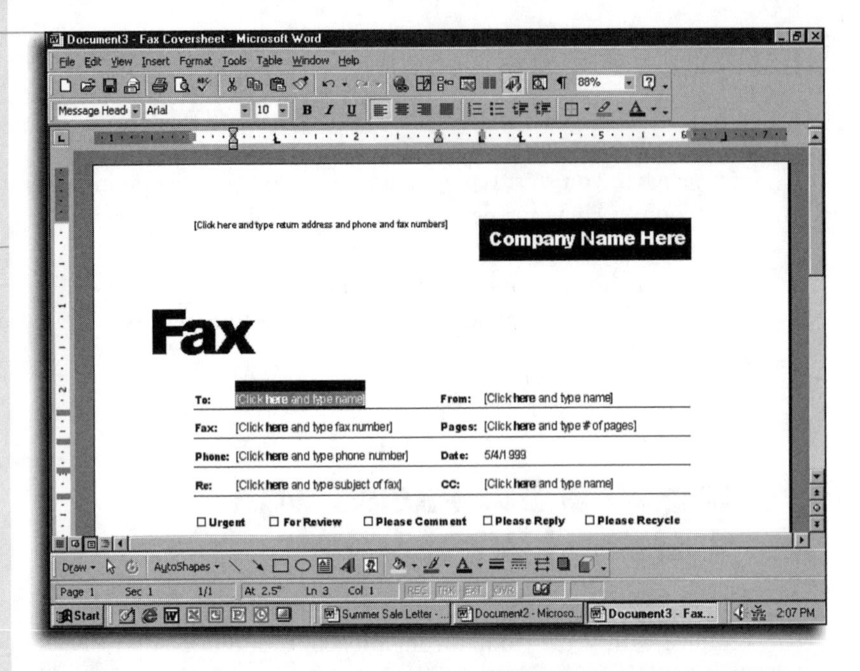

FIGURE 9.2

Click to replace these prompts with your own data; this template includes instructions for customizing your own fax cover sheet.

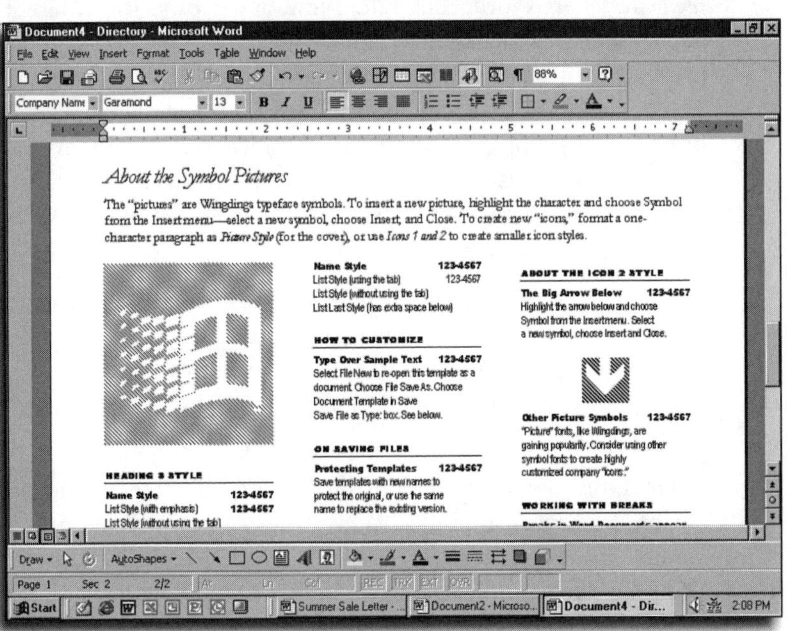

FIGURE 9.3

Sample text in this three-column Directory template includes tips on using icons as headings.

SEE ALSO

➤ *To learn how to manage document templates, see page 263*

Using Ready-Made Templates

To create a new document from a Word template, choose the **File** menu and then select **New**. The New dialog box shown in Figure 9.4 appears; it shows all the Word document templates available in your Templates folder, organized by category. (If you've added any templates of your own, they'll appear here as well.) Click a tab to look at the templates available in each category.

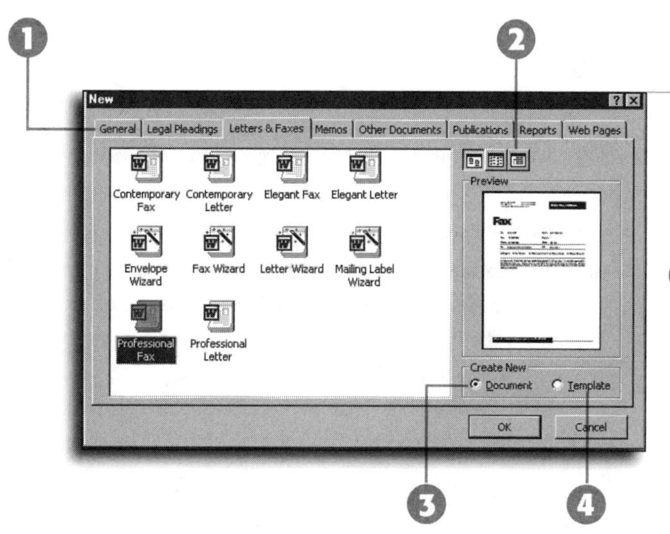

FIGURE 9.4

Pick a template from this dialog box. The preview box at right shows a thumbnail sketch of the selected template.

1. Each tab shows a different category of templates. To add a new tab, create a subfolder in the Templates folder and give it any name you like; to add templates in an existing category, create a subfolder with the same name as the category you see here.
2. Switch from large icons view to small icons or a list of file details.
3. Choose this default option to create a new document that contains all text and formatting options from the selected template.
4. Choose this option to make a copy of the template itself; then customize it and save the revised template under a new name.

In some of Word's default templates, you'll find generic text formatted using Word fields, which allow you to simply click to select the entire block of text and then type to replace it. In other cases, like the company name at the top of the Professional Memo template (Figure 9.5), you have to use the mouse to select the sample text and then replace it before you can use the document.

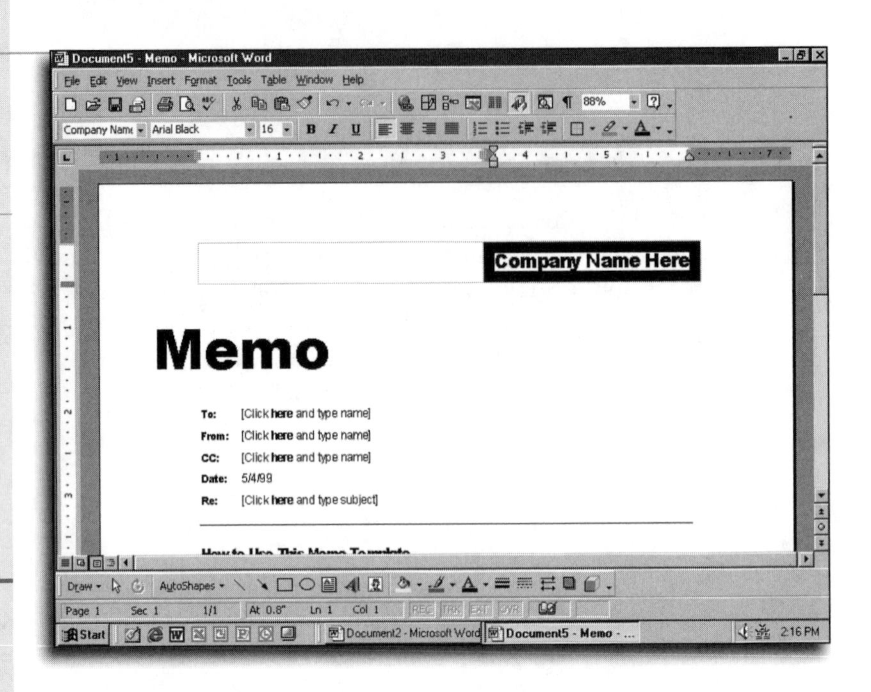

FIGURE 9.5

Select the "generic" text in a document template; it disappears as soon as you start typing.

Save templates in the right place

Be sure to save templates, including the Normal document template, in a location where Word can find them. By default, when you save a template, Word offers to store it in the same folder that holds your other templates. To set a different location for templates, pull down the **Tools** menu, choose **Options**, and click the **File Locations** tab. You can also specify an alternative location (usually on a network) where Word can find templates you share with other members of your workgroup.

Want to learn more about fields?

Fields contain special programming instructions that tell Word to automatically update the information when you create, save, or print a file. I don't have the space to provide details about this topic here; if you want to learn how to use fields in all sorts of documents, see Chapter 16, "Creating Dynamic Documents with Fields and Forms," in *Special Edition Using Office 2000*, published by Que.

As I mentioned earlier, in most cases, you should use Word's templates as a starting point for your own document. Don't just use the default graphics, typefaces, and other designs that come with a template—there are plenty of other Word users in the world, and they'll recognize it instantly. Do you really want friends, customers, and clients to see the same generic letters and memos from you that they get from everyone else?

Even after you customize a document template, be sure to proofread it carefully the first few times you use it. Pay special attention to headers, footers, and name and address information. Nothing is more embarrassing than sending a fax cover sheet that identifies you as an employee of Company Name Here. If you use a particular template regularly, turn to Chapter 12, "Using Templates and Styles," for instructions on customizing it for your own use.

SEE ALSO

➤ *To manage document templates, see page 263*

Creating Complex Documents with a Wizard's Help

Word 2000 offers an assortment of *wizards* designed to automate the process of creating new documents. These choices appear in the New dialog box alongside regular document templates; you can tell a wizard at a glance by its name (which invariably includes the word *Wizard*) and its distinctive icon (which includes a magic wand). Table 9.2 lists the wizards and what each one can do for you.

Wizards and templates work together

Most of Word's wizards work in conjunction with a matching set of templates. The Fax, Memo, Letter, and Résumé wizards, for example, let you choose from three templates in each category. If you customize any of these templates, you can make the wizard more useful.

Have the CD ready...

Only a few of the Word wizards are actually installed when you use Office 2000's default setup options. When you first try to use the wizards for creating agendas, calendars, résumés, newsletters, or legal pleadings, the Windows Installer program will prompt you to supply the necessary Office CD.

TABLE 9.2 **Word's Document Wizards**

Wizard Name	What It Produces for You
Memo	Produces inter-office memos in your choice of three styles; it fills in standard information including headers, footers, and address blocks.
Letter	Produces styles; it fills in basic information such as recipient name and address, plus signature block; you can replace sample body text with your own letter.
Fax	Creates cover sheets or faxes for an entire Word document; you can choose to use your fax software or print out for use with a fax machine.
Mailing Label	Creates one or several labels using standard Avery formats; you can pull information from your Windows address book.
Envelope	Creates one or several envelopes using standard formats; click a button to use names and addresses from your Outlook address book.
Agenda	Produces simple meeting agendas, including attendee lists, discussion points, and space for minutes.
Calendar	Creates a basic monthly calendar, using your choice of formats; one month per page.
Résumé	Produces chronological, professional, or other résumé formats; three standard designs; you can choose from a list of standard headings or add your own.
Newsletter	Produces an 8.5×11 newsletter in your choice of three designs; this template requires extensive customization to be useful.
Legal Pleading	Saves settings for each court in a custom template so you can reuse it later; this template is intended for use in law firms.

To use a wizard, simply follow the prompts. Most Word wizards include easy-to-follow online help. Choose options or fill in information on each of the wizard's dialog boxes, as in the Fax Wizard shown in Figure 9.6. Use the **Next** button as you complete each step, and click **Finish** when you're done.

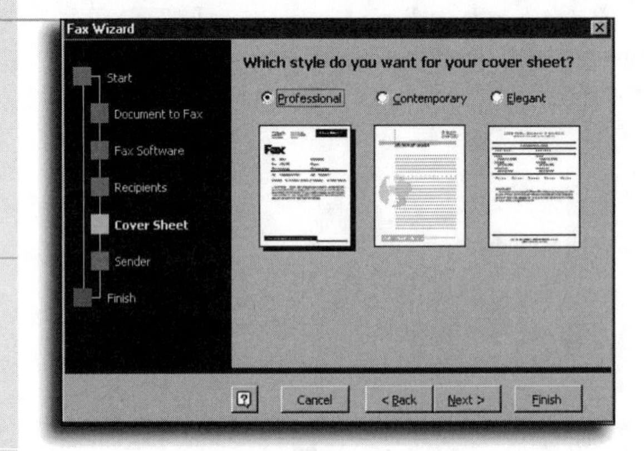

FIGURE 9.6

Wizards let you build documents by checking boxes and filling in blanks. Be sure to customize the fax cover sheet templates before using this one.

Opening a Saved Document

To open a saved document in any Office program, select the **File** menu and choose **Open**. When you select a document created by Word 2000, the process is straightforward. You may need to use special options, however, when you open a file created by another program or when you want to combine two or more files in a single document.

SEE ALSO

➤ *To learn more about opening and saving files, see page 31*

Working with Word 97

If you work for a large company that has decided to upgrade from Office 97 to Office 2000 over an extended period of time, it's possible that the upgrade process will take months, or even years. So what happens to shared files when some workers are using Word 97 and others have upgraded to Word 2000?

If you're lucky, there won't be any problems at all. Because Word 97 and Word 2000 use file formats that are almost identical, you can exchange files with Word 97 users without having to worry about converting files. Nor do you have to worry about losing data, although some types of advanced formatting will be affected if you use Word 97 to edit a file created in Word 2000.

In particular, data that is formatted using features that are new to Word 2000, such as nested tables and multilevel bulleted lists, will not survive the translation process. So if you use Word 2000 to create a document that contains a table within a table, a Word 97 user will be able to open that document, although the contents of the nested table will not look the same as in Word 2000. If the Word 97 user makes some changes to the document and saves it, the nested table will no longer appear correctly, even if you open the document in Word 2000.

If you know that another person will be using Word 97 to edit a document you're creating, you can save that file in Word 97 format. Pull down the **File** menu, choose **Save As**, and select Word 97 from the **Save as type** list. Word will warn you that you may lose formatting or data in the process. If you're not certain what the changes will be, save the file in Word 2000 format first, then save it in Word 97 format under a new name.

In offices where you have a significant number of Word 97 users, you can configure Word 2000 so that it always produces files that are completely compatible with Word 97.

Setting Word 97 Compatibility Options

1. Pull down the **Tools** menu and choose **Options**.
2. Click the Compatibility tab and select **Microsoft Word 97** from the list labeled **Recommended options for**.
3. Click the Save tab and choose **Word 97 (*.doc)** from the list labeled **Save Word files as**.
4. Also on the Save tab, check the box labeled **Disable features not supported by Word 97**.
5. Click **OK** to close the Options dialog box and save your changes.

Setting these options effectively disables all of Word 2000's new document-related features.

Other new features still work

Even if you've set Word 2000 to be compatible with Word 97, you can still use other new features. For example, you can create and edit Web pages and save them to Web folders.

Converting Files to and from Previous Versions of Word

In a large office, it's not unusual to find two, three, even four different versions of Word in everyday use by different workers. Sharing files in such an environment can be a nightmare unless you plan carefully.

Macintosh files may need a separate converter

If you have coworkers who use Office 98 for the Macintosh, you don't need to save your documents in a separate format; that version of Word uses the same format as Word 2000 and Word 97 for Windows. You will need separate converters to open files created by coworkers who use versions 4.x and 5.x of Word for the Macintosh, however. The Windows Installer may prompt you for the main Office 2000 CD the first time you try to use the converters.

Files originally created using version 2 of Word use the Word 2.x file format. Files created in Word 6.0 or Word 95 use a common file format generally referred to as Word 6.0/95. Files created in some versions of Word 97 and saved as Word 6.0/95 files actually use Rich Text File (RTF) format. Fortunately, you can open files in any of these formats in Word 2000 automatically and without requiring you to choose any special option.

If a coworker sends you a document created in a previous version of Word, you must be careful when saving your changes. If you save files using Word 2000's format, the person who originally created the document may not be able to open it.

When you edit a file that was originally created in one format and then attempt to save it in another, here's what is likely to happen:

Some features aren't available

When you open a file that was created in an earlier version of Word, some features simply won't be available. For example, if you try to draw a table within a table, you'll see a dialog box warning you that this feature is incompatible with the file format you're currently using.

- If you pull down the **File** menu and choose **Save**, Word will save the file using the same format in which it was originally created. You will not see a warning dialog box.
- If you choose **Save As** from the **File** menu, you can select **Word Document** from the **Save as type** box. When you then click the **Save** button, Word replaces the original file format. You may see a dialog box that warns you that you are about to change formats.

- When you open a document that you originally created in Word 2000 and attempt to use the Save As dialog box to save it in another format, Word first scans the document to see if it contains any features that will not translate correctly to the format you chose. If there are no problems, Word translates the file; if the document includes any Word 2000 formatting that may be lost in the translation, Word displays a dialog box like the one shown in Figure 9.7.

SEE ALSO

➤ *For more details on how to save Office files, see page 31*

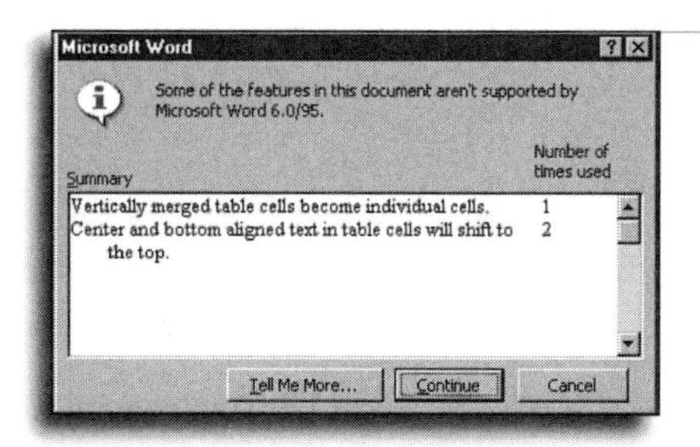

FIGURE 9.7
You'll see this dialog box if the file format you select doesn't support some of the formatting in your document.

Click **Continue** to convert the file to the previous format, with the consequences explained in the dialog box; click **Cancel** to try again using a different format.

SEE ALSO

➤ *To add Office components, see page 691*
➤ *To install patches and updates, see page 701*

Play it safe

If you see a warning dialog box when attempting to save a file in another format, check the box labeled **Create a copy of *filename* before modifying**, then click **Continue**. Word will save a version of your file in the same folder as the existing file, using the filename `Backup of filename` and changing the file type to Word Backup, with a *.wbk extension.

Converting Files to and from Other Document Formats

How do you exchange files with friends and coworkers who use word processors other than Word? Word 2000 can directly open files created in version 5 or 6 of WordPerfect, and can save files in the format of WordPerfect version 5. Word can also read and write files created in most versions of Microsoft Works. To exchange documents with a colleague who uses WordPerfect or Works, open the **File** menu, choose **Save As**, and then pick the appropriate version from the **Save as type** list.

Choose file formats carefully!

When you're saving a file in another format, make sure you choose the correct version, and be sure to test the transfer before you rely on it for an important file. When you're saving in WordPerfect format, for example, save a small test file using one of the WordPerfect options and send it to your intended recipient. If that person can open the file properly, translate the other files and send them along.

Recover text from any document

What happens when you simply can't open a file? Click the box labeled **List files of type** and choose the **Recover text from any document** option. This converter strips everything but text from the current file. You lose all formatting, but at least you won't have to retype all the text. Use this option to salvage text from damaged files or when you encounter a data file in a format that Word can't open.

What other file types can you open in Word 2000? Open the **File** menu, choose **Open**, and then click the box labeled **List files of type**. Entries in this list indicate which file formats Word can open. By default, Word can open plain text files, Web pages, files saved in Rich Text Format, Lotus 1-2-3 spreadsheets, and Excel workbooks. You need to install additional converters to open files created using Lotus Notes, Microsoft Works, or versions of Word other than Word 2000 or Word 6.0/95.

Combining Two or More Documents

From time to time, you will need to combine two or more Word documents into one. For example, say you've asked a coworker to help you write the introduction to an important report while you work on the details in the second half. Your coworker finished first and saved the work as a Word document on a shared network folder. You've now finished your half of the job. How do you bring the two documents together?

Combining Two Word Documents Into One File

1. Click to position the insertion point at the place in the main document where you want to add the new file.
2. Pull down the **Insert** menu and choose **File**.
3. Select the new file from the Insert File dialog box.
4. Click **OK** to insert the contents of the second file in the open document.

This option is an especially effective way to split a long document up so several different people can simultaneously work on individual parts of the file. When you get each part back, open a new, blank document and then insert each file in order.

Preventing Document Disasters

If you've turned to this section because you just lost a document, I might be able to help. I can definitely suggest some adjustments you can make to keep you from losing your work next time.

Turning On the AutoRecover Option

When you enable the *AutoRecover* option, Word saves your documents automatically at regular intervals while you work. (The default setting is every 10 minutes.) This feature is turned on automatically when you install Office. Word stores AutoRecover files in the Microsoft\Word subfolder of your Application Data folder; these files use a name like "AutoRecovery copy of <*filename*>.asd." When you exit Word normally, it deletes these files as part of the shutdown process.

If your computer shuts down unexpectedly and Word can't perform its cleanup duties, the most recent AutoRecovery files remain in place, one for each document you had open when your system crashed. When you restart your computer and open Word, Word will open any AutoRecover documents it finds, giving you a chance to bring back some or all of your work.

Don't forget to save

Using AutoRecover is a crucial way to keep from losing work in a power failure or computer crash, but it doesn't automatically save your files. Experienced computer users make a habit of saving all important files regularly while they work. Saving is an easy habit, regardless of which Office program you're using: Just press Ctrl+S every few minutes.

SEE ALSO

➤ *To set AutoSave and other essential Office options, see page 100*

Recovering a Document After Your Computer Crashes

Even if the AutoRecover option is enabled and properly configured, there's no guarantee you'll get your document back after a power failure. You'll lose whatever you typed between the last time Word saved the AutoRecover information and the time the power went out. You should be able to recover something, however.

When you restart your computer and open Word, it automatically loads any AutoRecovery files it finds. Look for the word *Recovered* in parentheses after the file's name in the title bar. To keep the recovered file, you must save it; if you close the document, Word discards all the recovered information. You cannot retrieve it again.

Don't save too quickly

Compare the recovered document with the saved version that's still on your disk to see which one is more recent. The file saved on disk may be more complete than the AutoRecovered version. If you can't be sure, save the recovered file under a new name, then open the original file and compare its contents with the recovered copy.

Choosing the Right Document View

Switch views with one click

Word's four viewing options are all available on the **View** menu. You can also switch between **Normal**, **Web Layout**, **Print Layout**, and **Outline** views using the four buttons in the lower-left corner of the document window, to the left of the horizontal scrollbar and just above the status bar.

Normal view lets you see styles

As Figure 9.8 shows, Normal view lets you see style information for every paragraph. To make this style area visible, pull down the **Tools** menu and choose **Options**. Click the **View** tab, and adjust the **Style area width** option at the bottom of the dialog box to a value other than zero. The style information is also visible in Outline view. To learn about styles, flip ahead to Chapter 12, "Using Templates and Styles."

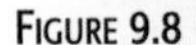

Word lets you choose one of four distinct views when you're creating or editing a document. Which view should you choose? The answer depends on what you're trying to do. Are you concentrating on writing? Trying to make your document look great? Organizing your thoughts? Word has a special view for each step in the writing process, as described in the following sections.

Entering and Editing Text in Normal View

Normal view is perfect for those times when you just want to get the words out of your head and you aren't concerned about exactly how they'll look when printed. Normal view shows you all text on the page, complete with character and paragraph formatting; graphics and other objects are hidden, and you see placeholders where page breaks, columns, and other Print Layout options should appear. Figure 9.8 shows this simplified view of a document.

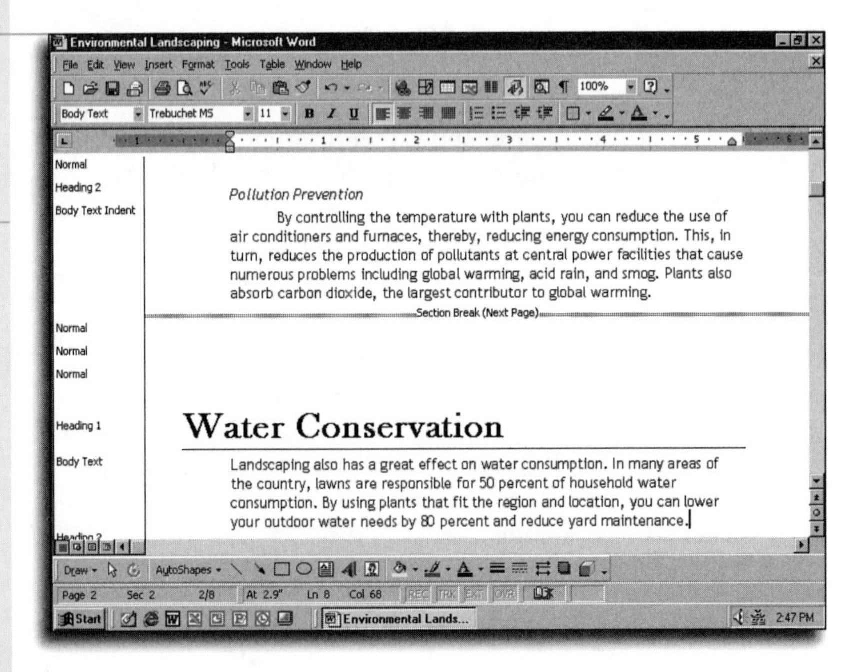

FIGURE 9.8

Normal view uses the entire window to display your document. It's perfect for quickly typing a first draft.

Previewing the Printed Page

When you select *Print Layout view*, you can see how much space is available in the margins on each side of the page. As you scroll through your document, you can see the bottom and top margins of each page as well. If you've put page numbers or a title on the page, those pieces will be visible, although they'll be grayed out. Print Layout view is particularly appropriate for tasks that involve fine formatting and precise placement of headers, footers, and other screen elements. Figure 9.9 shows what you see when you choose this view.

Why the name change?

In Word 97, Print Layout view went by a slightly different name: Page Layout. The name change reflects the fact that this view displays how your document will look on paper.

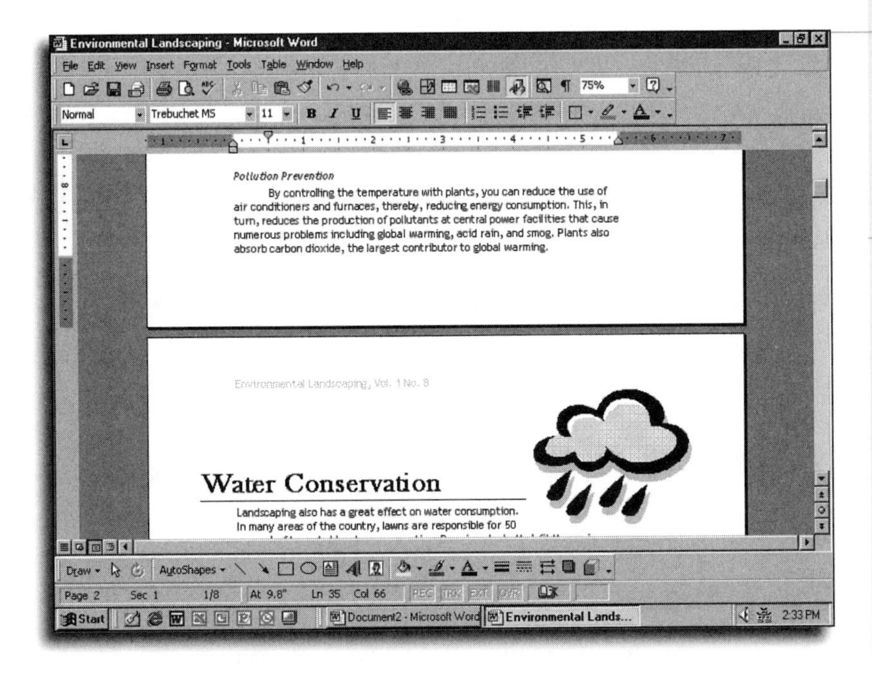

FIGURE 9.9

Print Layout view shows all four margins, adds a vertical ruler to help you find your place on the page, and displays headers and footers.

Organizing Your Thoughts with Outline View

Outline view is ideal for making sure your thoughts are well organized. When you use Word's built-in heading styles, you can switch to Outline view and collapse your document to see just its main points. The Outlining toolbar helps you collapse and expand each section (see Figure 9.10).

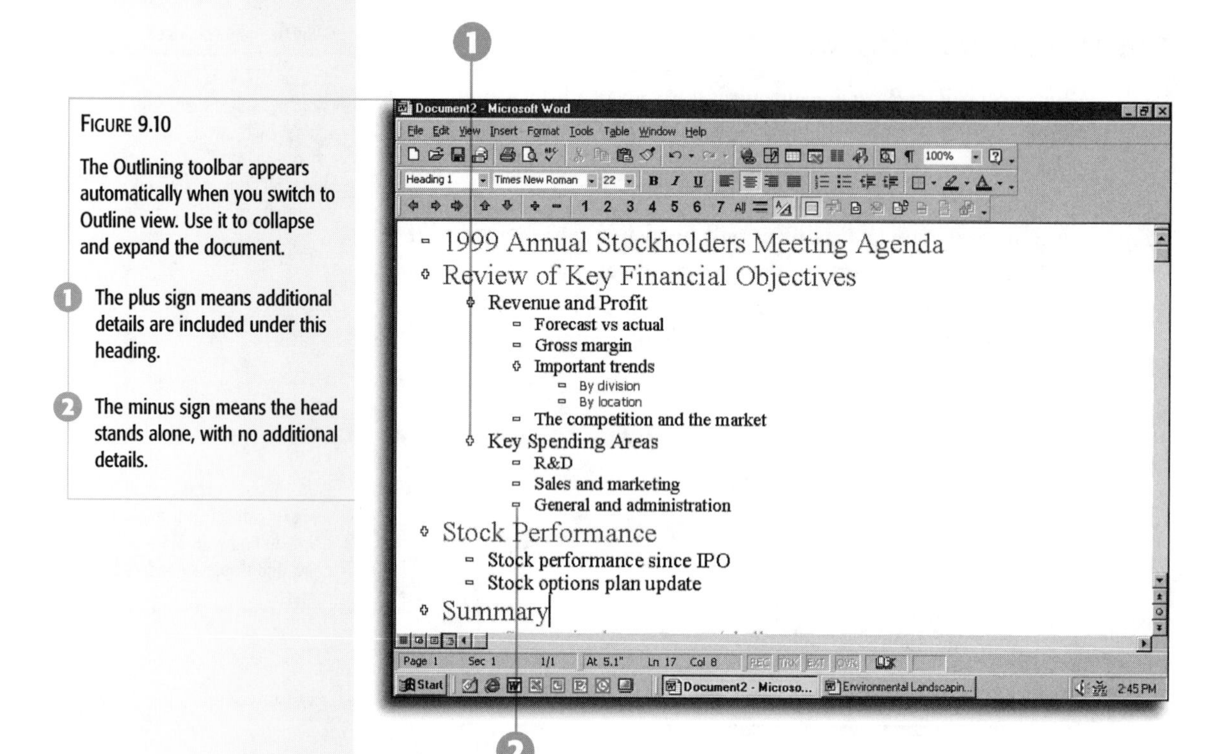

FIGURE 9.10

The Outlining toolbar appears automatically when you switch to Outline view. Use it to collapse and expand the document.

1. The plus sign means additional details are included under this heading.
2. The minus sign means the head stands alone, with no additional details.

Outline view makes editing easier

Want to rearrange paragraphs? Switch to Outline view; then point to the box in front of the section you want to move. Click and hold down the mouse button to select the paragraph and drag it to its new location. If you've used heading styles to organize your document, you can use this technique to move an entire section.

Optimizing Your Document for Online Reading

As the name implies, *Web Layout view* is the proper selection when you want to create Web pages and other documents that you expect to view onscreen and not on paper. The text in each paragraph is larger (for easy reading) and it wraps to fit the window instead of running off the edge of the screen.

Using the Document Map to Browse Headings

In any Word view, you can click the **Document Map** button to display a separate window just to the left of the document itself. As you can see from the example in Figure 9.11, the *Document Map* lets you see the headings in your document; click on a heading to jump directly to that section of the document.

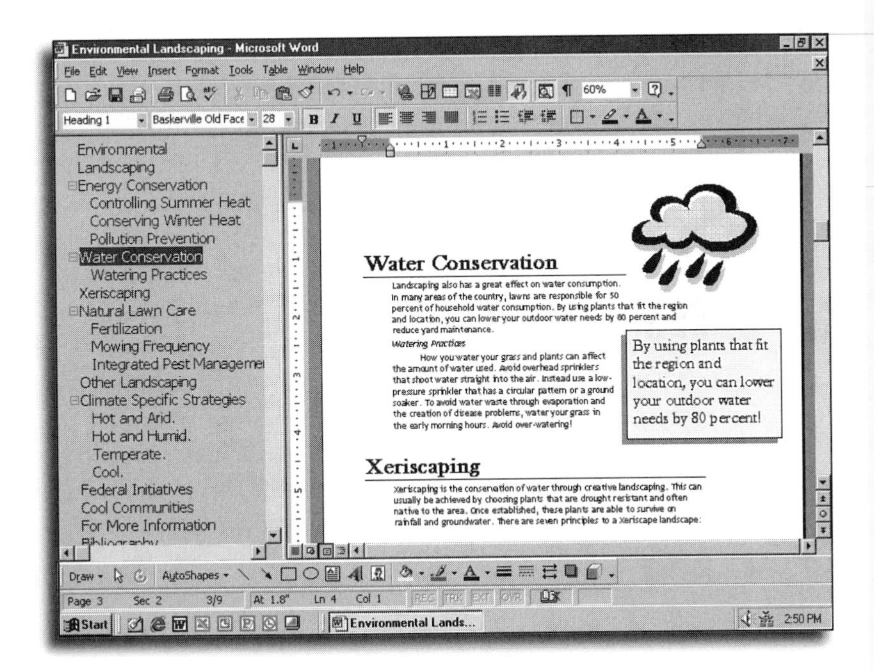

FIGURE 9.11

Use the Document Map (left) to see all the headings in your document.

Using Full Screen View to Clear Away Clutter

If toolbars, rulers, and other screen elements are too distracting, pull down the **View** menu and choose **Full Screen**. In this view, all you typically see is the document itself and a simple toolbar with one button; all other toolbars, menus, and other screen elements, including the Windows taskbar, disappear. Click the **Close Full Screen** button to switch back to the regular program window.

Each view uses separate settings

When you switch between views, Word remembers the Zoom settings for each one individually. So you might see Normal view at 75%, but when you switch to Print Layout view, you see your pages at 123%. Word remembers the view settings for each document when you close it so that it opens in the same view the next time.

Zooming In for a Closer Look

Regardless of which view you've selected, you can increase or decrease the size of the document displayed on the screen. Zooming in makes it easier to read or edit text when the words on the screen are too small to read easily. Zooming out lets you see the overall design of the page.

Use the Zoom control on the Standard toolbar to choose a predefined magnification from 10 percent to 500 percent normal

How does the Document Map work?

The Document Map requires that you use heading styles, which include a setting for outline level. Word includes nine built-in Heading styles: Heading 1, Heading 2, and so on. You can also define outline levels for any other style by changing the paragraph formats for that style, as described in Chapter 12.

size. If you are in Print Layout view, you can choose **Page Width** to expand the text so that it's as large as possible without running off the edge of the screen. Try **Whole Page** to fit the entire page on the screen, or **Two Pages** for a side-by-side view. To see more Zoom options, pull down the **View** menu and choose **Zoom**.

Customizing Word

If you add up all the customization options in Word 2000, the total comes to well over 600 settings, scattered throughout a handful of dialog boxes. The most important, though, appear on the dialog box shown in Figure 9.12. To display this 10-tabbed dialog box, pull down the **Tools** menu and choose **Options**.

SEE ALSO

➤ *To learn how to change where Office applications store files, see page 28*
➤ *For an overview of common Office customization options, see page 100*

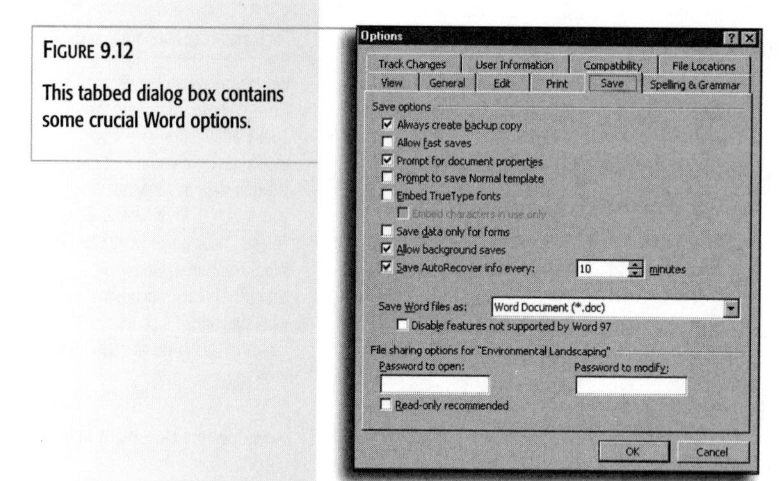

FIGURE 9.12

This tabbed dialog box contains some crucial Word options.

Many of the check boxes, lists, and other settings available here are similar to those found throughout Office. For example, click the **Spelling & Grammar** tab to dictate how Word handles spelling, including the availability of custom dictionaries. Enter your name, initials, and mailing address on the User Information tab; Word uses these details to tag comments you embed in a manuscript. Other options let you hide or show rulers, status bars, and other interface elements.

There are a handful of absolutely crucial options that are specific to Word, however. I recommend that every Word user check and adjust the customization options in Table 9.3 as soon as possible after installing Office 2000.

The Fast Saves option is dangerous

When you check Word's **Allow fast saves** option, Word simply adds your changes to the end of a file when you save it. That means text you deleted remains in the file, and anyone with even a small amount of technical knowledge can load the entire document and see what you thought you had deleted. The consequences could be disastrous in a contract, an employee performance review, or a legal pleading. I strongly urge you to clear the check mark from this box to avoid these possibilities.

Watch that document title!

Here's one very good reason to check the properties for every document you create. When you create a new document, add some text, and save it, Word automatically fills in the Title field with the first line of your document. If you later edit that document, Word doesn't change the Title. Say you start out writing an angry letter to your boss whose first line is "I quit!!!!!" Later, you calm down and delete that first line so that your letter simply says "Let's talk." The trouble is, Word captured that original first line in the Title field, and it will stay with the document—where anyone can read it—unless you specifically change it.

TABLE 9.3 **Common Word Options**

Location, Option Name	Description
General tab, **Recently used file list**.	Lets you see up to nine files you've opened most recently. Most users should set this to nine.
Edit tab, **Drag and drop text editing**.	Lets you copy and move text by dragging; most users should leave this option checked.
Edit tab, **Use smart cut and paste**.	Automatically adds spaces when you drag and drop words and sentences; clear this check box if you want precise control over positioning when editing.
Edit tab, **When selecting, automatically select entire word**.	Makes selecting text with the mouse easier; clear this check box only if you want pinpoint control over selections.
Save tab, **Always create backup copy**.	Automatically saves the previous version of a file whenever you save; most users should uncheck this option, because it wastes disk space.
Save tab, **Allow fast saves**.	All users should clear this check box; despite the name, this option doesn't really speed up saves, and it allows anyone to read information you think you've deleted from a file.
Save tab, **Prompt for document properties**.	I strongly recommend that all users check this option and enter at least a title for every document.
Save tab, **Prompt to save Normal template**.	Check if you want to avoid accidentally making changes to your Normal document template; if you have heavily customized styles, check this option.

continues...

TABLE 9.3 **Continued**

Location, Option Name	Description
Save tab, **Allow background saves**.	Lets you continue editing while Word saves a file; check this box only if you have a slow machine or routinely work with very large files.
Save tab, **Save AutoRecover info every *n* minutes**.	Automatically saves a copy of every open file at regular intervals of between 1 and 120 minutes; default of 10 minutes is good for most users.

CHAPTER

10

Editing Documents

- Use keyboard shortcuts to move through documents
- Select text using the mouse or keyboard
- Correct spelling mistakes automatically
- Undo mistakes
- Find (and replace) any text
- Build documents from boilerplate text
- Check your grammar

Moving Around in a Word Document

Knowing the right navigation shortcuts can dramatically increase your productivity as you edit in Word. I usually have to bite my tongue as I watch supposedly expert computer users hold down the arrow keys to move at a snail's pace through a Word document. Learn these mouse and keyboard shortcuts to help you move to the precise point where you want to be—quickly, without wearing out the arrow keys.

Using Keyboard Shortcuts to Jump Through a Document

Why take your hands off the keyboard? When you're editing text, the fastest way to move through the document is with the help of the keyboard shortcuts shown in Table 10.1.

TABLE 10.1 Moving Through a Document Using the Keyboard

To Do This	Press This Key Combination
Move to the beginning or end	Home and End of the current line
Move one word to the right or left, respectively	Ctrl+Right arrow or Ctrl+Left arrow
Move to the previous or next paragraph, respectively	Ctrl+Up arrow or Ctrl+Down arrow
Move up or down one window	PgUp or PgDn
Jump to the top or bottom of the document	Ctrl+Home or Ctrl+End

Three additional keyboard shortcuts are worth noting. Shift+F5 is one of my all-time favorites. When you press this key combination, Word cycles the insertion point through the last three places where you entered or edited text. Use this cool shortcut if you've scrolled through a long document and you want to jump back quickly to the place where you started.

Press Ctrl+G or F5 to pop up the **Go To** tab of the Find and Replace dialog box shown in Figure 10.1. Enter a page number to jump directly to that page. Use a plus or minus sign and a number to move back or forward the specified number of pages; for example, enter `+10` to move 10 pages ahead. You can also navigate by section, by line, or by using any of 13 different object choices. If you're browsing through a long document with lots of headings, for example, choose Heading from the **Go to what** list, and then click the **Next** and **Previous** buttons to jump from one heading to the next.

See more shortcuts

If you want Word to alert you to available keyboard shortcuts, pull down the **Tools** menu, choose **Customize**, and click the **Options** tab. Check the box labeled **Show shortcut keys in ScreenTips**, and Word will always display keyboard shortcuts along with ScreenTips for buttons and controls.

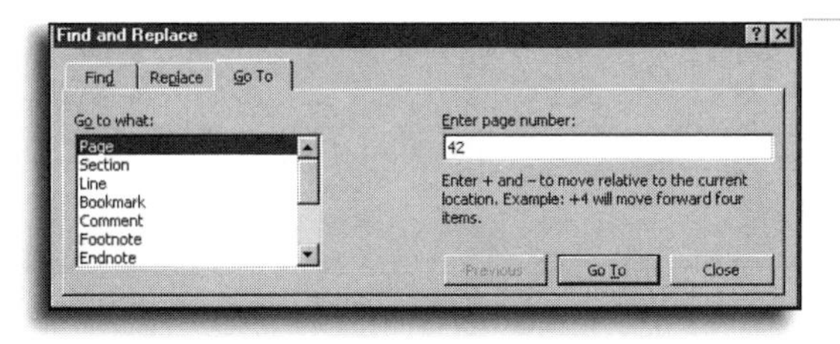

FIGURE 10.1
The Go To tab of the Find and Replace dialog box lets you jump through your document using the keyboard or the mouse.

And finally, after you've used the **Find**, **Replace**, or **Go To** tab of the Find and Replace dialog box, press Ctrl+PgDown or Ctrl+PgUp to jump to the next or previous instance. If you've used the Find tab to search for a string of text, for example, you can press Ctrl+PgDown to find the next occurrence of that text, even after you close the Find and Replace dialog box. This trick also works with objects you select from the **Go To** tab.

Prefer the mouse?

You can also pop up the **Go To** tab of the Find and Replace dialog box by double-clicking anywhere in the left side of the status bar, where you see information about the current page. If you let the mouse pointer rest over this region of the status bar, you see a ScreenTip to remind you of this feature.

Using the Mouse

The obvious way to move through a document, of course, is to use the *vertical scrollbar*. But you don't have to simply scroll through a document—at the bottom of the scrollbar, Word includes an extremely well hidden set of navigation controls that let you jump from point to point. This control, known as the *Object Browser*, consists of three buttons, as shown in Figure 10.2. Click the one in the center to choose how you want to move through the document—by page, by section, or by text you enter in the **Find** tab, for example. Click the **Browse by Page** button, for example, and then use the **Next** and **Previous** buttons to move a page at a time through your document.

Does that list of objects look familiar?

Scroll through the list of objects on the **Go To** tab of the Find and Replace dialog box, and you'll see the list is almost identical to those that appear when you click the Select Browse Object button at the bottom of the vertical scrollbar.

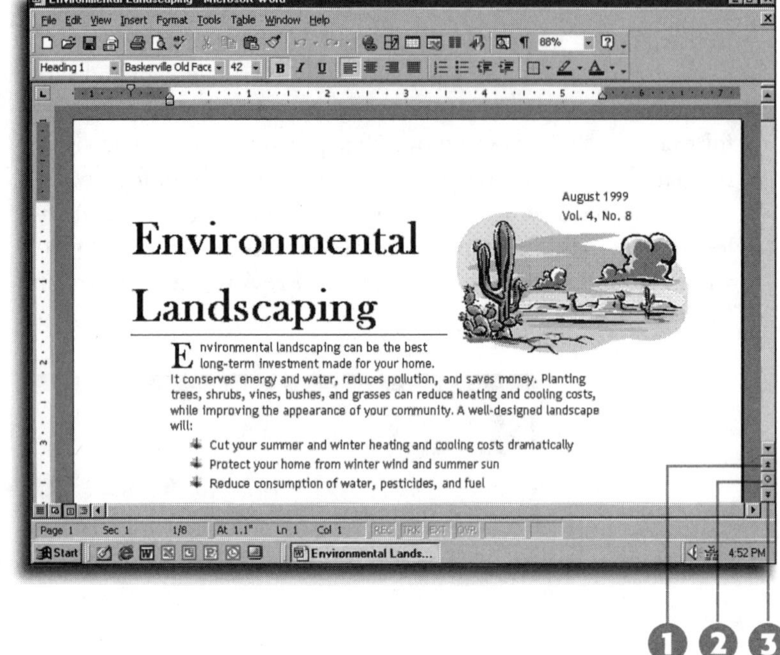

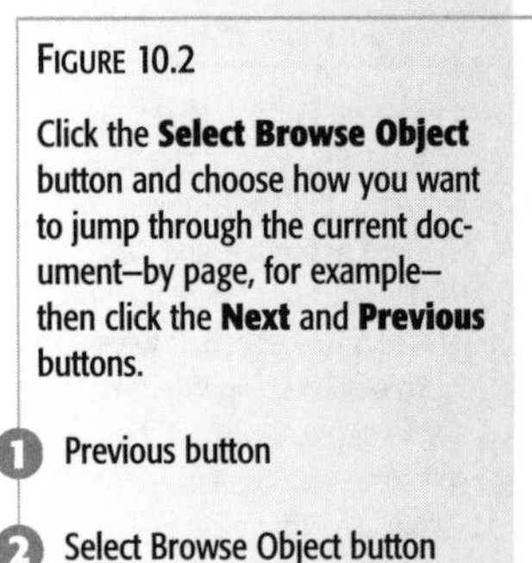

FIGURE 10.2

Click the **Select Browse Object** button and choose how you want to jump through the current document–by page, for example–then click the **Next** and **Previous** buttons.

1. Previous button
2. Select Browse Object button
3. Next button

Use the ScreenTips

Let the mouse pointer hover over the **Next** and **Previous** buttons to see where each one will take you. If you've selected **Browse by Page** from the **Object Browser**, for example, the ScreenTips read `Previous Page` and `Next Page`, respectively.

Or use the mouse...

If you prefer to use the mouse, it's easy to split a Word window. Aim the mouse pointer at the *split box*, just above the top of the vertical scrollbar. Click and drag to position the split bar in the document window.

Using Split Windows to See Two Views of One Document

Let's say you're working with a long document, and two far-removed sections deal with similar topics. You want to be sure that the material in both sections is in agreement, but you also want to avoid simply repeating the same paragraph. How do you look at the two sections side by side when they're so far apart? You can *split* the screen in two so that each window displays the same document but scrolls separately. Even though you're viewing it in two windows, you continue to work with just one copy of the document—any changes you make in one window appear in the other window immediately.

The easy way to create a split window is with the menus: Pull down the **Window** menu and click **Split**. When the pointer changes to a pair of horizontal lines with arrows above and below, drag the *split bar* down. Each window has its own ruler and its own set of scrollbars, which you use to move independently through the document. You can even set different zoom levels and use different views for the two windows, as I've done in Figure 10.3.

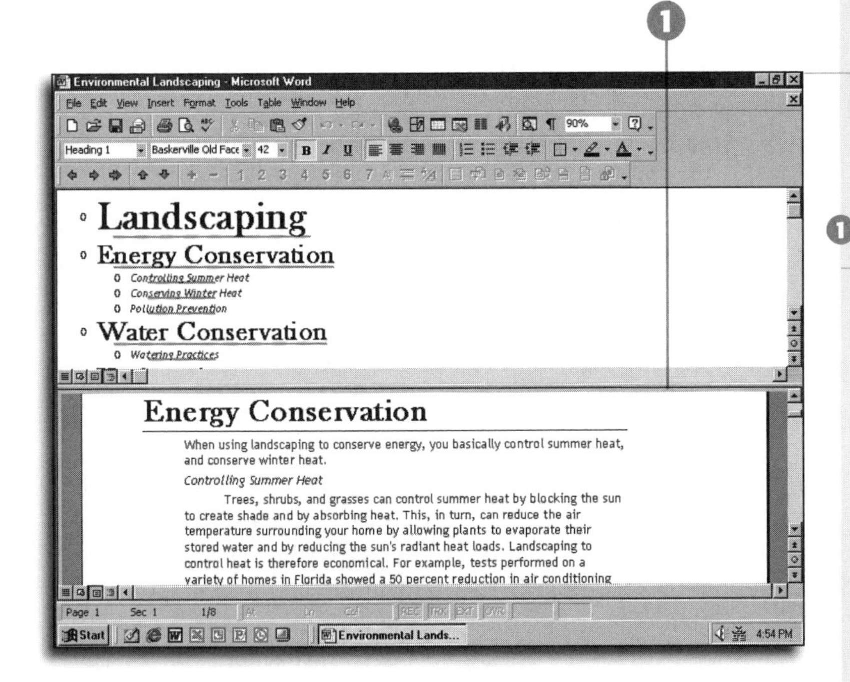

FIGURE 10.3

You can't be in two places at once, but you can work with a single document in two windows.

1. Split bar

To remove the split bar and work in a single window again, double-click the split bar or drag it to the extreme top or bottom of the document window.

Selecting Text in Word

Before you can move, copy, delete, or reformat text, you first have to *select* it. (You can tell when text has been selected in a document with default settings, because it appears in a dark bar, with white letters on a black background.) Selecting text using the mouse is easiest, but if you prefer to keep your hands on the keyboard, you can find plenty of shortcuts.

Selecting Text Using the Mouse

Word enables you to use an assortment of mouse techniques to select chunks of text.

To Select	Do This
A word	Point to the word and double-click.
A sentence	Hold down the Ctrl key, point to the sentence, and click.
A paragraph	Point to the paragraph and triple-click.
	OR
	Point in the margin to the left of the paragraph; when the mouse pointer turns into an arrow, double-click.
A whole document	Move the mouse pointer to the left margin until it turns into an arrow and then triple-click.

SEE ALSO

➤ *The techniques for selecting text in tables are different; see page 274*

You don't have to be precise to select an entire word using the mouse. Word assumes that when you drag the mouse pointer, you want to select entire words. As a result, when you aim the mouse pointer anywhere within a word and then drag the pointer left or right, the selection changes to include each new word. Most of the time, that's the correct action, because you typically want to move, copy, or format an entire word rather than a few characters within a word.

What if you really want to select the end of one word and the beginning of another? To override *automatic word selection* temporarily, hold down the Ctrl and Shift keys as you drag the selection.

Turning off automatic word selection

If automatic word selection bugs you, you can easily disable this feature. Pull down the **Tools** menu, choose **Options**, click the **Edit** tab, and remove the check mark next to the box labeled **When selecting, automatically select entire word**.

Selecting Text Using the Keyboard

If you're a speedy typist, nothing slows down your productivity more than having to take your fingers off the keyboard, find the mouse, click to select a block, and then move back to the keys. Every touch typist should learn to select text using the following keyboard shortcuts; in most cases, you can simply hold down the Shift key while you use the same shortcuts that you use to move through a document.

To Select	Do This
One or more characters	Hold down the Shift key as you press the left or right arrow keys one or more times.
A word	Move the insertion point to the beginning of the word; then press Ctrl+Shift+Right arrow.
To the beginning or end of the line	Press Shift+Home or Shift+End.
To the beginning or end of the paragraph	Press Ctrl+Shift+Up arrow or Ctrl+Shift+Down arrow.
To the beginning or end of the document	Press Ctrl+Shift+Home or Ctrl+Shift+End.
The whole document	Press Ctrl+A.

My favorite keyboard shortcut lets you quickly select a word, a sentence, a paragraph, or the whole document. Just move the insertion point where you want to begin selecting and then press the F8 key to turn on *Extend Selection mode*. (To see an onscreen reminder that you've turned on this feature, look in the center of the status bar at the bottom of the document window. If you see the letters EXT, Extend Selection mode is on.)

After you've pressed F8, you can press any key to extend the selection. If you press the period key, for example, Word extends the selection to the next period, which is usually the end of the sentence. Press the period key again to select to the end of the next sentence.

After pressing F8 the first time, you can extend the selection further. Press F8 a second time to select a whole word, a third time to select the entire sentence, a fourth time for the current paragraph, and a fifth time to select your entire document. To exit Extend Selection mode, press the Esc key. To deselect your selection, move any arrow key.

Careful with that selection!

If you inadvertently press any character on the keyboard, including the Spacebar, whatever you type replaces whatever is currently selected. To bring back the original selection, click the **Undo** button or press Ctrl+Z.

Entering and Deleting Text

When you start a new document, Word positions your insertion point at the top of the document, and all you have to do is type. In previous versions, Word only allowed you to enter text here; if you wanted to type elsewhere in your document, you had to press the Enter or Tab keys to move the insertion point. Word 2000 introduces a new feature called *Click and Type*, which lets you position the insertion point by double-clicking in a blank part of the page. Actually, this feature should be called "double-click and type," based on the way it works. Move the mouse pointer over the document and watch as it changes shape, adding lines on either side or beneath the pointer, and do the following:

- When you see lines beneath the pointer, double-click to position the insertion point on that line and change the paragraph formatting to centered.
- When you see lines to the right of the pointer, double-click to add a tab character on that line, and then start typing.
- When you see lines to the right of the pointer, double-click to position the insertion point at the end of that line, formatted for right alignment.

Frankly, I don't recommend that you use the Click and Type feature; you'll get much better results adding tabs and adjusting alignment yourself, using the techniques I describe in Chapter 11. If you don't want to be distracted by the Click and Type pointers, disable this feature completely: Pull down the **Tools** menu and choose **Options**; click the Edit tab, and clear the check box to the left of **Enable click and type**.

SEE ALSO

For full details on how to use tabs, indents, and paragraph alignment settings to arrange text on a page, see page 230

nO mORE cAPS lOCK mISTAKES

How many times has your finger slipped as you struck the Shift or Tab key, accidentally hitting the Caps Lock key and producing text like tHIS? Touch typists can go for a paragraph or even a full page before they notice that all the text has been entered incorrectly. Word 2000 is smart enough to detect when Caps Lock comes on inappropriately, automatically undoing the scrambled text and restoring Caps Lock to its correct setting.

Replacing Text As You Type

Normally, when you enter text, Word uses Insert mode—whatever you enter pushes any existing text out of the way to make room. In some versions of Word 97, pressing the Insert key, deliberately or inadvertently, toggles you into *Overtype mode*, in which each new character you type replaces the character immediately to its right. If you're a skilled touch typist and you press the Insert key by accident, you can wipe out massive amounts of work before you even realize anything is wrong.

To switch back to *Insert mode*, press the Insert key. If you regularly find yourself shifting into Overtype mode accidentally, follow these instructions to prevent the Insert key from performing this function.

Spotting Overtype mode

Word offers a subtle clue (maybe too subtle) that tells you when you've shifted from Insert to Overtype mode. In the center of the status bar at the bottom of the document window are five small indicator boxes. If the letters **OVR** are visible, you've switched into Overtype mode.

Disabling Word's Overtype Mode

1. Open the **Tools** menu and choose **Customize**.
2. Click the **Keyboard** button to open the Customize Keyboard dialog box (see Figure 10.4).
3. In the **Categories** list, select **All Commands**.
4. Scroll through the **Commands** list and select **Overtype**.
5. In the **Current keys** list, select the entry for the Insert key.
6. Click the **Remove** button.
7. Click the **Close** button.

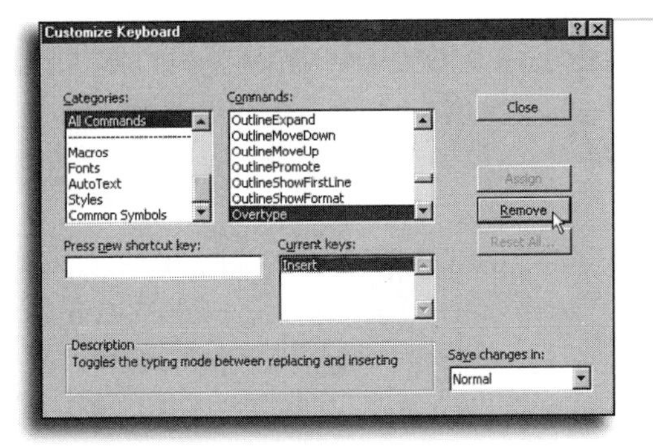

FIGURE 10.4

Click the **Remove** button, as I'm about to do here, to tell Word you don't want to switch into Overtype mode every time you press the Insert key by accident.

SEE ALSO

➤ *To create, edit, and use other keyboard shortcuts, see page 99*

Deleting Text

Keyboard shortcuts offer the fastest way to get rid of text. Touch typists should memorize these key combinations:

To Perform This Action	Use This Key or Combination
Delete the current selection; if no text is selected, delete the character to the left of the insertion point	Backspace
Delete the current selection; if no text is selected, delete the character to the right of the insertion point	Del (Delete)
Delete the word to the left of the insertion point or selection	Ctrl+Backspace
Delete the word to the right of the insertion point or selection	Ctrl+Del (Delete)
Cut the currently selected text and put it on the Clipboard	Ctrl+X

SEE ALSO

➤ *To learn how to cut and paste, see page 134*

Adding Symbols and Special Characters to Your Documents

Don't see the symbol you're looking for?

If you don't see the symbol you're looking for, close the Symbol dialog box, choose another font, and start over. Most TrueType fonts let you choose from a full set of extended characters, including accented upper- and lowercase letters.

If you use the standard U.S. keyboard layout, you can find all the letters of the alphabet, the numbers 0 through 9, and most punctuation marks on the keyboard. Often, though, you'll want to enter characters that aren't available on the keyboard: for example, accented characters from foreign alphabets, currency symbols other than the dollar sign, or copyright and trademark indicators.

If a character is not on the standard keyboard, Word considers it a symbol or a special character. The easiest way to insert any such character into the current document is to use the pull-down menus. First, position the insertion point where you want to add a symbol.

Adding Special Characters to a Document

1. Pull down the **Insert** menu and choose **Symbol** to pop up the dialog box shown in Figure 10.5.
2. To choose an available character from the current font, make sure **(normal text)** is selected in the drop-down list labeled **Font**.

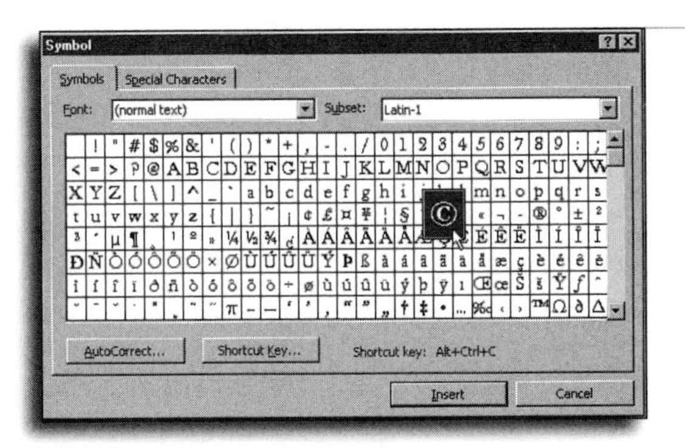

FIGURE 10.5
Click once to see a magnified view of any symbol; double-click to insert the symbol in your document.

3. For a magnified view of any character in the Symbol dialog box, click once on the character.
4. To choose a typographic character, such as the trademark or copyright symbol, click the **Special Characters** tab and select an entry from the list shown in Figure 10.6.
5. To add the symbol to your document, click the **Insert** button.
6. Repeat this process to add another symbol.
7. After you've finished inserting symbols or special characters, click the **Cancel** or **Close** button.

Instant symbols

Word's AutoCorrect feature lets you enter some special symbols directly from the keyboard. If you type `(tm)` or `(r)`, for example, Word automatically changes the entry to the trademark (™) or registered trademark (®) symbols. To see other such AutoText characters, pull down the **Tools** menu, choose **AutoCorrect**, and click on the **AutoCorrect** tab. There, you can find smileys, "frownies," and "who cares" faces, as well as some lines and arrows. If you want to remove any of these automatic substitutions, select the entry from the list at the bottom of the dialog box and click the **Delete** button.

Using Characters from Foreign Alphabets

If you have to type a word in French or Spanish, where do you get the accents and diacritical marks? You can find most of these characters in the Symbol dialog box, but if you use them regularly, there's a quicker method. Just press Ctrl plus the accent character you want to add; then press the letter you want accented. To create an *a* with an accent acute (á), for example, press Ctrl+', and then press A. For an *n* with a tilde above it (ñ), press Ctrl+~, and then press N. Table 10.2 lists keyboard shortcuts for common accented characters.

TABLE 10.2 Entering Accented Characters

To Produce	Press This Key Combination	Followed by This Key	Example
Accent grave	Ctrl+`	the letter	à, À
Accent acute	Ctrl+'	the letter	é, É
Accent circumflex	Ctrl+Shift+^ (caret)	the letter	ô, Ô
Tilde	Ctrl+Shift+~	the letter	ñ, Ñ
Dieresis (umlaut)	Ctrl+Shift+:	the letter	ü, Ü
Cedilla	Ctrl+,	c or C	ç, Ç
Inverted question mark	Alt+Ctrl+Shift+?	none	¿
Inverted exclamation point	Alt+Ctrl+Shift+!	none	¡

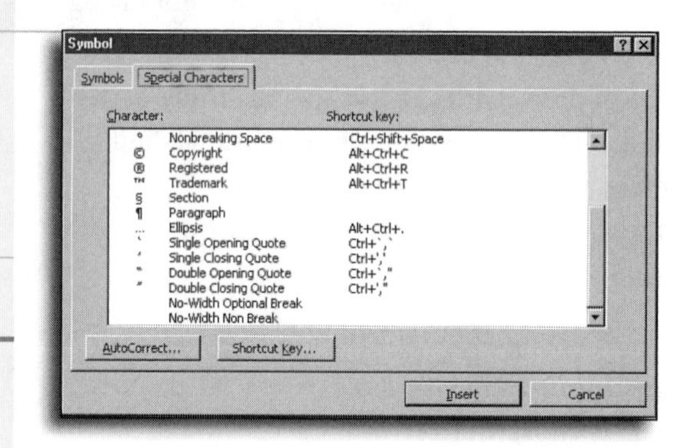

FIGURE 10.6

If you regularly use any of these special characters, memorize the keyboard shortcut listed to its right.

Correcting a stupid quote

Most of the time, smart quotes work as advertised, and they're truly smart. If you enter an apostrophe in front of a two-digit year–'99 or '05, for example–Word assumes you actually want an apostrophe, which curls in the opposite direction, and automatically corrects the entry for you. If you enter a contraction that begins with an apostrophe, though, such as 'tis, you'll need to fix the apostrophe yourself. Just press the single quote key twice before entering the word; then go back and delete the initial, incorrect punctuation mark.

Adding Wingdings and Other Graphic Embellishments

If you want to add whimsical characters or icons to your documents, open the Symbols dialog box and choose a different font from the **Fonts** list. The Wingdings font, for example, lets you insert happy faces, bombs, the peace symbol, and more. To insert one of these symbols, follow the steps titled "Adding special characters to a document" for the normal font.

Using Smart Quotes

You can use two kinds of quotation marks. Standard quotation marks are straight up and down and look the same at the beginning and the end of a quotation. Professionally published documents use *curly quotes* (see Figure 10.7), which use separate marks to signal the beginning and end of a quotation. By default, Word automatically inserts the correct curly quote when you enter a single or double quotation mark; because the program is intelligent enough to tell the difference between opening and closing quotation marks, this feature is called *smart quotes*.

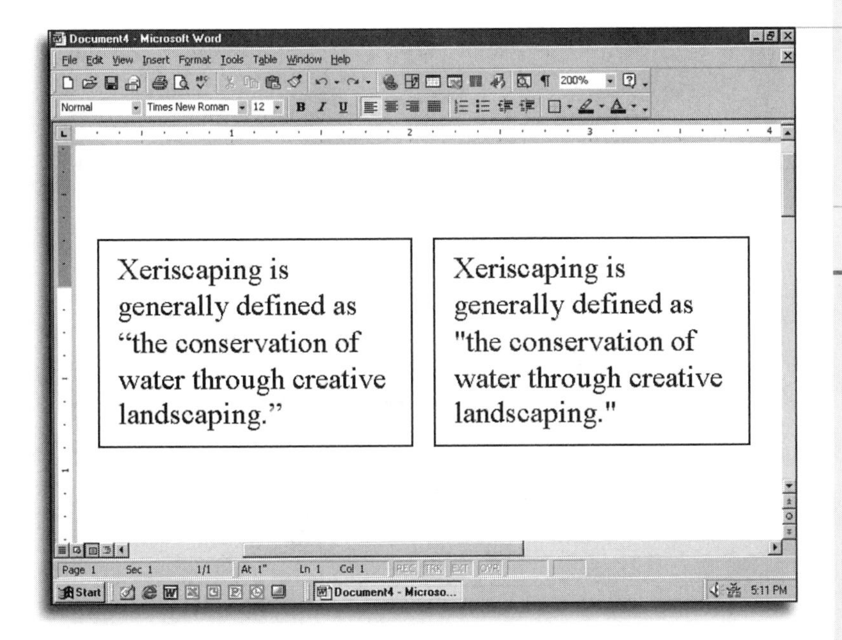

FIGURE 10.7
Smart quotes (like the ones in the box on the left) give your documents a more polished look than straight quotes (right).

Using a standard quote mark

What if you actually want a straight quote in your document? You use the plain character (called a prime or double prime) when indicating feet (') and inches (") in a document, for example. When you need to type a straight quote, just use this workaround: Immediately after you type the curly quote, click the **Undo** button on the Formatting toolbar or press Ctrl+Z. This action reverses the change and restores the straight quote.

Oops! Undoing (and Redoing) What You've Done

What happens when you inadvertently delete an important part of your document? Relax. You can put everything back the way it was by using Word's **Undo** button. Click once to undo your last action. Keep clicking, and the Undo button rolls back as many actions as you want, provided you don't close the document and reopen it. If you know you want to undo a lengthy sequence of actions, click the arrow at the right of the Undo button and then scroll through the drop-down list of steps Word can undo for you (see Figure 10.8). If you click the fifth step in the list, for example, Word automatically undoes the last five actions in a single motion.

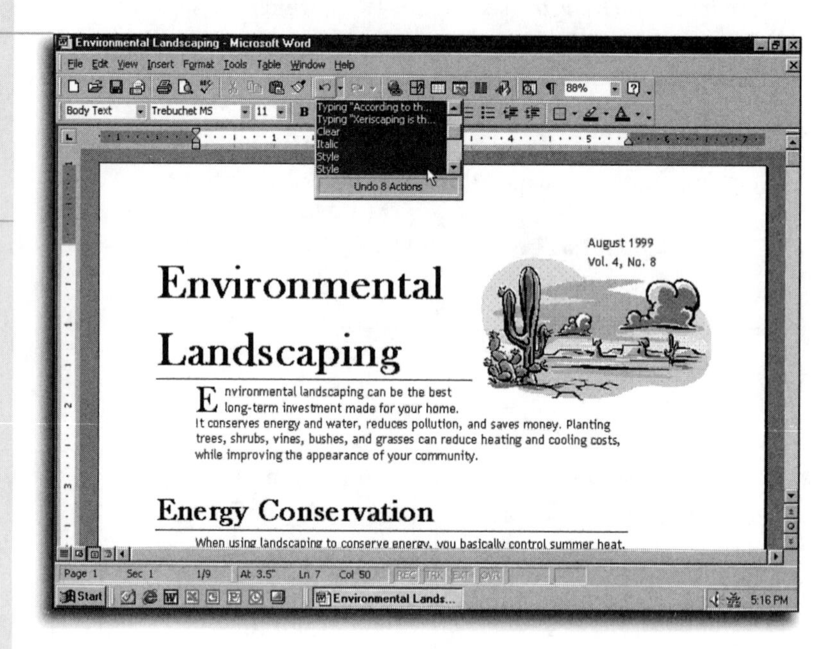

FIGURE 10.8

Word's Undo key can reverse the effects of 1, 50, or even hundreds of recent keystrokes and mouse clicks.

Don't wait too long to undo

Although you can use Undo to roll back changes, you can't pick and choose entries from the list. If you discover you inadvertently deleted a crucial sentence 10 minutes (and 179 actions) ago, the only way to get it back is to undo all 178 actions you've done since then. The list of descriptions on the Undo and Redo list isn't always helpful, either.

Use the matching **Redo** button and its keyboard shortcut Ctrl+Y when you change your mind after using the **Undo** button. In combination, the two buttons let you restore a chunk of text you deleted earlier in the current session, without losing other changes you've made since then. Save your changes first, so that you don't lose all your work if anything goes wrong. Then click the **Undo** button repeatedly to roll back your changes until the deleted text is visible again. Select the text, press Ctrl+C to copy it to the Clipboard, and then use the **Redo** button to return to the most recent version of the document. Now you can paste in the text you thought you'd lost forever, without losing all the changes you've made since then.

Adding Bookmarks, Jump Buttons, and Hyperlinks to Aid Navigation

Word *bookmarks* let you identify specific locations in a document by name. If you're creating an annual report for your company, for example, you can assign bookmarks to the portions of the document that contain the CEO's welcoming remarks, last year's financial results, and each document required by the U.S. Securities and Exchange Commission. When your CEO's assistant sends you the remarks, press F5 and pick the CEO_Remarks bookmark to quickly jump to that location so you can paste them in. After your document is complete, you can use the bookmarks to create *jump buttons* and *cross-references*; anyone reading the document in Word can click the jump text to move straight to the corresponding bookmark.

Adding a Bookmark

1. Click to position the insertion point at the place where you want to add the bookmark. If you want the bookmark to refer to a block of text, such as a heading or table, select the text or object.
2. Pull down the **Insert** menu and choose **Bookmark**. The dialog box shown in Figure 10.9 appears.
3. In the box labeled **Bookmark name**, type the name you want to use for the current location. The name must begin with a letter, and spaces are not permitted.
4. Click the **Add** button.

SEE ALSO

To learn how to add Web-style hyperlinks to documents, see page 64

To navigate through a document using bookmarks, choose one of the following two techniques:

- Open the **Insert** menu and choose **Bookmark**, and then select a name from the list and click **Go To**.

For more information...

Bookmarks and fields are especially useful when you're creating a table of contents or an index for a long document. For details on how to use these advanced features, pick up a copy of *Special Edition Using Office 2000* (also published by Que), and turn to Chapter 18, "Keeping Long Documents Under Control."

Should you make a selection?

How you plan to use the bookmark will determine whether you simply click or whether you make a selection first. If you want to use a bookmark primarily as a navigation aid, so that you can make it easy to jump to a specific location and begin reading, just click to position the insertion point–making a selection will only make the document harder to read when you use the bookmark. If, on the other hand, you expect you'll want to edit or copy the bookmarked text, or use it as part of a field, then make a selection first.

Managing bookmarks

Use this same dialog box to delete a bookmark–select its name from the list and click **Delete**. To change the location a bookmark points to, move to the new location, and then open the Bookmark dialog box, select the name, and click **Add**.

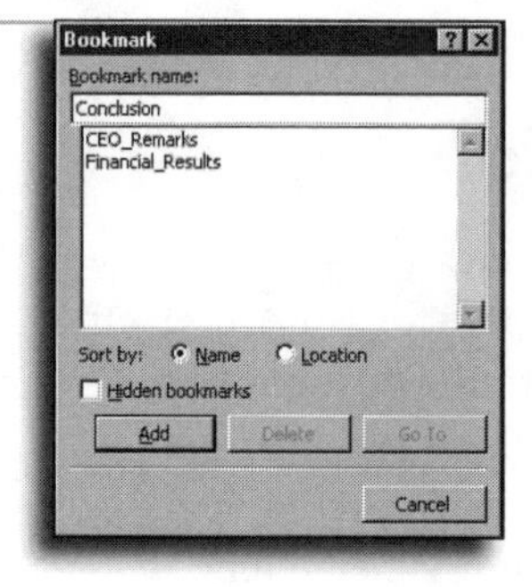

FIGURE 10.9

Use this dialog box to create a bookmark for the current location.

- Press Ctrl+G or F5 to open the **Go To** tab of the Find and Replace dialog box. Choose **Bookmark** from the **Go to what** list, and then select a specific bookmark from the list labeled **Enter bookmark name** and click the **Go To** button.

When you're editing a document that contains bookmarks, it can sometimes be helpful to make the locations of bookmarks visible. That shows you at a glance where you've added bookmarks instead of forcing you to repeatedly open the Bookmark dialog box. To show bookmarks, pull down the **Tools** menu, choose **Options**, and click the **View** tab. Check the box labeled **Bookmarks** and click OK. With this option enabled, Word places square brackets around bookmarks you assigned to an item; If you assigned a bookmark to a location, it appears as a gray I-beam, slightly larger than the insertion point.

Bookmarks work especially well in conjunction with Word fields. If you want to create a link that jumps straight to a location inside the current document, you can use a special field called a GoToButton.

Sort your bookmarks first

In a long document with lots of bookmarks, use the **Sort by** option in the Bookmark dialog box to control how the list appears. Click the **Name** option to see your list of bookmarks in alphabetical order; that's most useful if your bookmark names are descriptive and you're searching for a specific one. Click the **Location** option to see the list in the order they appear in the document.

The Bookmark box stays around

When you use either of these dialog boxes to jump to a specific bookmark, the dialog box stays on the screen. Move it out of the way if it covers the text you want to read.

No editing allowed

When you show bookmarks, the brackets appear on the screen, but they're not editable characters. You can't select them without also selecting the surrounding text, and they don't appear on paper if you print the document.

Creating a Jump Button

1. Create a bookmark for the location you want to jump to.
2. Click to place the insertion point where you want to create the jump button, pull down the **Insert** menu, and choose **Field**. The Field dialog box opens.
3. Scroll through the **Field names** list in the Field dialog box and choose **GoToButton**, as I've done in Figure 10.10.

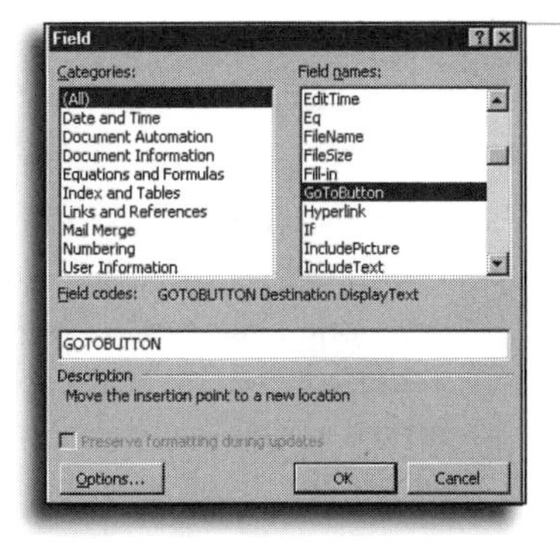

FIGURE 10.10
This dialog box gets you started with the GOTOBUTTON field; remember to create a bookmark first, or the Options button will be unavailable.

4. Click the **Options** button to display the Field Options dialog box (see Figure 10.11). Pick the name of the bookmark you created in step 1. Click the **Add to Field** button to insert the name in the box at the bottom of the dialog box.

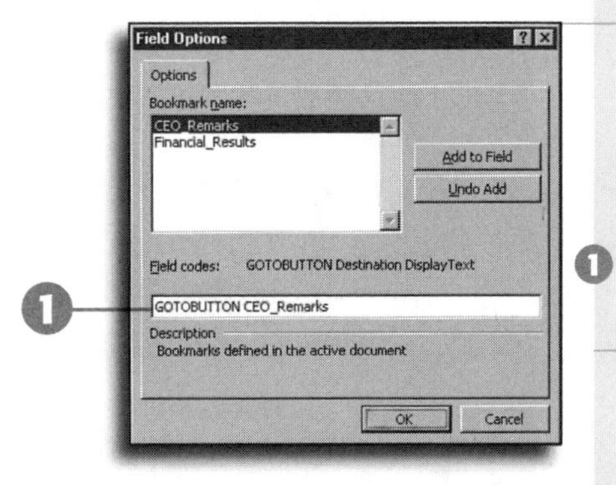

FIGURE 10.11
Use the GOTOBUTTON field to create a link to a bookmarked location; users can double-click the link text to jump to that location.

1 Click here to enter the text you want users to double-click.

5. Click at the end of the text box containing the GOTOBUTTON field and bookmark, and then type in any text you want to appear in the document—for example, `Double-click here to jump to CEO's Remarks.`
6. Click OK to close the Field Options dialog box and OK again to close the Field dialog box.

When you're creating a document that is primarily for online use, add cross-references to make it easy for readers to jump from one location to another. For example, you might add a sentence at the top of your annual report that says "Click here to jump to Remarks from the CEO"; by inserting a hyperlink-style cross-reference, you can make it much easier for your readers to navigate.

Use cross-references liberally

You can create cross-references to more than bookmarks. Use this dialog box to create clickable links to headings, figures, tables, and numbered paragraphs in legal documents, for example.

The cross-reference has two advantages over the GOTOBUTTON fields. First, they work exactly like hyperlinks, requiring only one click instead of two. Second, you don't have to manage them yourself. When you delete, move, or edit the item to which a cross-reference points, the cross-reference updates automatically. If you change the title of a section from "CEO Remarks" to "A Letter from the CEO," for example, your cross-reference will reflect the new title automatically.

Cross-references work only in one document

You can only create cross-references to items in the same document. If you want to cross-reference a figure or table in another document, you first have to combine the documents.

To create a cross-reference, you start by typing the text that introduces the cross-reference; then you insert one or more reference items.

Creating a Cross-Reference to a Bookmark

1. Click to position the insertion point at the place where you want the cross-reference to appear and type introductory text, such as `Click here to jump to` —make sure you include a space at the end.
2. Pull down the **Insert** menu, and choose **Cross-reference**. In the Cross-reference dialog box (see Figure 10.12), choose **Bookmark** from the drop-down list labeled **Reference type**.

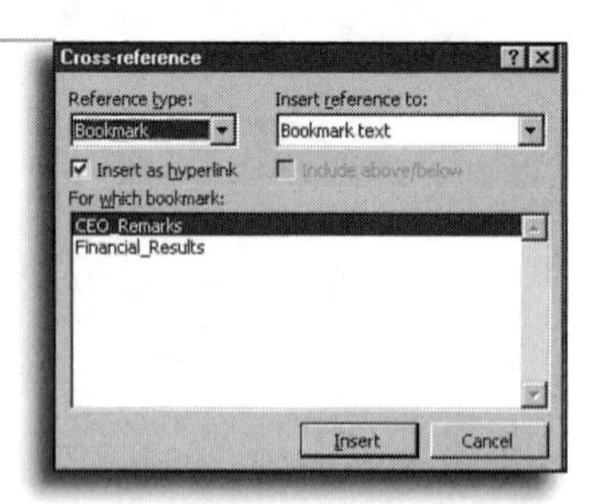

FIGURE 10.12

Use this dialog box to insert a clickable cross-reference to a bookmarked location.

3. If you want to change the format of the default cross-reference from the bookmark text to, say, the page number or the word "below," click the arrow to the right of **Insert reference to** and pick an item from the list.

4. In the box labeled **For which bookmark**, click the name of the bookmark you want to use.
5. To make sure users can jump to the cross-referenced bookmark, check the **Insert as hyperlink** box.
6. Click Insert to add the cross-reference to your document, and then click **Close** to put the dialog box away.

When you insert a cross-reference, users who open the document in Word will see the mouse pointer change to a small hand, just as it does in the Web browser, when the pointer passes over the cross-referenced text.

By changing the type of reference, you can add all sorts of smart navigational links to a document. When you open the Cross-reference dialog box, you can choose one of seven reference types to create. Use the procedures described above to work with all of them.

If you create a cross-reference and then edit, delete, or move the item it refers to, you need to update the cross-reference manually to make sure it still points to the correct location. For example, if you change the text in a heading and move it to a different page, you need to make sure that a cross-reference that points to that heading reflects both the updated text and the new page number. To update a single cross-reference, right-click and choose **Update Field** from the shortcut menu.

Choose the right cross-reference format

If your bookmark points to a location or a very large block of text, choose the page number or "above/below" choice rather than displaying the bookmark text. Those options let you insert a cross-reference that looks like this: "See the CEO's remarks on page 14" where the page reference (14, in this case) contains the hyperlink.

Cross-reference looks like gibberish?

Word inserts cross-references as fields, which are programming instructions that tell Word where to look for the information in the cross-reference. If you see a string that includes angle brackets and gobbledy-gook like {REF _Ref249586 * MERGEFORMAT}, Word is displaying field codes instead of field results. To hide the codes and show the field results instead, right-click the field code, and then click **Toggle Field Codes** on the shortcut menu.

...or update all codes at once

To update every field code in a document, including cross-references, press Ctrl+A to select the entire document, and then press F9, the shortcut for Update Fields.

Finding and Replacing Text and Other Parts of a Document

The longer and more complex a document, the more likely you'll need Word's help to find a specific section of the document. Have you used the same phrase too many times in the current document? Have you misspelled the name of a person or company? Where is the section that talks about second-quarter budget results?

To answer any of these questions, use Word's Find and Replace feature. In one simple dialog box, you can search for words or phrases. By clicking a different tab, you can search for information (or even special characters and formatting) and replace the found items. Day in and day out, it is probably the most valuable Word editing tool you can master.

Finding Text

You can easily find a word or phrase anywhere in your document by using Word's Find feature.

Finding Text in a Document

1. Press Ctrl+F (or pull down the **Edit** menu and choose **Find**). You see the dialog box shown in Figure 10.13.
2. Click in the box labeled **Find what** and type the text for which you want to search—a word, a name, a phrase, or a complete sentence.
3. Click the **Find Next** button to jump to the first occurrence of the text you entered.
4. Keep clicking the **Find Next** button to jump to each successive location in the document where the selected text appears.
5. Press Esc or click the **Cancel** button to close the Find and Replace dialog box.

Spelling doesn't count

If you're not sure of the correct spelling of the word you're looking for, enter your best guess. Click the **More** button, if necessary, and check the **Sounds Like** box in the bottom of the dialog box.

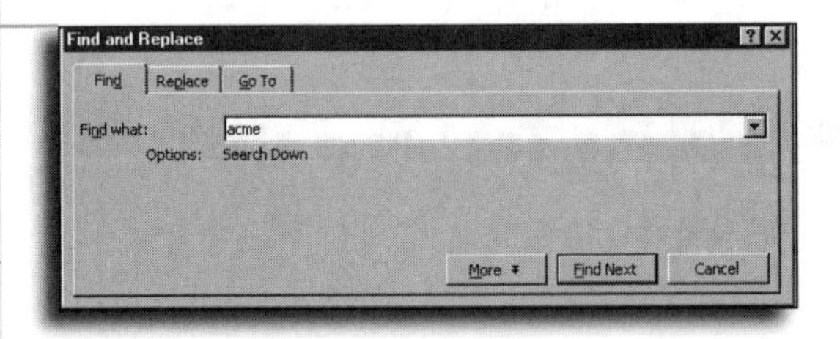

FIGURE 10.13

The Find and Replace dialog box lets you search for a word or phrase anywhere in your document.

If you want to restrict the search further, click the **More** button and select one or more of the check boxes in the bottom of the dialog box. For example, Word normally ignores the case of the text you enter in the **Find what** box. Turning on the **Match case** option forces Word to distinguish between upper- and lowercase letters. Use this option when you want to search for a

Deciphering Find options

Right-click and choose **What's This?** for a brief description of how you can use any of the options in the Find and Replace dialog box.

company or person's name that's also a common word—for example, to search a document for references to *Time* magazine without stopping whenever the word *time* appears. Check the **Find whole words only** option when you're looking for a word that could also be part of other words. For example, if you search for `Ed`, Word will stop on the words, `edition`, `Frederick`, and `suggested` unless you check this box.

Replacing Text

If you can find a piece of text, you can change it. That capability comes in handy if you've written a lengthy pitch for Acme Corporation and then discover the company's legal name is actually Acme Industries, Inc. Instead of searching through your document and painstakingly retyping the name each time it appears, let Word replace the existing text with the new text you specify.

Replacing Text in a Document

1. If the Find and Replace dialog box is visible, click the **Replace** tab. If this dialog box is not visible, press Ctrl+H or pull down the **Edit** menu and choose **Replace**.
2. Type the text you want to search for in the **Find what** box; type the replacement text in the box labeled **Replace with**. The dialog box should look like the one in Figure 10.14.
3. Click the **Find Next** button to jump to the first occurrence of the text you specified.
4. To replace the text in that location, click the **Replace** button. Word makes the substitution and moves on to the next spot where the search text appears.
5. To find the next occurrence of the search text without changing the current selection, click the **Find Next** button.
6. To change every occurrence of the selected text automatically, click **Replace All**.
7. Press Esc or click **Cancel** to close the Find and Replace dialog box.

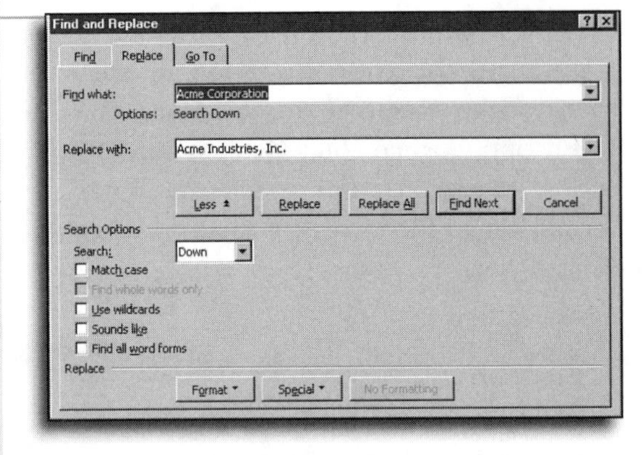

FIGURE 10.14

Use the Find and Replace dialog box to substitute one word or phrase for another automatically.

Don't close that box!

The Find and Replace dialog box, like the Spelling and Grammar dialog box, lets you edit your document even while it's open. Leave the dialog box open if you want, and click in the document editing window to add a new sentence or make another change. Click in the dialog box to resume working with it.

This dialog box has a memory

The Find and Replace dialog box remembers everything you searched for last time. That's good news if you want to repeat a search, but it can cause headaches when you search for plain text after you've searched for formatting and special characters. Look under the **Find what** and **Replace with** boxes to see whether any formatting is specified, and then click the **No Formatting** button to search for the text or special characters you entered, regardless of formatting.

Finding and Replacing Formatting and Special Characters

Sometimes you may want to search for (and replace) more than just text. For example, I might want to open a document, find every place where I've used Bold Italic, and change that formatting to Bold Underline. Or, if I've received a document that someone else formatted, I might want to remove all manual page breaks that were inserted. I routinely use the Find and Replace dialog box to change one style to another when I'm editing heavily formatted documents.

Two buttons at the bottom of the Find and Replace dialog box let you expand the scope of a Word search. Use these buttons to search for formatting (including fonts and styles) or *special characters* (such as tabs and paragraph marks). You can combine these attributes, searching for a specific word or phrase that matches the formatting you specify.

Look just below the **Find what** and **Replace with** text boxes to see whether you've selected any formatting to accompany the current selection in either box. To remove formatting, click in the appropriate box and click the **No Formatting** button.

One of the most common annoyances when you import a text document (such as an email message) into Word is how to deal with the unnecessary paragraph marks at the end of each line. Use the Find and Replace dialog box to make short work of this task—although it's not as simple as it looks at first glance.

Because two carriage returns mark the end of a paragraph in a text message, you first have to replace all the double paragraph marks with a placeholder character, then replace each paragraph mark with a space character, and finally turn the placeholder characters back to paragraph marks.

Stripping Hard Returns from a Text File

1. Open the text file in Word, or paste the text into a blank Word document.
2. Press Ctrl+H to open the **Replace** tab of the Find and Replace dialog box.
3. In the **Find what** box, enter `^p^p`. (That searches for two carriage returns in a row.) In the **Replace with** box, enter a nonsense phrase like `%%%`. Click **Replace All**.
4. Change the contents of the **Find what** box to `^p` and enter a space character in the **Replace with** box, and then click **Replace All**.
5. Reverse the actions in step 3: Enter `%%%` in the **Find what** box and `^p^p` in the **Replace with** box, and then click **Replace All**.
6. Click **Cancel** to close the dialog box and return to your document.

Using Word to Check Your Spelling

As you create or edit a document, Word automatically flags words it can't find in its built-in dictionary. When you click the **Spelling and Grammar** button, Word zips through the current selection or your entire document, stopping at each suspected misspelling and grammatical error. You can accept its suggestions, make your own corrections, or ignore the advice, if you want.

Back up your custom dictionary

All the Office programs share a complete dictionary, as well as a custom dictionary you build every time you check spelling. Normally, Word marks unfamiliar technical terms and proper names as misspelled; when you add them to your dictionary, all Office programs stop wasting your time by marking them as misspelled. If you've customized this dictionary file extensively, back it up! You can typically find the Custom.dic file in the C:\Windows\Application Data\Microsoft\Proof folder. (If you have a custom user profile, look for the Application Data folder that's specific to your profile.)

What the Spelling Checker Can and Can't Do

When Word checks the spelling of words in your document, it compares them with the contents of its built-in dictionary and your *custom dictionary*.

Word's spelling checker alerts you only when you use a word that isn't in its dictionary. If you've simply chosen the wrong word—typing `profit and less` instead of `profit and loss`, for example—Word does not flag the error. The moral? Spelling checkers are useful for catching obvious typos, but you should still proofread important documents carefully.

The spelling checker also flags doubled words, which is good news if you sometimes type `the the end`.

Edit the custom dictionary

Your custom dictionary is simply a text file, and you can add or delete words just by editing this file. Open the **Tools** menu, choose **Options**, click the Spelling and Grammar tab, and click the **Dictionaries** button. Select Custom.dic and then click the **Edit** button. Add, remove, or edit any entries you find here (for example, if you accidentally added a misspelled word to your list, delete it). Choose **File**, **Close** when you finish editing the file, and make sure to save your changes when prompted.

How to Check Your Spelling

A new feature in Word 2000 lets you automatically correct some spelling errors, even if they aren't in the AutoCorrect list. To turn this feature on, pull down the **Tools** menu, choose **AutoCorrect**, and check the box labeled **Automatically use suggestions from the spelling checker**. With this option enabled, Word automatically fixes a typo when you mistype a word for which the spelling checker finds only one suggested correction. For example, if you type `milennium`, Word automatically adds the second "l." But if you type `thim`, Word doesn't make a substitution, because it doesn't know whether you meant `them` or `thin` or `trim` or `him`.

Correct with care

I don't recommend this automatic spell-checking option unless you're an excellent proofreader. If your fingers slip off the home row, it's possible for Word to substitute a Word that has absolutely no relation to what you really meant to type. And because you won't see that wavy red line, you might not realize the "corrected" sentence makes no sense at all.

Word gives you two options for correcting spelling and typing mistakes. You can fix typos as you work, or you can simply get the words on the screen as fast as you can and clean up the misspellings later. Either way, Word marks mistyped words as you go, using wavy red underlines like those in the example in Figure 10.15.

To correct a typo right away, right-click the marked word and then make a selection from the pop-up menu you see in Figure 10.16.

Your choices are as follows:

- Use one of the suggestions—Word usually takes its best shot at guessing what you tried to type, offering one or more options. If the correct spelling is in this bold-faced list, select it.

Those red marks don't print

The red marks that flag possible misspelled words are visible only on the screen. They don't show when you print.

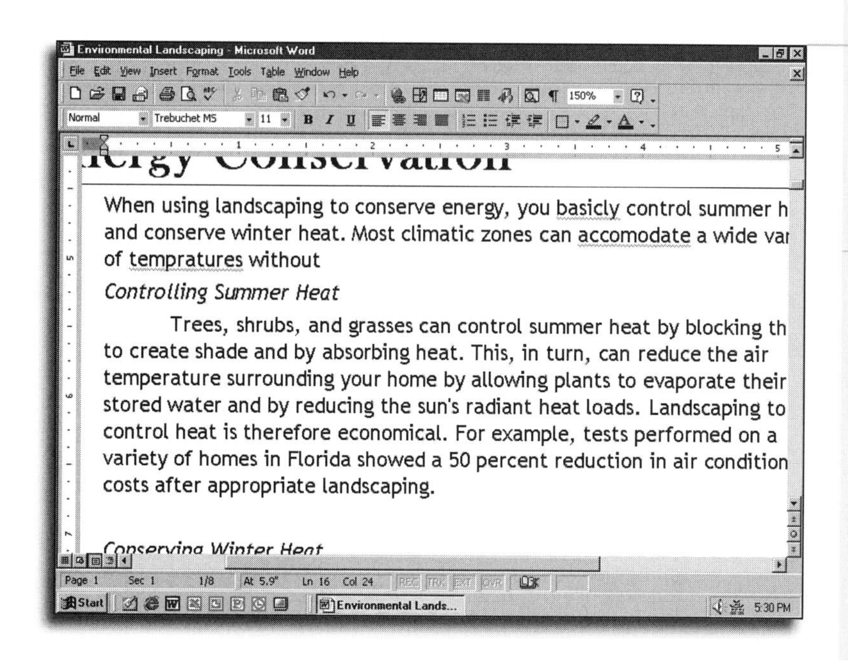

FIGURE 10.15

Word marks any words it can't find in its dictionary, including these obvious typos as well as proper names and some technical or specialized terms.

- Tell Word the spelling is correct—The word in question may be a foreign word or a proper name, or it just may not be in Word's dictionary. In either case, click the **Ignore All** choice, and Word stops flagging all future occurrences of that word in the current document.
- Add the word to your AutoCorrect list—If you regularly misspell the word in question, and the correct spelling is listed as a boldfaced entry at the top of the shortcut menu, add the word to your AutoCorrect list. Click **AutoCorrect** and choose the proper spelling from the cascading menu at right; from now on, Word will automatically substitute the word you chose for the one you mistyped.
- Add the word to your custom dictionary—Select **Add**, and Word will never again mark the selected word as misspelled.

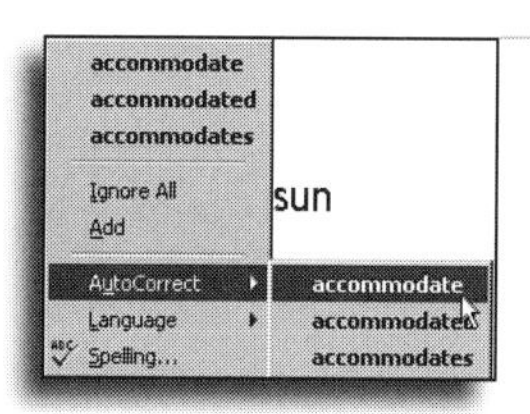

FIGURE 10.16

If you routinely misspell a word, use this menu choice, and Word fixes the typo automatically next time.

Turning Off the Spelling Checker

To some people, those red wavy lines are simply a distraction. If you feel that way, turn off Word's on-the-fly spell-checking. To do so, pull down the **Tools** menu, choose **Options**, and click the **Spelling & Grammar** tab. Remove the check mark from the box labeled **Check spelling as you type** at the top of the list. To hide the red marks only in the current document, check the box labeled **Hide spelling errors in this document**.

Even when automatic spell-checking is turned off, you can still use the spelling checker to look up a word, check a paragraph, or go through your entire document.

Checking the Spelling of Your Document

1. Select the text to check. If you don't make a selection, Word checks the entire document.
2. Click the **Spelling and Grammar** button on the Standard toolbar.
3. If any misspellings or grammatical mistakes appear in the selection, Word highlights the possible error and pops up a list of suggested alternatives, as shown in Figure 10.17.
4. If no errors appear in the selected text, Word offers to check the rest of your document (without mentioning that the highlighted text is spelled correctly). Click **Yes** to continue or **No** to return to the document.
5. After Word has finished checking the entire document, it pops up a dialog box telling you the spell check is complete. Click **OK** to return to the editing window.

FIGURE 10.17
When Word finds a possible misspelling, you can change it, ignore it, or add the word to your custom dictionary.

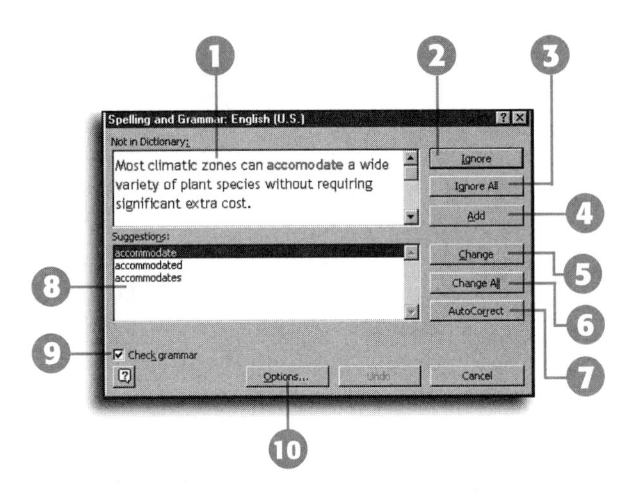

1. Click here to correct the word yourself if Word's suggestions aren't correct.
2. Tell Word to ignore this instance of this word.
3. Tell Word to ignore all instances of this word in the current document.
4. Click here to add this typo and its correction to the AutoCorrect list.
5. Select the correct spelling and then click here to fix the typo instantly.
6. Click here to fix every instance of this misspelling in the current document.
7. Add the word to your custom dictionary so that Word stops flagging it as misspelled.
8. If the correct spelling appears in this list, select it and then click **Change**.
9. Clear this check box to check only spelling, not grammar.
10. Click to set spelling options.

Saving Keystrokes with Automatic Data Entry Tricks

Does Office 97 have more Autos than a Ford factory? That's the way it seems sometimes. Word alone has AutoText, AutoComplete, and AutoFormat As You Type, which all fall under the general heading of AutoCorrect. The names may be confusingly similar, but each one of these AutoSomethings has a specific purpose: to fix obvious mistakes automatically and eliminate unnecessary keystrokes as you work.

How does AutoCorrect work? Word watches as you type, waiting for combinations of keys that it finds on the AutoCorrect list. In some cases, Word automatically replaces what you typed, usually so quickly that you don't even notice (if you type `teh`, for example, AutoCorrect changes it to `the` immediately). With AutoText entries, on the other hand, you have to press Enter or F3 after typing a shorthand name, at which point Word inserts whatever text you've assigned to that entry.

To see and adjust all the AutoOptions that are available, pull down the **Tools** menu and choose **AutoCorrect**. Each tab in this dialog box serves a slightly different purpose.

SEE ALSO

- *To learn how to add and remove AutoCorrect entries in any Office application, see page 41*
- *To learn about Word's AutoFormat feature, see page 245*

AutoCorrect: Fixing Typos On-the-Fly

Use Undo to reverse AutoCorrect

Anytime Word makes an AutoCorrect change, you can cancel the change by clicking the Undo button. When Word turns your (c) into a copyright symbol, for example, press Ctrl+Z or click the **Undo** button to change it right back, and then continue typing.

When you add an entry to the AutoCorrect list, Word makes the substitution without asking your permission. For this reason, AutoCorrect entries are generally limited to replacements for words that you know are incorrectly spelled. It's important to note that unformatted entries in your AutoCorrect list work throughout Office. So if you use the AutoCorrect list in Word to specify that you want `pgcinc` changed to `Paradise Garden Center, Inc.`, the same change will take place in Excel and PowerPoint.

AutoText: Inserting Boilerplate Text with a Click

If you create business documents, you probably find yourself using the same sentences and paragraphs over and over again. Word lets you automatically insert this kind of *boilerplate* text by defining a shorthand name for it and then using pull-down menus or a shortcut key to expand the shorthand name into the full text.

For example, your company might have a standard sales letter that you send out whenever a customer writes requesting information. You usually want to add a personal touch to these letters, but the first paragraph is invariably a standard one in which you tell the customer you're sending them a brochure. You could define an AutoText entry for that paragraph and assign the shorthand name `Brochure-letter` to it. Now, all you have to do is type that shorthand name and press Enter or F3 to stuff the entire paragraph into your document at the insertion point.

Entering days and months automatically

When you first install Word, the AutoText list includes more than 40 entries, most of them elements in common business letters. It also recognizes the days of the week and the months of the year, so if you type `febr` and press F3, `February` appears in your document. These entries appear in the AutoText menu, but not in the list of entries in the AutoText dialog box.

Adding an AutoText Entry

1. In the current document, select the text and/or graphics you want to insert into future documents. (If your entry is a paragraph, make sure that you include the entire paragraph in the selection.)
2. Pull down the **Tools** menu and choose **AutoCorrect**; then click the **AutoText** tab.
3. Check the **Preview** window at the bottom of the dialog box shown in Figure 10.18. If that entry is correct, type the shorthand name for your boilerplate text (in this case, `Brochure-letter`) in the box labeled **Enter AutoText entries here**.
4. If you want the AutoText entry to be available to all documents, choose **Normal (global template)** from the list labeled **Look in**. To assign the entry to another template, choose its name from the same list.
5. Click **Add** to save the new AutoText entry.
6. Click **OK** to close the AutoCorrect dialog box.

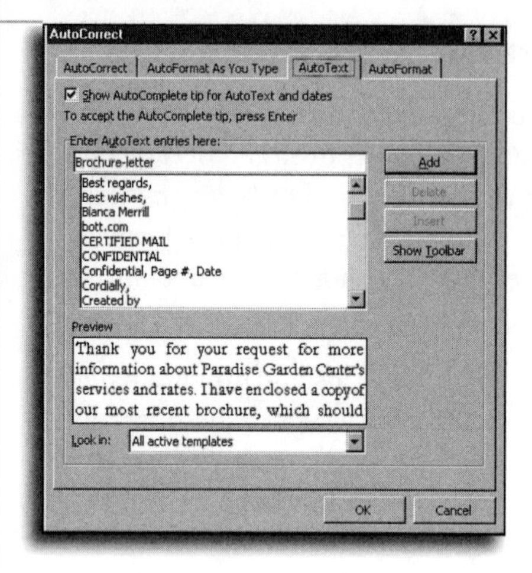

FIGURE 10.18

AutoText entries can be an entire document, a simple phrase, or a paragraph, like this example.

Turning off AutoComplete

When you type the first four letters of some (but not all) AutoText items, such as months, Word displays a pop-up tip that suggests the complete word or phrase. When you see this ScreenTip, you can press Enter or F3 to accept the suggestion and insert the AutoText entry. Just continue typing if you want to ignore the AutoText suggestion. To prevent these AutoComplete tips from popping up at all, clear the check box labeled **Show AutoComplete tip for AutoText and dates** at the top of the AutoCorrect dialog box.

After you've added an AutoText entry, you can use it in any document based on that template. When you store the AutoText entry in the Normal document template, it's available to all documents.

Entering Boilerplate Text Automatically

1. Position the insertion point in the document where you want to add the AutoText entry.
2. Type the name of the AutoText entry (you don't need to follow the name with a space).
3. If you've turned on the AutoComplete option, Word pops up a ScreenTip as soon as it recognizes what you've typed, even if you haven't finished typing the complete name. Press Enter to insert the AutoText item.
4. If AutoComplete is turned off, enter the shorthand name for your boilerplate text (`pr-close`, in this example) and press F3.
5. Word inserts the boilerplate text at the insertion point.

To change an AutoText entry, follow the preceding steps to create a new AutoText entry with the same name as the old one. Answer Yes when Word asks whether you want to redefine the entry.

To delete an AutoText entry, just highlight its name and click the **Delete** button.

AutoFormat As You Type

By default, Word changes some characters you type into a different format. For example, when you enter a fraction like 1/2, Word replaces those three characters with a single, neat publishing character—½. Any time you find Word changing what you've typed for no apparent reason, this feature is probably the reason.

To see all the formatting changes that Word can make automatically, pull down the **Tools** menu and choose **AutoCorrect**. Click the tab labeled **AutoFormat As You Type** (see Figure 10.19).

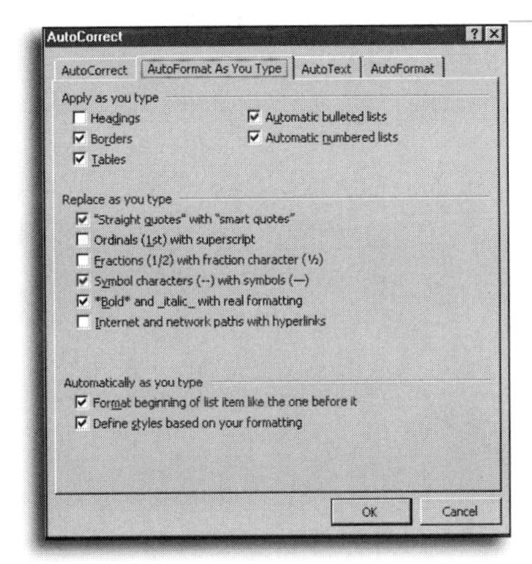

FIGURE 10.19
Adjust the AutoFormat options in this dialog box to match your preferences.

I like the way Word changes my straight quotes to the curly variety and changes a pair of hyphens to a dash, so I routinely leave these items turned on. I prefer seeing fractions as I type them, though, so I clear that check box. Also, because I usually create documents destined for paper rather than the Web, I turn off Word's option to convert Internet paths to clickable hyperlinks.

The following sections describe every one of these AutoFormat options and how they work. Most of these options are on by default when you first install Word 2000.

Setting the Apply As You Type Options

- **Headings**—Word tries to recognize and format headings for you, looking for blank lines and short sentences as its cues. For example, if you type the word Introduction at the beginning of a document and then press Enter twice, Word automatically converts it to a heading with the Heading 1 style. If you press the Tab key and then enter a heading and press Enter twice, word formats the text with the Heading 2 format. Use two tabs for Heading 3, three tabs for Heading 4, and so on. Clear this check box if you never want Word to add heading formatting.
- **Borders**—If Word sees you enter three or more characters that it recognizes as common borders, including hyphens, equal signs, and asterisks, it automatically creates a border along the bottom of the preceding paragraph when you press Enter. The border style matches the basic look of the punctuation you typed: a hyphen becomes a thin line, the row of equal signs is a double border, and tildes (~) or number signs (#) become decorative borders. Clear this check box to turn off automatic borders.

Automatic borders are tricky

To remove a border from a paragraph immediately after Word applies it, press Ctrl+Z or click the **Undo** button. If you've waited too long for Undo to be a practical option, click in the paragraph below the border, pull down the **Format** menu, choose **Borders and Shading**, and then choose **None** from the **Borders** tab.

- **Tables**—This is one of the least important in this dialog box. If you enter a row of hyphens and plus signs that resembles the column layout of a table (+---+----+-------+), Word will automatically create a table using those dimensions. Most people will never see this AutoFormat option in action, because it's so much easier to create a table using Word's table-drawing tools.
- **Automatic bulleted lists**—Word will turn paragraphs into a bulleted list for you if it thinks it recognizes a bullet character such as an asterisk, one or two hyphens, a greater-than sign (>), or an arrow created with ASCII characters (like -> or =>). If you enter an asterisk, for example, followed by a space or tab and some text, Word will convert the text you

entered to a bulleted list item; in addition, the new paragraph is also in bulleted list format. Enter more text to continue creating bulleted items, or press Enter twice to stop. Clear this check box if you never want Word to turn these characters into bulleted lists.

- **Automatic numbered lists**—Word will also turn paragraphs into numbered list format if it thinks that's what you want. This AutoFormat option kicks in when you type a number followed by a period, a hyphen, a closing parenthesis, or a greater-than sign (>), followed by a space or tab and some text. To end the list, press Enter twice.

Save formatting for later

When you're first putting a document together, use the asterisk character at the beginning of a line to create quick-and-dirty bulleted lists automatically. You can always go back and adjust the bullet formatting later.

Setting the Replace As You Type Options

- **"Straight quotes" with "smart quotes"**—Leave this box checked most of the time. Clear it only when you want to be certain that Word uses straight punctuation marks—for example, in a set of specifications that refer to measurements using feet (') and inches (").

SEE ALSO

For a full discussion of how Smart quotes work, see page 187

- **Ordinals (1st) with superscript**—Clear this box if you don't like the slightly old-fashioned look of these superscript characters, or if you routinely create documents at small point sizes, where these characters are nearly impossible to see properly.
- **Fractions (1/2) with fraction character (½)**—Fraction characters are only available for the most common fractions. If you regularly enter odd fractions, such as 7/32, this option will have no effect.
- **Symbol characters (--) with symbols (—)**—A very handy way to enter em dashes and en dashes; I strongly recommend leaving this box checked.
- ***Bold* and _italic_ with real formatting**—These conventions are popular among people who use text-based email programs. If you use Word to open an email message that

contains this type of pseudo-formatting, you'll see the real formatting. Clear this check box if you want to stick with plain text.

- **Internet and network paths with hyperlinks**—More people complain about this AutoFormat feature than any other. This option is turned on by default; if most of your documents are destined for output on paper, clear this check box.

Email addresses too!

Although the description in the AutoCorrect dialog box doesn't mention it, this option also applies to email addresses.

Setting the Automatically As You Type Options

- **Format beginning of list item like the one below it**—Use this option if you want the beginning of each item in a list to look the same. For example, if the first word in the previous item is bold, Word will turn on bold formatting when you start the next item. Clear this check box to use the default formatting instead.
- **Define styles based on your formatting**—This option automatically applies specific types of styles to new documents when you use certain types of manual formatting. For example, if you center a one-word heading and increase its point size, Word automatically applies the Title style. If you indent a paragraph, it will apply the Body Text Indent style when you press Enter. If you prefer to apply styles yourself, clear this check box.

Finish the formatting yourself

Although Word can automatically recognize the formatting at the beginning of the list item, it won't switch to a new formatting in the middle of the line. You'll have to change formatting options manually.

Automatic updates are even more confusing

Word includes two automatic style options. This one applies paragraph and heading styles the first time you use manual formatting. This option is not the same as the one that automatically updates styles when you change the formatting for a paragraph that includes that style. Confused? Jump ahead to Chapter 12, "Using Templates and Styles," for an explanation of what's going on.

SEE ALSO

➤ *To find out how to apply styles to your text, see page 250*
➤ *To learn how to format simple lists with bullets and numbers, see page 241*

Using Word to Sharpen Your Grammar

Just as Word automatically checks your spelling while you type, it also compares the words and sentences in your document with a set of common grammar rules. I routinely turn off the grammar checker, but I recommend using it if you feel your writing could use some help.

The grammar checker draws from an enormous list of grammar and style rules in 20 different categories. To see and customize the entire list, pull down the **Tools** menu, choose **Options**, click the **Spelling & Grammar** tab, and click the **Settings** button. Figure 10.20 shows a partial listing of the rules you can change.

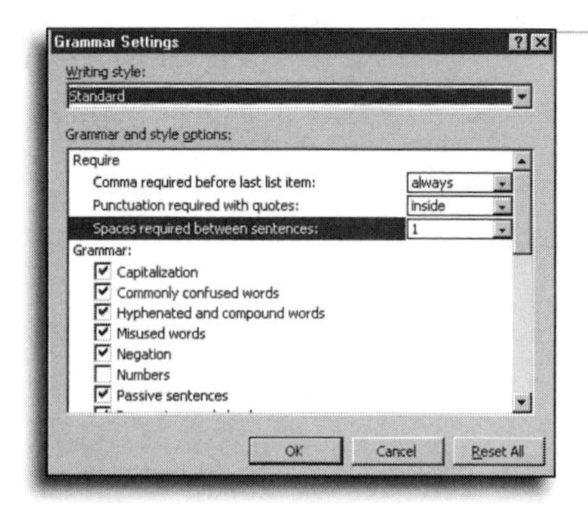

FIGURE 10.20
Word's grammar checker analyzes your writing and also handles basic style options, like the three at the top of this dialog box.

How the Grammar Checker Works

With the *grammar checker*, like the Word spelling checker, you can choose to check grammar as you write or do it all at once after you've finished with a document. On-the-fly grammar suggestions show up in your document with green wavy lines underneath the questionable text. When you right-click on one of these markers, you see a shortcut menu with three choices: Make the suggested change, if one is available; tell Word to ignore the phrase or sentence; or click the **Grammar** option to see a dialog box like the one in Figure 10.21.

Finding the Right Word

Sooner or later, every writer needs help finding exactly the right word. When you're stuck, use Word's built-in *thesaurus* to look up other words that might work in your current document. In previous versions of Office, you had to dig through several layers of pull-down menus to find the Thesaurus. In Word 2000, it's just a right-click away.

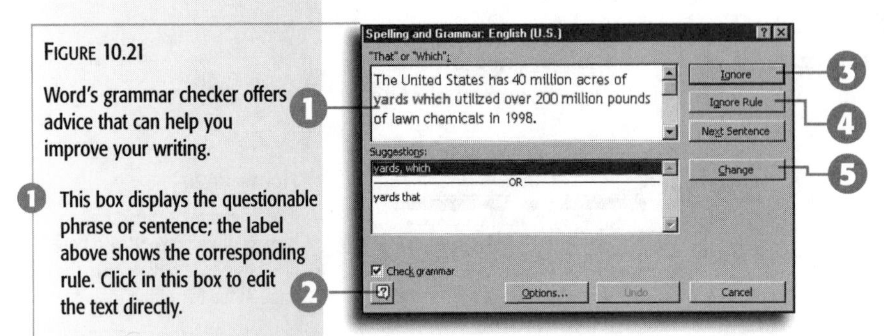

FIGURE 10.21

Word's grammar checker offers advice that can help you improve your writing.

1. This box displays the questionable phrase or sentence; the label above shows the corresponding rule. Click in this box to edit the text directly.
2. Click here to display a detailed explanation of the rule in the Office Assistant window.
3. Click here to ignore the rule, this time...
4. ...or throughout the current document.
5. Select a suggestion from the list and click here to make the change automatically.

To find a synonym, point to the word you want to look up (you don't need to select the entire word) and right-click. Click the **Synonyms** choice at the bottom of the shortcut menu to display a list like the one in Figure 10.22.

If you find a suitable word in the short list shown here, click it to replace the current word. To see more synonyms, click the **Thesaurus** choice, which lets you expand your search. This dialog box (see Figure 10.23) may also allow you to select related words or antonyms—words that are opposite in meaning to the one you selected.

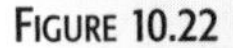

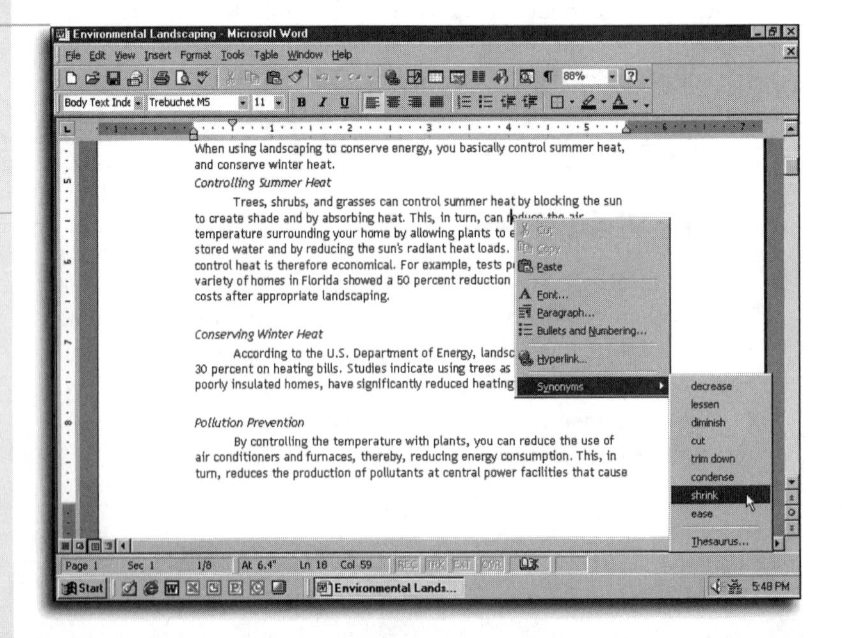

FIGURE 10.22

Use Word's thesaurus to search for a more appropriate word; these are the suggestions when you right-click *reduce*.

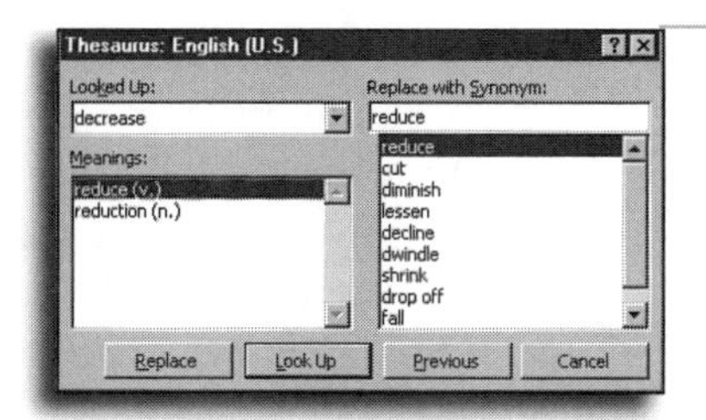

FIGURE 10.23

If one of the suggested synonyms is close, but not quite right, select that word and click the **Look Up** button.

Keeping Track of Changes in a Word Document

When you're truly collaborating with another person, though, you may pass the same file back and forth several times, with each of you making many small changes in each pass. How do you see all the changes that you and other people made to an original document?

For short documents, use the Highlight tool to call attention to a word or phrase that may need more work. Add comments when you want to ask questions and or add brief notes without typing text directly into someone else's work. For large documents, Word lets you track changes, automatically marking changes, additions, and deletions, no matter who made them. Later, you can review those changes, accepting the ones you want to keep and rejecting others to restore the original version of the document.

One at a time, please

Even if a Word document is stored in a shared network folder, only one person can edit it at a time. If you try to open a document that someone else is currently editing, you'll see a dialog box that allows you to open a read-only copy of the document; you can also ask Word to notify you when the other person has finished working with the document.

Highlighting Text

When sharing a Word document, use the Highlight tool to mark words, phrases, or entire paragraphs that you want to call to another person's attention. This tool works much like the markers you use on paper documents to highlight text: Just swipe the "pen" over the text you want to mark; the background color changes, but the text underneath remains visible.

Highlighters aren't just for comments

Although it's most common to highlight text in documents you're sharing with other people, you can use Word's Highlighter for strictly personal use. For example, while working on this book I used the yellow marker to highlight sections that needed additional research, and the green marker to indicate notes to myself that weren't intended for publication.

To begin marking text, click Word's **Highlight** button. The mouse pointer turns to a combination of an insertion point (an I-bar) and a pen. As long as that pointer is visible, you can drag it across any text to highlight it with a vivid color. Figure 10.24 shows the pointer and the marked text. To stop highlighting, press Esc or click the **Highlight** button again.

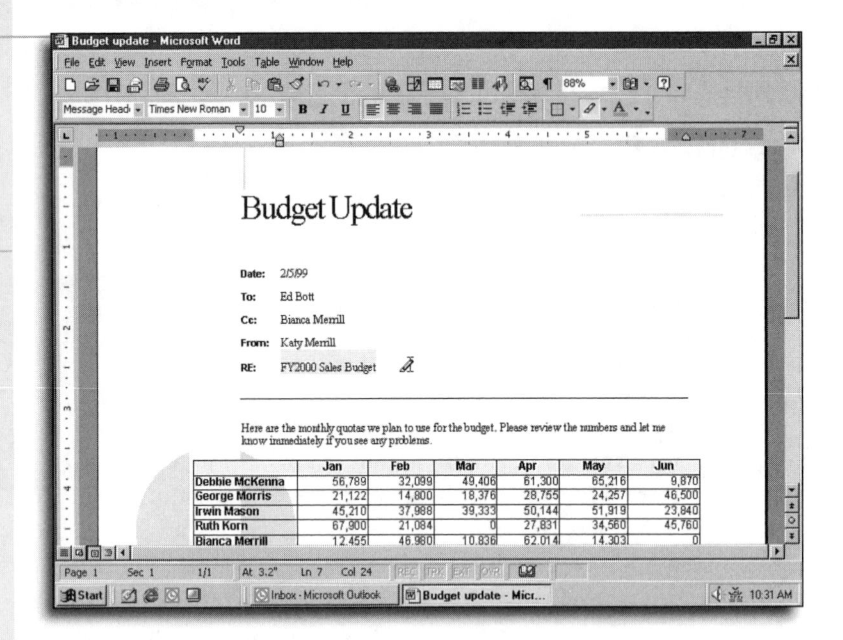

FIGURE 10.24

When the pointer turns to this marker, you can highlight any text. If you plan to print the document, be sure to choose a color that won't obscure the text.

Highlights don't work as well on paper

Highlighting works best when you're expecting someone to read the document online. If you plan to print it out on a black-and-white printer, the marked text turns to a dull gray, and it doesn't have anywhere near the same impact as that vivid yellow or fluorescent green. Of course, if you have a color printer, the results can be startlingly effective–and much easier and neater than highlighting each copy with a marker pen.

You can also highlight text by making a selection first, and then clicking the **Highlight** button. If you use this technique, the highlight affects only the selection; the pointer doesn't change shape, and you have to click the **Highlight** button again to mark another selection.

To change to any of Word's 15 marker colors, click the arrow to the right of the **Highlight** button and choose a color square from the box that drops down.

Adding Comments to a Word Document

Sometimes simply highlighting a section in a Word document isn't sufficient. If you're reviewing a draft of a report someone else prepared, you might have questions; if you're the original author, you might want to forestall a question by offering a quick explanation for why you used a particular word or phrase. Adding text directly into the document is a bad idea; instead, add a *comment* to your document.

When you add a comment to a Word document, three things happen:

- The text you selected (or the nearest full word) is highlighted in a faint yellow.
- Word adds a *comment reference mark* at the insertion point. This mark is automatically numbered and includes your initials.
- The *comments pane* opens at the bottom of the document window. Word inserts a *comment marker* that matches the one in the document and positions the insertion point there, waiting for you to enter your comment.

Figure 10.25 shows a Word document that contains several comments. Note that each comment reference mark is visible as long as the comments pane is open, and each piece of text that includes a comment is highlighted in yellow.

Inserting a Comment in a Word Document

1. Select the text you want to comment on.
2. Pull down the **Insert** menu and choose **Comment**. Or, if the Reviewing toolbar is visible, make your selection and click the **Insert Comment** button. Word adds a marker in your document, opens the comments pane below the document window, and moves the insertion point there.
3. Enter your comment and then click the **Close** button to hide the comments pane and return to your document.

Removing highlighting

To remove highlights from selected text, click the drop-down arrow to the right of the Highlight button, and choose **None**. To remove all highlights from a document, press Ctrl+A to select the entire document, and then click the drop-down arrow to the right of the Highlight button and choose **None**. To hide highlighting without removing it, pull down Word's **Tools** menu and choose **Options**, click the **View** tab, clear the check mark from the **Highlight** box, and click **OK**. You'll need to restore the check mark to make highlights visible again.

Use your full name in comments

If you and a coworker have the same initials and both of you add comments to a Word document, you'll be unable to tell who said what. The solution? Change your initials, at least for use with Word. Better yet, use your full first name or the first part of your email address. Open the **Tools** menu, choose **Options**, and click the User Information tab. Word identifies your comments using whatever you enter in the **Initials** box. Normally, this is your initials, but you can enter a name or other ID up to nine characters in length.

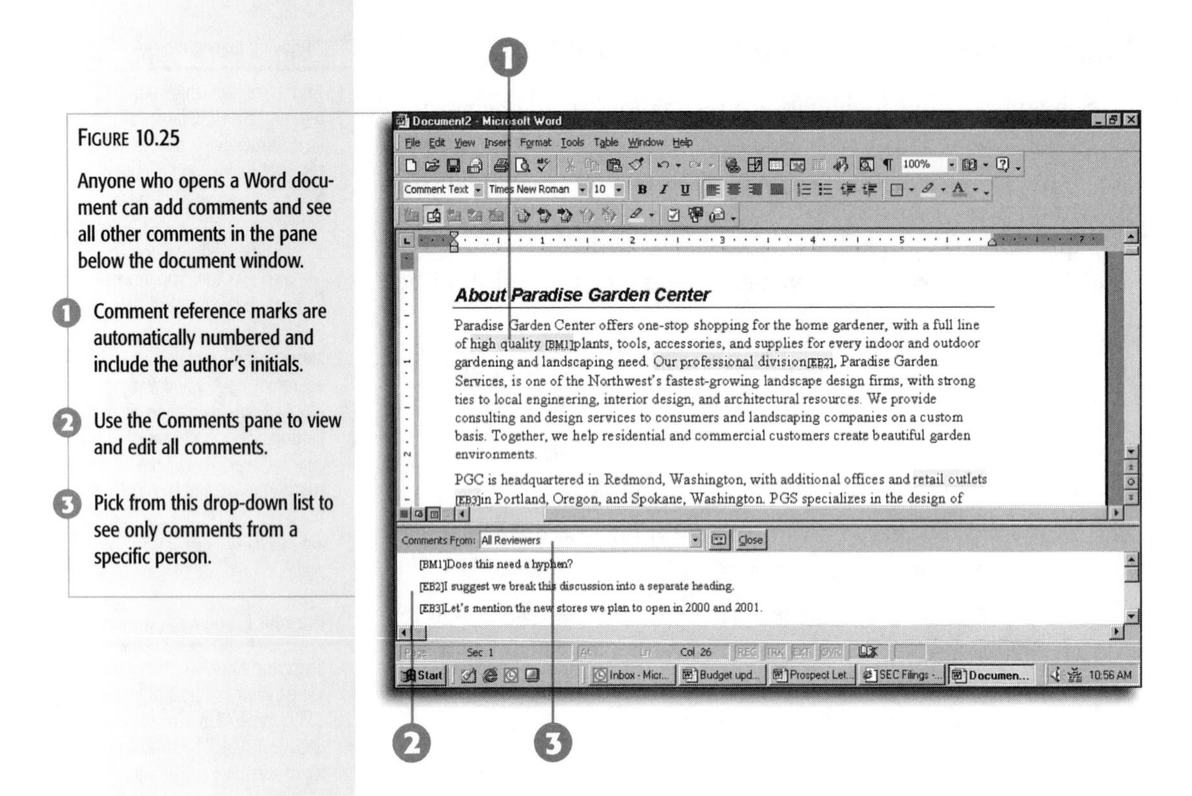

FIGURE 10.25

Anyone who opens a Word document can add comments and see all other comments in the pane below the document window.

1. Comment reference marks are automatically numbered and include the author's initials.
2. Use the Comments pane to view and edit all comments.
3. Pick from this drop-down list to see only comments from a specific person.

No selection necessary

Strictly speaking, you don't need to make a selection before you insert a comment–Word will automatically make a default selection for you. To attach a comment to a single word, just click to position the insertion point anywhere within that word (or at the beginning), and Word will automatically select it. But if your comment concerns a phrase, a sentence, or a whole paragraph, select it first so that other readers will be able to see the selection when they review your comments.

Double-click on any comment reference mark to jump to the associated entry in the comments pane, or select a comment to scroll the document to the associated marker. You can shift back and forth between the comments pane and your document when viewing or editing comments. To close the comments pane so you can see the full document again, click the **Close** button.

You don't need to open the comments pane to read individual comments in a document. Look for the faint yellow marks that indicate comments, and aim the mouse pointer at one of these marks. The pointer changes shape and you see a pop-up window containing the comment, like the one in Figure 10.26.

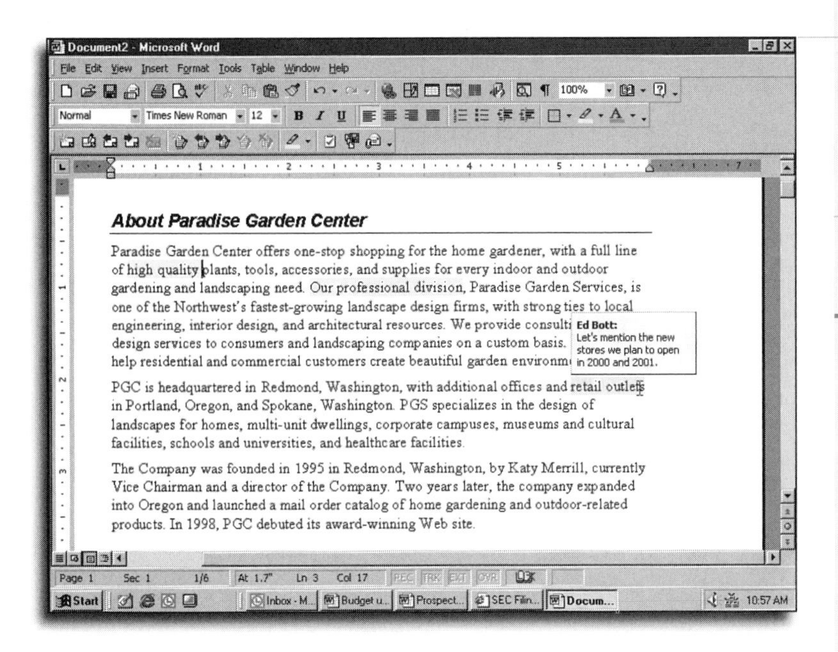

FIGURE 10.26

Point to the yellow text that indicates a comment in a Word document; after a second, the comment pops up.

To edit any comment, open the comments pane, click in the comment text, and make your changes. To remove a comment completely, select any portion of the text to which the comment is attached, and then right-click and choose Delete Comment from the shortcut menu. If the Reviewing toolbar is visible, use the **Delete Comment** button.

Turning on Revision Marking

Generally, you'll want to start with a first draft of a document, and then tell Word you want to track changes.

Tracking Changes in a Word Document

1. Open the document you plan to revise, pull down the **Tools** menu and choose **Track Changes**, and then **Highlight Changes**.

Force Word to show comment marks

Normally, closing the comments pane hides all comment reference marks. To make these indicators visible at all times, open the **Tools** menu and choose **Options**, and then click the **View** tab. In the **Formatting marks** section, check the **Hidden text** box. With this option on, Word shows comment reference marks even when the comments pane is closed.

Read all comments in order

When reviewing comments in a Word document or Excel worksheet, use the Next Comment and Previous Comment buttons on the Reviewing toolbar to move from one comment to the next.

Instant on

If you use revision marking often, try this very well hidden shortcut to bypass menus completely. Look on the status bar at the bottom of the Word document window; roughly halfway across, you'll see the grayed-out letters TRK in a small box. Double-click here to begin tracking changes. (The grayed-out letters turn black.) To stop tracking changes, double-click the same spot. Right-click on the same spot to pop up a shortcut menu with other options.

Hide revisions to make editing easier

When you're making extensive changes to a document, revision-tracking marks can be horribly confusing. To work with the document itself without being distracted by revision marks, clear the **Highlight changes on screen** box. After you finish editing, you can display the changes again and review each one, if necessary.

2. In Highlight Changes dialog box (see Figure 10.27), check the box labeled **Track changes while editing**.
3. If you want Word to track changes but hide the marks as you work, clear the check mark from the box labeled **Highlight changes on screen**.
4. Click **OK** to return to the document editing window.

Showing or Hiding Revisions in a Document

When you turn on revision tracking, Word retains normal formatting for all existing text in your document, but anything you add or delete from this point on gets special formatting, as shown in Figure 10.28.

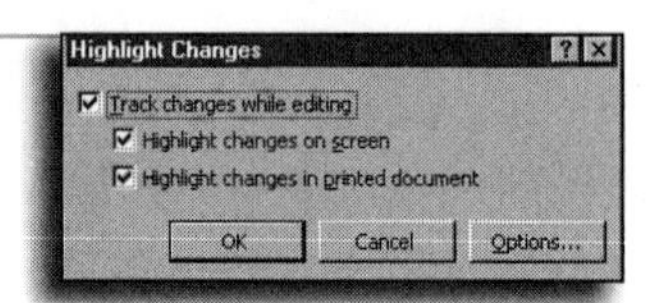

FIGURE 10.27

Check this box if you want Word to mark changes and deletions so you can see who did what in a shared document.

You can stop tracking changes at any time—pull down the **Tools** menu and choose **Track Changes**; then choose **Highlight Changes** and clear the check mark from the **Track changes while editing** box. (If the Reviewing toolbar is visible, just click the **Track Changes** button to toggle this feature on or off.) When you do so, all the revision marks remain in the current document; but if you add, edit, or delete any part of the document, your changes appear without special formatting.

Who made that change?

If you've turned on the option to highlight changes on the screen, ScreenTips identify the who, what, and when of each change. Point to the marked text to see who deleted, added, or reformatted it.

Quickly view the original document

If the Accept or Reject Changes dialog box is open, you can quickly switch between a view of the original document and the changed document. Choose the **Original** option in the **View** box to see the document with all changes hidden. Choose either of the other two options to see the document with its changes.

Accepting or Rejecting Changes in a Document

After you've passed a document around for several rounds of editing, someone has to produce a final version. If you drew that responsibility, you have three choices:

- Display the Reviewing toolbar and use the **Next Change** and **Previous Change** buttons to move through the document one change at a time. At each change, click **Accept Change** or **Reject Change** to remove all special formatting and leave only the version you want.

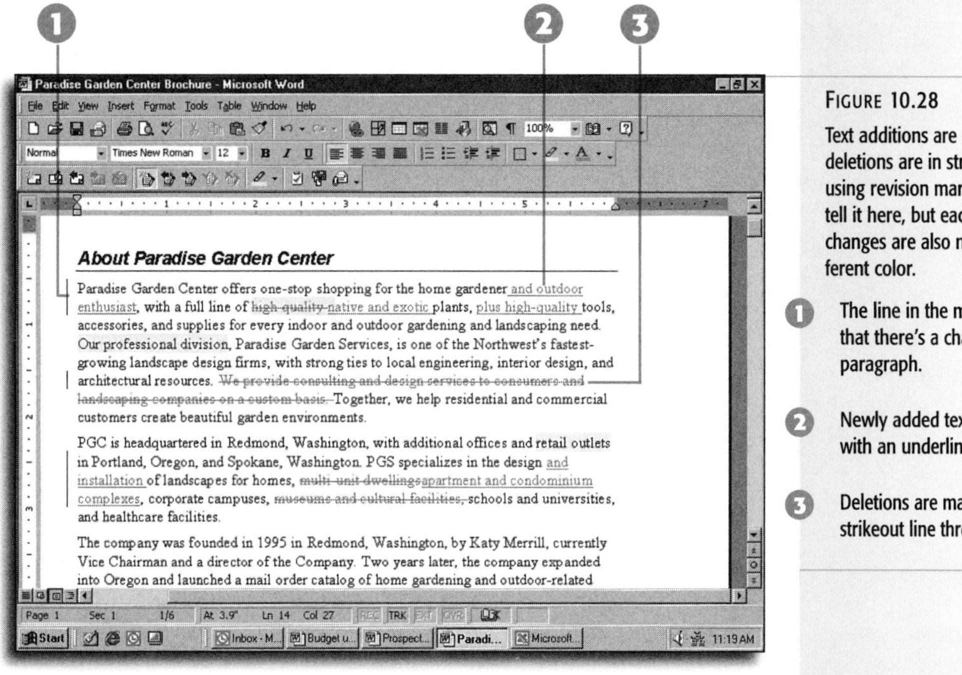

FIGURE 10.28

Text additions are underlined and deletions are in strikeout when using revision marks. You can't tell it here, but each author's changes are also marked in a different color.

1. The line in the margin tells you that there's a change in that paragraph.
2. Newly added text is marked with an underline.
3. Deletions are marked with a strikeout line through the center.

- Pull down the **Tools** menu and choose **Track Changes**, and then click **Accept or Reject Changes**. In the resulting dialog box (see Figure 10.29), click either **Find** button to move to the next or previous change. The Changes area at the left of the dialog box tells who made the change and when. Click **Accept** to incorporate the changes into the final document; click **Reject** to restore the original version and delete the change.
- To incorporate all changes into a document, pull down the **Tools** menu and choose **Track Changes**; then click **Accept or Reject Changes** and click **Accept All**. To restore the original document, click **Reject All**.

Changes are gone for good

When you accept and reject changes, Word keeps only the version you choose, permanently deleting the other one. If you want to maintain a history of the changes, make sure you save the final version under a new name.

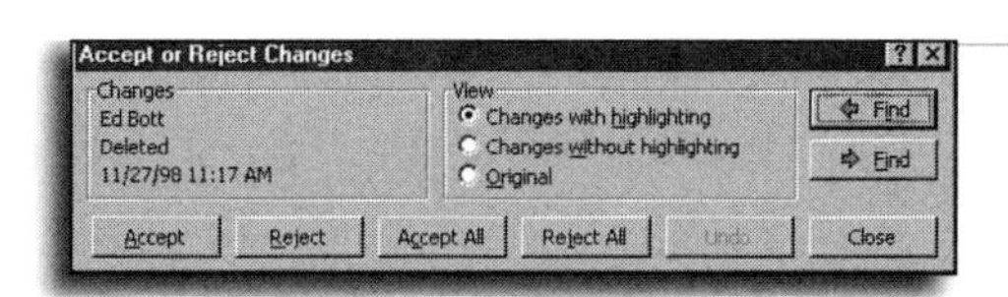

FIGURE 10.29

Use this dialog box to view all the changes in a document. You can accept or reject any or all of the changes.

CHAPTER

11

Formatting Documents in Word

Learn about formatting options in Word

Change your margins and paper size

Modify your fonts to add emphasis

Adjust line spacing and paragraph alignment

Create bulleted and numbered lists

Understanding Your Formatting Options

The goal of page design is to make documents easier to read. By carefully selecting fonts, varying the use of bold text and other attributes, and arranging blocks of text and graphics on the page, you create natural "entry points" that guide the reader through your document quickly and effectively.

Word lets you exercise pinpoint control over every part of a document's design, from the whitespace around pages to the placement of objects on the screen to the size and shapes of text. In general, you can use three formatting options to turn plain text into well-designed documents: *character formatting*, *paragraph formatting*, and page or section setup options.

Character Formats

Use font formatting to control the precise look of all the text in your document. You can choose separate fonts, adjust the size and style of the text, and use special effects such as underlining and strikethrough to accentuate words and paragraphs. Word also lets you choose colors and animated effects for text; these formatting options are most useful for Web pages and other documents designed for online viewing.

Word also includes an unusual character formatting option not available in other Office programs. Click the arrow to the right of the **Highlight** button on the Formatting toolbar and choose one of 15 colors; the pointer changes shape to resemble a highlighter pen, which you can swipe over text to change its color. Double-click the Highlight button to lock the pointer so that you can mark multiple blocks of text, and then click the button again or press Esc to restore the pointer to its normal shape. To remove highlighting, highlight the selection again, using the same color or the **None** option on the drop-down list to its right.

SEE ALSO

For more details on using Word's Highlight tool, see page 211

Typeface? Font? What's the difference?

At one time, the distinction between the terms typeface and font was clear. Today, that line has blurred somewhat, although the basic principles are still the same.

When you choose an entry from Word's drop-down Font list, you're providing only one piece of the information needed to describe the look of the selected text. Old-time typesetters and printers would insist that each item on that list is a *typeface*—the catchall term that describes the general shape and weight of the letters, numbers, and punctuation marks in that family. The *font*, they would argue, includes much more detail—not just the typeface, but also its size, weight (bold or demibold, for example), and style (such as italic). In this strict definition, Arial is the name of a typeface, and 12-point Arial Bold Italic describes a specific font.

Paragraph Formats

As the name implies, paragraph formats control the *alignment*, spacing, and arrangement of entire paragraphs. You can use indents to adjust margins on a paragraph-by-paragraph basis, and tab stops enable you to align text or numbers into columns.

SEE ALSO

➤ *For a detailed explanation of how to manage Word paragraph styles, see page 250*

Page/Section Setup Options

Open the **File** menu and choose **Page Setup** to adjust formats that affect the entire document. These settings define the margins at the top, bottom, left, and right of the page. They also allow you to specify what type of paper you plan to use for each document, how you want text oriented on the page, and whether you want headers or footers on each page.

SEE ALSO

➤ *To learn how page setup options can make your printed documents look better, see page 284*

Normally, page settings apply to your entire document. If you divide a document into sections, however, you can set different margins, paper sizes, orientations, headers, footers, and other page settings for each section. For example, you might create a letter that prints on standard letterhead paper, and include an envelope as part of the document file, so you can print both pieces at once. By adding a section break between the letter and envelope, you can specify a new paper source (#10 Envelope), with margins to match.

Direct Formatting Versus Styles

When you create a document from scratch, Word starts with the basic formatting options defined in the *Normal document template*, including all settings for the Normal character and paragraph styles. If you select text or click in a paragraph and apply other styles, Word changes the look of your document using the settings stored in those styles.

Serif versus sans serif

Typefaces come in all levels of complexity, but they can generally be divided into two broad categories: *serif* and *sans serif*. Serifs are the small decorative flourishes at the ends of some characters in some typefaces. Sans means "without," so a sans serif face has none of these decorations. Look at the tips of the capital T in the following type samples to see the difference clearly:

- This is a SERIF typeface.
- This is a **SANS SERIF** typeface.

Most designers agree that serif typefaces are the best choice for big blocks of text because they're easier to read, whereas sans serif typefaces are better for headlines and short paragraphs.

If you've used document *styles* to apply formatting, you can override these choices by choosing options from Word's **Format** menu. Font choices and other *direct formatting* options that you make in this fashion override character and paragraph styles. To see all the formatting options for a given block of text, including direct settings and named styles, choose the **Help** menu and select **What's This?** Aim the question-mark-and-arrow pointer at a character and click to see a window like the one in Figure 11.1.

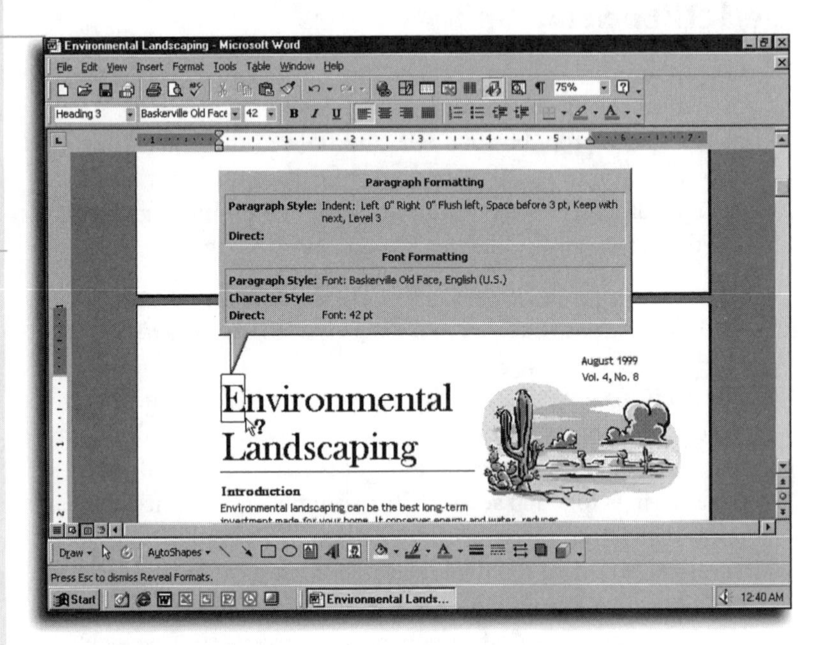

FIGURE 11.1

Use **What's This?** help to inspect all the formatting for a given part of your document. Direct formatting always overrides formatting applied by a named style.

Restoring Default Formatting

If you've mixed styles and direct formatting, trying to sort out which formatting is which can get hopelessly confusing. If you can no longer make heads or tails of the formatting in your document, you might want to reset formats to their defaults.

- To reset all paragraph format settings to those defined in the current style, position the insertion point within the paragraph and press Ctrl+Q.
- To reset any character formatting to the settings defined in the paragraph style, select the text and press Ctrl+Spacebar.

(This method also removes any character styles applied within the selected text.)

- To remove all formatting and reset the paragraph to the Normal style, press Ctrl+Shift+N.

SEE ALSO

- *For more details about Word's Normal document template, see page 154*
- *For instructions on how to change Word's automatic formatting options, see page 202*
- *To find general information on saving and reusing formats, see page 250*

Applying Multiple Formats with Themes

In previous versions of Word, the only way to save collections of formatting options was in named styles and templates. Word 2000 offers a new option called *themes*. These are collections of formats—including fonts, colors, bullets, graphics, and backgrounds—intended primarily for Web pages, email messages, and other online documents.

SEE ALSO

- *For a full explanation of the difference between templates and themes, see page 261*
- *To learn how to use themes with Web pages, see page 324*

Changing the Look of a Page

If you use the default settings in the Normal document template, Word assumes you want all your documents on 8½- by 11-inch letter paper with roughly an inch of whitespace on all four sides. You can adjust any of these settings, however, applying your changes to the entire document or to individual pages or *sections*. For example, you might format a letter for printing on your company's letterhead, and then create a section break and add the page settings for an envelope—which is a completely different size and prints at a different orientation. In this example, each section gets its own page setup settings.

Adding section breaks

Open the **Insert** menu and choose the **Break** command to create a dividing line between sections. Select **Continuous** if you want text to continue on the same page, with different margins and other page settings. Choose the **Next page** option when you want to insert a section break and start a new page, as you would when changing paper types. The **Even page** and **Odd page** options are most useful if you're creating a bound booklet.

Adjusting the Margins

You can leave extra room on the *margins* at either side, the top, or the bottom of your page; this option is especially useful if you want to leave room to write comments. You can also trim the margins to pack more words on the page, although that option may sacrifice readability.

To adjust the margins, pull down the **File** menu and choose **Page Setup**; then click the **Margins** tab (see Figure 11.2). You can set margins for all four edges, as well as the *gutter*, which is the inside of each page (the right side of a left-hand page and the left side of a right-hand page) when you're printing a book or other bound document. Click the box labeled **Mirror margins** to change the **Left** and **Right** boxes to **Inside** and **Outside** when printing documents you plan to bind book-style.

Zero is not an option

With most printers, you cannot set the margins to zero because standard laser and inkjet printers have an unprintable area that Windows doesn't let you use. If you try to set a margin to a value that is within the unprintable area, Word offers to change it to the minimum setting.

Type directly or spin

As with many Office dialog boxes, you can set the page margins by typing them directly into the boxes, or you can click the spinner buttons to nudge the value up or down in small increments–in this case, 0.1 inch at a time.

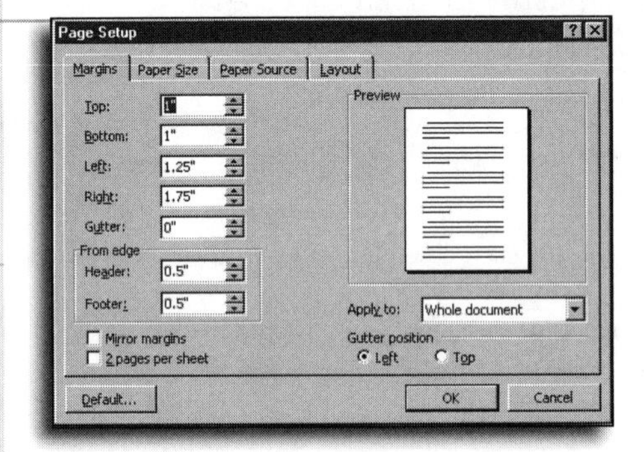

FIGURE 11.2

Click the **Margins** tab in the Page Setup dialog box to adjust the amount of whitespace around your pages.

Changing Paper Size and Orientation

You'll print most business documents on plain letter paper. But what do you do when you want to use legal-size paper or the A4 paper common in European offices? Or when you want to print a table in landscape mode, with the wide edge of the paper at the top and bottom of the page?

Mix and match margins

You can easily change margins and even paper size in the middle of a document. Just pick **This Point Forward** from the drop-down list labeled **Apply to**. Word inserts a section break (next page) at that point.

Changing Paper Size

1. Pull down the **File** menu and choose **Page Setup** to open Word's Page Setup dialog box.
2. Click the **Paper Size** tab (see Figure 11.3).

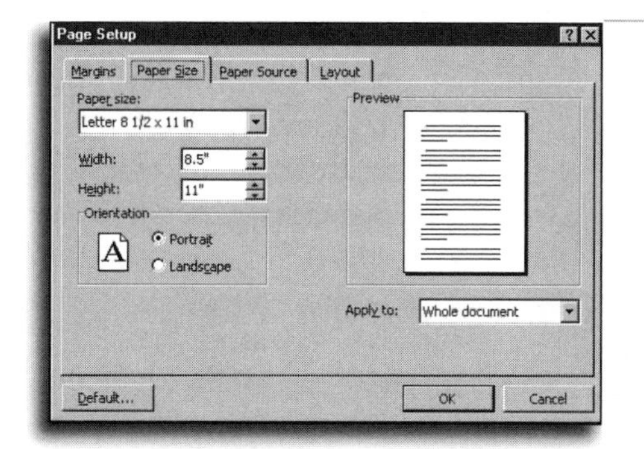

FIGURE 11.3
Use these options to change paper sizes and switch from Portrait (tall) to Landscape (wide) orientation.

3. The exact choices available in the **Paper size** list depend on the printer you've selected. Click the arrow to the right of the list to choose a predefined paper size.
4. If the paper size you want to use is not listed, choose `Custom size` from the bottom of the list and enter the dimensions of the paper in the boxes labeled **Width** and **Height**.
5. To use the selected paper size for all documents, click the button labeled **Default**.
6. Click **OK** to close the dialog box.

SEE ALSO

➤ *To learn how to send your document to the printer, see page 295*

Is your paper compatible?

Before you specify a custom paper size, make sure that your printer can handle it. Some printers require that you use a manual feed for nonstandard sizes, and thick papers such as the stock used for postcards or place cards can jam your printer. Read the printer's documentation if you're not certain.

Pick the right paper for each page

Does your office laser printer stock letterhead in one tray and plain paper in another? Use the Page Setup dialog box to tell Word which tray to use. You can find the specific options for your printer under the **Paper Source** tab. The exact choices vary by printer; on Hewlett-Packard LaserJets, for example, you can specify an upper or lower tray, a manual tray, or an envelope feeder. Alternatively, you can let the printer automatically select the correct paper source.

Starting a New Page

Sometimes you want to end the current page and force Word to start a new one—for example, to put a table on its own, separate page. Press Ctrl+Enter to add a manual page break; or pull down the **Insert** menu, choose **Break**, and then select **Page Break** from the Break dialog box.

Adding Emphasis to Text

By changing the appearance of words, numbers, symbols, and other text, you can dramatically enhance the readability of a document. (Of course, if you make lousy design decisions, you'll only make things harder on your readers. Check out a copy of *Wired* magazine if you don't believe me.) Fonts and font effects such as underlining can help the reader distinguish between headings and body text, or help draw the reader's eye to individual words or phrases within a paragraph.

Each view handles page breaks its own way

Page breaks look a little different, depending on the view you've selected. In Normal and Outline views, you see a dotted line, complete with the words `Page Break`, where you added the break. In Print Layout view, you see the end of the page just as it will look on paper. Word ignores page breaks in Web Layout view.

Choosing the Right Font

When you know exactly which font you want to use for a given chunk of text, the easy way is to select the text and then choose a font from the **Font** list on the Formatting toolbar. The *fonts* you've used most recently appear at the top of the list so they're easy to find; the rest of the fonts appear in alphabetical order. Use the **Font Size** list (just to the right of the font list) to make the font bigger or smaller.

Changing the current font

If you select no text at all, the font selection applies to anything you type at the insertion point. When you create a new document and immediately change fonts, for example, the change applies to all text until you change it again.

Other buttons on the Formatting toolbar let you add specific character formatting—bold, underline, or italic, for example.

Windows uses several kinds of fonts, but the most popular ariety is called TrueType. *TrueType fonts* are *scalable*, which means that Windows can stretch (scale) them into the exact size you specify, in virtually any size. They also look identical on the printer and onscreen. *Printer fonts* and *screen fonts*, on the other hand, usually come in a limited number of sizes and may cause problems when displaying or printing documents. If you choose a printer font that doesn't have a matching screen font, for example, Windows has to substitute an installed screen font when displaying the document, meaning what you see onscreen will not look the same as what you get from the printer.

Finding fonts

Windows gives you only five TrueType fonts for starters, and Internet Explorer adds a handful. Office 2000 adds several dozen fonts, and you can find dozens of extra fonts on the Office 2000 CD. Other programs come with fonts as well, and you can get more fonts for free or for a few dollars apiece. Or search the Web for a nearly infinite assortment of free and inexpensive fonts. If you want to increase your document design options, adding fonts is one of the best investments you can make.

When you want to add new fonts for ordinary documents, be sure to choose the TrueType variety. They're guaranteed to work with Word and other Office programs. TrueType fonts are preceded by a double T icon in the **Fonts** text box on the Formatting toolbar; a printer icon appears in front of fonts available with the current printer.

Before you choose a font, you probably want to have some idea what it will look like. The **Font** list itself can give you a pretty good preview of what each font looks like; pull down the **Font** list to see a list like the one in Figure 11.4.

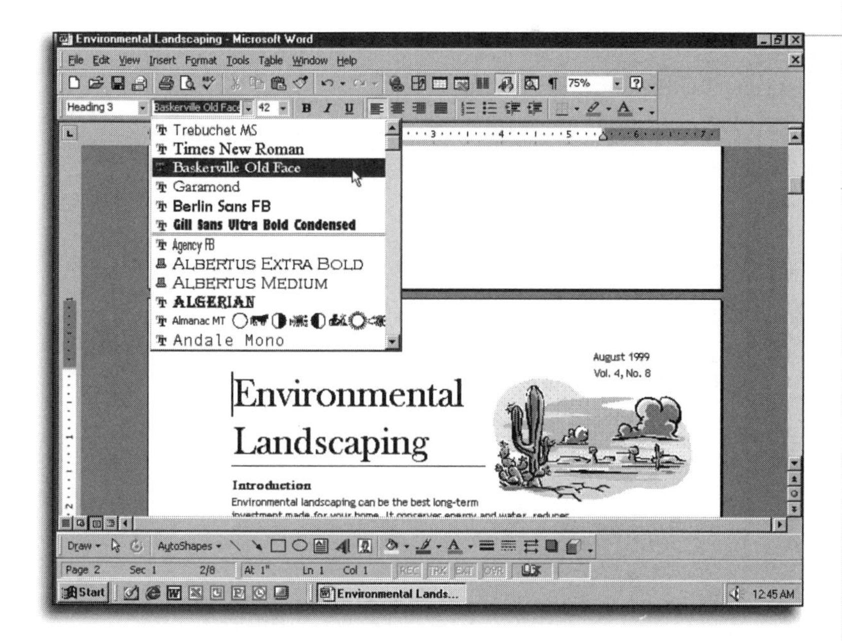

FIGURE 11.4
Unlike previous versions, Word 2000 shows you a sample of each font in this pull-down list.

If the sample in the Font list doesn't show enough to let you decide whether you want to use that font, look at a larger sample. When you make a text selection, the Font dialog box uses the selected text to preview what it will look like onscreen.

Changing Fonts

1. Select the text you want to change; then right-click the selection and choose **Font** from the shortcut menu. You see the Font dialog box shown in Figure 11.5.
2. Choose a typeface from the **Font** list. For a preview of what your text will look like, see the panel at the bottom of the dialog box.
3. Pick a font style: Bold? Italic? Both? Neither? The exact choices available depend on the font you selected.
4. Specify the font size (measured in points). You must enter a number between 1 and 1638 here. For most business documents, use 10 or 12 points for text.
5. Choose a text color from the drop-down list of 16 available colors and specify any additional font effects, if you want.
6. Click **OK** to change the look of the selected text.

Displaying a plain font list

If you have a slow PC and hundreds of fonts, the display of font samples might slow down your productivity. To tell Word that you prefer to see a simple list of fonts, pull down the **Tools** menu, choose **Customize**, click the **Options** tab, and clear the check mark from the **List font names in their font** box.

Go to the head of the list

You'll find fonts you've used most recently at the top of the Fonts list. That comes in handy when you have several hundred fonts installed on your system. Of course, you'll also find those fonts exactly where you would expect them in the alphabetical list.

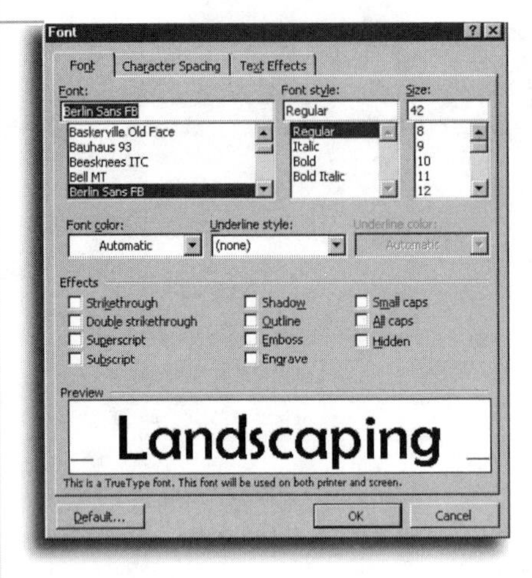

FIGURE 11.5

When you're not sure which font you want, use this **Preview** panel to see what your text will look like before you actually change it.

72 points = 1 inch

For more than 500 years, printers have used the point as a standard unit to measure the size of letters on a typeset page. There are approximately 72 points to an inch, so a 6-line paragraph set in 12-point type fills an inch, and a 72-point character is one inch tall.

Troubleshooting Font Problems

When you open a document created by a friend or coworker, it might not look the way that person intended. If the author used fonts that aren't installed on your computer, Word substitutes an available font for the one specified in the document. If the substitution is close enough, you may not notice the difference, but in other cases (especially with highly decorative fonts), the change can be downright ugly. To see details about substituted fonts, pull down the **Tools** menu, choose **Options**, click the **Compatibility** tab, and click the button labeled **Font Substitution**. The surest way to see the document with its proper formatting is to install the font on your computer. Otherwise, change the text formatting to a font that your PC can recognize. See the online Help topic "Specify fonts to use when converting files" for more advice.

Changing the Look of a Word or Character

Besides choosing the font, which dictates the shape and general appearance of characters, you can specify effects to be applied to that font. These options are independent of font selections; when you choose to underline the selected text, for example, underlining remains even if you change fonts. Click the **Bold** [B], **Italic** [I], or **Underline** [U] buttons to apply these common effects.

The following table lists additional font effects you can choose and what each one does:

Choose This Option	To Add This Effect
Strikethrough	Draws a line through text; often used in legal documents to indicate ~~deleted text~~.
Double strikethrough	Draws a line through text; often used in legal documents to indicate ~~deleted text.~~
Superscript	Displays a small character raised above normal text; for example, in the mathematical formula $a^2+b^2=c^2$.
Subscript	Displays a small character below normal text; for example, in the chemical formula H_2O.
Shadow	Adds some depth to the selected letters.
Outline	Shows only the edges of the selected text; the inside of each letter is white.
Emboss	Applies a 3D effect that's particularly effective for Web pages and other online documents.
Engrave	Applies another 3D effect, also primarily intended for Web pages.

SEE ALSO

➤ *For more information about applying effects to Web pages, including animation effects, see page 319*

Hiding Text

One of the *effects* available in the Font dialog box is **Hidden**. Select this font effect when you want the option to see text on the screen without seeing it on the printed page. Text formatted as hidden never prints out, and under most circumstances it's not visible on the screen either. To reveal *hidden text*, pull down the **Tools** menu, choose **Options**, click the **View** tab, and check the box labeled **Hidden text**.

Changing the Case of Selected Text

Two options in the Font dialog box let you specify **Small caps** or **All caps** for the current selection. You probably won't want to use the **All caps** setting with directly formatted text because you can retype the text more easily. Instead, this option is most appropriate with named styles. For example, you might create a Title style and store it in a document template; when you apply that template to a document, text formatted with that style automatically displays correctly. Several of Word's built-in Letter templates include styles that use this attribute, allowing you to type your company name or address and have it appear in all caps.

The **Small caps** option displays all the selected text as uppercase characters but uses a smaller point size for lowercase letters. This effect is a striking way to set off titles and headings so that they get noticed.

Some fonts are all caps already

Certain fonts include only capital letters in their character set. If you format text using the Algerian font, for example, lowercase and uppercase letters are identical. Whatever you type appears in caps regardless of other formatting options.

Change case instantly

One of my favorite keyboard shortcuts lets me quickly change a word from uppercase to lowercase and back, without deleting and retyping. If you select text first, this shortcut affects the selected text; otherwise, it applies to the word in which the insertion point appears. Press Shift+F3 to toggle from lowercase to mixed case (initial caps only) to all caps.

Arranging Text on the Page

By choosing the right fonts and applying other text formatting options, you can make words and sentences stand out on the page. When you design a document, arranging the words so that they fall in the right place on the page is equally important. Large headlines, for example, look better when centered between the left and right sides of the page, with ample white-space above and below. Summary information stands out on the page when it's indented slightly. If you want to leave room for changes in a draft of a document, you can add extra space between lines.

Word's paragraph formatting options let you set off text with extra spacing, stack your words neatly on top of each other, center words on the page, and control precisely when Word ends one page and begins a new one.

Adjusting Space Between Lines

For most documents, most of the time, you'll use the default single spacing. Some kinds of documents, though, are more readable when extra space appears between each line. (Double-spacing is especially useful if you expect someone to add comments and corrections to your work.) You can allow Word to adjust *line spacing* automatically, based on each line's font size and any graphics or other embedded objects. Or, to maintain precise control over the look of a page, you can specify an exact amount of space between lines.

Line spacing is for body text

Line spacing is most important in running text, when you have paragraphs that wrap around to multiple lines. To control space above and below headings, captions, and other one-liners, use paragraph spacing options instead.

Can't adjust paragraph settings?

Paragraph formatting options are not available in Outline view. To adjust these options, switch to another view, preferably Print Layout.

Changing Spacing Between Lines

1. Position the insertion point in the paragraph. Then pull down the **Format** menu and choose **Paragraph,** or right-click anywhere within the paragraph and select **Paragraph** from the shortcut menu.
2. In the Paragraph dialog box, click the **Indents and Spacing** tab.
3. To adjust line spacing, choose one of the following options:
   - Select **Single**, **1.5 lines**, or **Double** from the drop-down list labeled **Line Spacing**.
   - Select **Multiple** from the drop-down list labeled **Line Spacing**; then choose the number of lines in the box labeled **At**. You can enter a fraction, such as `1.25`; to use triple spacing, enter `3` here.
   - Choose **Exactly** from the **Line Spacing** list and enter the spacing you want (in points) in the **At** box. When you choose this option, Word maintains the precise line spacing you selected even if you increase or decrease the font size or insert graphics.
   - If you have large type or graphics mixed with small type, select **At Least** from the **Line Spacing** list. Enter the minimum spacing in the **At** box; make sure that this number is at least as big as the biggest type size you're using.
4. Click **OK** to close the dialog box.

Adjusting Space Before and After Paragraphs

Some people prefer to add space after each paragraph by pressing the Enter key twice. Don't! There's a better way to separate one paragraph from the next. To add space before or after a paragraph, right-click and choose **Paragraph** from the shortcut menu; then click the **Indents and Spacing** tab. The default setting in the **Before** and **After** boxes is 0 points; add space here to provide extra separation between paragraphs. For example, if you're using a 12-point font and you want to add half a line at the end of each paragraph, enter 6 points in the box labeled **After**.

Note that this setting is separate from the line spacing settings I described previously. If you've selected double spacing with 12-point text, and you add 6 points after each paragraph, the effect is to add 2 1/2 lines between paragraphs.

Paragraph spacing is most effective when used in combination with styles. Adding even a few points of spacing above and below headings, for example, can help them stand out from surrounding text.

SEE ALSO

➤ *For instructions on reusing paragraph and character formats, see page 140*

Aligning Text to Make It Easier to Read

For every paragraph, you can also choose how it lines up on the page. You have four distinct alignment choices. When should you use each one?

- **Left** —Because most Western languages read from left to right, this alignment is the most popular choice for text. Every line starts at the same place on the left edge and ends at a different place on the right, depending on how many characters are in each line.
- **Centered** —Use centered text for headlines and very short blocks of text. Do not center lengthy passages.

- **Right**—As you type, the text begins at the right edge, and each new letter pushes its neighbors to the left so that everything lines up perfectly on the right edge. Use this choice only for short captions alongside pictures or boxes, or when you want a distinctive look for a headline on a flyer or newsletter. Right alignment is also appropriate when numbering pages.
- **Justified**—When you choose this option, Word distributes extra space between words so that each line begins and ends at the same place on the right and left. *Justified text* works best with formatted columns, as in a newsletter. Don't use this setting in memos, because justified text with wide margins is hard to read.

One click handles a whole paragraph

The four alignment buttons on the Formatting toolbar let you change a paragraph's alignment with a single click. Because this setting applies to the entire paragraph, all you have to do is click anywhere in the paragraph and then click whichever button you prefer.

Indenting Paragraphs for Emphasis

When you set the margins for a document, they apply to every paragraph in that document (or in a section, if you've created multiple sections). Sometimes, though, you want to vary the relation between the text in one or more paragraphs and the white space in the document margins.

You might *indent* the first line to help make the beginning of a paragraph more noticeable. Indenting an important paragraph on both sides adds white space on the left and right so that it stands out from the rest of the page. Adding *negative indents*, which extend into the left margin, is a useful way to set off headings and lists. Finally, you might use a *hanging indent* to set off paragraphs in a list. Figure 11.6 shows examples of these three indent styles.

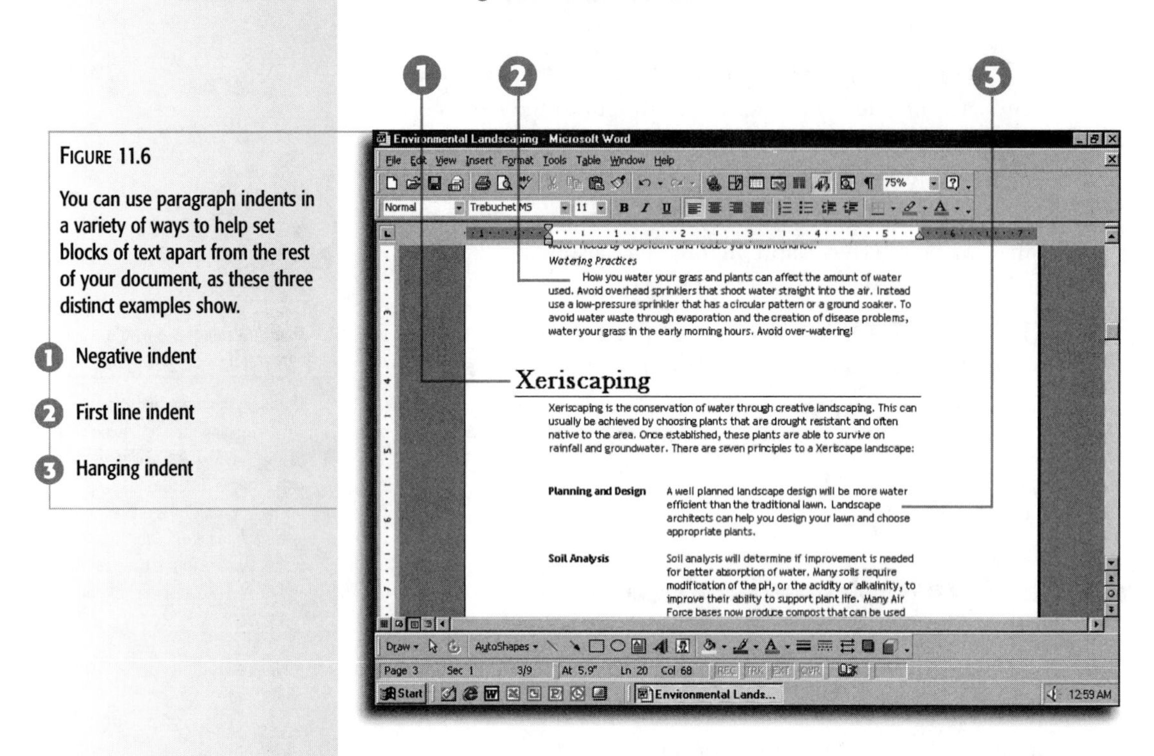

FIGURE 11.6

You can use paragraph indents in a variety of ways to help set blocks of text apart from the rest of your document, as these three distinct examples show.

1. Negative indent
2. First line indent
3. Hanging indent

Using the Ruler to Set Tab Stops and Indents

Hide the ruler

If your video display is set to a relatively low resolution (800 by 600 or less), Word's ruler takes up a significant chunk of the document editing window. To give yourself more room for editing, keep the ruler hidden until you need it. In Normal or Print Layout view, pull down the **View** menu and choose **Ruler** to show or hide the ruler.

What's the best way to add *tabs* and indents to your paragraphs? All the options are available in the dialog boxes that appear when you pull down the **Format** menu and choose **Tabs**. However, adjusting tab stops, indents, and even page margins is far easier with the help of Word's *ruler*, which sits just above the document editing window. Each of the small widgets on the ruler handles a specific alignment task. Because you can see the results instantly, this direct approach takes all the guesswork and most of the dialog boxes out of the process.

Figure 11.7 identifies each control on Word's horizontal ruler. See the following table for instructions on how to use these controls to set tabs and adjust indents.

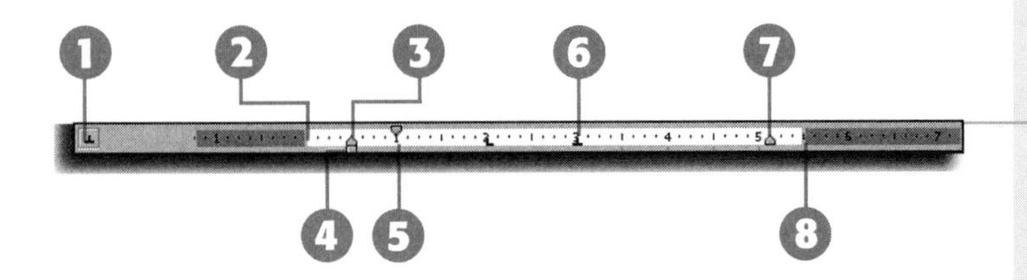

FIGURE 11.7

You don't need to memorize the names of these controls; let the mouse pointer rest over each one to see a descriptive ScreenTip.

1. Tab button
2. Left margin
3. Hanging indent
4. Left indent
5. First line indent
6. Tab stops
7. Right indent
8. Right margin

Ruler Control	How You Use It
Tab Button, Tab Stops	Click the button at the far left of the ruler to cycle through left, center, right, and decimal tab types (use ScreenTips to tell which is which). Select the type of tab you want to add and then click on the ruler to add the new tab stop. Drag a tab stop to move it; drag it off the ruler to remove it.
Left Margin, Right Margin	In Print Layout view, the white part of the ruler indicates the left and right edges of the document; the dark region shows the distance between the edge of the paper and both margins. To adjust page margins, aim the mouse pointer at the border between the dark and light areas; when the pointer turns to a two-headed arrow, click and drag.
Hanging Indent	To indent the second and subsequent lines in the current paragraph, drag the bottom triangle.
Left Indent	To indent the left side of the entire paragraph, drag this box. Both markers above it go along for the ride.
First Line Indent	To indent only the first line of the selected paragraph, drag the top triangle.
Right Indent	To indent the right side of the entire paragraph, drag this triangle.

Which paragraph is which?

Remember, tab and indent settings apply to the entire paragraph where the insertion point is located. To adjust indents for more than one paragraph, you must select the appropriate text. When you press the Enter key to start a new paragraph, it uses the ruler settings from the previous paragraph.

How the Tab and Backspace Keys Work

Most of the time, pressing the *Tab key* adds a tab character to your document, moving the *insertion point* to the next *tab stop*—a predefined location along the horizontal ruler within the current paragraph. In documents based on the Normal document template, default tab stops are located every half inch.

If you move to the beginning of a new paragraph and press the Tab key, the insertion point moves a half inch to the right. Keep pressing the Tab key to move the insertion point to the right, a half inch at a time. Press the Backspace key to delete the previous tab character and move the insertion point back to the previous tab stop. If you position the insertion point within a paragraph, the Tab and Backspace keys work the same way.

Where are the tab characters?

To see whether any tab characters appear in the current paragraph, click the **Show/Hide** button ¶. Tab characters look like small right-facing arrows, and they're positioned directly between the end of the text and the next tab stop.

In one specific circumstance, the Tab and Backspace keys behave differently. If you position the insertion point at the beginning of a paragraph that contains text and then press the Tab key, Word does not insert a tab character. Instead, that action adjusts the First Line Indent for the current paragraph, moving the beginning of the first line to the location of the first default tab stop. Leave the insertion point at the beginning of the paragraph and press the Backspace key, and Word removes the indent.

What happens if you press the Tab key again? Word moves the First Line Indent forward another tab stop and also creates a Hanging Indent at the first default tab stop. If you press Backspace at this point, you remove the First Line Indent, but the entire paragraph retains the Hanging Indent. Press Backspace again to remove the Hanging Indent. To make matters even more confusing, the Tab key reverts to its original behavior, adding a tab character at the beginning of the paragraph, if you've added your own tab stops to the current paragraph.

See tab characters (and more)

To see all the nonprinting parts of a document, including tabs, paragraph marks, and spaces, click the **Show/Hide** button ¶. This action is useful when you can't figure out why tabs aren't working properly. To choose which nonprinting characters to display, pull down the **Tools** menu, choose **Options**, click the **View** tab, and add or clear check marks as needed.

If you find this inconsistent behavior annoying, change it. Pull down the **Tools** menu, choose **Options**, click the **Edit** tab, and clear the check mark from the box labeled **Tabs and backspace set left indent**.

Positioning Text with Tabs

When you create a new tab stop, you define a point on the horizontal ruler. Each time you press the Tab key, the insertion point moves to the next tab stop. Of the five distinct types of tab stops, each is defined by the text alignment at that location. The most common use for tab stops is to allow you to mix and match different text alignments on the same line. For example, in a document footer you might set a center tab in the middle of the page and a right tab at the right margin; then you could enter a chapter number, press Tab to enter the chapter name and center it on the page, and then press Tab again to add a page number at the right margin.

The following table describes how each type of tab stop works:

Tab Alignment	How It Works
Left	Moves the insertion point to the tab stop; when you enter text, it extends to the right.
Center	Moves the insertion point and centers text you enter at the tab stop.
Right	Moves the insertion point to the tab stop; when you enter text, it extends to the left.
Decimal	Text or numbers align at the decimal point, with all other text extending to the left; this type is used most often to align columns of numbers in currency format.
Bar	Draws a vertical rule at the tab stop; pressing the Tab key does not move the insertion point. Generally, it's easier to use tables for a task like this.

SEE ALSO

➤ *To learn more about using Word tables, see page 268*

Normally when you press a Tab key, the insertion point simply moves to the next tab stop. You can tell Word to add a *leader* character, such as a row of periods, between the text and the tab stop; these characters are commonly used with tables of contents and invoices, where you want the reader's eye to clearly see the relationship between the entry at the left and the matching entry to its right.

Force Word to add a tab character

The Tab key also behaves differently in Outline view, where it promotes or demotes the current heading. To force Word to add a tab character in Outline view or at the beginning of a line in other views, where it would normally indent the paragraph, press Ctrl+Tab.

Alternatives to tabs

You might be tempted to just press the Tab key and keep pressing, but for most documents you should consider two alternative formatting options. For lining up columns of text and numbers, tables (with hidden borders) are easier to work with than tabs. Constructing a block-style résumé, for example, is a nightmare using tabs, but simple with tables. Likewise, simple paragraph alignment is easier, and the results are more predictable, when you use indents (described later in this chapter) instead of tabs.

As I explained earlier in this chapter, the quick way to set simple tab stops is to use the horizontal ruler. To set more complicated tabs or to adjust existing tab stops, pull down the **Format** menu and choose **Tabs**. You then see the dialog box shown in Figure 11.8.

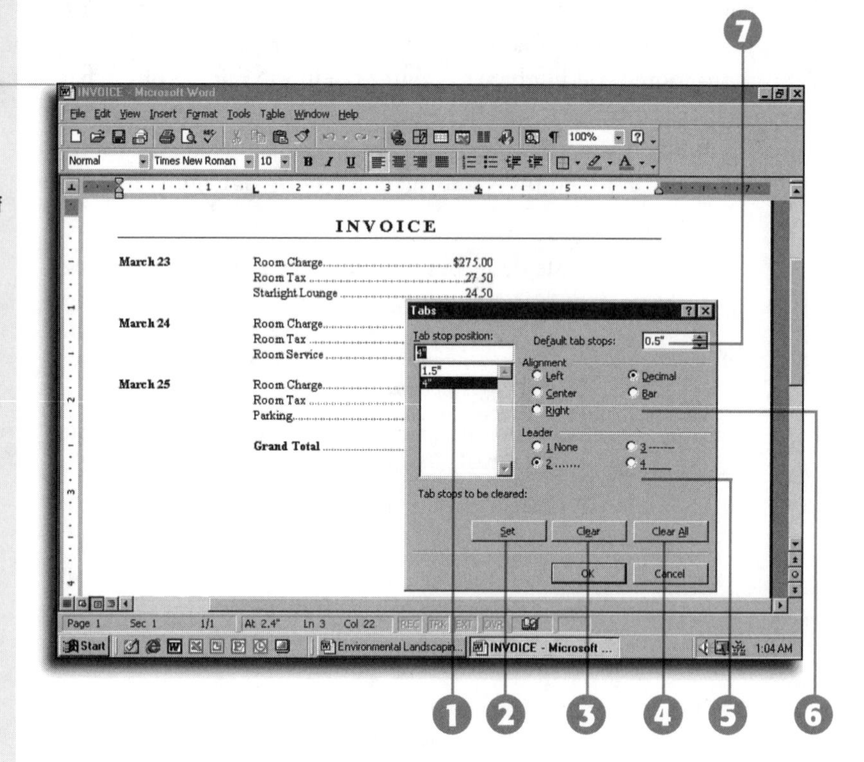

FIGURE 11.8

Leader dots and decimal alignment make it easy to read the column of numbers at the right of this invoice.

1. Select a tab stop from this box, then...
2. Click here to apply changes to the selected tab stop.
3. Click to clear the selected tab stop.
4. Click to clear all tab stops and start over.
5. Choose one of these leader characters to add a line or row of dots between text and a tab stop.
6. Choose an alignment style for the selected tab stop.
7. Use this spinner to adjust the distance between default tab stops.

Using Large Initial Caps for Emphasis

Professional designers often enlarge the first letter of a paragraph to make it easier for readers to find the beginning of a section. Because the larger initial letter drops below the base of the first line, designers call this feature a *drop cap*. Word enables you to create drop caps easily in documents you create. Click in the paragraph where you want to add a larger first letter, pull down the **Format** menu, and choose **Drop Cap**. You then see a dialog box like the one in Figure 11.9.

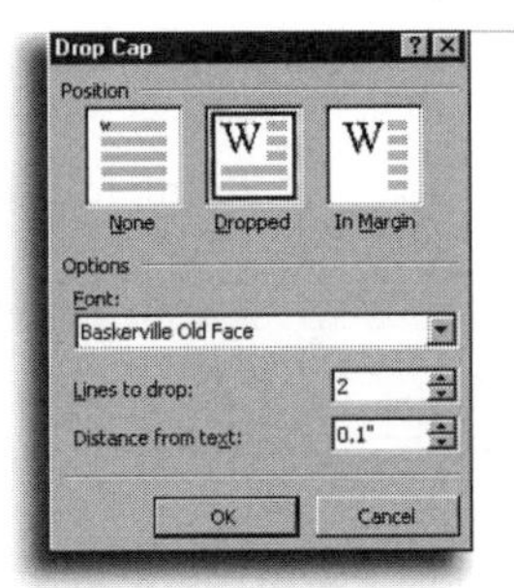

FIGURE 11.9
A drop cap should never be larger than the headline above it. In 12-point body text, a 3-line drop cap goes with a 36-point headline.

Choose a font, pick the number of lines you want the first letter to extend downward, and specify how much of a gap you want between the drop cap and the text. Click **OK** to add the drop cap.

Displaying Text in Multiple Columns

It can literally be exhausting to have to read page after page of text that runs the full width of a letter-sized page. That's why magazine and newsletter publishers often break stories into *columns*. You can do the same with Word documents. In fact, you can mix and match different column widths and arrangements within the same document, by using separate formatting for different sections.

Before you begin messing with columns, decide whether it's really worth the effort. Working with columns is complicated. You have to be painfully aware of where each section break is located and how the formatting behaves in each section. In many cases, it's easier to create a table with hidden borders, then fill it with text.

SEE ALSO

➤ *To get started with Word tables, see page 268*

Arranging Text in Multiple Columns

1. Position the insertion point at the spot where you want the columns to begin. To format a specific block of text, select it first.
2. Pull down the **Format** menu and choose **Columns**.

3. In the Columns dialog box (Figure 11.10), choose the number of columns you want to use. Use the spinner to choose a number, or click one of the five choices in the **Presets** box.

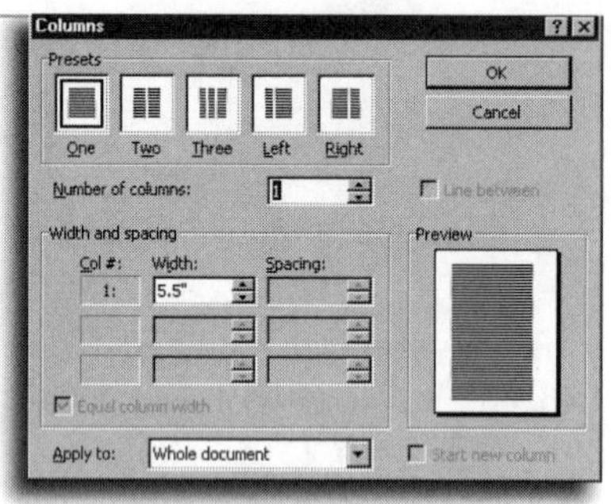

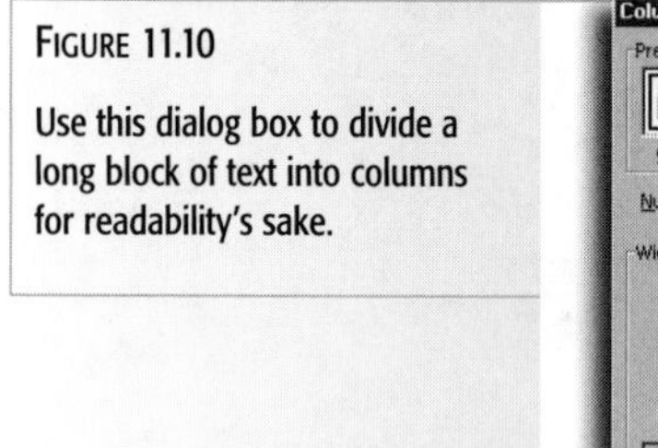

FIGURE 11.10

Use this dialog box to divide a long block of text into columns for readability's sake.

No more columns?

If you want to remove the column formatting from a block of text, just click the **One** column option in this dialog box.

4. To add a rule between columns, check the **Line between** box. Watch the Preview box to see the effect of your formatting.
5. Adjust the width of the columns, if you want. Clear the check mark from the **Equal column width** box if you want to format unequal columns.
6. In the **Apply to** box, choose the most appropriate option:
   - **Whole document**, as the name implies, formats the entire document using your column settings, regardless of whether you've selected any text.
   - **Selected text** adds a section break at the beginning and end of the current selection. The second break restores the column formats from the section before the selection.
   - **This point forward** adds a section break and applies the columns to any text that appears after this break, including text you've already entered.
7. Click **OK** to apply the formatting and return to the editing window.

Using Hyphens to Control Line Breaks

When your document includes sections with relatively narrow margins, a long word that falls at the end of a line may not fit. The result can be a line that's too short, making your document esthetically unpleasing and hard to read. To make more natural line breaks, tell Word you want it to make a pass through the document and automatically *hyphenate* words based on its dictionary. You can also go through a document manually, adding hyphens only where necessary. Choose this option when you want absolute control over the look of your document.

Save hyphenation for last

When you use Word's hyphenation options, it passes through your document adding optional hyphens, which only display when necessary. If you make additional changes to the document, the line breaks will change, and you'll need to run through the hyphenation routine again.

To turn on *automatic hyphenation*, Check the box labeled **Automatically hyphenate document** and click **OK**.

To manually insert hyphens, pull down the **Tools** menu and choose **Language**, then click the **Hyphenation** option. Click the **Manual** button. Word will walk you through the entire document, pausing at each instance where it would normally insert a hyphen if you chose the Automatic option.

Formatting Simple Lists with Bullets and Numbers

When you need to communicate effectively with other people, lists are among your most powerful tools. Whether the list items are single words or full paragraphs, bullet characters and numbers help set them apart from normal body text. Turning plain text into a list is one of the easiest things you can do to a Word document. After you've created a list, Word uses the same *bullet character* when you add new items, and if you rearrange items in a numbered list, Word renumbers the entire list automatically.

Creating a Bulleted List

To create a *bulleted list* on the fly as you type, just click the **Bullets** button on the Formatting toolbar. Type the first item in your list and then press Enter to add another bulleted item. The items in a list can be anything—numbers, words,

Automatic bullets

Unless you've turned off the **AutoFormat As You Type** option, Word automatically converts items to bulleted list format whenever you begin a paragraph with an asterisk (*) or a hyphen and press Enter.

phrases, whole paragraphs, even graphics. To stop adding bullets and return to normal paragraph style, click the Bullets button again.

To add bullets to a list you've already typed, first select the items in the list; then click the Bullets button. The default bullet is a simple black dot in front of each item.

SEE ALSO

➤ *For an explanation of how Word creates bulleted lists automatically, see page 202*

Changing the Default Bullet Character

When you first create a bulleted list, Word sets off each item with a big, bold, boring dot. If you would prefer a more visually interesting bullet, you're in luck. Word lets you choose from seven predefined bullet characters, or you can use one of hundreds of characters in any symbol font. For Web pages and other documents designed primarily for online viewing, you can also use a graphic as a bullet character.

Changing the Bullet Character in a List

1. Select the entire list; then right-click and choose **Bullets and Numbering** from the shortcut menu.
2. To use one of the seven predefined bullet characters, click the bullet style you want from the list (see Figure 11.11).

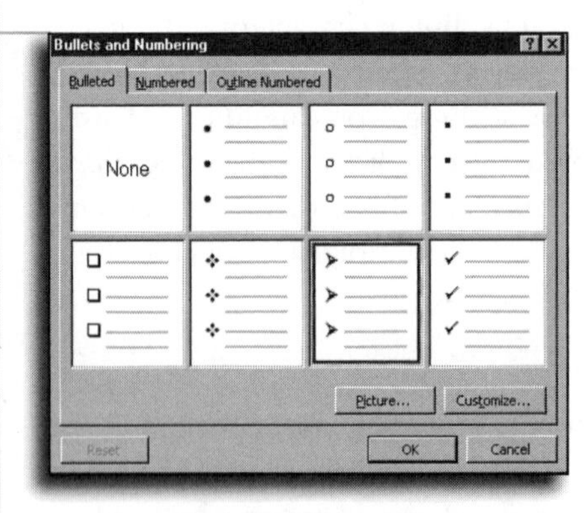

FIGURE 11.11

When you choose **Bullets and Numbering** from the shortcut menu, Word offers you these seven choices. Click the **Customize** button to select a new character.

3. To choose your own bullet character, click the **Customize** button. In the Customize Bulleted List dialog box (see Figure 11.12), choose the bullet type you want to replace; then click the button labeled **Bullet**.

4. Pick a character from the Symbol dialog box. (Choose a new font from the drop-down **Font** list, if necessary; the three Wingdings fonts, for example, are full of good candidates.)
5. Adjust the size, color, and position of the bullet, if necessary. The Preview window shows you how each change will affect the look of your list.
6. When you're satisfied, click **OK** to change the bullets in your list.

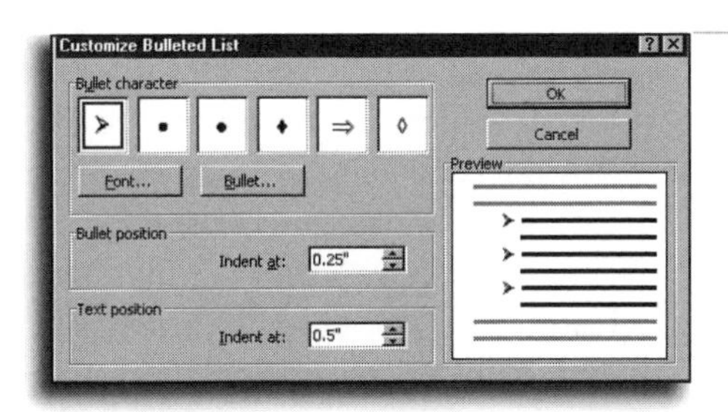

FIGURE 11.12
Choose any symbol to use as a bullet, and position it where you want it. Click the **Font** button to modify the size, color, and other bullet attributes.

To use a graphic as a bullet character, right-click on any item in the list. Choose **Bullets and Numbering** from the shortcut menu, then click the **Picture** button. Word opens a dialog box that lets you browse all the files in the Bullets subfolder. Pick any one to apply it to your list.

Most of the files in this folder have utterly inscrutable names, like Bd14565_. To see a small preview of each bullet, click the **Views** button in this dialog box and choose **Preview**.

Mix and match bullets

You can use different bullet characters within the same list. To change bullets for the entire list, make sure you select each line. After you click OK, if you discover that you inadvertently changed the bullet in only one line instead of the whole list, use Word's Repeat key right away. Select the rest of the items and press F4; that repeats your last action—which, in this case is the bullet character selection.

Graphic bullets are one size only

When you use a graphic as a bullet character, it appears at its actual size. That's ideal for text between 12 and 24 points, but downright ugly at smaller and larger sizes.

Creating Numbered Lists

Bullets signify that the items on the list are of equal importance. If the order of items in a list is important, as when you're writing step-by-step instructions, you should use a numbered list instead.

When you choose to number the items in your list, Word doesn't simply plop a number in front of each paragraph; instead, it adds a hidden numbering code. If you add a new item or move items around, Word automatically renumbers the list to keep each item in the proper order. You can't select the number or

Pick a number (or a letter, for that matter)

Although they're called numbered lists, the label is a bit misleading because Word also recognizes Roman numerals and letters as appropriate ways to order a list. You can begin a numbered list by typing `1`, `I)`, `a.`, or whatever style you want to use. Press the Spacebar or the Tab key; then enter the text you want for that item. When you press Enter, Word automatically converts the paragraph you just typed into numbered format and continues the list in the paragraph you're about to type.

edit it, although you can control the sequence of numbers and the starting point.

To start a *numbered list*, click the **Numbering** button on the Formatting toolbar and then begin typing. Word adds the numeral 1, followed by a period and an indent. Type whatever you want—a word, a sentence, or a whole paragraph. When you press Enter, Word begins the next paragraph with the next number in the sequence.

Changing Numbering Options

The basic format of a numbered list is a simple 1, 2, 3—but Word lets you choose another format if you want. You can switch to Roman numerals or capital letters, or you can add descriptive text to the bare numbers. If you're writing a list of instructions, for example, you might add the word `Step` before each number and a colon afterward, so your readers see `Step 1:`, `Step 2:`, and so on, in front of each item.

Changing the Format in a Numbered List

1. Select the entire numbered list, right-click, and choose **Bullets and Numbering** from the shortcut menu.
2. On the **Numbered** tab, pick a numbering format and click the **Customize** button to display the dialog box shown in Figure 11.13.

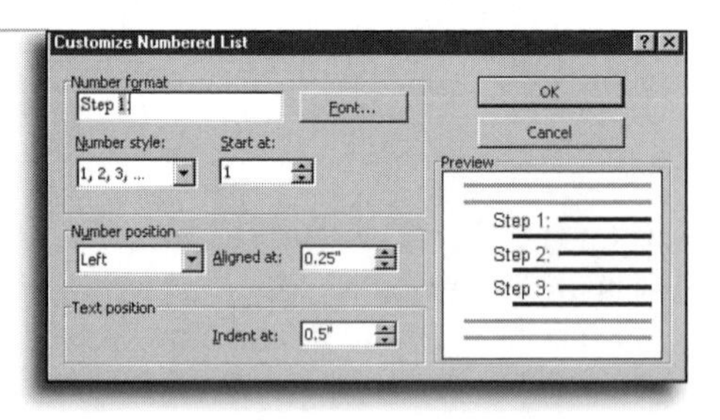

FIGURE 11.13

Replace Word's default numbering scheme with your own formats. Word takes care of the naming and numbering automatically.

3. To choose a predefined number format, choose an entry from the drop-down list labeled **Number style**. Choose a new font, position, or starting number, if you want.

4. To create a custom format that includes text, click in the box labeled **Number format** and add the text before the number field. Be sure to add a space after the text.
5. Click **OK** to save your new numbering format.

Rearranging and Editing Lists

Because bullet and number codes are contained in Word fields, you can easily rearrange, reorder, or expand items in a list. Here's how:

- *To move a list item to a new position*, first select the entire item, including the paragraph mark (¶). Then use the **Cut** and **Paste** shortcut menus, or simply drag the item to its new spot.
- *To add a new item to the end of the list*, move the insertion point to the end of the last paragraph in the list and press Enter.
- *To insert a new item*, click to position the insertion point at the beginning of the paragraph where you want to add the new item and then press Enter.
- *To skip or stop numbering*, right-click on the paragraph where you want to skip an entry, and choose **Paragraph** from the shortcut menu. (Switch to Print Layout view if necessary.) Click the **Line and Page Breaks** tab; then check the box labeled **Suppress line numbers**. This technique is especially useful when you want to add a comment in the middle of a long list.
- *To restore a list to plain text format*, select the entire list and click the **Numbering** button or the **Bullets** button.

Let Word Do the Formatting

Word's *AutoFormat* feature is a great idea that doesn't always work as promised. It's supposed to make your documents look great, effortlessly and automatically. Too bad it doesn't always work the way it's supposed to. The bigger the document, the

Restart when you create a new list

If your document contains a mix of numbered lists and text, Word can get confused. For example, if you insert a paragraph of explanation after an item in a numbered list, Word will start over at 1 when you resume the numbering. To control numbering, right-click the item that begins a group of numbered items and choose Bullets and Numbering from the shortcut menu. Click the **Restart Numbering** or **Continue Previous List** options on the Numbered tab.

Don't forget the paragraph mark!

To move a bulleted or numbered item properly, you must make sure that you've selected the paragraph mark (¶) at the end of the item. (Click the **Show/Hide** button on the Standard toolbar to make it easier to see paragraph marks.) If you don't select the entire paragraph, the bullet or numbering formatting stays where it is, and only the text moves.

more likely AutoFormat is to make some mistakes. The most common one is to apply the wrong style tag, turning body text into lists, for example. AutoFormat works best on short documents. It also works well on blocks of text, such as numbered lists and addresses.

Don't confuse AutoFormat with the AutoFormat As You Type feature. Although the two features share some of the same settings, they're completely independent of one another.

SEE ALSO

➤ *For details on how to use (or disable) Word's AutoFormat As You Type feature, see page 205*

When you use AutoFormat, Word works its way through your document from top to bottom, replacing standard quotes with *smart quotes*, taking out extra spaces and unnecessary paragraph marks, and so on. AutoFormat also tries to guess which style is best for each block of text. You can tell Word to skip one or more of these steps: Pull down the **Tools** menu, choose **AutoCorrect**, click the **AutoFormat** tab, and add or remove check marks as necessary.

To format the current document automatically, open the **Format** menu and choose **AutoFormat**. You then see a dialog box like the one in Figure 11.14. If you're feeling lucky, choose the **AutoFormat now** option. Word whizzes through your document, makes all its changes, and displays the newly formatted document in the editing window.

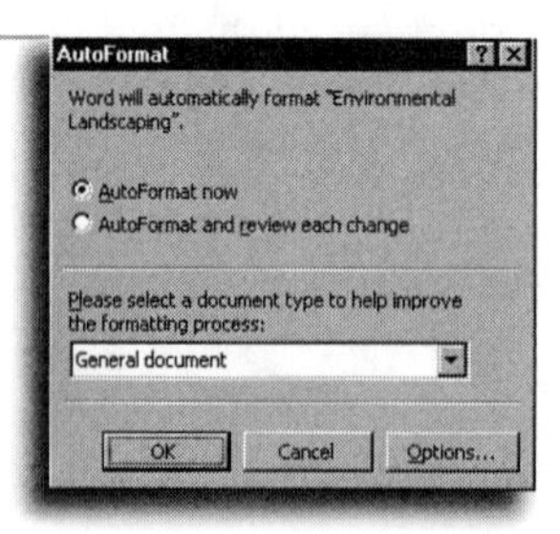

FIGURE 11.14

Use AutoFormat the fast way or the thorough way. Try the fast way first; if you don't like the results, click the Undo button and start over.

If you choose the second option, **AutoFormat and review each change**, Word formats the document and then asks if you want to accept, reject, or review the changes. Click the **Review Changes** button to begin reviewing the changes (as in Figure 11.15).

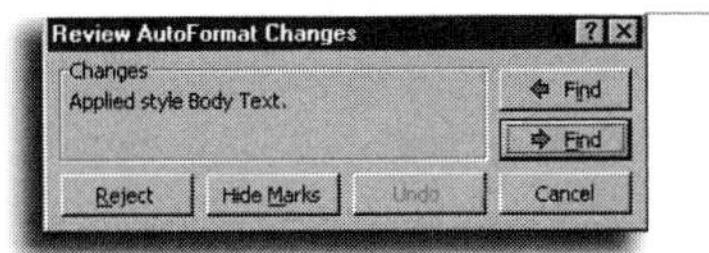

FIGURE 11.15
When you choose **Review Changes**, Word lets you say yes or no at every step of the process.

SEE ALSO

➤ *To learn how to use AutoCorrect, AutoFormat, and other common features, see page 41*

CHAPTER

12

Using Templates and Styles

Save and reuse formats with Word styles

Choose between character and paragraph styles

Let Word format paragraphs automatically

Create new styles from existing text

Use templates to change a document's design

Customize Word templates

Copy styles and settings to a new document or template

Formatting Documents with Styles

The letters, memos, reports, and faxes you create every day use many of the same elements—body text, headings, signatures, address blocks, and so on. Instead of formatting each of these elements from scratch when you start a new document, you can save format specifications, called *styles*, and reuse them any time. When you attach a saved style to a word or paragraph, the effect is the same as if you had applied formatting directly—fonts, colors, line spacing, tab stops, you name it.

Using styles offers two significant advantages over direct formatting. First, it makes even complex formatting tasks easy, bypassing all the check boxes, lists, and dialog boxes that you would otherwise have to use. Second, it lets you create and share consistent formatting for all documents you create; that's especially important in a corporate setting, where typefaces and other design elements can be as important as a company's logo in creating a visual identity.

Paragraph Versus Character Styles

Word enables you to create and use two types of named styles: paragraph styles and character styles.

Paragraph styles contain some character formats

Both paragraph and character styles can contain font and other character formatting. So what's the difference? When you apply a paragraph style, it affects every character in that paragraph, unless you've specified direct formatting. This option is most useful when you're trying to change the look of whole blocks of text. Use character styles when you want a particular word or phrase to stand out on the page or the screen. For example, in a press release template, you might define a Product Name style that adds bold and italic attributes to the Default Paragraph Font. Use that style every time you enter the name of the product you're writing about.

As the name implies, a *paragraph style* applies to an entire paragraph. A named paragraph style can include alignments, line spacing, tab settings, and other paragraph formatting options. It also contains character formatting, such as a default font and font size. When you create a document using the Normal document template, the default paragraph style is also called Normal. It uses 10-point Times New Roman, with single spacing and left alignment. When you apply the built-in Heading 1 style, the selected paragraph changes to 14-point Arial Bold, with 12 points of extra spacing before the heading and 3 points of extra spacing in addition to the single line spacing.

A *character style*, on the other hand, applies font, border, and language information to selected text or characters. When you use a character style, it overrides the font information contained in the paragraph style. When you enter a Web address in a Word document, for example, Word's AutoFormat As You Type feature applies the Hyperlink character style, which uses the Default Paragraph Font but displays the selection in blue, with a single underline.

You might want to create and use a custom character style for your company's name so that it always appears in the proper typeface and size. When writing this book, I used a custom character style to define words and terms that I planned to add to the Glossary. By redefining the Glossary style (a 60-second job), I was able to change the appearance of every Glossary entry when the book designer decided to use a different format.

Default paragraph font

Smart Word users base character styles on the Default Paragraph Font. That's the font specified by the underlying paragraph style. When you apply this type of character style to text, it adopts the same font as the underlying paragraph, while changing in size, color, or attribute to match the style you created.

SEE ALSO

- *For details on how you can customize the Normal document template, see page 154*
- *To find detailed explanations of all your paragraph formatting options, see page 230*
- *To learn how to add emphasis to text, see page 225*

What You Absolutely Must Know About Paragraph Marks

Word's Standard toolbar includes a button you won't find anywhere else in Office 2000. It's called the **Show/Hide** button ¶, and that ¶ symbol is a *paragraph mark*. When you click this button, you'll see that symbol in your document everywhere you've pressed the Enter key. You'll also see placeholders for tabs, spaces, and other normally invisible formatting characters.

After clicking the **Show/Hide** button ¶ for the first time, you may wonder how this extra clutter could possibly be useful. In fact, it's key to making sure formatting options remain as you intended when you move text from one place to another.

You must pay attention to paragraph marks for one important reason: Word stores all your paragraph formatting and styles in the paragraph marks. If you choose a paragraph style that instructs Word to display text in the Haettenschweiler font with

Show paragraph marks when moving blocks of text

Some Word experts recommend that you leave paragraph marks visible all the time you are working with Word. I consider that advice extreme, because it makes the text on your screen much harder to read. But I do recommend that you click the **Show/Hide** button ¶ to see all your paragraph marks whenever you plan to move one or more paragraphs. Make sure you move a paragraph mark only if you also want to move the formatting that goes with it.

Identifying the current style

If you position the insertion point within a word that is formatted with a character style, the **Style** box displays that style's name. If you haven't applied a character style at the insertion point, or if you select two or more words that are formatted with different character styles, the **Style** box displays the name of the current paragraph style. When you select text from two or more paragraphs formatted with different paragraph styles, the **Style** box is empty.

triple-line spacing, Word dutifully saves your instructions (along with any direct formatting) inside that paragraph mark.

Why does this information matter? Because if you copy or move that paragraph mark, you also move the styles and formats that go with it. On the other hand, if you don't include the paragraph mark in your selection, the text you paste changes to the style of the paragraph you paste it into.

Viewing Available Styles

Every document contains the styles stored in the template on which the document is based. When you create a new style or edit an existing one, you can choose to save the style only in the current document, or you can revise the template's style collection. To see which style is currently in use, look in the **Style** box at the left of the Formatting toolbar.

To see a list of available styles, click the drop-down arrow to the right of the **Style** box on the Formatting toolbar. The default list shows only the styles in use for the current document, plus a few standard styles. To see every style choice available in the current *document template*, including those not currently in use, hold down the Shift key when you click the drop-down arrow at the right of the **Style** list. The full list resembles the one shown in Figure 12.1.

SEE ALSO

- *Press Shift+F1 and click any character to see which styles and direct formatting are applied to it; see page 221*
- *To find details on how styles and templates work together, see page 259*
- *To find details on how to use the templates included with Word, see page 154*

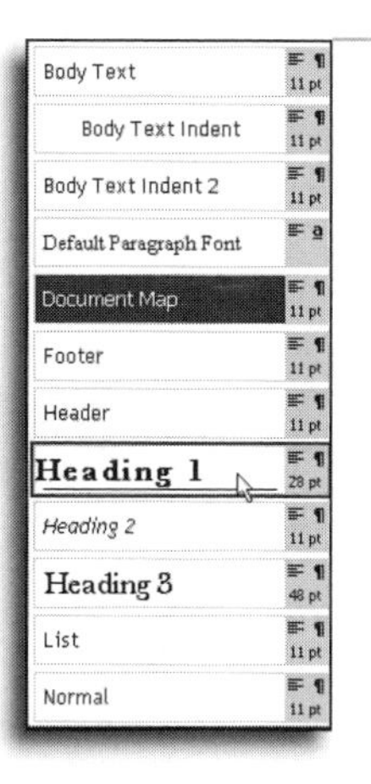

FIGURE 12.1

Hold down the Shift key to see a list of every available style; the icon at the right of each entry identifies the type of style and its size.

For complete details about each style, pull down the **Format** menu and choose **Style**. Figure 12.2 explains how to decipher the entries in this dialog box.

Applying Styles Using the Style List

The simplest way to apply a style to a document is with the help of the **Style** drop-down list on the Formatting toolbar. You can change the style for a text selection or a paragraph.

Using Styles to Format a Word Document

1. Position the insertion point where you want to change the style.
2. To choose a style that is already in use in the current document, click the arrow to the right of the **Style** list. To choose a new style that is available in the current document template (or in one of the *global templates*, such as Normal.dot), but is not yet in use, hold down the Shift key as you open the **Style** drop-down list.
3. Click a style from the list. Word applies the new formatting immediately.

You may have to wait for the Style list

Because the **Style** list displays styles in WYSIWYG (What You See Is What You Get) format, you may experience a brief delay when you display the entire style list for the first time. This delay is especially noticeable on slower computers when you use a template that contains a large number of styles.

Selections affect styles

If you position the insertion point in a word without making a selection and then choose a character style, Word applies that style to the entire word. If you make a text selection, Word applies character styles only to the selected words or characters. Paragraph styles always apply to the entire paragraph, regardless of whether you make a selection.

FIGURE 12.2
Use this dialog box to see and edit details about styles in the current document and template.

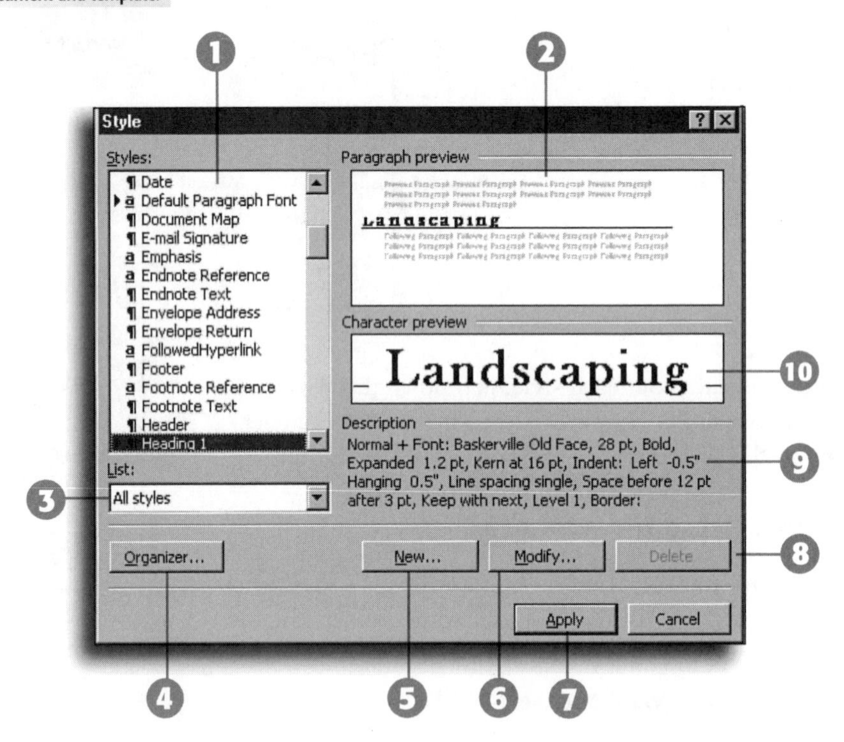

1. Select a named style from this list.
2. This box shows how the current paragraph will look if you apply the selected style. (Note that this preview shows the actual text from your document.)
3. Choose whether to display all available styles, only styles in use, or only user-defined styles.
4. Open a window that lets you move and copy styles and other elements between documents and templates.
5. Click to define a new style from scratch.
6. Open a dialog box that lets you modify any attribute of the selected style.
7. Apply a style to the current selection or paragraph.
8. Delete the selected style.
9. This description lists all font and paragraph settings for the selected style.
10. This box shows a sample of the character formatting stored in the selected style.

SEE ALSO

- *To learn how direct formatting and styles work together, see page 220*
- *To learn how to assign character and paragraph styles to keyboard combinations, see page 99*

Applying Styles Automatically

When you type certain kinds of text or paragraphs, Word automatically applies styles from the Normal document template. For example, if you type a title for your document and then press the Enter key twice, Word converts the title to the Heading 1 format. If the Office Assistant is visible and you don't have this option turned on, you see a dialog box like the one in Figure 12.3, which allows you to perform the change or turn off this option.

The quick Repeat key

One of my favorite Word keyboard shortcuts is the Repeat key. After you choose any Word command, you can repeat the command by pressing the F4 key. This shortcut is especially useful when you want to format a few widely separated paragraphs using the same style. Format the first paragraph using the steps shown here; then position the insertion point in the next paragraph you want to reformat and press F4.

FIGURE 12.3
The Office Assistant warns you when Word automatically applies styles based on the text you type.

SEE ALSO

- *To find a detailed explanation of how the Normal document template works, see page 154*
- *To learn how to customize the AutoFormat As You Type option, see page 219*

Saving Your Favorite Formats As Named Styles

Although the predefined styles in standard Word templates are useful starting points, sooner or later you'll want to create and edit formats for documents you've designed. Word lets you define a style by example, or you can modify the styles included with Word templates, including the Normal document template.

Automatic style updates

When you update an existing style, Word offers to apply further format changes automatically. Think carefully before you decide to allow automatic style updates. When you enable this feature, every manual formatting change you make applies instantly to other paragraphs formatted using that style. The results can be unsettling if you're not careful—in some cases, making a single word bold can cause your entire document to turn to bold type! If that happens, press Ctrl+Z to undo the change.

Defining a Style by Example

If you've formatted an existing document, you can easily save some or all of your settings as named paragraph styles so that you can reuse them later. (You cannot use these steps to create a character style; for that task, you have to open the Style dialog box.)

Creating a New Paragraph Style from a Formatted Document

1. Position the insertion point in the paragraph that contains the formatting you want to save.
2. Click in the **Style** box and enter the name of the new style.
3. Press Enter. If the style name you entered is not currently in use, Word creates the new style using the formatting of the current selection.
4. If you enter the name of a style that already exists in the current document or template, Word displays the dialog box shown in Figure 12.4. To redefine the existing style using the formatting of the current paragraph, choose the **Update the style to reflect recent changes** option. Click **OK** to save the change.

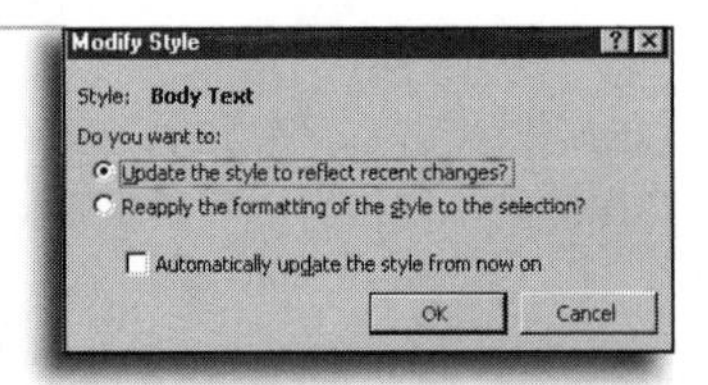

FIGURE 12.4

When you apply manual formatting and then enter the name of an existing style in the **Style** box, Word offers you these choices.

Modifying a Named Style

You can modify any character or paragraph style, including the Normal paragraph style. You can then choose precise formatting options for a style after you've created it.

Changing an Existing Style

1. Pull down the **Format** menu and choose **Style**. The Style dialog box opens.
2. Select an entry from the **Styles** list. Check the preview and description boxes at right to confirm that you've selected the correct style.
3. Click the **Modify** button. The Modify Style dialog box appears, as shown in Figure 12.5.

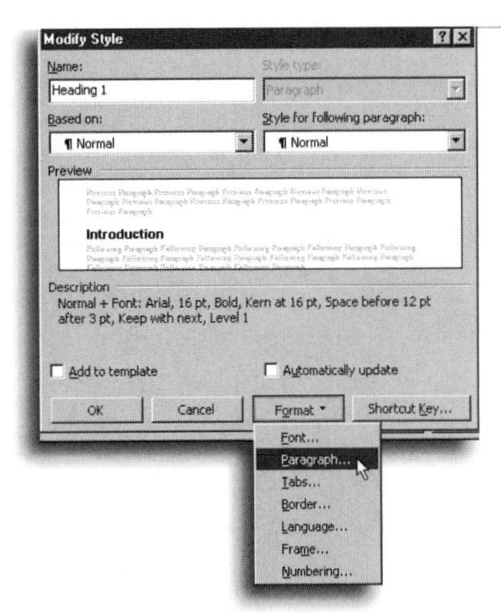

FIGURE 12.5
The Modify Style dialog box lets you change nearly any formatting option for the selected style.

4. Click the **Format** button and choose one of the following entries from the drop-down menu. For paragraph styles, all choices are available; for character styles, four of the seven entries are grayed out.

Font	Adjust the current font, font size, color, effects, and other options for character and paragraph styles.
Paragraph	Set line spacing, paragraph spacing, indents, and other paragraph options (not available for character styles).
Tabs	Set and edit tab stops (not available for character styles).

Border	Use rules and shading around the selected text or paragraph.
Language	Select a language for the selected text or paragraph; this setting tells Word which dictionary to use when spell-checking documents.
Frame	Choose size, text wrapping, and position options for text that appears in a frame (not available for character styles).
Numbering	Defines bullet and numbering options (not available for character styles).

5. Each choice leads to a different dialog box. Adjust formatting options as you like and click **OK**. Repeat steps 4 and 5 to set other formatting options, if you want.
6. Check the **Add to template** box if you want to save your changes in the current template and have them automatically applied to other documents based on that template. Leave this box blank if you want the style changes to apply only to text in the current document.
7. Click **OK** to save your changes and return to the Style dialog box. Click **Apply** to return to the editing window.

Basing One Style on Another

Managing large numbers of styles can quickly become a burden. For example, say you've defined 30 styles in the current document, a long and complex newsletter. Virtually all of them use the same font, but each one uses different point sizes, font effects, margins, tab stops, indents, and other basic changes. If you define the font separately for each style, what happens when you decide to give your document a different look by switching fonts? Changing each individual style could take hours, and there's a good chance you'll miss one.

On the other hand, if you group your styles into families, each built around a small number of base styles, you can change the overall look of the document by changing that one base style.

In Word's Normal document template, for example, many built-in styles are based on the Normal style. When you change the Normal style, all the other styles change automatically.

When one style is based on another, you can tell at a glance by looking at its description. Pull down the **Format** menu, choose **Style**, and select the name from the **Styles** list. The name of the base style appears at the beginning of the description, followed by a plus sign.

To change the style on which another style is based, follow the steps to modify a style and choose a new base style from the box labeled **Based on** in the Modify Style dialog box. Choose **(no style)** to use only the formatting options you specifically define.

Use the sample templates

For an excellent illustration of how to use base styles to organize a document, create a new document based on the Report template. Open the Style dialog box and look at the relationships between styles. The Chapter Subtitle style, for example, is based on the Chapter Title style, and all the heading styles start with a Heading Base style.

Specifying the Style of Following Paragraphs

Normally, when you apply a paragraph style, that style applies to succeeding paragraphs you create as well. This behavior makes sense for body text, but it's not the behavior you want for headings and other paragraphs designed to be used one at a time. In a newsletter, for example, you might want to follow each headline with an indented first paragraph, and follow that paragraph with normal body text.

Word allows you to handle some of this formatting automatically by specifying a style for the following paragraph. For example, you might define the Headline style so that it's always followed by a FirstPara style, which in turn is always followed by a Body Text style. Then, when you format the Headline, you can press Enter to apply the correct styles automatically to the rest of the article.

Collecting Styles (and Much More) in Document Templates

Templates make it easy to get started with new documents, but they also play an important role as a storage place for styles, macros, AutoText entries, and custom Word commands and toolbar settings. When you *attach* a template to a document originally created using a different template, Word can automatically update document styles whose names match those in the new template.

You can use this attribute of styles to make it easier for two people to work together even when they have different tastes in typography. Let's say your coworker absolutely adores the Arial Black typeface and uses it in every heading. You, on the other hand, find that typeface practically unreadable and vastly prefer Verdana Bold for headlines. How do you resolve the difference?

Each of you should create a template that contains the style you prefer, then save the template using the same name—say, MyStyles. When your coworker creates a document based on the MyStyles template, she'll use all her favorite styles and then send that document to you. When you open the document, Word will find the template of the same name in your Templates folder and automatically apply your favorite styles.

Template text is only for new documents

Document templates can contain boilerplate text that automatically becomes part of any new document you create using that template. When you attach a template to an existing document, however, Word ignores boilerplate text in the document and gives you access to styles and other document elements stored in the template.

Changing the Template for the Current Document

Document templates are powerful tools for maintaining a common corporate design standard, regardless of who creates the document. If one member of the corporate staff manages the design template, everyone who uses that template can be certain that documents will adhere to the standards. When you receive a new document template, copy it to your Templates folder and attach it to existing documents.

Missing template? No problem

What happens when you open a document that was created by someone else using a template that you don't have? Word stores all the formatting information for the styles used in that document within the document itself, which means you see the formatting as the author intended it. If the author updates the template, however, your copy won't reflect those updates.

Changing the Template for the Current Document

1. Click the **Tools** menu and choose **Templates and Add-Ins**. The Templates and Add-ins dialog box (see Figure 12.6) shows which template is currently associated with the document.
2. Click the **Attach** button to browse through a list of all available templates.
3. Select the template you want to use with the document and click the **Open** button.

4. If you want to open the attached template and update formatting every time you open the current document, check the **Automatically update document styles** box. Leave this box blank if you want to transfer styles and other templates to the document based on the current version of the template only.
5. Click **OK** to save your changes. The formatting of your document changes immediately.

FIGURE 12.6
Use this dialog box to change the look of a document by using styles stored in another template.

SEE ALSO
➤ *For a detailed list of Word's built-in templates, see page 157*

Viewing Styles in the Style Gallery

Word includes a built-in collection of templates, each of which is full of predefined styles. You may also receive templates from coworkers. Word's Help files say you can use the Style Gallery for a quick snapshot, but don't bother. If you must see what the Style Gallery is, be sure to save your current document first! Choosing a template from the Style Gallery can wipe out all the styles in your current document, without warning. Then pull down the **Format** menu and choose **Theme**, then click the **Style Gallery** button to see a close-up view of every template on your system, in the dialog box shown in Figure 12.7.

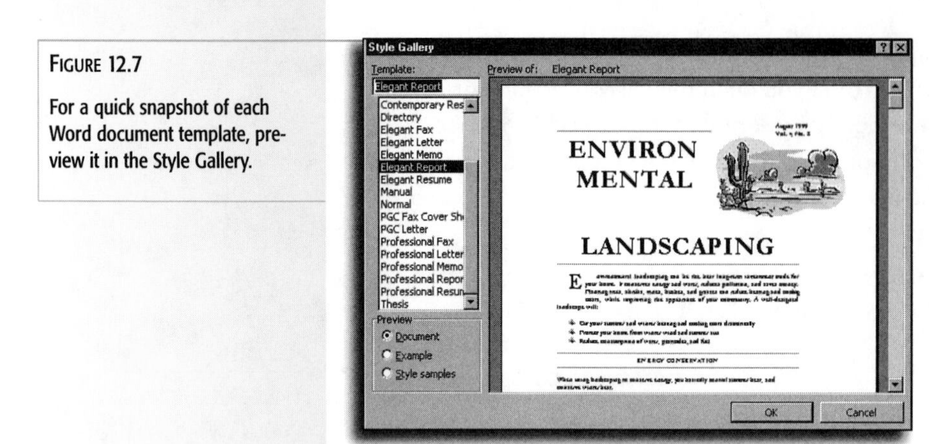

FIGURE 12.7

For a quick snapshot of each Word document template, preview it in the Style Gallery.

The three different views in the Style Gallery's Preview window allow you to do the following:

- See examples of how the styles within each template work so that you can modify them to meet your own needs.
- See each style in a single, alphabetical list.
- Preview what *your* document would look like if you used that style.

Unfortunately, the display in the Style Gallery window is so small that it's nearly useless, and many templates don't include a sample document or style samples.

Customizing the Normal Document Template

The Normal document template, Normal.dot, contains the styles, AutoText entries, macros, and toolbars that are available to all documents. When you first install Word, this file contains a huge collection of styles and a small number of AutoText entries. You can add all sorts of elements to Normal.dot, including new styles, custom toolbars, and as many macros and AutoText entries as you want. But you cannot delete built-in items from Normal.dot. If you create a new document based on Normal.dot, then pull down the **Format** menu and choose

Style, for example, you'll see a list of all the styles available; but the **Delete** button is grayed out. And if you try to open Normal.dot for editing, you'll discover it's a read-only file and no way exists to remove this attribute.

SEE ALSO

For instructions on how to change the default font and other attributes of the Normal document template, see page 154

Managing Styles and Templates

Although you can save a template in any folder, you should make it a habit to store document templates in one of two locations. For templates that you create and store for your own personal documents, use the default **User templates** location (typically the Application Data\Microsoft\Templates folder in your personal profile). When you pull down the **File** menu and choose **Save As**, and then specify **Document Template** from the **Save as type** list, Word automatically opens this folder so that you can save the template in the correct location. For easy access to templates your entire office uses, you can also specify a secondary location where you store templates that you share with other members of your workgroup. (You can find this **Workgroup templates** setting on the **File Locations** tab when you click the **Tools** menu and choose **Options**.)

Workgroup templates appear by magic

If you've specified a location for workgroup templates, any document templates you store there appear automatically in your list of new file types when you open the **File** menu and choose **New**. To add new tabs to the New dialog box, just create a subfolder either in your Templates folder or the workgroup templates location.

Creating a New Template

To create a new document template, start with a document. Although you can edit the template file later, most people find it easier to create styles, AutoText entries, and other document elements first and then save the file as a document template.

Saving a Word Document As a Template

1. Create the Word document you want to use as a template. Do not include any text unless you want that text to appear when you create a new document based on the template.
2. Pull down the **File** menu and choose **Save As**.
3. In the list labeled **Save as type**, choose **Document Template (*.dot)**.

4. Word switches to the Templates folder. Choose a subfolder within this folder, if you prefer.
5. Give the template a descriptive name.
6. Click **Save** to save the template.

Once a template, always a template

After you save a file in Document Template format, you cannot save it in any other format. When you open the template file for editing and you make changes, Word grays out the **Save as type** list to prevent you from inadvertently damaging a template. To save the document using another format, first create a new document based on the template.

Using Global Templates

When you store a style in a custom template, it's available only to documents that are based on that template. When you store styles and other items in the Normal document template, however, they're available to all Word documents. You can designate any template as a global template that works the same way. In the Templates and Add-Ins dialog box, click the **Add** button and choose the template you want to designate for use by all documents.

Use global templates to make certain that you always have key styles or macros available to you, regardless of whether the file you're working with is based on that template or not.

Customizing Word Templates

Most of the built-in Word templates are made to be customized. You can remove sample text and graphics, replacing them with names, logos, and other details appropriate for you or your company and adding text and graphics of your own. You can also adjust styles, change or delete AutoText entries, edit macros, and rearrange toolbars and menus for use with documents you create using the template.

The most straightforward way to customize an existing document template is to click Word's **File** menu and choose **New**; select a template from the tabbed dialog box, and then check the **Template** option in the **Create New** box. Click **OK** to create a new copy of the template you selected. This procedure makes certain that your original template remains undisturbed; as a result, you can feel free to experiment with the new copy, without fear that you'll damage an important file.

If you use a template that someone else has developed (or if you download a template from Microsoft's Web site), you may be frustrated to find that you can't select some words, nor can you even move the insertion point into certain blocks of text. That's usually a sign that the template is protected so that you don't overwrite anything crucial by mistake.

Protecting a template is common when the template is a Word *form*, which includes fill-in-the-blanks fields, usually in "Click Here" boxes into which you type new information. After each entry, you press the down arrow or the Tab key to jump to the next box. This technique is useful with invoice templates, for example, which often include *fields* that automatically insert the correct date and calculate totals based on the number of items and their unit cost.

Back up those templates!

Because templates are stored as files, you can easily create backup copies of templates. If you've created a library of custom templates, I highly recommend that you create backup copies in a safe place–preferably on a disk or tape stored in a different building, along with all your other important data files. In the event your system crashes or is stolen, you can restore your data and your template files.

Copying Styles and Settings Between Templates

If you design many documents, eventually you'll wind up with a large collection of templates. If you've saved a style in a special-purpose template, for example, you may want to make it available to all your documents. Or you may want to consolidate styles, AutoText entries, macros, and other document elements from several templates. To manage styles and templates, Word includes an all-purpose tool called the Organizer.

Although you can open the Organizer in several ways, the easiest way is through the Style dialog box.

More help with forms...

This book doesn't have enough room to cover the topic of Word forms; fortunately, Word's online help is excellent. For advice on how to create and use forms, search for the Help topic "Designing a Form." For detailed coverage of this and other advanced Word features, pick up a copy of *Special Edition Using Microsoft Office 2000*, published by Que.

Copying a Style from One Template to Another

1. Open a document that contains the style you want to copy to another document or template.
2. Pull down the **Format** menu and choose **Style**.
3. In the Style dialog box, click the **Organizer** button. The two-paned Organizer, shown in Figure 12.8, appears. Click the **Styles** tab, if it's not currently visible.

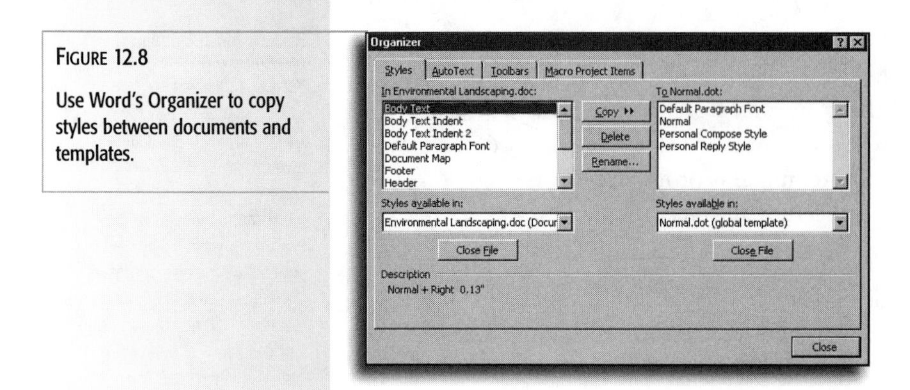

FIGURE 12.8

Use Word's Organizer to copy styles between documents and templates.

4. The left pane displays styles from the current document. If you prefer to see styles in the current template, select the template from the **Styles available in** drop-down list. (Be sure to use the left pane.)
5. By default, the right pane displays styles in the Normal document template. If you want to copy files to another template, click the **Close File** button beneath the right pane; when that button changes to **Open File**, click and open the template or document you want to use instead.
6. To copy a style, select its entry in the left pane and click the **Copy** button.
7. To manage styles in either pane, select the style and click the **Delete** or **Rename** button.
8. Use the other tabs to manage other document and template items. Click the **Close** button to save your changes.

Choose a document for one-shot jobs

Remember, you can store styles in documents or in templates. If you want to reuse a style from another document, and you don't expect to reuse the style in other documents, just copy it to the document rather than store it in a template.

CHAPTER

13

Using Tables

- Use tables to organize information into rows and columns
- Draw a table using Word's pen and eraser tools
- Convert text to a table with a few clicks
- Move and copy rows, columns, and cells
- Use Table AutoFormat to format a table quickly

Using Tables to Organize Information

How do you handle complex lists in which each item consists of two or more details—a price list, for example, or a time sheet or class schedule? Even experienced Word users are tempted to start pressing the Tab key to line up items in columns. Don't! Word tables are a far, far better tool to organize this kind of information into neat rows and columns. When you give each item its own row and break the details into separate columns, you wind up with an easy-to-read, information-packed table. With the help of tables, you can perform the following tasks:

- Align words and numbers into precise columns (with or without borders)
- Put text and graphics together with a minimum of fuss
- Arrange paragraphs of text side by side, as in a résumé
- Lay out a framed Web page
- Create professional-looking forms

Word tables include faint gridlines that help you see the outlines of the rows and columns when you're entering text. If you want, you can add borders, shading, and custom cell formats to give your tables a professional look. And if you've ever tried to line up columns using tabs, you'll appreciate how much easier you can work with tables.

Tables within tables

One of the coolest new capabilities in Word 2000 is that it lets you create nested tables, where one table is completely within a cell in another table. Why would you want to do that? Let's say you're creating a page for your annual report, and you want to position two tables on the page, with a caption under each one. Use one large table to define two large cells (one for each table) and two small cells (for the captions). Then create the tables inside the large cells. Voila! Instant page layout.

For more about forms...

Word includes some extremely slick features that let you build in fill-in-the-blanks forms by starting with tables and adding fields. There isn't room in this book to cover this extremely complex topic. If you want more details, pick up *Special Edition Using Office 2000* and turn to Chapter 16, "Creating Dynamic Documents with Fields and Forms."

Avoid using formulas in tables

Word tables allow you to perform basic mathematical calculations, including totals, averages, and counts. That's fine for simple sums (in fact, there's even a toolbar button for that formula), but the procedures for adding more complex formulas are daunting. Worst of all, you have to update the results manually if you change the numbers that go into a formula. If you need to perform calculations on data in a table, consider an embedded Excel worksheet instead (see Chapter 8).

How Word Tables Work

Like Excel worksheets, Word *tables* organize information into *rows* and *columns*. You add text (or numbers or graphics) inside *cells*; if you enter text that's wider than the cell, it wraps to a new line, increasing the height of the cell automatically. You can insert and delete rows and columns, or move entire columns by dragging from one location to another. You can also change column width and row height, or you can merge cells to form column headings and row labels. Figure 13.1 shows the parts of a typical Word table.

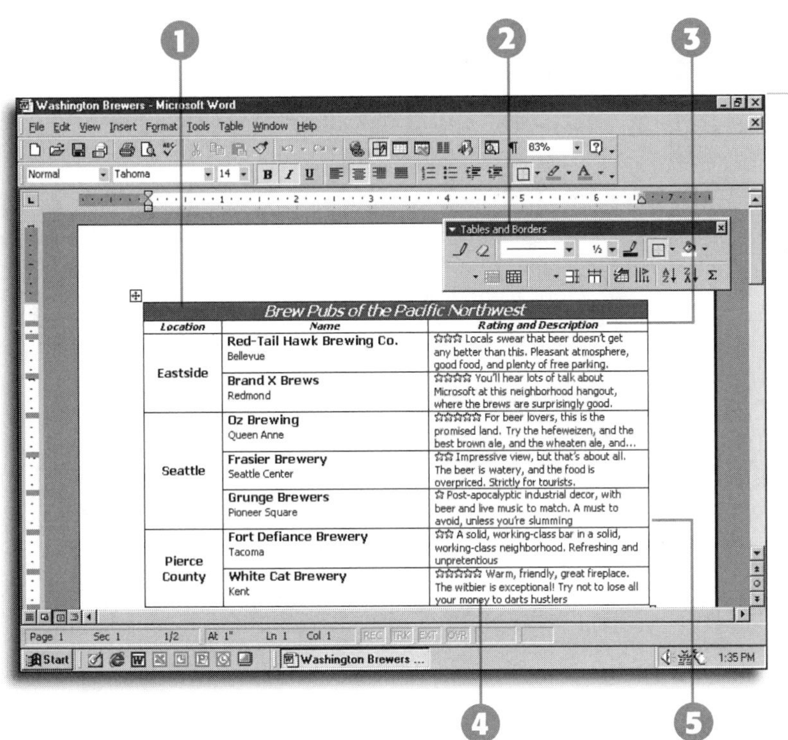

FIGURE 13.1

Use Word tables to organize information in easy-to-follow rows and columns.

1. Shading. Use shades of gray or colors to help add emphasis to rows and columns.
2. Tables and Borders toolbar. This toolbar contains buttons to help you create and edit tables.
3. *Heading*. Designate one or more rows to serve as labels for the columns below. With long tables, these headings appear at the top of every page.
4. Cell. The basic unit of a table. Each cell is formed by the intersection of a *row* and a *column*.
5. *Border*. Unlike the nonprinting gridlines, these lines show up when you print. You can adjust their thickness and location.

By default, Word tables include *borders*—lines that separate cells and define the boundaries of the table itself on the printed page. Using tables with borders is a good way to insert feature comparisons, price lists, and other tabular material in documents. Remove the borders to use tables as a way to arrange blocks of text and other objects on the page without having to fuss with columns and tabs stops.

You can make a Word table big enough for just about any practical purpose. A table can have up to 32,767 rows and 63 columns, although most Word tables are much smaller. If you need more room, use Excel instead.

SEE ALSO

- *To find details on how to set tab stops, see page 230*
- *To perform calculations on data in a table by using an embedded Excel worksheet, see page 143*

Turn off gridlines

If you want to hide all traces of a table, turn off gridlines after you've entered data. Pull down the **Table** menu and choose **Hide Gridlines** from the end of the menu. If gridlines are hidden, choose **Show Gridlines** to reveal them again. This command affects all tables in the current document.

Adding a Table to a Document

If you've struggled to create and adjust tables using previous versions of Word, you're in for a pleasant surprise when you tackle the same task in Office 2000. In fact, there are some subtle improvements that make creating and editing tables easier in Word 2000 than in Word 97. You can still put together a table from scratch, but using one of Word's many wizards to do the job is much easier.

Creating Tables Quickly with a Few Clicks

Watch the toolbars

When you select an entire row or column within a table, the buttons on the Standard toolbar change slightly. The Insert Table button disappears, replaced by the **Insert Rows** or **Insert Columns** button.

Click the **Insert Table** button on the Standard toolbar to quickly add an unformatted table at the current insertion point. When you click the button, a table grid (like the one in Figure 13.2) drops down from the toolbar. Drag the pointer down and to the right to select the number of rows and columns for your table.

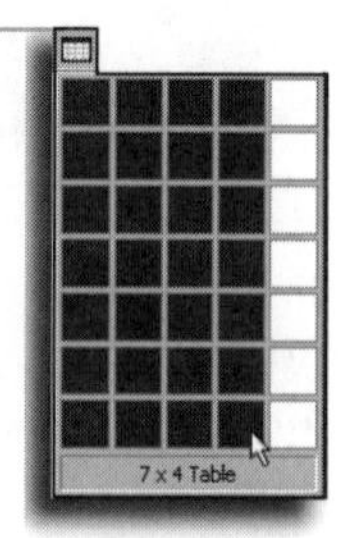

FIGURE 13.2

Click and drag to insert an unformatted table. The caption tells you this table will include seven rows of four columns each.

When you use the Insert Table button, the resulting table is completely unformatted. It fills the entire width of the current page (or, if you've inserted a table within a table, the complete width of the current cell). In this type of table, all columns are of equal size and all rows match the height of the font defined in the Normal paragraph style. If you're willing to go through the extra formatting steps, using this button is an acceptable way to add a few rows and columns to a document. But there's a much faster and easier way to create the exact table you want.

Drawing a Complex Table

For anything more complex than a few simple rows and columns, use Word's extremely effective Draw Table tool. Instead of dropping a simple rectangle in your document and forcing you to rearrange the cells to fit your data, this feature turns the mouse pointer into a pen, which you, in turn, use to draw the table exactly as you would like it to appear on the page.

Drawing a Table Within a Word Document

1. Click the **Tables and Borders** button on the Standard toolbar. Word switches into Print Layout view if necessary, displays the floating Tables and Borders toolbar, and changes the shape of the pointer to a pen.
2. Point to the place in your document where you want the upper-left corner of the table to appear.
3. Click and drag down and to the right until you've drawn a rectangle that's roughly the size you want your final table to be.
4. Use the pen to draw lines for the rows and columns inside the table. You don't need to draw full lines; as you draw, you'll see the lines "snap" to connect with those you've already drawn, as in Figure 13.3.
5. If you make a mistake, click the **Eraser** button. Drag the eraser-shaped pointer along the line you want to remove until the line appears bold; then release the mouse button to remove the line.
6. After you're finished, click the **Close** button to hide the Tables and Borders toolbar.

Don't worry about neatness when you're using the Table Drawing tool. After you have the basic outline of your table in place, you can use the Tables and Borders toolbar to give it a slick, professional appearance.

Don't worry about spacing

As you draw, rows and columns may appear in varying sizes, with uneven spacing between them. Don't worry. Just draw the proper number of rows and columns; then select some or all of them and click the **Distribute Rows Evenly** and/or **Distribute Columns Evenly** buttons to resize them all in one smooth motion. If you click in a single cell and click both buttons, Word makes your entire table symmetrical.

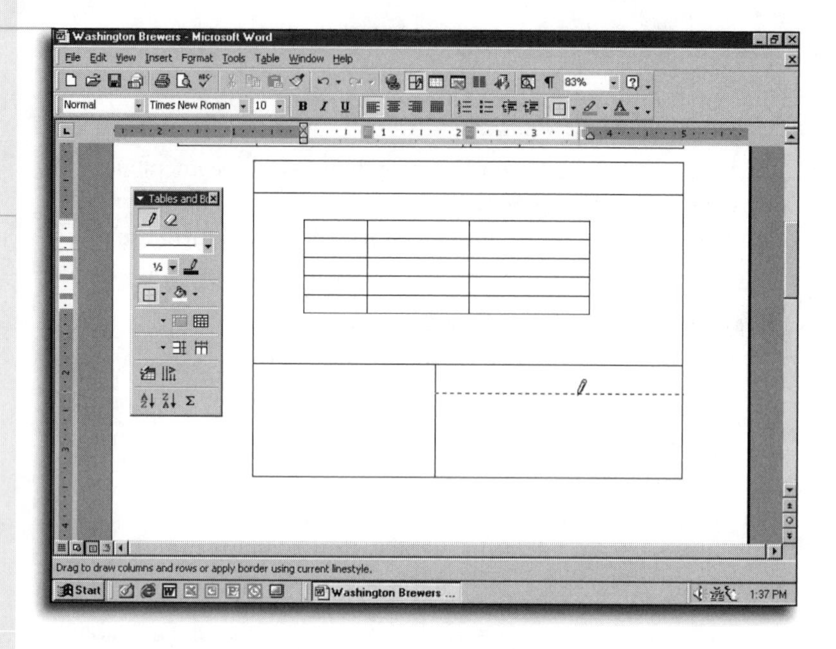

FIGURE 13.3

Use this pen-shaped pointer to draw the table you want, with merged cells for titles and headings and even nested tables.

Save your favorite table formats

If you regularly use the same type of table in documents, create a blank table and save it as an AutoText entry, complete with formatting and headings. To reuse the table, insert that AutoText entry into your documents whenever you need it.

SEE ALSO

➤ *To save a table with AutoText, see page 202*

Converting Text to a Table

What do you do when you've already entered text in a document and you know it would work better in a table? You don't need to cut and paste. Instead, you can convert the block of text to a table. This process will work extremely well if you simply want to put the text into a single column, with each paragraph in its own cell. To create multiple cells in each row, your text needs to be delimited with tabs, commas, or another separator character.

See the hidden codes

Click the **Show/Hide** button ¶ on the Standard toolbar to see tabs and paragraph marks when you're getting ready to convert text to a table. This step allows you to see easily whether you need to add another tab character to a row.

Converting a Block of Text to a Word Table

1. Select the entire block of text you want to convert. Make sure to include the paragraph mark for each row you plan to convert.

2. Click the **Insert Table** button on the Standard toolbar to surround the selected text with a table instantly.
3. If the one-button approach doesn't work (the columns are too wide, or the table doesn't have enough rows, for example), click the **Undo** button on the Standard toolbar and try again. This time, pull down the **Table** menu and choose **Convert, Text to Table**.
4. In the Convert Text to Table dialog box (see Figure 13.4), choose the separator character your text uses. Look in the **Number of columns** box; if the number displayed here doesn't match the number of columns you expect to see in the new table, click **Cancel** and make sure that the selected text contains no stray paragraph marks or tab characters.
5. If you want to apply automatic formatting options during the conversion process, click the **AutoFormat** button and adjust options as needed. Use the AutoFit options to let Word automatically adjust the width of each column during conversion.
6. Click **OK** to complete the conversion.

Separate items properly

If you want to split data into two or more columns per row, the data must include *separator characters* that define the end of each row and each item within the row. Word can use tabs, commas, or other characters as separators. If the text-to-table conversion doesn't give the expected results, you may need to edit your raw data to add or remove separator characters.

Convert a table back to text

To convert the contents of a table to text, reverse the process: Click in any cell and press Ctrl+A to select the entire table, then pull down the **Table** menu, and choose **Convert Table to Text**. Word lets you choose tab characters or paragraph marks to separate items in each row.

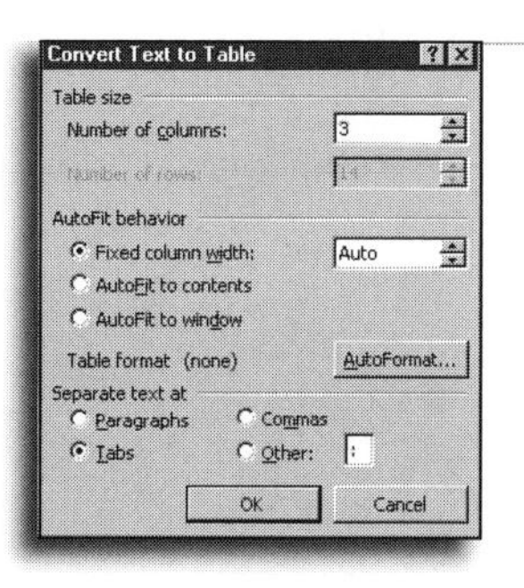

FIGURE 13.4

Before you convert text to a table, specify which character separates items in each row. Make sure that the number of columns matches the number you expect.

Working with Tables

Anything you can put in a Word document can also go into a table: text, numbers, symbols, or graphics, for example. You can even add automatic numbering to the items in a row or column of a table; select a column filled with text and click the **Numbering** button in the Formatting toolbar. As you move items around, they stay in the right sequence.

After you have your information neatly stashed in a table, you can rearrange it to your heart's content. You can move cells, rows, or columns; change the height of a row or the width of a column; even instruct Word to reformat your entire table automatically—all with a few mouse clicks.

SEE ALSO

➤ *To learn how to format simple lists with bullets and numbers, see page 241*

Selecting Cells, Rows, and Columns

Before you can rearrange, resize, or reformat a part of a table, you have to select it. Table 13.1 lists the specific techniques required to select parts of a table.

TABLE 13.1 Selecting Parts of a Table

To Select This Part of a Table	Do This
Cell contents	Drag the mouse pointer over the text you want to select.
Cell	Point to the inside left edge of the cell and click when the pointer turns to a solid arrow.
Entire row	Point and click just outside the left edge of the first cell in the row.
Entire column	Point to the gridline or border at the top of the column; click when you see a small arrow pointing downward.
Multiple cells, rows, or columns	Select a cell, row, or column; then click and drag to select additional cells, rows, or columns.
Whole table	Hover the mouse pointer over the upper-left corner of the table until you see a selection handle shaped like a cross, then click. Or, pull down the **Table** menu, then choose **Select** and **Table**.

Entering and Editing Data

To begin entering data into a table, just click to position the insertion point anywhere in the cell and then start typing. Don't press Enter unless you want to start a new paragraph within the cell; if Word runs out of room, it wraps the text within the cell. To move to the next cell, press Tab. (If you're already at the end of a row, this action moves the selection to the first cell in the next row.) To move to the previous cell, press Shift+Tab. Use the arrow keys to move up or down, one row at a time.

Moving and Copying Parts of a Table

Do you know how to move and copy text and objects in a Word document? If so, you'll have no problem moving and copying parts of a table. You can use the Windows Clipboard, or drag cells, rows, and columns from one place to another.

If you use the **Cut** or **Copy** menu commands (or their keyboard shortcuts) to place one or more cells, rows, or columns on the Clipboard, Windows adds a **Paste Cells**, **Paste Rows**, **Paste Columns**, or **Paste as Nested Table** command on the **Edit** menu. You can also find these options on right-click shortcut menus. To use drag-and-drop techniques, select the object you want to copy or move first; then drag it to its new location.

When you move or copy cells, the contents of the Clipboard replace the cells in the new location, possibly deleting existing data. When you move or copy rows or columns, existing rows and columns slide out of the way to make room, so you don't lose data.

SEE ALSO

To learn more details about cutting and pasting, see page 134

How to add a Tab character within a table

Pressing the Tab key moves from cell to cell within a table. If you want to insert a Tab character within a cell, hold down the Ctrl key and then press Tab.

Move the entire table

To move an entire table from one place to another, grab the handle at the top-left corner of the table and drag.

Changing Column Widths and Row Heights

One way to make a table more readable is to adjust its column widths so that each column takes up just enough room to accommodate the information in it.

To adjust the width of a column, point to the right border of the column; when the mouse pointer turns to a two-headed arrow, click and drag to the left or right. Hold down the Alt key while dragging to see column and table measurements in the ruler, as in Figure 13.5.

Don't use the ruler

When the insertion point is within a table, markers on the horizontal ruler define the margins and tab settings for each cell. Although you can adjust column and table widths using the rectangles, triangles, and other symbols, manipulating the table directly is far easier.

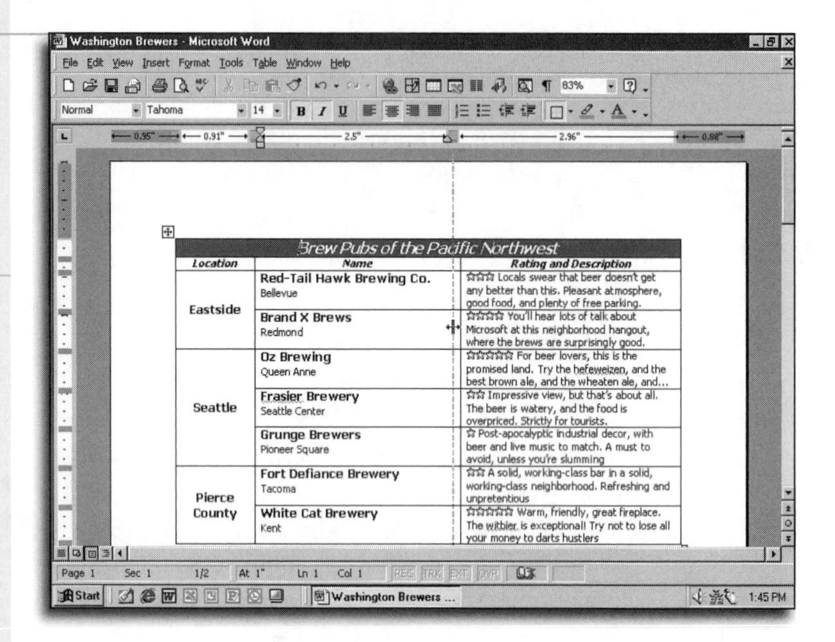

FIGURE 13.5

To change a column's width, point to the right border until the pointer changes to this shape and then drag. Hold down the Alt key as you click to see column and table measurements.

When you use the mouse pointer to reduce the width of a column, Word automatically increases the width of the adjacent column, and vice versa. If you want all your other column widths to stay the same, hold down the Shift key while you drag the ruler markers or the column boundaries; when you do so, the width of your table increases or decreases the same amount as the change you make in the selected column.

Adding and Deleting Rows and Columns

You can easily add or remove rows and columns in your table. If you're comfortable with Word's Table and Borders toolbar, use the Draw Table and Eraser tools to add and delete new rows within an existing table. Or follow the mouse- and menu-based procedures listed in Table 13.2.

Make your text fit perfectly

Want to adjust the width of your columns automatically according to what you've already typed in them? If you want to use AutoFit for the entire table, make sure to select the entire table. Then pull down the **Table** menu, choose **AutoFit**, and select one of the three options to fit to the table's contents, to the width of the cell or window, or to a fixed column width. Note that this choice may not work properly if your table contains any merged cells.

TABLE 13.2 **Table Editing Techniques**

To Perform This Action	Do This
Add a new row at the bottom of the table.	Click in the last cell of the last row; then press Tab.
Insert a row within the table.	Select the row just below where you want to insert a new row; then click the **Insert Rows** button, or right-click and choose **Insert Rows** from the shortcut menu.
Insert a column within the table.	First, select the column to the right of the place where you want to add the new column; then click the **Insert Columns** button, or right-click and choose **Insert Columns** from the shortcut menu.
Add a new column to the right of the last column.	Aim the mouse pointer just to the right of the top-right edge of the table until it turns to a down-pointing arrow. Click to select the column; then click the **Insert Columns** button, or right-click and choose **Insert Columns** from the shortcut menu.
Delete one or more rows or columns.	Select the row(s) or column(s), right-click, and choose **Delete Rows** or **Delete Columns** from the shortcut menu.

Merging and Splitting Cells

For part of an effective table design, you may want to use a single large cell that spans several rows or columns. This technique is a great way to add a title to the first row of a table; it's also the best way to label subgroupings within a table. (The example in Figure 13.1 at the beginning of this chapter demonstrates both of these techniques.)

If you know that your table needs to include this design element, you can add it when you create the table. Use the pen-shaped Draw Table tool to create rows or columns of the appropriate size and shape. On the other hand, if you've already created a table, you can merge two or more cells into a single larger cell.

Quickly add a new row

After you insert a row or column, you can easily add another in the same location. Just press F4 (the Office-wide keyboard shortcut for Repeat Last Action).

Modifying tables that extend beyond the margin

When you add a new column, it may extend well beyond the right margin. In Print Layout view, you cannot see the right edge of the table to resize the column and bring the table back within the page margins. Switch to Normal view and then use the *horizontal scrollbar* to see and modify the entire table.

Don't just press Delete

If you want to remove rows or columns, don't use the Delete key. Pressing this key simply clears the contents of the selected cells, leaving the basic structure of the table intact. To remove rows or columns, you need to pull down the **Table** menu, choose **Delete**, and pick the appropriate option. To delete more than one row or column at a time, you need to first make a selection.

Select the cells you want to merge, pull down the **Table** menu, and choose **Merge Cells**. To reverse the process and split a merged cell back into the original cells, open the **Table** menu and choose **Split Cells**.

Merging combines data into one cell

This is one of the rare cases where Word works better than Excel at handling a range of cells. When you merge cells in an Excel range, you wipe out the contents of all but the first cell in the selection. Word, on the other hand, combines the contents of the merged cells rather than wiping out your data.

Making Great-Looking Tables

Every table starts out as just a collection of cells, rows, and columns, with identical character formatting in each cell. To make a table easier to read, you need to resize rows and columns, reformat headings, add decorative borders, and use background colors and shading to set off individual sections. You can tackle each of these tasks individually, or you can use Word's Table AutoFormat feature to jump-start the process.

Letting Word Do the Work with AutoFormat

Any time the insertion point is within a table, you can open the **Table** menu and choose **Table AutoFormat**. Although I don't recommend that you use Word's AutoFormat feature for general documents, the Table AutoFormat feature usually works quite well. Because information is contained in neat rows and columns, Word can more easily analyze and format rows, columns, and headings automatically—and you can control each part of the process.

Study the Preview pane

Different formats are appropriate for different types of data; for example, some AutoFormats work perfectly with lists, and others give you your choice of grids. The Preview area in the Table AutoFormat dialog box shows you how each element of the table will look with the selected format. As you add and remove formatting options, the preview display changes.

Formatting a Table Automatically

1. Position the insertion point anywhere in the table.
2. Pull down the **Table** menu and choose **Table AutoFormat**.
3. Choose one of the prebuilt designs (see Figure 13.6).
4. Adjust other format options in this dialog box:
   - AutoFormat can add borders, adjust colors and shading, and resize columns. To skip any of these steps, clear the matching check mark in the section labeled **Formats to apply**.
   - To preserve the fonts you've already defined for the table, deselect the **Font** box.
   - AutoFormat assumes your table has labels in the first column and headings in the first row. If your table

doesn't include these elements, remove one or both check marks in the section labeled **Apply special formats to**.

- In tables that contain numbers, AutoFormat assumes the last row or last column contains totals. If this is not the case in the current table, deselect these check boxes in the section labeled **Apply special formats to**.
- The **AutoFit** feature doesn't work properly if you've merged cells to form a single cell in one row. Deselect this option if you have trouble.

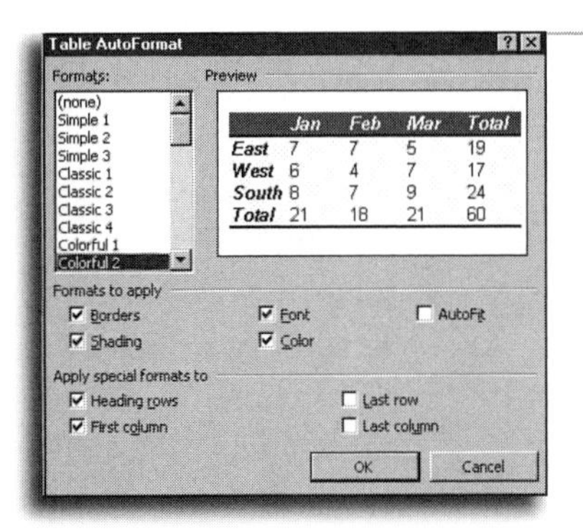

FIGURE 13.6
The Table AutoFormat feature gives you more than 30 different looks for your table.

5. Click **OK** to apply the selected formats to the entire table.

Adding Emphasis to Rows and Columns

Use lines and shading to help your readers follow along as they read items in the same row or column. This formatting step is especially important when you have wide rows and long columns filled with details. Format column headings in bold, easy-to-read fonts so that they stand out clearly from the details in each row.

Adding borders to a table is simple. Use the Tables and Borders toolbar to specify thick or decorative lines around the outside of the table, thin lines between rows and columns, custom borders to separate headings and totals, or colored borders anywhere.

Don't be afraid to experiment!

If the Table AutoFormat feature doesn't work when you try it, pull down the **Edit** menu, choose **Undo AutoFormat** (or press Ctrl+Z), and start again, choosing different options this time.

...or use the dialog box

All the choices on the Tables and Borders toolbar are also available in a three-tabbed dialog box. If you prefer dialog boxes to toolbars, click the **Format** menu and choose **Borders and Shading**.

Remove borders with another click

To remove an individual border, choose **No Border** from the list of **Line Style** options; then click the **Borders** button that corresponds to the border you want to change. To remove all lines around and within the selected cell or cells, click the **Borders** button; then click the **No Border** option at the far right of the second row.

Adding Custom Borders to a Word Table

1. Select the cells, rows, or columns where you want to add borders. If you simply click in the table without making a selection, Word assumes that you want to add borders to the current cell only.
2. Click the **Tables and Borders** button to display the Tables and Borders toolbar.
3. Click the **Line Style** button and choose the look you want for your borders.
4. Click the **Line Weight** button and choose a border thickness. The default setting is a relatively thin 1/2-point line.
5. Click the **Border Color** button. Choose the default setting (Automatic) for printed documents; select one of 16 available colors if you plan to use your table in a Web page or send it to a color printer.
6. Click the drop-down arrow to the right of the **Borders** button to display all 10 available combinations of borders; if you plan to set multiple borders, click the horizontal bar just above the two rows of buttons and drag the Borders menu off the toolbar so that it "floats."
7. Click the button that corresponds to the border you want to adjust. The **All Borders** button adds a line to all sides of all cells in the current selection, and the **Bottom Border** button is useful for putting a thin double line under headings or under the last row before totals.
8. If necessary, select another cell or cells and repeat steps 3 through 7.

To add a gray or colored background within one or more cells, first select the cells, rows, or columns; then click the arrow to the right of the **Shading Color** button on the Tables and Borders toolbar. The palette includes 40 choices, most of them representing various shades of gray.

Aligning a Cell's Contents

Individual cells within a table can contain practically anything, from text to graphics to another table. How you align each cell's contents makes a big difference. For example, in the top row of a table that contains headings of varying depth, you might want to center the text both vertically and horizontally. In a column of numbers, you might choose right-alignment.

To set *alignment* for one or more cells, first make a selection, then right-click and choose **Cell Alignment**. A second toolbar cascades out from the shortcut menu, as shown in Figure 13.7. Click a button to choose one of nine combinations of vertical and horizontal alignment.

Identifying the right color

Let the mouse pointer hover over the squares in the color palette to see the name of each one in a ScreenTip. For the sake of readability, avoid using more than a 20 percent gray background behind ordinary text.

That menu is really a toolbar

For complex columns that require lots of formatting, drag the Cell Alignment menu into the Word window, where it will float, toolbar-style.

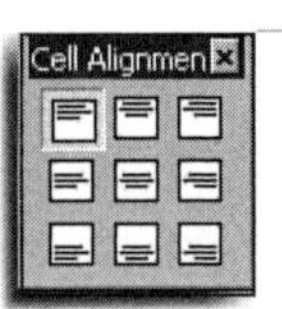

FIGURE 13.7

Select one of these nine options to align the contents of selected cells horizontally and vertically.

Working with Long Tables

Two special format settings can help make reading and following long tables easier. First, if your table includes column headings and you expect it to print on two or more pages, tell Word you want to repeat the headings on subsequent pages. Select the row or rows that you want to repeat; then pull down the **Table** menu and check the **Heading Rows Repeat** option.

Second, if your table includes some cells whose contents wrap to two or more lines, you can prevent those rows from splitting across page breaks. Select the cell or cells (or the entire table), pull down the **Table** menu, and choose **Cell Height and Width**. Click the **Row** tab and clear the check mark next to the box labeled **Allow row to break across pages**.

You must use the first row for headings

Word assumes that the first row of your table includes headings. If this assumption is correct, just click anywhere in that row before you define headings to repeat on subsequent pages. If you want to use multiple rows, select them before choosing the **Headings** command. You must include the first row in your selection; otherwise, the command is grayed out and unavailable.

CHAPTER

14

Putting Your Work on Paper

Print titles and other information in headers and footers

Add page numbers to the printed page

Preview pages before you print

Print multiple copies of a document

Cancel a print job

Troubleshoot printer problems

Preparing Your Document for the Printer

In every Office program, the Standard toolbar includes a **Print** button that sends the entire current document to the default printer. When you click this button, you get one copy, using the default settings. That's fine for simple memos, but if you're planning to print a long Word document, do your readers a favor and add a few finishing touches first.

Page numbers, chapter titles, and section names help readers understand how a document is organized. You can add these and other milestones to long Word documents, enabling readers to find their way more easily around the printed page.

Format your first page with care

Word lets you create custom headers and footers that apply exclusively to the first page of your document. Create a blank header and footer if you've created a custom title page, or if your document is in letter format and you plan to print the first page on letterhead. I cover these and other options a little later in this chapter.

When this sort of information is at the top of the page, it's called a *header*; at the bottom of the page, it's a *footer*. You can put just about anything in a header or footer, but most often you use these spaces for information such as titles, page numbers, dates, and labels (like "Confidential" or "Draft"). Usually, you don't need to add these details to short documents such as one-page letters and memos or to documents that you expect will be read online.

Adding Information at the Top and Bottom of Each Page

Word's default document settings include space for a header and footer 1/2 inch from the top and bottom of each page. Before you can add text or graphics to a header or footer, you first have to make these editing boxes visible. Pull down the **View** menu and choose **Header and Footer** (see Figure 14.1). Word switches to *Print Layout view*, if necessary, and displays the Header and Footer toolbar.

FIGURE 14.1
When you make the header and footer visible, Word switches to Print Layout view, and the text of your document appears in gray.

You can enter any type of data in a header or footer box, including text, text boxes, drawings, pictures, tables, and hyperlinks. You can also change typefaces and sizes, realign text, and adjust the space between the header or footer and the body of your document.

While you work, the Header and Footer toolbar floats nearby with buttons you can use to navigate through your document, or to insert page numbers, dates, and other information. Table 14.1 shows the buttons that are useful for working with headers and footers.

TABLE 14.1 Buttons on the Header and Footer Toolbar

Button	What It Does
	Jumps from header to footer and vice versa
	Inserts the page number
	Inserts the number of pages
	Formats the page number

continues…

TABLE 14.1 Continued

[icon]	Inserts the date
[icon]	Inserts the time
[icon]	Shows or hides the document text
[icon]	Finds the previous header or footer (useful if you've created a special header for the first page or for a section)
[icon]	Finds the next header or footer
[icon]	Creates the same header/footer as the previous section
[icon]	Opens the **Layout** tab of the Page Setup dialog box
Close	Hides the Header and Footer boxes and toolbar; returns to the previously selected view

Use graphics for a sophisticated look

Headers and footers aren't limited to text. You can add graphic elements, such as a company logo, to any header or footer.

Field codes keep page numbers accurate

When you click the **Insert Page Number** or **Insert Number of Pages** button, Word actually inserts a field code in the header or footer. As you edit a document and it gets longer or shorter, Word keeps track of the total page count. When you view or print a document, Word updates the numbers on each page as needed. Date and time fields work the same way.

One of the most popular uses for a document footer is to keep a running total of pages in the current document (`Page 16 of 30`, for example), automatically updating this information as you make a document longer or shorter.

Adding Page Numbers to a Document

1. Pull down the **View** menu and choose **Header and Footer**.
2. Click in the **Footer** box.
3. Type `Page` and press the Spacebar.
4. Click the **Insert Page Number** button [icon].
5. Press the Spacebar, type `of`, and press the Spacebar again.
6. Click the **Insert Number of Pages** button [icon].
7. Select and format the text you entered, if you want.
   Click the **Close** button to return to the main body of the document.

Positioning Headers and Footers

Headers are always at the top of the page; footers are always at the bottom. You can't change these facts, but you *can* change the space between where the header ends and where your document begins—if, for example, you want to squeeze more lines of text onto each page. You can also add space between the end of the text on each page and the beginning of the footer.

To reposition and resize headers and footers, use the *vertical ruler* at the left side of the document window.

Changing the Size of a Header or Footer

1. Click the **View** menu and choose **Header and Footer** to display the Header and Footer boxes.
2. To the left of the header or footer you want to change is a white region that defines its height. Aim the mouse pointer at the top or bottom of this part of the vertical ruler (called the *margin boundary*) until the pointer changes to a two-headed arrow, as shown in Figure 14.2.
3. Drag the margin boundary to change the size of the header or footer.
4. Use the buttons on the Formatting toolbar to change the alignment of your header or footer (centering the text, for example). Two tabs are set up in a header or footer, by default: a center-aligned tab and a right-aligned tab. To create a footer that has a title on the left and page numbers on the right, type the title, press the Tab key twice, and then enter the page number.

SEE ALSO

➤ *For a detailed explanation of how tabs work, see page 236*

Displaying the vertical ruler

If you can't see the ruler, it's just hidden. Switch to Print Layout view; if you still can't see the ruler, pull down the **View** menu and choose **Ruler** to bring it back. If it's still not visible, click the **Tools** menu, choose **Options**, click the **View** tab, and check the box labeled **Vertical ruler (Print view only)**. Then use the Header and Footer toolbar to switch to the header or footer you want to change.

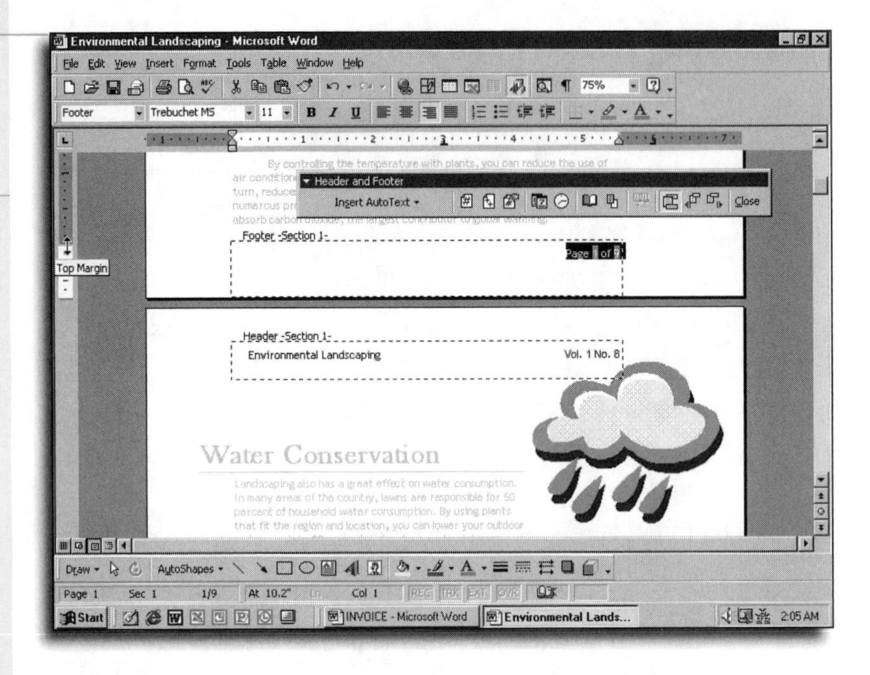

FIGURE 14.2

Use the vertical ruler to change the size and position of a header or footer.

Giving Printed Documents a Professional Look

Do you want the exact same header and footer on every page? Maybe not. If you've created a custom title page, the header and footer would mess up its careful design. Likewise, if you're planning to print on both sides of the paper and bind your work in book format, you might want to set up different headers and footers on left and right pages, with the title of your report on the right page header only, for example. (Look at this book to see an example of different headers for left and right pages.)

Word lets you handle both instances with ease. To pop up the Page Setup dialog box (shown in Figure 14.3), just click the **Page Setup** button on the Header and Footer toolbar.

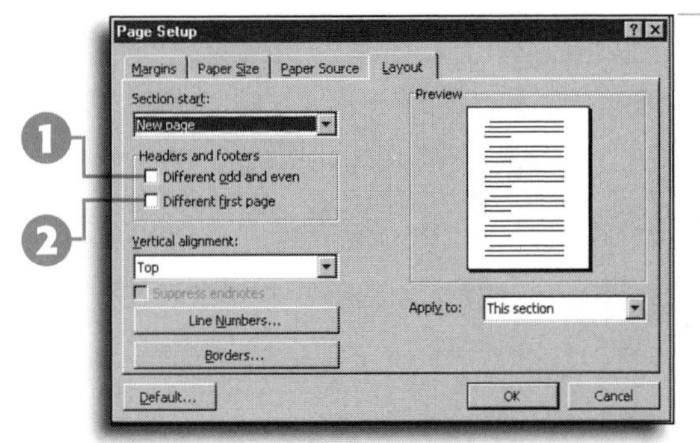

FIGURE 14.3

The Page Setup dialog box lets you tell Word where you want your headers and footers to appear.

1. **Click here to set up separate headers and footers for left and right pages.**
2. **Click here to set up a separate header or footer for the first page of a document or section.**

Which header is which?

Look at the top of the header or footer box to see at a glance which header you're currently working with. A simple Header or Footer label means you have only one of each. If you've set up additional headers or footers, you see different labels for each one–First Page Header or Even Page Footer, for example.

If you've created separate sections in a long document, you can use different headers and footers for each section. By default, each section uses the same header information as the previous section. Click the **Same as Previous** button to toggle this setting on and off.

Use the navigation buttons on the Header and Footer toolbar to jump back and forth between different headers and footers, like the ones you've created for left and right pages. In Print Layout view, double-click the header or footer area to activate it at any time and double-click anywhere on the page (outside the header or footer area) to return to the text of your document.

Adding Page Numbers Only

If all you want to do is number the pages in your document, you don't have to hassle with headers or footers. When you pull down the **Insert** menu and choose **Page Numbers**, Word creates a footer (or a header, if you prefer) in your document and then adds a page number to it. You can control the process by using the dialog box shown in Figure 14.4.

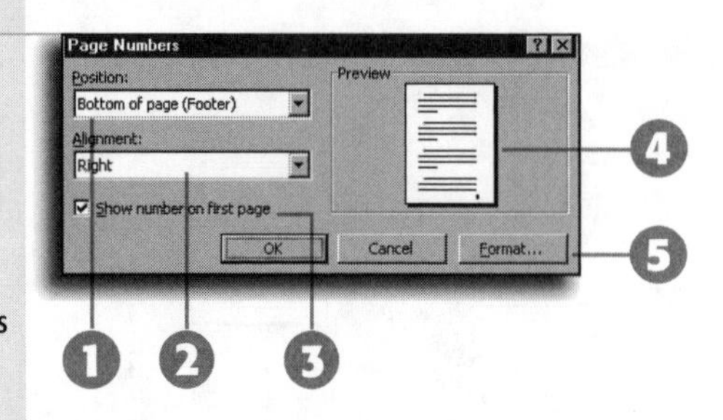

FIGURE 14.4

Choose the **Insert** menu and then select **Page Numbers** to add page numbers quickly to any document.

1. Click here to position numbers on the top or bottom of the page.
2. Tell Word how to align the page numbers: left, right, or centered.
3. Clear the check mark here to hide the first page number.
4. This box shows you where the numbers will appear on the printed page.
5. Click to display the Page Number Format dialog box, and pick a numeric format. If you're happy with a simple 1, 2, 3, skip this step.

You can't add numbers in Outline view

The **Page Numbers** command is grayed out and unavailable when you're working in Outline or Online Layout view. Switch to Normal or Print Layout View and try again.

Adding Today's Date to the Printed Page

Some documents are made to be updated regularly. When I'm immersed in a complex project, for example, I update a status report and print a fresh copy to share with my coworkers every day. How can they tell yesterday's version from today's? To make it easy on everybody, I add a footer to the document and then insert a code that automatically displays the current date and time every time I open or print the document.

To add today's date or time to a header or footer, click the **Insert Date** or **Insert Time** buttons. (You can add both a date and a time.) To choose a special format for the date or time field, pull down the **Insert** menu and choose **Date and Time**. You then see a dialog box like the one in Figure 14.5. Pick a format and click **OK** to enter the current date or time at the insertion point. Check the box labeled **Update automatically** to insert the date or time as a field. You can use this feature in the text of any document, too, but it's particularly useful in headers and footers.

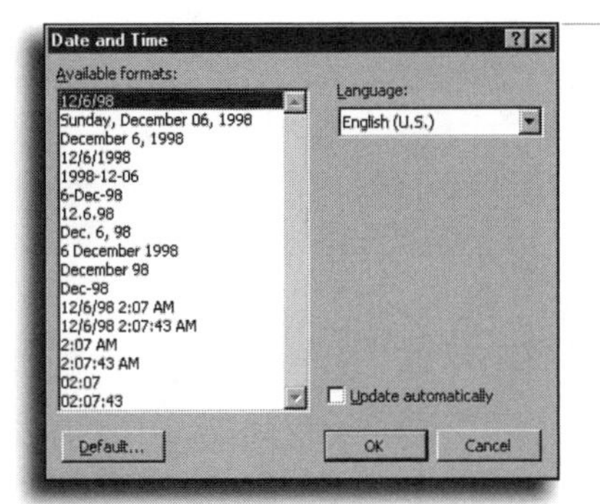

FIGURE 14.5
Insert a field that displays the current date and time in any of these formats.

Before You Print, Preview!

I don't like surprises. I especially hate that surprised feeling I get when I pull a 48-page report out of the printer and discover that I forgot to add headers and footers to the document.

Before I send a document to the printer, I *always* click the **Print Preview** button. You should, too. With a single click, you get to see *exactly* what your printed output will look like—no surprises.

The Big Picture: Seeing Your Entire Document at Once

The Print Preview screen (see Figure 14.6) is dramatically different from the normal document editing window. The Standard and Formatting toolbars vanish, and only the Print Preview toolbar is visible. Using this view, you can look at the pages in your document just the way they'll appear when printed, complete with graphics, headers, footers, and page numbers.

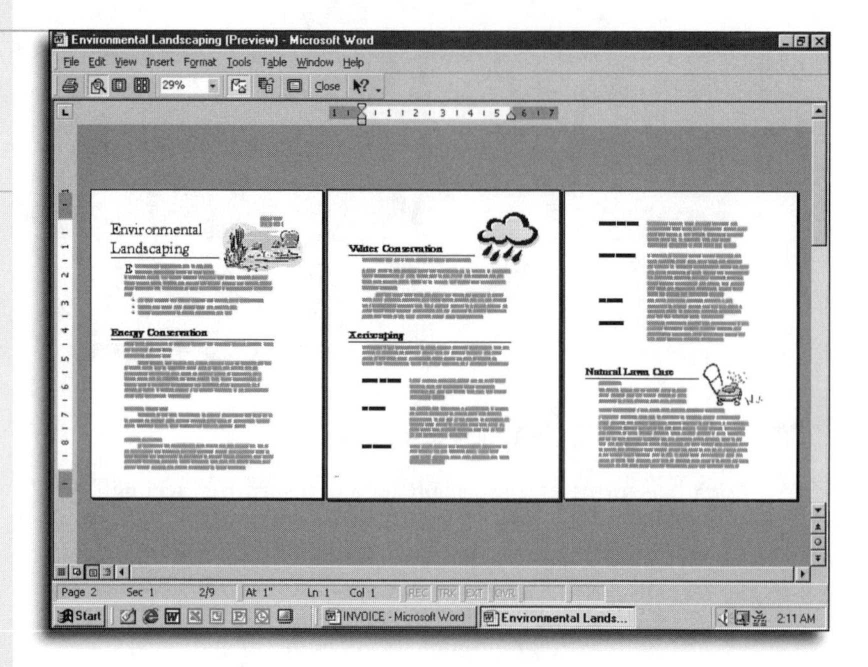

FIGURE 14.6

Use Print Preview to see exactly what your document will look like before you send it to the printer.

You can preview one page or an entire document. Zoom in for a quick look at the details; then zoom out to see several pages at once. If you find a mistake, or you just don't like the way one of your pages looks, you can fix it right there. The Print Preview toolbar lets you choose whether to view, zoom in, or even edit your document in Print Preview mode.

- Click the **One Page** button to fill the window, from top to bottom, with just the page you're looking at right now.
- Click the **Multiple Pages** button to view two or more pages side by side in the preview window.
- Use the **Zoom Control** to choose a specific magnification; choices on this drop-down list let you select one or two pages, or zoom the current page to full width.
- Click the **Toggle Full Screen View** button to hide the title bar, menu bar, and taskbar, leaving only the Print Preview toolbar and the document you're previewing. (Click the **Close Full Screen** button to return to Normal view.)

Selecting Multiple Pages view is a great way to see the overall layout of a document—where graphics are placed and where headlines fall, for example.

Previewing an Entire Document

1. Click the **Print Preview** button to switch to Print Preview mode.
2. Click the **Multiple Pages** button and hold down the left mouse button. Drag the mouse pointer down and to the right to select the number of rows and the number of pages in each row, as in Figure 14.7.
3. Release the mouse button to display the number of pages you selected.
4. If your document contains more pages than the view you selected, use the scrollbars or the Page Up and Page Down keys to move through the document.
5. Click the **Close** button to return to the normal document editing window.

How many pages can you preview at once?

The answer depends on the video resolution you've selected. At 1,024×768, for example, you can see up to 50 pages at once, in 5 rows of 10 pages each. At 800×600 resolution, you can see only 24 pages at a time, in 3 rows of 8 pages each. To change display resolutions, open the Display option in the Windows Control Panel, click the **Settings** tab, and move the **Screen Area** slider.

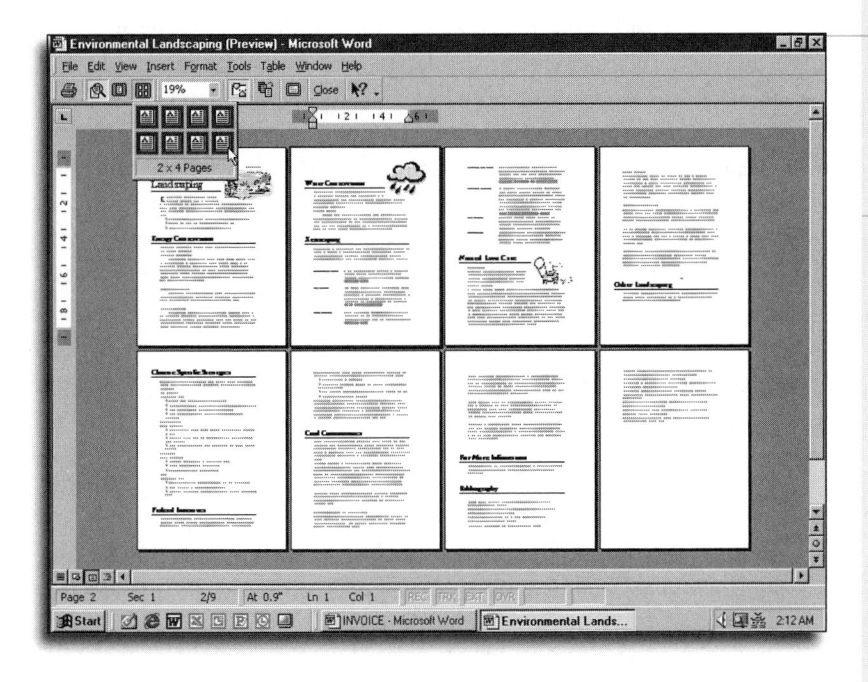

FIGURE 14.7
Click the Multiple Pages button and drag to select the number of pages you want to preview at once.

Switching to Close-Up View

In Multiple Pages view, you can quickly tell where a headline falls on a page. When you use this view of a document, you can also zoom in for a close-up look at any text, graphic, or other part of the document.

If you see an I-beam insertion point when you pass the mouse pointer over any page, click the **Magnifier** button. You then see a dark border around the current page. Click to select another page.

When you point to the selected page, the pointer changes to a magnifying glass with a plus sign in the center. Click on any part of the page to zoom to 100 percent magnification. The mouse pointer changes to a magnifying glass with a minus sign in the center. Click again to return to Multiple Pages view.

Avoid editing in Print Preview mode

I recommend using Print Preview's editing mode only when you want to fix a mistake in a big headline or move a graphic from one page to another. To change body text, switch back to Normal or Print Layout view, where text is easier to read and all of Word's editing tools are available.

Making Quick Changes in Preview Mode

Normally, Print Preview is simply a way to look at your document and verify that it's ready for printing. However, you *can* edit a document while displaying it in Print Preview mode. You can move whole chunks of text, reformat characters or paragraphs, adjust margins, or even insert a graphic. To switch into editing mode, click the **Magnifier** button on the Print Preview toolbar. Now you can click on any region in any page to move the insertion point and edit the document. Click the Magnifier button again to switch backto Print Preview mode.

Undo lets you experiment

With Word, you can easily experiment with features like the Shrink to Fit button. If you don't like the results of this or any formatting decision, just click the **Undo** button (or press Ctrl+Z) to cancel the changes and restore your previous document formatting.

What to Do When Your Document Is One Page Too Long

It's Murphy's Law of Long Documents: The last page invariably contains only two or three lines of text. When you spot this common design problem, click the **Shrink to Fit** button on the Print Preview toolbar. Word adjusts the size of the type you've used in your document to squeeze those last few lines onto the previous page. Don't expect miracles, though, especially if your document is heavily formatted or filled with graphics. Shrink To Fit works best on simple memos and letters.

Sending Your Document to the Printer

After you're satisfied that your document will print correctly, you can click the **Print** button. Whether you use the button on the Print Preview toolbar or click its twin on the Standard toolbar, the effect is the same: You get one copy of your entire document, and the job goes to your default printer.

If you want to print more than one copy, use a different printer or paper tray, or select just a few pages, don't click the Print button. Instead, pull down the **File** menu and choose **Print**, or use the Ctrl+P keyboard shortcut. In either case, you see the Print dialog box, shown in Figure 14.8.

One of the most impressive improvements in Word 2000 is its capability to print multiple pages on a single sheet of paper. In the Print dialog box, click the **Pages per sheet** drop-down list and choose 2, 4, 6, 8, or 16 pages. If your vision is sharp enough, you can probably read a document with 2 or even 4 pages per sheet. Any more than that, however, and your printout is useful mostly as a way to see thumbnails of a document's layout.

Perfect for road trips

Paper is heavy, so use Word's capability to print two pages per sheet to cut your load down to size when you want to print out a lengthy report and review it on an airplane. Better yet, print on both sides of the page and cut the number of sheets of paper to a quarter of the original count.

Canceling a Print Job

When you send a document to the printer, it doesn't always go directly there. Word can send pages to the printer faster than most printers can print; if the printer you're trying to use is connected to a network, your coworkers can add even more congestion. Depending on how your system is configured, the print job may actually end up in the print queue, a temporary disk file that Windows uses to keep the flow of information from outpacing the printer's for print jobs. Windows sends each job to the printer as quickly as the printer can handle it.

To check the status of a Word document after you send it to the printer, click the **Start** button, choose **Settings**, and then open the **Printers** folder. Click the printer icon to see a list of documents waiting to be printed. The list includes information about each waiting job, including who sent it to the printer.

FIGURE 14.8
Don't click the Print button. Choose the **File** menu and then select **Print** to print extra copies or set other options.

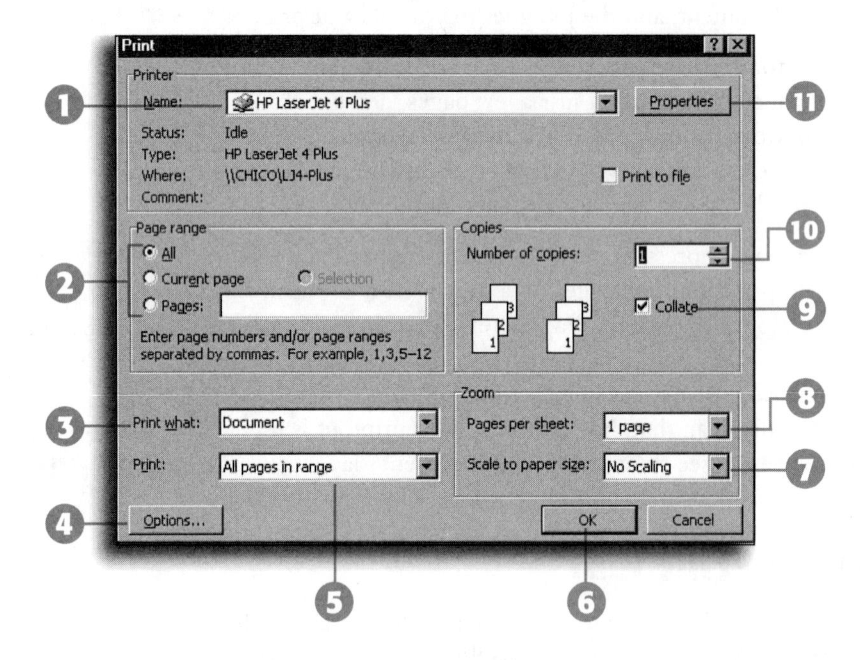

1. Make sure that the correct printer is selected. Click the drop-down arrow to pick another printer.
2. Print just the current page, a group of pages, or the whole document.
3. Options on this list let you print document properties, comments, and other information.
4. Adjust printing options, including which paper tray to use.
5. If you're printing two-sided copies, choose odd or even pages from this list.
6. Send the job to the printer.
7. Scale the page so it fits properly on a different paper size than the one for which it was designed.
8. Print multiple pages on a single sheet of paper.
9. Click here to print each copy in page order instead of printing two copies of page 1, two copies of page 2, and so on.
10. Use this spinner to adjust the number of copies.
11. Configure Windows printer options.

On most networks, you can't delete someone else's waiting print job (nor can your coworkers delete yours, unless the network administrator has granted them the right to manage printers). On most networks and on printers attached directly to your computer, you can delete your own print jobs—if you catch them before they get to the printer.

To kill a print job that's waiting in a Windows 95 or Windows 98 *print queue*, select the document and right-click; then choose **Cancel Printing**. (On Windows NT systems, choose **Cancel**.) You can also pause and resume print jobs using this shortcut menu.

Open the print queue instantly

Did you just send a long document to the printer by mistake? Look for a printer icon in the notification area at the right side of the taskbar. That's the shortcut to the print queue, and if you're fast enough on the draw, you might be able to stop the job before it reaches the printer.

Troubleshooting Printer Problems

If you click the Print button and your document never emerges from the printer, check the following list of common printer problems and solutions.

Windows offers Troubleshooting help

When you have trouble printing, Windows can help track down the problem with its built-in troubleshooter. Open the **Start** menu and click **Help**. Click the **Contents** tab and open the **Troubleshooting** topic. Select the **Printing** topic and follow its step-by-step procedures.

Printer Doesn't Produce Pages

The most common cause of printer problems is a bad connection or a printer that isn't turned on. Before you call tech support, run through this checklist:

- Is the printer connected to your PC? (Check the plugs on either end of the connection, just to be sure.)
- Is the printer plugged in and turned on?
- Is the Windows printer driver installed? Is the printer set up as the default printer?
- Did you choose the correct printer in Word's Print dialog box?
- Is the printer out of paper? Is the paper jammed? Click **Start**, **Settings**, **Printers**, right-click the printer's entry in the Printers folder, choose **Properties**, and click the **Print Test Page** button to see whether the problem is with Windows.
- Do you see any error messages on the printer's front panel? If so, try turning the printer on and off to clear its memory and then try printing again.

Can't read the printout?

When pages finally do come out of your laser printer, is the text faint, washed out, or illegible, or do you see streaks? If so, it may be time for a new toner cartridge.

Printing Takes Too Long

If your pages take too long to come out of the printer, the cure may be to replace your printer with a faster model. However, if you simply want to get back to work more quickly, configure Word to print in the background instead of taking over the entire system while printing.

Open the **Tools** menu, choose **Options**, and click the **Print** tab. Make sure that a check appears in the box next to the **Background printing** option. This setting slows down print jobs, but it does allow you to continue working with the next document.

Wrong Fonts Appear on Printed Pages

If the fonts you see onscreen don't match the ones on your printed pages, the problem is in the fonts you've selected. If your printer doesn't know how to use those fonts, you have to change the formatting to another font that your printer can use.

When you select a font from the font list, look for a TT symbol alongside the name. *TrueType fonts* always display the same onscreen as they do on the printed page. A small printer icon next to the font name means the font is built into your printer. If you don't have a matching screen font installed, what you see on the screen will not match what the printer puts on the page (although the printer will use the font name you've selected). If no symbol appears next to the font name, it's a screen font only, and your printer may or may not print it the way it appears onscreen.

Print Options Are Not Available

If Word doesn't display the Print dialog box, that's its way of telling you that you have a problem with the default printer; most often, this problem means you need to install a printer. Open the Printers folder and make sure that your printer driver is properly configured.

Can't solve your printer problem?

If you're stumped by a printer problem in Windows 98, try using the built-in Windows troubleshooters to find a solution. Click the **Start** button, choose **Help**, click the Troubleshooting topic, and select **Print** from the collection of Windows 98 Troubleshooters.

CHAPTER 15

Letters, Labels, and Envelopes

- Make your own custom letter templates
- Create single letters with the Letter Wizard
- Use mail merge to construct custom letters
- Print envelopes and labels

Creating Letters Using Word

Even a simple letter consists of many parts: address blocks, subject lines and salutations, body text, and complimentary closings, for example. If you position and format each of these elements individually, you're wasting valuable time, and chances are your letters won't look their best. If you apply styles from ready-made templates instead, Word handles the routine formatting chores so that all your letters have a consistent look and you can concentrate on writing. Use Word's *Letter Wizard* to automate some of the drudgery.

What should you do when you need to produce a stack of letters that look like they were written one at a time? Word's *mail merge* feature is tricky to master, but if you pay attention to the details, you can personalize a generic letter with a list of names, addresses, and other details. The results can help you look professional, organized, and credible.

SEE ALSO

➤ *To learn more about mail merges, see page 305*

Customizing Letter Templates

Faxes and memos, too

Word includes prebuilt templates for fax cover sheets and memos that closely resemble the letter templates I discuss in this section. You can use the same techniques to customize these templates so you can create these common document types quickly and easily.

Although it's possible to create a letter from scratch using Word's Normal document *template*, you'll have much better results if you start with one of Word's three prebuilt letter templates. Each includes the following helpful elements:

- Commonly used letter styles, including Inside Address, Mailing Instructions, Salutation, and Signature.
- AutoText entries for the Salutation, Closing, and other useful fields, many of them available with a right-click in the template.
- Click-and-type placeholder fields that let you type essential information—like the recipient's name and address—in exactly the right place.

Unfortunately, each of these generic templates also includes sample text that you need to get rid of before you can truly call the letter your own. For example, there's a "Company Name Here" heading in the Professional Letter template shown in Figure 15.1. Rather than replace these generic elements every time you create a new letter, customize the template and save it under a new name.

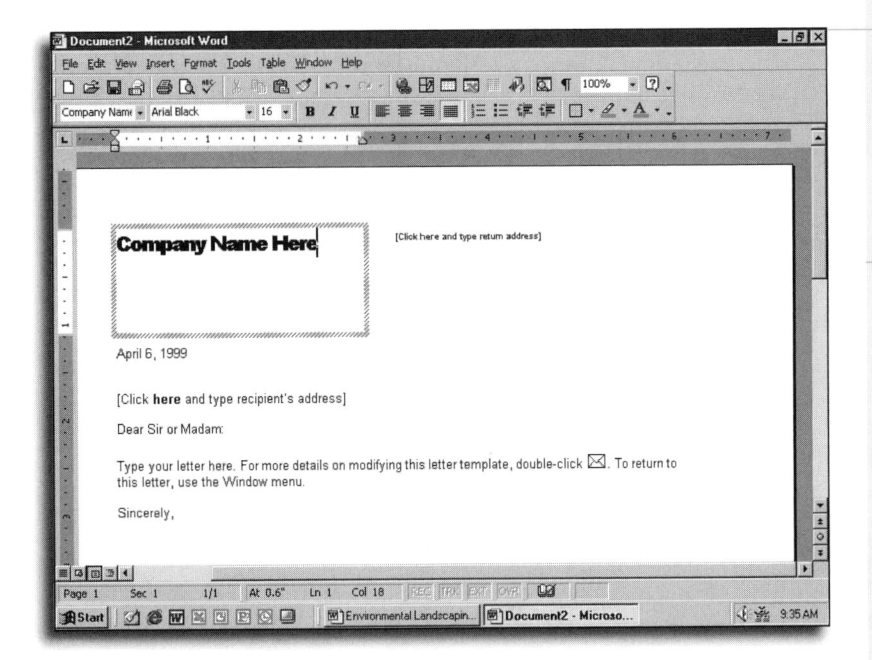

FIGURE 15.1
The default Professional Letter template includes blocks of generic text like the Company Name Here heading. Change these placeholders and save the template under a new name.

You don't need to go through every step in the following checklist, but I highly recommend that you spend the time now to customize these letter templates. If you write even one letter a week, you'll save countless hours over the course of the next year, and it only takes a few minutes of up-front work now.

In fact, customizing a letter template will help your letters stand out in a crowd. If you're sending an important fax, letter, or résumé, do you really want to risk the possibility that your recipient will toss your letter in the trash because he's insulted you used a canned Word template? Your correspondence should convey the message that you're hard-working, thorough, and creative. This is a good place to start.

Pick a letter style

This example uses the Professional Letter template, but you can also customize the Elegant Letter or Contemporary Letter templates. Use the same techniques as described here. In the Contemporary Letter template, make sure you replace the background graphic with one appropriate for your business.

Just add graphics

Would you like to include your company logo in this letter template? If the logo is available in a graphics file format that Word can recognize, go ahead and insert it in the text box that contains the company name.

Move the text boxes later

Because both the company name and return address fields are enclosed in text boxes, you can move them anytime you want. For now, leave them where they are.

Why change the DATE field?

All the ready-made Word letter templates use the DATE field to automatically insert the current date into each new letter. That sounds great, but it's guaranteed to cause problems when you look at a saved letter next week or next month. Because Word automatically updates the DATE field each time you open a saved file, you won't be able to tell when you originally created the letter. Changing this field to CREATEDATE tells Word to lock in the current date the first time you save the letter. Next month, when you open the saved letter, the field is still there, but the date accurately reflects its creation date.

Customizing a Letter Template

1. Open the **File** menu and choose **New**. Click the **Letters and Faxes** tab and click to select the Professional Letter template. Under the **Create New** heading, choose the **Template** option and click **OK**. Word opens the document template for editing.
2. Select the **Company Name Here** text from the box at the upper-left, and replace it with your own company name. Don't change the font or font size. (You'll have a chance to adjust this and other formatting options later.)
3. Click the return address placeholder in the top-left corner and replace its contents with your return address. Note that this is a text box, so you can press Enter at the end of each line. Don't change any font formatting here, either.
4. Right-click the date *field* and choose **Toggle Field Codes** from the shortcut menu. Change the DATE text in this field to CREATEDATE, and then right-click and choose **Toggle Field Codes** again.
5. Right-click the Salutation—the text that begins with "Dear"—and inspect the list of AutoText entries. If you want to add a custom entry of your own to this list, type the text (including punctuation) over the existing salutation; then right-click, choose **Create AutoText**, and use the Create AutoText dialog box shown in Figure 15.2 to enter the text you want to see on the shortcut menu.
6. Delete all but the first sentence ("Type your letter here.") from the sample body text in the letter. Be careful not to delete the paragraph mark, which contains the paragraph style for this text.
7. Right-click on the Closing block and inspect the AutoText list. If you want to add a new entry, use the same technique as in step 5.

SEE ALSO

➤ *For an explanation of how styles work, see page 250*

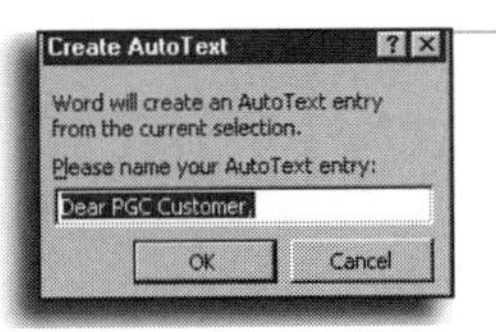

FIGURE 15.2
To add your own custom entries to the AutoText list for a letter field, enter the text itself in the letter, and then add the menu text in this dialog box.

8. Click on the Signature placeholder and type your name. Click on the Signature Job Title placeholder and click your job title, or delete the placeholder if you don't want to include a job title with each letter. Again, don't change font formatting for either of these elements.
9. To delete the sample AutoText entry, choose the **Tools** menu, click **AutoCorrect**, and click the **AutoText** tab. Select **Gallery Example** from the list of entries and click the Delete button.
10. To change the default font or font size (or both) for the letter, pull down the **Format** menu and choose **Font**. Click the **Font** tab and select a font name and size from the list, then click the **Default** button. Click OK if you see a warning dialog box.
11. To save your new template, pull down the **File** menu, choose **Save As**, and give it a descriptive name. By default, Word saves the template in the correct folder so that it appears on the General tab when you choose the **File** menu and click **New**.

Default = Normal

Clicking the **Default** button actually changes the formatting associated with the Normal style for your new template. Because many other styles in the letter templates are based on the Normal style, changing this one setting is the best place to start when you want to change the look of your letter template consistently. You may need to tweak other styles manually as well, if those styles include a specific font name.

Using the Letter Wizard

Like all wizards in Office 2000, the Letter Wizard takes you step by step through the letter-writing process. There are four ways to start the Letter Wizard. Each technique gives you a slightly different set of options, but only one lets you produce a truly great-looking letter:

- Open a blank document and type `Dear`, followed by a name and a colon or comma, and then press Enter. This option works only if the Office Assistant is visible. Choose **Get help with writing the letter** to start the Letter Wizard. This option is easy, but it produces less than satisfactory results because you're limited to Word's built-in templates.

...or replace the built-in templates

If you customize one of Word's built-in letter templates and save your changes using the same name and location as the built-in version, you can use your custom versions directly in the Word Letter Wizard. The exact location varies depending on your language settings; with a U.S. English version, for example, you'll find these templates in C:\Program Files\Microsoft Office\Templates\1033.

Start a letter with Outlook

If you want to write a letter to a contact whose name and address are already in your Outlook Contacts folder, the Letter Wizard can help. Click the contact's name in Outlook, pull down the **Actions** menu, and click **New Letter to Contact**. That starts the Letter Wizard, with the contact's name and address already filled in for you.

Is the recipient's name and address already stored in your Microsoft Office address book?

If you're sending a letter to someone whose information is already stored in the Microsoft address book, on the **Recipient Info** tab, choose the **Address Book** icon in the **Click here to use Address Book** field and double-click the name you want. That person's information is then filled in automatically. Unfortunately, you can't choose fine details, such as the contact's job title, nor can you easily switch between the home and business addresses.

SEE ALSO

➤ *To learn how to get answers from the Office Assistant, see page 72*

- Pull down the **File** menu, choose **New**, and click the **Letters and Faxes** tab. Select the **Letter Wizard** icon and click **OK**. This option lets you choose to create a single letter or a group of letters using Word's Mail Merge tools. You can do better.
- Start with a new blank document, pull down the **Tools** menu, and choose **Letter Wizard**. This option dumps some basic text on the page, then forces you to go through the entire wizard to build the letter. Skip this option, too.
- Pull down the **File** menu, click **New**, and select the custom letter template you created in the previous section. Click **OK** to create a new letter based on this template, and then choose **Letter Wizard** from the **Tools** menu. The wizard starts with the defaults you entered in your template. This is by far the most productive way to use the Letter Wizard.

The Letter Wizard's four tabs let you add elements to your letters using four categories. Begin on the **Letter Format** tab. Click **Next>** or **<Back** to move between tabs across the top of the wizard to fill in Recipient Info, Other Elements, and Sender Info (see Figure 15.3). After you've entered all the information, click **Finish** to create and view the letter.

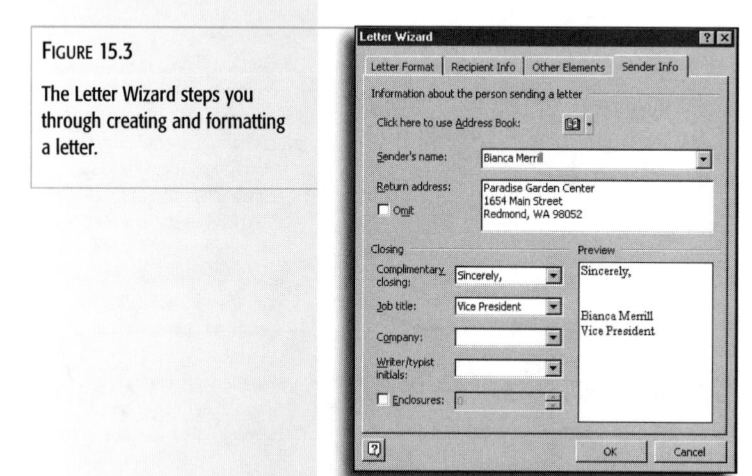

FIGURE 15.3

The Letter Wizard steps you through creating and formatting a letter.

SEE ALSO

➤ *To learn how to use the Outlook address book, see page 614*

What Is Mail Merge and How Does It Work?

Mail merge is a powerful process you can use to create individualized letters, labels, or envelopes for a group of people without typing separate letters.

Mail merge is a three-step process. First, you create the form letter that everyone will receive, with placeholders to mark the spots where you want personalized data to appear. Next, you create or open a file that contains the recipients' names, addresses, phone numbers, and so on. Finally, you combine (or merge) the two files into custom form letters. Use the Mail Merge Helper to walk you through this process step by step.

Creating the Form Letter

The first step in creating personalized form letters is to create the generic letter that all recipients will receive. You can use a custom template or the Letter Wizard to create the letter, or you can open an existing letter and adapt it for use in your mail merge.

Although it's possible to create a mail-merge letter by starting with a completely blank document, this option is usually more trouble than it's worth. If your ultimate goal is to create a stack of letters, you're much better off starting with a letter template.

After you create the letter, you can define it as a mail merge *main document*, which means that you define the document as the form letter you plan to send to all recipients.

Defining a Mail Merge Main Document

1. Open or create the generic letter that all recipients will receive. Leave blanks where you want to add personalized information, such as the recipient's name.

Return to the wizard to make changes

If you want to return to the Letter Wizard after the letter is created, choose the **Tools** menu and select **Letter Wizard**. Return to the page to which you want to make changes. Click **OK** after you've finished making changes.

Do even more with mail merge

If you're willing to dig deep into Word, you can use mail-merge capabilities to create all sorts of documents besides letters and envelopes. For example, you can take a database full of product and price information and merge it into a Word document to create a price list or catalog. For details on using advanced mail-merge features, see *Special Edition Using Microsoft Office 2000,* Chapter 17, "Merging Data and Documents."

A word about fields

Word's mail-merge features depend on fields—placeholders within Word documents that change dynamically and automatically. Some fields are simple, like the DATE field that substitutes today's date every time you open or print a document. Other fields add "smarts" to a document—for example, you can add an ASK field to a mail-merge letter so that every time you run the merge, it stops and lets you add personalized information. To learn much more about fields, check out Chapter 16, "Creating Dynamic Documents with Fields and Forms," in *Special Edition Using Microsoft Office 2000.*

Returning a mail merge document to a normal document

When you create a mail merge main document, Word adds hidden information to the file. If you want to remove all mail-merge features from a document, choose the **Tools** menu, select **Mail Merge**, and then choose the **Create** button in the **Main document** section of the Mail Merge Helper. Click **Restore to Normal Word Document**.

2. Choose the **Tools** menu and select **Mail Merge**. The Mail Merge Helper appears, as shown in Figure 15.4.
3. Under step 1, **Main document**, click the **Create** button and select **Form Letters** from the drop-down menu that appears. Choose **Active Window** to indicate that the form letter is on the active document.

SEE ALSO

➤ *To learn more details about opening a saved document, see page 36*
➤ *For more information on how to work with letter templates, see page 300*

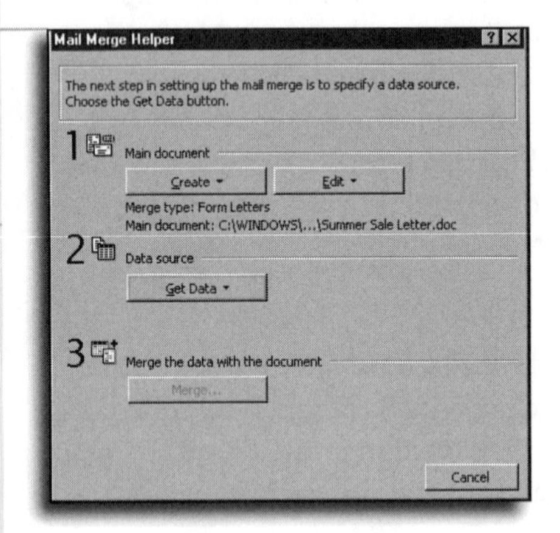

FIGURE 15.4

The Mail Merge Helper steps you through the process of creating and generating custom letters.

Ask for help about fields

Word fields can supercharge a mail-merge operation. For example, the **Fill-in** field lets you pop up a dialog box every time you run the mail merge so that you can enter custom details, such as a product name. Or use the **If...Then...Else...** field to specify a different discount for customers based on their zip code or a key you use to identify your best customers. If you think a field might be helpful but you're not sure what it does, look in the on-line help for a topic called "Word fields for use in mail merge."

After you define a document as a mail-merge main document, the Mail Merge toolbar appears. This toolbar appears only when you're working with a mail merge document. Table 15.1 shows the tools in this toolbar and describes their use.

TABLE 15.1 Using the Mail Merge Toolbar

Tool	Description
Insert Merge Field	Displays a list of the fields in your data source and lets you insert one into the main document.
Insert Word Field	Inserts a Word field that performs advanced merge functions.
«» ABC	***View Merged Data*** toggles between display of field codes in your main document and the data entered in the selected record.

Tool	Description
	First Record, Last Record, Previous Record, Next Record When you click the View Merged Data button, these buttons let you flip through the records in your data source to preview how the results will look, spotting possible problems before they occur.
	Mail Merge Helper Hide the Mail Merge Helper dialog box when you're editing documents or data, and then click this button to display it again quickly.
	Check for Errors identifies potential merge errors in your document by simulating the merge process, by performing the merge and reporting on each error as it occurs, or by logging errors in a new document.
	Merge to New Document combines the main document and the data source in a new Word document so that you can review the results before printing. This action happens immediately, with no confirmation steps.
	Merge to Printer merges the main document and the data source directly to a printer.
	Mail Merge displays the Mail Merge dialog box. You can choose used for customizing merge results.
	Find Record lets you enter search criteria and find the next matching record in your data source.
	Data Source lets you directly edit records in the data source, using a data form. This button is only available from the main document.

...or go to a specific record

The blank **Go To Record** box in the center of the VCR-style controls on the Mail Merge toolbar lets you type in a specific record number. Press Enter to preview the data from that record number in your data source file.

Don't merge to the printer

I strongly recommend that you avoid clicking the Merge to Printer button. This option gives you no control over the output, and if anything goes wrong with a printer, you'll have to rerun the merge to repeat the job. Instead, merge the results to a new Word document, and then print them in batches so that you can control the output.

Merge works with email, too

One of Word's merge options lets you choose email as an output source. Click the **Mail Merge** button and choose **Electronic mail** from the **Merge to** list. The resulting messages will go into your Outlook Outbox and will be sent the next time you connect with your outgoing mail server.

Telling Word Where to Find Names and Addresses

After you create and save the letter you plan to send to everyone, you're ready to identify the *data source*—the file that contains the information you want to merge. When you're creating a stack of form letters, the data source contains the names and addresses of the people to whom you plan to send your letter. The following are the most common data sources:

- An existing address book list (such as your Outlook Contacts Folder)
- A Word document containing names, addresses, and other data in table format

Prepare your data source first

You don't have to have a data source before you start the Mail Merge Wizard, but it sure makes the process easier. For very simple merge jobs, you can actually use the Mail Merge Helper to create a data source, and then fill it with names and other data using a simple Word data form. If your list includes more than a dozen names, though, you'll be better off using Outlook or Excel.

- A text document containing data in delimited format
- An Excel list
- A table in a database created by Access or another program

SEE ALSO

➤ *For an overview of the Outlook Contacts folder, see page 614*
➤ *To learn more about lists, see page 419*

Opening a Mail Merge Data Source

1. Switch to your mail merge main document and click the **Mail Merge Helper** button.
2. Click the **Get Data** button.
   - To select an external file, such as an Access database or Excel file, click **Open Data Source** and browse for the file. You may see an additional dialog box asking you to specify a data range or a table name.

SEE ALSO

➤ *For more details on how to work with Excel lists, see page 420*

   - To use your Outlook Contacts Folder, click **Use Address Book**. If you're using Outlook 2000, choose Outlook Address Book from the resulting dialog box and click **OK**.
3. To verify that you've imported the data correctly, click the **Edit** button under the Data Source heading. Click the data file to view all the records in a standard data form, like the one in Figure 15.5.

Personal address book?

In Office 97, Outlook created multiple address books. Beginning with Outlook 2000, you'll typically have only one address book. To grab records from your Outlook Contacts Folder, choose Outlook Address Book and ignore the other choices.

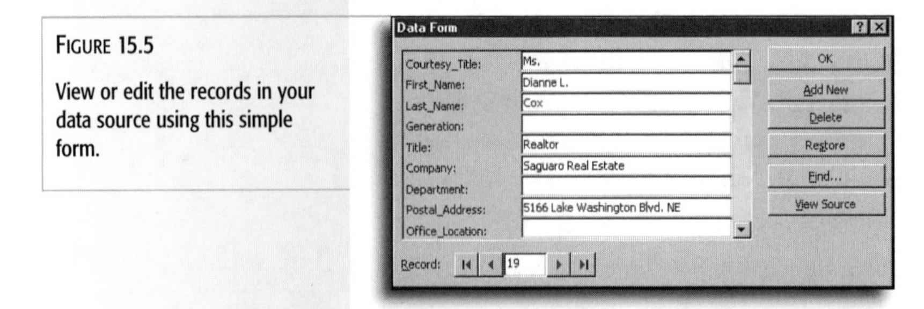

FIGURE 15.5

View or edit the records in your data source using this simple form.

4. Click **Cancel** to close the Mail Merge Helper dialog box and return to the main document.

Telling Word Where to Place the Data on Each Letter

With your main document and your data source in place, you can now begin to place data fields in your main document. If the letter includes an address block, for example, you'll want to add the First_Name, Last_Name, Street_Address, City, State_or _Province, and Postal_Code fields from the Outlook Address Book.

Inserting Merge Fields into a Main Document

1. In the main document, click to position the insertion point at the place where you want to add the first merge field.
2. Click the **Insert Merge Field** button [Insert Merge Field] on the Mail Merge toolbar to display a drop-down list of fields from the data source; click the name of the field you want to insert. The field name appears in the document, surrounded by double angle brackets, as in Figure 15.6.
3. Repeat steps 1 and 2 until you've finished adding all the merge fields you want.

Previewing Mail Merge Results

At this point, you've defined your data source and your main document, but you can't be certain that they'll work together smoothly. So before you send the job to the printer (and possibly waste a few hundred sheets of paper), let Word show you what the finished result will look like. To do so, click the **View Merged Data** button on the Mail Merge toolbar. Click the **Next Record** button a few times to see more than just the first *record*.

Use this preview to check for major mistakes, such as using the wrong field (First_Name, when you really wanted Last_Name, for example). Also check to make sure you don't have blank spots caused by missing data. To return to the main document and correct any merge mistakes, click the **View Merged Data** button again.

What's ~~~_virtual_ file_~~~.olk?

If you see that bizarre filename after selecting your Outlook Address Book as the data source, don't panic. Word converts the address book to a temporary file for use during the merge and then deletes the file after the merge is complete. Just remember that any changes you make to your Outlook Contacts Folder after attaching this data source won't appear in your merged document!

Don't forget punctuation

When placing fields in a main document, don't forget to place punctuation exactly as you want it to appear. For example, you'll probably want to add a comma and a space between the City and State_or_Province fields, with another space before the Postal_Code field.

You can't edit a merge field directly

You can't enter, select, or edit the bracket characters on either side of a merge field. Word has to enter them for you. And although you can enter or delete characters within a merge field, you shouldn't try. Editing these fields manually will usually mess up your merge. To edit a merge field, drag the mouse pointer to select the entire field, and then use the **Insert Merge Field** button.

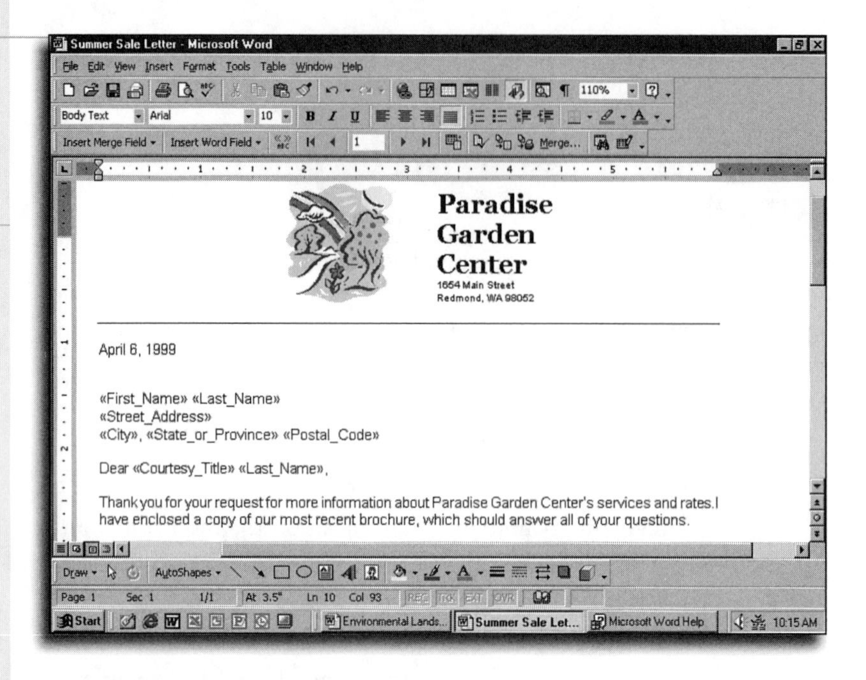

FIGURE 15.6

Merge fields look like this in your main document. Remember to add spaces and punctuation as needed between fields.

Performing the Merge

When you're satisfied, that the merge looks right, you're ready to combine the data source and main document into a new Word document.

Merging to a New Document

1. From the main document, click the **Mail Merge** button. You'll see the dialog box shown in Figure 15.7.
2. In the **Merge to** box, select **New document**.
3. Adjust any other options, and then click the **Mail Merge** button. Your merged document appears in a new window, with a generic name like `Form Letters1`.
4. Scroll through the document to make sure everything is correct. If it passes inspection, pull down the **File** menu and then click **Print** to send the job to the printer.
5. Save the new merged document under a new name.

What should you do with blanks?

In general, you'll want to suppress blank records in your merge. For example, if there's no data in the Country field for most records, why add the extra space in the address block? You'll want to show blanks if you're merging data to a form where position counts–a preprinted postcard, for example.

Try printing in batches

For really big merge jobs, cut the work down to size. In the Merge dialog box, use the **From** and **To** boxes to limit the number of records you merge at once. To keep the merged file manageable, try 1 to 100, then 101 to 200, and so on.

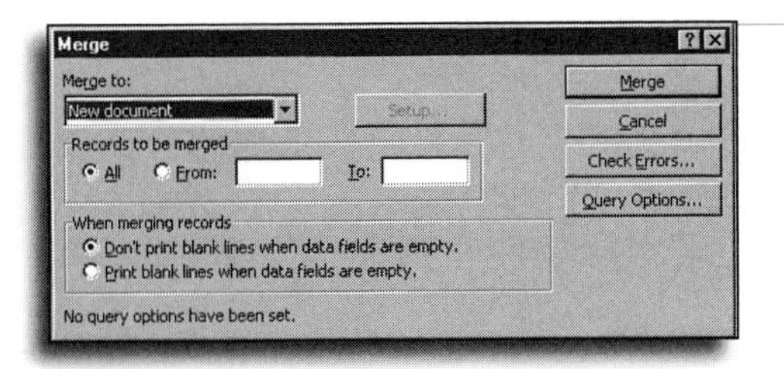

FIGURE 15.7

Use options in the Merge dialog box to choose the output source and to cut a big job down to size by printing a selected number of records.

Filtering Your Mailing List

Sometimes, you may have a long list of names in your data source, but you want to send letters to only a specific group of people. For example, if you want to announce that you've opened a new regional service center in Boston, you probably will want to send the letter only to contacts in Massachusetts or the Northeast. Why waste the postage notifying your customers in California and Arizona?

When performing a merge, Word allows you to *filter* your data source so that only records that meet specific criteria are merged into the main document. You can also sort your data by any field you choose; that option might save you money if you can qualify for lower postage rates.

Should you save that file?

After you've printed a merged job, I recommend you save the finished document until you're certain the documents have made it to their ultimate destination. If you drop a box of letters in a puddle on the way to the post office, you'll be glad you had a backup file.

Some queries don't need filters

If you've used Microsoft Query to access data from an external database, it's possible to define the filter directly in that query rather than in Word. If you regularly use information from large network databases like Oracle or SQL Server, pick up a copy of *Special Edition Using Microsoft Word 2000*.

Filtering Your Mailing List

1. Open your main document and click the **Mail Merge** button.
2. In the Merge dialog box, click the **Query Options** button.
3. In the Query Options dialog box (see Figure 15.8), click the **Filter Records** tab.
4. Click the drop-down arrows to pick the appropriate values in the **Field**, **Comparison**, and **Compare to** list boxes in the top row. To find all customers in Massachusetts, for example, specify `State_or_Province Equal to MA`.
5. To enter multiple criteria, use succeeding rows. Choose **And** to specify that a record must match all criteria; choose **Or** to choose a record that matches any of the criteria. Click **Or**, for example, if you want to filter for addressees based in Massachusetts or Vermont or New Hampshire.

6. Click **OK** to close the Query Options dialog box. Then click the **Merge to New Document** button to send the merged results to a file.

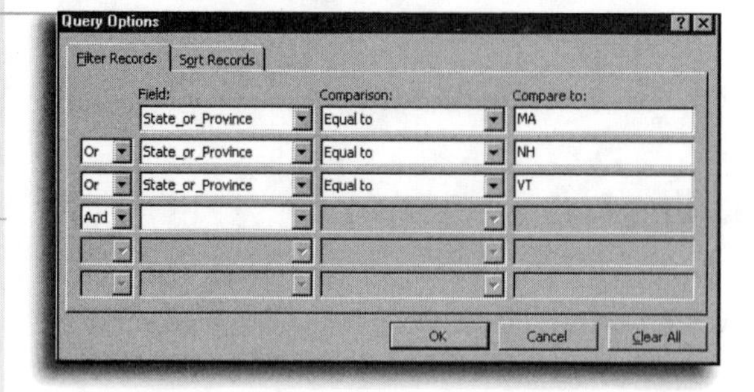

FIGURE 15.8

Use the Query Options dialog box to choose a specific set of records from a longer list.

Removing merge criteria

To remove *merge criteria* so that you can enter new criteria or use the entire data set, open the Merge dialog box again, click the **Query Options** button, and click **Clear All**.

Choose your fonts

You can use any fonts on an envelope–a large font for the delivery address and a smaller one for the return address, for example. Click the **Options** button and then click the **Envelope Options** tab to specify these settings.

Word remembers your address

You have to enter your address only once. Word remembers the return address you entered the previous time whenever you create an envelope. It also uses styles to insert addresses and then automatically picks up the correct addresses when you reopen the Envelopes and Labels dialog box.

Creating Envelopes and Labels

There's nothing quite as pathetic as receiving a perfectly printed letter, with gorgeous fonts and graphics, in an envelope where the sender scrawled the address by hand. Unless, of course, it's the pitiful sight of watching someone run an envelope through a typewriter when a laser printer is right alongside. After you learn how easy it is to create envelopes and labels with Word, you'll never need that typewriter again.

Printing a Single Envelope

You can create a single envelope from information on a letter or in its own document.

Creating a Single Envelope

1. Open the letter for which you want to create an envelope and select the recipient's address.
2. Choose the **Tools** menu, select **Envelopes and Labels**, and click the **Envelopes** tab. The selected text appears in the **Delivery address** box, as shown in Figure 15.9.
3. If necessary, type your address in the **Return address** box.
4. The default, format is a standard U.S. #10 envelope. To select a different format, click the **Options** button.

5. Choose **Add to Document** to insert the envelope at the top of the active document. Click **Print** to send the envelope directly to the printer.

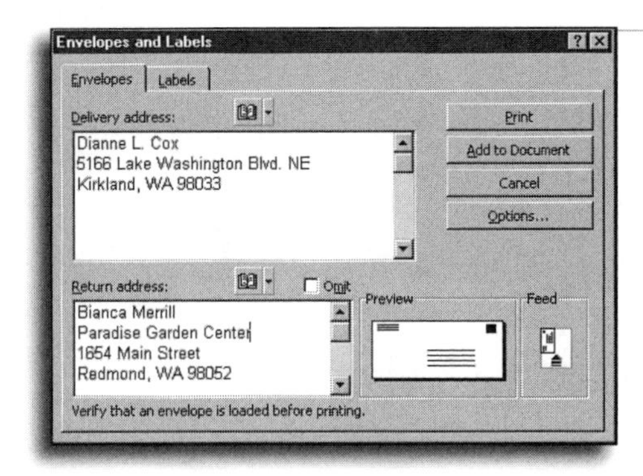

FIGURE 15.9

You can create single envelopes on a separate document or add them to an existing document.

How does it know?

See the tiny graphic to the right of the return address? That tells you how to insert the envelope into your printer for the correct results. Word uses information from the Windows printer driver to pick up this information. If it's wrong (and it usually isn't), click the **Options** button, and then adjust settings on the **Printing Options** tab.

Use barcodes for special handling

In the United States, you can help your letters get delivered faster by printing a *POSTNET bar code* on the envelope. When your letter gets to the post office, the automatic sorting equipment is trained to look for these bar codes and process them directly. Click the **Options** button, click the **Envelope Options** tab, and then check the **Delivery point barcode** box to speed up the mail.

Follow the numbers

Word supports an astonishing number of preprinted label formats, including those from Avery, the most popular label maker of all. Look for the product code on the box of labels and match it to the Word label format.

Printing Labels

Word users can take advantage of three main label printing options. You can print a single label, a sheet of the same label, or labels that correspond to a mail merge data source.

Printing a Single Label or Sheet of Labels

1. From any document, choose the **Tools** menu, select **Envelopes and Labels**, and click the **Labels** tab. The Envelopes and Labels dialog box appears (see Figure 15.10).
2. In the **Address** box, enter the information you want to appear on the label.
3. In the **Print** box, select **Single label**, and then enter the row and column number for the label on which you want to print. This technique allows you to use a sheet of preprinted labels repeatedly without wasting any.
4. Click the **Options** button and specify the manufacturer and product number for the style of labels you're using; then click **OK**.
5. To send the label directly to the printer, click the **Print** button. To create a new Word document with the correct formatting for your label, click the **New document** button.

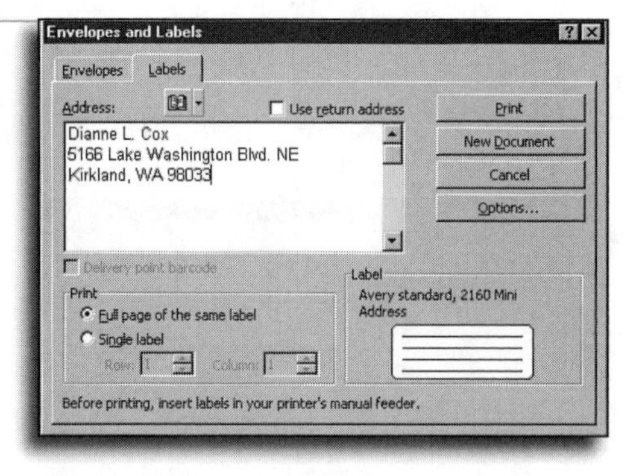

FIGURE 15.10

Quickly print a single label or a sheet of the same label from the Envelopes and Labels dialog box.

Select your text first

If you select a block of text in a document, Word automatically uses this text in the Envelopes and Labels dialog box. For labels, this text could be anything, not just an address. Select a report title, for example, to print a label for use on the outside of a binder.

Try manual feed

This dialog box also allows you to specify a paper tray. For printing a single label, you'll usually want to specify manual feed, so you can insert the correct sheet of labels when prompted.

Creating Multiple Labels

Earlier in this chapter, I showed you how to use mail merge to create custom letters. Use the exact same techniques to combine a data source with a label layout to arrange the addresses on the page in exactly the right position for printing. This procedure is essential if you're planning a mass mailing of newsletters or packages that are too large to fit in envelopes.

1. Define a label format and layout (main document).
2. Create or identify the location of the data source.
3. Insert data fields into the label format (main document).
4. Generate individual customized labels (or merge the data with the document).

Using Mail Merge to Create Labels

1. Create a new, blank document, pull down the **Tools** menu, and select **Mail Merge.** In the Mail Merge Helper dialog box, click the **Create** button and select **Mailing Labels** from the drop-down list.
2. In step 2 of the Mail Merge Helper, click Get Data and choose a data source, using the same techniques as described earlier in this chapter.
3. After you select a data source, Word displays a dialog box. Click the **Set Up Main Document** button to display the Label Options dialog box, as shown in Figure 15.11.

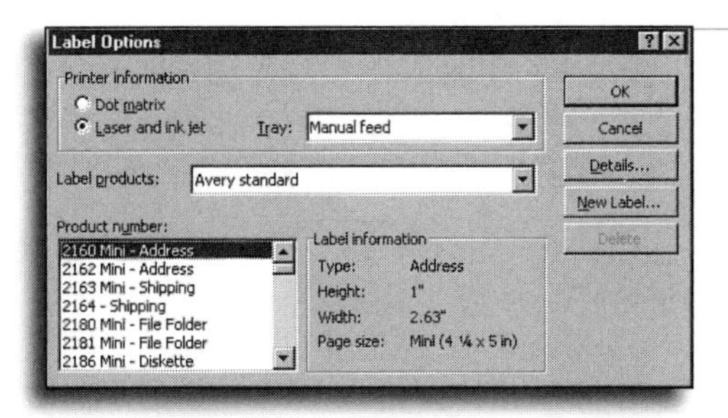

FIGURE 15.11

Select printer settings and label types on the Label Options dialog box.

4. Select the appropriate printer and label types, and click **OK**. The Create Labels dialog box appears.
5. In the Create Labels dialog box, define the label layout. Click the **Insert Merge Field** button to add the first field, and repeat this procedure until all merge fields are in place. Click **OK** to return to the Mail Merge Helper. Choose **Close** to view the label document.
6. Click the **Merge to New Document** button to combine the data source and label layout in a new Word document.
7. Click the **Print** button to send the labels to the printer.

Use the barcodes here, too

Click the **Insert Postal Bar Code** button to add bar codes to your labels. Word will ask you to specify the field that contains the zip codes for lookup. It will also display a warning message on the label layout to show you where the bar code will print.

CHAPTER

16

Creating Web Pages with Word

Learn about Word's Web authoring tools

Design your Web page for maximum readability

Use a wizard to build a complete Web site

Change the look of a page

Add frames to help you navigate on a Web site

Use tables and text boxes to position text and graphics

Is Word the Right Web Tool for You?

As I pointed out in Chapter 4, "Creating and Publishing Web Pages," Word 2000 is an excellent starting point if you want to create a general-purpose Web page. When you're getting ready to create a single Web page or an entire Web site, ask yourself these questions:

- Are you thoroughly comfortable with Word and its editing techniques? If so, you'll find it easy to begin creating Web pages, and you'll be able to use Word's familiar editing tools, including AutoCorrect and AutoText.
- What kind of page are you trying to create? If your pages will contain simple text, graphics, and hyperlinks, Word is up to the challenge. If you need to use advanced features, such as *scripts* and *dynamic HTML*, you'll need to use a more advanced program, such as FrontPage 2000.
- Will you need to add and remove pages from the site regularly? Creating new Web pages in Word and linking them to existing pages can become tedious if you have to do it often. Word is fine for sites in which you plan to update the content on a fixed number of pages, but FrontPage is a better choice if you expect your site to grow and change over time.
- Are you responsible for managing a Web site, either on your company's intranet or with an Internet service provider? FrontPage has superb tools for managing graphics, tracing and fixing broken hyperlinks, and keeping track of pages that need additional work. If you need to coordinate Web pages produced by several people, you'll be frustrated by Word's stripped-down capabilities. If you are charged with managing a Web site, I recommend that you upgrade to the Premium Edition of Office, which includes FrontPage 2000.

SEE ALSO

➤ *For an overview of how you can use each Office program (including FrontPage) to create Web pages, see page 56*

Word 2000 includes a handful of useful *templates* and a wizard that walks you through the process of creating a Web page. With Word's help, you can create reasonably sophisticated Web pages in a short period of time. You don't need to start from scratch to create a Web page, either; if you've already created a Word document, you can save it as a Web page with a single menu choice.

"Borrow" Web page designs

If you see a Web page and you like its overall design, it's perfectly okay to borrow that design. You can open any existing Web page in Word and replace its text and graphics with your own words and pictures. Avoid the temptation to steal copyrighted images, however. It's easy to copy a graphic image from another site and use it on your own page, but that doesn't make it right or legal.

Designing Documents for the Web

The only real rule of Web page design is that there are no rules. If you surf the Web long enough, you'll see an astonishing array of designs, ranging from the dullest of plain text displays (every word in 12-point Courier) to outrageous color combinations (pink on chartreuse, anyone?). As in printed designs, your audience and your message should dictate your design. A Web site for a traditional corporation should stick with simple typefaces and colors, for example. On the other hand, a dull design would never do if your target audience is young and hip; in that case, it's perfectly okay to add some jarring, edgy fonts, colors, and other design elements.

If neither your audience nor your message demands an out-of-the-ordinary design treatment, your main goal should be to make your pages easy to read. To that end, I recommend you observe the following basic principles of graphic design:

- Make sure the text contrasts with the background. The most readable combination is dark text on a cool, light background. Avoid plain white backgrounds, which tend to cause eyestrain. Also avoid colors that are too bright—red and yellow are especially glaring.
- Use subheads to break up large blocks of text and help readers find information quickly. Readers confronted with a wall of dense text may decide it's too much work and not even try to read your carefully selected words.
- Avoid long lines of text. When text stretches from one side of the page to the other, it can be visually tiring for readers, because they don't have a resting spot for their eyes.

Light on dark?

Experienced graphic designers know that white text on a dark background can be an effective way to draw attention to a small amount of text. Avoid using this format for an entire page, and make the font size at least 1 point larger than you would use if you were displaying the same text in black on a light background.

- If you're creating several related pages, use similar layouts and graphic elements on all of them. A consistent graphic design should place frames, headings, and visuals in the same place on each page. Stay away from ransom-note typography, too—choose two complementary fonts, one for headings and another for backgrounds, and stick with them.
- Use graphics sparingly. Your page doesn't have to be visually dull, but overloading a page with gimmicky, gratuitous graphics makes it hard to figure out which pieces are important. If you're publishing a page on a Web server where you expect other people to connect over dial-up connections, big graphics take a long time to download and can annoy your audience.

Does your audience have the same fonts?

Unusual fonts can add pizzazz to printed documents, but they rarely work on Web pages. To be safe, stick with the fonts included with Windows and Internet Explorer–Arial, Times New Roman, Impact, Comic Sans, and Tahoma are always safe choices.

Getting Started with the Web Page Wizard

If any of the wizards in Word 2000 deserves an award for "most improved," the Web Page Wizard is it. In fact, this wizard's name is misleading—by following the wizard's prompts, you can create an entire Web site with a default page that contains hyperlinks to all other pages you create. Choose from a variety of formats, with a consistent set of fonts and graphics based on themes. Like other templates that include dummy content, you'll need to replace the text and graphics after you create your pages using the Web Page Wizard.

Before you begin using the Web Page Wizard, it's a good idea to sketch out the basic structure of your new Web site. What do you want your home page to look like? Do you want other pages linked from this one? If so, what sort of basic design do you want for each linked page? For example, if you're putting together a set of pages to show off products at your small business, you might want to use the home page to list each product category, then create a separate page for each of those categories, plus one more page to include answers to frequently asked questions.

Using the Web Page Wizard

1. Pull down the **File** menu and choose **New**.
2. Select the **Web Pages** tab on the New dialog box and double-click the **Web Page Wizard**.
3. Click the **Next** button to move past the introductory text and view the first step of the wizard. In the **Web site title** box, enter a name for your new Web site. By default, the wizard uses the name you specify here to create a new folder in your My Documents folder.
4. Click **Next** to choose a navigation style for your default page. In the dialog box for this step (shown in Figure 16.1), the wizard asks whether you want to add a *frame* to your default page or create a separate page with links to your other pages.

Use the default location

Resist the temptation to change the location specified in the first step of the Web Page Wizard unless you're certain of the consequences. The default setting organizes all your new pages in one folder; after you finish with the wizard, you can easily move this folder to a new location.

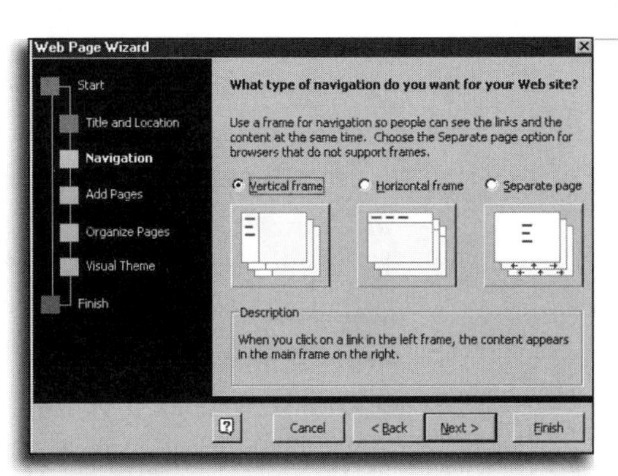

FIGURE 16.1
When using Word's Web Page Wizard to build a simple Web site, you can choose from two frame styles for your opening page.

- **Vertical frame** is your best choice if you're planning to add more than three or four pages to your Web site. In this design, all the linked pages appear in a navigation bar at the left of the page; when the user clicks one of the links in this frame, the page appears to its right. The vertical bar generally remains unchanged regardless of what page is shown in the main browser window.
- **Horizontal frame** is the right choice if your Web site is simple—with no more than three or four linked pages. In this design, the pages that appear when the

Not sure where to put that frame?

If you make the right decision about where to place a frame now, the Web Page Wizard will take care of a lot of tedious formatting for you. If you change your mind later, however, don't despair–you can always add a new navigation frame to your default page, then move the navigation links from the current frame to the new one, and finally delete the old frame. You'll need to do some shuffling to arrange the hyperlinks properly if you switch from a left frame to a top frame, but it's not all that difficult.

When in doubt, add extra pages

If you're not sure what you're going to do with your Web site, toss in a handful of extra blank pages. It's easier to delete links from your default page than it is to add pages later.

user clicks a link are easier to read because they use the browser's full width. As with the vertical frame, the horizontal frame generally remains unchanged regardless of what page is shown in the main browser window.

- **Separate page** uses no frames at all. This design is appropriate if you expect that anyone who reads your default page will want to choose only one of your linked pages. If you think users will want to explore several pages, use a frame instead, to make navigating easier.

5. Click **Next** to choose your lineup of pages. If you thought about this before you started, you can make short work of this step. The default page lineup consists of a Personal Web Page and two blank pages, but the choices in this dialog box give you many more options. You can add more blank pages, choose from specific page templates, or import Web pages you've already created. If you make a mistake (or if you want to remove the default pages), select an entry from the list and click the **Remove Page** button.
   - **Add New Blank Page** creates a new page with absolutely nothing on it, and adds a hyperlink on the default page.
   - **Add Template Page** shows the Web Page Templates dialog box, which lets you add one of Word's ready-made Web page designs to your site. When you make a selection by clicking the name of a template in the list, you can see what that type of page looks like in the Word window behind the dialog box, as shown in Figure 16.2.
   - **Add Existing File** lets you browse for pages you've already created and add them to your new Web site. If you've already saved a collection of Word documents, Excel workbooks, or PowerPoint presentations in Web format, you can add them here, along with a Table of Contents page to make it easy for other people to open them by clicking a hyperlink.

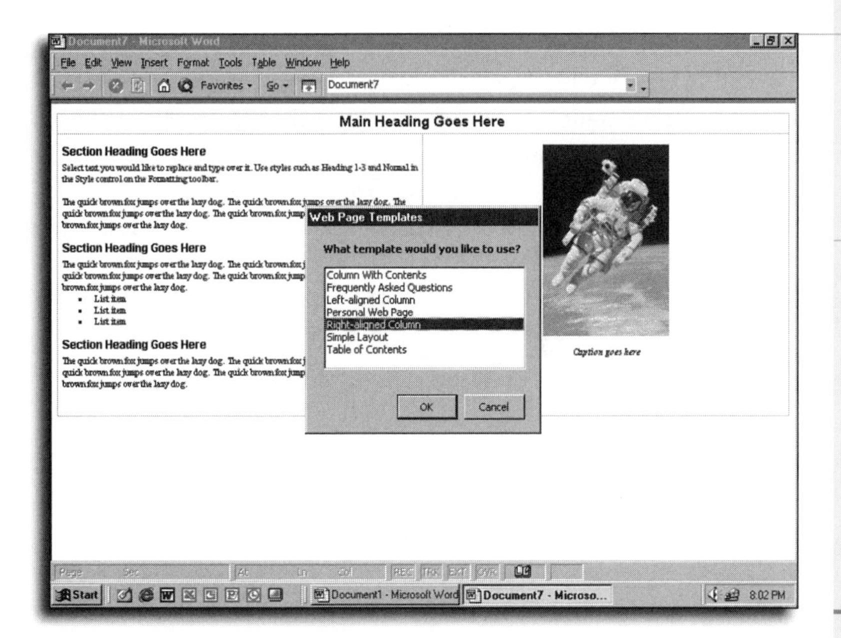

FIGURE 16.2

The templates available from this dialog box include dummy text and graphics that you'll need to replace. The Word window shows a full-sized preview of each page.

6. Click **Next** to specify the order of pages in your site and give each page a title. Select any page and use the **Move Up** and **Move Down** buttons to change the order in which it appears in the navigation frame. By default, each page has a dull generic name, like `Personal Web Page` or `Left-aligned Column 3`; select each page in turn, click the **Rename** button, and enter a more descriptive name. When you're finished, the dialog box should look something like the one in Figure 16.3.

Trouble opening a file?

If you try to add an existing file to your Web site but find that the page opens in Excel, PowerPoint, or FrontPage instead, try this trick: Click the **Add Existing File** button to open a Browse window, then select the name of the file you want to add and right-click. From the shortcut menu, choose **Open in Microsoft Word**.

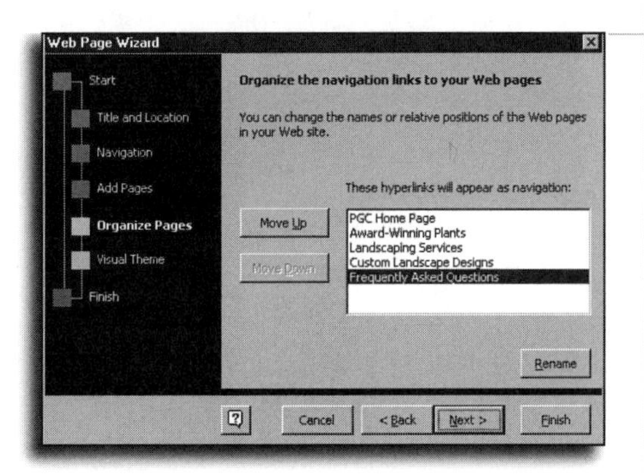

FIGURE 16.3

Change the names of pages in your new Web site from their dull defaults to descriptive titles that make it easy to fill in content later.

7. Click **Next** to display the final step of the Web Page Wizard, which lets you choose a *theme* to give your Web site a consistent look. If you want to add a theme, click the **Browse Themes** button to display the dialog box shown in Figure 16.4. As you can see from this example, themes consist of fonts, bullets, backgrounds, and color schemes. Select a theme and click **OK**.

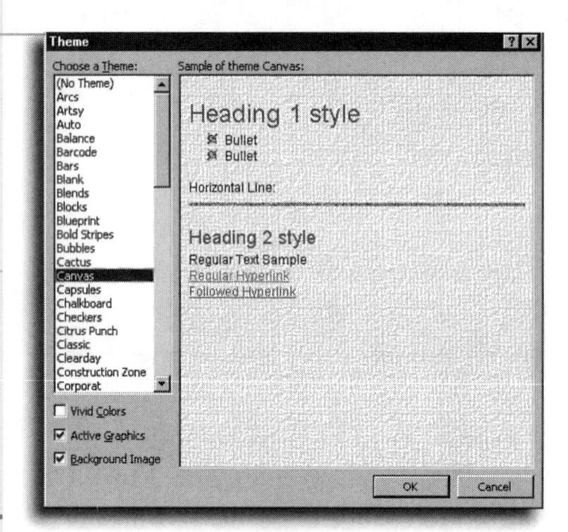

FIGURE 16.4

Choosing a theme replaces the harsh white background and default fonts with the colors and graphics shown in this preview window.

Put the default page at the top

The page at the top of the list will always be your home page; choose this page carefully, because it's more trouble than it's worth to change this page after you finish with the Web Page Wizard. The order you specify for other pages determines in what order the hyperlinks appear on the home page. After you create your Web site, you can change the order of these links just by dragging them around on the default page.

Did you forget a page?

While using the Web Page Wizard, you can click the **Back** button at any time to rerun an earlier step. Use this option to add or remove pages, for example, especially if you decide that you didn't add enough pages to your site. Going back doesn't undo any of your other changes.

8. Click **Finish** to save all the pages you've created in the location you specified in step 3. Word loads and saves each page, then finishes by loading the new Default.htm page, ready for you to begin editing.

SEE ALSO

➤ *For more details about how Office saves Web pages, see page 57*
➤ *To publish your pages to a Web server using Web Folders, see page 57*

After running the Web Page Wizard, you can begin editing your new Web site instantly. Figure 16.5 shows what the default page might look like. Select the dummy text and placeholder graphics on this page and replace them with your own text, pictures, and drawings. To edit other pages in your site, click the hyperlinks.

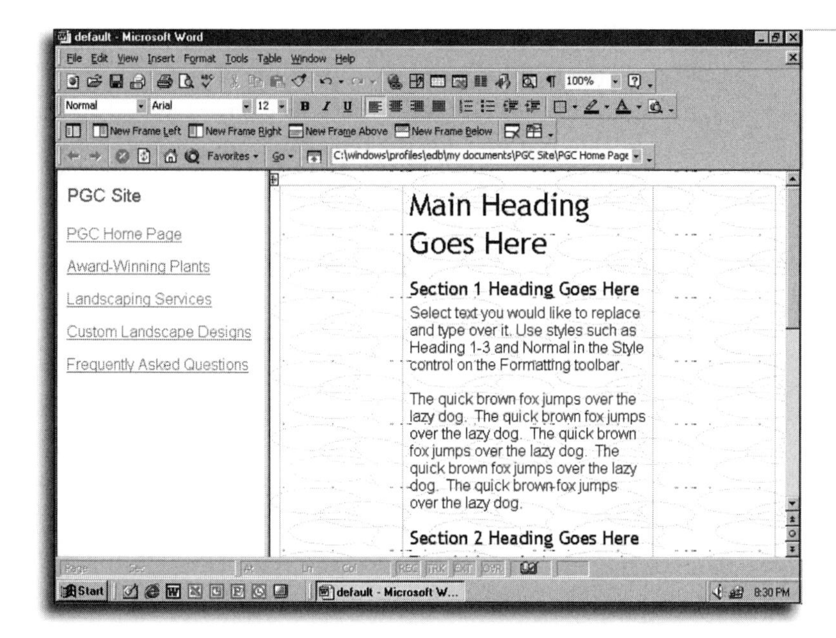

FIGURE 16.5
Replace the dummy text and pictures in these template pages with the real text and graphics you want to appear in your Web site.

Adding a Page to an Existing Web Site

Although the Web Page Wizard is a wonderful way to get started, it has one serious limitation. After you create your Web site, you can't use the wizard to go back and add new pages. It's possible to use the wizard to create a new Web site, then import pages from your existing site—but it's usually less effort to create a new page from scratch and then link it to the default page for your site.

To create a simple Web page, skip the Web Page Wizard and use any of Word's ready-made Web templates; to add a Word document or Excel workbook to your site, save it as a Web page. In either case, make sure to save it in the same folder as your existing Web site.

Keep it simple

Feel free to delete items you don't need from your new Web site, but avoid the temptation to do too much manual formatting on individual pages. In general, you should stick with the fonts and colors from the theme you selected to ensure that your new site has a consistent look.

Adding a New Web Page to a Site

1. Pull down the **File** menu, choose **New**, and click the **Web Pages** tab on the New dialog box.
2. Select one of the ready-made Web pages (the list is the same as the options available in the Web Page Wizard) and click **OK**.
3. Change the text and graphics on the page if you want, then pull down the **Format** menu, choose **Theme**, and select the same theme you used for the rest of the site. Click **OK** to save your choice.
4. Pull down the **File** menu and choose **Save**. Click the **Change Title** button, if necessary, and give the page a descriptive title. Enter a filename for your new page, choose the folder that contains your Web site, and click **Save**.
5. From the **File** menu, choose **Open** and select the default page (Default.htm) from the folder that contains your Web site. Click to position the insertion point where you want to add a hyperlink to the page you just created. (You may need to press the Enter key once or twice to add enough space.)
6. Type the text you want to use for your new hyperlink and select it, then click the **Insert Hyperlink** button .
7. In the Insert Hyperlink dialog box (see Figure 16.6), click **Recent Files** and choose the Web page you just created from the top of the list. Click **OK** to create the hyperlink.
8. Save your default page.

Or drag and drop...

If you don't want to mess with dialog boxes, you can drag a file onto your Web page and create a hyperlink. Just remember to drag with the right mouse button, then choose **Create Hyperlink Here** from the shortcut menu that appears when you release the mouse button. To edit the text that appears on your page, right-click and choose **Hyperlink**; then click **Edit Hyperlink** and add your text in the **Text to display** box.

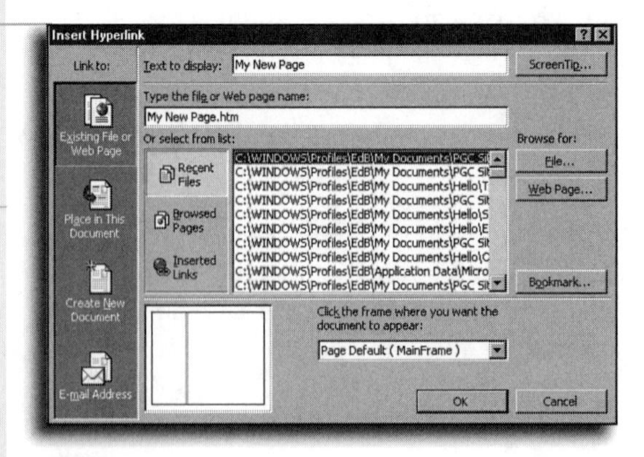

FIGURE 16.6

Use this dialog box to create a hyperlink to a new page on your site.

SEE ALSO

For more details on how to use hyperlinks in Word and other Office programs, see page 64

Editing Web Pages in Word

With a few exceptions, anything you can put in a Word document will work on a Web page as well, and you can use all of Word's editing tools and techniques to work with Web pages. A handful of features won't work at all—for example, if you break a section into two columns, it will display in columns inside the Word window, but when you view the page in a browser you'll see one very wide column. (Don't despair—there is a clever solution that lets you create the illusion of columns on a Web page, as I'll explain shortly.) Most of the other incompatibilities affect odd character-formatting options, such as embossed text, or floating objects, such as drawings and pictures. To read a full list of the incompatibilities you might encounter when saving a Word document as a Web page, ask the Office Assistant to display the Help topic "What happens when I save a document as a Web page?"

Changing the Appearance of Text

To change the format of text in a Web page, use the exact same techniques you use with other types of Word documents. Just like a memo or report, you can mix direct formatting, character styles, and paragraph styles. For example, you can format headings using the Heading 1, Heading 2, and Heading 3 styles. To change the color of text, select a word, phrase, or entire paragraph, then click the arrow to the right of the **Font Color** button, and choose the color you want to use from the palette.

To change the font of selected text, use the **Font** and **Font Size** controls on the Formatting toolbar. For more options, pull down the **Format** menu and select **Font** (or right-click the selected text and choose **Font** from the shortcut menu). Some font options are not available when you work with Web pages:

When in doubt, preview!

Word (like all Office programs) includes a menu choice that is indispensable when you're creating and editing Web pages. Pull down the **File** menu and choose **Web Page Preview** when you want to quickly check what your page will look like in a browser. If the results aren't what you expect, change the formatting and try again.

For example, as Figure 16.7 shows, you can't use special effects such as emboss, shadow, and engrave, because they don't have HTML equivalents.

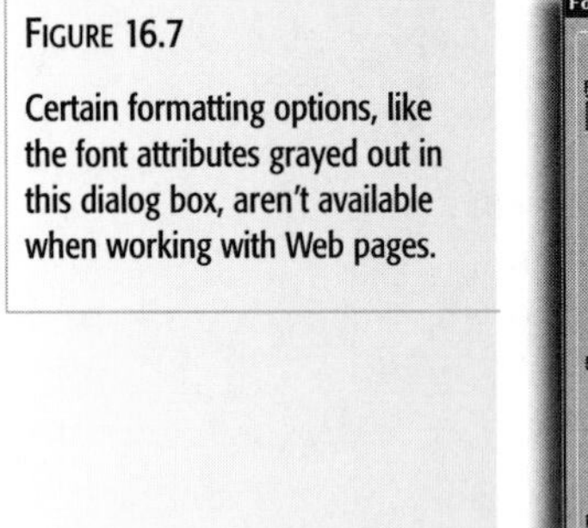

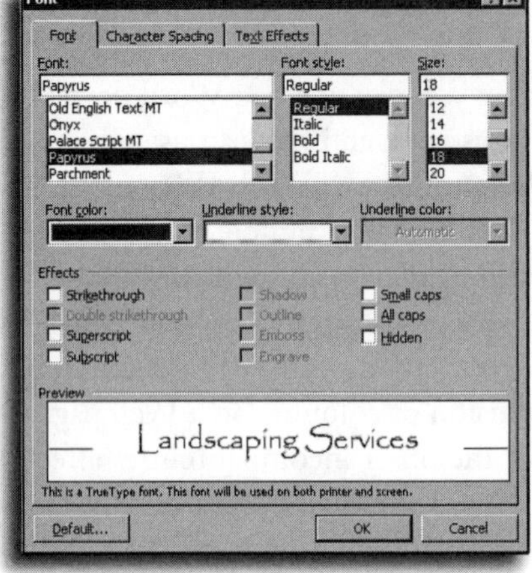

FIGURE 16.7

Certain formatting options, like the font attributes grayed out in this dialog box, aren't available when working with Web pages.

Subdividing Web Pages with Frames

Word warns you when formats won't work

What happens if you create a normal Word document that uses formatting not available in Web pages? When you choose the option to save your document as a Web page, Word displays a dialog box that tells you exactly which formatting will be changed.

The Web Page Wizard offers an easy way to create a default page with frames for navigation. You can also add frames to any Web page and use them for a variety of purposes. When you want to work with frames, I highly recommend that you use the Frames toolbar. If this toolbar isn't visible, right-click any toolbar or the main menu bar and choose **Frames** from the pop-up list.

Using buttons on the Frames toolbar, you can add a new frame on the top, bottom, left, or right side of a page. To get rid of a frame on an existing page, click the **Delete Frame** button.

The Frame Properties dialog box lets you change the way a particular frame looks and acts. For example, by default Word does not add a line between the frame itself and other sections of the page. But if you click the **Frame Properties** button, and then click the **Borders** tab, you see the dialog box shown in Figure 16.8. Using these options, you can make the line between frames visible, change its thickness and color, and specify whether you want anyone viewing the page in a browser to be able to change the width of the frame. This option is especially useful for users running at low display resolutions that want to be able to see more of the main page in the browser window.

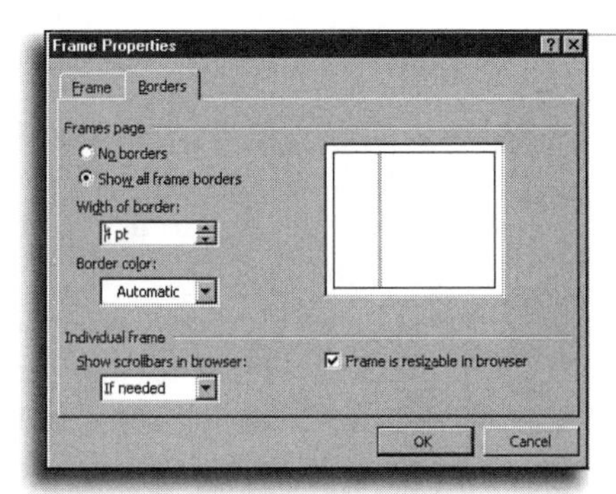

FIGURE 16.8
Choose these options to display a line between frames and allow anyone viewing the page to re-size the frame.

Arranging Text and Graphics on a Web Page

When laying out text and graphics on Web pages, your secret weapons are *tables* and *text boxes*. Using either of these tools, you can arrange items exactly as you want them. Tables are especially helpful when you want to align text and graphics, which can be tricky on a page you plan to save for use on the Web.

As I noted earlier, for example, you can't add columns to a Web page, but you can insert a table to create a column-like effect. (If you look carefully at most of the templates created by the Web Page Wizard, you'll see that they typically include a table.)

To insert a table on your Web page, use any of the standard Word procedures. For example, you can use the **Insert Table** button to add a table with standard widths, or click the **Tables and Borders** button to use the more powerful table drawing tools.

SEE ALSO

➤ *For full instructions on how to create and format tables, see page 270*

Where should your frame go?

Generally, frames at the top of a page contain information about the site itself, such as your company name or logo. The advantage of using a frame in this location is that the logo never disappears, even when the user is scrolling through a long page. Frames on the left are typically used for navigation. Frames at the bottom of a page are best for small navigation shortcuts, especially buttons that return you to the home page or to the top of the page. It's extremely rare to see a frame on the right side of a page.

Gridlines and borders

You can display or hide the gridlines on a table by choosing the **Table** menu and then selecting **Show Gridlines** or **Hide Gridlines**. This menu choice only affects the editing window; when you view the page in a browser, gridlines are never visible. If you want your table to have borders, right-click in any cell, choose **Borders and Shading** from the shortcut menu, and click the **Page Border** tab.

A text box is a container for text and graphics. When you add a text box to a Web page, you can resize it and position it anywhere you want. To add a text box to a page, click the **Text Box** button on the Drawing toolbar and drag the box to the position where you want it to appear (after you create the text box, you can drag it to another location if you prefer).

One of the most effective ways to position graphics on a page is to insert pictures in table cells or text boxes. Word automatically resizes the table cell to fit the picture, and by dragging the sizing handle in the lower-right corner of each image you can make sure each one is exactly the same width. To insert a picture, click to position the insertion point in the table cell or text box where you want to add the picture, then pull down the **Insert** menu and choose **Picture**. Select the source of the picture—a file, for example, or a scanner—and Word does the rest.

The example page in Figure 16.9 shows a simple two-column table that includes graphics in the cells on the left, with corresponding text in the cells on the right. This sort of table is especially effective for price lists.

FIGURE 16.9

Insert pictures into table cells to position them precisely on the page.

Inserting Lines

Adding lines to your Web page can help you organize information and make it more visually appealing. Horizontal lines also help to set off sections of a page.

Inserting a Horizontal Line

1. Click to position the insertion point where you want to add the line.
2. Pull down the **Format** menu and choose **Borders and Shading**; click the **Borders** tab, and then click the **Horizontal Line** button.
3. The Clip Gallery opens, showing the choices of lines available to you, as shown in Figure 16.10. Scroll through the list until you find one you like, and then click to display the Clip Gallery shortcut menu and choose **Insert Clip**.

Use hyperlinks in a table

You can add hyperlinks to text or graphics in a table as you would any other text or graphics on a Web page. This technique can be useful if you want to create a navigation bar using pictures instead of text. Create a one-column table with one row for every picture you want to insert, add pictures to each cell, then click each picture in turn and use the **Insert Hyperlink** button to link the picture to another page.

Use themes to format a line

When you use themes to apply a design to a Web page, Word includes a line design as part of the package. If you've inserted a different line, pull down the **Format** menu, choose **Theme**, and reapply the theme you selected earlier. Word automatically changes the line you just inserted.

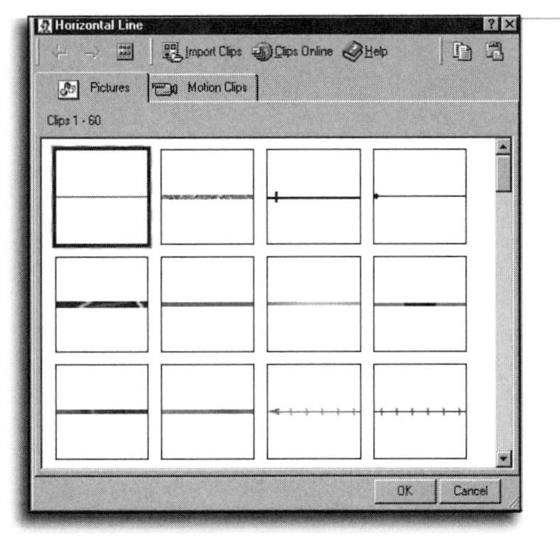

FIGURE 16.10
Use a line to help organize the content on your Web page.

PART III

Using Excel 2000

CHAPTER

17

Getting Started with Excel

- Enter numbers, text, and dates
- Find and replace data
- Select and work with ranges of data
- Let Excel automatically fill in dates, numbers, and more
- Move from cell to cell
- Learn how rows, columns, and cell addresses work
- Resize and rearrange worksheet windows
- Work with multiple worksheets and workbooks

Working with Worksheets and Workbooks

Get ideas from sample worksheets

Unlike Word and PowerPoint, which are packed with sample documents and presentations, Excel offers few ways to get started. When you dig into Excel's Setup options, you find prebuilt invoice, purchase order, and expense report templates. You'll find additional templates on Microsoft's Web site; open Excel's **Help** menu, choose **Office on the Web**, and search for templates.

The basic building block of Excel is the worksheet—a two-dimensional grid whose rows and columns define individual cells. Within each cell you can enter numbers, text, date and time information, or references to other cells. Most importantly, cells can contain mathematical and logical formulas that calculate and display results based on data you enter. Formulas in a worksheet can draw from Excel's enormous library of built-in *functions* to perform everything from elementary arithmetic to sophisticated number-crunching, including statistical and financial analysis. To visually explain the relationship between numbers, you can also display data in an Excel worksheet as a chart.

A well-designed worksheet can be as simple as a list of names or checkbook transactions, or as complex as the financial model for a major multinational corporation. In either case, you begin with a blank sheet.

Excel closes Book1 if you don't use it

If you start Excel by opening a saved worksheet, Excel skips the step of creating a new blank workbook. Likewise, if you launch Excel and immediately open a saved worksheet, Excel closes the blank Book1 workbook.

When you start Excel by using its shortcut on the **Start** menu, the program automatically opens a new, blank Excel workbook with the temporary name Book1. To create another new workbook, click the **New** button, or use the keyboard shortcut Ctrl+N. Each new workbook gets a similar generic name—Book2, Book3, and so on.

When you save a worksheet, you actually save it in an Excel workbook, which can hold multiple worksheets. By default, each new Excel workbook starts out with three blank worksheets; you can add new worksheets, delete an existing one, and rename or rearrange worksheets to suit your needs.

An index tab at the bottom of each worksheet identifies the sheet by name. When you open a new workbook, each sheet has a generic name: Sheet1, Sheet2, Sheet3, and so on. Later in this chapter, I'll explain how to change the label on each tab to be more descriptive.

SEE ALSO

➤ *To find detailed explanations of how to use formulas and functions, see page 363*
➤ *For instructions on how to transform worksheet data into charts, see page 443*

Working with Cells and Cell Addresses

Each worksheet consists of 256 columns and 65,536 rows. Gridlines separate rows and columns, and at the intersection of each row and column is a cell. Most worksheets use only a fraction of the 16,777,216 available cells (256×65,536).

Each cell has a unique cell address, formed by combining the column heading and the row heading. Because Excel uses letters to identify columns and numbers for rows, the top-left cell in the worksheet is A1.

When you open a new worksheet, A1 is the active cell. If you start typing, you begin entering data in that cell. To make another cell active, point to it and click, or use the arrow keys to move there.

As you move around in a worksheet, you can always identify the active cell by the dark box that encloses it; if you've selected a range of cells, the active cell is the one light-colored cell in an otherwise dark selection. The address of the active cell appears in the Name box at the left of the Formatting toolbar, as in the example in Figure 17.1.

Spreadsheet, worksheet–no difference

Is it a *worksheet* or a *spreadsheet*? There's no difference, really. Excel refers to each two-dimensional collection of rows and columns as a *worksheet* (often abbreviated to just *sheet*); Lotus 1-2-3 users are accustomed to referring to these building blocks as *spreadsheets*. Lotus users may also be used to the terms *notebook* and *page*; in Excel, these elements are known as *workbooks* and *worksheets*.

After Z comes AA...

How does Excel identify columns after all 26 letters in the alphabet are used? By switching to double letters: AA, AB, AC, and so on, to AZ. Next comes BA, BB, BC, and so on. The last column in every Excel worksheet is IV; although it looks like the Roman numeral 4, it's really just the last entry in the sequence that begins after HZ, with IA, IB, and IC.

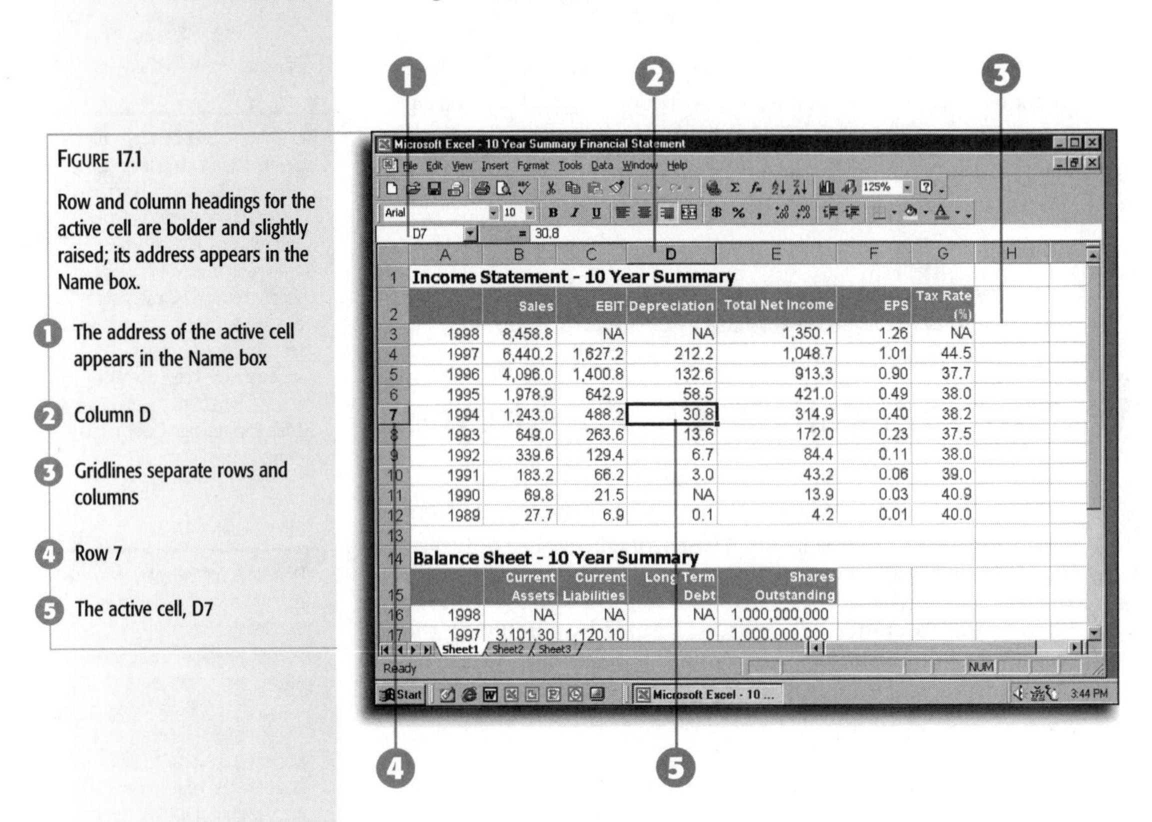

FIGURE 17.1

Row and column headings for the active cell are bolder and slightly raised; its address appears in the Name box.

1. The address of the active cell appears in the Name box
2. Column D
3. Gridlines separate rows and columns
4. Row 7
5. The active cell, D7

Entering and Editing Data

Should you edit in the cell or the formula bar?

You can click in the formula bar to begin entering data in the active cell, or you can click in the cell itself; the contents are identical regardless of which option you choose. Most people find it easier to enter and edit text and numbers directly in the cell. Use the Formula bar for long text items and mathematical equations or formulas, especially if you expect you'll need to use Excel's online help.

Entering data in a cell is easy: Use the mouse or the arrow keys to make the cell active, and then begin typing. Whatever you type appears in two places simultaneously: in the cell itself and in the Formula bar, just above the column headings.

As soon as you begin typing, two small boxes—a red X and a green check mark—appear to the left of the Formula bar. Depending on where you've chosen to begin entering data, a blinking insertion point, just like the ones in Word and PowerPoint, appears in the Formula bar or in the cell, as in the example in Figure 17.2.

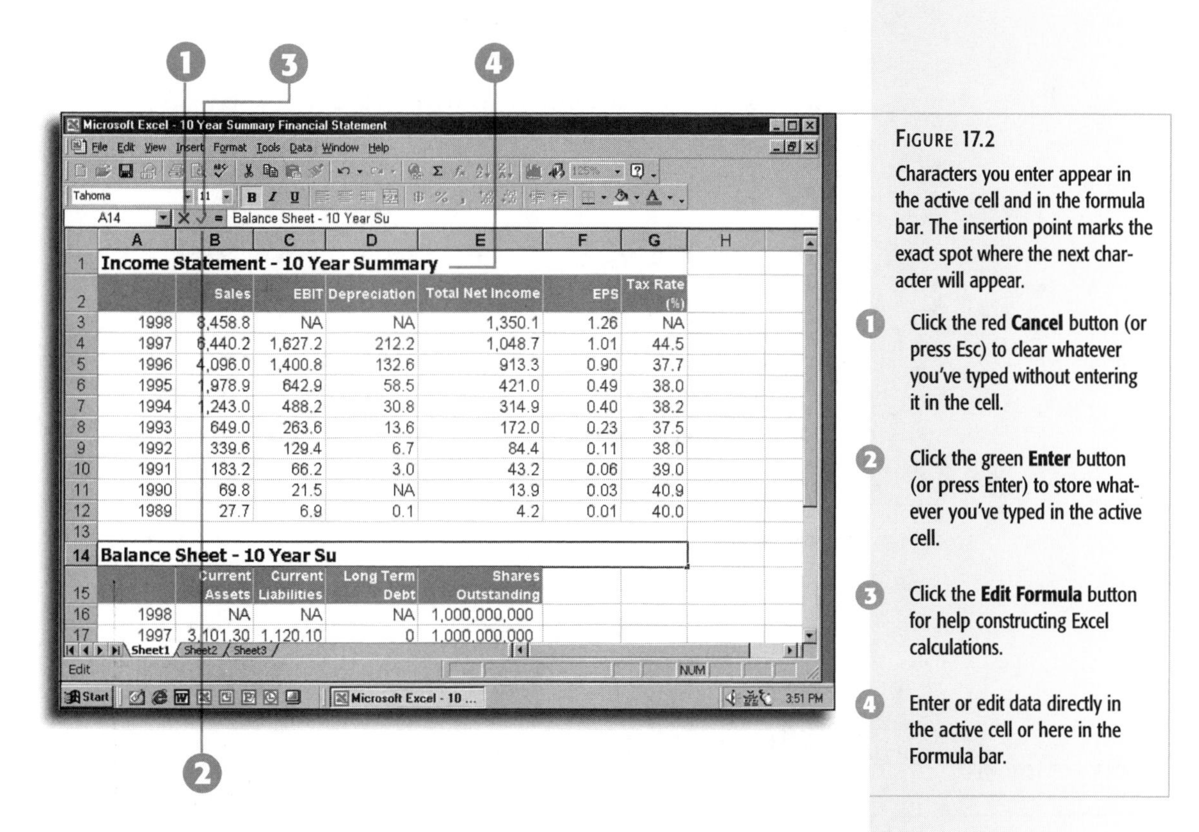

FIGURE 17.2

Characters you enter appear in the active cell and in the formula bar. The insertion point marks the exact spot where the next character will appear.

1. Click the red **Cancel** button (or press Esc) to clear whatever you've typed without entering it in the cell.
2. Click the green **Enter** button (or press Enter) to store whatever you've typed in the active cell.
3. Click the **Edit Formula** button for help constructing Excel calculations.
4. Enter or edit data directly in the active cell or here in the Formula bar.

If you hit the wrong key while you're typing, press Backspace to fix your mistake. To cancel whatever you've typed, press Esc. Are you entering a lengthy series of text items in a column? Press Enter to insert the data in the active cell and move down to the next cell in that column. Or press the right arrow key to record the entry in the cell and move one cell to the right.

When you enter data into a cell, Excel automatically formats it using the rules shown in Table 17.1.

TABLE 17.1 **How Excel Formats Data**

When You Enter This Type of Data	Excel Formats It As	Examples
Numbers only	Number (including percentage and currency signs)	42 $999.95 34.8%
Letters only, or a combination of letters and numbers	Text	Travel Expenses 12 #10 Envelopes 5% Discount
Anything that looks like a date or time	Date/Time	5/23/99 3:30 AM April 15
Anything beginning with an equal sign	Formula	=2+2 =F124*.0825 =SUM(D4:D15)

SEE ALSO

➤ *For more information on how to enter and edit formulas, see page 364*

Editing a Cell's Contents

Forcing a number to display as text

Excel's automatic formatting can cause unintended consequences when you enter ambiguous data. For example, if I'm building a worksheet that includes odds for this year's Kentucky Derby contenders, I might enter **8/5** in one cell. When I do, however, Excel interprets the entry as a date and converts it to the date code for August 5 of the current year. To force Excel to display the number as typed, enter an equal sign and enclose it in quotation marks: **="8/5"**. Or enter the value 1-2-3 style by starting with an apostrophe: **'8/5**.

To edit the contents of a cell, use one of the following techniques:

- Double-click on the cell and move the insertion point to the place where you want to add or edit characters.

  OR

  Click to make the cell active. Then click in the Formula bar and position the insertion point for editing.
- To select characters within a cell, double-click in the cell, position the insertion point at one side of the characters you want to select, and then drag to make the selection.
- To select a word within a cell, double-click in the cell and then double-click the word. (This technique also works with cell references, numbers, and other entries that aren't, strictly speaking, words.)

- To edit one or two characters within a cell, double-click on the cell and then click to position the insertion point at the place in the text where you want to make a change. Use the Backspace or Del keys to clear the characters, type the correct contents, and press Enter.
- To clear (erase) the contents of a cell, select the cell and then press the Del key.
- To replace the contents of a cell completely, click on the cell to make it active, type the new contents, and press Enter.

Finding and Replacing Data

Excel's search-and-replace features work with both text and numbers, but they're most useful in lists. Press Ctrl+F (or pull down the **Edit** menu and choose **Find**) to open an easy-to-use dialog box that lets you search the current worksheet for text or numbers. You can also replace one string of text or numbers with another. If you use an Excel worksheet to maintain a list of names and phone numbers, for example, how do you update a group of phone numbers all at once when the area code changes from 818 to 626? The procedure is nearly the same as in Word or PowerPoint, although there are a few Excel-specific options.

Replacing Cell Contents in a Worksheet

1. Choose the **Edit** menu and select **Replace** (or press Ctrl+H) to open the dialog box shown in Figure 17.3.
2. Type the cell content that you want to replace (`818`, in this example) in the **Find what** box and press Tab (not Enter) to move to the **Replace with** box.
3. Type the content with which you want to do the replacing (`626`, in this example) in the **Replace with** box. (Don't press the Enter key.)
4. If necessary, clear the check mark from the box labeled **Find entire cells only**. With this option checked, Excel won't find the area code you're looking for if it's embedded in a phone number like 818-555-1234.

Warning: Don't use the Spacebar to clear a cell

Beginning Excel users often try to clear the contents of a cell by pressing the Spacebar. Although that action appears to have the desired effect, it actually replaces the cell's contents with a space character. If you calculate averages or counts, the space causes Excel to display the wrong result. To clear the contents of a cell properly, select the cell and press the Del key, or right-click and choose **Clear Contents**.

Use the Undo button to recover from data disasters

Have you inadvertently deleted the contents of a cell or range? Take a deep breath and then click the **Undo** button or press Ctrl+Z. Most of the time, this action brings back the data you accidentally wiped out. If you've performed several tasks in the meantime, click the **Undo** button repeatedly to "roll back" your changes. Don't wait too long, though; unlike Word, which stores an unlimited number of changes, Excel can undo only the 16 most recent actions.

5. Click **Find Next** to search through your list for the next record containing the value you entered. Normally, Excel searches from right to left and top to bottom; hold down the Shift key and click **Find Next** to search in reverse order.
6. Click **Replace** to change the value in the selected cell and move to the next matching record, or click **Find Next** to move to the next match without making a change. To change every instance without being asked for confirmation, click **Replace All**.
7. If you used the **Replace All** option, the dialog box closes automatically. Otherwise, click **Close** to exit the Replace dialog box.

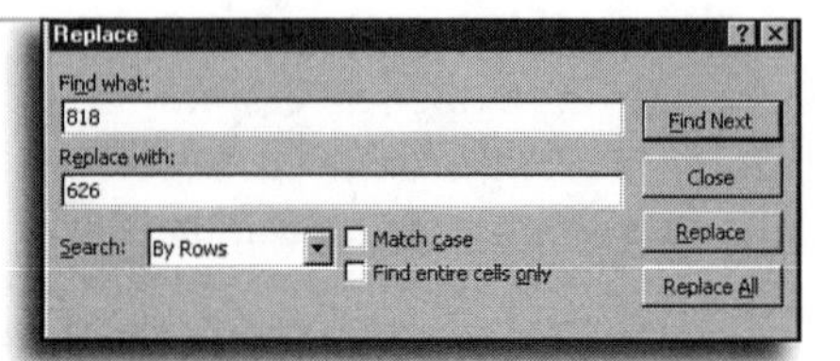

FIGURE 17.3

If you want to replace values in only a small portion of your list, select that range before you open this dialog box.

Pay attention as Excel works

Search-and-replace operations can have unintended consequences. For example, if you ask Excel to replace all instances of 818 with 626 in your name-and-address list, you fix all phone numbers that begin with 818, but you also change the zip code 81850 and the phone number 555-8181 (because both of these examples contain 818). If you have this problem, immediately click the **Undo** button and try again. Scrolling through your worksheet immediately after executing a search-and-replace action is always a good idea; if you see unexpected results, you don't risk losing data. Even better, make a backup copy of your worksheet under a new name before you make wholesale changes.

Working with More Than One Cell at a Time

Instead of entering, editing, and formatting data in one cell, you can select a group of cells to work with all at once. Any selection of two or more cells is called a range, and you can dramatically increase your productivity by using ranges to enter, edit, and format data. For example, if you highlight a range and click the **Currency Style** button, all the numeric entries in that range appear with dollar signs and two decimal places. You can even create a descriptive name (like Totals) for a range and then use that name to make formulas and cell references easier to understand.

The most common way to select multiple cells is to highlight a contiguous range. In this type of selection, all cells are next to one another; by definition, a contiguous range is always rectangular. If a range is 3 cells deep and 4 cells wide, for example, it contains 12 cells. But cells in a range don't have to be contiguous. You can also define a perfectly legal range by selecting individual cells or groups of cells scattered around the worksheet.

Excel uses two addresses to identify a contiguous range, beginning with the cell in the upper-left corner and ending with the cell in the lower-right corner of the selection. A colon (:) separates the two addresses that identify the range. For example, the range A1:F27 would refer to an area of your worksheet starting at the upper left with cell A1 and working its way downward and to the right to cell F27.

SEE ALSO

- *To learn how you can change the way cells appear, see page 387*
- *To learn how to apply names to cells and ranges, see page 378*

Selecting Ranges

As you'll discover in later chapters, selecting a range is a crucial first step for a variety of actions, including sending a worksheet to a printer and creating or editing a chart. To select a range, use any of the techniques described in Table 17.2:

TABLE 17.2 **Selecting a Range**

To Select	Use This Technique
A contiguous range	Click the cell at one corner of the range and drag the mouse pointer to the opposite corner.
A noncontiguous range	Select the first cell or group of cells, hold down the Ctrl key, and select the next cell or group of cells; continue holding the Ctrl key until you've selected all the cells in the range.
An entire row or column	Click the row or column heading (see Figure 17.4).
Multiple adjacent rows or columns	Select the first row or column, and hold down the mouse button while dragging through the rest.
Multiple nonadjacent rows or columns	Select the first row or column, hold down the Ctrl key, and select additional rows or columns.
All cells in the current worksheet	Click the Select All button in the upper-left corner of the worksheet (see Figure 17.4).

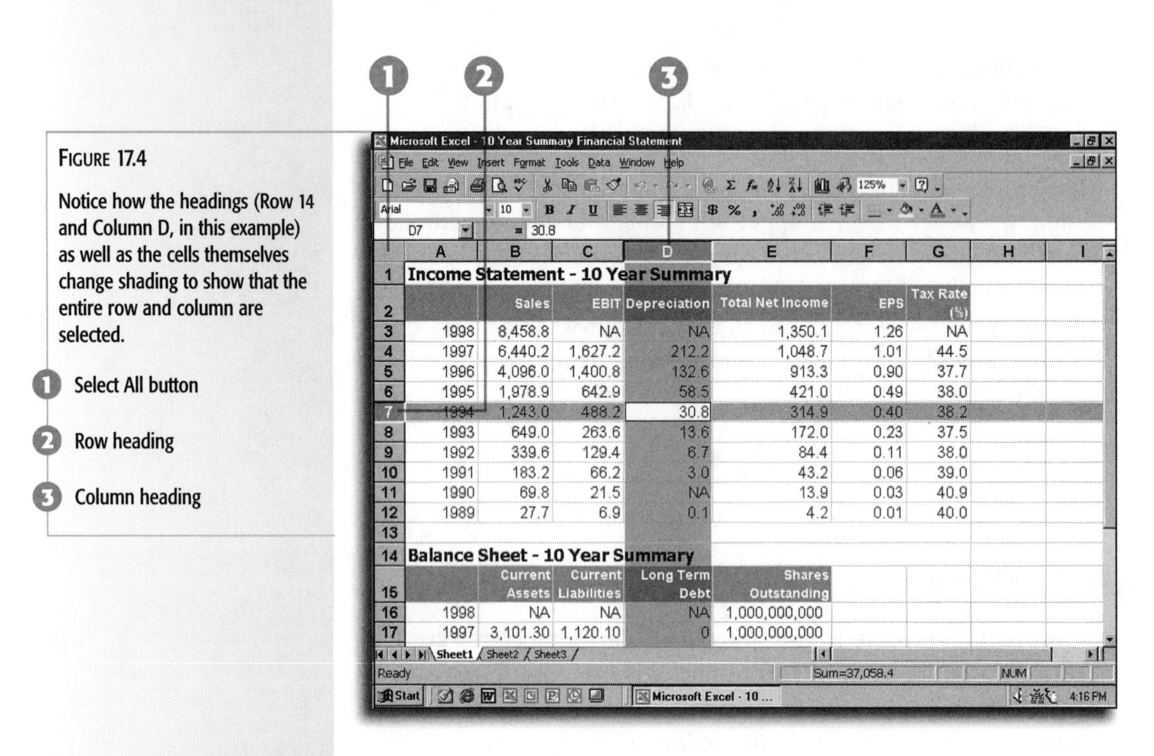

FIGURE 17.4

Notice how the headings (Row 14 and Column D, in this example) as well as the cells themselves change shading to show that the entire row and column are selected.

1. Select All button
2. Row heading
3. Column heading

Shift to select a large range

If the range you want to select occupies more than one screen, try this shortcut. Click the top-left cell in the range and then use the scrollbars to move through the worksheet until you can see the lower-right corner of the range. Hold down the Shift key and click the final cell you want to include to select the entire range.

How to Move Around in a Range

To enter data only within a specific range, select the range first. After you've selected a range, pressing the Enter key moves the active cell down to the next cell within the range. When you reach the bottom row of the range, pressing Enter moves the active cell to the top of the next column in the selection. When you reach the lower-right corner of the range, pressing Enter moves you back to the upper-left corner. To move within the range from right to left, one row at a time, press Tab; press Shift+Enter and Shift+Tab to move in the opposite direction.

Entering the Same Data in Multiple Cells

You've created a new worksheet, and you want to fill a number of cells with exactly the same data. For example, you might want to enter zero values in cells where you intend to enter values later. You could enter the data in the first cell and then copy it to all the others, but there's a faster way to fill all those cells at once.

Entering Data in Multiple Cells Simultaneously

1. Select the range of cells into which you want to enter data. The range need not be contiguous.
2. Type the text, number, or formula you want to use in all selected cells, but don't press Enter.
3. Hold down the Ctrl key and press Enter. The data appears in all cells you selected.

Automatically Filling in a Series of Data

Nothing is more tedious than entering a long sequence of numbers or dates in a column. So let Excel handle the drudge work. As the name implies, its AutoFill feature can automatically fill in information as you drag the mouse through a range. You can use AutoFill to enter the days of the week, months of the year, any series of numbers or dates, and even custom lists that you create.

Before you can use AutoFill, however, you need to learn to recognize Excel's fill handle. Select any cell or range, and you'll see a thick border around the selection. Look in the lower-right corner of the selection for a small black square. That's the fill handle. When you point at the fill handle, the mouse pointer turns to a thin black cross. Drag in any direction (up or down in a column, left or right in a row, or through a contiguous range) to begin filling in values.

In Figure 17.5, for example, I've begun creating a cash flow statement. I started by entering row labels in Column A, and now I want to add a label for each month, so I can enter a full year's worth of data. Rather than type in each month manually, I entered `January 1999` (Excel formatted the date automatically for me) and dragged the AutoFill handle to the right to fill in additional months using the same format.

What kind of list can you create using AutoFill? The answer depends on what you enter in the first cell (or two or three cells). Table 17.3 lists examples of what you can expect when you use AutoFill.

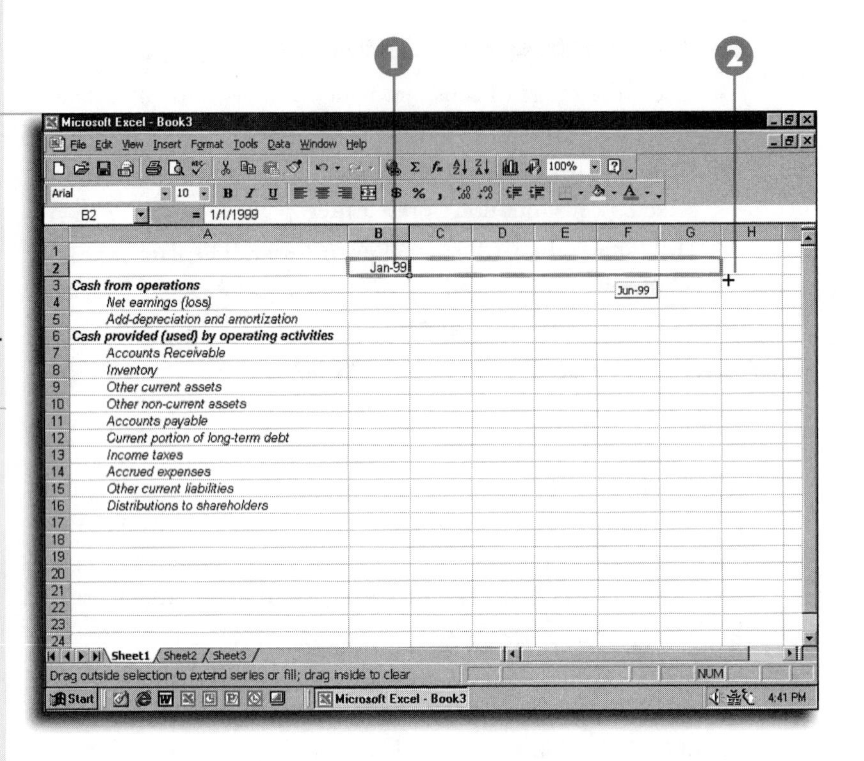

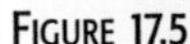

FIGURE 17.5

As you drag, Excel automatically fills in values in your series–dates, in this example.

1. Click here...
2. ...and use this fill handle to enter dates automatically.

TABLE 17.3 Using AutoFill to Create a List

Start with This Value	To Fill in This List	Examples
April	Months	April, May, June...
Jan	Abbreviated months	Jan, Feb, Mar...
Thursday	Days of the week	Thursday, Friday, Saturday...
30-May	Date series	30-May, 31-May, 1-Jun...
Q3	Calendar quarters	Q3, Q4, Q1, Q2...
Chapter 1	Any text plus a number	Chapter 1, Chapter 2, Chapter 3...

When you click the fill handle and drag, the selection gets bigger and includes more cells. When you release the mouse button, Excel fills every cell in the selection with values.

AutoFill sequences repeat

What happens when you reach the end of an AutoFill sequence? It begins repeating. If you start with January, for example, and extend the selection 13 or more cells, the months reach December and start over again at January.

Automatically Filling in a Series of Dates As Column Labels

1. Click in the cell above the first column and enter the first item in the list, `Jan`.
2. Click in the cell that contains `Jan` to make it active, and then point to its fill handle. When the mouse pointer turns to a black cross, hold down the left mouse button and drag the selection to the right across the row.
3. As you drag, watch for ScreenTips, which display the values AutoFill will enter in the selection.
4. When the selection includes 12 cells, release the left mouse button.

If you enter a single number in the first cell and then drag the fill handle, Excel simply repeats the value in every cell you select. AutoFill behaves the same way if you enter text, like `ABC`. To force AutoFill to enter a simple series of numbers, hold down the Ctrl key as you drag—you'll see a plus sign next to the fill handle to signal that you've changed to a new AutoFill mode. Your list starts with the original number and increases by one throughout the selection.

What do you do when you want to count by twos, tens, or millions? If you select two or more cells at the beginning of a list that uses a special increment (like 2, 4, 6, or 10, 20, 30) and then drag the fill handle, Excel uses that increment to AutoFill the selected area. You can also enter a date series such as every other day or every fourth month. So if you want to count by 10s, enter the numbers `10` and `20` in adjacent cells, and then select *both* cells and drag the fill handle to extend the selection; AutoFill adds `30`, `40`, `50`, and so on. If you enter `Jan` and `Mar` in adjacent cells, then select both cells and drag the AutoFill handle, Excel adds `Jul` and `Oct` and starts over with Jan.

AutoComplete and AutoCorrect

When you're entering a long list of text entries into a column, Excel's AutoComplete feature can be a help or a hindrance. As you type, Excel compares the opening characters with other entries in cells directly above the active cell. If the first two or

Create a custom list

Do you have a list you use regularly, such as departments in your company or product codes? Add your custom list to Excel, and you can use AutoFill to insert it in any row or column, anytime. Select the worksheet range (column or row) that contains the list. Click the **Tools** menu, choose **Options**, click the **Custom Lists** tab, and then click the **Import** button. Your list is now available in any Excel worksheet. To use the custom list, enter the first list item and then use the fill handle to complete the list.

three characters match another entry, Excel assumes that you want to repeat that entry and fills in the rest of the cell with the matching text it found in a previous cell. If the new text is indeed what you wanted to enter, press Enter (or any arrow key) to insert the AutoComplete entry in the cell. Or keep typing what you actually want to enter in the cell.

Frankly, I find this feature a nuisance because I run the risk of accidentally entering data I didn't intend to enter. For that reason, I routinely disable the AutoComplete feature.

Disabling Excel's AutoComplete Feature

1. Pull down the **Tools** menu and choose **Options**.
2. Click the **Edit** tab.
3. Clear the check mark from the box labeled **Enable AutoComplete for cell values**.
4. Click **OK** to save the changes and continue editing.

SEE ALSO

➤ *To learn how to configure other automatic data entry features, AutoCorrect and AutoFormat, see page 41*

Moving and Copying Data

When you want to move the contents of a cell or range a short distance, just drag the selection and drop it in the new location. For more complex moving and copying tasks, Excel gives you an assortment of tools. Most notably, you can open the **Edit** menu and choose **Paste Special**, which lets you choose how to transfer information stored on the Clipboard and even lets you transform data as you move it. (I'll cover this command later in this chapter.)

SEE ALSO

➤ *To learn how to use the Windows Clipboard to move and copy data, see page 134*
➤ *To find an explanation of how cell references in a formula change to reflect a new location and how to deal with the consequences, see page 376*

Dragging Data from One Cell to Another

You can use basic drag-and-drop techniques to copy and move cells. If you're willing to learn a few advanced techniques, you can even transform data as you move it from place to place.

Moving or Copying Data with the Mouse

1. Select the cell or contiguous range you want to move or copy (you can't drag a noncontiguous range), and point to the thick border around any edge of the selection. The mouse pointer changes to an arrow.
2. Click and drag to move the selection to a new location. As you drag, you see the outline of the cell's borders along with the mouse pointer, and a ScreenTip identifies the address of the destination cell or range.
3. To copy rather than move a cell or range, hold down the Ctrl key while you drag the selection. The plus sign along-side the mouse pointer is a visual cue that you're about to copy rather than move.
4. Drop the selection in its new location.

As is true elsewhere in Office, you can hold down the right mouse button when dragging cells from one place to another. When you release the button, a shortcut menu (see Figure 17.6) lets you tell Excel exactly what you want to do with the data.

FIGURE 17.6
Hold down the right mouse button when you drag a selection from one place to another; then use this shortcut menu to choose how to paste the results.

Of the other choices that appear on the menu when you right-click and drag, **Copy Here** and **Move Here** are self-explanatory, as are the options that let you shift cells out of the way so that you can paste data without erasing the contents of existing cells.

Two other options on this menu are especially useful. Let's say you've created a worksheet with one column that calculates totals for several rows. If you simply copy that range of totals and paste it elsewhere, Excel copies the formulas, and you see error codes instead of numbers. Instead, hold down the right mouse button, drag the range to its new location, and choose **Copy Here as Values Only**. In this case, Excel converts the formulas to their results and pastes in the totals as numbers. This technique is also useful if you want to convert a cell or range from a formula to a value—just paste the values over the original cells.

Use the **Copy Here as Formats Only** choice to quickly transfer cell formatting (fonts, shading, borders, and so on) without copying the contents of the cells.

Shift with care

When you choose any of the Shift options, Excel moves the contents of only the row or column at the destination. If you right-drag a single cell from D4 to B3, and choose **Shift Down and Copy**, for example, Excel moves the current contents of B3 to B4, B4 to B5, and so on down the column, without disturbing the contents of any other column. That can make a major mess of a carefully organized worksheet. If you use this option and the results aren't what you intended, press Ctrl+Z to undo the move or copy and start over.

Cutting, Pasting, and Transforming Data

One of the most powerful ways to move data on a worksheet is to use the Paste Special menu to manipulate information on the Windows Clipboard. Copy the contents of one or more cells to the Clipboard, open the **Edit** menu, and then choose **Paste Special**—you'll see the dialog box shown in Figure 17.7. With just a few clicks, you can transform or transpose data.

Say, for example, you're planning next year's budget and you want to increase a range of numbers by 10 percent. You could create a new column and fill it with formulas, but transforming the range is much easier.

Copying one cell to many cell locations

When you copy one cell to a range, it fills that entire range. This technique is extremely useful when you're adding formulas to a highly structured worksheet. To total every column in a budget worksheet, for example, just create the **SUM** formula under the first column, copy the formula to the Clipboard, select the range that includes the cells below all the other columns, and paste. Excel adjusts each formula so that it totals the cells above it.

Transforming a Range of Numbers with the Clipboard

1. Click in any blank cell and enter the value you want to use when transforming the existing data. In this case, you can enter `1.1` because you want to increase the values by 10 percent.
2. Press Ctrl+C to copy the value to the Windows Clipboard.
3. Select the range you want to transform.
4. Click the **Edit** menu and choose **Paste Special**.
5. In the Paste Special dialog box, choose the **Multiply** option. If blank cells appear in the selected range, check the box labeled **Skip blanks**.

Copying without borders

Figure 17.7 shows another option that's incredibly useful when copying or moving data in a range that contains borders. If your range has a border around every outside cell but none on the inside, copying a cell from the middle of the range to any edge will mess up your borders. Use Paste Special and check the **All except borders** option and your borders remain exactly the way you designed them.

6. Click **OK**. Excel multiplies the selected range by the constant on the Clipboard, increasing each number by exactly 10 percent. Thus, if the original values were 2500, 3250, and 4000, the new values would be 2750, 3575, and 4400.

FIGURE 17.7
Use the Paste Special menu to add or subtract two columns of numbers, or to multiply or divide a range of numbers by a value you copy to the Clipboard.

Inserting and Deleting Cells, Rows, and Columns

When you first set up a worksheet, you probably won't get the arrangement of rows and columns just right. That's okay; you can always insert or delete cells, rows, and columns to redesign your worksheet on-the-fly. When you insert or delete parts of a worksheet, Excel moves and renumbers adjacent cells, rows, and columns. For example, if you delete Row 12, Row 13 moves up and becomes Row 12, Row 14 moves to Row 13, and so on.

Inserting or Deleting Cells, Rows, or Columns

1. Select the cells you want to insert or delete.
2. Point to the selection, right-click, and choose **Insert** or **Delete** from the shortcut menu.
3. If you selected one or more entire rows or columns, Excel inserts or deletes the selection immediately. Adjacent rows or columns slide up or to the left, respectively, to fill the space left behind when you delete.
4. If you selected one or more cells, you see a dialog box like the one shown in Figure 17.8. Choose one of the available options and click **OK**. Excel inserts cells or deletes the selection and rearranges the remaining cells according to your instructions.

Paste Special is versatile

Use the other options in the Paste Special dialog box to copy a constant amount to the Clipboard and add that value to or subtract it from a range of numbers. You can also use Paste Special to flip the contents of a row into a column, and vice versa. Just click the **Transpose** option on the Paste Special dialog box; then click **OK**.

Don't use Delete to clear cells

If you want to simply erase the data in one or more cells without disturbing the position of other cells in the worksheet, don't use the Delete command on the shortcut menus. Instead, select the cells, right-click, and choose **Clear Contents** from the shortcut menu. Or press the Del key, which has the same effect.

FIGURE 17.8

When you select a cell and choose **Delete**, Excel asks how to rearrange the worksheet. When inserting cells, you can choose to shift cells down or to the right.

Shift cells with care

When you choose **Shift cells left** or **Shift cells up**, Excel rearranges only the cells in the selected rows or columns. This change is fine if you're working with a list that occupies only a single row or column, but it can make a mess of a carefully designed worksheet that includes many rows or columns. Be careful when choosing this option–and use the Undo command if the results aren't what you intended. If you choose **Entire row** or **Entire column**, Excel deletes the rows or columns in which the selected cells appear, just as if you had selected the entire row or column.

Deleting a cell can break formulas

When you delete a cell, range, row, or column, Excel removes every trace of data. Any formula that refers to a deleted cell no longer displays the correct results; instead, you see `#REF!` in the cell where the formula appears. This error message means Excel has lost track of a cell reference and can't calculate the correct value for the formula. To fix the problem, you have to edit the formula.

SEE ALSO

➤ *For full details and expert tips on debugging worksheet formulas, see "Troubleshooting Formulas" in Chapter 21, "Using Formulas and Functions," of* Special Edition Using Microsoft Office 2000.

Moving Around in a Worksheet

Moving from cell to cell in a worksheet isn't complicated; you point and click, use the scrollbars, or tap the arrow keys. The basic techniques are the same ones you use to move around in a Word document. The arrow keys and scrollbars respond just as they do in other Windows programs. If you're a touch typist, you can use the keyboard to navigate through a worksheet in precise movements. Table 17.4 lists Excel's most useful keyboard shortcuts.

TABLE 17.4 Using the Keyboard to Move the Active Cell

To Do This	Press This
Move to beginning of row	Home
Move up/down one window	Page Up/Page Down
Go to the top-left corner of the worksheet	Ctrl+Home
Go to the bottom-right corner of the part of your worksheet that contains data	Ctrl+End
Jump to the next/previous worksheet	Ctrl+Page Up, Ctrl+Page Down
Move to a specific cell or area of the worksheet	F5 or Ctrl+G (GoTo); type the cell address
Move the active cell from left to right or top to bottom in a selected range	Tab
Move the opposite direction in a selected range	Shift+Tab

Navigating with the Go To Key

Excel's Go To key offers a number of useful shortcuts to move around a worksheet. You can jump straight to a named range, return to a cell you previously selected, or select all cells in a worksheet that match criteria you specify.

To open the Go To dialog box, pull down the **Edit** menu and choose **Go To**. You'll see the dialog box shown in Figure 17.9.

To jump to a specific cell or range, type its address in the box labeled **Reference**. To make it easy to retrace your steps, Excel keeps track of cell addresses you enter here, including the cell you started from. To return to any of these addresses, select the entry from the **Go To** list and click **OK**.

The list of references in the Go To dialog box also includes any named ranges in the current workbook. To jump to one of these ranges, select its name from the list and click **OK**. Because Excel saves range names with the workbook, that list is always available when you open the Go To dialog box; on the other hand, Excel discards the list of recent addresses each time you close the workbook.

Understanding how the End key works

When you press the End key, you don't move to the end of the current row, as you might expect. Instead, pressing this key turns on End mode, an unusual (and occasionally confusing) way to move through the current worksheet. Press End followed by an arrow key to jump along the current row or column, in the direction of the arrow, to the next cell that contains data, skipping over any intervening empty cells. Press End and then Home to go to the last data-containing cell in the current worksheet. Press End and then Enter to move to the last cell in the current row. Press End again to turn off End mode.

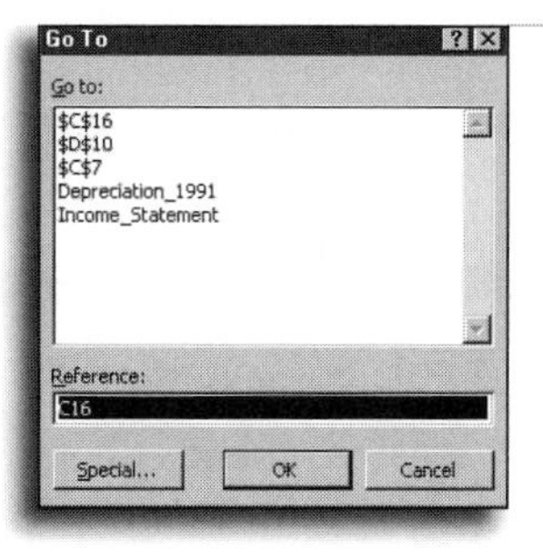

FIGURE 17.9

Use the Go To dialog box to jump to cells or named ranges you've visited recently. You can also type any cell address in the box labeled Reference.

SEE ALSO

➤ *For more details on how to move around using range names, see page 381*

The Go To dialog box is especially useful when you're designing or troubleshooting a large worksheet and you want to quickly view or edit a group of cells with common characteristics. Open the Go To dialog box as usual, and then click the **Special** button to display the dialog box in Figure 17.10. When you select one of these options and click **OK**, Excel selects all the cells that match that characteristic.

Keyboard shortcuts

Excel and Word share a pair of keyboard shortcuts for the Go To dialog box. Press F5 or Ctrl+G in either application to pop up this handy navigational aid without pulling down menus.

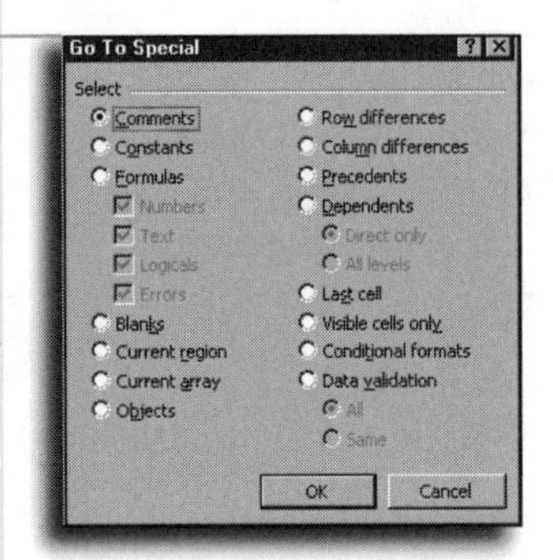

FIGURE 17.10

Choose any of these options, and then click OK to quickly select all matching cells in the current worksheet.

Choose **Comments**, for example, to select all cells containing comments. Click the **Last cell** option to jump to the last cell on the worksheet that contains data or formatting. To view and edit all formulas you've entered in a specific region of the worksheet, first select the range, then pop up the Go To Special dialog box, and choose the **Formulas** option. To see only formulas that contain logical functions, clear the **Numbers**, **Text**, and **Errors** check boxes.

When you select cells using the Go To Special dialog box, the effect is the same as if you had selected a range by pointing and clicking. You can move from cell to cell using the same techniques as you would with any range—using the Tab and Enter keys, for example.

Online help

Excel provides excellent online help for each of the options in the Go To Special dialog box. Click the question mark button at the right of the title bar, and then point to each option to see a detailed description of what it does.

Customizing the Amount of Data You See

Use the Zoom button on the Standard toolbar to change the view of your worksheet. Click in the box and enter a number from 10 percent to 400 percent. Smaller numbers let you see the overall design of a worksheet, although editing ordinary text is difficult when the size drops below 25 percent. In contrast, you can use larger magnifications for a close-up view of data.

The Zoom control allows you to resize your worksheet so that the data you select fills the entire worksheet editing window. After you make a selection, click the drop-down arrow to the right of the Zoom list and choose **Selection** from the bottom of the list. Excel resizes the selection automatically. To return to normal view, click the **Zoom** button again and choose **100%** from the drop-down list.

Locking Row and Column Labels in Place

As you build your worksheet, you use labels at the top of columns and the beginning of rows to identify the data in each column or row. For example, a typical annual budget worksheet might arrange data into one row for each budget category, with values for each month appearing in columns from left to right. In this model, a label at the beginning of each row indicates the category, and a label at the top of each column identifies the month. This design is useful, but if the data in your worksheet occupies more than a single screen, row and column labels can scroll out of view, making it difficult to track which data goes in each row and column.

To keep the row and column labels visible at all times, freeze the labels into position. In Figure 17.11, for example, notice that you can see the row titles in column A at the left, as well as the columns for July, August, and beyond at the right. As you click the horizontal scrollbar, columns on the left of the data area scroll out of view, but the row labels remain visible.

Use the mouse wheel to zoom

If you have a Microsoft IntelliMouse, you can use the wheel to zoom in and out of your worksheet. Hold down the Ctrl key and spin the wheel down to zoom out; spin the wheel up to zoom back in.

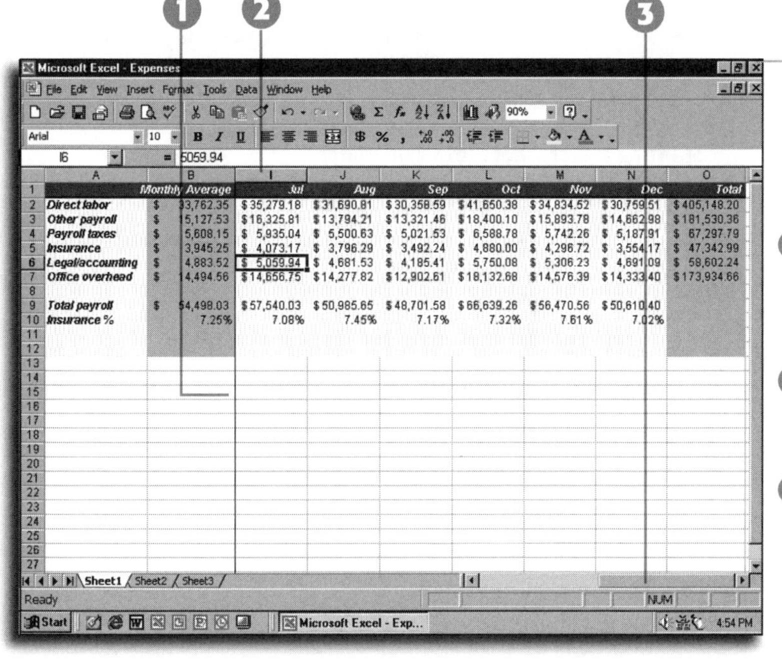

FIGURE 17.11

When you freeze rows or columns in place, you can scroll through the worksheet without losing your place.

1. The solid line indicates a frozen pane; columns to the left of this vertical line don't move as you scroll.
2. Notice that some column letters are missing; they've scrolled past the frozen columns.
3. Use this horizontal scrollbar to move left and right through the worksheet.

Freezing Row and Column Labels into Position

1. Click in the cell below the row and to the right of the column you want to lock into position. To freeze the first two columns and the first row, for example, click in cell C2.
2. Pull down the **Window** menu and choose **Freeze Panes**. You then see a solid line setting off the locked rows and columns from the rest of the worksheet.
3. Use the scrollbars to move through the data in your worksheet. The panes are locked only on the screen; if you print the worksheet, rows and columns appear in their normal positions.
4. To unlock the row and column labels, pull down the **Window** menu again and choose **Unfreeze Panes**.

For lists, lock column titles only

If your worksheet consists of a long list, lock in the labels for columns only. Click in column A, just below the row that contains your column labels. Then pull down the **Window** menu and choose **Freeze Panes**.

SEE ALSO

➤ *To learn how to repeat row and column labels when printing a worksheet that runs over multiple pages, see page 408*

Splitting the Worksheet Window

Freezing a row or column is the right solution when you want to see only your row and column labels. However, you can also split your worksheet into separate panes to scroll through different regions of a worksheet and see the data side by side.

Splitting a Worksheet into Two Panes

1. Aim the mouse pointer at one of the two split boxes. One is just above the vertical scrollbar, and the other is to the right of the horizontal scrollbar.
2. When the mouse pointer changes to a double line with two arrows, click and drag in the direction of the worksheet to display the split bar.
3. Release the split box and click on the split bar; then drag in either direction to snap the bar into place at a row or column boundary. The results are shown in Figure 17.12.
4. Drag between panes to move or copy text and other objects.
5. To remove multiple panes and return to a single editing window, double-click the split bar, or click the bar and drag it off the worksheet window.

Use up to four panes

The split bar divides the window into two panes, horizontally or vertically. You can drag both split bars onto the worksheet to create four panes. Each pane includes its own scrollbars for moving around.

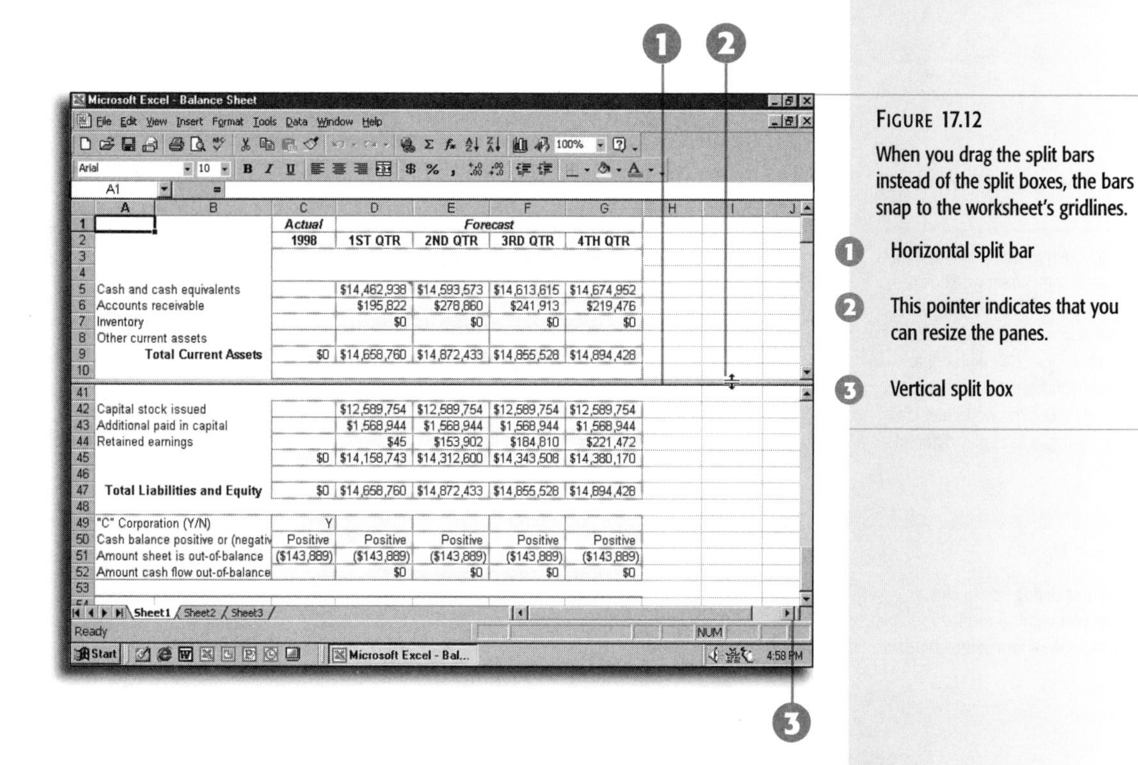

FIGURE 17.12

When you drag the split bars instead of the split boxes, the bars snap to the worksheet's gridlines.

1. Horizontal split bar
2. This pointer indicates that you can resize the panes.
3. Vertical split box

Arranging Worksheet Windows

You can open, view, and edit multiple Excel workbooks simultaneously. Unlike Excel 97, which forced you to view all workbook windows within a single program window, Excel 2000 gives each workbook its own window and its own button on the Windows taskbar, making it much easier to switch between open workbooks. You can also choose to view multiple workbooks within the same window, as in Excel 97.

After opening a workbook window, you can open one or more windows in the same workbook. This technique allows you to work with multiple worksheets simultaneously; it's also useful when you want to view different regions of the same worksheet without scrolling. To open a new window in the current workbook, pull down the **Window** menu and choose **New Window**. Each window you create gets its own taskbar button. To cycle between open workbook windows, press Ctrl+F6. To cycle through all open Windows, including workbooks as well as documents created by other programs, use the standard Windows shortcut, Alt+Tab. You can switch to a specific workbook window by clicking its taskbar button or choosing its entry from the list in the **Window** menu.

The number of windows is not limited

You can open as many windows as you like in the current workbook. The title bar for each window displays the workbook title, followed by a colon (:) and a number that indicates you have multiple windows open. Use the worksheet tabs in each window to display different worksheets.

Displaying two or more worksheets or workbooks simultaneously in the same Excel window can make it easier to compare and manage worksheets. To position windows in this manner, pull down the **Window** menu and choose **Arrange**. You'll see the dialog box shown in Figure 17.13. If you've opened multiple windows in a single workbook, check the box labeled **Windows of active workbook** to arrange only those windows, ignoring all other open workbooks.

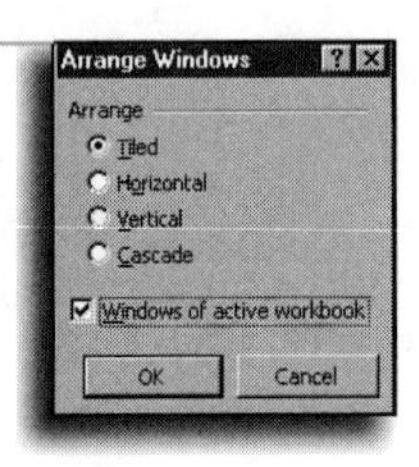

FIGURE 17.13

Use this dialog box to choose how you want to display multiple workbook or worksheet windows.

The four choices in this dialog box work as follows:

Tiled	Divides the current Excel window into rectangles of equal size and arranges all open workbook or worksheet windows within those spaces.
Horizontal	Stacks all open workbooks or worksheets in equal-size windows from top to bottom in the Excel workspace.
Vertical	Creates windows of equal size and arranges them from side to side in the Excel workspace.
Cascade	Arranges workbook windows in a fanned stack, with the title bar of each window visible.

Working with Multiple Worksheets

Storing multiple worksheets within a workbook is an effective way to keep projects organized. One of the most common scenarios is a consolidated company budget or profit-and-loss statement; within a single workbook, create a separate worksheet for each department's numbers, and then create one summary worksheet that consolidates totals for each line item and calculates a grand total.

This section includes instructions that can help you manage multiple worksheets.

Switching Between Worksheets

To move from one worksheet to another, just click on the index tab of the sheet you want to work with. If you can't see all the tabs in the current workbook, use the arrow buttons to the left of the worksheet tabs to scroll left or right.

To select multiple worksheet tabs simultaneously, hold down the Ctrl key as you click on each tab. To select all the worksheets in the current workbook, right-click on any worksheet tab and choose **Select All Sheets** from the shortcut menu. When you've selected more than one sheet, you'll see the word `Group` in brackets in the title bar for that window. When you've selected multiple worksheet tabs, any data you enter will appear in the corresponding cells on each worksheet in the group. Likewise, any formatting choices you make—resizing columns, for example, or applying a numeric format—will affect all the grouped worksheets identically. To remove a sheet from a group, hold down Ctrl and click on its tab.

Moving, Copying, Inserting, and Deleting Worksheets

Although each new workbook starts with a set number of blank worksheets, you can add, copy, delete, and rearrange worksheets at will. In every case, the easiest way to manage a collection of worksheets is with the help of the mouse.

Change the default number of sheets in a new workbook

When Excel creates a new workbook, it automatically fills the workbook with three blank worksheets. To change this default setting, open the **Tools** menu, choose **Options**, click the **General** tab, and enter any number between 1 and 255 in the box labeled **Sheets in new workbook**. Choose a smaller setting if you rarely use multiple sheets in a workbook, or a larger one if you regularly create complex workbooks, such as consolidated budgets.

Adding a New Worksheet to a Workbook

1. Point to any sheet tab and right-click.
2. From the shortcut menu, choose **Insert**.
3. Select the **Worksheet** icon in the Insert dialog box.
4. Click **OK**. The new sheet appears to the left of the sheet to which you originally pointed.

Deleting a Worksheet from a Workbook

1. Point to the tab of the worksheet you want to delete and right-click.
2. Choose **Delete** from the shortcut menu.
3. Excel displays a confirmation dialog box before permanently deleting the worksheet. Click **OK** to delete the worksheet.

Moving a Worksheet Within a Workbook

1. Point to the tab of the worksheet you want to move and hold down the left mouse button. The mouse pointer changes into the shape of an arrow with a sheet of paper, and a small triangular marker appears at the top of the sheet tab.
2. Drag the mouse pointer along the sheet tabs until the black marker is over the location where you want to move the worksheet.
3. Release the mouse button to drop the worksheet in its new location.

Copying a Worksheet Within a Workbook

1. Point to the tab of the worksheet you want to copy; hold down the Ctrl key and hold down the left mouse button. The mouse pointer changes to the shape of a sheet of paper with a plus sign on it. A small triangular marker appears at the top of the sheet tab.
2. Continue to hold down the Ctrl key and drag the mouse pointer to the left or right until the black marker is over the location where you want to copy the worksheet.
3. Release the mouse button to create a copy of the selected worksheet.

Moving or Copying a Worksheet to Another Workbook

1. Open the target workbook into which you plan to move or copy the worksheet. You can skip this step if you want to move or copy the worksheet to a new workbook.
2. Switch to the workbook that contains the worksheet you want to move or copy, point to the worksheet tab, and right-click.
3. Choose **Move or Copy** from the shortcut menu.
4. In the Move or Copy dialog box (see Figure 17.14), select the name of the target workbook from the drop-down list labeled **To book**. To move or copy the sheet to a new, empty workbook, choose **(new book)**.
5. If you want to, use the list labeled **Before sheet** to select the location where you want the new worksheet tab to appear.
6. By default, using this dialog box moves the selected worksheet to the target workbook. To leave the original worksheet in place, check the box labeled **Create a copy**.
7. Click **OK** to complete the move or copy.

Each worksheet copy gets a generic name

When you copy a worksheet within a workbook, the new copy uses the same name as the old sheet, tacking on a number in parentheses at the end of the name. If the original worksheet is named `June`, for example, the new sheet is called `June (2)`. If you create an additional copy, it is called `June (3)`.

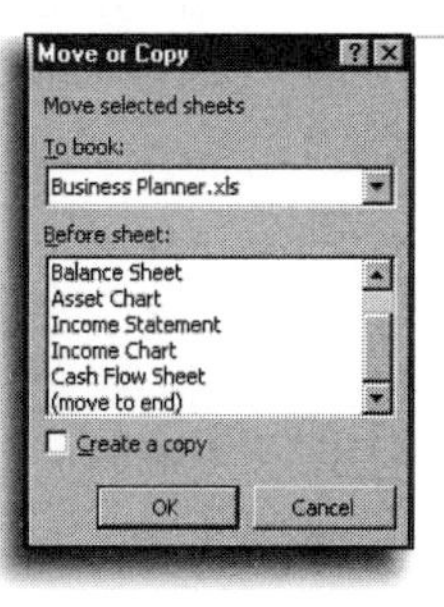

FIGURE 17.14
Use this dialog box to move or copy a worksheet to any open workbook, or create a new workbook on-the-fly.

Hiding and Showing a Worksheet

In some workbooks, you might want to hide a worksheet, either to remove the temptation for coworkers to tamper with its data or simply to reduce clutter. This technique is especially useful when a worksheet contains data you use in formulas on other worksheets but rarely need to edit. Pull down the **Format** menu, choose **Sheet**, and select **Hide** from the cascading menu. If the current workbook contains any hidden sheets, use the **Unhide** choice on the same cascading menu to reveal the hidden sheets once again.

Renaming a Worksheet

You'll find navigating through workbooks with multiple worksheets easier if you replace the default worksheet labels (Sheet1, Sheet2, and so on) with descriptive names such as "Sales Forecasts" or "Marketing Department Expenses." To rename a worksheet, double-click on the **Worksheet** tab (or right-click on the tab and select **Rename**). Type a new name and press Enter.

Worksheet names always fit on the tab

You don't need to resize the worksheet tab when you enter a longer or shorter name; it changes size to accommodate the new label.

Naturally, you must follow a few rules to name your worksheets:

- You're allowed 31 characters for each tab.
- Spaces are allowed.
- You can use parentheses anywhere in a worksheet's name; brackets ([ ]) are also allowed, except as the first character in the name.
- You can't use any of the following characters as part of a sheet name: / \ ? * : (slash, backslash, question mark, asterisk, or colon). Other punctuation marks, including commas and exclamation points, are allowed.

CHAPTER

18

Building Smarter Worksheets with Formulas and Functions

Use formulas to analyze and summarize data

Learn how to enter a formula using the keyboard or the mouse

Examine Excel's built-in functions

Enter error-free functions

Add a column automatically

Use labels and names to make worksheets easier to read

Using Formulas for Quick Calculations

Designing the basic row-and-column structure of your worksheet and entering data are only the first steps. To really take advantage of Excel's number-crunching capability, you can create *formulas* that help you analyze and summarize all that data. Excel formulas let you perform simple arithmetic, complex calculations, and logical tests. Better yet, they allow you to update the underlying numbers or create alternative scenarios, instantaneously recalculating the results without tedious retyping.

What Can You Do with a Formula?

You can use Excel formulas to manipulate numbers and text. For example, with a column of numbers, you can calculate a total for the entire column and then determine the average value of all the numbers in the column. For good measure, you can also determine the highest and lowest numbers in the list.

Why would you want to do that? Let's say your worksheet includes monthly sales figures for each of the sales people in each of your regional offices. The data is stored in the range of cells defined as B2:M20. You want to see the highest and lowest monthly results, along with an average of all the numbers. To do so, pick a blank area of the worksheet and enter the following formulas in adjacent cells: `=MAX(B2:M20)`, `=MIN(B2:M20)`, and `=AVERAGE(B2:M20)`.

You can also use formulas to calculate percentages, to combine text from different cells, and even to display different labels based on the results of another calculation. In the sales worksheet, for example, you might want to display the word `Bonus` next to the name of any salesperson whose average sales exceeded the target entered in your worksheet.

Instant calculations

There's a fast and easy way to see totals, averages, minimums, maximums, and other calculations, without having to enter formulas. Select a range of numbers and then look in the right side of the status bar at the bottom of the worksheet window, where you should see `SUM=`, followed by the total of the selected cells. Right-click anywhere on the status bar to display a shortcut menu that lets you choose a different calculation, including `Average` and `Count`.

How Formulas Work

A formula can use any combination of numeric values, references to cells and ranges (either by address or by name), mathematical operators, *functions* (predefined Excel formulas that handle specific tasks), and even other formulas. (Skip ahead to the next section for a detailed look at the difference between formulas and functions.)

When you enter a formula into a worksheet cell, you must follow these rules:

- A formula always begins with an equal sign.
- You can use any of these *arithmetic operators* as part of a formula: addition (+), subtraction (–), multiplication (*), division (/), percent (%), or exponentiation (^).
- You can use *logical operators* to compare two values and produce the result TRUE or FALSE. Logical operators include equal to (=), greater than (>), less than (<), greater than or equal to (>=), less than or equal to (<=), and not equal to (<>).
- Use an ampersand (&) to combine, or *concatenate*, two pieces of text into a single value.
- You can substitute a cell address for any part of a formula, and Excel substitutes the contents of that address just as if you had typed it in directly. So the formula =A1+B1 tells Excel to read the contents of A1 (or the result of a formula in that cell), add it to the contents of B1, and then display the result.
- To control the order of calculation, use parentheses. Arguments in parentheses are resolved first. If you don't use parentheses, Excel performs mathematical operations in the following order: exponentiation, followed by multiplication and division, followed by addition and subtraction. Check the order of operators carefully because it can have a significant effect on results. For example, =3+4*5 is 23, whereas =(3+4)*5 is 35.

Don't forget the equal sign

If you leave off the equal sign before a formula, Excel assumes you've entered a text label and displays exactly what you typed. If you enter **2+2**, without an equal sign, that's what you see in the cell instead of the result of the calculation, which of course would be 4.

Nest parentheses for complex calculations

Some of the most useful calculations combine several formulas within a single cell. Excel allows you to *nest* parentheses within parentheses; just make sure that each open (left) parenthesis includes a matching close (right) parenthesis in the proper position. When you enter a parenthesis in a formula, Excel uses color coding to display other matched sets of parentheses in the same formula.

How to Enter a Formula

When you enter text or numbers in a cell, Excel assumes you're entering a *value* (sometimes referred to as a *constant*). The program displays values exactly as you type them, adjusting the display only if the cell includes any formatting settings. When the first character you type is an equal sign, however, Excel knows you're entering a formula. Excel stores the formula in the cell, but it displays the *result* of the formula. When you type `=950-21`, you're telling Excel, "Subtract 21 from 950 and show the result in the cell." If you select the cell, you see the formula itself displayed in the *Formula bar*, where you can click to edit. Figure 18.1 shows an example.

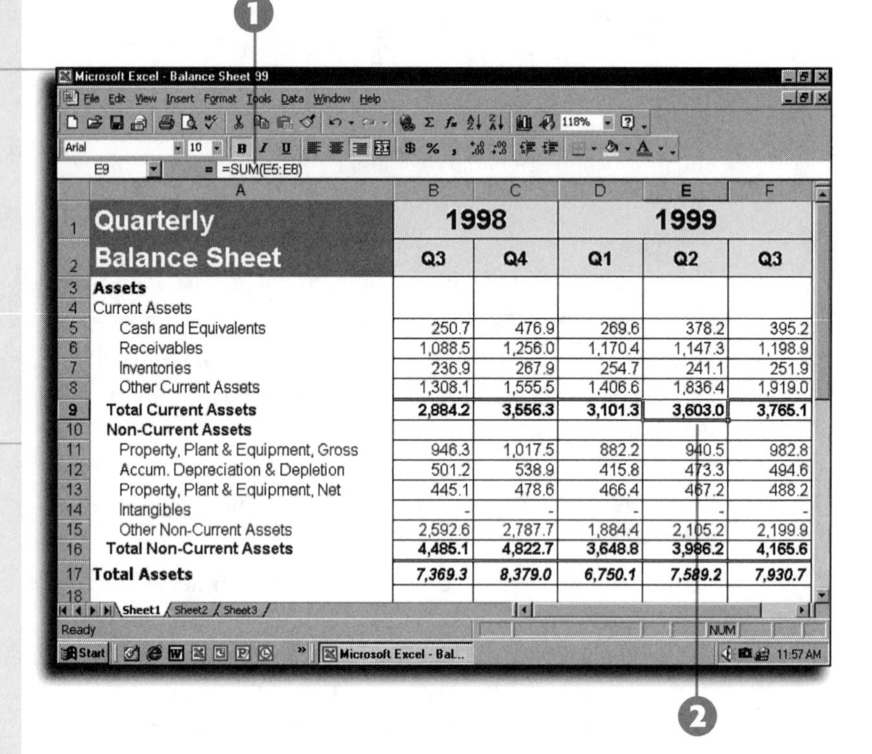

	A	B	C	D	E	F
1	Quarterly	1998		1999		
2	Balance Sheet	Q3	Q4	Q1	Q2	Q3
3	Assets					
4	Current Assets					
5	Cash and Equivalents	250.7	476.9	269.6	378.2	395.2
6	Receivables	1,088.5	1,256.0	1,170.4	1,147.3	1,198.9
7	Inventories	236.9	267.9	254.7	241.1	251.9
8	Other Current Assets	1,308.1	1,555.5	1,406.6	1,836.4	1,919.0
9	Total Current Assets	2,884.2	3,556.3	3,101.3	3,603.0	3,765.1
10	Non-Current Assets					
11	Property, Plant & Equipment, Gross	946.3	1,017.5	882.2	940.5	982.8
12	Accum. Depreciation & Depletion	501.2	538.9	415.8	473.3	494.6
13	Property, Plant & Equipment, Net	445.1	478.6	466.4	467.2	488.2
14	Intangibles	-	-	-	-	-
15	Other Non-Current Assets	2,592.6	2,787.7	1,884.4	2,105.2	2,199.9
16	Total Non-Current Assets	4,485.1	4,822.7	3,648.8	3,986.2	4,165.6
17	Total Assets	7,369.3	8,379.0	6,750.1	7,589.2	7,930.7

FIGURE 18.1

When you enter a formula, Excel displays the calculated result in the cell. Look in the Formula bar to view or edit the stored formula.

1. This formula is stored in the active cell.
2. Excel displays the formula's result in the cell.

When you see a cell that begins with the number sign (#), that's Excel's way of telling you that it cannot calculate a result for your formula. You may see any of seven possible error codes. To remove the error message and display the results you expect, you have to fix the problem either by editing the formula or changing the contents of a cell to which the formula refers.

Table 18.1 lists the error codes you see when an Excel formula isn't working properly, along with suggested troubleshooting steps. (Some of the explanations in this table refer to functions and arguments, two basic building blocks of Excel that I cover in more detail later in this chapter.)

TABLE 18.1 Common Formula Error Codes

Error Code	What It Means	Suggested Troubleshooting Steps Displayed
#DIV/0!	Formula is trying to divide by a zero value or a blank cell.	Check the divisor in your formula and make Sure it does not refer to a blank cell. You may want to add an error-handling =IF() routine to your formula, as described later in this chapter.
#N/A	Formula does not have a valid value for argument(s) passed.	#N/A means "No value is available." Check to see whether you have problems with LOOKUP functions.
#NAME?	Formula contains text that is neither a valid function nor a defined name on the active worksheet.	You've probably misspelled a function name or a range name. Check the formula carefully.
#NULL!	Refers to intersection of two areas that don't intersect.	You're trying to calculate a formula using intersection of two ranges that have no common cells. Redefine one or both ranges.
#NUM!	Value is too large, too small, imaginary, or not found.	Excel can handle numbers as large as 10^308 or as small as 10^-308. This error usually means you've used a function incorrectly—for example, calculating the square root of a negative number.

continues...

TABLE 18.1 **Continued**

Error Code	What It Means	Suggested Troubleshooting Steps Displayed
#REF!	Formula contains a reference that is not valid.	Did you delete a cell or range originally referred to in the formula? If so, you see this error code in the formula as well.
#VALUE!	Formula contains an argument of the wrong type.	You've probably mixed two incompatible data types in one formula—trying to add text with a number, for example. Check the formula again.

Using Functions to Create More Powerful Formulas

Asking Excel to do only simple addition or multiplication is like hiring a Harvard MBA to balance your checkbook. Yes, you can and will use simple Excel formulas to add columns of numbers, but its biggest asset is its repertoire of mathematical, financial, statistical, and logical functions. Excel 2000 can crunch numbers using more than 200 functions, from simple averages to complex trigonometric formulas.

How Functions Work

An Excel *function* is simply a specialized formula that Excel has memorized. Every function includes two parts: the function name (such as AVERAGE) and the specific values the function uses to calculate the result. These values are called *arguments*, and the order in which Excel performs the calculation is called the *syntax*.

Depending on the function, an argument might be text, numbers, logical values, or a cell or range address. You can also use other formulas and functions as arguments. Some arguments are required, and others are optional. Arguments always appear to the right of the function name, inside parentheses; Excel uses commas to separate multiple arguments.

The examples below illustrate the syntax of some commonly used functions. Bold type means the argument is required. An ellipsis (...) means that the function accepts an unlimited number of arguments.

=AVERAGE(number1,number2, ...)

=PMT(rate,nper,pv,fv,type)

In the AVERAGE function, you need to replace **number1**, **number2**, and so on, with values that Excel can use to perform the calculation. If you enter **=AVERAGE(5,10)**, for example, Excel displays the result of 7.5. More likely, however, you'll use a worksheet range as the argument for this function. If you store a year's worth of monthly sales totals in cells B20 through M20, for example, you can enter **=AVERAGE(B20:M20)** to calculate the average monthly sales.

More complicated functions demand that you fill in just the right information. To calculate the monthly payment on a loan, for example, you use the PMT function. This function requires (in order) the interest rate (**rate**), the number of payments (**nper**), and the present value (**pv**, the amount of the loan). The last two arguments—future value (fv) and the type of loan (type)—are optional.

Although you can use numbers and text as arguments in mathematical and logical functions, you typically use references to other cells and ranges instead. When you change the data in the referenced cells, the results of the formulas change automatically. With proper worksheet design, you can create "*what if*" scenarios that let you quickly see the results of different scenarios.

The example in Figure 18.2 shows how you can use a worksheet to quickly calculate loan payments for different interest rates and principal amounts. I've entered labels in column A and then used the adjacent cells in column B to enter the principal amount, interest rate, and loan period. Beneath those cells, I've entered a formula that calculates a monthly payment based on the contents

Sometimes no argument is needed

Some functions are so simple that they don't require any arguments. If you type **=TODAY()** in a cell (complete with the empty parentheses), Excel displays today's date in the cell. Whenever you open a worksheet that contains this function, Excel checks the date from your computer's clock/calendar and updates the value in that cell. You, in turn, can use that result for more calculations, such as the number of days that have passed since you received a payment.

Caps or lowercase? Doesn't matter.

Although Excel's help screens typically display function names in capital letters, the names are not case sensitive. Use any combination of capital and lowercase characters; when you enter the formula, Excel converts its name to capitals.

of those cells. To see how a different interest rate or loan amount would affect the payment, just enter the new amount in the box; Excel recalculates the payment automatically.

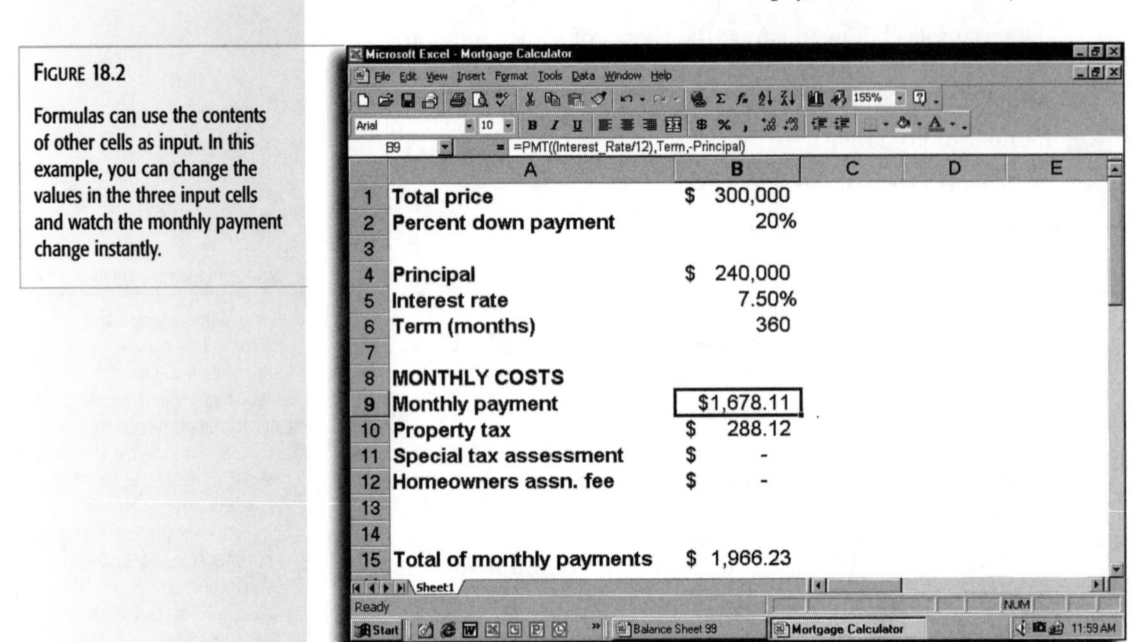

FIGURE 18.2

Formulas can use the contents of other cells as input. In this example, you can change the values in the three input cells and watch the monthly payment change instantly.

What You Can Do with Functions

You can find hundreds of predefined functions in Excel, including esoteric ones designed for financial analysts and statisticians. Table 18.2 includes a sampling of the most commonly used functions; to see the complete list, use the Formula Palette, described later in this chapter.

TABLE 18.2 Commonly Used Functions

Function	What It Does	Examples
SUM(*number1*, *number2...*)	Calculates the total of all the values in parentheses.	**=SUM(C4:C24)** Displays the total Of all the numbers in cells C4 through C24.

Function	What It Does	Examples
AVERAGE (*number1*, *number2…*)	Calculates the average of a group of values.	**=AVERAGE(C4:C24)** Displays the average of all the numbers in cells C4 through C24, ignoring blank cells.
COUNT(*value1*, *value2…*)	Counts the number of cells that contain numeric values.	**=COUNT(C4:C24)** If every cell in this range contains a value, the result will be 21.
MAX(*number1*, *number2…*) and MIN(*number1*, *number2…*)	Finds the highest and lowest value within the list.	**=MAX(C4:C24)** Displays the highest numeric value in the list, ignoring text labels and blank cells.
MONTH (*serial_number*) and WEEKDAY (*serial_number*)	Displays only the month or day of the week for a given date. (You type a date; Excel automatically converts it to a serial number.)	**=WEEKDAY(9/29/2005)** Sunday=1, Monday=2, and so on; apply Custom format Dddd to a cell, and you see this date falls on a Saturday.
PROPER(*text*) and UPPER (*text*)	Capitalizes you type—just the first letters, or all text, respectively.	**=PROPER("macmillan computer publishing")** Changes the first letter of each word to a capital letter—in this case, Macmillan Computer Publishing.
ROUND (*number*,*num_digits*)	Rounds off to a given number of digits.	**=ROUND(3.1415926,2)** Rounds to two decimal places, or 3.14.
TODAY()	Displays today's date in this cell.	**=DATEVALUE ("12/25/2001")-TODAY()** Calculates the number of days between now and Christmas, 2001, displaying the result as a number.

Why is that date in the cell?

If you use the formula shown here, you may see an odd date in the cell, rather than the number of days, as you expect. That's perfectly normal, as I explain in Chapter 19, "Formatting Worksheets." Excel mistakenly applies a date format to the cell that contains the number; if you change the cell to the General format, Excel displays it in a way that makes more sense.

Use IF to avoid error codes

One common use of the IF function is to avoid seeing the **#DIV/0!** error code in your worksheet. The formula **=IF(A8=0,0,A7/A8)**, for example, tests the value of A8 before performing a calculation. If A8 is equal to 0, Excel displays 0 as the result of the formula; if the value of A8 is other than 0, Excel performs the division operation.

SEE ALSO

➤ *To find instructions on how display data using Custom formats, see page 392*

Using Logical Functions

Some of the most useful functions are the *logical functions*. You can find countless practical uses for Excel's most popular logical function, *IF*. The following is the syntax of the IF function:

```
=IF(logical_test,value_if_true,value_if_false)
```

Let's say you've created a worksheet that you use to create invoices. You want to reward your best customers with a 10 percent discount, and you want Excel to apply the discount automatically.

Normally, you would use the SUM function in the cell where you display the grand total. If you use the IF function instead, you can ask Excel a simple true-or-false question: Did this customer spend more than $1,000 this month? Then you provide two sets of instructions—one for Excel to use if the answer is yes, the other if the answer is no.

The IF function uses three arguments: the logical test, the value if true, and the value if false; the first two arguments are required, but the third argument is optional. In the invoice example, assuming that the subtotal was in cell D24, you would fill in the following formula: **=IF(D24>1000,D24*90%,D24)**. The first argument, the logical test, checks to see whether the value in D24 is greater than 1,000. If that condition is true, Excel uses the second argument and calculates 90 percent of the subtotal, effectively passing along a 10 percent discount. If the logical test is false, Excel uses the third argument and displays the value shown in cell D24.

Using the Formula Palette to Avoid Errors

If you know the exact syntax of a function, you can enter the function and its arguments in the active cell; just remember to start with an equal sign. But what do you do when you're not sure which arguments go with a specific function? Use Excel's Formula Palette to help you enter the function and all its arguments.

To open the Formula Palette, you must first position the insertion point in the cell where you want to add a formula.

Using the Formula Palette to Enter Functions

1. Click the **Edit Formula** button (the equal sign just to the left of the Formula bar). Excel inserts an equal sign in the Formula bar, positions the insertion point to its right, and opens the Formula Palette just below the Formula bar.
2. If the name of the function you want to use appears in the **Function Box**, click to enter it into the Formula bar. To see additional choices, click the drop-down arrow to the right of the **Function Box**.
3. To choose from a master list of all available functions, choose **More Functions** from the bottom of the drop-down list. The Paste Function dialog box shown in Figure 18.3 appears.

The Function Box replaces the Name box

Opening the Formula replaces the Name box with the Function Box. When you first use Excel, this list includes the 10 most popular functions; as you use the Formula Palette, the list fills with functions you've entered. The one you worked with most recently is always the current selection in the **Function Box**.

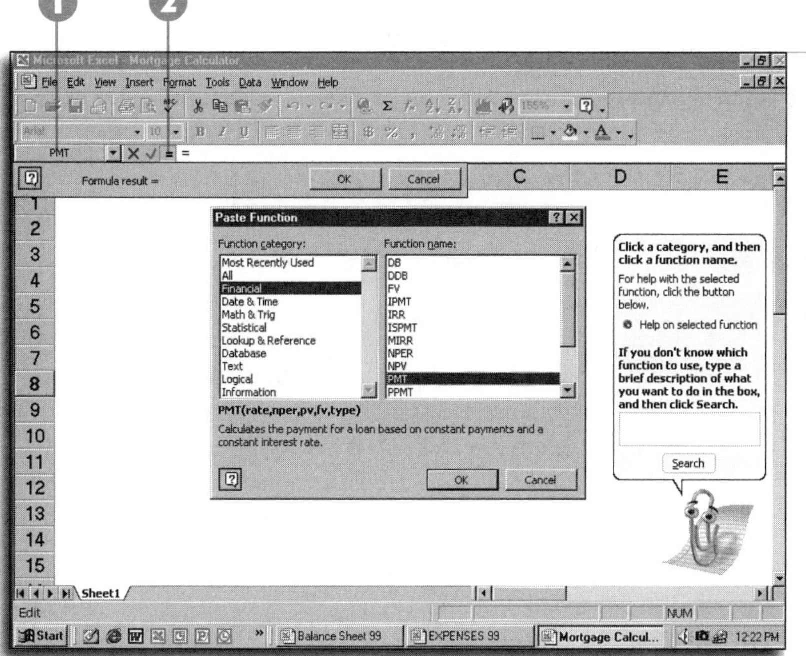

FIGURE 18.3

Excel organizes its built-in functions—nearly 300 of them—into this list. If you're not sure which function is the right one, ask the Office Assistant for help.

1. Edit Formula button
2. Function Box

Read the quick explanations

At the bottom of the Paste Function dialog box is a brief explanation of what the selected function does. The formula's syntax also appears here. To read extra details about a function, click the **Office Assistant** button in this dialog box and then choose **Help on selected function**.

4. Select a category from the list on the left, choose a function from the matching list on the right, and then click **OK**. Excel adds the function to the Formula bar and expands the Formula Palette to show separate text boxes for each argument, as shown in Figure 18.4.

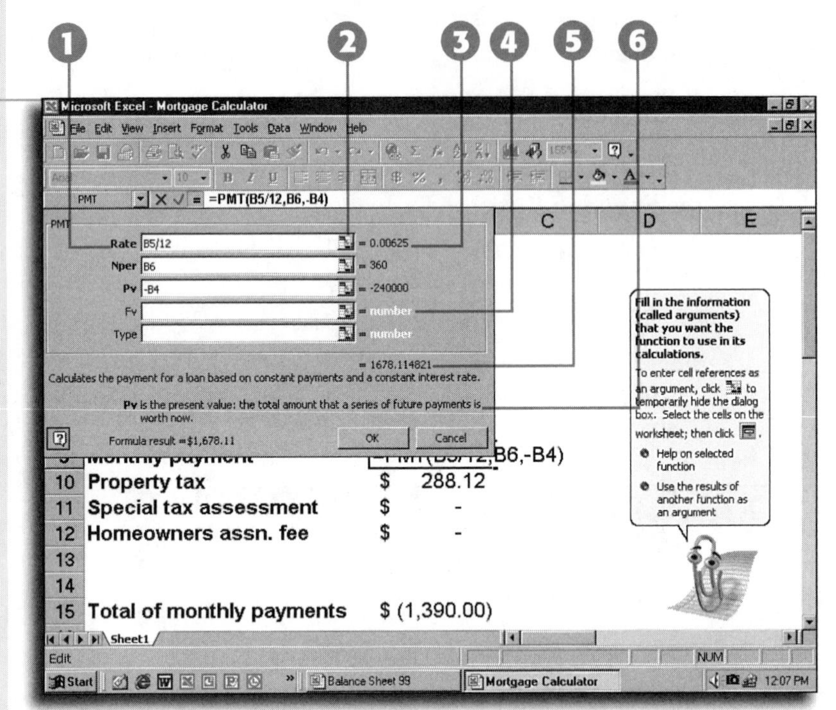

FIGURE 18.4

Watch the messages in the Formula Palette for help and feedback. If you enter incorrect data for an argument, you see a warning to the right of its input box.

1. Argument name (bold text means the argument is required).
2. Click this **Collapse Dialog** button to roll the dialog box out of the way while you select a cell or range; click again to restore the dialog box to full size.
3. Everything to the right of the equal sign shows the current value of the argument, using the contents of the cell address or range if you've entered one.
4. Argument type
5. This help text explains the function and the selected argument.
6. Check the result of the formula here as you enter arguments.

5. Click within the first argument box and fill in the required data. To add cell references by pointing and clicking, first click the **Collapse Dialog** button to roll most of the Formula Palette up and out of the way. Next, select the cell or range to use for the selected argument, and then click the **Collapse Dialog** button again to continue.
6. Repeat step 5 for other required arguments and optional arguments.
7. After entering all required arguments, click **OK** to paste the complete function into the current cell, or click **Cancel** to start over.

SEE ALSO

➤ *To find step-by-step instructions on how to select cells and ranges for automatic entry in formulas, see page 342*

Formula AutoCorrect: Excel's Built-in Proofreader

Sometimes typing a formula or function directly is faster. But what if your fingers slip on the keyboard, or you forget a crucial piece of punctuation? That's where Excel's Formula AutoCorrect feature comes in. When you enter a formula directly, Excel proofreads your work before pasting it into the active cell. This feature checks for common typing mistakes and suggests a correction, if possible. For example, if you forget the closing parenthesis for a function, Formula AutoCorrect offers to add it. You can accept or reject the suggested correction.

Formula AutoCorrect looks for misplaced operators (such as an extra equal sign at the beginning of a formula), mismatched parentheses, extra spaces and decimal points, and other common typing errors. When you make one of these common formula mistakes, you see a dialog box like the one shown in Figure 18.5.

Entering functions within functions

To use a function as an argument within another function, click to position the insertion point within the box for that argument and then select the function from the **Function Box**. When you work with *nested functions* like this, Excel displays matching sets of parentheses with color-coding in the Formula bar to help you see which set of arguments belong with each function.

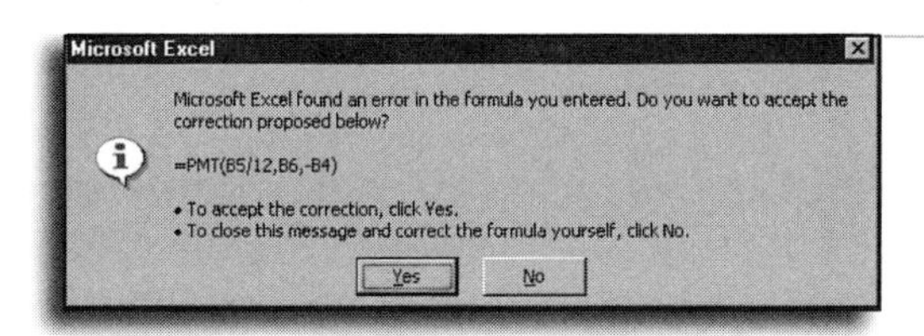

FIGURE 18.5

Excel's AutoFormat feature doesn't find every mistake, but it can suggest corrections for several common formula errors.

Adding Rows and Columns Automatically

The one Excel function that you'll probably use more than any other is SUM. In fact, you can even find an **AutoSum** button [Σ] on the Standard toolbar. To add up a column or row of numbers automatically, click in a blank cell beneath any column of numbers (or at the end of a row of numbers); then click the **AutoSum** button. Excel inserts the SUM function with the argument already filled in. Use the fill handle to adjust the selected range, if necessary, then click the **Enter** box in the Formula bar or press Enter to store the formula in the active cell.

Excel monitors the data you enter

When entering constants, you can include the percent operator (%) and minus signs with numeric data. Look to the right of the input box to see how Excel interprets the data you entered. If the data is not of the type required by the argument, Excel displays the word `Invalid` to the right of the input box.

Color-coded arguments

When you click to edit a cell that contains a formula with references to cells or ranges, you'll see a different color-coding for each reference. Look at the referenced ranges on the worksheet, and you'll see the same colors there, too. Excel uses these colors to let you see (and edit) each reference at a glance. Use the mouse to move or extend the color-code ranges and Excel automatically incorporates your changes in the formula.

Another AutoSum trick

To calculate totals for several adjacent rows or columns automatically, select the cells directly beneath the columns or to the right of the rows and then click the **AutoSum** button. Excel plugs in the SUM formula for each row or column, just as if you had added each one individually. When you use the **AutoSum** button this way, you do not see any confirmation dialog boxes.

One cell leads to another

One of the simplest Excel formulas is a direct reference to another cell. If you click in cell I24, for example, and enter the formula =A5, Excel displays the value of cell A5 in cell I24. Use this technique when you want to create input cells where you type data that you'll use throughout the worksheet. You can then use custom formatting to display the same data in different ways in other cells, without retyping the data in more than one place.

Entering Cell and Range References

When you create formulas, you choose exactly how to enter references to cell and range addresses. To enter a cell address in a formula, type its column letter and row number, with no separation between them. (Don't worry about capital letters; if you enter `a52` in a formula, Excel converts the entry to `A52` when you press Enter.)

To specify a range of data, enter the address of the cell that defines the top-left corner of the range, followed by a colon (:) and the address of the cell that defines the lower-right corner of the range. Enter `B2:M20`, for example, to refer to all the cells in columns B through M that are also in rows 2 through 20. To refer to all the cells in a row or column, use only the single coordinate. Thus, `2:2` refers to all the cells in row 2, and `C:E` includes all the cells in columns C through E.

You can also enter any cell or range reference in a formula by pointing and clicking. Start typing the formula and then click in the worksheet to enter the reference to a single cell. Drag through several cells to select a range and insert it into a formula.

Relative Versus Absolute References

The first time you move or copy a formula, you might be surprised to see that Excel automatically changes some cell references in your formula. Is this a bug? Not at all; it's an example of how Excel formulas help you build powerful worksheets without a lot of typing.

By default, cell and range references within a formula use *relative addresses*. Although Excel stores the exact location of the cells to which the formula refers, it also takes careful note of where those cells are located in relation to the cell that contains the formula. When you copy or move that formula, Excel automatically adjusts cell references to reflect their position relative to the new location.

Let's say you have a column of numbers in cells B1 through B20, and you've created a formula in B21 that totals those cells:

`=SUM(B1:B20)`. If you copy that formula to cell C21, Excel assumes you want to total the numbers in column C, so it adjusts the formula accordingly, to `=SUM(C1:C20)`. If you move a formula three rows down and five columns to the right, Excel adds three to each row number and counts five letters higher in the alphabet for each cell or range address in the new formula. Thus, a reference to D5 changes to I8.

What happens when you store a scrap of crucial information, like the current interest rate, in one particular cell? You want all formulas on your worksheet to use the value entered in that cell whenever they make an interest-related calculation. If you use relative references, every time you move or copy a formula that refers to this cell, the reference points to the wrong address. The solution? Use an *absolute address* to tell Excel not to adjust the reference when you move or copy a formula.

To specify an absolute address, use dollar signs within the cell address. When you type `$A$4` as part of a formula, for example, Excel looks for the value in cell A4 even if you move the original formula or copy it to another location.

You can mix and match relative and absolute addresses in a formula, or even in the same address. For example, `$A4` tells Excel to leave the column address at A when you move or copy the formula, but adjust the row address relative to the new location.

Relative to absolute, and back again

When you enter a cell or range reference in the Formula bar, you can quickly switch between relative, mixed, and absolute addresses without typing a single dollar sign. Place the insertion point in a cell reference or select a range reference; then press F4 to cycle through all four variations for the selection.

Using 3D References to Cells on Different Sheets

To refer to cells and ranges on other worksheets within the same workbook, follow the same rules as described in the preceding section, but preface the cell or range address with the name of the sheet followed by an exclamation point. If you have a sheet named Budget, for example, you can refer to the top-left cell of that sheet by entering `=Budget!A1` on any other sheet in the same book. You can also add references to cells or ranges on other sheets by pointing and clicking, just as you would on the active sheet. Click the appropriate sheet tab; then select the desired cell or range of cells. When you use this technique, Excel automatically enters the sheet name, exclamation point, and cell references.

Using Labels and Names to Demystify a Worksheet

Understanding how a worksheet works can be a daunting task. That's especially true when you're looking at a worksheet that someone else designed, or even one that you put together months ago and haven't looked at recently.

When you enter formulas into a worksheet, you typically point, click, and type to add references to cell and range addresses. Excel has no trouble calculating the result of `=SUM(G1:G24)*A5`. However, the meaning of that formula isn't obvious to you or me until we examine the data in all the referenced cells. To make formulas (and worksheets) easier to understand, you can enter easy-to-understand formulas using the labels on rows and columns within a worksheet instead of cell addresses. If you want to refer to cells that aren't in a labeled range, you can assign names to cells and ranges; named cells that contain formulas or constant values, like interest rates or discount formulas, can easily be plugged into other formulas on any worksheet within a workbook.

Every important cell on your worksheet—especially the ones in which you plan to change data to test different "what if" scenarios—should have a name, not just a number. On an invoice worksheet, for example, you can name one cell SalesTax Rate and another InvoiceTotal. Then, in the TotalAmount cell, you can replace those confusing cell addresses with the easy-to-understand formula **`=InvoiceTotal*SalesTaxRate`**. This formula is far easier to understand than **`=H42*B7`**.

Use named ranges instead

When you name a range, Excel uses that name throughout the entire current workbook. To use information stored in a cell or range on one sheet as part of a formula on another sheet, give the first cell or range a name. Switch to the second sheet and create the formula using the named range.

Names use absolute addresses

When you name a cell or range, that name attaches itself to the absolute address you specify. If you move or copy a formula containing a reference to the named range, the reference continues to point to the original address rather than adjust to a new relative address.

Use range names to select regions quickly

Even if you don't use named ranges in formulas, they can make navigating easier. You can jump to a cell or select an entire named range, just by choosing its name from the **Name** box to the left of the Formula bar.

Using Labels to Make Formulas Easy to Understand

When you use labels formula, pull to identify a region within a worksheet, Excel lets you create easy-to-use formulas by referring to the intersections of rows and columns. The worksheet in Figure 18.6, for example, uses months of the year as column labels and expense categories as row labels. To refer to the value at the intersection of a row and column, enter the two labels (the order doesn't matter), separated by the *intersection operator*, a space. Thus, `=Jan Insurance` refers to cell C5, which is at the intersection of the column labeled `Jan` and the row labeled `Insurance`.

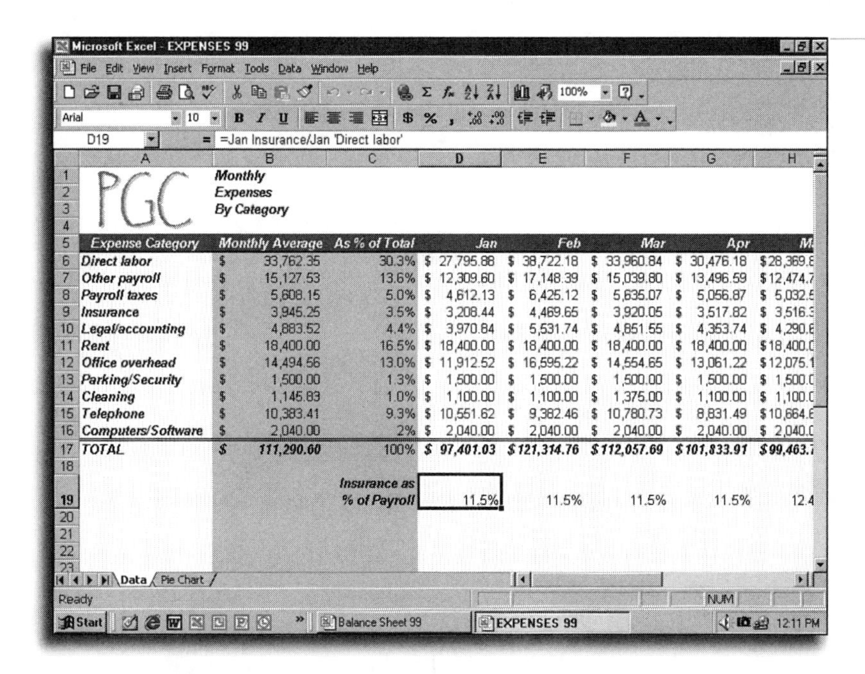

FIGURE 18.6
The formula shown here divides the contents of C5 by C9; using row and column labels makes understanding its purpose much easier.

How to Name a Cell or Range

Using labels doesn't require any effort beyond setting up your worksheet in the first place. Creating named cells or ranges, however, takes a little extra work. The easiest way to name a cell or a range is to use the **Name** box, located just to the left of the Formula bar (see Figure 18.7).

Use single quotation marks for labels with spaces

As the example in Figure 18.6 illustrates, row and column labels may contain spaces. To use these labels in formulas, be sure to enclose them in single quotation marks ('). If you use double quotation marks, Excel's Formula AutoCorrect feature offers to correct the entry for you.

Naming a Range

1. Select the cell or range you want to name.
2. Click in the **Name** box to highlight the entire cell address.
3. Type a legal name for the cell or range. (The list of rules appears in the next section.)
4. Press Enter to add the name to the list in your worksheet.

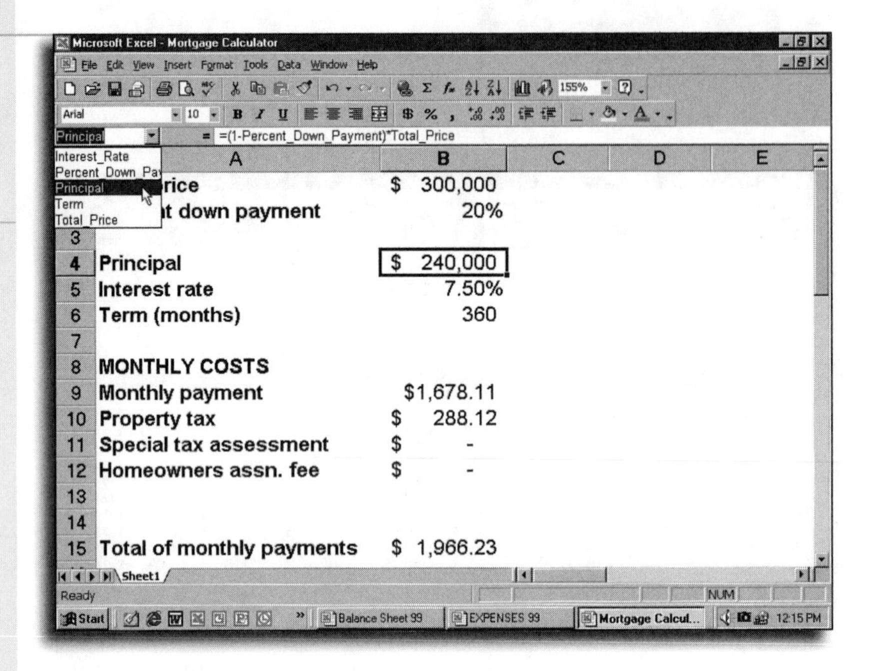

FIGURE 18.7

Select one or more cells. Then click in the **Name** box and type the name you want to use for the selected range.

Fill in formulas faster

In previous versions of Excel, you could use the drop-down list of range names to fill in formulas, too. In Excel 97 and Excel 2000, that's not possible because **the Function Box** hides the **Name** box when you edit a formula. To add a named range while editing a formula, pull down the **Insert** menu, click **Name**, and choose **Paste**. Choose the name from the Paste Name dialog box and click **OK**.

Is That Name Legal?

Excel follows strict rules that govern what you can and can't use to name a cell or a range. (And just to keep things confusing, the rules are completely different from the ones for naming a file or a worksheet tab.)

- You can use a total of up to 255 characters (but for the sake of clarity you should keep range names much shorter than that).
- The first character must be a letter or the underline character. You can't name a cell `1stQuarterSales`, but `Q1Sales` is okay.
- The remaining characters can be letters, numbers, periods, or the underline character. No other punctuation marks are allowed.
- Spaces are forbidden. If you try to name a cell `Sales Tax Rate`, Excel responds with an error message, but `Sales_Tax_Rate` is okay.

- A cell or range name cannot be the same as a cell reference or a value, so you can't name a cell `Q1` or `W2`, nor can you use a single letter or enter a number without any punctuation or letters.

One range can have several names

Yes, you can assign more than one name to the same cell or range. You might want to use different names if you intend to use a constant value in several formulas for different purposes, and you want the names to explain the purpose of each formula using slightly different wording.

Changing a Name or the Item to Which It Refers

Use the **Name** choice on Excel's **Insert** menu to manage names of cells or ranges in a workbook. The Define Name dialog box (see Figure 18.8) lets you add a new name to an existing range or change the reference for an existing name.

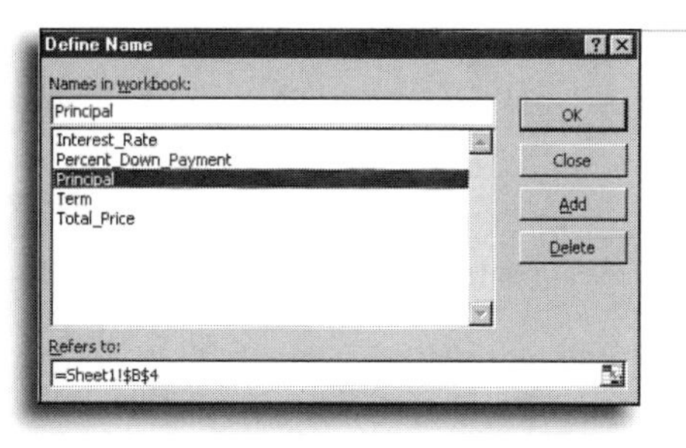

FIGURE 18.8

Choose a name from the list shown here; then select a new cell or range to redefine the name.

Changing a Named Range

1. Pull down the **Insert** menu, choose **Name**, and click **Define**.
2. In the Define Name dialog box, select the cell or range name from the **Names in workbook** list.
3. Select the contents of the **Refers to** box.
4. Click in the worksheet to select the new cell or range. Use the **Collapse Dialog** button, if necessary, to move the dialog box out of the way.
5. Click the **OK** button to change the name of the range and close the dialog box.

Creating Links Between Worksheets

You can use Excel *links* to share data between cells or ranges in one worksheet and a location in the same workbook or in a completely different workbook. Just as a formula tells Excel to display the results of a calculation, a link tells Excel to look up data from another location and use it in the active cell.

You might want to consolidate data from different sources into one worksheet. For example, you can use separate sales-tracking worksheets for each month of the year, with a single year-to-date worksheet that consolidates the monthly results. Or you might use separate worksheets to analyze budget information for each division in your company, with a master worksheet that ties all the numbers together. Linked cells help you avoid repetitive data entry.

Establishing a link may seem a bit tedious, but you do it only once. After you establish the links, you never have to go through this process again, and data you enter in one location automatically appears in all linked locations.

Linking Data Between Worksheets

1. Open all the related workbooks.
2. In the *source* worksheet (the one that has the information you want to reuse in your master worksheet), select a cell you want to link, and press Ctrl+C to copy it to the Clipboard.
3. Go to the master worksheet or workbook (called the *target* or *destination*), and select the cell in which you want to insert that information.
4. Pull down the **Edit** menu and choose **Paste Special**.
5. In the Paste Special dialog box, choose **Paste Link**.

SEE ALSO

➤ *To find details about how Excel and other Office programs use the Windows Clipboard, see page 134*

➤ *For step-by-step instructions on how to create and use hyperlinks, see page 64*

CHAPTER

19

Formatting Worksheets

Use cell formats to make worksheets easier to understand

Display dates and times correctly

Change fonts and add emphasis to cells

Wrap and slant text

Save and reuse formats using named styles

Add borders and colors to sections

Use conditional formatting to change the display of a cell's contents

Format a worksheet automatically

How Excel Displays Cell Contents

What you type in a cell is not always the same as what Excel displays; if you enter a formula, for example, you see the results of the calculation rather than the formula stored in the cell. When you enter numbers, dates, or text, Excel looks for specific instructions on formatting options such as decimal places, currency symbols, and the order of days, months, and years in a date. Thus, if you click in a cell and enter `2`, you might see `$2.00` or `200%` or `January 2, 1900`, depending on the formatting assigned to that cell. Formatting instructions also tell Excel which fonts, colors, and other attributes to use when displaying the characters in a cell or range.

Buttons on the Formatting toolbar let you apply some Office-standard formatting options, such as choosing a font or changing a range of cells to **Bold** [B], **Italic** [I], or **Underline** [U].

To see the full assortment of Excel formatting options, pull down the **Format** menu and choose **Cells**, or right-click the active cell of a selection and choose **Format Cells** from the shortcut menu. To choose a specific group of formatting options, click one of the six tabs in the Format Cells dialog box (see Figure 19.1).

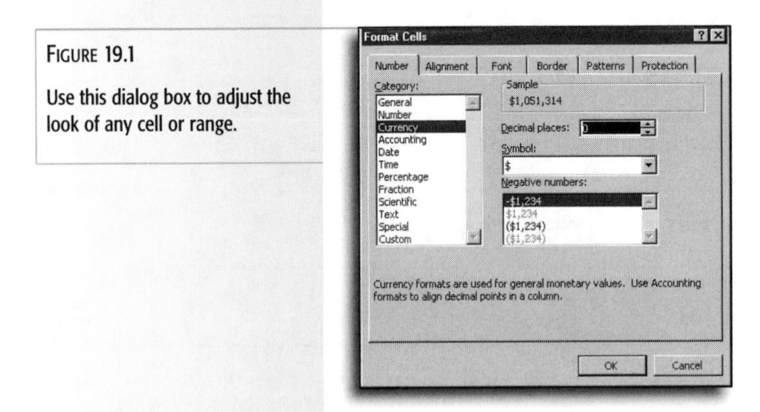

FIGURE 19.1

Use this dialog box to adjust the look of any cell or range.

Table 19.1 describes the options available on each of the tabs in the Format Cells dialog box.

TABLE 19.1 Cell Formatting Options

Click This Tab	To Set These Formatting Options
Number	Specify the number of decimal points and whether to use a currency sign or percent symbol, and other options. Don't be misled by the name—this tab also lets you format dates and text labels.
Alignment	Choose how you want cell contents to line up. By default, numbers are right-aligned in the cell and text is left-aligned. Options let you display text at an angle or wrap long entries on multiple lines within a cell.
Font	Define the font name, size, style, and color of each character in the cell. The default Excel font is 10-point Arial.
Border	Draw lines around and within cells, to set off totals or enclose a range within a box; choose line styles and colors.
Patterns	Add background colors and/or shading—to set off titles and totals, for example.
Protection	Lock the contents of cells or hide formulas to prevent you or anyone else from accidentally changing the contents of a cell; password protection is optional.

SEE ALSO

➤ *To find instructions on how to select cells, ranges, or an entire worksheet, see page 352*

Using the General Number Format

When you create a new worksheet, every cell starts out in the General format. If you don't specify any other formatting, Excel usually displays the exact text and/or numbers you entered; in cells that contain a formula, the General format displays the results of the formula using up to 11 digits (if the number contains a decimal point, it counts as a digit).

To remove all number formats you've applied manually and restore a cell to its default General format, right-click and choose **Format Cells** from the shortcut menu, then click the **Number** tab and choose **General** from the **Category** list.

Indent to set off lists

You can indent the contents of a cell by up to 15 characters. This type of formatting is useful when you have a column of items that falls into categories; format the category names normally, then use a five-character indent to set off items underneath each category.

Mix and match fonts

Excel lets you mix fonts and font attributes on different characters or words in a single cell.

Borders versus gridlines

Don't confuse borders and gridlines. Gridlines are the faint lines of a single thickness that define the borders between cells; they're visible onscreen but usually don't print. Borders, on the other hand, can be formatted to practically any size, shape, and color, and they're intended to set off regions of a worksheet when printed.

How Excel rounds off

In cells formatted with the General format, if the cell is not wide enough to show the entire number, Excel rounds the portion of the number to the right of the decimal point. If the portion of the number to the left of the decimal point won't fit in the cell or contains more than 11 digits, you see the number in scientific notation.

Applying Number Formats Automatically

Although every cell starts out in General format, it doesn't stay that way. When you enter data in a format that resembles one of Excel's built-in formats, Excel automatically applies cell formatting to the cell.

Your country determines your currency

The advice here applies to Excel users in the United States. If you've used the **Regional Settings** option in the Windows Control Panel to specify a different currency symbol, Excel uses those settings as the default when you enter currency values. To specify a different currency–if, for example, your worksheet includes a column of values in Yen as well as some in U.S. dollars–choose a Currency format, and then choose the Yen symbol from the **Symbol** drop-down list on the **Number** tab of the Format Cells dialog box.

- If the data starts with a dollar sign and contains only numbers afterward, Excel applies the Currency format, with two decimal places, regardless of how many decimal places you entered.
- If you enter data that begins or ends with a percent sign and contains only numbers otherwise, Excel applies the Percent format with up to two decimal places.
- If you enter a value that matches any of Windows' date and time formats, Excel converts the entry to a date serial value and formats the cell using the closest matching Date format. If the date you enter includes only the month and day, Excel uses the current year.
- If you enter a number that includes a comma to set off thousands or millions, Excel applies the Number format using the thousands separator and up to two decimal places.

To override any of these automatic number formats, pull down the **Format** menu and choose **Cells**; then select a new format.

Avoiding Common Errors

When does 2+2=5? Anytime you're not careful to match display formats with the numbers you've entered. Let's say you've entered `2.3` in cells A1 and B1; in cell C1, you've entered the formula `=A1+B1`. Finally, you've formatted all three cells to show no decimal places. When Excel performs the calculation, it uses the *actual* amount stored in the cell, not the truncated version you see. But it displays the results without decimal points, exactly the way you specified in the cell format. The sum of the two cells is 4.6, but Excel rounds the result to 5 for display using the no-decimal format.

To prevent this type of rounding from making it look like your worksheet contains errors, try to match the number of decimal places displayed with the number of decimal places you've entered in the row or column in question.

What happens when the number you enter is too long to fit in the active cell? Excel deals with the data in one of the following three ways:

- When you enter a number that is only a few characters wider than the current cell, Excel automatically resizes the column. It does not resize a column if you have already set the column width manually, or if you enter data that includes letters.
- In cells using the default General format, Excel uses scientific notation to display large numbers, if possible.
- If not enough room is available to display the number in scientific notation, or if you've chosen a format other than General, Excel displays a string of number signs (####) in the cell. You have to make the column wider before you can see the number.

SEE ALSO

➤ *For an explanation of error messages you might see when using formulas, see page 365*

Changing the Way a Cell's Contents Display

As I noted previously, Excel makes its best guess at the correct formatting when you enter data in a cell. You're not stuck with that choice, however; you can change the format of any cell using dozens of built-in options so that its contents display exactly the way you want them to appear. Use number and date formats, for example, to precisely control the number of decimal points and whether months and days are spelled out or abbreviated. If you can't find the precise format you're looking for, Excel lets you create your own custom format.

Add a disclaimer when you round

If you must use rounded numbers in a worksheet, indicate that fact in a footnote on charts and reports you plan to present to others. Rounding can cause apparent mistakes, and anyone who sees your worksheet, chart, or document may make judgments about your accuracy if totals, for example, don't add up to 100 percent.

Deciphering scientific notation

When you type a number that contains more digits than will fit in the current cell width, Excel rounds the number, if necessary, and displays it in scientific (exponential) notation, such as 8.23+E09. To convert the number to its decimal equivalent, move the decimal point to the right by the number after the *E* (if a minus sign appears before the *E*, move the decimal to the left). Add extra zeros as needed. In this example, because the number after the E is 9, the decimal point moves 9 places to the right and the number displayed is actually 8,230,000,000.

Special formats for values less than zero

Negative numbers often appear in parentheses, or in red (as in red ink), and sometimes in both. You can also define special formats that control what appears in a cell when the value is 0. Turn to the end of this chapter for instructions on how to use conditional formatting, which lets you use a cell's contents to define its appearance.

Plan ahead when formatting

You can format a cell or a range even if those cells are empty. Later, when you enter data into those cells, the contents will pick up the correct formatting.

Open the Format Cells dialog box instantly

One of Excel's most useful keyboard shortcuts is the one that instantly opens the Format Cells dialog box: Ctrl+1. When I'm formatting a large or complex worksheet, this key combination saves hundreds of mouse clicks. Even if you normally prefer to use the mouse, this keyboard shortcut is worth memorizing.

Some formats are automatic

When you first type in a cell, Excel watches what you enter and applies some types of formatting automatically. If you start with a dollar sign or finish with a percentage sign, for example, Excel automatically applies the Currency and Percentage formats.

Setting Number and Text Formats

When you type a number and press Enter, how should Excel display it? You have dozens of choices, all neatly organized by category on the **Number** tab of the Format Cells dialog box.

Setting Number, Date, and Text Formats

1. Click to activate the cell you want to format or select a range.
2. Pull down the **Format** menu and choose **Cells**.
3. In the Format Cells dialog box, choose an entry from the **Category** list on the left.
4. If the category you selected includes predefined display options, select one from the **Type** list. Adjust other format options (currency symbol, decimal point, and so on), if necessary.
5. The **Sample** box in the upper-right corner of the dialog box shows how the active cell will appear with the selected format settings. Click **OK** to accept the settings and return to the editing window.

Table 19.2 lists the available format categories and describes what each one does.

TABLE 19.2 **Cell Formatting Categories**

Choose This Category	To Format Cells Using These Settings
General	The default format displays numbers as entered, up to 11 digits, including a decimal point and negative sign; Excel also has a 15-digit precision limit.
Number	Displays the number of decimal places you choose, as well as an optional separator for thousands; choose from four formats for negative numbers.
Currency	Displays values using selected currency symbol, number of decimal places, and format for negative values.
Accounting	Like the Currency format, except currency symbols are aligned in columns and you can't choose a format for negative values.

Choose This Category	To Format Cells Using These Settings
Date	Uses one of 15 formats that determine whether and how to display day, date, month, and year, and whether to display a leading zero (as in 05-08-99) to help you line up columns properly.
Time	Uses one of eight formats that determine whether and how to display hours, minutes, seconds, and AM/PM designators.
Percentage	Multiplies the cell value by 100 and adds a percent symbol; you specify the number of decimal places.
Fraction	Stores numbers in decimal format but displays as fractions in one of nine formats; to display stock prices using 8ths, 16ths, and 32nds, select **Up to three digits** from the **Type** box.
Scientific	Displays numbers in scientific notation; you select the number of decimal places.
Text	Displays cell contents exactly as entered, even if the cell contains numbers or a formula.
Special	Lets you enter long and short U.S. zip codes, phone numbers, and social security numbers; adds hyphens and parentheses as necessary.
Custom	Start with a built-in format and use symbols to define your own display rules; instructions are in the Help topic titled "Custom number, date, and time format codes."

Five buttons on the Formatting toolbar represent convenient formatting shortcuts. Select a cell or range and then click the button to apply the appropriate formatting immediately. See Table 19.3 for descriptions of these buttons.

TABLE 19.3 **Formatting Toolbar Button Descriptions**

Button Name	Button	Description
Currency Style	$	Click to apply the default Currency style.
Percent Style	%	Click todisplay the selection as a percentage with no decimal points.

continues...

New Y2K formats

Excel includes two new Year 2000–compatible date formats that use four digits for the year. See "Excel and the Year 2000" later in this chapter.

Watch those percentages!

Be careful how you enter percentages into your worksheet. If you format a cell using one of the **Percentage** options and then enter a number like `7`, it appears as **`700%`** (and your calculations are off by two decimal points). To enter percentages into a worksheet, remember to use the percent sign (`7%`) or add the decimal point (`.07`).

Entering fractions without hassle

To enter a number as a fraction and store its decimal equivalent in the cell automatically, enter `0` and a space first. If you don't, Excel converts some fractions to dates (5/8, for example, becomes May 8) and others to text. When you enter `0 5/8` into a cell formatted with the General format, Excel correctly stores the number as **`0.625`** and displays the fraction you entered, changing the cell format to Fraction.

Mastering the tricky Text format

When you format a cell using the Text format, whatever you enter in the cell appears exactly as you typed it. However, if you apply the Text format to cells that already contain numbers or formulas, the display may not change as you expect. To reset the display, click in the cell, press the F2 key, and then press Enter.

TABLE 19.3 **Continued**

Button Name	Button	Description
Comma Style	,	Click to add a thousands separator and display the selection with two decimal points.
Increase Decimal	+.0 .00	Each click adds one decimal point to the format of the selected cell(s).
Decrease Decimal	.00 +.0	Each click removes one decimal point from the format of the selected cell(s).

Setting Date and Time Formats

Currency and Percent keyboard shortcuts

To apply the Currency format to the current selection, press Ctrl+Shift+$. To format the selection in Percent format, press Ctrl+Shift+%.

Recovering from date disasters

If you accidentally apply a Date or Time format to a cell that contains a number, the result usually makes no sense at all. For example, if your worksheet contains a list of transactions with dates and numbers, you might want to format all the dates at once. If you accidentally select one of the cells that contains the number `$42.95`, Excel displays some variation of the following date and time: February 11, 1900, 10:48 PM. Fortunately, the number you entered is unchanged; choose the correct Number format to display the cell's contents correctly.

When you type a simple date or time into a cell, Excel converts the value into a format you might not recognize. This serial date format is the key to Excel's capability to perform calculations using date and time information.

When you click in a cell and enter any data in a recognized date or time format, Excel converts it to a whole number.

- If you enter a date, Excel converts it to a whole number that counts the number of days that have elapsed since January 1, 1900. Thus, the serial date value of `August 24, 1999` is 36396.
- When you enter a time (hours, minutes, and seconds), Excel converts it to a decimal value between 0 (midnight) and 0.999988 (11:59:59 PM). If you enter a time of `10:00 AM`, for example, Excel stores it as 0.416667.
- If you combine a date and time in a single cell, Excel combines the serial date and time values. Thus, Excel saves `August 24, 1999 10:00 AM` as 36396.416667.

Most of the time, you don't even need to be aware of these transformations. They happen instantly, and Excel automatically applies the default Date or Time format to your cell so that it displays correctly. You can choose a different Date or Time format to change the way the date appears in the cell without changing the stored value; for example, to save space in a column of dates, you might choose a format that displays only the month and date and not the year.

This complex transformation actually takes place for a good reason. In serial format, dates and times represent values that Excel can readily use in calculations. Using date values stored in this format, you can enter formulas that calculate how many days are left until a project's scheduled completion date, how many months have elapsed since an employee was hired, or the average number of minutes required to complete a task. If you enter dates in cells C1 and C2, for example, you can quickly calculate the difference between them using the formula `=C1-C2`.

Shortcuts for Date and Time formats

You don't need to open a dialog box to apply Date and Time formats to data. If you've inadvertently reformatted a cell, row, or column that should display dates or times, you'll see the serial numbers instead. Use these keyboard shortcuts to reset the display: Ctrl+Shift+# for the default date format; Ctrl+Shift+@ for the default time format.

Excel and the Year 2000

It's impossible to enter dates before January 1, 1900, in an Excel worksheet. Dates after December 31, 1999, however, are no problem—in fact, you can enter any date through December 31, 9999 (that's a serial date value of 2958465, if you want to try it for yourself).

As the name suggests, Excel correctly handles Year 2000 (Y2K) issues. But avoiding Y2K problems takes your cooperation. Most Y2K problems crop up when you enter or import data that includes only two digits for the year. When you enter or import dates in this format, Excel converts the year to four digits, using the following rules:

- Excel converts the two-digit years 00 through 29 to the years 2000 through 2029. Thus, if you enter or import the value `3/14/04`, Excel stores it as serial value 38060, or March 14, 2004.
- Excel converts the two-digit years 30 through 99 to 1930 through 1999. When you enter or import the value `9/29/55`, Excel stores it as serial value 20361, or September 29, 1955.

If you're using a display format that shows only two years, you may not realize that Excel has stored the wrong data, but any calculations you make may be off by a full century. For example, if you are preparing an amortization table for a 30-year mortgage with a start date of 2/1/00, Excel will correctly interpret the date as being in the year 2000; but if you manually enter the end date as 2/1/30, Excel will assume you meant 1930, and your calculations won't work. Enter the date as `2/1/2030` instead.

Always use four digits

To avoid inadvertently entering or importing incorrect data, get in the habit of entering years in four-digit format: 5/23/2005. Excel will always store this date correctly, regardless of the Date format you've chosen for display purposes.

Creating Custom Cell Formats

You can access literally hundreds of built-in formats for displaying numbers, dates, and text in cells. If the exact format you need isn't in that collection, create a custom format of your own. Custom formats let you specify the display of positive and negative numbers as well as zero values; you can also add text to the contents of any cell. Use a custom format to add text to the result of a calculation, for example, so that negative numbers include the word `deficit`.

To create a custom number format, open the Format Cells dialog box, click the **Number** tab, and choose **Custom** from the bottom of the **Category** list. You then see the list of choices shown in Figure 19.2. Enter custom format codes in the **Type** box. To modify an existing format, apply that format to the selection and then select its entry from the bottom of the **Type** drop-down list.

Get help for creating custom number formats

This book isn't large enough for me to explain all the custom codes that Excel uses as part of a custom number format. Fortunately, excellent online help is available. Click the **Office Assistant** button and search for `Create a custom number format`. Hyperlinks and jump buttons in this topic offer detailed instructions on how to create any type of custom format.

For a more in-depth discussion of Custom number formatting, see Chapter 20, "Advanced Worksheet Formatting," in *Special Edition Using Microsoft Office 2000*, also published by Que.

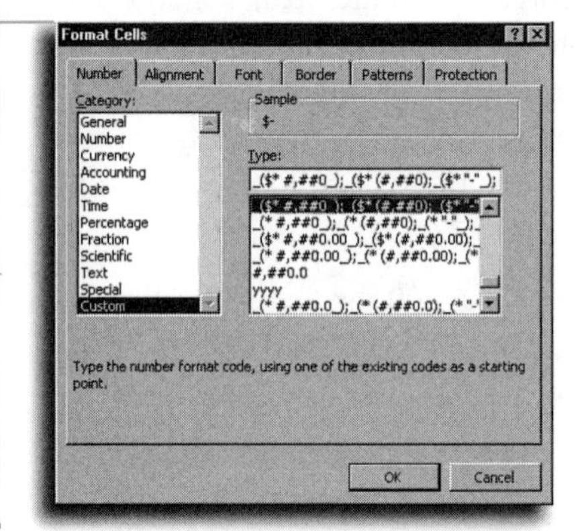

FIGURE 19.2

Excel's online Help includes excellent instructions for creating and editing your own custom number formats in this dialog box.

Formatting a Worksheet

When you first create a worksheet, every cell uses the same fonts, every row is the same height, and every column is the same width. If you enter numbers, text, and formulas, your calculations may work perfectly, but anyone looking at the worksheet will have to struggle to see the distinction between headings, data,

Change the way zeros display

Normally, when you enter a zero value in a cell, it picks up the formatting assigned to that cell. In a column formatted with the Currency format, for example, that means you'll see `$0.00`. You can use custom formats to make these values appear as a dash instead; open the Format Cells dialog box, choose **Custom** from the **Category** list, and pick one of the two options near the bottom of the **Type** list that begin with `($`.

and totals. With Excel's extensive selection of formatting tools, you can redesign a worksheet to make its organization crystal clear.

When I'm designing a worksheet, I use the following checklist to make sure that it's as easy to understand as possible:

- Double-check the formatting for every cell, especially those that contain numbers, dates, and dollar amounts; make any necessary adjustments.
- Make sure that all columns align properly.
- Make headings and titles bigger and bolder so that they clearly define what type of data is in each row and column. Bold, italic, and white type on a dark background are especially effective in titles.
- To really make the bottom line pop off the page, use the **Borders** button to add an emphatic double underline above a row of totals. Add thinner borders to set off subtitles.
- For worksheets intended for online viewing, use the **Fill Color** drop-down list to add light shading throughout the **data** section. Soft yellow shading is easier on the eyes than the default white background.
- Use the **Sheet** tab in the Page Setup dialog box to turn off the normal Excel gridlines. You'll be amazed at how uncluttered the worksheet looks without these distracting lines.

Changing Fonts and Character Attributes

Fonts are one of your most effective tools for designing easy-to-follow worksheets. The default font (10-point Arial) is fine for basic data entry, but you may want to choose smaller fonts when you need to squeeze more data onto printed pages, and you'll certainly want to beef up headings and totals with larger, bolder fonts.

Mix and match formatting within a cell

You can apply different fonts, font sizes, colors, and other formatting to different words or characters in the same cell. Use this feature to highlight a company name in your logo font, for example. Using this feature is also a useful way to insert trademark and copyright symbols or to emphasize key words in labels. To see your changes instantly, edit in the cell rather than in the formula bar.

Use the dialog box for fine formatting

The **Font** tab of the Format Cells dialog box offers some formatting options not found on the toolbar, such as strikethrough and double underline. When you add custom formatting, you automatically clear the **Normal font** check box. Check here to clear all formatting and restore the cell to Excel's default style.

Excel lets you apply font formatting to an entire cell, or you can select individual words, numbers, or characters in a cell and format them differently.

Formatting Fonts in a Cell or Range

1. Select the cell or range. To format one or more characters within a cell, click the cell to make it active; then click within the cell or in the formula bar and select the character(s) you want to reformat.
2. To change fonts, choose a font from the drop-down list on the Formatting toolbar. Use the **Font Size** drop-down list to change the size of the selection.
3. Click the **Bold** [B], **Italic** [I], or **Underline** [U] buttons to change font effects. You can combine any of these effects.
4. For additional font options, right-click the selection and choose **Format Cells** from the shortcut menu. If you've selected part of the current cell's contents, you see the **Font** tab of the Format Cells dialog box as shown in Figure 19.3.
5. Click **OK** to apply the changes to the selection and close the dialog box.

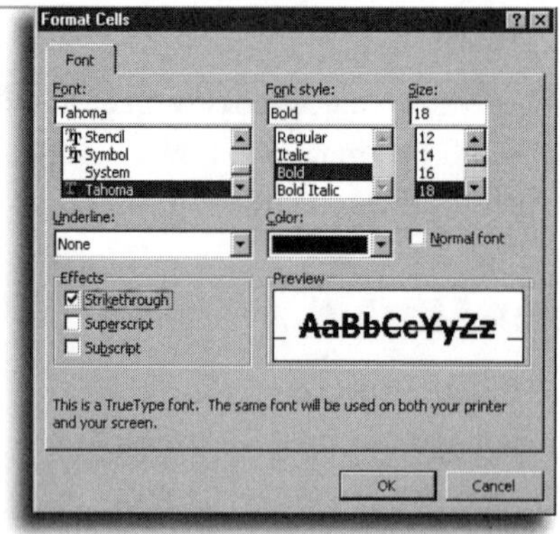

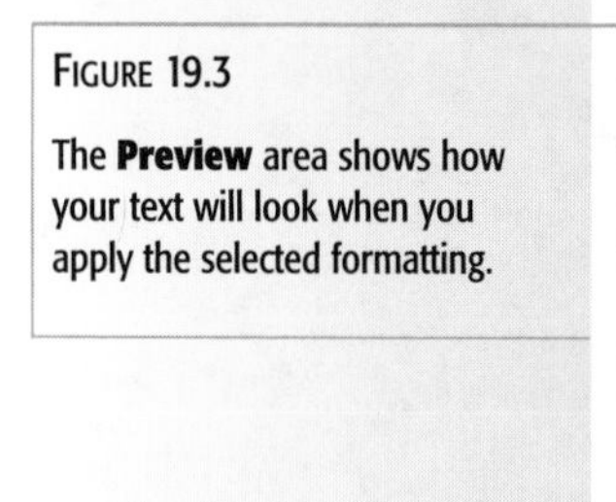

FIGURE 19.3

The Preview area shows how your text will look when you apply the selected formatting.

Entering international currency symbols

If your worksheets track global stock markets and monetary funds, you may need to insert special characters that don't appear on the standard U.S. keyboard—such as the symbols for a pound (£) or yen (¥). Select the Currency format and then look at the **Symbol** drop-down list, where you can choose any currency from Albanian *Leks* to Polish *zlotys*.

Aligning, Wrapping, and Rotating Text and Numbers

What do you do when the text in a cell is too long to fit comfortably? That's a particular problem with the headings above columns—for example, in a worksheet that includes a column with the heading `Average Sales Price` over a column of numbers in Currency format. Making the column wide enough to accommodate the text isn't an acceptable option, because you want the column to be just wide enough to display the numbers neatly. The solution? Have Excel wrap the text in the heading cell to a second or third line.

Formatting Text to Display in Multiple Lines

1. Select the cell or range you want to reformat.
2. Right-click and choose **Format Cells**.
3. Click the **Alignment** tab and check the **Wrap text** box.
4. If your column headings include a mix of long and short labels, choose **Center** from the **Vertical** drop-down list. Headings formatted this way seem to "float" instead of sitting on the bottom of the cell.
5. Click **OK** to apply the new format. Now, instead of disappearing from view when they reach the right edge of the cell, your text wraps to create additional lines in the same cell.

Wrap text as you enter it

You can control exactly where each line breaks in a cell, rather than relying on Excel to break at the first available point in a long line. To wrap text to a new line, press Alt+Enter. If you use this technique when you first enter the text in a cell, it automatically turns on wrapping for that cell.

You can also change the orientation of text within a cell to any angle, including straight up or down. Changing the orientation can save space and give your data a professional look when you have narrow columns with lengthy titles. Open the Format Cells dialog box, click the **Alignment** tab, and drag the control in the **Orientation** section up or down to the desired angle. You can combine wrapped text and slanted headings to good effect, as shown in Figure 19.4.

Using Borders, Boxes, and Colors

You can create a distinctive identity for sections of a worksheet by using borders, boxes, and background colors. Choose thin lines, thick lines, and double lines on any side of any cell or range. You can also add colorful backgrounds (and change the font formatting to complementary colors).

To instantly apply borders or colors, first select a cell or range, then click the **Borders**, **Fill Color**, or **Font Color** buttons on the Formatting toolbar. Click the arrow to the right of each button to choose a specific option from the drop-down list.

Choose the right colors and shading for each section

Dark backgrounds and white type help worksheet titles stand out. Soft, light background colors make columns of numbers more readable; be careful not to add so much color that the text becomes hard to distinguish. Use alternating colors or shading to make it easy for the eye to tell which entries belong in each row, even on an extra-wide worksheet that contains many columns of data.

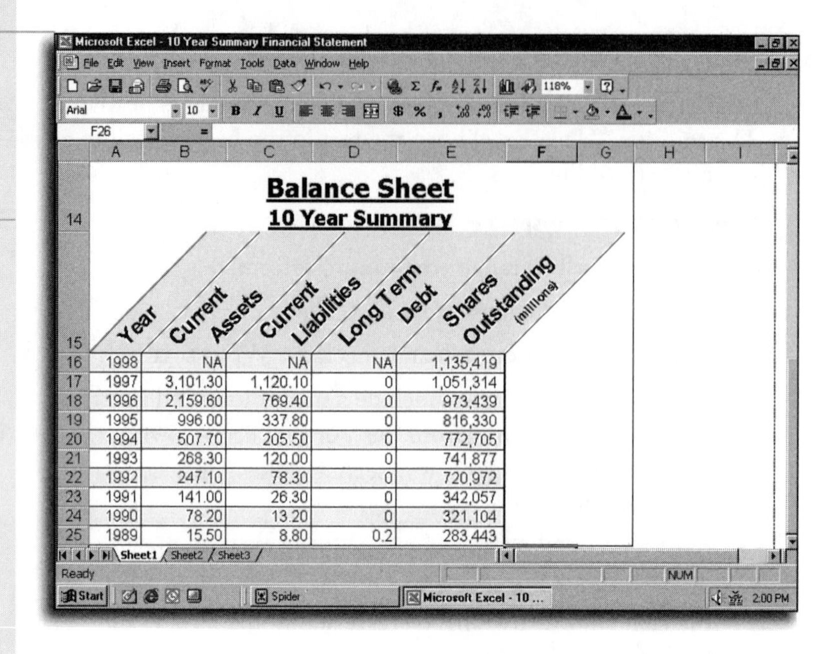

FIGURE 19.4

Wrapping text in these cells and changing the orientation to 45 degrees gives this table a professional appearance.

To fine-tune borders and colors, first select the cells or range you want to format; then right-click and choose **Format Cells**. Click the **Border** tab (see Figure 19.5) to add and remove lines around the selection.

Use different borders in the same cell

You can mix and match line styles and colors, even on different borders of the same cell. In an accounting worksheet, for example, you might want a double line below the last row of data and just above the totals, with single lines between each row of data.

Merging Cells

How do you center a heading over several worksheet columns? When I worked with my first spreadsheet program years ago, I remember having to pad cells with space characters to create the illusion that a heading was centered over several columns. With Excel, I can use the **Merge and Center** button on the Formatting toolbar to make short work of this task. This technique is useful when your worksheet includes years and quarters, as in the example in Figure 19.6.

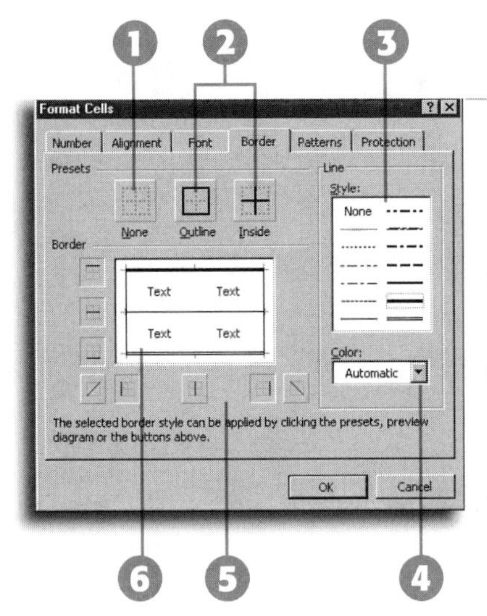

FIGURE 19.5

Use borders, boxes, and colors to distinguish sections of your worksheet.

1. Click here to clear all cell and range borders.
2. These preset selections add borders around the entire range or just the inside.
3. Choose a line style–thick, thin, doubled, dotted, or dashed–before you add any lines.
4. Choose a different color for the border, if you like.
5. Add one line at a time, on the left or right, top or bottom of the cell, or diagonally. Click again to remove the line.
6. This **Preview** window shows you how your borders will look. Click any line to change its style or remove it.

Centering a Heading over Several Columns

1. Select the cells over the columns where you want to center the heading.
2. Click the **Merge and Center** button. The text from the leftmost cell is now centered within the range you selected.
3. To change the text, click in the cell and begin typing. You can also change the alignment of the merged cells to left or right, without changing the merge.

You may encounter problems when you try to cut and paste merged cells, or when you attempt to sort a list that contains a merged cell. To restore the merged cells to their normal position on the grid, click to make the merged cell active, then right-click and choose **Format Cells**. Click the **Alignment** tab and clear the check mark from the **Merge cells** box.

Look before merging

When you merge cells, Excel uses only the contents of the top-left cell and deletes the contents of all other cells in the selection. Be sure you're not inadvertently deleting important data when you try this.

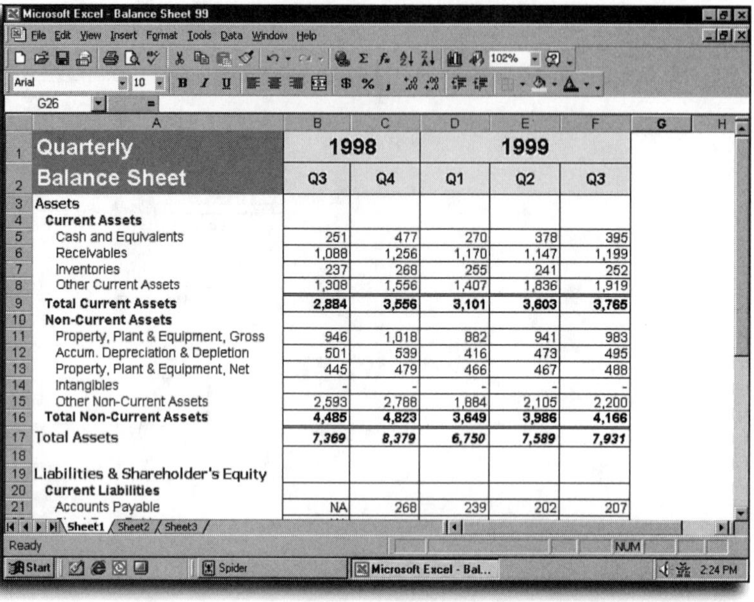

FIGURE 19.6

Merge several adjacent cells and center them to make it clear that a heading applies to several rows or columns.

	A	B	C	D	E	F
1	Quarterly	1998		1999		
2	Balance Sheet	Q3	Q4	Q1	Q2	Q3
3	Assets					
4	Current Assets					
5	Cash and Equivalents	251	477	270	378	395
6	Receivables	1,088	1,256	1,170	1,147	1,199
7	Inventories	237	268	255	241	252
8	Other Current Assets	1,308	1,556	1,407	1,836	1,919
9	Total Current Assets	2,884	3,556	3,101	3,603	3,765
10	Non-Current Assets					
11	Property, Plant & Equipment, Gross	946	1,018	882	941	983
12	Accum. Depreciation & Depletion	501	539	416	473	495
13	Property, Plant & Equipment, Net	445	479	466	467	488
14	Intangibles	-	-	-	-	-
15	Other Non-Current Assets	2,593	2,788	1,884	2,105	2,200
16	Total Non-Current Assets	4,485	4,823	3,649	3,986	4,166
17	Total Assets	7,369	8,379	6,750	7,589	7,931
18						
19	Liabilities & Shareholder's Equity					
20	Current Liabilities					
21	Accounts Payable	NA	268	239	202	207

Changing Row Height and Column Width

On a fresh new worksheet, every row is the same height, and every column is the same width. As you design and fill the sheet with data, however, you'll probably change the size of rows and columns. A column that contains only two-digit numbers doesn't need to be as wide as one that's filled with category headings, for example.

Excel takes care of some of these adjustments automatically. Rows automatically adjust in height when you change the font size of the text within the cells, for example. When you enter a number that's a few characters too wide to fit in the current cell, the column expands to accommodate. You can also adjust row heights and column widths manually.

- Double-click the right border of a column heading (the alphabetic label above the column) to automatically adjust column width to accommodate the widest entry in that column. Double-click the bottom border of a row heading (the numeric label to the left of the row) to resize a row to accommodate the tallest character in that row.

Don't just center headings

On the **Alignment** tab of the Format Cells dialog box, click the **Horizontal** drop-down list in the **Text alignment** section. Choose **Left (Indent)** and pick the number of characters you want to indent the current cell. This option is useful to distinguish subheadings from headings at the beginning of a row, as in Figure 19.6. Right-click this list and choose **What's This?** to see detailed descriptions of other options.

Use Excel's Shrink to fit option

You can make a quick adjustment when the contents of a cell are just a bit too large to fit. Right-click the cell, choose **Format Cells**, and click the **Alignment** tab. Check the **Shrink to fit** box. Excel automatically adjusts the font size to fill the column width.

- To drag a column to a new size, point to the thin line at the right of the column heading until the pointer changes to a two-headed arrow. Hold down the mouse button, drag the edge of the column until it's the width you want, and release the button.
- To drag a row to a new height, point to the bottom of a row heading and click when you see the resize pointer. Hold down the mouse button, drag the edge of the row until it's the height you want, and release.
- To set a precise row height or column width, pull down the **Format** menu. Choose **Row** and click **Height**, then enter any number between 0 and 409 points. Use the **Column** and **Width** menu options to enter any number between 0 and 255 characters.
- To change the standard width for all columns in the current worksheet, pull down the **Format** menu, choose **Column**, click **Standard Width**, and enter the new column width (in characters) in the dialog box. The new width will not apply to columns whose width you have already reset.

Adjust several rows or columns at once

To adjust more than one row or column at a time, make a selection first. You can change the width of multiple columns, for example, even if they're not adjacent to one another.

Watch the ScreenTips

As you drag to resize a row or column, ScreenTips show you the new height of the row (in points) or the width of the column (in characters). If you've selected multiple rows or columns, Excel adjusts all of them to the size shown in the ScreenTip.

You can hide a row or column by dragging it until its height or width is 0. Or use the pull-down **Format** menu, choose **Row** or **Column**, and click **Hide**. To make a hidden column or row visible, select the columns or rows on either side of the hidden one; then pull down the **Format** menu, choose **Row** or **Column**, and click **Unhide**.

To resize a column or row to fit the size or length of text automatically, make a selection, click **Format**, choose **Row** or **Column**, and then choose **AutoFit** or **AutoFit Selection**.

Reusing Your Favorite Formats

Creating the perfect formatting for a section can be a time-consuming process. When you find a format you want to reuse, save it. Just like Word, Excel lets you collect your favorite formats and store them in reusable styles.

Saving a Cell Format As a Named Style

1. Select a cell that contains the formatting you want to save.
2. Click the **Format** menu and choose **Style**. The dialog box shown in Figure 19.7 appears.
3. Type a name in the **Style name** box.
4. By default, all cell formatting options are included with the style. Clear the check mark from any of the boxes below the style name to remove that option from the style.
5. Click the **Modify** button to open the Format Cells dialog box and adjust any formatting options, if necessary.
6. Click the **Add** button to save the style in the current workbook.

What's in a (style) name?

You can use any combination of letters, numbers, and spaces in a style name; to make sure you can read the full name from the drop-down list, however, keep its total length to 30 characters or less.

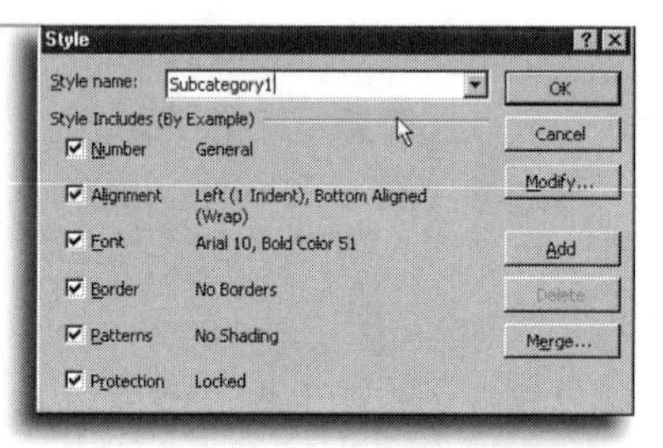

FIGURE 19.7

Want to reuse a complicated cell format? Save it as a named style and then apply it when you need it.

To use a named style instead of direct formatting options, click the **Format** menu and choose **Style**. Choose a style name from the drop-down list and click **OK**.

Copy styles between workbooks

Styles are available only to worksheets in the workbook where you save them. However, you can copy styles between workbooks, as long as both are open. First, open the workbook containing the styles you want to copy. Next, open the workbook where you want to use the styles, pull down the **Format** menu, choose **Style** to open the Style dialog box, and click the **Merge** button. In the Merge Styles dialog box, pick the name of the workbook containing the styles. After you click **OK**, your styles will be available in the current workbook, too.

SEE ALSO

➤ *To learn how to copy formats between cells quickly using Excel's **Format Painter** button, see page 140*

Changing Default Formatting for New Worksheets

Every time you start Excel or whenever you click the **New** button, you get a blank workbook that uses Excel's default settings. If you want to use different fonts, row heights, or column sizes for each new workbook, you can change settings for the default workbook. To do so, create a new workbook template and save it in the XLStart folder.

Changing Default Workbook Formats

1. Create a new workbook or open an existing workbook whose settings you want to use as Excel's defaults.
2. To change the style of all cells in the workbook, modify the General style, as described in the previous section. Add other named styles and macros. If you want to include text, graphics, and other content or formatting on any worksheet, you can do so.
3. Pull down the **File** menu and choose **Save As**. In the **Save as type** box, choose **Template**.
4. In the **File name** box, enter `Book`. (Excel adds the .xlt extension automatically.) Do not save the file in the Templates folder; instead, save it in the C:\Program Files\Microsoft Office\Office\XLStart folder. (The exact location of this folder may be slightly different, depending on your version of Windows.)
5. Click **OK** to save the template. Any future workbooks you create will include the formats and content in this template.

Adjusting Formatting Based on a Cell's Contents

Sometimes you may want the numbers or text displayed in a cell to act as an alarm. In a sales worksheet, for example, you might want to pay special attention to the row of totals, displaying a cell's contents in bold red letters when it falls below a certain target and in bright green when the number is above the monthly goal.

Excel 2000 lets you define conditional formatting that works exactly that way. This feature is tricky, so it's a good thing that along with the dialog box you see in Figure 19.8, the Office Assistant appears to offer help. Pull down the **Format** menu and choose **Conditional Formatting** to get started.

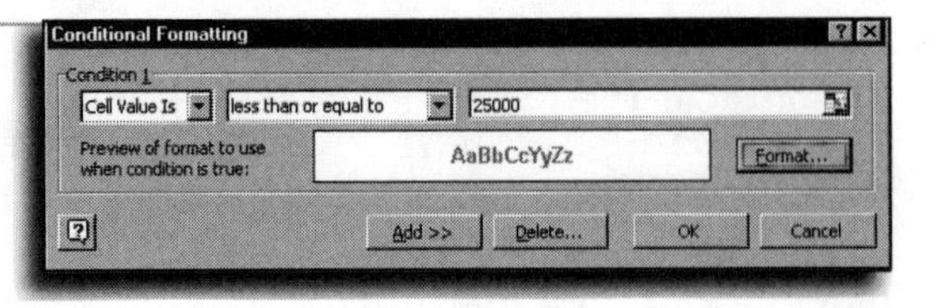

FIGURE 19.8

Use conditional formatting to change the appearance of certain cells based on comparisons you define.

To order Excel to display the contents of a cell using a special format, you first have to create a condition. Use drop-down lists in the **Condition** section to compare the cell values with the contents of another cell or with a value. For example, you could define a condition "Cell value is greater than or equal to 20,000," and Excel would apply the special formatting if the value is 30,000 but leave the standard format in place if the value is only 15,000. You can also enter a formula in this box to have Excel compare the cell's contents against a calculation.

Using a Calculation to Format a Cell's Contents

1. Select the cell or range where you want to apply the formatting; then pull down the **Format** menu and choose **Conditional Formatting**.
2. In the **Condition 1** box, use the drop-down lists to define the comparison you want to make. In this example, Excel applies the formatting only if the cell contents are less than or equal to 25,000.
3. Click the **Format** button to open a stripped-down version of the Format Cells dialog box.
4. Define the special format you want to use when the cell's contents match the condition you defined and then click **OK**. (Although you can't tell from this illustration, the sample text is bright red.)

Your format choices are limited

When defining a conditional format, you must use the same font and font size as the underlying format, but you can choose a different font style (bold italic, for example), adjust the text and background colors and shading, and use underlining or strikethrough.

5. To create a second or third conditional format, click the **Add>>** button and repeat steps 2-4 for **Condition 2** and **Condition 3**.
6. Click **OK** to apply the new formatting options to the selected cell or range.

Using AutoFormat for Quick Results

Like Word's matching feature with the same name, Excel's AutoFormat promises to turn your worksheet instantly into a work of art. When you apply AutoFormatting to simple worksheet ranges with easily identifiable headings, totals, and other elements, the feature works pretty much as advertised. If your worksheet is more complex, however, you'll probably be dissatisfied with the results.

How Excel selects ranges automatically

When you use AutoFormat or other table-based options (such as sorting a list), Excel uses the current selection. If you don't make a selection, Excel uses the current region, which is the block of filled-in cells that extends in all directions from the insertion point to the next empty row or column, or the edge of the worksheet. For that reason, when you design a worksheet, you should always include at least one blank row and column to mark the border of every separate data entry block.

Formatting a Worksheet Automatically

1. Select a range. If you skip this step, Excel selects the current region.
2. Pull down the **Format** menu and choose **AutoFormat**. The dialog box shown in Figure 19.9 appears.
3. Pick one of the built-in formats. Each entry in the list includes a preview, with the name of the format just below it.
4. To enable or disable specific types of automatic formatting, such as borders or fonts, click the **Options** button and add or remove check marks.
5. Click **OK** to see the results.

Experimenting is okay

You don't take any risks by using the **AutoFormat** option. If the results are unsatisfactory, click the **Undo** button or press Ctrl+Z immediately to restore the previous worksheet formatting. Then select a smaller range or a different set of format options and try again.

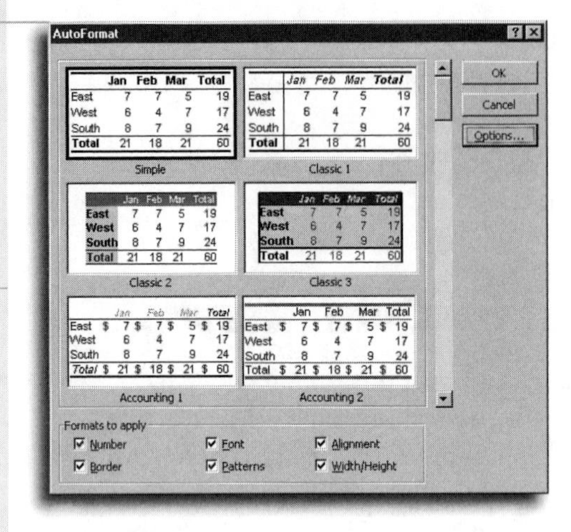

FIGURE 19.9

AutoFormat is most effective when you use it on small, well-defined ranges. Choose the options at the bottom of the dialog box to determine what types of changes to apply automatically.

SEE ALSO

➤ *To learn more about AutoCorrect, AutoFormat, and other common features, see page 41*

CHAPTER

20

Printing Worksheets

Learn why you shouldn't use Excel's Print button

Preview the page before you print

Specify sheets and ranges to print

Add titles and page numbers to worksheets

Control exactly which data goes on which page

The Secrets of Perfect Printouts

After you've debugged every worksheet formula and formatted each row and column to perfection, how do you get the results to look good on paper? That task isn't as easy as it sounds. By their very nature, worksheets sprawl in every direction, and your data will rarely fit perfectly on ordinary letter paper without some formatting help from you.

Excel gives you several powerful tools that let you preview how your worksheet will look on the printed page. If necessary, you can divide the worksheet into smaller sections and give each of these regions its own page. You can shrink rows and columns to a size that will fit on the page, repeating row and column headings to make the display of data easier to follow. You can even force Excel to fit your data into the exact number of pages you specify.

Whatever you do, though, don't just click the Print button.

What Can Go Wrong When You Print

Rewire the Print button

I feel so strongly about the inadvisability of using the Print button that I've reassigned it on my Standard toolbar. The change is simple: Follow the procedures outlined in Chapter 6, "Customizing Office," to customize the toolbar, drag the Print button off the toolbar, and drop the Print... button in its place. The ellipsis after the Print command means that when you click the button, Excel opens the Print dialog box instead of blindly starting to print pages.

On Excel's Standard toolbar is a **Print** button that lets you bypass all dialog boxes and print the current worksheet (or the current *print area*) using default settings. I strongly recommend that you avoid clicking this button to start printing. Why? Here are just a few of the things that can go wrong when you send a worksheet to the printer without first checking your print settings:

- The 13 columns in your budget worksheet don't quite fit on the page, so the last two or three months wind up on a page of their own, separated from the rest of your data.
- One or two columns aren't wide enough to display the data entered there, so you see a string of pound signs (####) instead of the numbers you expect.
- You've edited your worksheet since you last defined the print area, and now your printout doesn't include the row that includes your grand totals.

- Your default printer is set for portrait orientation, but all your pages were designed to be printed sideways, using landscape orientation.
- You've inadvertently selected the wrong printer, so you have to walk to another building to track down your hard copy.

Using Print Preview to Guarantee Best Results

If you shouldn't use the Print button, how should you go about putting your worksheets on paper? The best way to get perfect printouts every time is to preview your pages first.

Open the worksheet you plan to print and click the **Print Preview** button. Excel switches from editing mode to a Print Preview window like the one in Figure 20.1.

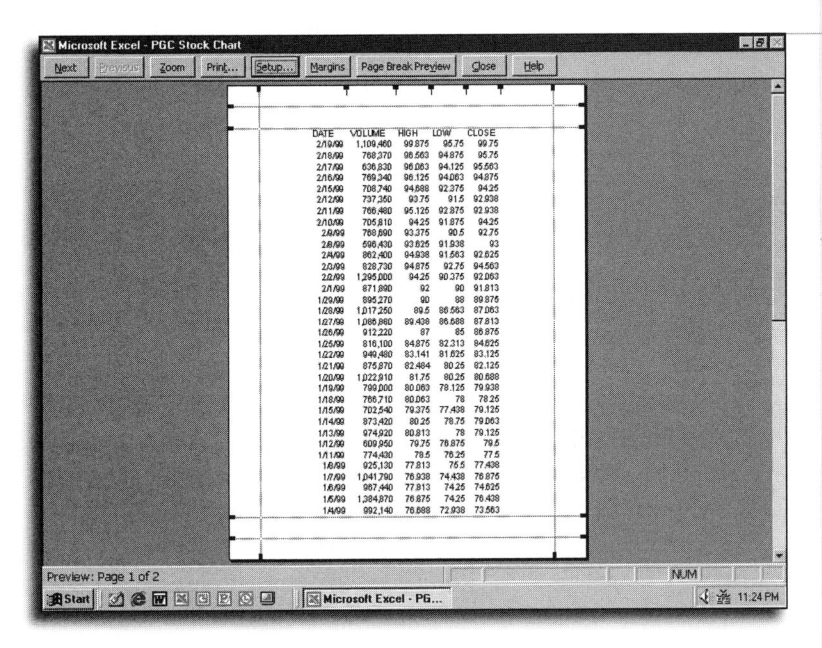

FIGURE 20.1
The status bar at the bottom of the Print Preview window lets you see at a glance how many pages the printed worksheet will use.

To fix a typo or change the formatting of a cell's contents, you need to switch back to editing mode. However, you can handle all basic page-formatting tasks directly from the Print Preview window. The tools listed in Table 20.1 can help you make adjustments.

Word's Print Preview is better

Excel's Print Preview window is useful, but it doesn't offer the same flexibility as Word's identically named feature. You can't display multiple pages in the preview window, for example, nor can you click a button to edit a heading quickly.

TABLE 20.1 Tools Used in the Print Preview Window

Button	What It Does
Next, Previous	Jumps from page to page. The status bar in the lower-left corner shows the current page and the number of pages your printout will occupy.
Zoom	Toggles between full-page view and actual size.
Print...	Sends the current job to the printer.
Setup...	Has the same effect as choosing Page Setup from the File menu. Adjust most page-related options here.
Margins	Displays markers that indicate page margins, row and column borders, headers, and footers. Click and drag to adjust any of these settings visually.
Page Break Preview	Overlays page numbers on the entire worksheet to indicate which data will appear on each page. Click the thick dotted lines to adjust page breaks manually.
Close	Exits the Print Preview display and returns to the worksheet editing window.
Help	Provides context-sensitive help and step-by-step instructions.

Preparing Your Worksheet for the Printer

When you're building a worksheet, paper is often the last thing on your mind. You're more concerned with making sure that the formulas are correct, that data is arranged into proper rows and columns, that columns are wide enough to show the numbers inside, and that all your data shows up in the right bars on your charts.

When you finish building a worksheet, switch into Print Preview mode to see a quick snapshot of how it will look on the page. The first thing you'll notice is that Excel tries to identify the proper region to print. If you don't specifically define an area to be printed, Excel assumes that you want to print all the data in

Use Print Preview for small jobs, too

If the worksheet you're getting ready to print is a simple one-page job, use the Print Preview button to check that the print area is properly selected. For a job that doesn't spill onto a second page, the **Next** and **Previous** buttons should be grayed out. If they're not, click the **Close** button, pull down the **File** menu, clear the settings for **Print Area**, and try again.

the currently selected worksheet or worksheets, starting with cell A1 and extending to the edge of the area that contains data or formatting.

Selecting the Print Area

If you're satisfied with the default selection, you can continue formatting your worksheet for printing. If the default selections are not quite what you had in mind, you can select a specific area to be printed.

Printing a Range of Data

1. Select one or more ranges to print. The selected ranges do not have to be *contiguous*, but they must be on the same worksheet.
2. After you make your selection, pull down the **File** menu and choose **Print.**
3. In the Print dialog box, choose **Selection** from the **Print what?** area.
4. Click the **Preview** button to confirm that the current selection is what you want to print. Adjust any other formatting options in the Print Preview window.
5. Click the **Print** button.

SEE ALSO

➤ *To find instructions on how to select contiguous and noncontiguous ranges, see page 342*

Using a Defined Print Area

If you regularly print a complex worksheet that contains multiple nonprinting regions, you may get tired of selecting the same area every time you're ready to print. To force Excel to use a defined print area as the default for a worksheet, first select the range you want to designate as the *print area*. (The range need not be contiguous, but each worksheet in a workbook gets a separate print area.)

Page breaks are (barely) visible when editing

While you create and edit your worksheet, Excel provides subtle indicators of where pages will break. Fine dashed lines identify the rows and columns where Excel will break for a new page when printing.

You may print more than you expect

An option in the **Print what?** area of the Print dialog box lets you choose **Entire workbook**. Think twice before checking this option, especially if you've added formulas, supplementary tables, or other supporting calculations away from the main data area or on a separate worksheet. Because Excel considers every bit of data when it defines the default print area, you may need to specify the print area more precisely.

The print area doesn't update automatically

When you define a print area, Excel prints only that area when you click the Print button. Printing only a certain area can lead to embarrassing mistakes if you've added data to your worksheet since you defined the print area. Whenever you add rows or columns or otherwise redesign a worksheet, recheck the print area.

Switch print areas on-the-fly

To override the defined print area temporarily, first select the range you want to print. Then pull down the **File** menu, choose **Print**, click the **Selection** option, and click **OK** to send the selection to the printer.

To set the selected range as the print area, pull down the **File** menu, choose **Print Area**, and select **Set Print Area** from the cascading menu. To delete the print area selection and start over, use the **Clear Print Area** command on this same menu.

When you define a print area, Excel uses that region as its new default when you click the Print button or use the Print Preview window. If you define a print area on each worksheet, you can select **Entire workbook** from the **Print what?** region of the Print dialog box to preview or print the selected ranges on all the sheets in your workbook.

Extra Items You Can Print

Excel's Print dialog box lets you specify extra items you want to include with your printout—as well as a few options you might want to avoid printing. To see all these options, pull down the **File** menu, choose **Page Setup**, and click the **Sheet** tab in the Page Setup dialog box (see Figure 20.2).

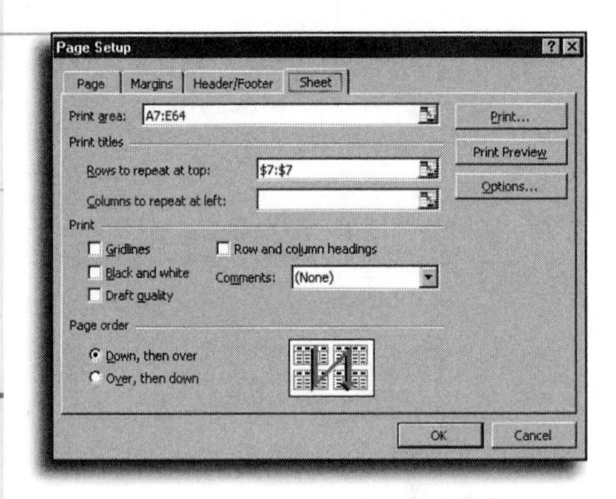

FIGURE 20.2
Use these options to adjust the look of your worksheet.

Select the current print area

When you define a print area, Excel creates a named range in the current worksheet. This way, you can easily select the current print area: Just click the arrow to the right of the **Name Box** and choose **Print Area** from the drop-down list. If you define other named ranges, you can select them instead and then print only that range. This technique lets you quickly print different regions on a worksheet.

Table 20.2 lists the options available for each worksheet.

TABLE 20.2 **Worksheet Print Options**

Print Option	What It Does
Gridlines	*Gridlines* help you identify individual cells when you're editing a worksheet; use borders to set off data areas for printouts. Check this box to print out a quick-and-dirty draft copy.

Print Option	What It Does
Comments	*Comments* are notes you attach to individual cells. They don't normally print; if you tell Excel to include them, you can print them on a separate sheet or as they appear on the screen.
Draft quality	Printing a heavily formatted worksheet can take a long time, especially on an inkjet printer. This option saves time by printing all the text and numbers but skipping gridlines and graphics.
Black and white	If you format data in color for the screen, you may end up with an unsatisfactory black-and-white printout. This option optimizes color settings for printing; it can also speed up print jobs on color printers.
Row and column headings	Sometimes, you may want to print out a worksheet with its reference points; *column headings* identify letters and *row headings* identify numbers in cell addresses.
Print titles	If the data in your worksheet spans several pages, you may lose your points of reference, such as the headings above columns of data. Identify the **Rows to repeat at top** of each page or the **Columns to repeat at left** of each page.
Page order	The graphic to the right of this option shows whether your sheet will print sideways first, then down, or the other way around. Set this order if you've set up page numbering.

Choosing Paper Size and Orientation

To pick a paper size and orientation, pull down the **File** menu and choose **Page Setup**. Click the **Page** tab to choose from available options.

Check your printer's default orientation

The default orientation for most printers is portrait, but many financial worksheets are designed for landscape mode. When these settings are mismatched, your data is spread over two or three pages instead of being neatly arranged on one page as you intended. You can save time (and paper) if you preview, or at least check the orientation carefully, before you print.

Most printers in the United States hold regular letter-size paper: 8.5×11 inches. Some have trays that hold legal paper (14 inches long). Most printers can also handle special paper sizes, as long as you're willing to feed it in manually. Choose the correct paper size; then choose between **Portrait** and **Landscape** orientation.

Centering a Worksheet on the Page

Excel's default printing options do a downright lousy job of positioning data on the page. Unless you intervene, your data will appear in the top-left corner of the printed page. The effect is especially ugly when you select a small range as your print area. In most cases, printed worksheets look best when you center data on the page.

Centering Worksheet Data on the Printed Page

1. Click the **File** menu and choose **Page Setup**.
2. Click the **Margins** tab to display the Page Setup dialog box shown in Figure 20.3.
3. If the data range you plan to print is relatively shallow—less than half a page deep—check only the box labeled **Horizontally**, and leave the **Vertically** box unchecked. This setting centers the sheet between the left and right margins but starts it near the top of the page.
4. For larger worksheets that fill up all or most of the page, check the box labeled **Horizontally** as well as the box labeled **Vertically.**
5. Click the **Print Preview** button to see how your printed page will appear or click the **Print** button to send the job directly to the printer.

Labeling the Printout with a Header and Footer

Any worksheet that spans more than one page should include a *header* or a *footer* (or both). Use headers and footers to number pages, identify the worksheet, specify the date it was created, list the author, and so on.

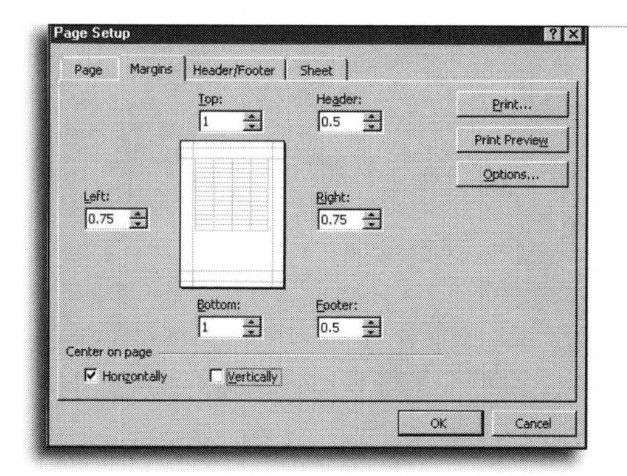

FIGURE 20.3
If your worksheet doesn't fill the entire page, use the **Center on page** options to arrange it properly.

When you pull down the **File** menu, select **Page Setup**, and click the **Header/Footer** tab, you get access to all sorts of useful options for these labels (see Figure 20.4). Excel includes a set of preconfigured headers and footers that mix page numbers, worksheet names, dates, and your name.

SEE ALSO

To find out what to do if your name doesn't appear in the list of predefined headers and footers, see page 101

Adding Row and Column Labels

A standard sheet of letter paper in portrait orientation has room for 49 rows and 9 columns of text or numbers formatted using Excel's default fonts, font sizes, row heights, and column widths. In landscape mode, you can fit up to 35 rows in 14 columns across the page (using Excel's default settings). If your worksheet contains more data than these values, tell Excel that you want each new page to include one or more rows or columns (or both) that you use as titles for the data. If the first column of your worksheet contains the names of employees, for example, with columns that extend to the right across several pages, you can select the column of employee names as the titles to repeat at the left of each page.

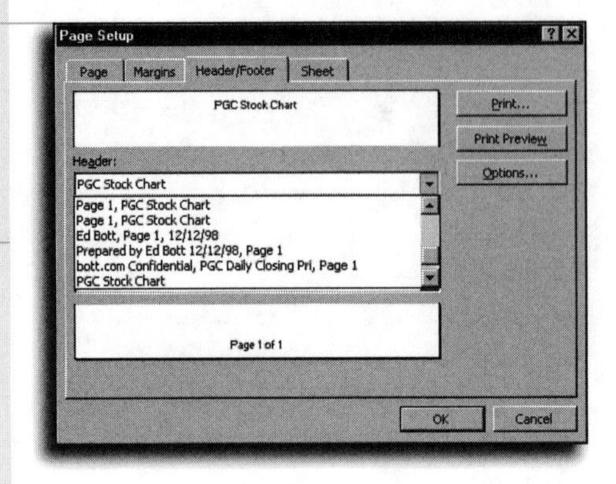

FIGURE 20.4
Excel's ready-made assortment of headers and footers includes a surprising number of personalized choices.

Adding Titles to Rows and Columns on Printed Worksheets

1. Click the **File** menu, choose **Page Setup**, and click the **Sheet** tab.
2. To specify a row that you want to repeat at the top of each new page, click in the box labeled **Rows to repeat at top**. To use a column for titles, click in the box labeled **Columns to repeat at left**.
3. Click in any cell in the row or column you want to use as your title. You don't need to select the entire row or column. If you select multiple cells, Excel uses all rows or columns as titles.
4. Click the **Print Preview** button to see how your titles will look on the page or click **Print** to send the job to the printer immediately.

Leave the dialog box open while you select

You can select cells in the current worksheet while this dialog box is open. When you click in the worksheet, Excel adds the cell reference for the cells you select to the box where the insertion point is located. To move the dialog box out of the way temporarily, click the **Collapse Dialog** button at the end of either text box before selecting a cell. Click the button again to restore the dialog box to full size.

Controlling the Contents of Each Page

When you click the Print button, Excel automatically inserts *page breaks* to divide the worksheet into sections that will fit on the paper size you specified. Excel doesn't analyze the structure of your worksheet before inserting page breaks; it simply adds a dividing line at the point where each page runs out of room. If your worksheet extends over more than one page, you might want to insert page breaks precisely where you need them.

Inserting Page Breaks

If you know exactly where you want your pages to break, you can force Excel to start a new page at a specific point. To insert a manual page break, select the cell below and to the right of the last cell you want on the page; then pull down the **Insert** menu and choose **Page Break**. To remove the page break, select the same cell and choose **Remove Page Break** from the **Insert** menu. To remove all manual page breaks from the current worksheet, select the entire sheet and pull down the **Insert** menu and choose **Reset All Page Breaks.**

Horizontal and vertical page breaks

To add only a horizontal page break, select a cell in column A; to add only a vertical page break, select a cell in row 1.

Although you can use the **Insert** menu to add and remove page breaks, there's a better way: Switch to *page break preview* to see all your page breaks and adjust exactly where each one will appear. From the Print Preview window, click the **Page Break Preview** button on the toolbar; from the worksheet editing window, pull down the **View** menu and choose **Page Break Preview**. In this view, you see your entire worksheet, broken into pages exactly as Excel intends to print it, with oversize page numbers laid over each block. Figure 20.5 shows how a sample worksheet looks in this view.

To adjust page breaks in this view, point to the thick dashed line between two pages and drag it in any direction. Move the solid line between rows or cells to change the print area.

Worksheet's Too Big? Force It to Fit

If you know exactly how many pages you want to use for your printed worksheet, Excel can accommodate your request. With a few clicks, you can reduce your printout to as little as 10 percent or as much as 400 percent of its normal size. Making the *scale* smaller lets you squeeze more rows and columns onto each page. But how do you know what value to put in the scaling box? You don't need to know. Just tell Excel to fit your worksheet in a specific number of pages.

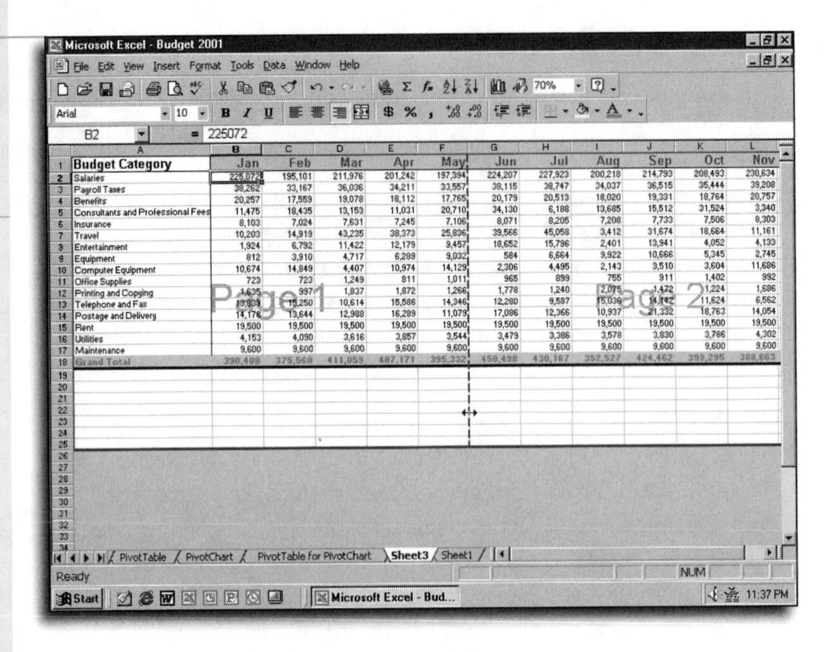

FIGURE 20.5

The page numbers show the order in which pages will print; drag the thick lines to adjust the print area and page breaks.

Printing a Worksheet on a Specific Number of Pages

1. Pull down the **File** menu and choose **Page Setup**.
2. Click on the **Page** tab to display the dialog box shown in Figure 20.6.

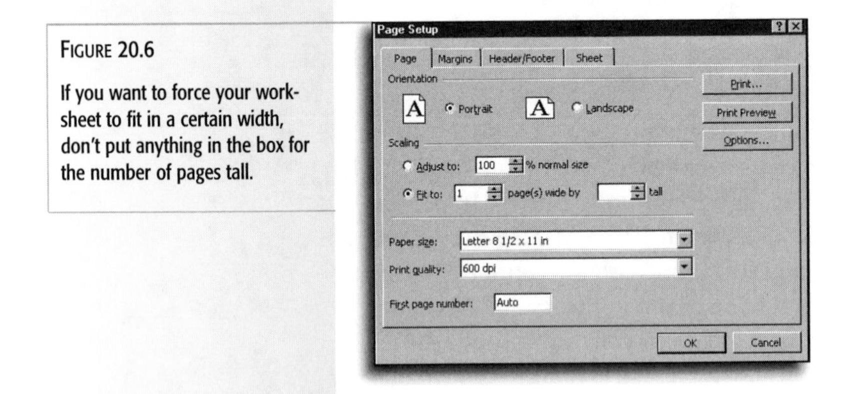

FIGURE 20.6

If you want to force your worksheet to fit in a certain width, don't put anything in the box for the number of pages tall.

3. In the section labeled **Scaling**, select the option that begins **Fit to**.
4. Use the spinner controls to adjust the number of pages you want the printout to occupy; leave one of the numbers blank if you want Excel to adjust only the width or height of the printout. In this example, Excel forces the worksheet to fit in a space no more than **1 page(s) wide**.
5. Click **Print Preview** to see what your worksheet will look like when printed.
6. Click **Print** to send the worksheet to the printer.

CHAPTER

21

Managing Lists and Databases

- Create a list on a worksheet
- Sort lists in a specified order
- Find and filter data in a list
- Use data-entry forms to manage information in a list
- Add subtotals to a sorted list of numbers
- Create and edit PivotTables
- Format PivotTables

Creating a List on a Worksheet

Excel 2000's row-and-column structure makes it an ideal tool for organizing related information into a *list*. Unlike the notes you scrawl on the back of an envelope or numbered lists you create with Word, however, Excel lists must adhere to strict formatting guidelines.

On an Excel worksheet, a list is a group of consecutive rows of related data. Each column within a list is a *field*, and each row is a *record* of data; the labels in the top row represent the names of the fields. Within each field, you can enter text, numbers, dates, formulas, or hyperlinks. Excel does not impose any additional restrictions on the type of data you can enter in a list.

PivotCharts are new

Previous versions of Office introduced the PivotTable report, which allows you to summarize lists by dragging and dropping fields on a sheet. PivotChart reports are new in Office 2000, and if you use charts, they will change your life. You'll find full details at the end of this chapter.

Excel or Access?

For basic list-management tasks, such as sorting and searching, Excel is an appropriate, easy-to-use tool. For large and complex databases, however, you'll want to use more powerful database-management software. Access, part of the Office 2000 Professional package, is a better choice when you need to combine data from multiple tables, create sophisticated reports, or build applications that let multiple users work with a database simultaneously. For more details on how to use Access, pick up Que's *Special Edition Using Microsoft Office 2000.*

Use Excel's list-management features to sort data alphabetically, numerically, by date, or by a custom order. You can search for a specific piece of information within a list, or use filters to find groups of data that match criteria you specify. For complex lists, Excel can automatically create outlines that let you summarize groups of records, and in lists that contain numeric data, you can add subtotals as well. For large, complex lists, use *PivotTable* and *PivotChart* reports to perform complex data-analysis tasks by dragging labels on the page.

To begin creating a list, pick a blank row and start typing. You can also create an Excel list by importing information from an external database.

SEE ALSO

➤ *For more information about connecting to external databases, pick up a copy of* Special Edition Using Microsoft Excel 2000, *also published by Que Corporation.*

Creating a List on a Worksheet

1. Create a new workbook or open an existing workbook, and then select a blank worksheet. (To add a blank worksheet to an existing workbook, pull down the **Insert** menu and choose **Worksheet**.)
2. Enter a name for each field in the first row (also called the header row). Apply any text formatting, if you like.

3. Start entering data beginning on the row directly below the header row. Enter formulas if you want to create *calculated fields*.

SEE ALSO

➤ *To learn how to enter a formula, see page 365*

To make Excel's list-management features work properly, follow these basic guidelines when creating lists:

- Create only one list per worksheet.
- Create one *header row* with a unique label for each column.
- Don't leave any blank rows or columns in your list. When you sort or search, Excel ignores data that appears below a blank row or to the right of a blank column.
- Use distinctive text formatting (bold italic, for example) to make the column labels in your header row stand out from the rest of the list.
- Don't use a row of dashes or underline characters to separate your header row from the list itself. To add a line between the header row and the rest of the list, use borders instead.

SEE ALSO

➤ *To learn how to add borders to a worksheet, see page 395*

- Don't add spaces before or after entries in your list. Stray spaces can cause problems with sorts and searches.

Begin your list anywhere

You can begin your list in any cell on the worksheet; you don't have to start in the first column or the first row.

Don't forget the header row

Normally, Excel uses the column labels in the first row to identify field names. Creating a header row makes it easier to see the structure of the list. You must have a header row if you want to enter data using forms or use the AutoFilter feature to find groups of records. You don't need a header row to sort records, however; if your list doesn't include column labels, be sure to check the **No header row** option when you sort.

Sorting Data

To quickly *sort* a list, first click in the column by which you want to sort, then use either of two buttons on Excel's Standard toolbar, depending on whether you want to sort using *ascending* order (A–Z or 1–10) or *descending* order (Z–A or 10–1). When you click **Sort Ascending** [A↓Z], Excel selects all the data in your list and sorts it alphabetically, using the column that contains the active cell. Click **Sort Descending** [Z↓A], to sort in reverse order, using the same column.

Performing a One-Column Sort

1. Click any cell in the column on which you want to sort.
2. Click **Sort Ascending** to sort in A–Z or 1–10 order; click **Sort Descending** to sort in reverse order.

Sorting by More Than One Field

Don't forget Undo!

If sorting your list doesn't produce the results you want, choose the **Edit** menu and select **Undo**, or click the **Undo** button to restore your list to its previous order.

Sometimes a single-column sort isn't sufficient to rearrange your list in the order you desire. In a list of names that includes several people with the same last name and different first names, for example, you'll need to sort first by last name and then by first name. With a list of sales results, you might want to sort by product name, in ascending order, and then by date, in descending order. In these cases, you'll need to use Excel's Sort dialog box to specify more than one field.

Sorting without a header row

If your list doesn't include a header row, pull down the **Data** menu, select **Sort**, and then select **No header row**. Use the column addresses (Column A, Column B, and so on) to specify the sort criteria.

To sort by more than one field, pull down the **Data** menu and choose **Sort**. Excel lets you specify up to three fields for your sort order, using ascending or descending order for each one.

Sorting a List by More Than One Field

1. Click anywhere in your list.
2. Pull down the **Data** menu and select **Sort** to display the Sort dialog box, as shown in Figure 21.1.

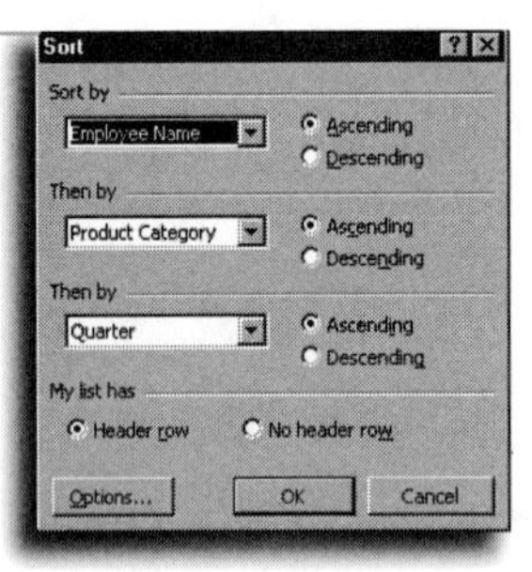

FIGURE 21.1

The Sort dialog box lets you sort by up to three fields at a time.

3. Choose the field name you want to sort first from the **Sort by** drop-down list. Select **Ascending** or **Descending** order.
4. Select the second sort field in the first **Then by** drop-down list. Click to select **Ascending** or **Descending** order.

5. If you want to specify a third sort field, select the name of that field in the final **Then by** box. Click to indicate **Ascending** or **Descending** order.
6. Click **OK** to perform the sort.

Using a Custom Series to Sort Lists

By default, Excel's sort options reorder your data alphabetically or numerically. However, a basic A–Z or 1–10 sort isn't always appropriate. For example, your list may include a text field that identifies the month in which an investment matures. Using the default sort order would put the month names in alphabetical order, beginning with April, followed by August and December, and ending with September. In this example, instead of in alphabetical order, you want to see your list in calendar order.

Excel's collection of built-in lists includes the months of the year and days of the week, fully spelled out or abbreviated. You can also create your own custom list, including product codes and department names. Use any custom list to define a sort order that is different from the default alphabetical or numerical order.

SEE ALSO

➤ *To learn how to create custom lists, see page 345*

Sorting a List Using a Custom Series

1. Click anywhere in your list.
2. Pull down the **Data** menu and select **Sort**. The Sort dialog box appears.
3. Identify up to three field names you want to sort by.
4. Click the **Options** button in the lower left-hand corner of the Sort dialog box to display the Sort Options dialog box (see Figure 21.2).

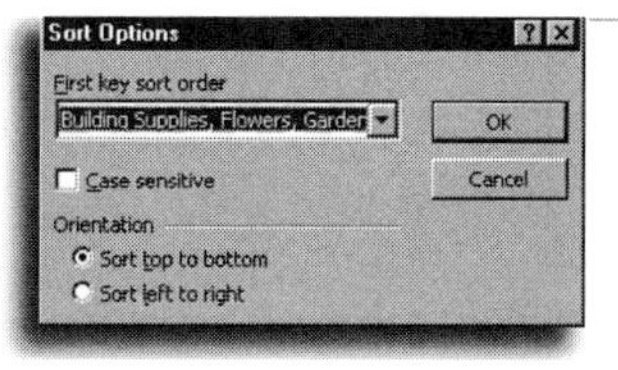

FIGURE 21.2
Use a custom list instead of the default alphabetical order to sort in the precise order you prefer.

Performing a case-sensitive sort

By default, the sorting process does not look at the case of your letters to perform the sort. If you want Excel to separate lowercase text from uppercase text, when you choose the **Data** menu and select **Sort**, click **Options** and then check the **Case sensitive** option. With this option enabled, words beginning with lowercase letters appear before those beginning with capital letters.

Narrow the search

When you use the Find and Replace dialog boxes, Excel searches for the specified information on the entire worksheet. To narrow the search to the list (or a portion of it), select a range before you begin the Find or Replace operation.

5. Click the down arrow in the **First key sort order** list box and select the appropriate series.
6. Click **OK** to confirm the new sort order you've selected; then click **OK** again to perform the sort.

Searching for Data in a List

After a list has grown in size to fill a hundred or more rows, how do you locate specific information within the list? The simplest way is to use Excel's Find and Replace tools: Press Ctrl+F to open the Find dialog box, which helps you locate a specific piece of information anywhere within a worksheet; press Ctrl+H to open the Replace dialog box, which lets you update your list, one record at a time or all at once.

SEE ALSO

➤ *For details on how to use Excel's Find and Replace dialog boxes, see page 341*

Excel also includes two specialized tools that let you extract details from a list instead of jumping to a record. Use *filters* to hide all records except those that match criteria you specify. Use the Lookup Wizard when you want to add a fill-in-the-blanks region on your worksheet that lets you type in one piece of information (a part number, for example) and find related information (such as the product name associated with that number) from the list.

Using AutoFilter to Find Sets of Data

Use filters to sift through an Excel list and view a selection of the records in that list. In a list that contains hundreds or thousands of rows, defining a filter helps you see a small number of related records together, making it easier to compare rows and identify trends.

Excel filters a list using *criteria* you specify. For example, in a list of stock prices you might want to see all records where the entry in the Symbol field is KO. A menu choice lets you find the top 10 (or bottom 10) entries in a list, based on the contents of a single field. Or, create a custom filter that uses multiple criteria, such as a price that is greater than or equal to 90 but less than 100. You can also combine criteria from multiple columns, filtering only records that match all the criteria you specify.

The simplest type of filter is an *AutoFilter*. As the name implies, this Excel option lets you define criteria using drop-down lists, then automatically apply the filter to your list.

Combine criteria for maximum effect

Although you're limited to only two criteria when you use AutoFilter's Custom option, you can easily work around this limitation by using Excel's capability to filter on criteria for two or more columns at once. Make a copy of the column you want to use in your filter, and specify a second set of criteria in the AutoFilter box for that column.

Using AutoFilter to Find a Group of Records

1. Click anywhere in your list. (This step isn't necessary if Excel recognizes that your worksheet contains a single list with headings.)
2. Pull down the **Data** menu, select **Filter**, and then choose **AutoFilter**. A drop-down arrow appears to the right of each column heading in your list, as shown in Figure 21.3.

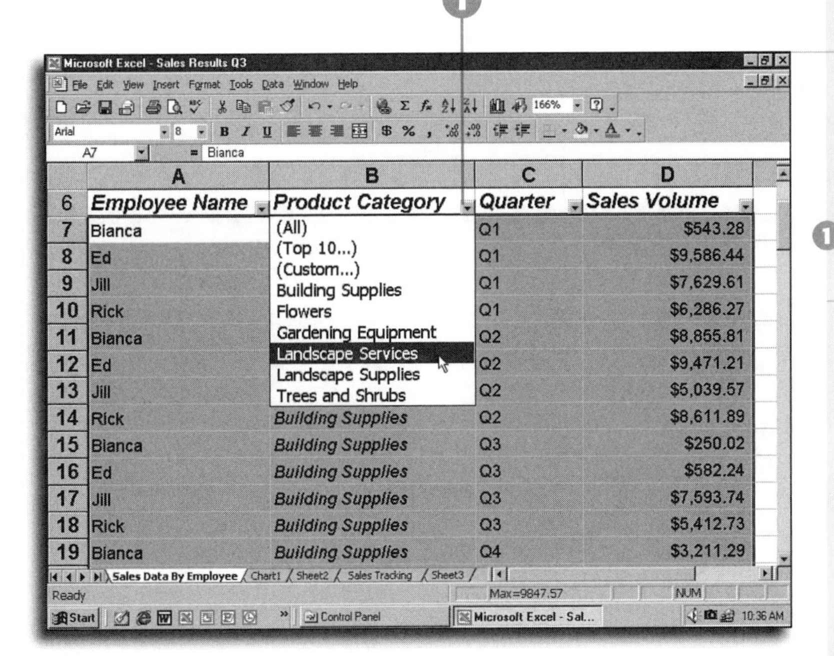

FIGURE 21.3

The drop-down list arrows display all unique values in a column when AutoFilter is turned on.

1. AutoFilter drop-down list arrow

3. Choose the column that contains the information you want to use in your filter criteria, then click the drop-down arrow to the right of the column label.

Each list is unique

Excel generates the list of values for each AutoFilter arrow by identifying unique values within that column, then displays the list in ascending order. That makes it easy to define the right criteria, and impossible to enter a value that isn't in the list.

Top 10 is for numbers only

The Top 10 (or Bottom 10) selection works only with numeric fields. If you choose this option for a field that contains only text, Excel beeps and refuses to display the Top 10 AutoFilter dialog box. For fields that contain a mix of numbers and text, Excel ignores the text values.

4. Choose a value from the drop-down list, or choose one of the options defined in Table 21.1. Excel applies your criteria immediately, filtering out all rows except those that contain the value you selected, as shown in Figure 21.4.

TABLE 21.1 AutoFilter Options

Select	To
All	Show all records in the list. Use this option to remove AutoFilter criteria from a column and show all records.
Top 10	Show the highest or lowest numeric values in a list. Don't be misled by the name—you can enter any number between 1 and 500; you can choose **Bottom** or **Top**; and you can specify percent as well. For example, you might use this type of AutoFilter to display the bottom 25 percent of a group by price, or the top five salespeople based on sales totals.
Custom	Use comparison operators (covered in the next section) to define criteria. You can also combine two criteria using this option.
Blanks	Display only records that contain no data in the selected column.
NonBlanks	Hide records that contain no data in the selected column.

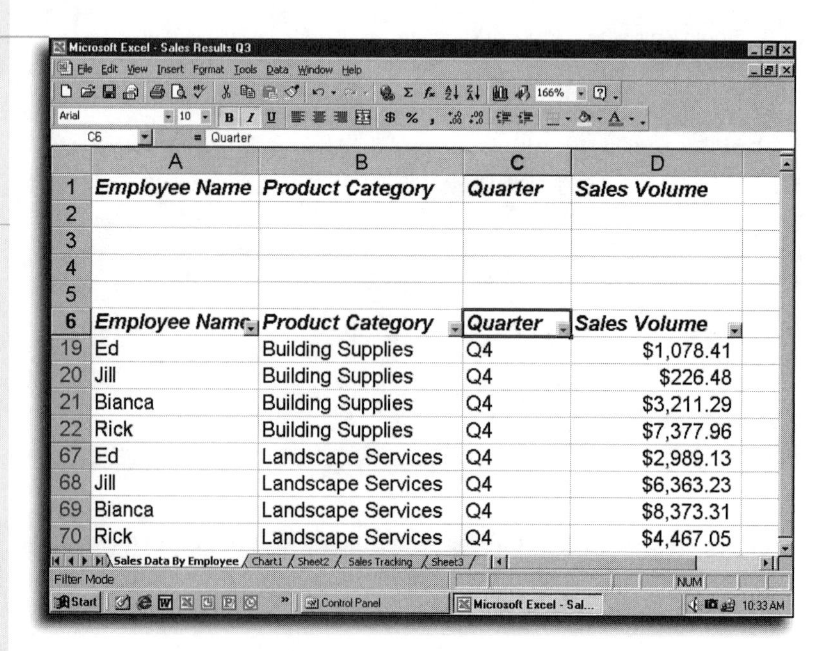

FIGURE 21.4

Look at the row numbers in this filtered list. Records that don't match the AutoFilter criteria are hidden.

To restore a list to its original, unfiltered display all view, pull down the **Data** menu, select **Filter**, and click **AutoFilter**. The drop-down arrows disappear.

Using Comparison Criteria to Create Custom Filters

The AutoFilter drop-down list lets you select a specific value and display only records that match that value. But what if you want to see records that are greater or less than a particular value? How do you search for text that begins with a given letter or contains a specific text string? To create more complex criteria like these, use the **Custom** option on the **AutoFilter** drop-down list. The following comparison operators are available:

- Equals/does not equal
- Is greater than/is less than
- Is greater than or equal to/is less than or equal to
- Begins with/does not begin with
- Ends with/does not end with
- Contains/does not contain

You can also combine two criteria for a single field using the *logical operator* and; or use the or operator to tell Excel that you want to see records that match either of the criteria you specify.

Creating Custom AutoFilter Criteria

1. Make sure AutoFilter is turned on.
2. Click the arrow next to the column heading for the field you want to use for your filter criteria. Select **Custom** from the drop-down list to display the Custom AutoFilter dialog box, as shown in Figure 21.5.

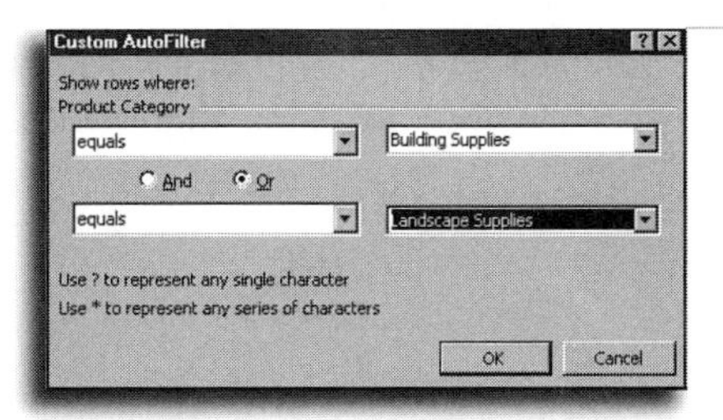

FIGURE 21.5
I used the Custom AutoFilter dialog box to combine two criteria for more precise results.

A blue arrow means AutoFilter is on

When you apply a filter to a list, Excel changes the color of the drop-down arrow for the field you selected. To remove or change AutoFilter criteria, click the blue arrow.

Delete rows with care!

When you apply an AutoFilter and then delete one or more rows from a filtered list, you can undo your action only as long as you keep AutoFilter selected. After you remove AutoFilter, the change is permanent—the **Undo** button is grayed out.

Excel doesn't store AutoFilter criteria

When you remove AutoFilter from a list, Excel discards any custom criteria you've created. To reapply those same AutoFilter criteria later, you'll have to re-enter them by hand.

3. Select a comparison operator for the first set of criteria.
4. Click in the box to the right of the comparison operator and enter the comparison data, or select an entry from the drop-down list of all unique values in the field.
5. Add a second set of criteria, if you like. Click **And** to select only records where both criteria are true; click **Or** to show records that satisfy either set of criteria.
6. Click **OK** or press Enter to display the group of records that meet the specified criteria.

Using the Lookup Wizard

Simple search tools work just fine when you want to track down a stray bit of data in a table, but they're not appropriate when you regularly need to look up the same type of information. If you store a list of part numbers, product names, and prices in an Excel table, for example, you might want to create a form that lets you quickly look up a specific value from one field and find the corresponding value from another field in the same row.

In Figure 21.6, I've created a lookup formula that lets me enter a specific value in cell B1; Excel then finds that value in the Date field, reads the value from the Daily Sales column in that row, and displays the result in cell B2. Writing the formula wasn't difficult, because I used an Excel add-in called the Lookup Wizard, which is included on your Office 2000 CD. (The Windows Installer may ask you to supply this CD the first time you try to use the Lookup Wizard.)

No wizard? No problem

If you don't see the **Wizard** choice when you pull down Excel's **Tools** menu, you'll need to install the Lookup Wizard add-in. From the **Tools** menu, choose **Add-Ins**, then check the **Lookup Wizard** box. If you haven't used this wizard previously, you may need to supply the Office 2000 disk to complete the setup process.

Creating a Lookup Form on a Table

1. Open the **Tools** menu, choose **Wizard**, and then select **Lookup**.
2. Define the range you want to look in—in this example, the entire list, including the header row.

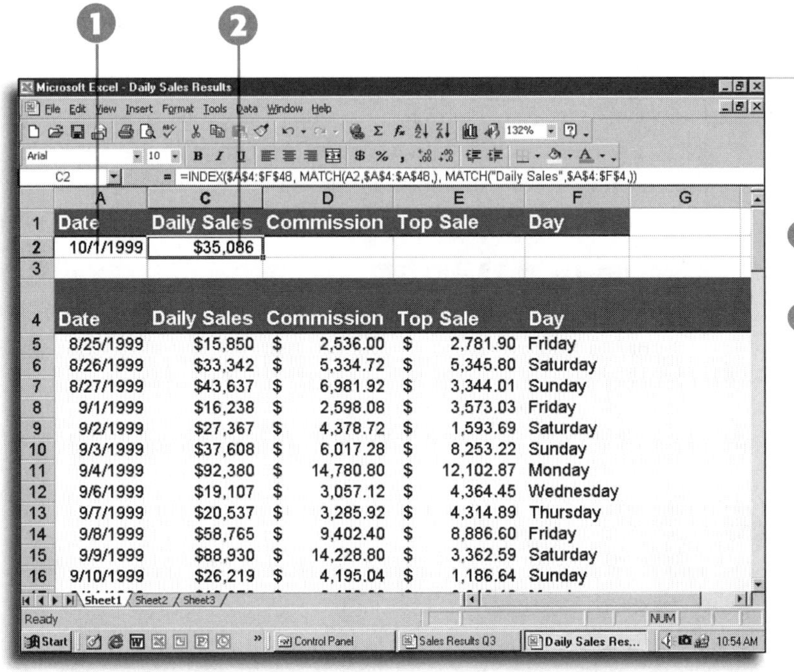

FIGURE 21.6

Use the Lookup Wizard to add a data-entry cell and lookup formula to your worksheet.

1. Enter the information you want to look up in this cell.
2. Excel displays the result of the lookup here, using a formula the wizard creates.

3. Choose the row and column labels that define the cell you're searching for.
4. The next step in the wizard lets you add just the formula into your worksheet or specify that you want to position the lookup parameters in your worksheet, as I've done in Figure 21.7.

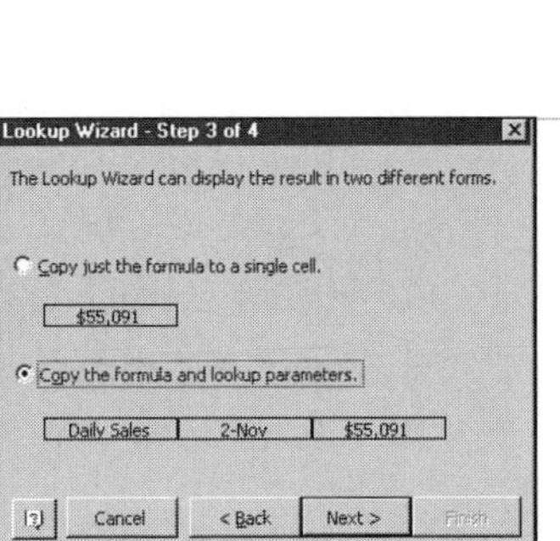

FIGURE 21.7

The Lookup Wizard lets you add a formula or a lookup form to your worksheet.

5. Follow the wizard's prompts to position formulas and lookup cells on the worksheet. Add explanatory labels, if necessary.

Use the wizard for lookup formulas

Why would you want to add just a lookup formula to your worksheet? You might want to create a separate list that automatically performs lookups, such as sales tax rates for different zip codes, when you enter data. Each time you enter a zip code, Excel uses the lookup formula to find the matching tax rate and calculate the correct total.

Put your lookup formula in the right place

Be careful where you place a lookup formula on your worksheet. If you position the formula alongside a list, you could accidentally hide or even erase the formula when you filter or delete records. For best results, add a few rows above the list and place the lookup formula there.

Using Forms to Enter and View Data

Data forms provide a simple method of entering data into an Excel list. The Excel data form creates a text box based on your list's column headings. When you enter data in the form, Excel fills in the correct columns, adding rows to the end of the list, if necessary.

Adding Records with a Data Form

1. Click any cell in the list. If you're entering the first record, enter a row containing column headings and click any cell in that row.
2. Pull down the **Data** menu and select **Form**. The data form appears, as shown in Figure 21.8.

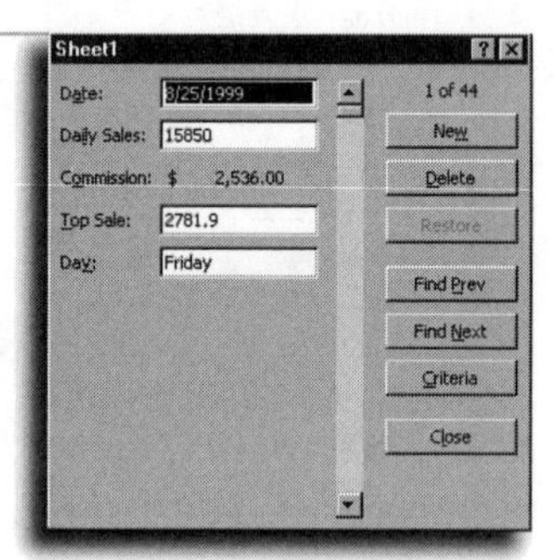

FIGURE 21.8

Data forms let you work with a list one record at a time, using a form like this one to show the contents of each row.

3. To add a record to a list that already contains data, click the **New** button; a blank form appears.
4. Enter your data into the fields on the form. Press Tab to move from one field to the next; press Shift+Tab to move to the previous field.
5. Press Enter when the record is complete. A blank form for the next new record appears.
6. Click **Close** or press Esc to return to the worksheet.

Error messages when adding records

If you see the error message `Cannot Extend List or Database`, Excel can't add a new record because you've run out of blank rows below your list. Select one or more rows beneath the list, right-click the selection, and choose **Insert** from the shortcut menu. Better yet, move the data from beneath the list to a separate worksheet.

Viewing and Finding Records with a Data Form

Use the data form to view records in your list. To move through the list one record at a time, click the up- and down-arrows in the scrollbar to the right of the data fields. Click above or below the scrollbar handle to move 10 records at a time in either direction.

You can also use the data form to locate specific records by entering criteria that identify data in your list.

How many records?

As you move between rows using a data form, the status message in the upper-right corner displays the record number and the total number of records in the list.

Locating Records Using the Data Form

1. Open a data form and click the **Criteria** button. Excel clears the data from the form and displays a blank box for each field in the list.
2. Enter criteria in the box next to the field in which you want Excel to search. To narrow your search, you can enter criteria in multiple fields, as shown in Figure 21.9.

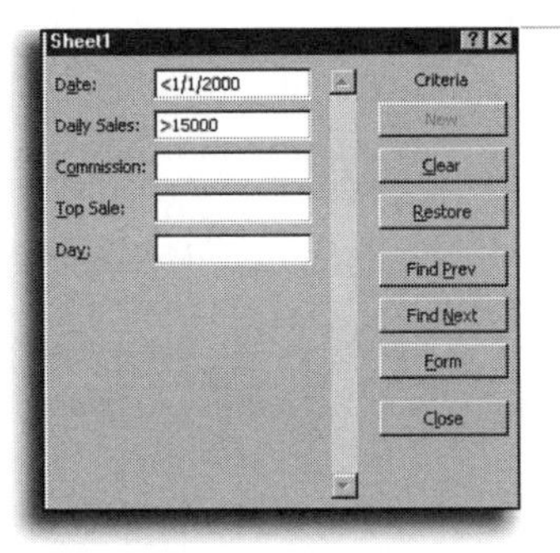

FIGURE 21.9
After you enter criteria for one or more fields, click Find Next to begin searching.

3. Click **Find Next** to move through the list looking for records that match the criteria you entered. If Excel can't find a matching record, you'll hear a beep. Click **Find Prev** to search in reverse order through the list.
4. Click **Clear** to erase all your criteria and start a new search. Click **Restore** to reuse the criteria you entered previously.
5. Click **Close** to return to your worksheet and close the data form.

From Form to Criteria

When you begin searching for data using a form, Excel changes the status message in the upper-right corner of the form. The function of other buttons changes slightly as well. To resume viewing records with the data form, click the **Form** button.

The cell remains the same

As you move through a list using a data form, the active cell doesn't change. When you close the data form, Excel returns you to the cell that was active when you opened the data form, without regard to the records you viewed using the form.

Deleting Records with the Data Form

When you view data using the data form, you can delete records. The effect is the same as if you had deleted all cells from that record in the list, then shifted the remainder of the list up.

Editing Records with the Data Form

Changes you make to data in the data form appear in the corresponding list as soon as you move to another row. You can access the data form by clicking anywhere in the list, choosing the **Data** menu, and then selecting **Form**. Locate the record you want to change, edit your data, and click **Close** when you are finished.

Deleting multiple records at once

Using a data form, you can delete only one record at a time. To delete multiple records in one step, return to the list, select the rows to delete by holding the Ctrl key as you select the row number, choose the **Edit** menu, and select **Delete**.

Sorry—no can Undo

If you delete a row by mistake in data form view, you'll see a confirmation message warning you that you're about to delete the record permanently. Believe it! When you delete a record using a data form, the **Undo** command is not available to restore the original data.

Restoring data to undo changes

If you change a record using a data form and then decide you don't want to make the changes after all, you can click the **Restore** button. This option is available only if you haven't moved to the next record and entered your changes into the worksheet.

Updating calculated fields in the data form

When you change a number in the data form that is used in a calculated field, you won't see the change in the calculated result immediately, because Excel waits to recalculate fields until you move to another record. To update the calculation, press Enter and then click **Find Prev**.

Creating Subtotals

Simple summaries can sometimes make a lengthy list of numbers easier to understand. In a list of sales figures, for example, with each row representing daily sales for each sales representative, you might want to display total and average sales for each person. You can do the job manually—inserting extra rows and headings, and then adding calculations to total subgroups within your list. It's much, much easier, however, to let Excel insert automatic *subtotals* with just a few clicks.

Excel can automatically insert subtotals into a continuous list at each change of data within a column you specify. Excel groups your data by the field you specify, inserts a subtotal row, and adds a formula that performs the calculation you specify. After you insert subtotals, they update automatically as data changes.

Inserting Subtotals into a List

1. Sort the list by the column by which you want to group your data.
2. Click anywhere in the list, pull down the **Data** menu, and select **Subtotals**. Excel displays the Subtotal dialog box (see Figure 21.10).

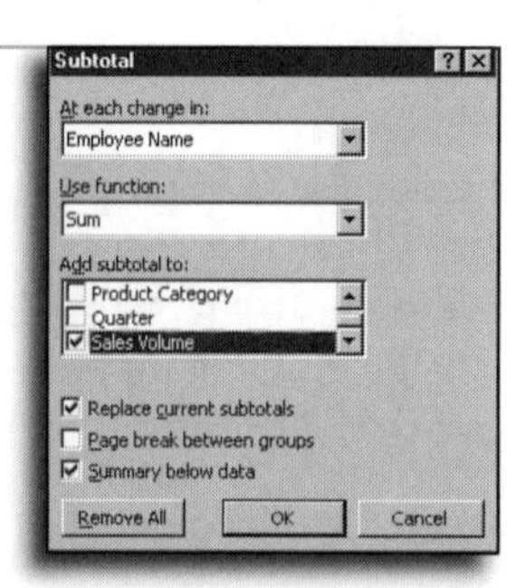

FIGURE 21.10

Use this dialog box to automatically insert summary rows into your worksheet.

3. From the **At each change in** drop-down list, select the field by which you want to group your list. Make sure this is the same field you used to sort the list in step 1.
4. From the **Use function** drop-down list, select the type of summary calculation you want Excel to perform. The default is SUM.
5. In the **Add subtotal to** list, check the names of the columns for which you want to calculate subtotals. If necessary, clear the check mark from the box next to columns you don't want to summarize.
6. If you want summary rows to appear above the data rows for each group, clear the **Summary below data** box. Check this box to add summaries below the data rows.
7. Click **OK** to add the subtotals to your worksheet and close the dialog box.

SEE ALSO

For details on using SUM, AVERAGE, and other functions to summarize data, see page 370

Showing and Hiding Subtotals in Outline View

When Excel creates subtotals, it automatically groups your data and displays it as an outline. Each level of detail appears at a different level within the outline—for example, details in level 3, subtotals in level 2, and grand totals in level 1. By showing and hiding those levels, you can quickly jump between detailed and summary views of the same data.

Figure 21.11 shows all the outline symbols on a worksheet to which I've added automatic subtotals. The outline buttons appear to the left of the worksheet. Each level of the outline is numbered, with dots below indicating row-specific levels.

Sort before you subtotal

This is the single most important step in making subtotals work properly. You must sort your list by the column you want to subtotal. If you sort by any other column first, you'll wind up with inaccurate calculations–and probably a mess.

More than totals

Don't let the name fool you. When you insert subtotals into a list, you can choose from any of 11 different summary functions. Use this feature if you want to quickly calculate minimum and maximum values (such as a high and low stock price) or averages, for example. You can also insert statistical tests for your list, such as variance and standard deviation.

Grand totals appear automatically

When you insert subtotals, Excel adds a grand total of all groups at the bottom of the list. Note that the grand total uses the same function as the subtotals; if you calculate an average for each group, the grand total will be the average of all entries in your list.

How subtotals work

Automatic subtotals are a tremendous timesaver, but there's nothing magic about them. When you use this feature, Excel just inserts a formula using the SUBTOTAL function. You can insert this function yourself, but it's much easier to do it automatically using the **Subtotals** menu.

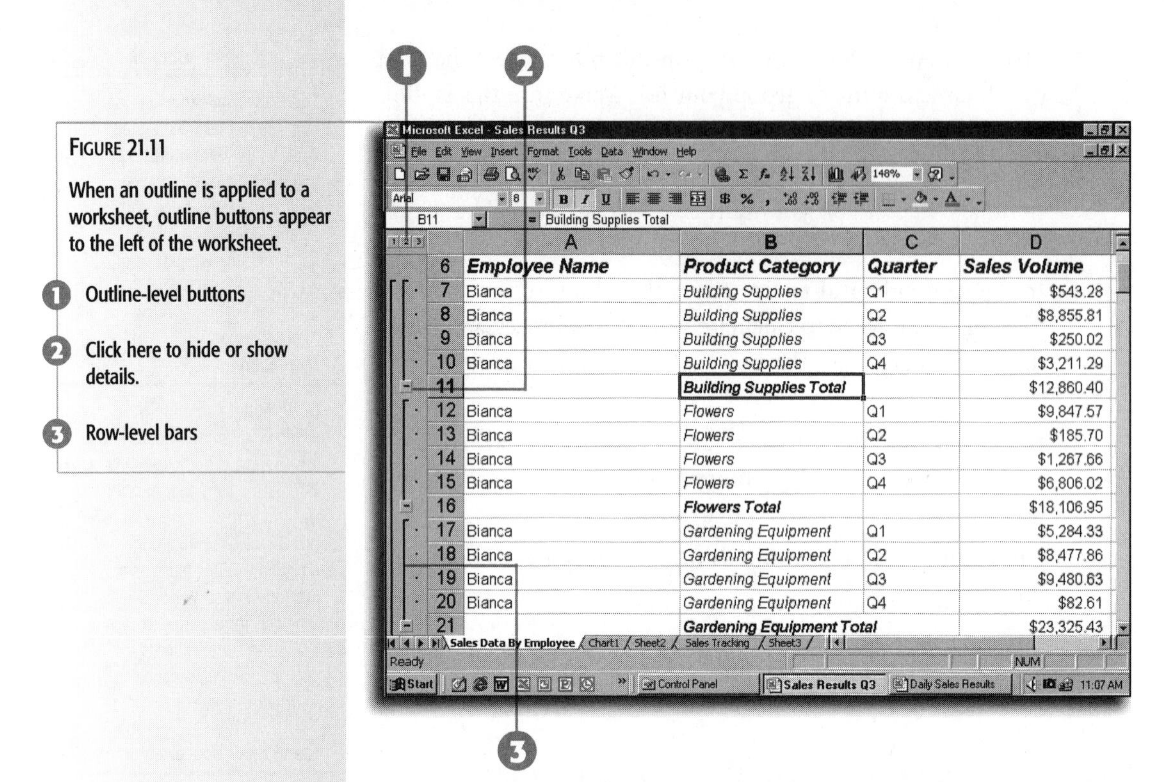

FIGURE 21.11

When an outline is applied to a worksheet, outline buttons appear to the left of the worksheet.

1. Outline-level buttons
2. Click here to hide or show details.
3. Row-level bars

Click the minus sign to the left of a summary row to hide the detail rows associated with that group. A plus sign (like the one in Figure 21.12) means that details are hidden and only summary information is visible; click to show the details.

To display or hide any level of detail, click the corresponding + or – button.

Want to hide the outline symbols?

When you use automatic subtotals, Excel adds outline symbols to your worksheet. To hide these symbols without removing the subtotals, pull down the **Tools** menu, choose **Options**, click the **View** tab, and clear the check mark from the **Outline symbols** box. Restore the check mark to display the symbols again.

Displaying all data and subtotals

To display all data and subtotals, click the highest number level indicator at the top of the outline. To show only the summary rows, click a lower number.

Removing Subtotals

When you use automatic subtotals, Excel keeps track of summary rows and lets you easily remove them.

Removing Automatic Subtotals

1. Click anywhere in your list.
2. Choose the **Data** menu and select **Subtotals**.
3. Click the **Remove All** button.

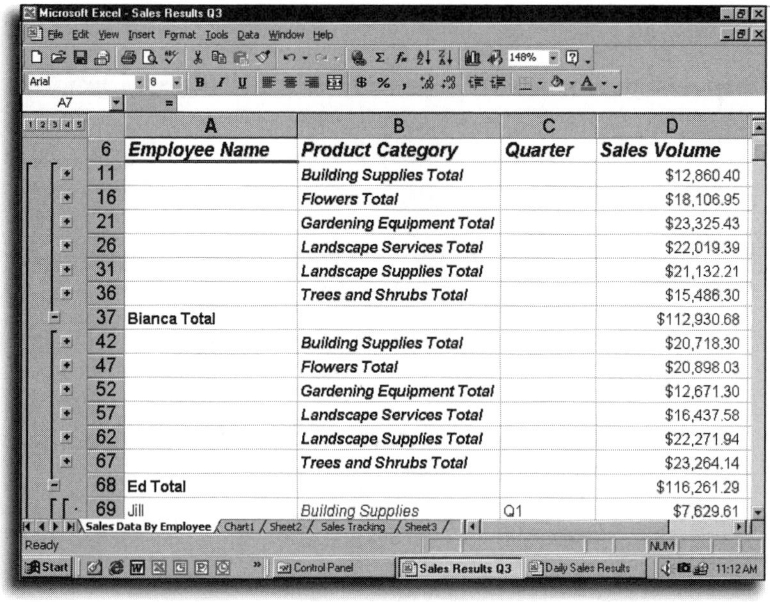
Microsoft Excel - Sales Results Q3
File Edit View Insert Format Tools Data Window Help
Arial
A7
A B C D
6 Employee Name | Product Category | Quarter | Sales Volume
11 Building Supplies Total $12,860.40
16 Flowers Total $18,106.95
21 Gardening Equipment Total $23,325.43
26 Landscape Services Total $22,019.39
31 Landscape Supplies Total $21,132.21
36 Trees and Shrubs Total $15,486.30
37 Bianca Total $112,930.68
42 Building Supplies Total $20,718.30
47 Flowers Total $20,898.03
52 Gardening Equipment Total $12,671.30
57 Landscape Services Total $16,437.58
62 Landscape Supplies Total $22,271.94
67 Trees and Shrubs Total $23,264.14
68 Ed Total $116,261.29
69 Jill Building Supplies Q1 $7,629.61
Sales Data By Employee / Chart1 / Sheet2 / Sales Tracking / Sheet3
Ready
NUM
Start
Control Panel
Sales Results Q3
Daily Sales Results
11:12AM

FIGURE 21.12

Collapse levels using outline buttons to condense a detailed worksheet into an easy-to-read summary report.

Creating and Editing PivotTables and PivotCharts

PivotTables and *PivotCharts* are powerful tools for automatically summarizing data. The starting point for either report is a list that contains multiple fields. By dragging fields around on a PivotTable page, you tell Excel exactly how you want to summarize the data. PivotCharts let you manipulate the same data visually.

Figure 21.13 shows a simple PivotTable, built using data from the list I used earlier in this chapter. Unlike subtotals and outlines, which modify the structure of your list to display summaries, PivotTables and PivotCharts create brand-new elements in your workbook. As you edit the list data, your PivotTables and PivotCharts change as well, and you can easily change the structure of a PivotTable or PivotChart without affecting the data in the underlying list.

Puzzled by PivotTables? Try again...

If you tried to create or edit a PivotTable in an earlier version of Excel and gave up in frustration, try again. The interface you use to create and edit PivotTables in Excel 2000 is dramatically easier than its Excel 97 counterpart, especially when it comes to changing a PivotTable on-the-fly. And if you're a whiz with charts, you'll flip over PivotCharts, which are completely new in Excel 2000.

Much more to PivotTables

In this book, I'll show you how to get started with PivotTables and PivotCharts, but there isn't enough space to cover the many techniques you can use to make the most of these powerful analytical tools–including the ability to publish PivotTables in Web pages. For more detailed instructions and expert advice on how to create, format, and modify PivotTables and PivotCharts, pick up a copy of *Special Edition Using Microsoft Excel 2000*, or *Special Edition Using Microsoft Office 2000*, both published by Que.

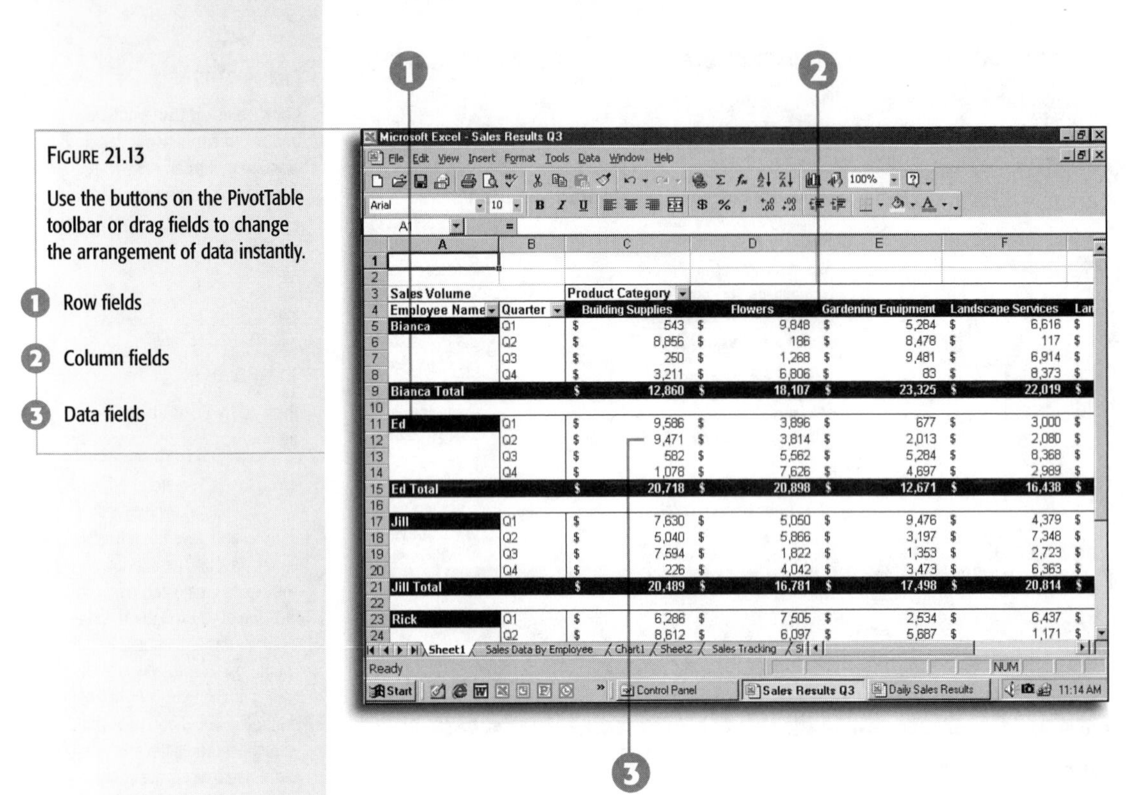

FIGURE 21.13

Use the buttons on the PivotTable toolbar or drag fields to change the arrangement of data instantly.

1. Row fields
2. Column fields
3. Data fields

When in doubt, right-click

You'll find countless PivotTable options when you right-click an object. For example, you can hide or show grand totals, change the numeric format of data, and change the calculations Excel makes on the data–from a simple count of items to a sum, average, or even a custom formula.

Row fields and *column fields* define how you want Excel to group your list. Data fields define the pieces of information you want to summarize. Page fields let you further refine the way you view data by displaying the PivotTable for each item in a group as though it were on its own virtual page. You can use multiple row or column fields, or both, in a PivotTable, and you can specify which *summary action* you want Excel to perform on the data fields—the sum or average or count of all related values, for instance.

The PivotTable in Figure 21.13 uses Employee Name and Quarter as the row fields, Product Category as the column field, and Sales Volume as the data field. Each row displays a unique value from the columns defined as row fields; likewise, each column shows each unique value from the column I defined as a column field. At the intersection of each row and column in the

PivotTable, Excel calculates the total value from the Sales Volume field for all rows that match that combination of unique values. Using this view, I can see each employee's quarterly performance at a glance; I can easily tell who had a good year and who didn't do so well, and I might be able to determine how each employee does with each product in my line.

Now watch what happens when I drag the Product Category heading to a row field and drag the Quarter heading to the page field, as shown in Figure 21.14. Excel recalculates the data instantly. Using this view of the data makes it easy for me to focus on products instead of people. By selecting Q4 from the page field list, I can break down that quarter's total sales for each product by employee, and I can make management or marketing decisions if I see a total that's lower than it should be.

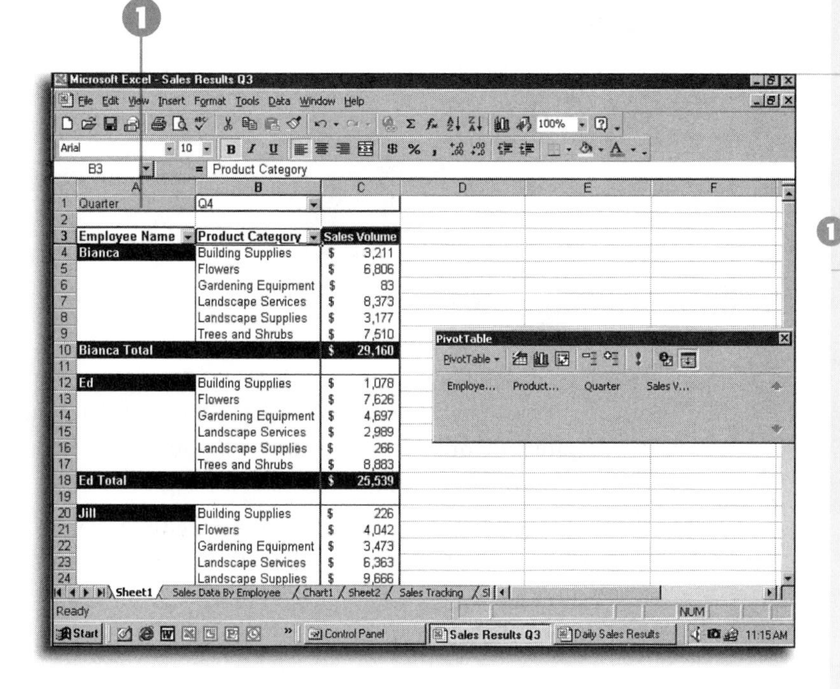

FIGURE 21.14

By dragging fields on the page, you can create a completely different summary of your data.

1 Page field

To create a PivotTable from an existing list, start with Excel's PivotTable Wizard.

Updating a PivotTable

When you change the layout of a PivotTable, Excel automatically recalculates the results. If you edit data in the underlying table, however, the results may not appear in the associated PivotTable right away. To be certain that the PivotTable reflects all recent changes, pull down the **Data** menu and choose **Refresh Data**.

Using the PivotTable Wizard

Excel provides an excellent tool for getting started with PivotTables. The PivotTable Wizard steps you through the process of creating a new PivotTable or PivotChart. After you finish with the wizard, you'll be able to lay out your data directly on the worksheet.

Feel free to experiment

Because PivotTables and PivotCharts have no effect on your existing list, you can freely experiment with different PivotTable layouts. Use the **Undo** button to roll back any changes you make in a PivotTable layout. If you want to start over, just run the PivotTable Wizard again.

Creating a PivotTable

1. Click anywhere in your list. If you want Excel to build your PivotTable from a subset of the data in your list, select the range first.
2. Pull down the **Data** menu and select **PivotTable and PivotChart Report**. The PivotTable and PivotChart Wizard appears, as shown in Figure 21.15.

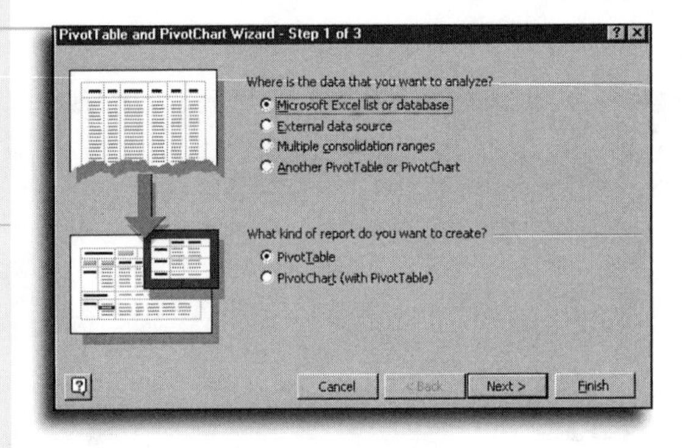

FIGURE 21.15

Use the PivotTable Wizard to specify the location of the data you want to summarize.

3. Specify that your data is located in an Excel list and that you want to create a PivotTable rather than a PivotChart. Click **Next** to move to step 2.
4. In step 2 of the Wizard, Excel asks you to specify the range in which your data is located. The default selection is your current list, or any range you selected before starting the Wizard. Adjust the selection, if necessary, and click **Next**.
5. In its third and final step, the Wizard asks you where you want to place the PivotTable. Choose the default option, **New worksheet**.

Using external data for a PivotTable

In corporate environments, PivotTables are often based on data stored in external databases. If you choose the **External data source** option, Excel starts the Microsoft Query program and prompts you for details about the format and location of the database. Excel then uses this query as the source for the PivotTable or PivotChart.

6. Click **Finish** to close the Wizard and create a blank PivotTable. Excel jumps to the new worksheet and displays the PivotTable toolbar, as shown in Figure 21.16.
7. Drag field buttons from the PivotTable toolbar and drop them into the appropriate regions in the layout. You must have at least one row or column field, and you must specify a data item.

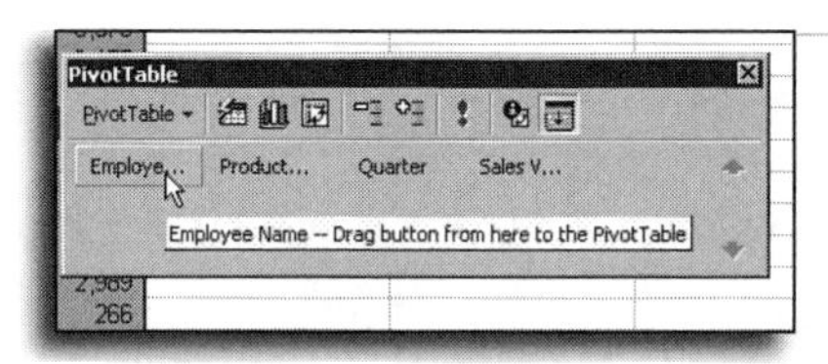

FIGURE 21.16
Use the field labels on the PivotTable toolbar to create the layout. ScreenTips like this one provide instructions as you work.

Creating a PivotChart

A PivotChart is a chart based on data in a PivotTable. In previous versions of Excel, you had to first build a PivotTable, and then manually create a chart from its data. In Excel 2000, building a PivotChart literally takes one click (in fact, it happens so quickly you may think you've skipped a step). Just as with its row-and-column–based counterpart, you can edit a PivotChart by dragging field labels on a chart sheet. When you change the layout of a PivotChart, Excel automatically rearranges the corresponding data in your PivotTable, and vice versa.

To create a PivotChart from an existing PivotTable, first click in the PivotTable, then click the **Chart Wizard** button. The PivotChart appears on a new chart sheet, as shown in Figure 21.17.

To change the arrangement of data in the PivotChart, drag field buttons from the PivotTable toolbar and drop them in one of four areas on the PivotChart. Category fields go below the chart, and series fields appear at the right of the chart. Drop data items directly into the body of the chart. If you want to add a page field, drag it to the region above the chart.

Where to place a PivotTable

The PivotTable Wizard offers the option to place a PivotTable or PivotChart on an existing worksheet. In general, you should avoid this option because of the risk that changes you make to the design of your list will affect your PivotTable, or vice-versa. If you must place the PivotTable on your main worksheet, your safest option is to position it below and to the right of your working area.

Using the PivotTable toolbar

The PivotTable appears automatically when you create a PivotTable. Click the **Close (X)** button to hide the toolbar; to display the toolbar after hiding it, pull down the View menu, select **Toolbars**, and click **PivotTable** from the list of available toolbars.

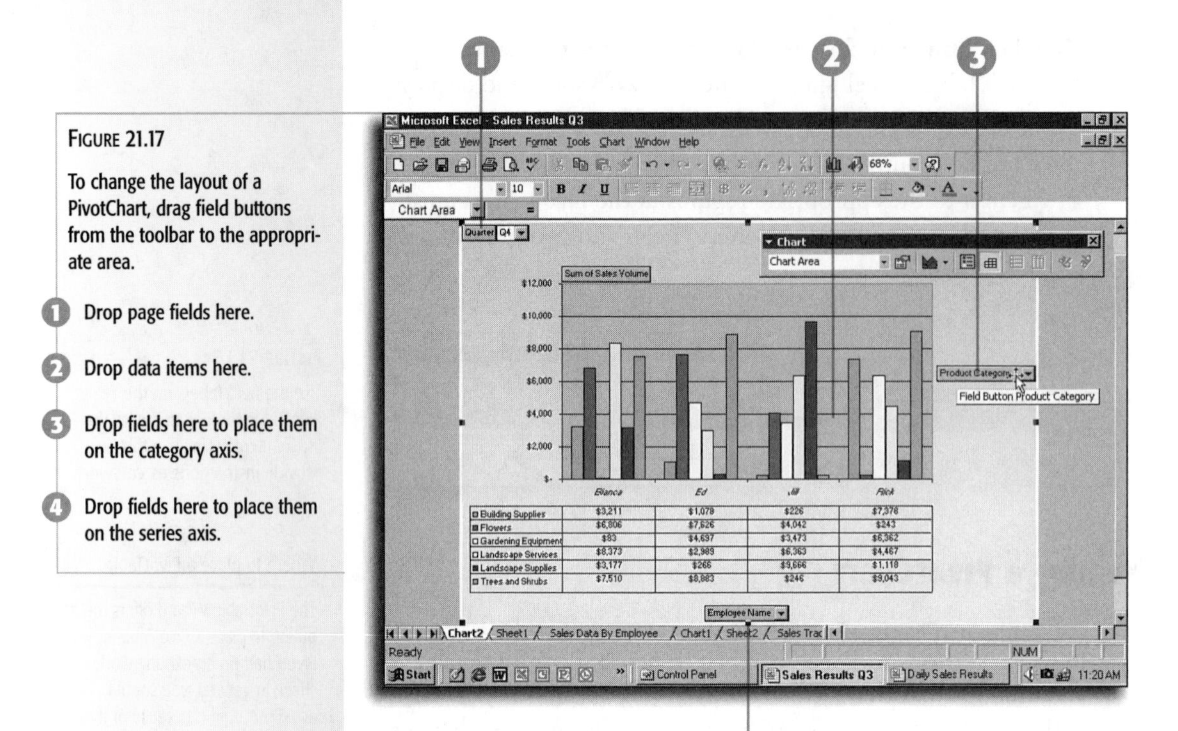

FIGURE 21.17

To change the layout of a PivotChart, drag field buttons from the toolbar to the appropriate area.

1. Drop page fields here.
2. Drop data items here.
3. Drop fields here to place them on the category axis.
4. Drop fields here to place them on the series axis.

Every chart needs a table

When you use the WIzard to create a PivotChart from scratch, Excel places the chart on its own sheet and creates a corresponding PivotTable. You cannot create a PivotChart without adding a PivotTable to your worksheet as well.

Double-duty button

You'll find the **Chart Wizard** button on Excel's Standard toolbar and on the PivotTable toolbar. Use either button to create a PivotChart with one click. Click the button again to open the Chart Wizard and either change chart types or adjust chart options.

Editing the Layout of a PivotTable

After you create a PivotTable, it's easy to rearrange fields and data items. Drag fields from one place to another to change the display of data. Right-click to display shortcut menus that let you adjust formatting and other options for each field. Table 21.2 lists common procedures for editing PivotTables.

TABLE 21.2 Editing a PivotTable

If You Want To	Then Do This
Change the list to which the PivotTable points.	Click the **PivotTable Wizard** tool on the PivotTable toolbar. Click **Back** to return to step 1 and make the required changes. Click **Finish**.

If You Want To	Then Do This
Change one or more fields that define rows, columns, pages, or data items.	Drag a field button from the Pivot Table toolbar and drop it on the layout; drag the existing field off the layout. Click **Finish**.
Remove a field from the PivotTable layout.	Drag the field button off the layout; when the pointer icon changes to include a red X, release the mouse button.
Change the order of fields in rows, columns, or the data area.	Drag the field button and drop it in the correct location on the layout.
Change the summary function used in the data area.	Right-click the field button in the top-left corner of the PivotTable and choose **Field Settings** from the shortcut menu. Select the function from the **Summarize by** list.

Formatting PivotTables

When you first create a PivotTable, it picks up the generic look of a default worksheet, with plain 10-point Arial formatting for details and headings alike. To make your PivotTable more compelling, use Excel's formatting features to add emphasis to text and backgrounds or shading to cells, rows, and columns.

SEE ALSO

➤ *To learn more about worksheet formatting, see page 383*

You can format numbers and text in a PivotTable by selecting cells individually and choosing formatting options as you would in a normal worksheet. However, if you redefine your PivotTable later, you will lose this formatting. To apply formatting that will last, right-click any cell in the data items area and choose **Field Settings** from the shortcut menu. Click the **Number** button and choose a format from the dialog box.

To make PivotTables look their best, take advantage of Excel's AutoFormat capability. After you've created a PivotTable, click the **Format Report** button on the PivotTable toolbar. You'll

Use the ScreenTips

As you drag field buttons around on PivotTable and PivotChart layouts, watch the ScreenTips. These informative messages tell you exactly what each object is and what will happen if you release it in a given area.

Hiding field buttons

You can't hide field buttons on a PivotTable, but you can remove clutter from a PivotChart. If you're happy with the chart layout, click the **PivotChart** buttons on the PivotTable toolbar and choose **Hide PivotChart Field Buttons**. Use the same menu choice to display the buttons again.

Rename sheet tabs

When you create a PivotTable or PivotChart on a new worksheet, Excel assigns a generic name to the new sheet. To make your worksheets easier to understand, right-click the tabs and give the sheet a new name that helps identify it.

Undo AutoFormat

If you don't like the AutoFormat you've applied to a PivotTable, it's easy to undo the changes. First, right click any cell in the PivotTable, choose **Table Options** from the shortcut menu, and clear the check mark from the **AutoFormat table** box. Next, click the **Format Report** button to open the AutoFormat dialog box again. Scroll to the bottom of the list. Select the option labeled **None** and click OK.

see a dialog box like the one in Figure 21.18, containing more than 20 collections of ready-made formats. Select any format and click OK to apply the changes to your PivotTable.

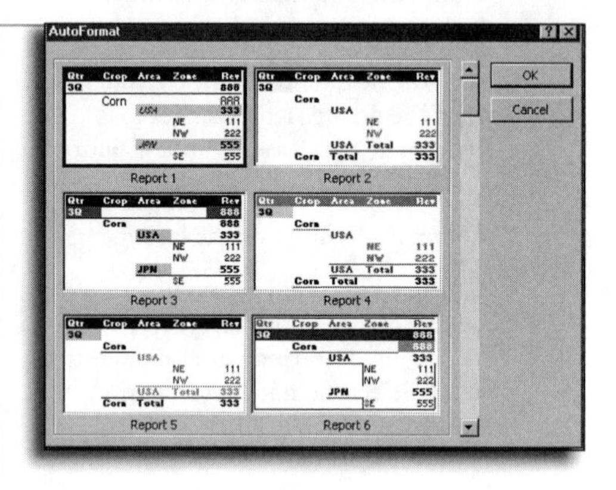

FIGURE 21.18

Use these predefined PivotTable formats to instantly make a drab table easier to understand.

CHAPTER 22

Creating and Editing Charts

Use the Chart Wizard for instant results

Choose the perfect chart type for your data

Add details to your chart

Print your chart

Convert your chart for use on a Web page

How Excel Charts Work

There are two ways to look at data in an Excel worksheet: as raw numbers, arranged in rows and columns, or as *charts*. While those rows and columns are essential for organizing the data and performing calculations, it's difficult—and sometimes impossible—to analyze the information and see patterns simply by staring at a sea of numbers.

Keep a link to your chart

You can copy any Excel chart object and paste it into a Word document, a PowerPoint presentation, or a Web page. If you use the Clipboard to simply paste the chart, you'll usually end up with a graphics file that you will need to update the next time your data changes. Pull down the **Edit** menu and use the Paste **Special** command to copy a linked chart that updates automatically when you change your worksheet.

Charts help you graphically represent numeric data in a way that lets you spot patterns at a glance. By summarizing data and displaying comparisons over time or across categories, charts help you emphatically answer tough questions: Which division sold the most last year? How much of an effect did that harsh winter have on heating costs in the first quarter? Have my golf scores improved since last summer?

SEE ALSO

➤ *To learn how to analyze data using PivotCharts, see page 435*

When you create a chart, Excel links the data you select to its graphic representation on the chart. Later, if you change the numbers or text in the worksheet's data range, the columns, pie slices, and other graphic elements on the chart will change, too.

Elements of an Excel Chart

Use the ScreenTips

As you work with Excel charts, pay attention to the ScreenTips that pop up when the mouse pointer passes over objects. ScreenTips identify virtually every chart element; within the plot area, they identify the name of the data series and point, as well as the precise value of each data point.

Although you can choose from dozens of different Excel chart types, most charts share common elements. Each row or column in your worksheet, for example, makes up a *data series*. Each value within the series is called a *data point*. If the range you select for your chart includes worksheet headings, Excel will use them as *labels* along the *category axis* or *value axis*. The stacked-column chart in Figure 22.1 shows most of the common elements you'll encounter as you work with charts.

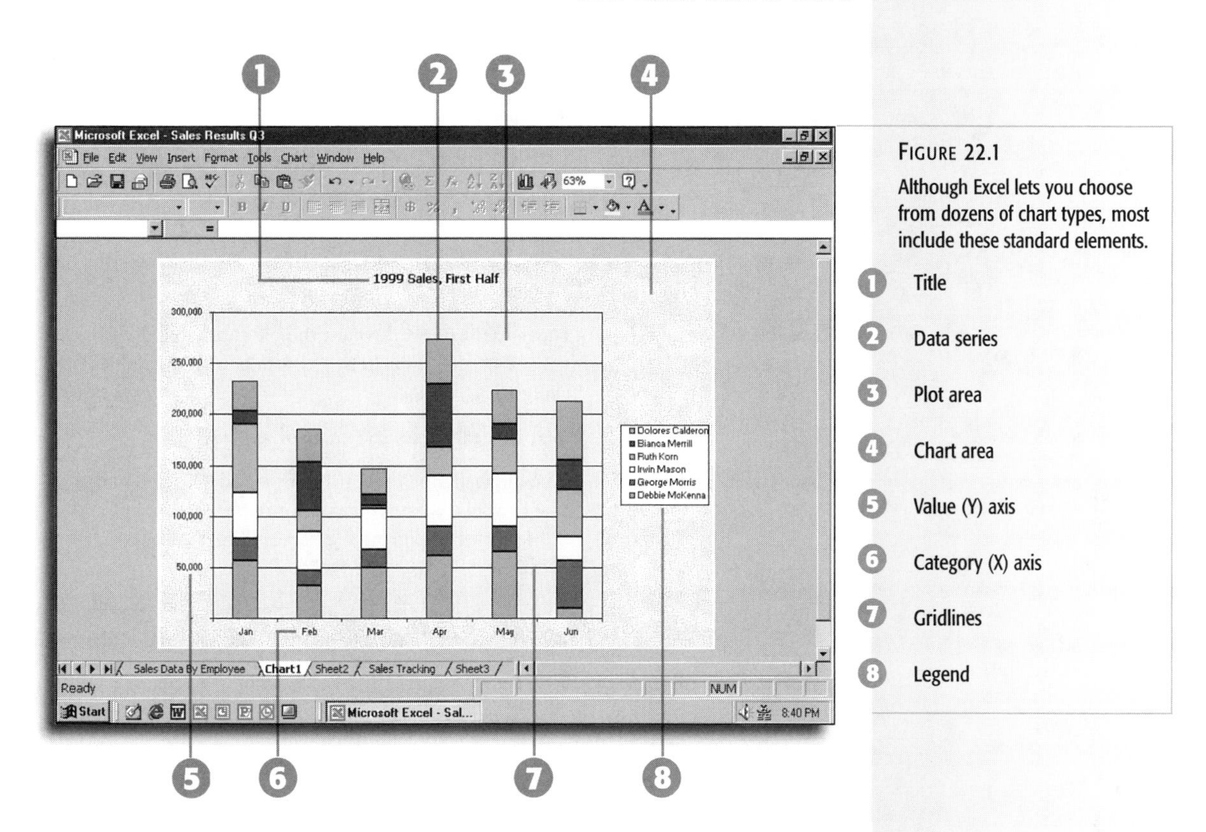

FIGURE 22.1

Although Excel lets you choose from dozens of chart types, most include these standard elements.

1. Title
2. Data series
3. Plot area
4. Chart area
5. Value (Y) axis
6. Category (X) axis
7. Gridlines
8. Legend

Table 22.1 lists the elements you can expect to find in most Excel charts.

Use two axes to compare data

You can create *secondary axes* for categories and values. These are especially useful when you're comparing data with very different values. When you create a secondary value axis, the labels appear on the right of a column chart.

TABLE 22.1 **Common Excel Chart Elements**

Object Name	Description
Category (X) axis	This axis (usually horizontal) arranges your data by category—by time, for example, or by division or employee.
Value (Y) axis	This axis (usually vertical) tells Excel how to plot the worksheet data. In the default column chart, for example, taller columns represent bigger numbers.
Data series	Excel converts the data from rows or columns in your worksheet into groups of chart elements; each point in the series becomes a single data marker, such as a column, a pie slice, or a point along a line.

continues...

Rows to columns, and vice versa

When you select the data source, Excel chooses whether to plot data by rows or by columns. If the default setting isn't correct, click the **Series in Rows** or **Series in Columns** button to reverse these settings. With some chart typesand data, making this switch could render the chart incomprehensible; click the **Undo** button.

When should you add a title?

Add a chart title when you want to provide a descriptive label for the entire graphic. If you plan to paste the chart in a highly formatted Word document or PowerPoint presentation, though, you might want to add the chart title using Word or PowerPoint instead. That way, when you change your document or presentation design, the title can be changed as well.

Arrange your data with care

Charts work best when you have a well-organized worksheet range, with only one row of headings and no blank columns or rows. Make sure the range you select includes all the data to be charted, as well as the labels you'll use for the categories. If the range you plan to chart ends with a row or column of totals, don't include those totals in your selection, or the totals will create one column or pie slice that overwhelms all the others in the chart.

TABLE 22.1 Continued

Object Name	Description
Labels	Labels identify items on the category axis and define the scale of the value axis; you can also add labels to data series.
Legend	A color-coded key that identifies data series or categories.
Gridlines	Lines that extend through the plot area to help you see the connections between data points and values or categories.
Title	Text that identifies the chart or axes.
Chart area	The chart area is the entire chart and every element. You can select fonts for the entire chart here and add borders and background effects, such as colors or textures.
Plot area	The plot area is the area that includes all data series. Right-click to define borders and background effects for this region.

Selecting Data to Chart

Before creating a chart, you first have to enter the numeric data and row and column headings you want Excel to use. When you begin creating a chart, Excel will use the current selection as the data source. If the active cell is in a list and you haven't selected a range, Excel will attempt to use the entire list. The range you select for chart data does not have to be contiguous. For example, to create a pie chart you might want to select a row of column labels and a row of totals, ignoring the detail rows in between.

SEE ALSO

- *To learn more about organizing lists, see page 421*
- *For details on how to select ranges, see page 342*

Excel uses a set of common-sense rules to decide which rows and columns contain data and which contain labels. Most of the time, the default settings will be correct. If they're not, use the

Chart Wizard to adjust the range used for data series or category axis labels.

Creating a Default Chart

The quickest way to create a chart in Excel is to use a *default chart*. Because the chart's style is predefined, all you have to do is select your data and press a key (or click a toolbar button).

Creating a Default Chart

1. Open the worksheet that contains the data you want to chart.
2. Select the range that contains the data you want to chart. Make sure you include the row and column labels.
3. Press F11. The completed chart appears on a new chart sheet.

Data series are color coded

When you click a chart's data series, Excel selects the corresponding range on the worksheet that contains the data source. Each range is color-coded, just like range references in formulas. If you extend or change the selected range, the plotted data on the chart will change as well.

Column charts are the default

Unless you specify a different default chart type, Excel will always assume you want to create a column chart. It's easy to switch to a different chart type after you've created a chart.

Choosing the Right Chart Type

Excel lets you pick from 73 different chart types in 14 distinct categories. There are also 20 custom chart types, and you can add your own chart types to this list as well. How do you decide which chart type to use? The type of data you're planning to plot usually dictates what type of chart you should choose.

To see trends over a period of time, for example, use a line chart; when you plot daily sales or stock prices over a period of two or three months, you can see at a glance whether the line is moving up, moving down, or remaining flat. On the other hand, you would use a pie chart, like the one in Figure 22.2, to see what percentage of your monthly departmental budget goes to payroll, insurance, office supplies, and other categories.

The list of built-in Excel chart types includes several *combination charts*, which mix two chart types in a single graphic. In the Stock category, for example, you'll find combination charts that let you plot high, low, and closing stock prices on a line, with trading volume in columns. In this case, you use two value axes, one to the left of the chart area, the other to the right. Figure 22.3 shows one such chart, complete with some advanced elements like custom backgrounds and a trend line.

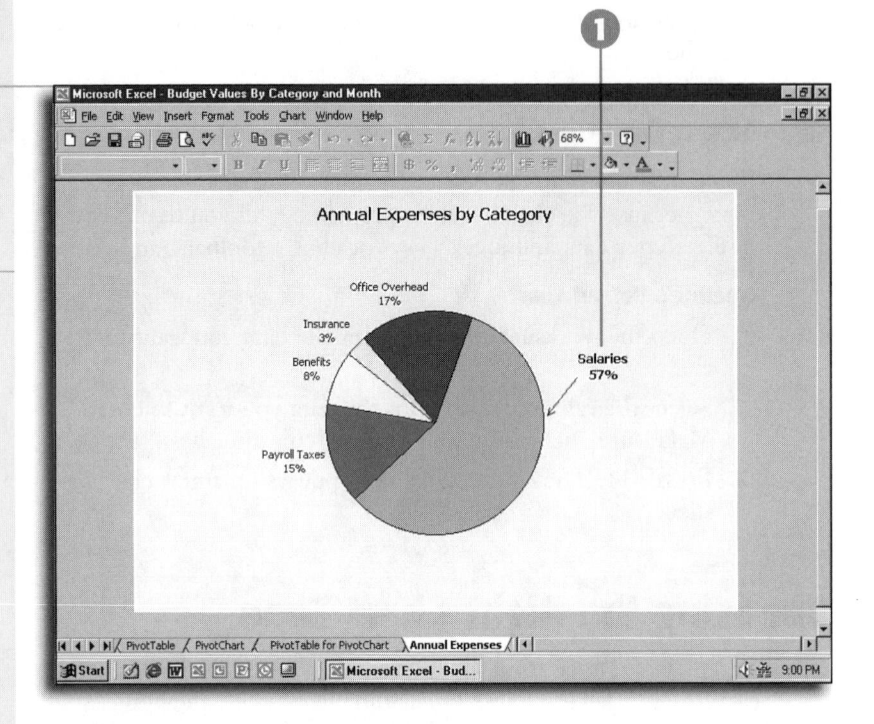

FIGURE 22.2

Pie charts show how each piece of data contributes to the whole.

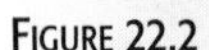
1 Data labels

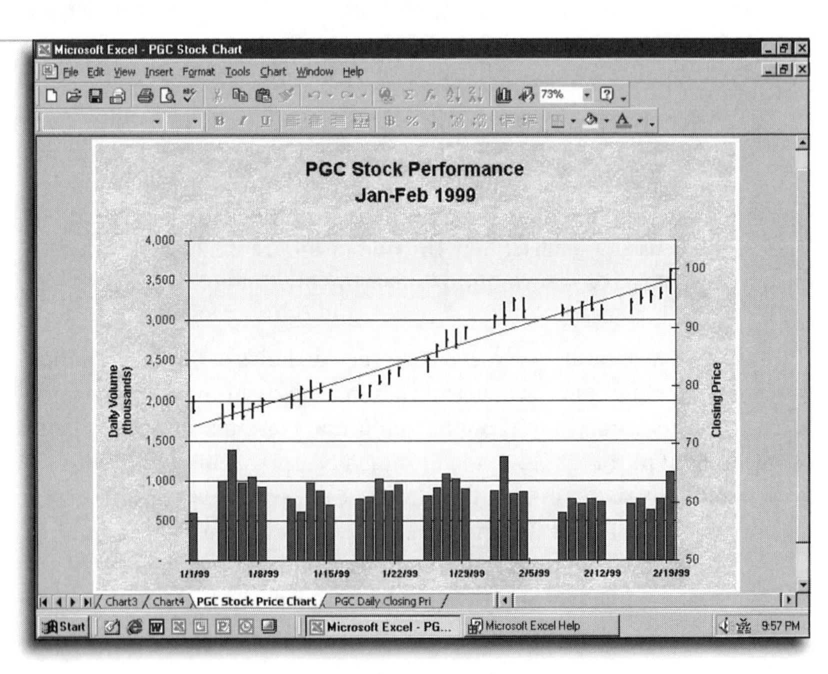

FIGURE 22.3

Combination charts enable you to plot more than one type of information.

Choosing the Best Chart Type for Your Data

When you start the Chart Wizard, the first step is to specify what type of chart you want to create. You can easily change an existing chart to a new type; click the **Chart Type** button on the Chart toolbar to select from the list in Figure 22.4. Table 22.2 lists all the Excel chart categories and describes how you can best use them.

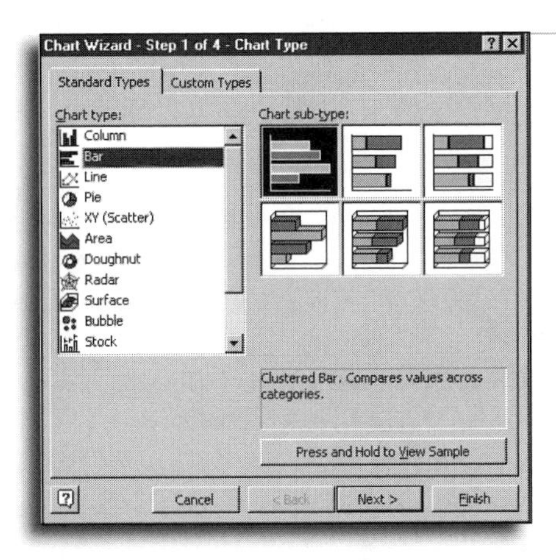

FIGURE 22.4
Choose a chart type from Excel's enormous collection, or save a custom type of your own choosing.

TABLE 22.2 **Standard Chart Categories**

Chart Type	How You Use It
Column	Comparison between values in one or more series, often over time. For example, you can show how much revenue each of your sales people brought in over the past year. Stacked column charts further divide the total for each column, so you can also measure how each sales person did with individual product lines.
Bar	A column chart turned on its side, with values along the horizontal axis and categories on the vertical axis. De-emphasizes time comparisons, and highlights winners and losers.
Pie	Shows the relative size of all the parts in a whole—for example, the ethnic composition of a city. Pie charts have no X or Y axis, and only one data series can be plotted.

continues...

Column chart do's and don'ts

Choose a column chart when you want to show changes over time or comparisons among different items. Avoid this chart type if each series includes so many data points that you'll be unable to distinguish individual columns.

Pie chart do's and don'ts

Use pie charts when you have only a few numbers to chart and you want to show how each number contributes to the whole. Avoid this chart type when your data series includes many low numbers that contribute a very small percentage to the total. In this case, individual pie slices will be too small to compare.

Line chart do's and don'ts

Choose a line chart when you have many data points to plot and you want to show a trend over a period of time. Avoid this chart type when you're trying to show the relationship between numbers without respect to time, or when you have only a few data points to chart.

Arrange stock data properly

If you're trying to plot stock prices and volume traded, make sure you have your data arranged correctly. The Office Assistant will display an error message if you have too few columns, or if they are in the wrong order.

X, Y, and Z axes explained

In the default column chart type, the Y-axis is the vertical one and the X-axis is the horizontal one. Direction isn't important, though; what matters is what type of data you plot along each axis. In any chart, the X-axis contains categories. On a 2D chart, the Y-axis is for values. In 3D charts, the values go on the Z-axis, with the Y-axis reserved for a different series of data.

TABLE 22.2 Continued

Chart Type	How You Use It
Line	Displays a trend, or the relationship between the values over a time period. When you plot daily high temperatures on the value axis and use the category axis as the time scale, the dips and rises in the line show when the weather is getting warmer or cooler.
Area	Shows lines for parts of a series, adding all the values together to illustrate cumulative change. Use this chart type, for example, to show how each division of your company contributes to total sales over time.
Stock	As seen in the *Wall Street Journal*. With days along the horizontal axis, and high/low/close prices on the vertical axis, you can track whether a stock is climbing or plunging in value. Use one of the combination chart types in this category to plot volume traded, as well.
Cone/Cylinder/Pyramid	Glitzed-up versions of standard column and bar charts.
XY (Scatter)	Shows correlation between different series of values—usually used for scientific analyses.
Doughnut/Radar/ Bubble/Surface	Strictly for specialists and advanced data-analysis tasks.

Saving and Reusing Custom Chart Types

If you've carefully customized a chart, you can add its settings to the list of *custom chart types*. Later, when you choose that chart type, Excel will apply all your option and format settings to the current chart. This is a particularly handy way to maintain a consistent style across charts with a company.

Saving a Custom Chart Format

1. Select the chart whose settings you want to save.
2. Click the **Chart Type** button on the Chart toolbar, right-click on the chart and choose **Chart Type** from the shortcut menu.

3. Click the **Custom Types** tab; under the heading **Select from**, choose **User-defined**. Excel filters the list to display only the Default chart type and other custom chart types you've previously created.
4. Click the **Add** button to display the dialog box shown in Figure 22.5.

Change default chart types

If you want to use a custom chart type as your default instead of the standard Column chart, open the Chart Type dialog box, select the chart type you want to use, and click the **Set as default chart** button.

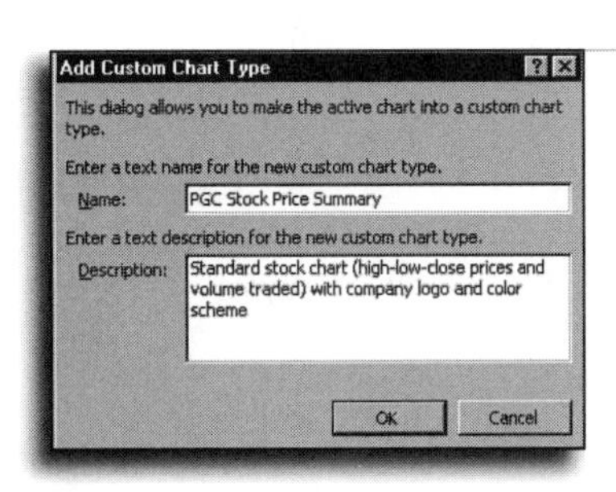

FIGURE 22.5

Make sure you add a descriptive name and comments to help explain what settings are in a custom chart type.

5. Enter a name and description for your chart type.
6. Click **OK** to save the new chart type.

To create a chart using a custom chart type, select its entry from the list, just as you would a standard chart type.

Pick a chart, any chart

If you're not sure which chart type to use, feel free to experiment. If you don't like the results, click the **Back** button to try another option.

Creating a Basic Chart with the Chart Wizard

Excel's Chart Wizard walks you through all the details of creating and displaying a chart. When you click the **Chart Wizard** button on the Standard toolbar, Excel launches a simple process that helps you build a chart in four steps.

Click, don't type

Although you can type a range name directly in the Chart Wizard dialog box, it's far more accurate to use the mouse than to bother with typing a range address. Just point to the first cell in the range you want to select, and then click and drag to select the range. As soon as you click the mouse, the Chart Wizard will zoom out of the way, returning when you stop dragging.

Creating a Chart Using the Chart Wizard

1. Click the **Chart Wizard** button. You'll see the dialog box shown in Figure 22.6.
2. Select a category from the list labeled **Chart type**, and then click the icon for the corresponding **Chart sub-type** that best represents the type of chart you want to create. Click **Next>**.

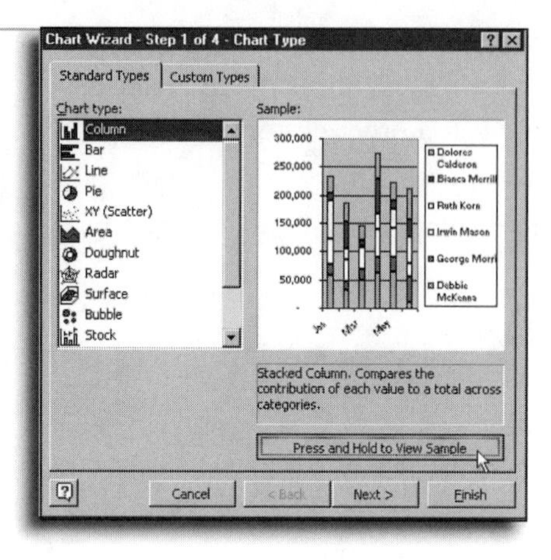

FIGURE 22.6

If you selected a range of data before starting the Chart Wizard, click and hold the button below the chart types to see a preview of your data.

SEE ALSO

➤ *For advice on which type of chart to choose for different types of data, see page 447*

3. In step 2 of the Chart Wizard, confirm that the correct range is selected. If you didn't select a range, or if you want to adjust the data source for the chart, select a new range, and click **Next>**.

4. In the next step of the Chart Wizard, adjust formatting options using any of the six categories in the multi-tabbed dialog box shown in Figure 22.7. You can add a title and label the axes, position the legend that explains what each data marker represents, and add other details that help make your chart more readable.

SEE ALSO

➤ *For details on how to adjust chart formatting, see the next section.*

5. In the final Chart Wizard step, select where you want to place your chart. If you want your data and chart on the same worksheet, click **As object in** and then choose the name of the sheet where the data is stored. To give the chart its own sheet, click the **As new sheet** option. Type a new name for the sheet, if you want.

6. If you want to review your choices or make any changes, click the **Back** button. Click **Finish** to close the Chart Wizard and insert the chart in your workbook.

Keep it simple

You can agonize over every detail of your chart, but Isuggest that you use the Chart Wizard's default settings and ignore most of the details on your first pass through the wizard. You can restart the Chart Wizard after you've created your chart, and most of the choices will be much clearer when you see what it looks like in your worksheet.

Move the dialog box

If the Chart Wizard is in the way of the cells you want to select, click the tiny **Collapse Dialog** button to the right of the box labeled **Data range**. The entire dialog box will roll up out of your way, showing only the title bar and the data-entry box. Click the same button to restore the Chart Wizard to its full size.

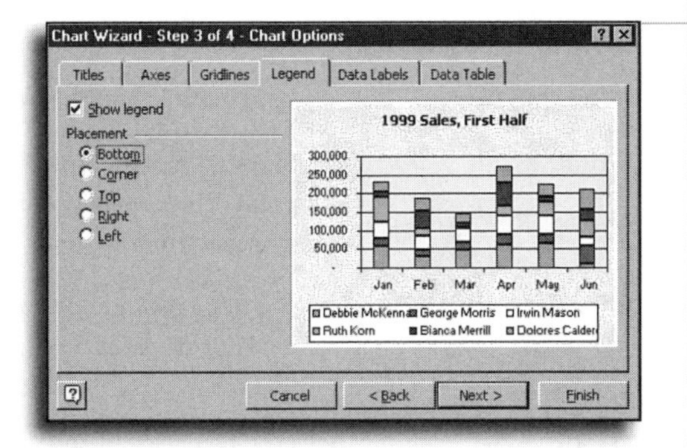

FIGURE 22.7

As you add title text and adjust other chart options, the preview window changes to show how your chart will look.

Formatting Chart Elements

Although the default chart settings are generally acceptable, you'll probably have to tinker with various elements to get a chart to look precisely the way you want it. Excel offers a broad range of chart options that let you control the look of the chart and plot area. To adjust individual chart objects, you'll need to first select the object (the chart title or the category axis, for example), and then change its properties.

Adjusting Chart Options

Step 3 of the Chart Wizard displays a tabbed dialog box that lets you adjust various chart options. After you create a chart, you can display the same dialog box by right-clicking on the chart area and choosing **Chart Options** from the shortcut menu. Table 22.3 summarizes the options available on each of the six tabs. (Note that not all of these options are available for every chart type.)

TABLE 22.3 **Chart Formatting Options**

Choose This Option	To Adjust This Formatting
Titles	Create titles that appear on the top of the chart or next to any axis.
Axes	Check **Automatic** to allow Excel to format and display the axes that are appropriate for the chart type you've chosen.

continues...

Where should your chart go?

It doesn't matter whether you give a chart its own sheet or put it on an existing worksheet. I find it's easier to jump between the data and the chart without scrolling if I put the chart in a separate sheet within the workbook. But either way, the links between the data you've charted and the graphic representation on the page are dynamic—as you change the numbers, the chart will change, too.

Restart the wizard anytime

If you're not satisfied with the results from the Chart Wizard's default settings, just go through the process again. Simply select the chart and then click the Chart Wizard button again. Go through each of the wizard's four steps, making whatever changes you feel like, and click **Finish** to see the new chart.

Use the Chart Objects list

It can be extremely difficult to select a chart object by pointing to it, especially on a small chart with many elements. There's a simple shortcut: Pick any chart object from the drop-down Chart Objects list at the left of the Chart toolbar.

Do you need titles?

Although you don't have to give every chart a title, it's a good idea to help viewers figure out exactly what they're looking at. If the arrangement of data along each axis isn't immediately apparent, you can add explanatory text here, too. Open the Chart Options dialog box, click the **Titles** tab, and add titles for the chart and axes, if you wish.

Arranging the legend

If you don't need to show a legend (perhaps because you want to label each column or pie slice individually), remove the check mark from the **Show legend** box. If you do plan to use a legend, the **Placement** options control where it first appears within the chart. You can drag the legend on the chart to position it more precisely later. The Graph toolbar has a Legend toggle button.

Resetting number formats

When you choose a number format within a chart, Excel clears the check mark from the box labeled **Linked to source**. To re-establish the link so the data on the chart uses the same number format as the data on the worksheet, check this box again.

TABLE 22.3 **Continued**

Choose This Option	To Adjust This Formatting
Gridlines	Show or hide lines that help readers see where data points cross category or value axes. Watch the Preview window to see the effect of various options.
Legend	A chart *legend* identifies each *data marker* according to its color or pattern on a chart. Options on this tab let you move or reformat the legend.
Data Labels	Use *data labels* for Excel to display charted worksheet values, category labels, or percentages next to each point in a data series.
Data Table	Display a worksheet-style table directly in your chart to show the plotted worksheet data alongside the chart itself.

Changing the Way Numbers Appear

Normally, numbers that appear in Excel charts use the same format as the source data in the worksheet to which they're linked. If you change the format of the numbers in the chart, you break the link to the format in the worksheet. You might want to do exactly that—for example, if numbers in your worksheet use Currency format with two decimal places, but you don't want to see a dollar sign or decimals in your chart.

Change Number Formats on a Chart

1. Right-click the chart object (value axis or data labels, for example) and choose **Format** from the shortcut menu.
2. Click the Number tab, and then click a format in the **Category** list. If necessary, select the exact format from the list labeled **Type**.

SEE ALSO

➤ *For a full explanation of Excel number formats, see page 388*

3. Adjust any options (decimal places or currency symbols, for example). Check the results in the Sample box just below the Number tab.
4. Click **OK** to apply the new format to your chart data.

Changing Text Formats and Alignment

You can change the appearance of any text item on a chart. As with worksheet cells, Excel lets you change fonts as well as font sizes and character attributes. You can choose different colors for the text and its background. To keep labels from running into one another on any axis, rotate text to an angle.

To adjust font options for all text in your chart, right-click on the chart and choose **Format Chart Area**. Click the **Font** tab of the resulting dialog box and adjust formatting as necessary.

To change text formatting for any other text object, first select the object. Right-click and choose **Format** from the shortcut menu. Click the **Font** tab and adjust options as desired.

To rotate text on any axis, right-click on the axis and choose **Format Axis** from the shortcut menu. Click the **Alignment** tab to display the dialog box shown in Figure 22.8.

Lock down your font size

By default, text in an Excel chart is scalable—that is, as you resize the entire chart, the text gets larger or smaller so it remains in proportion with the rest of the chart elements. If you have carefully designed a text element and you don't want its font size to change, turn off automatic scaling. Right-click on the object and click the **Format** menu. On the Font tab, clear the check mark from the box labeled **Auto scale**.

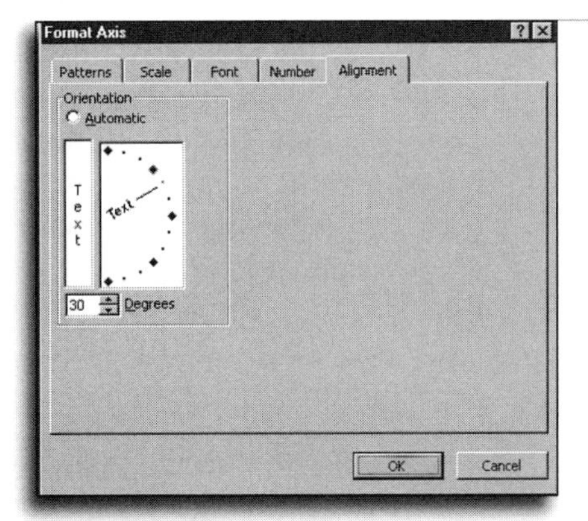

FIGURE 22.8
Use this dialog box to change the scale of numbers on the value axis.

Click the slim text box at left to display the text so that it reads from top to bottom. To align the text at an angle, click in the right-hand box and drag the line up or down (or use the spinners to choose a precise angle over a range of 180 degrees); the text in the box changes alignment to show how it will appear in your chart. Click the **Offset** box to set the distance between the axis labels and the axis itself; the higher the number, the more distance between the two points.

Careful with those sizes!

Use the **Format Chart Area** menu choice to apply the same font to all text in your chart, but avoid the temptation to choose a size as well. In most cases, you'll want to specify different font sizes for different items, such as the chart title, axes, and legend.

Adding Background Colors, Textures, and Pictures

The default background for charts is a boring white, but you can spice up any chart by adding patterns, textures, gradient fills, or even pictures to the chart area, the plot area, individual data series, or the legend. In 3D charts, you can also add images to the walls and the floor.

These features use the Drawing tools that are shared by all Office programs. If you've designed a Web page in Word or a PowerPoint presentation, you can use the same backgrounds in Excel charts and paste those charts into your document or presentation.

SEE ALSO

➤ *For instructions on how to add background colors, pictures, textures, and gradients to Excel charts, see page 122*

Changing the Scale and Spacing of Axes

To make your chart easier to read, you might also want to adjust the *scale* on the value axis. Normally, the values on this axis start with 0 and extend to a number past the highest number in your data series. You might want to change the scale to start at a higher number so that you can more easily see the difference between data points. In the chart in Figure 22.3, for example, the stock prices plotted in the axis on the right range from a little over 70 to just under 100. Rather than use that range, however, I chose a range of 50 to 100 so that the high-low-close bars wouldn't bump into the columns below.

Adjusting the Scale on the Value Axis

1. Right-click on the value axis and choose **Format Axis**.
2. Click the **Scale** tab to display the dialog box shown in Figure 22.9.
3. Enter the high and low values for the axis in the boxes labeled **Minimum** and **Maximum**. Note that when you change the default numbers, Excel automatically clears the checkmarks in the **Auto** column.

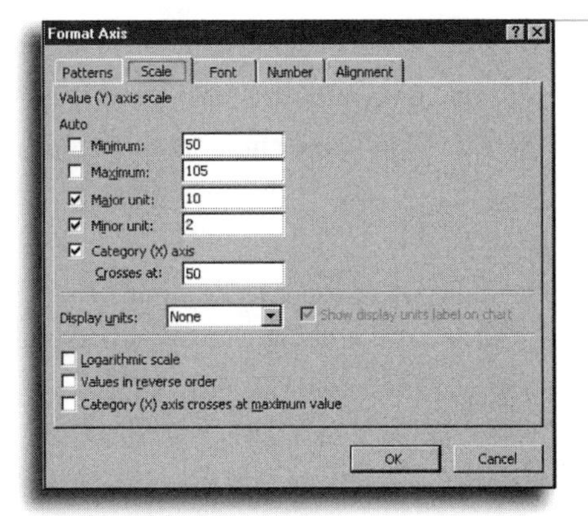

FIGURE 22.9
Use this dialog box to change the scale of numbers on the value axis.

4. If you want to make large numbers—thousands or millions, for example—easier to read, choose an option from the drop-down list labeled **Display units**. If you choose **Thousands**, for example, Excel will display `$340,000` as `$340`.
5. Click **OK** to apply the change to your chart.

Editing a Chart

The easiest way to change a chart is to rerun the **Chart Wizard** by clicking its toolbar button. The wizard's dialog boxes pick up your current chart settings and let you change chart types, edit the source data, apply new formatting, or change the location of your chart. This section covers techniques that aren't available in the Chart Wizard.

Tell the reader when you're rounding

By default, when you change the display units for the value axis, Excel adds a label alongside the axis to let the reader know that the numbers are actually larger than they appear. If you don't like this clutter, clear the check mark from the box labeled **Show display units label on chart**. But make sure you add an explanatory note somewhere on the chart to alert readers that you've truncated the numbers.

Moving and Resizing Charts

If you chose to insert the chart as an object in an existing worksheet, it sits in its own layer on top of your data. Select the chart by clicking anywhere on it, pointing to any part of the chart area, and clicking and dragging to slide the chart object into a new position. As you slide to any edge of the window, the worksheet scrolls in that direction.

To resize a chart object, use a slightly different technique.

Working with chart objects

When you move or resize cells underneath a chart object on a worksheet, Excel moves or resizes the chart as well. To change this link between chart and cells, right-click on the chart object and choose **Format Chart Area** from the shortcut menu. Click the **Properties** tab and choose one of the three options under **Object positioning**.

Resizing a Chart Object

1. Click once on the chart border to select the Chart Area.
2. You'll see eight small sizing handles along the border—one on each side and one in each corner. Point to any of these black squares until the pointer turns to a two-headed arrow.
3. Drag the handle in any direction to adjust the size and shape of the chart. Excel will adjust the scale of all the elements on your chart to match.

Adding Data to an Existing Chart

When you want to change the data source for an existing chart, your easiest option is to rerun the Chart Wizard. Use the dialog box in step 2 of the wizard to reset the data range and the location of each series.

To add a single series to a chart that's embedded on a worksheet, select the range that contains the data and headings and drop it directly on the chart. Excel adds the data to the plot area, complete with new category labels and legend items, if necessary.

Or use the Clipboard...

If you copy a worksheet range to the Clipboard, you can choose **Edit**, **Paste** from the chart window to add the series to an existing chart.

Additional Customization Options

Excel lets you add an enormous number of attention-getting elements to charts. For example, you can add text boxes and labels to data markers to explain anomalies in your data or call attention to key numbers.

SEE ALSO

➤ *To learn how to add text boxes and drawing objects to a worksheet, see page 124*

The chart in Figure 22.10 demonstrates several of these formatting options. By default, a basic pie chart shows a simple pie with a legend explaining what each slice means. To give the chart more impact, slide out one slice of the pie and replace the legend with explanatory labels that include the percentage for each slice.

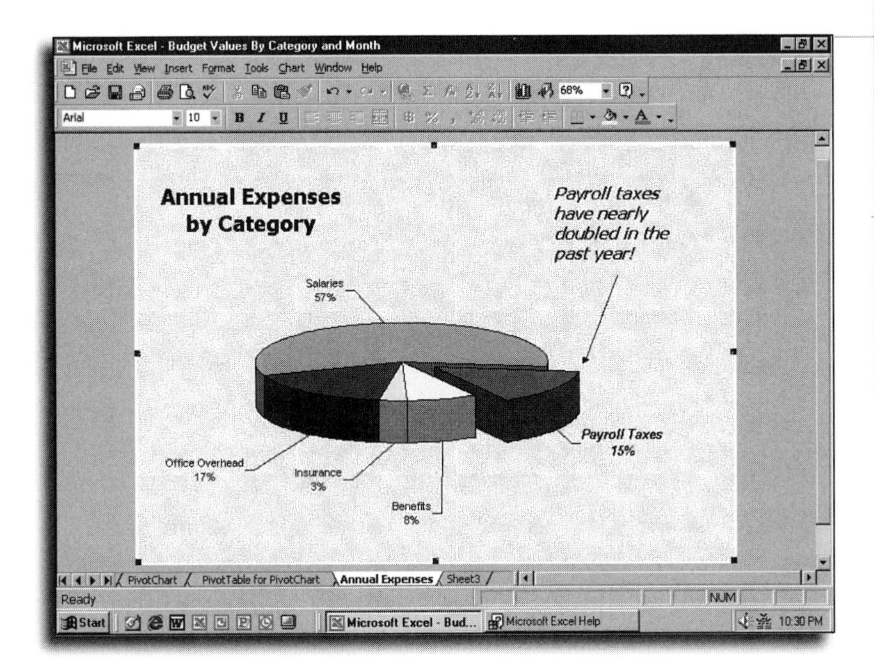

FIGURE 22.10
Using Excel's many formatting options, I changed the dull default pie chart to this more attention-getting version.

Customizing a Pie Chart

1. Click anywhere on the chart to select the entire pie, and then click on the slice you want to pull out. Click and drag the slice out of the pie as far as you want.
2. To hide the legend, right-click and choose **Clear** from the shortcut menu.
3. Click on any blank area in the chart to clear the selection, and then right-click on the pie and choose **Format Data Series**.
4. In the Format Data Series dialog box, click on the **Data Labels** tab; choose the **Show label and percent** option.
5. Click on the **Options** tab. In the box labeled **Angle of first slice**, click the up and down spinners to bring the selected slice closer to the front. The Preview window shows you where the slice will appear.
6. Click **OK** to save the changes and return to your worksheet.

Use data labels anywhere

You can use data labels with any type of chart. Just right-click on the data series, choose **Format Data Series** from the shortcut menu, and choose the appropriate options on the **Data Labels** tab.

Printing Charts

When it's time to print your chart, you have two options: You can print the chart along with the worksheet data, or print it on a page by itself. For financial presentations, you may want to see the worksheet data along with the charts, but most of the time you'll want to print just the charts.

How you go about getting ready to print depends on where the chart is located in your workbook.

To Print a Chart That's Embedded in a Worksheet

1. Choose **View**, **Page Break Preview** to see where your pages will break. If you don't like the layout, you can move or resize the chart object, or change the page breaks.
2. To force the worksheet to print using a given number of sheets of paper, first make sure to select the range you want to print. Click the **Print Preview** button to switch to Print Preview mode.
3. Click **Setup** to display the Page Setup dialog box.
4. Click the Page tab and enter the appropriate numbers in the area labeled **Fit to *X* page(s) wide by *X* tall**.
5. Click **Print** to display the Print dialog box. If all print settings are correct, click **OK**.

SEE ALSO

➤ *For detailed instructions on how to print worksheets, see page 406*

Printing a Chart Sheet

1. Click to select the chart sheet, and then choose **File**, **Page Setup**. Click the Chart tab to see the dialog box shown in Figure 22.11.
2. By default, Excel checks the **Use full page** option, which may cause the chart to stretch more in one dimension (width or height) than in another. To maintain the proportions of your chart, choose the **Scale to fit page** option instead.

Resizing a chart on a chart sheet

If you create a chart on its own sheet, Excel doesn't add sizing handles. To resize the chart area of a chart sheet, you must first choose **File**, **Page Setup**; click the **Chart** tab and choose the **Custom** option. Click **OK** to return to the chart sheet. Follow the same steps if you want to move the chart.

Use this technique with embedded charts, too

To print an embedded chart on a worksheet, click to select the chart and follow the same procedures as you would for a chart sheet. Don't forget to preview.

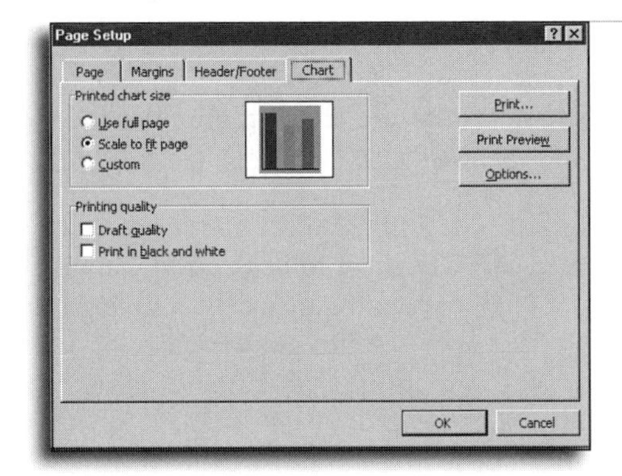

FIGURE 22.11
Use these options to control exactly how your printed chart will look. Remember to preview before printing.

3. In the **Printing quality** section, check the box labeled **Print in black and white** only if you want to replace colors with patterns instead of gray tones.
4. Click **Print** to display the Print dialog box. If all print settings are correct, click **OK**.

How will your color chart print?

Although your screen can display your chart in color, that won't matter if you're printing to a black-ink printer. Always preview your selection before you print it–if your default printer is a black-and-white model, the preview screen shows the colors translated to shades of gray. You may want to replace some colors or play with patterns to make the chart more legible.

Converting a Chart for Use on a Web Page

You have several choices to make when adding an Excel chart to a Web page. Do you want to create a new Web page or add the chart to an existing page? Do you want to convert the chart to a graphic file, or do you want to make the chart interactive, so that anyone who views the page in a browser window can change the underlying data and redraw the chart? Finally, do you want to add a title above the chart in your Web page?

SEE ALSO

For more details on how to save worksheets and other documents for use on the Web, see page 57

Saving a Chart for Use on a Web Page

1. Open the workbook that contains the chart and select the chart or chart sheet.
2. Pull down the **File** menu and choose **Save As Web Page**.
3. Choose **Selection: Chart** to specify that you want to save only the selected object and the entire workbook.

Compatibility notes

If you choose to make a chart interactive, only users with Internet Explorer 4.01 or later will be able to work with the chart data. Users of Netscape Navigator, other non-Microsoft browsers, or Internet Explorer 2.0 and 3.0 will see an error message. Also, interactivity doesn't give viewers the ability to save the page; they can only experiment with the data as long as the page is open in the browser window.

4. Check the **Add interactivity** button to insert the chart using the Web Chart Component. Leave this checkbox clear to save the chart in graphics file format.
5. Click the **Change** button to give the chart a label on the Web page.
6. Choose a folder and filename and click **Save**. If the page name already exists, a dialog box will ask you if you want to replace the existing page or add the chart to the end of the existing page. Choose either option to finish.

CHAPTER 23

Analyzing Data and Sharing Workbooks

- Use scenarios for sophisticated what-if analyses
- Use Goal Seek to get the result you're looking for
- Lock cells and worksheets to prevent changes
- Add comments to a workbook
- Share workbooks with coworkers
- Track changes in shared workbooks to see who did what

Using Scenarios to Perform What-If Analyses

When you use an Excel workbook to analyze historical data, you have the luxury of relying on numbers that aren't going to change. When you know how much you sold and how much you spent last quarter, it's easy to construct a formula to describe the overall results. But what do you do when it's time to prepare a forecast of what might happen next quarter? Because the numbers aren't in yet, you have to make your best estimate of sales and expenses, and hope you're right. Predicting the future is never easy; just ask anyone who's ever handicapped a horse race or invested in the stock market.

One of Excel's advanced workbook-design features is ideal when you need to prepare forecasts. After you create your basic worksheet layout, you can define different *scenarios* and enter data separately for each one. By switching between scenarios, you can watch the bottom line change—and even change the bars and columns in charts.

Scenarios help you plan the future when you're uncertain about some of the assumptions that go into your worksheet. Excel experts call this *what-if analysis*. As the owner of a ski resort, for example, you might prepare a forecast with different scenarios to answer questions such as "What if we don't get any snow before Thanksgiving?" and "What if we get a big storm over Christmas and no one can drive up from the city?" By plugging in different sets of numbers, you can prepare for the best-case and worst-case scenarios.

Scenarios take very little room

Using scenarios in a workbook makes efficient use of disk space. If you created a workbook roughly 100KB in size, then created two copies and modified each one to show different scenarios, you would use a total of 300KB in space—and you would have a hard time keeping track of the differences between them. In contrast, each new scenario adds only a tiny amount of data to the workbook, and it's easy to switch back and forth between scenarios.

The first step in the process is to create a worksheet that includes all the basic data you want to use in your comparison. Then, you select specific cells you want to change as part of each scenario. (The *changing cells* are usually part of one or more formulas in the sheet.)

In Figure 23.1, for example, I've designed a worksheet to calculate monthly mortgage payments based on a purchase price, down payment, interest rate, and the term of the loan. After shopping around, I've found three different loan packages to compare. By setting up three scenarios, I can quickly switch from one scenario to the next and compare the monthly payment and total interest over the life of the loan.

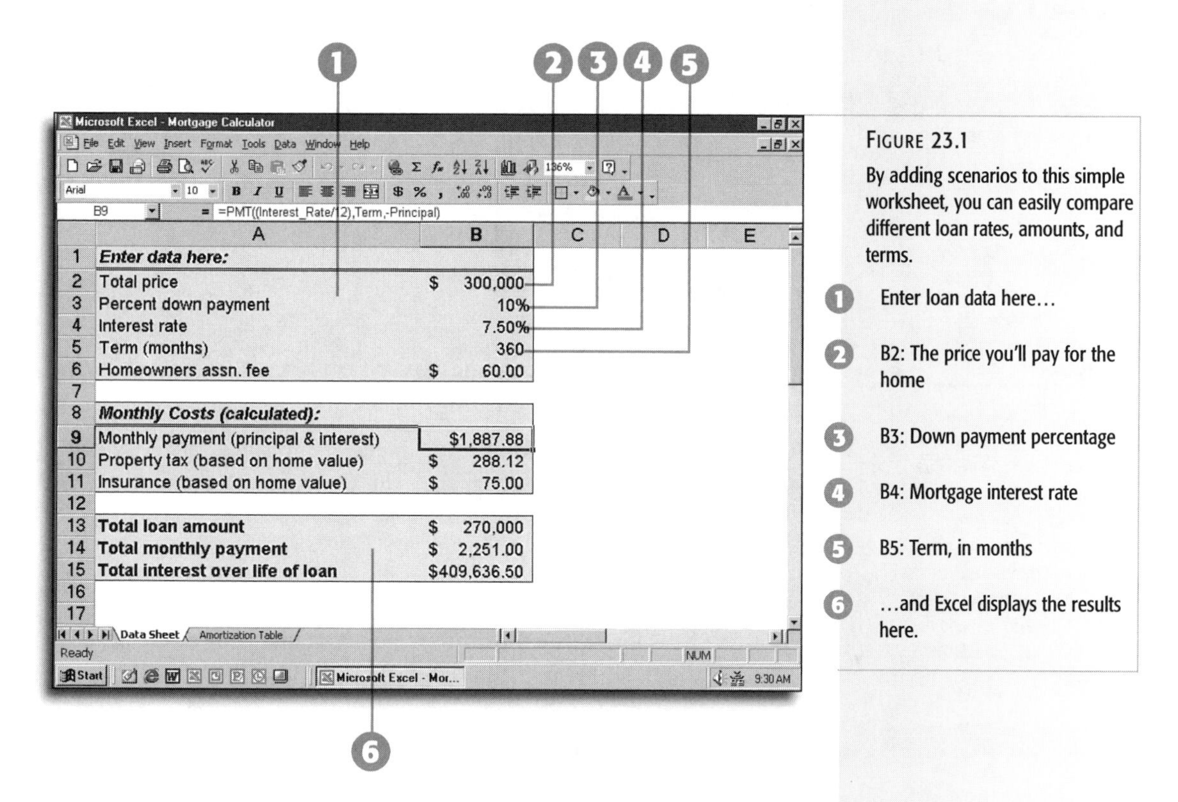

FIGURE 23.1

By adding scenarios to this simple worksheet, you can easily compare different loan rates, amounts, and terms.

1. Enter loan data here...
2. B2: The price you'll pay for the home
3. B3: Down payment percentage
4. B4: Mortgage interest rate
5. B5: Term, in months
6. ...and Excel displays the results here.

Creating Multiple Scenarios in a Single Worksheet

1. Select the cells that will change in each scenario. In Figure 23.1, for example, select cells B3, B4, and B5. (Leave B2 the same, because the price of the home is a constant in all scenarios.) This step is optional; however, if all your scenarios involve changes to the same cells, then selecting the cells first is much more convenient. Pull down the **Tools** menu and select **Scenarios**.
2. In the Scenario Manager dialog box, click the **Add** button to display the Add Scenario dialog box shown in Figure 23.2.

Scenarios can use different cells

You don't have to change the same cells in each scenario; you can use a different set of cells in each scenario, if you want. However, I strongly recommend that you use the same set of changing cells when comparing scenarios; unless you understand exactly what happens when you switch scenarios, the results could be extremely confusing.

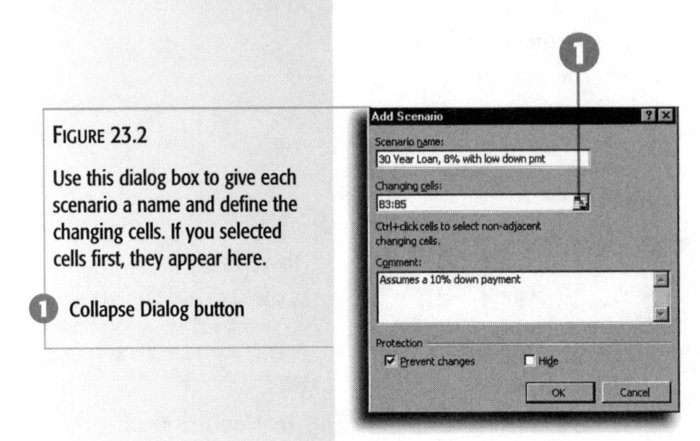

FIGURE 23.2

Use this dialog box to give each scenario a name and define the changing cells. If you selected cells first, they appear here.

1 Collapse Dialog button

Be descriptive

You will use the scenario name you enter here to view and edit scenario information later, so make this name descriptive. `Best case` and `worst case` are good names, but `Best case, with 20% sales growth in 2002` is even better. Use the **Comment** section of the Add Scenario dialog box to add even more details.

3. In the **Scenario name** box, type a name that describes the scenario you're creating.
4. Make sure the **Changing cells** box contains the cells you selected; if necessary, click the **Collapse Dialog** button and change the selection.

SEE ALSO

➤ *For more details on how to select cells in a dialog box, see page 343*

5. By default, the **Comment** box contains your name and the date you created the scenario. Edit this comment if you want to describe the scenario in more detail, then click **OK**. The Scenario Values box appears, as shown in Figure 23.3.

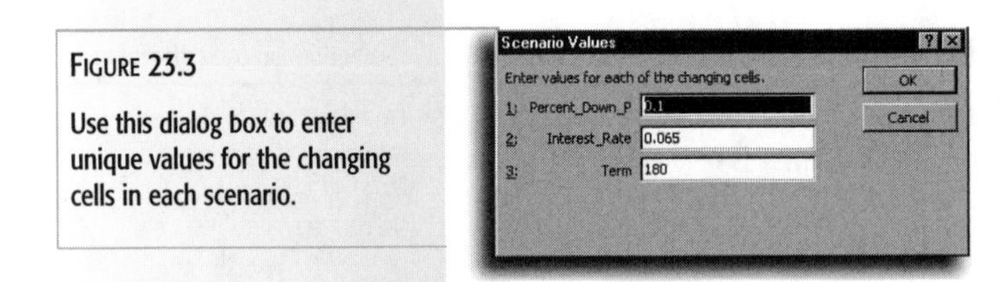

FIGURE 23.3

Use this dialog box to enter unique values for the changing cells in each scenario.

6. Enter the value you want to use for each of the changing cells in this scenario. Because this worksheet contains named ranges, the example shows cell names rather than addresses, making the task even easier. (If the cells contain data, the dialog box displays their current values.) Click **OK** to return to the Scenario Manager dialog box.

7. Repeat steps 2–6 to create additional scenarios. When you finish, the dialog box should look something like the one in Figure 23.4.

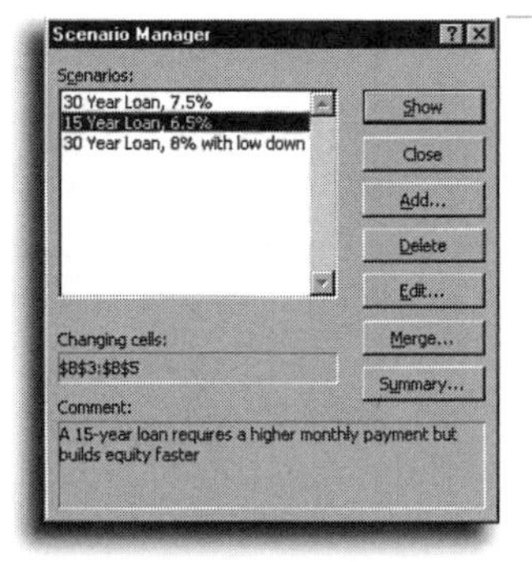

FIGURE 23.4
Select a scenario and click the **Show** button to see the worksheet with that scenario's values.

8. Select any scenario and click the **Show** button at right (or double-click the scenario name) to show the worksheet using those values. Other buttons let you add, remove, and edit scenarios.

After creating scenarios, you can add new scenarios or change existing ones using the same set of dialog boxes. Pull down the **Tools** menu and choose **Scenarios**. To create a new scenario, click the **Add** button. To edit an existing scenario, select its name in the **Scenarios** list and click the **Edit** button.

Prevent changes?

If you want to prevent changes to your scenario or hide multiple scenarios in a workbook, checking the **Prevent changes** or **Hide** box here isn't enough; you also need to protect your entire worksheet. Skip ahead to the section "Restricting Data Entry in a Worksheet" for more details.

Watching the data change

You might have to drag the Scenario Manager dialog box out of the way to see the changed values in your worksheet. If you want to edit the worksheet, however, you must close the dialog box.

Using Goal Seek to Find the Right Value

After you've constructed a worksheet and built all your formulas, you may discover that you can't easily get the answer you're looking for. In the mortgage payment worksheet shown previously in Figure 23.1, for example, the formulas are designed to produce the total monthly payment when you enter the price and loan details.

But what if you want to calculate how much home you can afford based on a maximum monthly payment? You could construct a new formula. Or, you could use the trial-and-error method, entering different home prices until you find the right one. But the fast and easy way is to use Excel's *Goal Seek* tool to do the calculations in one operation.

Using Goal Seek to Find a Value

1. Open the worksheet that contains the formula you want to work with, then pull down the **Tools** menu and select **Goal Seek**.
2. Fill in the three boxes in the Goal Seek dialog box to match the results you're trying to achieve. In Figure 23.5, for example, I asked Excel to set cell B14, which contains the total monthly payment, to `2000`, my maximum monthly budget, by adjusting the purchase price in cell B2.

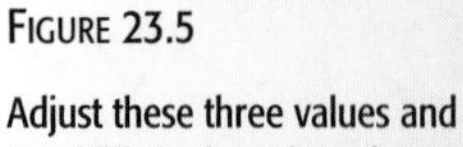

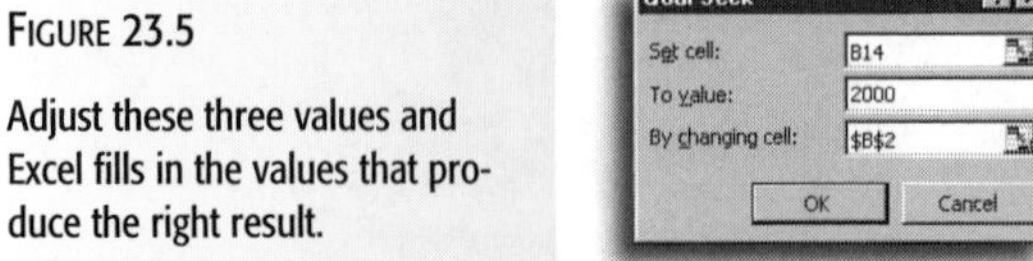

FIGURE 23.5

Adjust these three values and Excel fills in the values that produce the right result.

3. When you click **OK**, Excel runs through all possibilities and displays the Goal Seek Status dialog box, as shown in Figure 23.6. If you look at the worksheet itself, you'll see the values have changed to reflect the result you were looking for.

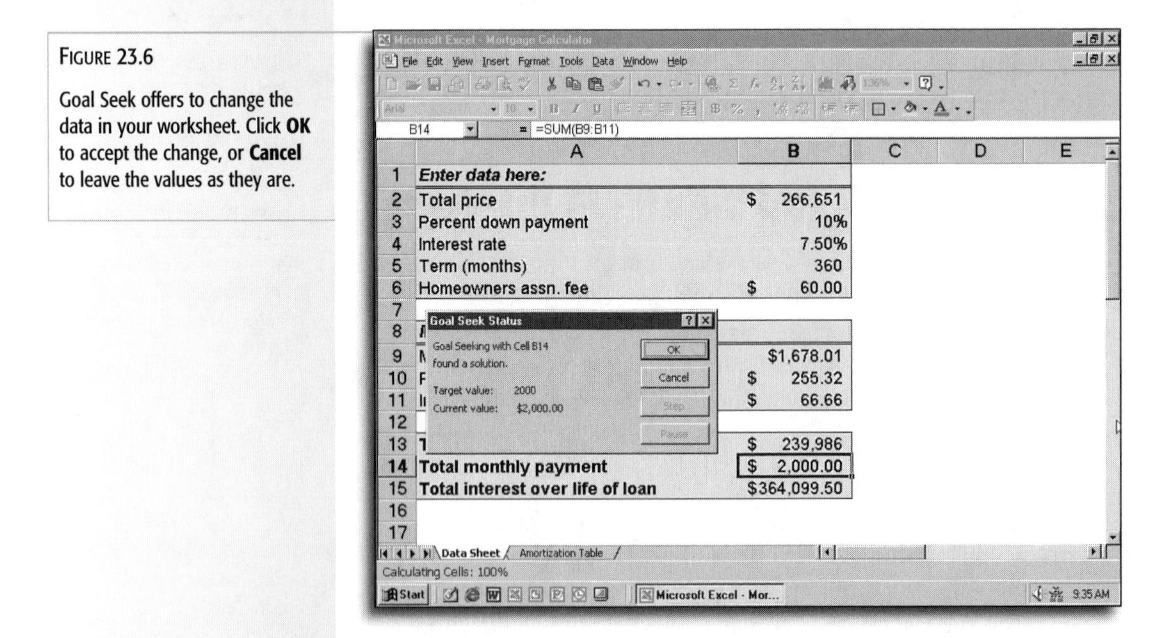

FIGURE 23.6

Goal Seek offers to change the data in your worksheet. Click **OK** to accept the change, or **Cancel** to leave the values as they are.

4. Click **OK** to incorporate the changed data into your worksheet; click **Cancel** to close the dialog box and restore the original data.

Restricting Data Entry in a Worksheet

When you carefully design a worksheet, the last thing you want to do is accidentally wipe out formulas or crucial data later. This consideration is especially important when creating worksheets you intend to share with other people. Excel lets you *lock* individual cells, then turn on worksheet *protection* so that nobody can make changes without entering a password. Use this feature when you want to allow other people to open a shared workbook over the network without allowing them to make changes. It's also a useful way to turn a worksheet into a data-entry form: By locking all cells in the sheet except those where you want users to enter data, you ensure that other users will enter their data in the proper cells.

Protecting a worksheet is a two-step process. The first step is to unlock the cells in which you want to allow data entry. By default, all cells in a worksheet are locked. The second step is to enable protection for the entire worksheet. By default, protection is off for all new worksheets you create.

Protecting Cells for Data Entry

1. Display the worksheet you want to protect.
2. Select the cells in which you want to allow editing; hold down the Ctrl key as you click to select multiple cells.

SEE ALSO

➤ *If you need a refresher course on how to select multiple cells, see page 343*

3. Pull down the **Format** menu, select **Cells**, and click the **Protection** tab. Clear the **Locked** check box. Click **OK**.
4. Pull down the **Tools** menu, select **Protection**, and choose **Protect Sheet**.
   - Check the **Contents** box to prevent changes to cells that are marked as Locked.

Use the Web instead

Does your company have an intranet? If so, publishing a workbook as a Web page is much easier than locking a workbook, and anyone can view its contents using a browser, even if they don't have Excel. For more details, see Chapter 4, "Creating and Publishing Web Pages."

Start by locking every cell

By default, every cell on a new worksheet is locked, so all you need to do is unlock the cells in which you want to allow data entry. If you've already changed the locked status of some cells, here's how to make sure you're starting with a clean slate: Press Ctrl+A to select every cell in the worksheet, then use the Format Cells dialog box and check the **Locked** box. Now you can safely unlock just the cells you want to work with.

- Check the **Objects** box to prevent users from moving or editing graphic objects (including charts).
- Check the **Scenarios** box if you've set up multiple scenarios and you don't want users to be able to edit them. Users will still be able to switch to different scenarios, but the **Edit** and **Delete** buttons in the Scenario Manager dialog box will be grayed out.

5. Enter a password if you want to restrict the ability of unauthorized users to remove protection, and then click **OK**.

To remove protection from a worksheet so that you can change the contents of cells, move objects, or edit scenarios, pull down the **Tools** menu, select **Protection**, and then choose **Unprotect Sheet**. Enter the password, if necessary, and click **OK**. After making changes, don't forget to turn on protection again!

Do you really need a password?

If your goal is to prevent accidental changes to a worksheet, you don't need to use a password. Adding protection without using a password is a handy way to keep you from accidentally damaging a worksheet by moving a chart or formula. Just remove protection when you want to make changes.

Tracking Changes in Shared Excel Workbooks

If you're collaborating with other people on an Excel workbook, Excel lets you track changes in much the same way you do with Word. If the workbook is in a shared network folder, two or more people can open it simultaneously and change formulas, add or delete cells, insert comments, and print reports.

SEE ALSO

➤ *For details on how to track changes in Word documents, see page 211*

Some changes aren't allowed

When you set up a workbook so that changes are tracked, you lose the ability to make some types of changes. For example, you can't merge cells, delete a worksheet, add a hyperlink, or insert or edit a chart. For a full list of these restrictions, search for the Help topic, "Limitations of Shared Workbooks."

Embedding Comments in an Excel Worksheet

Excel lets you add *comments* to a worksheet, in the form of pop-up notes, each attached to an individual cell.

To add a comment to a worksheet, select any cell, then right-click and choose **Insert Comment** from the shortcut menu. (If the Reviewing toolbar is visible, use the **Insert Comment** button.) You'll see a box like the one in Figure 23.7.

One at a time, please...

You can't comment on a range of cells–if you try, Excel attaches the comment to the current cell within that range.

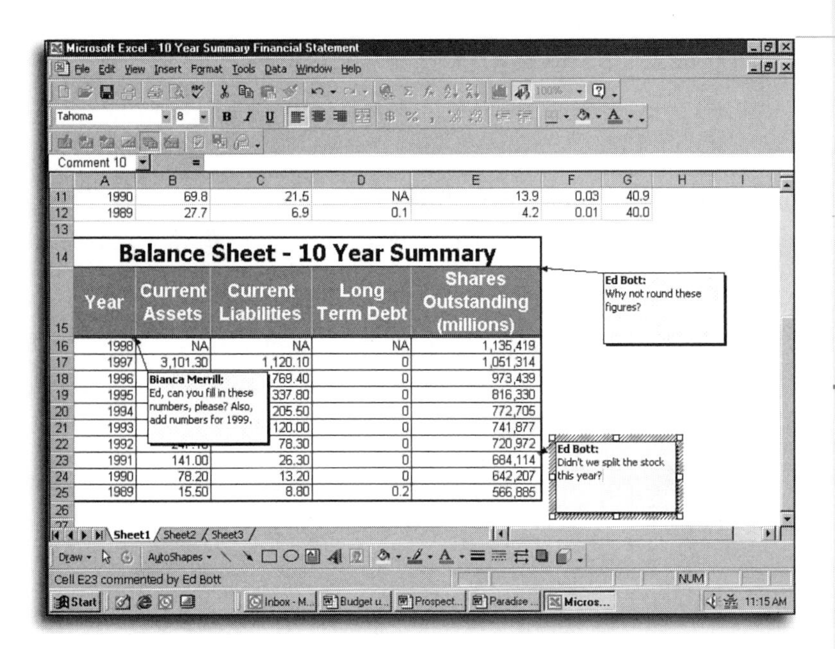

FIGURE 23.7

Enter your comments here. The red triangle in the upper-right corner indicates the cell has an attached comment.

After you add a comment to a cell, a tiny red triangle called a *comment indicator* appears in the cell's upper-right corner. When you move the mouse pointer over a comment indicator, the comment pops up; move the pointer away, and the comment disappears.

What if you don't want to make comments obvious? If you've added comments strictly for your own use and you don't want other people to see them when they view or edit the worksheet, pull down the **Tools** menu, choose **Options**, and click the **View** tab. The **Comments** section includes these three choices:

- **Comment & indicator**—Makes all comments in the current workbook visible, regardless of where the mouse pointer is located.
- **Comment indicator only**—The default setting; a red triangle appears in each cell, and the comment pops up when the pointer passes over.
- **None**—Hides all comment indicators and suppresses pop-up comments. Use the buttons on the Reviewing toolbar to jump from comment to comment, or right-click any cell with a comment to use shortcut menu choices.

Format comments as you like

Although cell comments look like simple sticky notes, they're actually objects in the *drawing layer*, with special properties that allow them to appear and disappear when you use the comment-related menus and buttons. You can format these notes in several eye-catching ways: Right-click the note board and choose **Format Comment**, then change fonts and background colors, add borders, and change text alignment within the note.

Show a selection of comments

Let's say you've created a worksheet that you want to pass along to several other people for review. You've used more than a dozen comments to document your assumptions, but you want to make sure the reviewers see three of them in particular. By default, each cell with a comment has a comment indicator; right-click the indicators for the comments you want to emphasize and choose **Show Comment** from the shortcut menu. To hide the comment again, right-click and choose **Hide Comment**. These per-comment settings work independently of the global settings for a workbook.

Telling Excel Which Changes to Track

To begin tracking changes in a worksheet, you have to specifically enable this feature. Doing so also shares the workbook.

Sharing workbooks is a complex topic

If you plan to share a workbook occasionally, I can help you get started. But if shared workbooks are a key part of your work, you'll need more information than is provided here to help you truly explore this complicated feature. I suggest you pick up a copy of *Special Edition Using Excel 2000*, also published by Que.

Tracking Changes in a Workbook

1. Open the workbook in which you want to track changes.
2. Pull down the **Tools** menu, select **Track Changes**, and then choose **Highlight Changes**. The Highlight Changes dialog box appears, as shown in Figure 23.8.

FIGURE 23.8

Check the top box to track changes to your workbook; all other options define which changes are visible.

3. Check the **Track changes while editing** box.
4. By default, Excel highlights all changes made by all users. To hide some changes while still keeping track of them, select from the three drop-down lists in the dialog box. To hide all changes, clear the check from the **Highlight changes on screen** box.
5. Click **OK** to begin tracking changes. You must save the workbook to complete this operation.

Restrict your view of changes

It's possible to keep a running list of all changes to a workbook over a long period of time. For example, an accounting manager might want to track changes to the master P&L workbook throughout the year, so she can tell when each change was made. In this instance, the list of changes can become overwhelming. Use options in the Highlight Changes dialog box to make the workbook easier to read. For example, click the **When** drop-down list and specify the first day of the current month to see only recent changes.

Reviewing Changes in a Workbook

After you enable the option to track changes in a workbook, changing the contents of any cell adds a thin blue border around the cell and adds a blue flag in its top-left corner. If you've specified that you want to highlight changes, moving the mouse pointer over a changed cell pops up a ScreenTip showing who made the change, when the change was recorded, and specifically what was changed, as you can see in Figure 23.9.

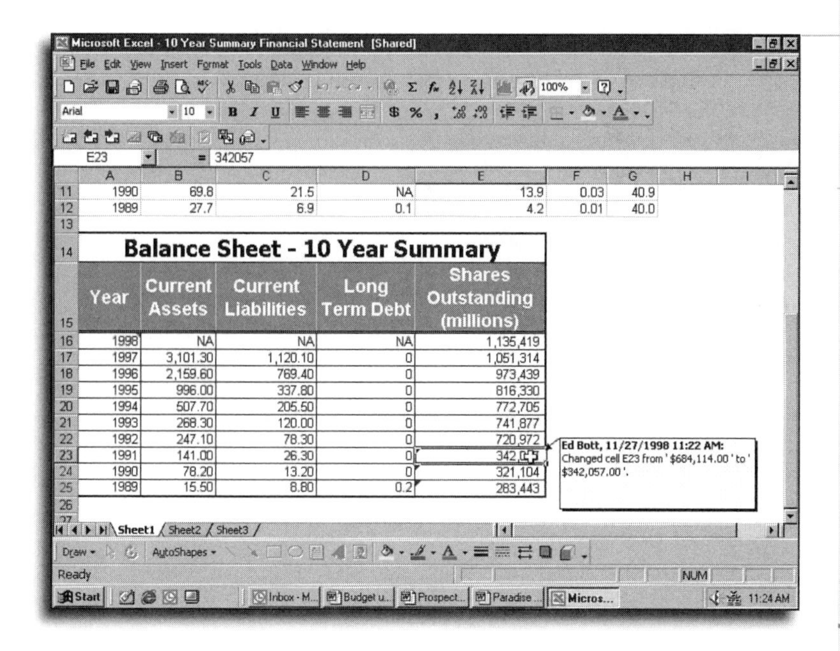

FIGURE 23.9

ScreenTips show details of all changes you and others make in a shared workbook.

You can use the change history as a way of tracking changes so that you have an audit trail. You can also share a workbook as it goes through drafts, then incorporate some or all changes into a final version.

Incorporating Changes into a Workbook

1. Open the workbook that contains the changes you want to review.
2. Pull down the **Tools** menu, choose **Track Changes**, and then click **Accept or Reject Changes**. If Excel prompts you to save your workbook, click **OK**.
3. In the Select Changes to Accept or Reject dialog box, choose which changes you want to review. By default, Excel shows you all changes you have not yet reviewed; you can restrict the list to changes made after a certain date, in a specific range of cells, or by a specific person. After making your selections, click **OK**.
4. Use the Accept or Reject Changes dialog box, shown in Figure 23.10, to move through your workbook one change at a time. The dialog box displays details about the change.

Viewing the change history

Excel keeps track of the who, what, and when of workbook changes in the *change history*. To see all these details in a single list on its own worksheet, pull down the **Tools** menu, choose **Track Changes**, click the **Highlight Changes** menu option, and check the **List changes on a new sheet** box. Excel doesn't automatically update this list, so you must save your workbook and choose this option immediately to see the full history.

Changes are permanent

When you accept or reject changes to a shared workbook, Excel eliminates the item from your change history. If you want to maintain an audit trail showing all changes to a workbook, track changes without going through the accept-or-reject step. Excel always displays the most recent changes in your workbook.

Click the **Accept** button to incorporate the change, or click **Reject** to restore the original cell contents.

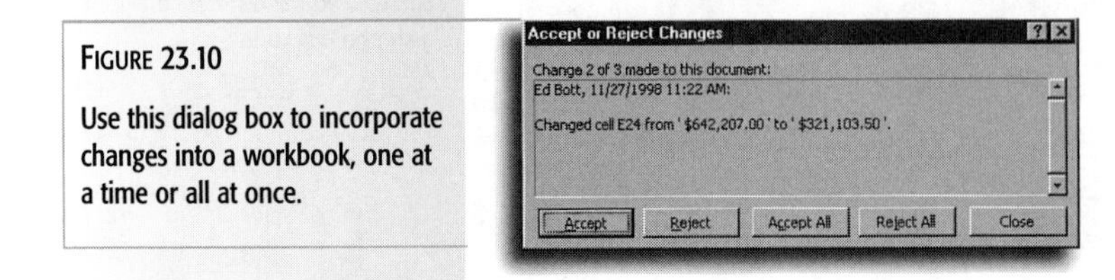

FIGURE 23.10

Use this dialog box to incorporate changes into a workbook, one at a time or all at once.

PART

IV

Using PowerPoint 2000

CHAPTER

24

Creating a New Presentation

- Use PowerPoint to create a presentation
- Learn how to get started
- View your presentation in different ways
- Add and edit slides
- Delete, copy, rearrange, and hide slides
- Add comments to your PowerPoint slides

How PowerPoint Works

Who says slide shows have to be sleep-inducing? When they're put together with style, electronic *slide shows* can be powerful tools for selling products and ideas. The most common use of PowerPoint is to create *presentations* that turn your computer into a cross between an overhead projector and a slide carousel, with some intelligence tossed in. But PowerPoint is also a great tool for creating paper-based presentations, where each "slide" occupies a single page. Unlike previous versions, PowerPoint 2000 also lets you easily design presentations for use on the Web—instead of standing in front of an auditorium and clicking from one slide to the next, Web presentations let your audience zip through your slide show at their own pace.

Anatomy of a PowerPoint Presentation

PowerPoint presentations are a good way to communicate ideas simply and effectively. For complex topics that are rich with details, such as a scientific paper or an annual report, Word is the appropriate choice. PowerPoint is intended for less complex messages. A PowerPoint presentation is ideal for simple lists and talking points, or for the electronic version of a brochure or flyer; if you're planning to speak in front of a crowd, a PowerPoint slide show gives your audience visual cues that help them follow along while you speak.

If you've used previous versions of PowerPoint, you'll notice a dramatic change the first time you start PowerPoint 2000. Instead of forcing you to switch between three different views to work with different parts of your presentation, the new *Normal view* of a presentation (shown in Figure 24.1) includes all the basic components—slides, notes, and an outline—on one screen.

- Every PowerPoint presentation consists of basic units called *slides*. Although these slides have the color and depth of the 35mm version, they're really more like overhead transparencies, because you can add and remove text, graphics, charts, and other objects whenever you want.

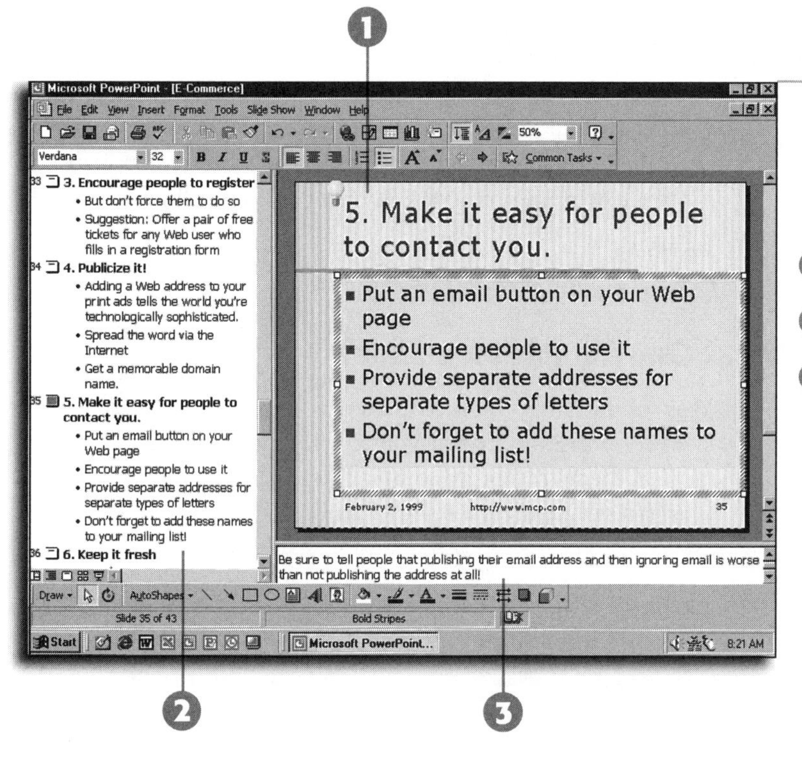

FIGURE 24.1

PowerPoint's Normal view includes most of the information you'll need to assemble a presentation.

1. Slide
2. Outline
3. Notes

- You can attach notes (sometimes referred to as *speaker notes*) to each slide. Whatever you type here doesn't appear on the screen when you deliver your presentation. As the name implies, notes are for your reference—use them to remind you of details that you want to mention while delivering the presentation.
- Every presentation also includes an *outline*. The top-level heading for each slide in the outline corresponds to the slide title, and bullet points on each slide appear as second-level headings.
- The arrangement of words, graphics, and other objects on each slide is called a *layout*. You can start with a blank layout, but PowerPoint includes 24 fill-in-the-blanks versions you'll use most often. These ready-to-use slides incorporate placeholders for titles, bulleted lists, pictures, charts, and other objects, alone and in combinations.

Let Word and PowerPoint work together

PowerPoint doesn't let you do much formatting with notes, but Word does. If you want to print out a version of your presentation that includes a half-sized version of each slide with its accompanying speaker notes on each page, pull down the **File** menu, choose **Send To**, and click the **Microsoft Word** option. Experiment with different layouts, and then use Word's editing and formatting capabilities to make your printed pages look their very best.

Edit the outline or the slides

Should you work with the outline or the slides? It doesn't matter. When you change the title or bullet points on a slide, the text in your outline changes automatically; if you change the text in your outline, the effect is the same as if you had edited the slide directly. Use whichever view is more comfortable for the task at hand.

- Even aesthetically challenged writers like me can put together slick-looking PowerPoint presentations with coordinated colors, matching fonts, and tasteful background images. All these components are bundled into collections called design templates. By attaching a design template to your presentation, you can change its overall look instantly.

SEE ALSO

➤ *For details on how to change the formatting of slides, see page 498*

What Can You Put on a Slide?

Most of the time, you'll create a new slide using one of PowerPoint's 24 built-in layouts. That may sound like a lot, but most of them are simply combinations of a handful of basic *placeholders*, like the ones shown in Figure 24.2.

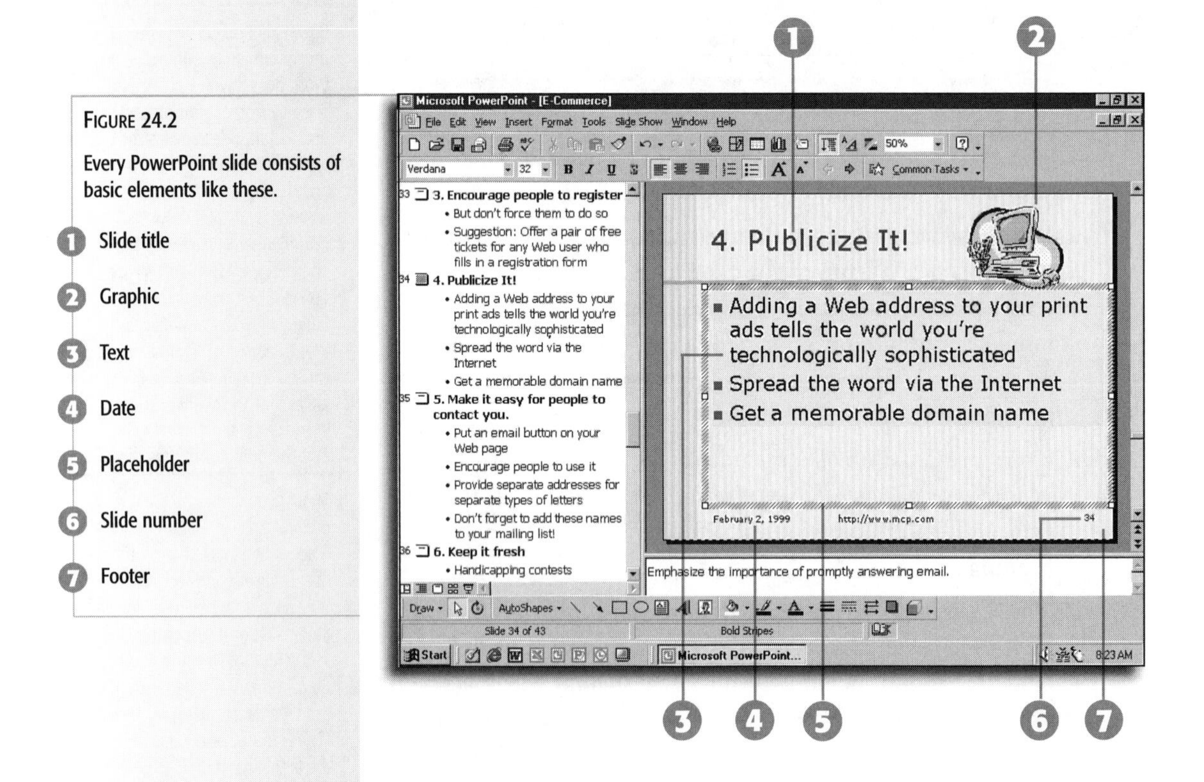

FIGURE 24.2

Every PowerPoint slide consists of basic elements like these.

1. Slide title
2. Graphic
3. Text
4. Date
5. Placeholder
6. Slide number
7. Footer

- Practically every slide layout has a title, and for good reason: These are the main points in your presentation. You might omit the title if you're creating a blank slide to leave onscreen when you want the undivided attention of your audience, or if your slide includes a full-screen video clip.
- Bulleted lists are the most common way to present ideas or talking points quickly and effectively. You can also add numbered lists or simple, paragraph-style text blocks.
- When you have a lot of information to display, tables are the best way to use the limited space on each slide. The neat, clean grid makes it perfect for comparisons of different options.
- The best way to effectively convey numeric information is with a well-designed chart. Pie charts, bar charts, or a column chart—combined with simple titles and text labels—can tell a compelling story.
- Showing one text-heavy slide after another can make your audience feel like they're the ones doing all the work. Mix a few carefully chosen graphics into your presentation, such as a dramatic picture or a clever cartoon, and you'll often get a better response. Select from one of the dozens of *clip-art* images included with Office, or find your own.

SEE ALSO

➤ *To learn how to add graphics from the Office Clip Gallery, see page 131*

- Besides text and graphics, you can also add objects to any slide. Objects in the standard layouts include media clips (sound or video, for example) and organization charts. You can also insert a Word document or Excel worksheet as an object on a slide.
- Finally, a slide may or may not include any of the following elements along the bottom: the date and time (generally in the lower left), a footer (usually in the middle), and a slide number (generally in the lower right).

Recognizing placeholders

When you add text to a slide, it sits inside a placeholder, which is normally not visible; when you click in the text itself, you can easily identify this region by the thick dashed line around it. Slide titles, tables, and graphics use placeholders, too. Use the mouse to resize and move the placeholders on any slide.

A little clip art goes a long way

Because it's so easy to add clip art and change fonts, most inexperienced PowerPoint users over-embellish presentations, making the resulting slide shows look cluttered and amateurish. Fight the temptation to overuse clip art. Use graphics sparingly, and only when they help make your point.

Objects should be your last resort

PowerPoint's **Insert** menu lets you choose from a huge assortment of elements to add to slides. Your choices include pictures from a variety of sources, movies, sounds, and even CD audio tracks. You'll find additional choices in the dialog box that appears when you click **Object**, but most of these items are strictly for experts. Whenever possible, stay away from this menu and stick with the built-in menu choices instead.

Getting Started

To launch PowerPoint, click the PowerPoint icon on the Programs menu. When PowerPoint starts, it graciously presents you with a menu of four options that let you create a new presentation or open an existing one.

Skip the Startup screen

If you'd rather skip the Startup screen and use the Office-standard Open dialog box instead, check the box labeled **Don't show this dialog box again**.

Creating a Presentation Using the AutoContent Wizard

As its name suggests, the *AutoContent Wizard* guides you through the process of starting a PowerPoint presentation on a selected topic, complete with a set of slides that contain generic content. The ready-made slides include helpful instructions and placeholders that you can replace with your own words, pictures, tables, and charts.

To begin, choose the **AutoContent Wizard** option and click **OK**. In this three-step interview process, the Wizard first offers you a choice of 24 topics, arranged by category. (Your options may be different from the ones in Figure 24.3, but you get the idea.)

Replace that generic text!

The AutoContent Wizard is convenient, but remember that every PowerPoint user in the world has access to the same generic templates. If you try to pass off a canned presentation in front of an audience that includes other PowerPoint users, they'll recognize the templates instantly—and you'll lose credibility. Use the wizard's templates as a starting point, if you want, but make sure to replace that generic text with your own ideas.

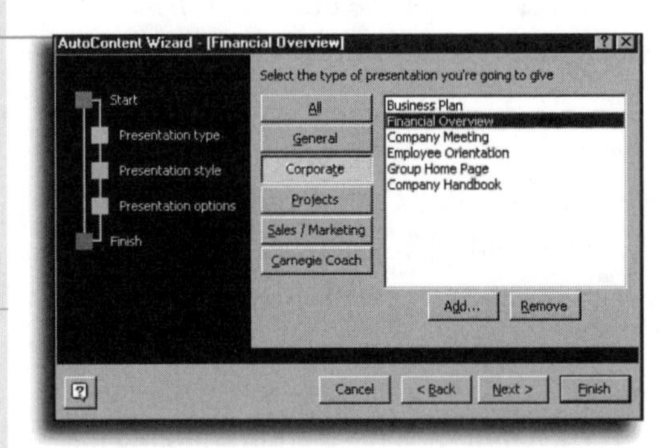

FIGURE 24.3

Replace the generic text in these ready-made presentations, add some relevant charts and pictures, and you've cut your preparation time in half.

After selecting a topic, click **Next** and tell PowerPoint what type of output you plan to use. Will you deliver your presentation on a computer screen or save it to a Web site? On 35mm slides? Or as overheads? Click **Next** again, and give your presentation a short, snappy title. Enter a footer, if you want, and check or clear the boxes that add the date and slide number to each slide.

When you click **Finish**, PowerPoint merges its canned content with the information you supplied, and you can begin working with the presentation.

If you regularly create presentations that follow a standard *template*, you can add them to the AutoContent Wizard, and you can also remove templates that you don't find helpful.

Customizing the AutoContent Wizard

1. Create a new presentation or open an existing one. Make sure it contains only the generic text and design elements you want to see in all new presentations based on this template.
2. Pull down the **File** menu and choose **Save As**.
3. Give the new template a descriptive name. Then, in the **Save as type** box, select **Design Template** from the drop-down list. Click **Save**.
4. Pull down the **File** menu again, and this time click **New**.
5. Click the **General** tab, select **AutoContent Wizard**, and click **OK**.
6. In the AutoContent Wizard, click the **Next** button to jump to the first step, Presentation Type. Select the category to which you want to add the new template, and then click the **Add** button.
7. In the Select Presentation Template dialog box, pick the template you just created and click **OK**. PowerPoint adds the template to the selected category.
8. Press Esc or Cancel to close the AutoContent Wizard.

Creating a Presentation Using a Template

If none of the canned samples in the AutoContent Wizard meets your needs, you can still let PowerPoint give you a head start on your next presentation. From PowerPoint's startup screen, choose **Design Template** and click **OK**. If PowerPoint is already open, pull down the **File** menu, choose **New**, and click the **Design Templates** tab. In either case, you'll see the dialog box shown in Figure 24.4.

Rerun the AutoContent Wizard anytime

If you've already started PowerPoint, the only way to restart the AutoContent Wizard is to pull down the **File** menu, choose **New**; click on the General tab, select the AutoContent Wizard template, and click **OK**.

PowerPoint saves templates in the correct folder

When you save a presentation as a Design Template, PowerPoint automatically saves it in the folder that contains all your other custom templates. When customizing the AutoContent Wizard, don't use any other folder.

You can remove templates, too

Use these same techniques to remove items from the AutoContent Wizard. Just select the templates you no longer want to see in the list, and then click the **Remove** button instead of **Add**.

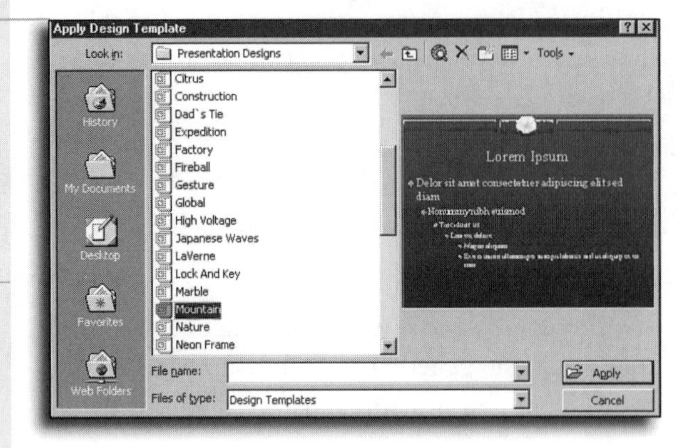

FIGURE 24.4

When you choose a template from this list, PowerPoint begins a new blank presentation using the backgrounds, colors, and other design elements shown in the preview at right.

What's in a design?

A design template includes a background, font specifications for the title slide and other slides in the presentation, a default bullet character for lists, and a handful of other settings–title locations, footers, slide numbering, and so on.

Most templates aren't installed

Only a few of PowerPoint's built-in design templates actually make it onto your hard drive as part of a Typical installation. The first time you try to use one of the extra templates, you'll need to supply the Office 2000 CD–when you do, the Office Installer adds all the extra templates.

PowerPoint includes a hefty selection of *design templates* with names that don't always offer a clue as to what the design looks like. For a better idea of what you can expect from a design template, select its entry from the list and look in the Preview pane to the right.

SEE ALSO

➤ *For more details on installing Office 2000, see page 691*

When you find a template you like, click **OK**. PowerPoint creates a new presentation and displays the New Slide dialog box. You must specify what kind of slide you want to start the presentation with, and then you'll have to add slides to the presentation one at a time.

SEE ALSO

➤ *For more details on how to select a slide layout, see page 488*

Creating a Blank Presentation

To start a presentation with a completely clean slate, use any of the following options:

- From the PowerPoint startup screen, choose **Blank presentation**.
- If PowerPoint is already open, pull down the **File** menu, choose **New**, select **Blank presentation** from the **General** tab, and click OK.
- Click the **New** button on the Standard toolbar.

Just as when you start a new presentation using a design template, PowerPoint creates a new blank presentation and asks you to choose the layout type for your first slide. The design of your new presentation is about as dull as you can imagine, with a plain white background, text formatted in Times New Roman, and generic round bullets.

If you regularly create PowerPoint presentations, you probably already have a custom design template, with your company logo in just the right location, custom fonts for titles and text, perhaps even custom transitions between slides. If you want to start with this standard design every time you click the New button, it's easy to do so. Just replace PowerPoint's basic blank presentation with your own.

Choose a new design anytime

You can apply a new design to any presentation at any time, using PowerPoint's collection of built-in templates. Click the **Common Tasks** menu on the Formatting toolbar, and then choose **Apply Design Template**. Pick a template from the dialog box (using the Preview pane to quickly identify each layout) and click **Apply** to replace the existing design with the new one. If you don't like the results, press Ctrl+Z to undo the change and try again.

Creating a New Default Presentation

1. Create or open the presentation you want to use as the basis for all new, blank presentations. Remove all text unless you want it to appear as part of each new presentation.
2. Pull down the **File** menu and choose **Save As**. In the **Save as type** box, click **Design Template**.
3. Click in the **File name** box, type `Blank Presentation`, and click **Save**.

Opening an Existing Presentation

If you want to open a presentation you previously created and saved, choose the **Open an existing presentation** option in the startup dialog box. The list just below it includes the nine presentations you've worked with most recently; select a file from that list and click **OK**, or choose **More Files** and click **OK** to display the standard Open dialog box.

Restore the original blank design

If you change your mind and decide you want to start over with PowerPoint's original blank design, just delete the file you created. Open the **File** menu, choose **New**, right-click the **Blank Presentation** entry, and click **Delete**.

Different Ways to View Your Presentation

As I noted earlier, the Normal view is new in PowerPoint 2000. Because this view displays the outline for your presentation, plus a close-up view of the current slide and its notes, there's normally no need to switch between views for routine tasks. In some cases, however, a different view can make it easier to work with your presentation. The Slide Sorter view, for example, lets you see your entire presentation at a glance; it's the easiest way to work when you want to quickly rearrange slides in a large presentation.

To switch to a different view of your presentation, use any of the five buttons in the View Bar at the lower-left corner of the PowerPoint window. You can return to Normal view at any time by choosing **Normal** from the **View** menu, or by clicking the **Normal View** button on the View Bar.

Customize Normal view

You can resize any of the three panes in Normal view. Click and drag on the edge of any pane to make it larger or smaller–for example, you can drag the top border of the Notes pane up to give yourself a little extra room for speaker notes. The other panes resize automatically to accommodate your change.

Zoom in for a close-up view

Whenever you want to take a close look at a slide, use the Zoom icon on the Standard toolbar. You can choose a specific percentage, but your best choice is the last entry in the Zoom drop-down list. Choosing **Fit** adjusts the size of the slide so it uses the maximum space available while still showing all elements on the slide.

Organizing Your Thoughts in Outline View

In earlier versions of PowerPoint, switching to Outline view was the only way to see a presentation in its outline format. In PowerPoint 2000, by contrast, the basic arrangement of Outline view is nearly identical to that of Normal view; the outline pane is larger, while the slide and notes panes are considerably narrower.

Work in Outline view when your presentation is large and complex, with a great deal of text that isn't easy to work with in Normal view. To switch into Outline view, click the **Outline View** button in the View Bar.

When you're working with a presentation outline, the buttons on the Outlining toolbar can be enormously helpful. With one click of the **Collapse All** button, for example, you can collapse the entire outline to see just the slide titles and use the **Move Up** and **Move Down** buttons to rearrange slides with ease.

Use Word outlines, if you want

If you've already created an outline in Word, you can import it into PowerPoint and get a head start on your presentation. From Word, open the document that contains the outline, pull down the **File** menu, choose **Send To**, and click **Microsoft PowerPoint**. From PowerPoint, open the **File** menu, choose **Open**, and in the **Files of type** box choose **All Outlines**. When you import a Word outline, text formatted with the Heading 1 style turns into the title of a new slide. Text formatted as Heading 2 or higher turns into bullet points.

Working with a Single Slide

Slide view zooms in on a single slide to allow you to get a slightly better view of graphics and other details. Despite the name, Slide view is nearly identical to Normal view, with the slide pane expanded, the outline pane collapsed so only slide numbers show, and the notes pane hidden. To switch into Slide view, click the **Slide View** button in the View Bar.

Jump from slide to slide

In Normal, Outline, and Slide views, use the double arrow buttons at the bottom of the vertical scrollbar to quickly move up or down, one slide at a time.

Using Slide Sorter View to Rearrange a Presentation

Unlike Outline view and Slide view, which are simply slight variations on Normal view, Slide Sorter view offers a completely different perspective on a presentation. As Figure 24.5 shows, this view lets you see the entire presentation at once—or at least as many slides as will fit at the screen resolution you've selected. In this view, you can easily change the order of slides, add or delete slides, preview and edit the transition effects that occur when you move from one slide to the next, and work with animations on each individual slide.

Watch the toolbars

The Slide Sorter toolbar is only visible when you switch to this view. It includes buttons and menu choices that help you manage transitions and animations. Most other toolbars, including the Formatting toolbar, are disabled in Slide Sorter view.

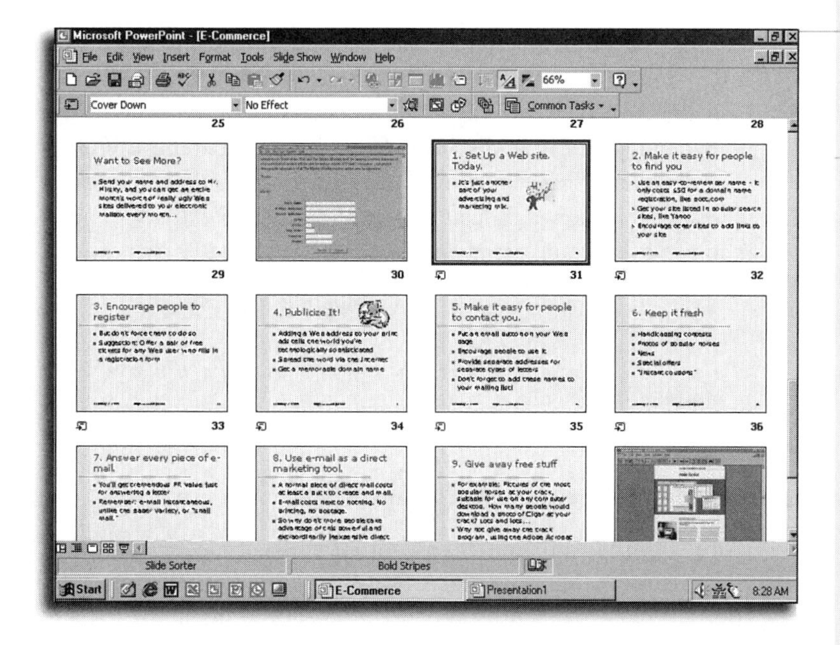

FIGURE 24.5
Slide Sorter view makes it easy to see the big picture.

To switch to Slide Sorter view, click the **Slide Sorter View** button in the View Bar, or pull down the **View** menu and choose **Slide Sorter**.

Adding Notes

The bullet points on an individual slide help your audience focus on your message. When you want to jot a reminder (or even a

Let your audience make notes

If you're planning a presentation and you want your audience to be able to take notes on your presentation, try printing handouts. You can't see this view on the screen, but you can choose it from the Print dialog box. If you select three slides per sheet, each printed page will show a stack of three slides, with lines to the right of each one for audience members to write their own notes. Pull down the **File** menu, choose **Print**, and select **Handouts** from the **Print what?** list; choose 3 from the **Slides per page** list and click **OK**.

Or see the entire show...

If you want to view your entire presentation, starting with the first slide, open the **Slide Show** menu and click **View Show**. After the show is finished, you'll return to the same view as when you started.

detailed script that includes everything you want to say when that slide appears on the screen) use the notes pane in Normal or Outline view.

PowerPoint includes a Notes Page view that you can use for a close-up look at the notes for an individual slide. Unlike all other views, you won't find a button for this view; instead, the only way to switch to this view is to open the **View** menu and then click **Notes Page**. In this view, you can add notes within a text placeholder, and you can edit using all of PowerPoint's formatting tools.

Previewing Your Presentation

At any point during the process of creating a presentation, you may want to preview the show itself. To see the presentation starting with the currently selected slide, just pick a slide (in any view) and click the **Slide Show View** button on the View Bar. Press the spacebar or click the left mouse button to move through the show a slide at a time. Press Esc to exit. When the show is over, you'll return to whichever view you were using when you started the show.

SEE ALSO

➤ *To learn all the keyboard and mouse techniques you can use to move through a presentation, see page 519*

Adding and Editing Slides

Although the AutoContent Wizard is a useful way to kick-start the creative process, you may find that you're more comfortable filling in a blank canvas. When you select the Blank Presentation or Design Template options from the PowerPoint start-up screen, you'll end up at the dialog box shown in Figure 24.6. The next step is to choose the appropriate slide layout.

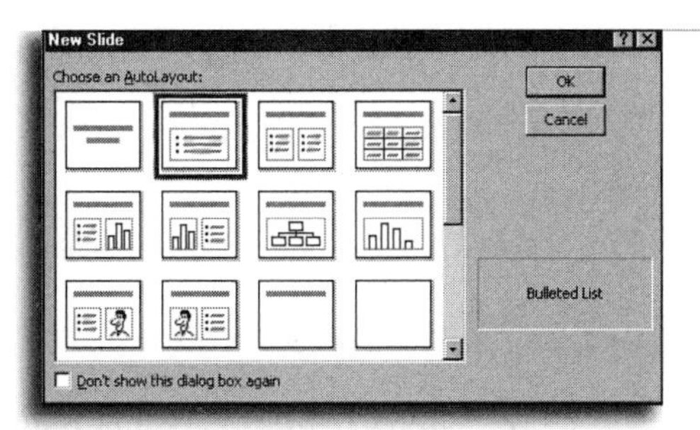

FIGURE 24.6
To add a new slide, select one of these 24 layouts and add your own text and graphics.

The options in the New Slide dialog box are officially known as AutoLayouts. In this example, you can tell that the Bulleted List option is selected, because it has a thicker frame than the rest of the slides. Watch the text to the right of the layout as well, to see a description of the one you've selected. After you select a layout, click **OK** to add the new slide to your presentation.

When you add a new slide, each object on the slide is contained in its own placeholder. With the obvious exception of the Blank layout, every choice includes one or more of these fill-in-the-blanks boxes. To add text in a placeholder box, just click. To add a table, picture, chart, media clip, or other object, double-click.

Build your own layouts

If you don't find a layout you like, pick the closest match, and then resize, remove, or replace any of its parts until you have the right mix.

Change your mind? No problem...

To change a slide layout after you've created it, click the **Common Tasks** menu on the Formatting toolbar (or the Slide Sorter toolbar, if you've switched to that view) and choose **Slide Layout**. Pick a different layout, and PowerPoint will do its best to rearrange text and other objects to suit the new layout. If the layout you choose doesn't include the objects already on your slide, don't worry–you won't lose anything. You may need to rearrange objects to fit the new layout, however.

Creating Titles

Most presentations begin with a *title slide*, which includes the title of the presentation, the speaker's name, and other introductory details. Other slides in a presentation may also be title slides—you might use a title slide to introduce different portions of a very long presentation, for example—but in most cases, you'll have just one title slide in a presentation, and it will serve as the first slide.

PowerPoint treats title slides differently from other slides in a presentation—they pick up their formatting from the Title Master, for example, whereas other slides get their formatting from the Slide Master. Title slides generally don't have bullet points, and they generally do have a subtitle.

To add a title slide to a presentation, click the **Common Tasks** menu on the Formatting toolbar, and then choose **New Slide**; the Title Slide layout is first in the list.

Title slide? Slide title?

Don't be confused by the terminology. A title slide is, in most cases, a slide that introduces a presentation. A slide title, on the other hand, is usually the first line on a slide.

To enter a title for an individual slide, just click in the title placeholder and begin typing. To change the position or formatting of titles within a presentation, use the title master.

SEE ALSO

➤ *For more information on how to work with title masters, see page 500*

Working with Bulleted Lists

More than half of PowerPoint's built-in slide layouts include text boxes that are already formatted with the default bullet character for the design layout you've selected. To add a bulleted list to a slide, just click in the text box and begin typing.

The fastest way to work with bulleted lists is in the outline pane. Enter each main topic you plan to cover as the title of a slide, and then press Enter; PowerPoint assumes you want to enter another slide title at this point, but if you press Tab instead, you can enter the first bullet. Press Enter to move to the next line and the next bullet. When you reach the end of the bulleted list, press Enter and then Shift+Tab to enter the title of the next slide.

Press Enter to add a new bullet

When entering text on a slide layout that includes bullets, just press Enter to add a new bullet. Don't press Enter after the last bullet on a slide, though, or you'll end up with an extra bullet. If you press Enter by mistake, press the Backspace key to remove the spare bullet.

Outline view is ideal for bullets

Use the Tab and Shift+Tab keys to shift items up or down in the outline's hierarchy. Press Tab a second time, for example, to begin entering a bulleted list underneath a top-level bullet. Or, if you decide that one of your bullet points is important enough to warrant its own slide, just position the insertion point on that line and press Shift+Tab. Click and drag to move an individual bullet (or an entire slide, for that matter) up or down in the outline.

Editing and Formatting Text

To enter text directly on a slide, click in the text placeholder and begin typing. You can also add and edit text in the outline pane, and every character you enter will appear immediately in the slide to the right. If you try to enter more text than a placeholder will accommodate, PowerPoint automatically tries to shrink the text to fit within the confines of the placeholder. First, it tries to reduce the spacing between lines. If that doesn't work, it shrinks the size of the font.

If you type more text than will fit on one slide, a light bulb will appear at the bottom of the slide. Click on the light bulb, and the Office Assistant displays a dialog box that lets you choose whether to create a second slide, or to move each of the bullet points on the current slide into its own slide.

For perfect designs, turn off Auto Fit

Automatically fitting text sounds like a slick trick, but it can make a mess of your design and make your slides hard to read. To be certain that all font sizes stay exactly as you designed them, turn off this feature. Pull down the **Tools** menu, choose **Options**, click the **Edit** tab, and clear the box labeled **Auto-fit text to text placeholders**.

After you've typed a title or text in a slide, you can select a different font or apply special text attributes such as bold, italic, or a different color. The buttons on the Formatting toolbar—Font, Bold, Italic, and so on—work the same here as in other Office programs. Any formatting options you choose apply to the current selection; if you position the insertion point within a word without making a selection, font selections and other formatting options apply to the entire word.

- To make text larger or smaller, click the **Increase Font Size** or **Decrease Font Size** buttons. Keep clicking until you're satisfied.
- To add more pizzazz to a title, click the **Shadow** button. These so-called drop shadows create the illusion that your letters are floating above the surface.
- Click the **Numbering** or **Bullets** buttons to quickly add or remove these attributes from the selected text. For more control over how PowerPoint numbers each item, or to change a bullet character, right-click the text you want to change and choose the appropriate menu option.

Click the borders to format all text

To apply text-format changes to all the text inside a placeholder, click the shaded border that defines the placeholder. You can also select some or all of the text inside a frame by dragging the mouse over the words, just as you would in Word and the other Office programs.

PowerPoint applies some formatting automatically, changing fractions (1/2) and ordinals (1st, 2nd, and so on) to publishing characters, such as ½, 1st, and 2nd. It also converts straight quotes to curly quotes, and (like Word) it's smart enough to recognize when you're trying to type a two-digit year with an apostrophe ('99), automatically changing the single quote in front of that number into an apostrophe, with the curl pointing in the correct direction. And PowerPoint shares the AutoCorrect list with other Office programs, so that when you type `(c)`, it turns the text into a copyright character ©.

Undo AutoFormatting, once or for good

You can undo any of these AutoFormatting and AutoCorrect options by pressing Ctrl+Z or clicking the Undo button. To turn off all of PowerPoint's AutoFormat options, pull down the **Tools** menu, choose **Options**, click the **Edit** tab, and remove the check mark from the **AutoFormat as you type** box.

SEE ALSO

For detailed instructions on how to control AutoCorrect and AutoFormat options, see page 41

As you enter and edit text, PowerPoint checks your presentation for common spelling errors and style mistakes, such as fonts that are too small or bulleted items that don't begin with a capital letter. A wavy red line underneath a word indicates a possible spelling error. In some cases, PowerPoint changes your text automatically as you type. In other instances, a light bulb icon appears next to each possible style error (even if you've chosen to hide the Office Assistant). Click the light bulb to see a message that describes the style option that triggered the warning, with an option to fix it automatically.

Adding Pictures and Clip Art

Set your personal style

To see a full list of the style options PowerPoint checks, pull down the **Tools** menu, click **Options**, click the **Spelling & Style** tab, and then click the **Style Options** button. To turn off style checking, clear the check mark from the box labeled **Check style**.

You can use the full array of Office drawing tools (available on the Drawing toolbar) to spice up a slide with your own graphic images. Using these tools, plus choices on the **Insert** menu, you can add pictures, text boxes, and AutoShapes, set colors for text and backgrounds, draw shadows, and more.

To insert clip-art images into a slide, use the Office Clip Gallery.

SEE ALSO

➤ *To learn how to work with the Drawing toolbar, see page 116*
➤ *For details about using the Clip Gallery, see page 131*

Deleting, Copying, Rearranging, and Hiding Slides

Take it from me: You won't create a perfect presentation by starting at the beginning and working straight through to the end. Nor should you even try. Concentrate instead on getting your words, graphics, charts, and other presentation elements in place, and then step back and rearrange the slides so they make sense.

Switch to Slide Sorter view

Deleting slides is easiest when you start in Slide Sorter view, but you can also get the job done in the outline pane. In Normal view, for example, click the number of the slide you want to get rid of, and then press the Delete key.

- To delete a slide, select it and press the Delete key (or pull down the **Edit** menu and choose **Clear**).
- To move a slide, switch to Slide Sorter view, and then click the slide and drag it to its new position. You can also select the slide by clicking its number in the outline pane and dragging it up or down.
- To copy a slide, right-click its thumbnail (in Slide Sorter view) or the slide number in the outline pane in all other

views, and then choose **Copy** from the shortcut menu. To paste in Slide Sorter view, right-click the blank space between the slides where you want to place the slide and choose **Paste**. In other views, right-click the slide number just before the spot where you want to place the new copy and choose **Paste**.

- To add a new slide to a presentation in Slide Sorter view, click between the slides where you want to add the new slide; in other views, select the slide just before where you want the new slide to appear. Then pull down the **Insert** menu and choose **New Slide**.

PowerPoint also lets you mark specific slides as hidden. When you hide a slide, it's visible in all views except Slide Show view—in other words, your audience won't see it when you run the slide show. To hide a slide, switch into Slide Sorter view, select the slide you want to hide, and click the **Hide Slide** button. *Hidden slides* are easy to spot in this view—you know the slide won't be shown in the presentation because the *Not* sign appears over the slide number.

PowerPoint also includes a handy utility that lets you quickly copy one or more slides from one presentation to another.

Hidden slides = instant answers

Why on earth would you want to hide a slide? Use this trick when you anticipate that your audience might ask questions about your presentation. If there's a topic you don't want to bring up yourself, you can still be prepared in case it comes up during a Q&A session. Prepare a slide with detailed answers, facts and figures, or even a chart, and then hide it. If the question comes up, unhide the slide and give your answer.

Copying Slides Between Presentations

1. Open the presentation where you want to add the slide (or slides).
2. Switch to Slide Sorter view and click between the slides where you want the imported slides to appear.
3. Pull down the **Insert** menu and choose **Slides from Files**. You'll see the Slide Finder dialog shown in Figure 24.7.
4. Click the **Browse** button, locate the file containing the slides you want to copy, and click **Open**. Click the **Display** button to see all slides in the presentation you selected.

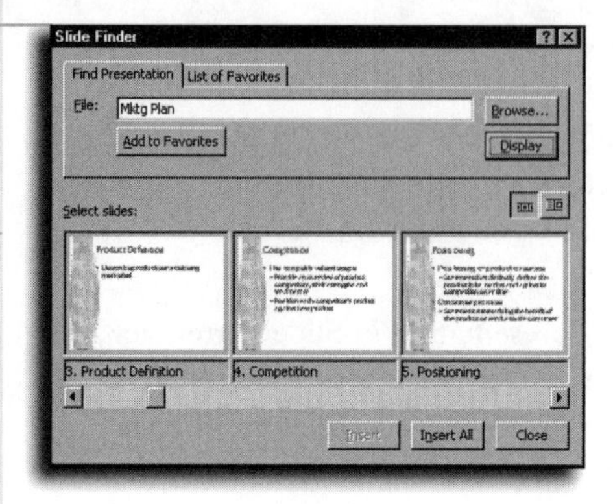

FIGURE 24.7

Use this dialog box to quickly copy slides from one presentation to another.

5. Click each slide you want to add, in turn, and click **Insert**, or click **Insert All** to copy every slide in the presentation.
6. Click **Close** to return to the original presentation and begin working with the slides you imported.

Switch between titles and thumbnails

Use the two buttons just below the **Display** button to toggle between a scrolling view that shows *thumbnails* for every slide and a list that shows slide titles, with the selected title visible in the Preview pane at the right.

Build your own custom shows

PowerPoint includes a capability that lets you create one large slide show and create several custom shows out of it, by hiding slides and saving each variation under its own name. If you're intrigued by this advanced presentation-building technique, check out *Special Edition Using Microsoft Office 2000;* Chapter 34, "PowerPoint Essentials," it contains full instructions on how to do it.

Adding Comments to PowerPoint Slides

In PowerPoint, comments behave much like their Excel counterparts, appearing as yellow sticky notes that are visible only when you view the slide itself. Use comments when you're collaborating with authors while creating a presentation. They can also be useful within a presentation—to flag important points for follow-up, for example.

SEE ALSO

➤ *For more details on using comments in Excel, see page 470*

Adding Comments to a PowerPoint Presentation

1. Select the slide where you want to add the comment.
2. Pull down the **Insert** menu and choose **Comment**. If the Reviewing toolbar is visible, click the **Insert Comment** button. PowerPoint creates a text box and enters your name at the beginning of the note.
3. Enter the information you want to appear in the note, and click anywhere outside the comment box to return to your slide.

To show all comments in the current presentation, open the **View** menu and choose **Comments**; if the Reviewing toolbar is visible, click the **Show All Comments** button. Other users can open the presentation and add their own comments as well; each author's name appears at the top of the comment. In both Excel and PowerPoint, this text is inserted automatically, but you can change the name after creating the note.

Comments are flexible

Comments you add to a PowerPoint slide are actually AutoShapes that appear in the drawing layer. You can reformat a comment or even change its shape in either program. To change a comment from a boring box to a starburst, for example, pull down the **View** menu and choose **Comments** to make all comments visible. Select the comment you want to change, click the **Draw** menu on the Drawing toolbar, and choose **Change AutoShape**. Pick a different shape—in this case, choose from the **Stars and Banners** menu—and the comment changes from a yellow sticky note to the new shape. You can resize the comment, move it, and change fonts as well.

CHAPTER 25

Making Great-Looking Presentations

- Create a consistent look for your presentation
- Add a logo or graphic to every slide
- Make sure your colors look right
- Give charts and bulleted lists zing with animation effects

Creating a Consistent Look for Your Presentation

A typical PowerPoint presentation can run for 20, 30, even 40 or more slides. Obviously, formatting each slide individually would be a nightmare—and changing formats on each slide, one at a time, would be even more daunting. Fortunately, PowerPoint makes it easy to create a consistent design that guarantees your entire presentation uses the same background graphics, color schemes, bullet styles, fonts, and other design elements.

To change the look of every slide in your presentation, you have to edit only one or two master slides. When you apply a new design template to an existing presentation, you replace these master slides with a new one, instantly applying the new look to your presentation.

Use the master slides whenever possible

When you apply a design template to your presentation, PowerPoint automatically positions titles, text, and other objects in consistent locations on each slide. You can move objects individually, but I strongly recommend you avoid doing so unless you absolutely have to. If you reposition the text placeholder on a handful of slides, the effect on your audience is jarring when you begin presenting–the text appears to jump all over the screen instead of appearing in one predictable location. It's a subtlety of design, but your audience will notice.

Applying a New Design to a Presentation

The easiest way to give a presentation a complete makeover is to apply one of PowerPoint's custom design templates to it. By doing so, you replace all the master slides with professional designs whose graphics, colors, fonts, and other elements are guaranteed to look good.

Applying a New Design

1. Click the **Common Tasks** menu on the Formatting toolbar and choose **Apply Design Template**.
2. In the Apply Design Template dialog box (see Figure 25.1), select a design. Use the **Preview** pane at right to see what the graphics and text formatting look like.
3. Click **Apply** to change the design of your presentation and return to the PowerPoint editing window.

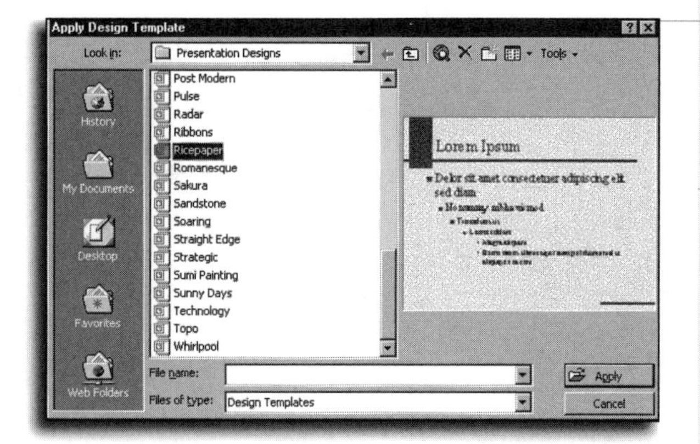

FIGURE 25.1
The Preview pane at right gives you a rough idea of what each design template looks like.

Using Master Slides

With one exception, every formatting option in a PowerPoint presentation is stored in one of four *master slides*. (I discuss the exception—color schemes—later in this chapter.) These masters control the position and appearance of objects on each slide—backgrounds, fonts, bullets, and color schemes, for example—as well as the look of printed notes pages and handouts. You can customize a master to change formatting or add images and boilerplate text, like a corporate logo or company slogan that you want to appear on all slides.

To see all master slides in a presentation, pull down the **View** menu, click **Master**, and choose one of the following four options:

- The *Slide Master* contains formatting options for slides based on any layout except the Title Slide. As the example in Figure 25.2 shows, it contains a Title Area at the top and an Object Area in the center that determines formatting for bulleted lists and other text. Three placeholders along the bottom of the slide contain footer information, including the date/time and slide number.

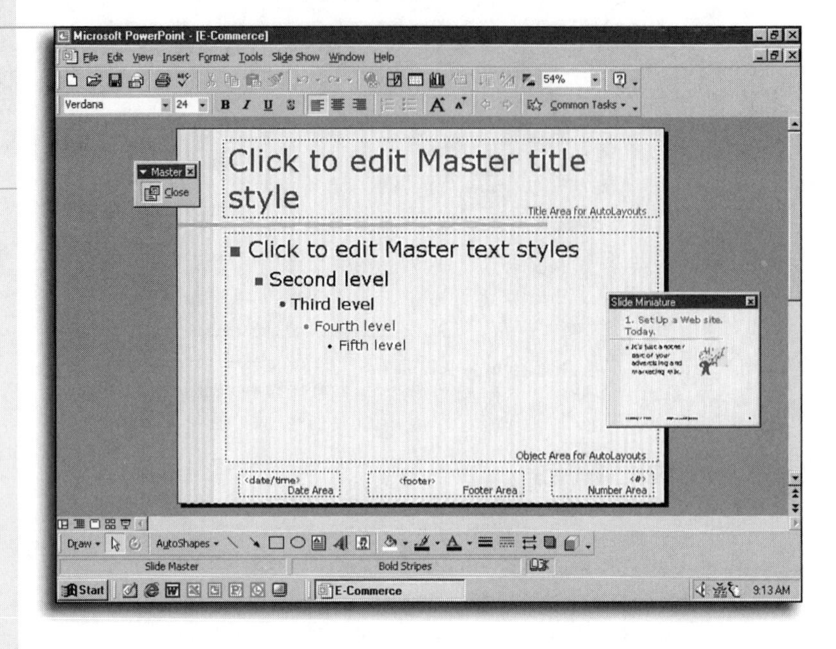

FIGURE 25.2

This Slide Master is the key to virtually all PowerPoint formatting options.

Don't bother with the Title Master

If your presentation has only one title slide, it's usually easier to edit that slide directly than to change the Title Master. When should you change the Title Master? Only if you want to save the presentation as a new design template or if you want to borrow the design for use in another presentation.

Use the Print dialog box instead

When you open the Handout Master for editing, you see a toolbar that lets you set the number of slides that print on a default layout. Don't bother. It's much easier to change the arrangement of slides on printed handout pages using the Print dialog box. Choose **Handouts** from the **Print what?** list, and then pick the number of slides you want on each page.

- The *Title Master* stores formatting for any slide you create using the Title Slide layout—typically just the first slide of your presentation. Similar to the Slide Master, it contains a Title Area and three placeholders for the date/time, slide number, and footer. The Subtitle Area placeholder stores formatting for a subtitle (often used for the presenter's name and affiliation).
- The *Notes Master* lets you adjust the look of printed notes pages. You can change the size of the Slide Object or the Notes Object, and you can choose new fonts for notes, headers, and footers.
- There's rarely a need to edit the *Handout Master* unless you want to remove one of the boxes from the header or footer.

Using and Customizing the Title Master

For most presentations based on a design template, you don't need to do anything to the Title Master. One exception is when you're working with an extremely long presentation; in that case, you might want to break up individual sections by inserting a new title slide at the beginning of each one.

SEE ALSO

➤ *To learn how to add a new slide, see page 488*

If you started your presentation using the Blank Presentation option, you soon discover that no Title Master is available; the menu choice is grayed out. If you're determined to keep working with the blank layout, complete with white background, it's easy to add a Title Master. Pull down the **View** menu, select **Master**, and choose **Slide Master**; then press Ctrl+M, the shortcut for adding a new slide in PowerPoint.

How text works on master slides

PowerPoint ignores any text you type into the Title, Subtitle, or Object (bulleted text) placeholders. If you type text into the date/time, footer, or slide number placeholders, PowerPoint repeats the text on all title slides. So if you want the slide number on each title slide to say "Slide *n*", click once on the slide number placeholder and type the word `Slide` in front of the <#>; don't forget to leave a space between them.

Using and Customizing the Slide Master

When you use a design template, all your formatting decisions are made for you—typefaces, font sizes, colors, and so on. By editing the Slide Master, you can customize the design for every type of slide except those based on the Title Slide layout. The most common formatting changes are to text and bullet characters.

Restore missing pieces

If you accidentally delete one of the five placeholders on the Title Master or Slide Master, it's easy to bring it back. Pull down the **Format** menu, choose **Master Layout**, and check the box next to the missing placeholder. Click **OK** to return to the master slide. You may have to click and drag the new placeholder to return it to its proper location.

Changing Font Formatting on the Slide Master

1. Pull down the **View** menu and choose **Master**, and then click **Slide Master**.
2. Click to position the insertion point in the part of the slide whose formatting you want to change. Click in the Title Area to change the title font; choose one of the five levels of bullet formats to change all bulleted text at that level.
3. Use the controls on the Formatting toolbar to change font, font size, or attributes.
4. To tighten or loosen the space between each bulleted item, pull down the **Format** menu and choose **Line Spacing**. Try adding a few tenths of a line at a time before or after a paragraph; double spacing isn't usually practical, given the limited space on a PowerPoint slide.
5. Click **Close** on the Master toolbar to save the changes and return to your presentation.

Selecting text makes no difference

It doesn't matter whether you make a selection in the Slide Master when formatting. Your changes will apply to all the text in that part of the slide, regardless of whether you've made a selection.

Changing Bullets in a Presentation

1. Pull down the **View** menu, choose **Master**, and click **Slide Master** to open the Slide Master for editing.
2. Right-click the line that reads **Click to edit Master text styles**, and choose **Bullets and Numbering** from the shortcut menu. The dialog box shown in Figure 25.3 appears.

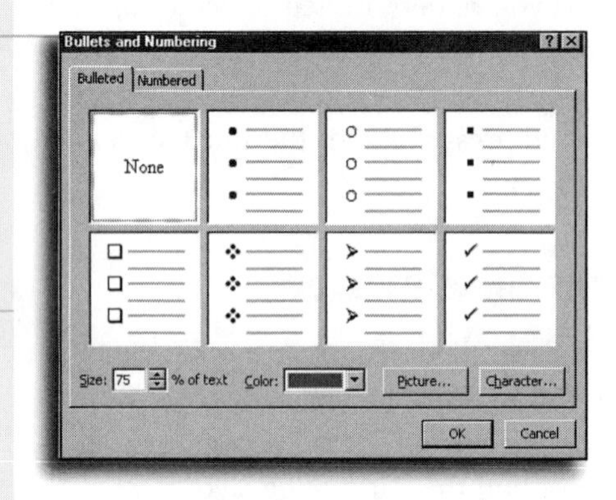

FIGURE 25.3

Change the default bullets from dull dots and dashes to any of these characters—or click the buttons at lower right to choose from different fonts or graphic bullets.

3. To use one of the seven available bullet characters, click in the box that contains the character. To choose another bullet from a Windows font, click the **Character** button and look through the greatly expanded list of characters there.
4. If you'd prefer to use a graphic for the bullet character, click the **Picture** button. PowerPoint pops up a special dialog box (based on the Clip Gallery) containing more than 150 bullet characters. If you find one that matches your presentation, select it and click **OK**.
5. Click **OK** to apply the new bullet character to your Slide Master.
6. Repeat steps 2 through 5 for the remaining bullet levels, if you wish.

Keeping titles in sync

When you change font formatting for the title placeholder on the Slide Master, you also change the formatting on the Title Master. This guarantees that you won't be embarrassed by a mismatched font when you flip from the title slide to subsequent slides in your presentation. The Slide and Title Masters do not share paragraph formatting, however. If you change the alignment of the title placeholder on the Slide Master, for example, the corresponding element on the Title Master remains unchanged.

Pick a bullet size

No, not .38 caliber. When you choose a character from a Windows font (like WingDings), you can increase or decrease it from its standard size. If you like the bullet character but it's just a bit too small, try increasing it to 125% of normal. This trick isn't available for picture bullets.

Adding Logos and Graphics

Branding is crucial to maintaining a corporate identity. If you're giving a sales presentation, one effective way to keep your audience focused on your company's identity is to add your logo to each slide. You don't need to be a Fortune 500 company, either; a memorable logo can make even a one-person shop look powerful and professional. If you've hired a graphic artist to design your logo, you can easily import the resulting file into PowerPoint.

Adding a Logo to a Presentation

1. Pull down the **View** menu, choose **Master**, and select **Slide Master**.
2. Open the **Insert** menu, select **Picture**, and then choose **From File**. Select the graphics file from the Insert Picture dialog box and click **Insert**.
3. Use the buttons on the Picture toolbar to crop and format the picture, to change its contrast and brightness, or to add borders.
4. Position the logo where you want it to appear. Make sure it's out of the way of the areas where text will typically appear in placeholders.
5. Click the **Close** button on the Master toolbar to save your changes and return to the presentation.

SEE ALSO

For more information on working with pictures, see page 130

You can also use the Clipboard to copy and paste pictures into a presentation. This approach is especially useful if the picture you want to reuse is in another PowerPoint presentation or is part of a Word document. After copying the graphic to the Clipboard, follow the same steps as outlined above, but choose the **Edit** menu and select **Paste** instead of inserting the image from a file.

Using Headers and Footers

If you're an experienced Word user, you're accustomed to seeing headers at the top of a document and footers at the bottom. In a PowerPoint presentation, these elements behave a bit differently.

- *Headers* appear only on notes and handout pages.
- You can add custom text, such as your company's name, a slogan, or Web address, in a *footer* at the bottom of each

Or use a logo just on the title

If your good taste overwhelms your commercial sense and you decide your audience doesn't need to see your logo on every slide, consider adding it just to the title slide. Use the techniques outlined here to add a graphic to the title slide in your presentation. If you have a standard design template you use for all business presentations, add the logo to the Title Master so that it appears automatically when you apply the template to an existing presentation.

Or use a link...

Use the drop-down arrow on the **Insert** button to create a link to the graphic file containing the logo. This technique lets you update every presentation that contains the logo file automatically, just by replacing the old file with a new one; however, you have to remember to keep the logo file with your presentation, or your audience will see an ugly placeholder character.

Pick a date format carefully

Use date codes in the footer when you want the date to show the last time you updated the presentation. Choose a fixed date if you're planning a major presentation—at a trade show or company meeting, for example—and you want the date on the slides to match the date of the big event.

slide. This footer is completely separate from the one that appears on notes and handout pages.

- The Slide Master includes a placeholder that lets you add the date and time, in your choice of formats. This value can be a code that updates automatically every time you print or save the presentation, or it can be a fixed value.
- The Slide Master also includes a placeholder for the slide number, which is normally hidden.
- You can show, hide, or edit the date/time, slide number, and footer placeholders on a single slide, or edit the Slide Master so that these elements change on all slides at once.

Use the Wizard

In the last step of the AutoContent Wizard, you can choose whether to show the date and slide number. By default, these boxes are checked; make sure to clear the check marks if you don't want to see one or both of these elements.

Move a footer anywhere on a slide

Although this dialog box refers to a footer, don't be confused by the label. You can move this placeholder to any location on a slide–including the top. In general, though, you want to leave titles at the top and footers at the bottom of a slide.

Customizing a Slide Footer

1. To adjust the footer on a single slide, first select the slide. If you want to change the footer on all slides in the presentation, select any slide.
2. Pull down the **View** menu and choose **Header and Footer**. You see the dialog box shown in Figure 25.4.

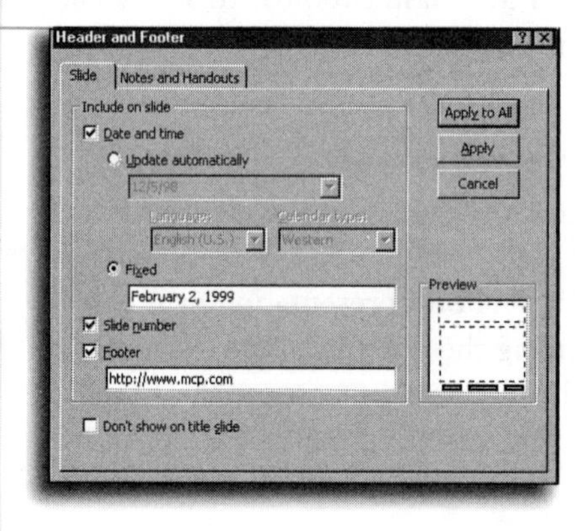

FIGURE 25.4
Use this dialog box to create a custom footer, with or without the date, time, and slide number.

3. Check the **Date and time** box if you want to see this information in the footer. If you want this information to change every time you save the presentation, check the **Update automatically** box and choose a format from the drop-down list. Otherwise, choose **Fixed** and enter the exact date.

Hide footers on graphic pages

Hiding a date, slide number, or other footer information on a single slide is a good idea when the slide contains a picture, graphic, or other large image. In this case, you don't want the footer to fight with the rest of the content on the slide.

4. To control whether or not numbers appear on your slides, check or clear the **Slide number** box.
5. If you want to add text at the bottom of the slide—a Web address, for example—check the **Footer** box, and then click in the text box and enter the content you want to appear.
6. Click **Apply** to change the footer on the currently selected slide only. Click **Apply to All** to save your changes on the Slide Master so that the footer text appears on all slides in your presentation.

If you want to change the location of the date/time field, the slide number, or the footer text, do so on the Slide Master, not on each individual slide. Pull down the **View** menu, select **Master**, and then choose **Slide Master**. Click the **Number Area**, **Date Area**, or **Footer Area** boxes and drag them to a new location, or use the handles on any side or corner to resize them.

Removing Master Elements from a Single Slide

The Slide Master defines background graphics, footers, and other elements for every slide in the presentation, but there are times when you don't want these elements to appear on an individual slide. Maybe you want to show a completely blank slide in the middle of your presentation so that you can answer questions, or maybe you want to show a picture of your new Southwest regional office, without the distraction of the background graphic and footer.

To hide *all* the Slide Master elements on a single slide, leaving only the title and text placeholders, right-click anywhere on the slide and choose **Background** from the shortcut menu. Check the box labeled **Omit background graphics from master**, and then click **Apply**.

Using Color Schemes

As I mentioned at the beginning of this chapter, there's one additional piece of every design that isn't stored in master slides. A *color scheme* consists of eight colors, one for each major type of

Enter anything you want in this box

There's no limit on what you can enter in the date box when you choose the **Fixed** option. Take advantage of this flexibility if you want to add a note to your presentation's footer. For example, you could add the word `CONFIDENTIAL` or `DRAFT` in this box. It's not a date, but PowerPoint accepts and displays the entry anyway.

When should you number?

For presentations you plan to use exclusively as electronic slide shows or on the Web, slide numbers are unnecessary. Numbers are most useful when you plan to print slides on paper, on overhead transparencies, or on slides. In each of these cases, you'll appreciate the numbers if you drop the presentation and have to put it back together in a hurry.

What about the title slide?

In most cases, you want title slides to be uncluttered, so it makes sense to leave the footer off this slide. If you really want to apply your changes to the title slide, however, be my guest: Clear the check mark from the box labeled **Don't show on title slide**.

It's an all-or-nothing proposition

If you've added a logo or other graphic to a Slide Master, there's no easy way to hide it while still showing the background graphic for the slide, or vice versa. You can use the Header and Footer dialog box to hide footer information, but PowerPoint treats all the graphics on the master slide as a single element to hide or show.

element in a presentation. These aren't just a random selection, either. They're carefully selected to complement one another so that your text is readable, especially when viewed on a large screen in an auditorium.

Just as you can change any detail on a master slide, you can change all the colors in the current presentation by changing the color scheme. PowerPoint begins by suggesting that you select one of several sets of matched colors from the Standard tab in the Color Scheme dialog box. If you don't like any of those, you can pick from a selection of 127 colors by clicking the **Change Color** button on the **Custom** tab. And if none of those suit your fancy, you can create your own color using any combination of colors your display adapter can show.

Careful with those buttons!

Don't click the **Apply to All** button. Doing so will hide the background graphics and other Slide Master elements from every slide in your presentation. Fortunately, the mistake is easy to fix: Press Ctrl+Z (or click the **Undo** button) to undo your action and start over.

Why reinvent the wheel?

It's possible to customize color schemes, but I don't recommend it. Using the ready-made schemes offers a huge variety of choices, all of them tested and certified by professional designers. If you're an artist, you can ignore this advice; but if you're a businessperson, your audience probably won't appreciate your experiments in color.

Choosing a New Color Scheme

1. If you want to change colors on a single slide, select that slide; to change the color scheme for an entire presentation, select any slide. Right-click the slide background and choose **Slide Color Scheme** from the shortcut menu.
2. In the Color Scheme dialog box (see Figure 25.5), select one of the available color schemes in the list at the left.

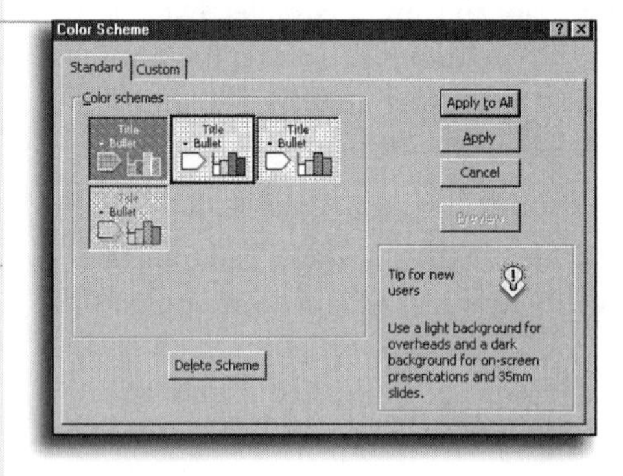

FIGURE 25.5

Each design includes a handful of ready-made color schemes, all guaranteed to be aesthetically pleasing and easy to read.

3. To see what your presentation will look like with the selected scheme, click the **Preview** button.
4. To see the full assortment of colors in the selected scheme, click the **Custom** tab. As the example in Figure 25.6 shows, each color is automatically assigned to specific types of

Slide the dialog box out of the way

Previewing the color scheme changes the colors in your presentation immediately. You may need to move the dialog box out of the way to see the changes, however.

objects—title text, fills, and hyperlinks, for example. The miniature slide in the lower-right corner shows all your colors as you work.

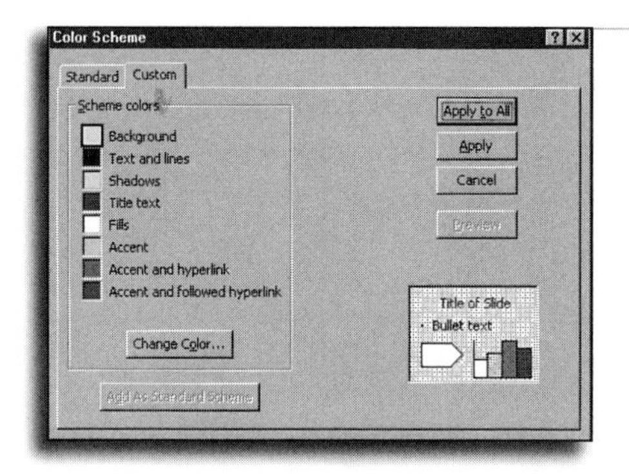

FIGURE 25.6
Use this tab to see how the color scheme applies specific colors to each type of object in your presentation.

5. To save the new color scheme with the Slide and Title masters so that it changes the entire presentation, click **OK**, and then click **Apply to All**. If you want to use the new background only with the current slide, click **Apply**.

PowerPoint uses the colors in your scheme throughout the presentation. For example, if you click the Fill Color, Line Color, or Font Color buttons on the Drawing toolbar, you see only the eight colors in the current scheme. Go ahead and change the colors of an element—as long as you stick with these choices, the colors will work well together.

On most slide elements—especially text—you want to use a solid color. But slide backgrounds are much more interesting when they have some variety, such as shading or a texture. A special type of shading called a *gradient fill* is one of the most impressive and professional-looking effects you can add to a slide. You can also add textures or even photographs as a slide background.

To add a fill effect to your presentation, pull down the **Format** menu and choose **Background**. Click the down arrow beneath the **Background fill** box, and click **Fill effects**. In the Fill Effects dialog box (see Figure 25.7), click the **Gradient** tab, and choose any combination of shade styles and variants to get precisely the effect you're looking for.

Get ideas from design templates

For examples of truly interesting background effects, check out the design templates included with PowerPoint. The Artsy design template, for example, shows how to create an interesting gradient fill from two otherwise drab colors. Other templates, like the Ricepaper design, shows how to use textures for excellent results.

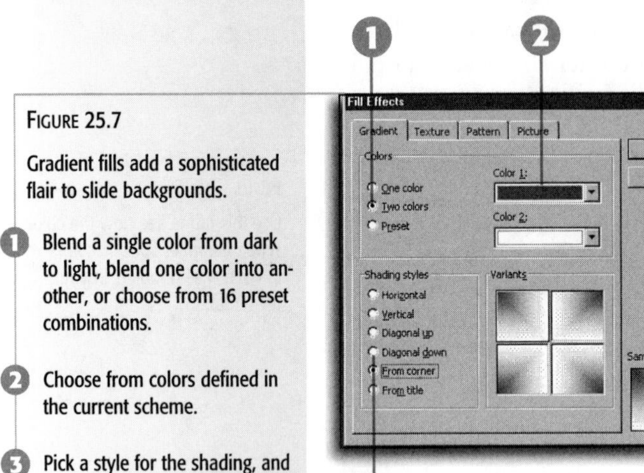

FIGURE 25.7

Gradient fills add a sophisticated flair to slide backgrounds.

1. Blend a single color from dark to light, blend one color into another, or choose from 16 preset combinations.
2. Choose from colors defined in the current scheme.
3. Pick a style for the shading, and then click one of the variations at the right.

After you select a new background, click **Apply** to modify just the current slide. Click **Apply to all** to save the changes as part of the Slide and Title masters so that they appear as the background on every slide in your presentation.

Animating Text and Objects on a Slide

What can you animate?

You can animate practically anything on a PowerPoint slide, including titles, bullet points, and even the columns, lines, and bars on charts.

Animation by any other name...

PowerPoint refers to the special visual and sound effects associated with text and other objects on the active slide as *animation*. If you've been using PowerPoint 95, you might know this feature by its old name: a *build*. The two names refer to the same thing (although PowerPoint 2000 includes far more interesting animation effects than those earlier versions).

Even the most seasoned presenter understands this basic fact of public speaking: Minds wander. It doesn't matter how good a speaker you are or how interested your audience is in your subject matter. To minimize distractions, you need to synchronize what's on the screen with what you're saying. It certainly won't do to let your audience race ahead (and ignore what you're saying right now) by putting all your bullet points on the first slide.

If you've ever used an overhead projector as a presentation aid, you know the low-tech way to reveal one bit of information at a time: Cover the transparency with a piece of paper, and slide it down a bit each time you want to reveal a new item. PowerPoint lets you achieve a far more sophisticated version of the same effect with titles, bullet points, chart objects, and other objects on your slides.

To add animation to a single slide, click in the bulleted text that you want to animate. Click the **Animation Effects** button to display the Animation Effects toolbar, with its eight ready-made effects. It also includes a **Custom Animation** button that lets you choose a practically limitless number of custom animations.

When you switch to Slide Sorter view, you see a much longer list of preset animations. Despite the large number of animation categories, however, there are really only two basic animation methods: Your words either fly onto the screen fully formed, or they materialize out of thin air and take shape onscreen. Some effects also include attention-getting sounds.

Adding "Flying" Bullet Points

1. Switch to Slide Sorter view, and select the slide or slides you want to animate.
2. Pick the animation you prefer from the **Preset Animation** drop-down list. Fly From Right, for example, causes each bulleted item to careen in from the right side of the screen and take its normal place on the slide.
3. As soon as you choose an animation effect, look at the first slide you selected to see a preview of the effect. Click the **Animation Preview** button to see it again.

Do you want sound with your animation? Although there are many more animations in the drop-down Preset Animations list, the short list on the Animation Effects toolbar includes some interesting and useful variations. For example, the Drive-In, Flying, Camera, LaserText, and Typewriter animations all have accompanying sound.

If none of the prebuilt animations on the toolbar strike your fancy, click the **Custom Animation** button and use the dialog box shown in Figure 25.8 to create your own. There are literally thousands of combinations you can use to animate just about anything on a slide. In this example, I've convinced PowerPoint to unveil each set of columns in a chart from the bottom up and from left to right, accompanied by a drum roll. It's a very effective way to display this type of chart.

Select several slides at once

In Slide Sorter view, all the Windows-standard techniques apply: Hold down the Ctrl key as you click to select a group of slides, one at a time. To select a consecutive group of slides, click the first one, and then hold down the Shift key and click the last one in the group. Press Ctrl+A to select all the slides in your presentation.

From the home office in Nebraska...

PowerPoint 2000 includes a preset animation that uses the Top 10 format made wildly popular by David Letterman. This animation shows the last bullet point on the slide, then the next to the last, and so on. If the Animation Effects toolbar is visible, click the preset animation called **Reverse Text Order Effect**. In Slide Sorter view, choose **Reverse Order** from the **Preset Animation** list.

Web effects require an extra step

If you want your transitions and animations to appear when your presentation is viewed in a Web browser, you need to take one extra step. Pull down the **Tools** menu, click **Options**, and click the **General** tab. Click the **Web Options** button, and check the **Show slide animation while browsing** box.

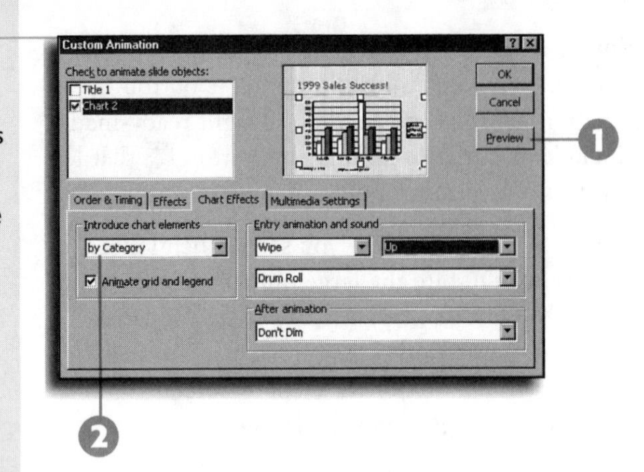

FIGURE 25.8

PowerPoint can animate text, multimedia objects, and charts, as in this example.

1. Click the **Preview** button to see what your animation will look like.

2. This option unveils each set of columns, from left to right. To show last year's numbers, followed by this year's results, choose **By Series** instead.

CHAPTER

26

Planning and Delivering Presentations

Use special effects to help your slides flow gracefully

Add sound to your presentation

Practice your pitch with PowerPoint's built-in stopwatch

Master the shortcuts for running a slide show

Print slides, handouts, and notes pages

Using Special Effects to Create Transition Slides

Want to be a PowerPoint expert?

For more information on how you can use animations, transitions, and multimedia to build spectacular PowerPoint presentations, pick up a copy of *Special Edition Using Microsoft Office 2000* and read Chapter 37, "Adding Graphics, Multimedia, and Special Effects."

How many transitions?

Although the list of transitions includes 40 entries, strictly speaking, there are only 12 types of transitions, each with several variations. What they all have in common is the gradual transformation from one slide to the next.

If you expect to hold the attention of your audience, you need to make sure your presentation flows smoothly, with each new slide shifting gracefully into the foreground while the old slide recedes. One way to ensure that your presentation goes swimmingly is to carefully select the *transitions* between slides. Just as you plan the way that words and bulleted items appear on each slide, you can plan the way slides come and go on the screen.

In the film world, editors win Oscars for creating graceful transitions between scenes. Sometimes a scene briefly "fades to black" before the next one appears. Occasionally, you see a brief overlap between two scenes. In PowerPoint presentations, transitions help convey different moods just as they do in the cinema. You might want a more abrupt transition if you're trying to project a snappy, rapid-fire image, and a more relaxed transition when your message is upbeat and informal. In all, you can choose from more than 40 distinct transitions to smoothly shift between slides.

Applying a Transition to One Slide

The easiest way to apply a transition to a slide is to switch to Slide Sorter view. Select the slide to which you want to apply the transition, and then use the Slide Transition Effects drop-down list to choose one of the available transitions from the following groups:

SEE ALSO

➤ *For more details about using Slide Sorter view, see page 487*

- **Blinds**—Just like window coverings, these come in the horizontal or vertical variety, gradually opening until you see the entire new slide.
- **Box**—A square shrinks into the center of the slide or grows to show the entire slide.

- **Checkerboard**—Small squares cover the new slide and disappear either sideways or downward.
- **Cover**—The new slide "flies" in from the top, bottom, sides, or corners, and covers the previous slide.
- **Cut**—An abrupt transition, lacking the grace of most of the others.
- **Dissolve**—Tiny dots that make up the new slide gradually take over the previous one.
- **Fade Through Black**—A familiar Hollywood "fade-in" effect. The new slide materializes from black.
- **Random bars**—Thick and thin lines (vertical or horizontal) gradually display the new slide.
- **Split**—Think of it as pulling curtains over your slide, vertically or horizontally.
- **Strips**—The new slide reveals itself by covering the previous one in a diagonal direction with a jagged edge.
- **Uncover**—Unlike Cover, where the new screen flies in all at once, Uncover does a little striptease, peeling off the onscreen elements gradually, in whichever of eight directions you choose, as the new slide reveals itself.
- **Wipe**—Slowly reveals the new slide, as if you were gradually sliding a dark cover sheet from in front of a picture.

In Slide Sorter view, the tiny Transition icon under each slide is your indication that a transition has been applied to that slide, as in Figure 26.1. (You also see an icon for animations.) To see a quick preview of the transition or animation for a given slide, just click one of these icons.

When you assign a transition to a slide, it takes place as soon as the slide appears. There's no way to control how a slide leaves the screen, except by defining a transition for the next slide in the presentation.

Do you feel lucky?

If you select **Random Transition** from the list of available effects, you see different transitions for different slides every time you run the show. That's a nearly foolproof recipe for annoying your audience. Most experts agree that you should pick one transition and use it exclusively throughout your presentation; it's all right to pick a few exceptions for dramatic effect, but use them sparingly.

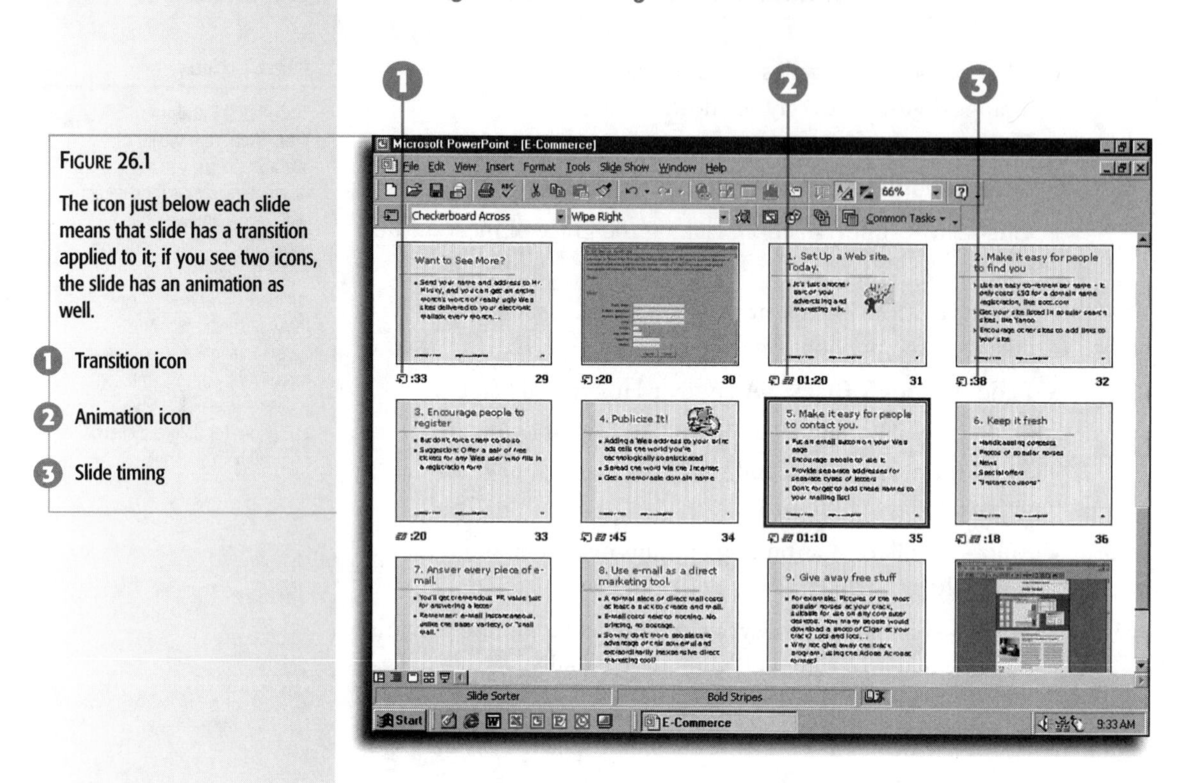

FIGURE 26.1

The icon just below each slide means that slide has a transition applied to it; if you see two icons, the slide has an animation as well.

1. Transition icon
2. Animation icon
3. Slide timing

Applying a Transition to a Group of Slides

To assign the same transition to a group of slides, switch to Slide Sorter view and Ctrl+click or Shift+click to select multiple slides then pick a transition from the Slide Transition Effects drop-down list. You see a preview of the transition on one of the selected slides.

If you want to apply the same transition to all the slides in a presentation, there's no need to make a selection. Pull down the **Slide Show** menu, and click **Slide Transition**. In the Slide Transition dialog box, choose an effect and click the **Apply to All** button.

Careful with this option!

If you've applied different transitions to one or two slides for dramatic effect, don't use the **Apply to All** button. This feature does exactly what it says, replacing every transition in the presentation with the one you select here.

Controlling Transition Speed

You say you selected just the right transition, but on your speedy desktop PC those checkerboard squares whiz by too quickly for anyone to notice? Not a problem.

Changing the Speed of Transitions

1. Switch to Slide Sorter view and select the slide whose transition you want to adjust. (If you've applied the same transition to all slides, select any slide.)
2. Click the **Slide Transition** button on the left of the Slide Sorter toolbar to display the Slide Transition dialog box shown in Figure 26.2.

FIGURE 26.2
Take your choice of transitions. The puppy in the preview window shows you what the transition effect will look like.

3. Click each of the speed options—**Slow**, **Medium**, **Fast**—and watch the preview screen (the one showing alternating pictures of a dog and a key) for an idea of how fast they go.
4. Click **Apply** to change the speed of the transition for the selected slide. Click **Apply to All** to change the speed of all transitions in the presentation.

Two PCs? Plan ahead

The transition speed you choose depends on the speed of your computer. If you create the presentation on your fast desktop PC but use a slower notebook computer to display it, the results might not be what you expect. Be sure to test the transition on the PC you plan to use to give the presentation before you step on stage.

Adding Sounds to Transitions

If you choose them carefully, sounds can add the equivalent of punctuation to your slide transitions. They can also serve as a form of comic relief—combining an animation effect with the sound of screeching tires, for example, will probably get a laugh from your audience. As with all PowerPoint effects, these are best used sparingly.

Add your own sounds

If you've found a sound that will work in your presentation, scroll to the bottom of the **Sound** list and click the **Other Sound** choice, and then click the file that contains the sound. Want Groucho Marx or Darth Vader to introduce a slide? You'll find a tremendous collection of sound clips from classic movies and TV shows at `http://www.dailywav.com`.

Who owns that clip?

It's easy to lift graphics from magazines and Web sites or to "borrow" a sound clip or image you find on the Internet. For informal presentations–a departmental status meeting, for example–these can add a lot of fun, and you usually don't need to worry about copyright issues when you reuse someone else's material for personal use. For formal presentations, however, especially those you plan to publish on the Web, pay close attention to copyright issues. If you're thinking about using a copyrighted image (such as a Dilbert cartoon) or a sound clip (say, something from *Star Wars*) without permission, think again–or you're likely to receive a letter from a lawyer.

CD Audio requires extra preparation

If you're planning to deliver your presentation from a notebook computer, make sure it has a CD-ROM drive that is properly configured to play audio CDs. And don't forget to tell the audio-visual specialist at the presentation venue that you need to connect the notebook PC 's audio output to the sound system. That configuration may require special cables.

You can add sounds to a presentation the hard way, by using the Clip Gallery in combination with PowerPoint's built-in slide layouts. The easy way to add standard sound effects, however, is to include them as part of a transition. You can choose from 16 sounds in the PowerPoint transition list, including applause, gunshots, and a drum roll.

Adding Sound to a Transition

1. Switch to Slide Sorter view and select the slide to which you want to add sound.
2. Click the **Slide Transition** button on the left of the Slide Sorter toolbar to display the Slide Transition dialog box.
3. Choose a sound from the drop-down **Sound** list.
4. Click **Apply** to add the sound to the selected slide. Don't click the **Apply to All** button unless you want the audience to storm the stage and rip the audio cables from the back of your PC.

Using CD Audio

You can use recorded audio (such as a *narration*) or a track from a music CD as a dramatic way to introduce a slide or presentation. You can even use this technique in combination with a series of timed animations to run a dramatic series of slides, complete with audio, before you take the stage.

Adding CD Audio to a Presentation

1. Insert the audio CD into the CD-ROM drive. If the Windows CD Player program begins playing automatically, close it.
2. Switch to Normal or Slide view, and select the slide during which you want to begin playing music.
3. Pull down the **Insert** menu, choose **Movies and Sounds**, and select **Play CD Audio Track**.
4. In the Movie and Sound Options dialog box (see Figure 26.3), choose the number of the track or tracks you want to play. To use just one track, enter the same number in the **Start** and **End** boxes. Click **OK**.

FIGURE 26.3
PowerPoint automatically calculates how much time it will take to play the tracks you select from an audio CD.

5. PowerPoint displays a message asking whether you want your sound to play automatically in the slide show. If you want the CD track to start the moment this slide hits the screen, click Yes. If you pick No, you have to click the CD icon on the slide before the music will play.
6. A CD icon appears in the center of the slide. Move it to a less obtrusive location, if you want. Your CD audio track is now ready.

Use a CD for background music

Attach a CD track to the title slide of your CD and use it as the background sound while your audience is arriving. To keep the music playing, check the **Loop until stopped** check box.

Rehearsing Your Presentation

When you're in the audience, trying desperately to stay awake through a presentation, your worst nightmare is the speaker who simply stands up and reads his slides. If you're on the podium, your worst nightmare is that you'll forget your own name. As the speaker, you can prevent both problems with even a modest amount of preparation and rehearsal.

The great Sir Laurence Olivier advised beginning actors to concentrate on two things: memorize your lines, and don't bump into the scenery. You have to depend on your own coordination to avoid tripping on the podium, but PowerPoint has a powerful tool that can help you prepare for the presentation itself. Switch to Slide Sorter view and click the **Rehearse Timings** button. Script in hand, you go through a dry run of the presentation, preferably more than once, and PowerPoint times how long each slide takes. When you're finished, you get a report you can use to fine-tune your show so that it fits in the allotted time.

Remember to bring the right CD

PowerPoint doesn't identify the actual CD in the CD-ROM drive; it only knows to play the tracks you've specified, no matter which CD may be in there. If you forget to put a CD in the drive when running a presentation, PowerPoint continues as if there were no track(s) to be played.

The first slide comes up, showing a running digital stopwatch in a small dialog box (see Figure 26.4). Start talking through the presentation, just as you would in front of a live audience, and PowerPoint keeps track of your progress. Click the left mouse button when you're ready to move to the next slide.

FIGURE 26.4

PowerPoint keeps a running total of your time as you rehearse. Flub a slide? Don't worry–just click the Repeat button and start over.

1. As you rehearse, PowerPoint tracks the total time of your presentation here.
2. This clock tells you how much time you've spent on the current slide.

When does the timing begin?

PowerPoint starts timing as soon as the first slide appears. On some systems, loading the presentation can take 10 seconds or more, but PowerPoint doesn't count that time. As soon as you see your title slide, start talking.

If the phone rings, or you need to clear your throat, click the **Pause** button to stop timing the current slide without losing the timings for the entire show. If you make a mistake, you don't have to start the entire presentation over. Click the **Repeat** button to reset the clock to 0:00 for the current slide; the elapsed time resets properly, too.

When you click to advance past the final slide, PowerPoint displays a dialog box similar to the one in Figure 26.5. It reports the total length of the presentation and asks whether you want to record the slide timings so that you can see them in Slide Sorter view. If you're satisfied with the rehearsal results, click Yes.

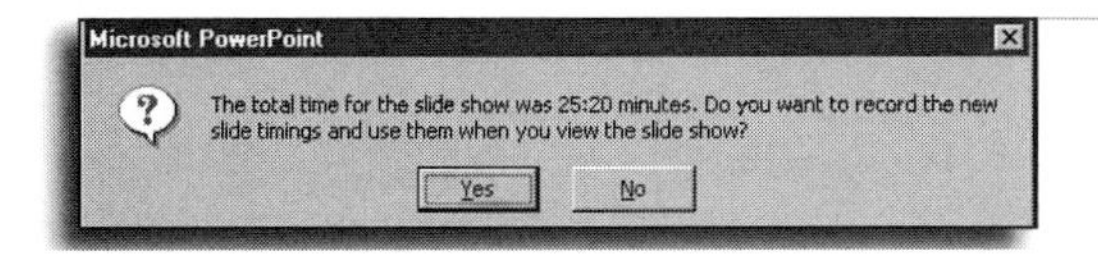

FIGURE 26.5
If you want to restart the clock and run through your presentation once more, click No.

When you return to Slide Sorter view, each slide has a time stamp under it. Now is a good time to fine-tune your presentation. Did the whole thing take too long? Where can you cut out a few seconds or minutes? Adjust your script accordingly, and try again until you fill the time allotted to you perfectly, without rushing the finish.

Let PowerPoint set the pace

If you tend to ramble in front of a crowd, consider letting PowerPoint force you along, by automatically advancing to the next slide using the intervals you set during rehearsal. (Click the Slide Transitions button and tell PowerPoint to advance automatically after a certain time.) Of course, the trick here is to cut your patter appropriately and keep up with PowerPoint so that you don't end up five slides behind at the end!

Delivering the Perfect Presentation

After you've created the perfect presentation, all that's left is, well, the difficult part. Remember to breathe, smile, relax, and make eye contact with your audience. If you've rehearsed properly, you'll be basking in an enthusiastic ovation before you know it.

Running a Slide Show

For the main event, you want to display your presentation as a slide show, minus all the PowerPoint toolbars and menus, without even the Windows Taskbar to get in the way. To start the slide show, click the **Slide Show** button on the View Bar, or pull down the **Slide Show** menu and click **View Show**.

PowerPoint includes an overwhelming number of shortcuts you can use to jump from slide to slide, but you don't have to memorize them all. Instead, pick the mouse or keyboard techniques that work best for you from the following list:

Quick jumps

To return to the first slide in the presentation, press Home. To jump to the end of the presentation, press End. To go to a specific slide number, type the number and press Enter.

On with the show...

Accidentally switching back to your PowerPoint window, with its toolbars and menus, can ruin the professional image you've tried so hard to convey. To eliminate this possibility, save your presentation as a slide show; pull down the **File** menu, choose **Save As**, and pick **PowerPoint Show** from the **Save as type** list. Create a shortcut to this file on your desktop, and use this icon to run your show. All the standard navigation techniques work, but Esc drops you back to the Windows desktop instead of the PowerPoint window.

Hide slides to trim a presentation

Hidden slides have another handy use as well. If you need to cut a presentation short at the last minute because your time slot shrunk from 30 minutes to 15 minutes, quickly switch into Slide Sorter view and hide the slides you want to omit. When you run the slide show, you skip right by them. Make sure to unhide the slides when you're finished with the one-time show.

Slide Show Action	Keyboard Shortcut	Mouse Shortcut
Advance to the next slide, or perform the next animation on the current slide	Enter N (for Next) Page Down Right Arrow Down Arrow Spacebar	Click the left mouse button, or right-click and choose **Next** from the shortcut menu.
To move to the previous slide, or activate the preceding animation on the current slide	Backspace P (for Previous) Page Up Left Arrow Up Arrow	Right-click and choose **Previous** from the shortcut menu.
End a presentation	Esc	Right-click and choose End Show from the shortcut menu.

While you're in the midst of your presentation, it's sometimes useful to blank the screen. You might want to do this if you plan to deliver some unprepared remarks, and you want the audience to focus on you, not on the slide that's currently visible.

- To display a black screen, press **B** or the period. Press either key again to display the current slide again.
- To display a white screen, press **W** or the comma. Press either key again to display the current slide again.

Working with Hidden Slides

In the previous chapter, I explained how to hide slides within a presentation. This technique is useful when you want to be prepared with answers to a specific question or supporting details for another slide, but you want to divulge those details only if you have to.

How do you "unhide" a hidden slide while delivering a slide show? Jump to the slide immediately before the hidden slide and press **H**.

Writing or Drawing on Slides

No matter how clear your presentation, there may be times when you need a pen or a pointer to highlight an important fact on a slide. If you're presenting the financial results for the most recent quarter, for example, you might want to circle or underline numbers that are unusually low or high.

Annotating a Slide Show

1. During the slide show, right-click anywhere on the screen, choose **Pointer Options**, and click **Pen**. The standard arrow pointer changes to the shape of a pen.
2. Click the left mouse button and drag to draw circles, underlines, or any other freeform lines.
3. To change the color of your markings from the default black to any of eight other colors, right-click and choose **Pointer Options**. Click **Pen Color**, and select a color from the cascading menu.
4. To erase all marks on the current slide, press **E**.
5. Press **Esc** to change the pointer back to its normal shape and quit annotating.

Slide numbers will give you away

Avoid numbering slides if you want your hidden slides to remain a secret. When you hide slide 6, your audience will see you jump from 5 to 7, and some joker is certain to ask what's on the missing slide.

No text, please

PowerPoint's annotation tools are strictly for freehand drawing. You can't enter text when a slide show is in progress, and trying to do anything more than simple scribbles is more effort than it's worth.

Ctrl+P pops up a pen

If you use PowerPoint's annotation capabilities often, memorize this keyboard shortcut: Ctrl+P pops up a pen whenever you're running a slide show. Press Ctrl+A to turn the pencil pointer back to normal.

Printing Your Presentation

In general, PowerPoint's capabilities are biased toward the sort of flash you can only get from a computer monitor. But even in the most sophisticated slide show, there's still a place for paper. There are three circumstances in which you might want to commit your presentation to the printed page:

- You find yourself in a place where setting up a computer is impractical or even impossible. If you're meeting a client over lunch, for example, it might be difficult to find room for a computer. Instead, pass out printed copies of your slides.
- When delivering an electronic slide show, it can help to pass out copies of your slides as *handouts*. Unlike printed slides, which appear full size on the page, you can print several slides on each page to conserve space.

Annotations are temporary

As soon as you move on to the next slide, annotations disappear. There is no way to save annotations with a presentation.

When should you hand out handouts?

In some cases, you might want to save your handouts for the end of your presentation. Using handouts in this fashion keeps your audience from jumping ahead while you deliver your pitch but still allows them to refer to the printed version after you leave.

- Have you taken extensive notes that you plan to use when delivering your presentation? Print out the *notes pages* and keep them in front of you so you don't miss any key details.

If you set up your presentation for onscreen viewing, you needn't go through the page setup dialog box again—PowerPoint will print your slides in *landscape mode* (sideways) and your notes or handout pages in *portrait mode* on letter-sized paper.

For all printing tasks, pull down the **File** menu and choose **Print**. The exact options available in the Print dialog box may vary depending on your Windows version and type of printer, but you should see a dialog box that resembles the one shown in Figure 26.6.

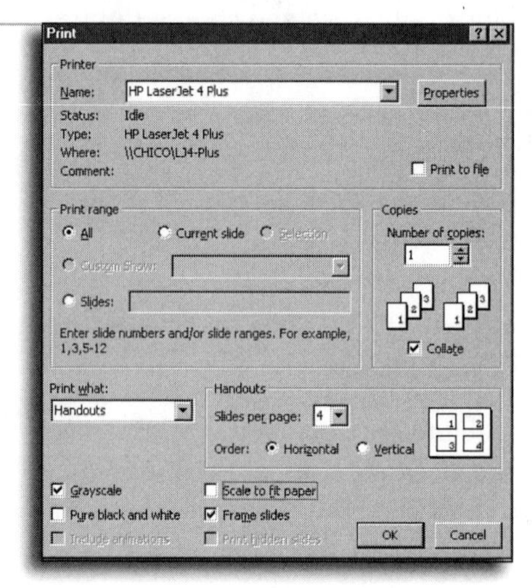

FIGURE 26.6

If you plan to print your presentation on a standard laser printer, make sure you've checked the Grayscale option.

Test your color printer first

Printing on some color printers–especially professional quality laser printers–can be tremendously expensive; even on a simple color inkjet printer, each page can take a minute or two and use precious ink. Before you print a long presentation, try a sample page or two first. When you're satisfied the output looks right, print the entire presentation.

Printing a Presentation

1. In the **Printer** section at the top of the dialog box, double-check that you've selected the correct printer.
2. In the **Print range** section, specify which slides you want to print. Use the default setting (**All**) to print the entire presentation; other settings let you specify slides by number or those you've selected.

3. If you want to print more than one copy, choose a number in the **Copies** box and decide whether you want to *collate* copies—printing each set in page order.
4. Use the drop-down list labeled **Print what?** to specify which parts of your presentation you want to print. If you choose the **Handouts** option, use the box at the right to specify the number of slides you want on each page.
5. PowerPoint does a remarkable job of getting the options at the bottom of the dialog box correct. If you select a black-and-white printer, for example, the **Grayscale** option is automatically selected. Change these options only if you're certain it's necessary.
6. Click **OK** to begin printing.

Do you really need to collate?

Checking the **Collate** box is convenient, but it can slow down printing dramatically, especially on color printers. If you're producing many sets of a long presentation filled with complex graphics, consider doing the collating yourself; it takes only a minute or two to arrange the sets by hand, and you can save 30 minutes or more by letting the printer produce multiple copies of each page.

Careful with those options

By definition, you don't want your audience to see hidden slides, so check the **Print hidden slides** box only if you want to add these slides to notes pages. If your presentation includes animations, PowerPoint automatically prints them on a single slide unless you specifically choose the **Include animations** option. Be careful—if you use many animations, this option can turn a 20-page printout into a hundred pages or more!

CHAPTER

27

Automating Your Presentation

Create a self-running presentation

Record a narration to go with your slide show

Add automatic timings for perfect pacing

Package a presentation for use on another computer

Create slide shows that work in any Web browser

Creating a Self-Running Presentation

Who says you have to be physically present to deliver a perfect presentation? With the right preparation, you can package a PowerPoint presentation so it runs completely unattended. As long as you have a computer and monitor handy, your presentation can stand in for you at a trade show or in a store; some creative Office users even set up self-running presentations in a lobby as a way of greeting guests and introducing a company or its products.

To create a self-running presentation, you'll use the same techniques as if you were planning to present the slides yourself, paying special attention to transitions and slide timings. To help the show run smoothly, you can add background music, sounds, or a recorded narration.

For playback, take your choice of two techniques: Use the Pack and Go Wizard to compress your presentation into a file that will run on any Windows computer, even if PowerPoint is not available; or save the presentation in HTML format to play it back in any Web browser.

SEE ALSO

➤ *For more information on how you can create effective slide transitions and add multimedia to a presentation, see page 512*

Adding Voice Narration

Use a narration for your own notes

A voice track doesn't have to be for an outside audience. If you plan to deliver the presentation in front of a live audience, consider recording a voice track to help you rehearse and to remind you of all the details you need to cover.

If you can't be there in person to deliver a presentation, you can still add a personal touch by recording a *narration* in your own voice. Even the simplest soundtrack can add interest and interactivity to a self-running presentation. For example, saying "touch the screen or click the mouse to advance to the next slide" is far friendlier than a cold message on the screen. If you send a presentation file to someone else via email, or post it on a network server for coworkers to play back, a voice narration allows your virtual audience to experience the presentation exactly as you intended it.

Don't confuse narrations with simple voice recordings. PowerPoint maintains narrations as an integral part of the presentation. If the PC you use to perform the presentation includes a microphone, a sound card, and sufficient disk space, you can keep a permanent record of the presentation—complete with slide timing, audience comments, and even your witty ad libs—by recording a narration. It's the easiest way to take notes.

Can you repeat the question, please?

If you record a narration while delivering a presentation, remember that your PC's microphone may not pick up questions and comments from your audience. Get into the habit of repeating each question before you give your answer.

Recording a Narration

1. Open the presentation to which you want to add a narration, switch to Normal, Slide, or Slide Sorter view, and select the first slide in the presentation.
2. Pull down the **Slide Show** menu and choose **Record Narration**. PowerPoint displays the Record Narration dialog box shown in Figure 27.1.

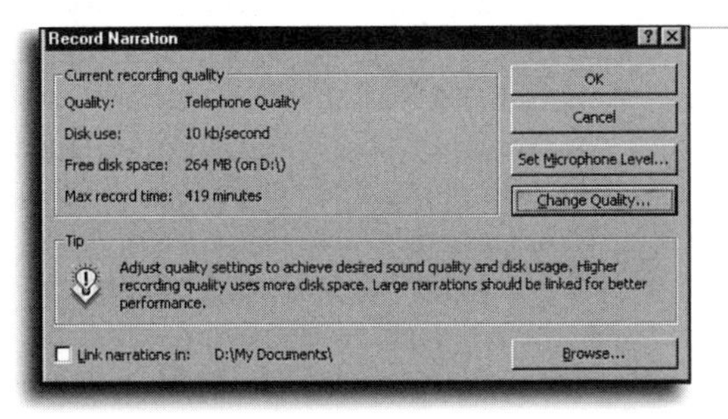

FIGURE 27.1

At the default setting, even a 10-minute recording occupies 6MB. Increasing the quality of the recording takes even more space.

3. Click the **Change Quality** button to adjust recording quality. Choose **CD Quality**, **Radio Quality**, or **Telephone Quality** from the **Name** list, or choose from dozens of different formats in the **Attributes** list.
4. If you haven't used the narration recorder on this PC before, click the **Set Microphone Level** button and use the Microphone Setup Wizard to automatically calibrate the mike as you read a sentence aloud.
5. Click **OK** to start the presentation and begin recording your narration. As you record, PowerPoint uses its Timer feature to keep track of the time you spend on each slide.

When in doubt, experiment

Choosing **CD Quality** may sound tempting, but you'll need well over 100MB of free disk space for a 10-minute talk–and you may not hear the difference. Before you settle on a format, try recording and playing back some test narrations at different quality settings, and then use the one that offers the best balance between sound quality and disk consumption.

SEE ALSO

➤ *For more details on how to use PowerPoint's Timer, see page 517*

Take a breather

You don't have to deliver your narration flawlessly from start to finish. To take a break, right-click the screen and choose **Pause Narration** from the shortcut menu. To pick up where you left off, right-click again and choose **Resume Narration**.

When you finish the presentation, PowerPoint stores your narration with the presentation, and then asks if you want to store the slide timings as well. If you want to be able to replay the presentation with the narration synchronized to the slides, you *must* click **Yes**. If you click **No**, PowerPoint saves the narration so that you can listen to it, but you'll have no way to know which slide was on the screen at a given point in the narration.

To play back the presentation using the narration, run the presentation normally. If you want to view the presentation without the narration, open the **Slide Show** menu, choose **Set Up Show**, and check the **Show without narration** box.

Adding and Editing Hyperlinks

PowerPoint allows you to turn any text or graphic object on a slide into a *hyperlink*. Although you can add hyperlinks to any presentation, they're especially useful when you're creating a presentation that you want other people to be able to run. For example, say you've prepared a presentation explaining your company's new insurance options. You might add three hyperlinks to a slide that introduces the three options, and then let the person viewing the presentation click to jump to the portion of the show that explains the selected option.

Jump to a Web page

If the PC you're using to deliver a presentation is connected to the Web, or if you've published the presentation itself to a Web page, you can use hyperlinks to connect to other Web pages.

Hyperlinks can point just about anywhere—to a specific slide, to the first or last slide in a presentation, or to the next or previous slides. You can even open a Word document or Excel worksheet or play a sound file.

You can use the same techniques you use in other Office programs to add hyperlinks to Web pages or other slides in a presentation. Select the text or graphic to which you want to attach the hyperlink, and then click the **Hyperlink** button on the Standard toolbar. But you'll have much better results if you use PowerPoint's special techniques instead.

SEE ALSO

➤ *For instructions on how to use Office-standard techniques to add hyperlinks, see page 64*

Adding a Hyperlink to a Slide

1. In Normal or Slide view, select the text or object you want to serve as the hyperlink.
2. Pull down the **Slide Show** menu and select **Action Settings**. The Action Settings dialog box appears, as shown in Figure 27.2.
3. Choose the **Mouse Click** tab if you want the link to work when clicked; choose the **Mouse Over** tab if you want the hyperlink to fire when the user passes the mouse over the link.

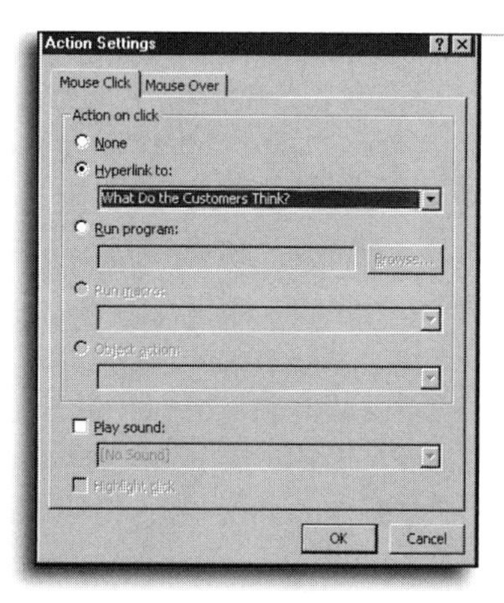

FIGURE 27.2
Use this dialog box, found only in PowerPoint, to create custom hyperlinks. This link jumps to a specific slide.

4. Pick an action from the list of available options. To jump to a specific slide, for example, choose **Hyperlink to**, and then select **Slide** from the drop-down list and pick the slide number or title you want the hyperlink to jump to.
5. Click **OK** to save the hyperlink and return to the slide.

To edit or remove a hyperlink, click to select the text or object that contains the link, and then pull down the **Slide Show** menu and choose **Action Settings**. Select another option, or click **None** to remove the hyperlink.

Why use Mouse Over?

Most of the time, you'll choose the Mouse Click option for hyperlinks. Under rare circumstances, the Mouse Over option is useful. For example, you could attach small sound files to two or more links on a page so that the person viewing the show could hear a message by pointing. Or you could set up three slides, each containing an identical set of three hyperlinks on the left and different explanatory text on the right. When the person viewing the show passes the mouse over a link, the slide would change, but it would appear as though the text had popped up.

Hyperlinks work only in a show

When you're editing slides, don't be surprised to find that your hyperlinks don't work. That's perfectly normal. Run the slide show to test the links.

Use masters for foolproof buttons

If you inadvertently leave Action Buttons off even a single slide, your audience won't be able to move to the next slide. To place Action Buttons on every slide in a presentation, add them to the Slide Master. Pull down the **View** menu, choose **Master**, and then click **Slide Master**.

Using Action Buttons

When you set up a presentation to run on its own, PowerPoint disables all the normal mouse and keyboard techniques you use to move from slide to slide. If you want your audience to control the pace at which they move through the presentation, add *Action Buttons* that let the viewer click to move to the next (or previous) slide, jump to the start or end of the presentation, or perform any of several other custom actions.

Action Buttons do the same work as hyperlinks, with two significant advantages: First, all the functions of Action Buttons are predefined, so you don't need to do any extra work. And second, Action Buttons use standard shapes that resemble the controls on a VCR, making them especially easy for your audience to understand (and probably easier to use than the typical VCR).

Adding Action Buttons to a Slide Show

1. Open the presentation and select the slide or master to which you want to add Action Buttons.

SEE ALSO

➤ *For details on how to work with masters, see page 499*

2. Pull down the **Slide Show** menu and choose **Action Buttons** to display the palette of buttons shown in Figure 27.3.

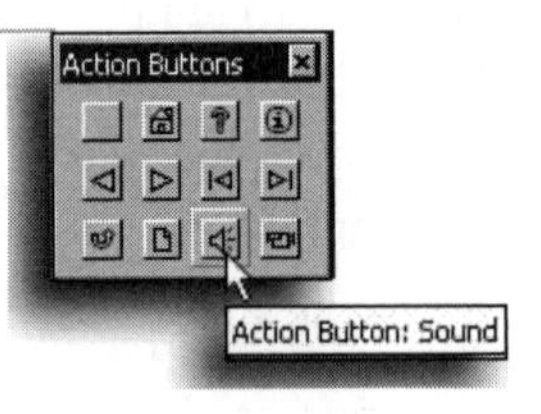

FIGURE 27.3

Action buttons enable the viewer to control the pace of the presentation.

3. Click the Action Button you want to add, and then draw the shape on your slide in the position where you want it to appear.

Action Buttons = AutoShapes

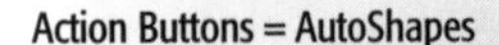

If you know how to use AutoShapes, you have a head start in working with Action Buttons. In fact, if you display the Drawing toolbar in PowerPoint and click the **AutoShapes** menu, you'll see the same set of shapes.

4. The Action Settings dialog box opens, allowing you to adjust the options for the button you just added. If you chose the Back, Forward, Home, Return, Beginning, or End buttons, click **OK**.
5. Repeat steps 2–4 to add more buttons to the slide.

Most of the Action Buttons include predefined actions that fire when the user clicks the button. You can insert a pair of buttons on the Slide Master to go to the next or previous slide. If you don't want your audience to be able to go backward, just add a Next Slide Action Button in one corner.

Do-it-yourself actions

Several of the choices on the Action Buttons menu don't actually do anything. If you click the **Help** button (with a question mark icon) or the **Information** button (with a bold I as its icon) PowerPoint pops up the Action Settings dialog box, but you have to do the work. If you've set up a slide with extra information or helpful details, click **Hyperlink to**, choose **Slide** from the drop-down list, and pick the slide you want to display.

Setting Timings for Each Slide

Sometimes you want to hide the computer, keyboard, and mouse, place the monitor in a prominent location, and let a slide show run completely unattended. If you've created a presentation for use at a trade show, for example, you might want to have it run nonstop. That way, anyone who walks up to the counter can stop and watch for as long as you can hold their attention.

SEE ALSO

➤ *For more information about how to add timings to a presentation, see page 517*

If you've created *timings* by adding a narration or using PowerPoint's rehearsal features, you can use them as part of an unattended slide show. You can also add timings manually to each slide. For a slide show in a lobby or at a trade show, you might want each slide to appear for 15–20 seconds—long enough to let passers-by read the information, but not so long that they'll become bored.

Setting Automatic Timings for a Slide Show

1. Open the presentation you want to automate and switch to Slide Sorter view.
2. Pull down the **Slide Show** menu and choose **Slide Transition**. The Slide Transition dialog box appears (see Figure 27.4).

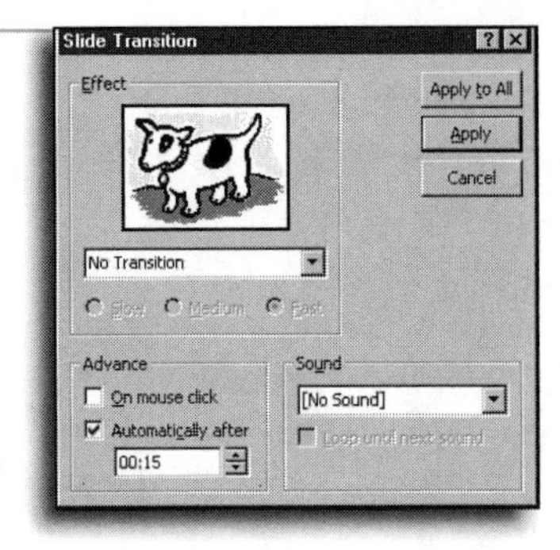

FIGURE 27.4

To switch slides automatically in an unattended presentation, set a value in the **Advance** box. In this case, the slide is visible for exactly 15 seconds.

Set one timing for all, then adjust

When creating automatic timings for an unattended presentation, always start by applying a timing to all slides, and then adjust individual slides as needed. This practice ensures that you don't inadvertently skip a slide and cause the presentation to stop unexpectedly.

3. In the **Advance** box, choose the **Automatically after** option and enter the time, in minutes and seconds, that you want to use for most slides in your presentation—00:15 is 15 seconds, for example.
4. Click **Apply to All** to add the selected timing to every slide in the presentation.
5. To adjust timings for individual slides, select one or more slides, and then pull down the **Slide Show** menu, choose **Slide Transition**, and repeat step 3. This time, however, click the **Apply** button to set the timings only for the selected slide or slides.
6. Run the slide show to ensure that it works as expected. Make any necessary adjustments in timing, and then save your changes.

Have the CD handy

The typical Office 2000 Setup options do not install the Pack and Go Wizard. The first time you select this menu option, the Windows Installer runs and offers to install the feature for you. Be sure you have the CD handy, so you can complete the installation.

Packaging a Presentation for Use on Another Computer

The simplest way to take a presentation on the road is to carry it on a portable computer. That way, you can test it before you leave, and when you arrive at your destination all you need is an external monitor to begin the show. But what if that option isn't available? In that case, use PowerPoint's Pack and Go Wizard to assemble all the pieces of your presentation onto a floppy disk. When you package a presentation using this wizard, it includes the fonts you specified, as well as linked graphics and sound files.

It also includes a PowerPoint viewer, so you can easily deliver a presentation on a computer without worrying about whether PowerPoint is installed.

Packaging a Presentation

1. Open the presentation you want to pack, and run through it to make sure all slides display properly, including graphics and multimedia files.
2. Pull down the **File** menu, choose **Pack and Go**, and begin following the wizard's prompts:
   - Select which presentation you want to pack; the default is the current presentation.
   - Choose the destination drive; the default is A:\, but you can specify any location, including a folder on your hard drive or a Zip disk.
   - Check the **Embed TrueType fonts** option if your presentation uses any fonts other than those included with Windows. Leave the **Include linked files** box checked unless you're certain you don't want to bring along external graphics or sound files.
   - Specify whether you want to include the *PowerPoint Viewer*. This option adds more than 2.5MB to the total size of your packed presentation.
3. Click **Finish** to begin compressing the presentation and transferring it to the destination you specified. If your presentation is too large to fit on a single floppy disk, the wizard breaks it into multiple files and asks you to insert as many disks as are needed.

PowerPoint copies two files to the floppy disk or other location you specified—one is a setup file called Pngsetup.exe; the other is the compressed file containing your presentation, with the extension *.ppz. If you chose to include the PowerPoint Viewer, it's in the compressed file along with the presentation.

Don't skip the wizard

Even if you're certain a computer with PowerPoint will be at your destination, I suggest you use the Pack and Go Wizard when you want to transport a complex presentation. Yes, you can copy the presentation file to a disk or send it via email, but you run the risk of ruining your presentation by leaving crucial support files, including graphics, at home. The wizard guarantees that you'll pick up every detail.

Try email instead of a floppy disk

If you're planning to deliver your presentation at a remote destination, skip the floppy disk option. Instead, consider saving the packed presentation to a location on your hard disk, and then send it to an associate at the remote location via email. Using this option gives your coworker a chance to test the packed file on the computer you'll use for the presentation, and you don't have to remember to carry a stack of floppy disks with you.

No Viewer? Don't panic...

If you skip the option to include the Viewer files and then discover that the presentation machine doesn't include a copy of PowerPoint, don't panic. Connect to the Internet and download a copy of the PowerPoint Viewer from Microsoft's Web site, `http://officeupdate.microsoft.com`.

Running a Packed Presentation

1. On the destination computer, insert the floppy disk containing the presentation files; if you sent the files using another method, copy them to a folder on the hard disk.
2. Click the **Start** button, choose **Run**, and enter the command `A:\Pngsetup`. (If the files are in a different location, substitute that location for the drive letter in this command.)
3. In the Pack and Go Setup dialog box, enter the destination where you want to store the uncompressed presentation files, and then click **OK**.
4. PowerPoint unpacks the files and asks you if you want to run the presentation. Click **Yes** to begin running the presentation immediately. (If the machine on which you're installing the slide show does not have a working copy of PowerPoint, skip ahead to the next section to install the PowerPoint Viewer.)
5. To run the presentation again, find its file icon in the location you specified in step 3. Right-click and pick **Show** from the shortcut menu.

Don't choose C:

Unfortunately, the default location when you unpack a presentation is C:\, which is a terrible place to copy files. That's especially true if you chose to include the PowerPoint Viewer, which consists of 17 files in all. I recommend you create a folder such as C:\PNG first, and then uncompress the files to that location. After that process completes, you can move the folder to any location you want.

To run a slide show from the PowerPoint Viewer, double-click **the PowerPoint Viewer** icon (on most machines, Pptview is the name of the program icon). Figure 27.5 shows the resulting dialog box. Click the **Options** button and check boxes in the **Presentation Settings** section if you want to run the presentation continuously—if you're showing it unattended at a trade show booth, for example. You can also use automatic timings and choose whether you want to play back a narration. Select the presentation you want to run from the file list above, and then click **Show**.

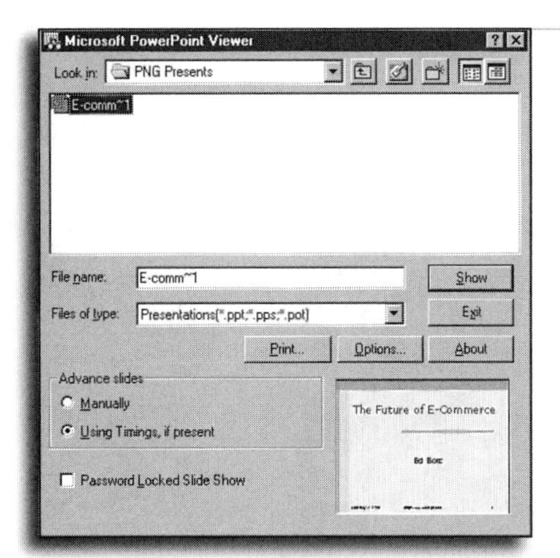

FIGURE 27.5

Use the PowerPoint Viewer to run presentations you transfer with the Pack and Go Wizard.

Creating Presentations for the Web

So far, I've been talking exclusively about saving and showing presentations using PowerPoint's native format. But you can deliver a show to anyone anywhere—even an audience of millions. All you have to do is save your slides as a Web page.

Using this option is an incredibly easy way to share a presentation with other people. You can send the resulting presentation as an email message, which the recipient can then open in any browser. Or you can post your show to a Web site and let anyone with access to that site see your slides in an easy-to-navigate format.

After you've finished creating and editing all the details of your presentation, pull down the **File** menu and choose **Save as Web Page**. PowerPoint displays a specially modified version of its Save As dialog box. If you click the **Save** button, your presentation will look like the one shown in Figure 27.6 when you open it in a browser window.

SEE ALSO

➤ *For details on how to save and manage Web pages in Office, see page 57*

Use HTML for portable presentations

If you find the Pack and Go Wizard unbearably complicated, consider saving your presentation as a Web page instead. If you set options carefully, the results are almost indistinguishable from those you get when you view the show using PowerPoint, and all you need is a browser to deliver your message.

Test in different browsers

Anytime you put together a Web-based slide show, be sure to try it out in your browser first. If you expect that other people who view the show will use different browsers, such as Netscape Navigator, ask them to check it out as well. It's easier to fix mistakes if you find them before you've posted a lengthy presentation to the Internet.

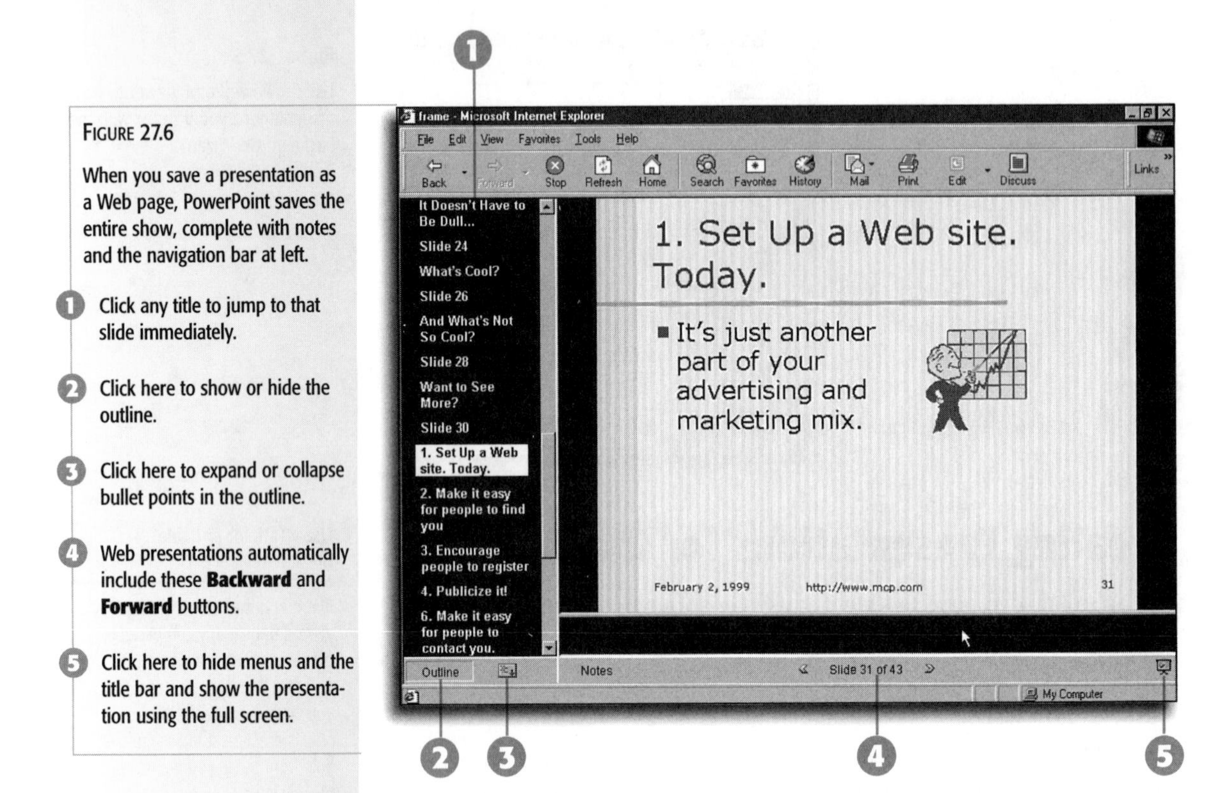

FIGURE 27.6

When you save a presentation as a Web page, PowerPoint saves the entire show, complete with notes and the navigation bar at left.

1. Click any title to jump to that slide immediately.
2. Click here to show or hide the outline.
3. Click here to expand or collapse bullet points in the outline.
4. Web presentations automatically include these **Backward** and **Forward** buttons.
5. Click here to hide menus and the title bar and show the presentation using the full screen.

To set custom Web viewing options, click **Publish**, and adjust settings in the Publish as Web Page dialog box, shown in Figure 27.7. For example, if you're planning to put a presentation on a Web site where many users of Netscape Navigator will want to see it, choose the **All browsers listed above** option in the **Browser support** box.

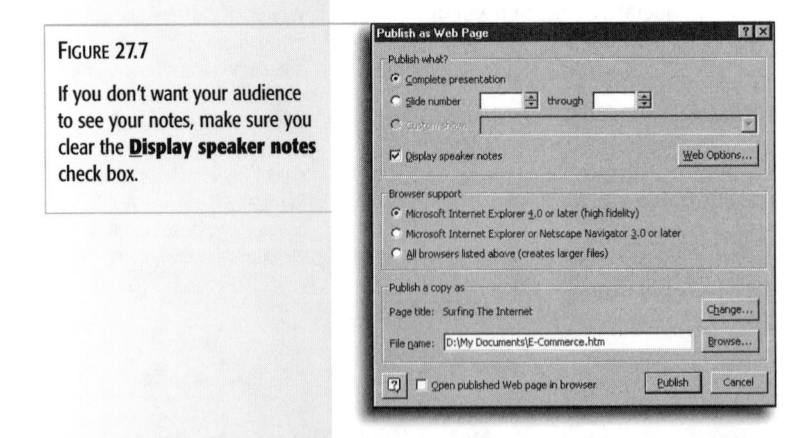

FIGURE 27.7

If you don't want your audience to see your notes, make sure you clear the **Display speaker notes** check box.

Click the **Web Options** button to set still more options for your presentation, including where you want to store supporting files and whether you want to add navigation controls. The options you set here become the default for future Web-based presentations.

PART

V

Using Outlook 2000

CHAPTER

28

Outlook Basics

Learn how to configure Outlook properly

Understand your email options

See your schedule at a glance on the Outlook Today page

Use the Outlook Bar to move among folders

Create and manage Outlook items

Create new Outlook items automatically

Keep your Outlook file from growing too large

Find information when you need it

Getting Started with Outlook

By default, Office 2000 automatically installs Outlook, but it doesn't finish the job. Why? Because three different sets of program files actually make up Outlook 2000, and you have to tell Outlook which configuration you want to use before it installs the right set of files. In essence, Outlook can be any of three different programs, and you have to pick one before you can get started. Outlook offers three configurations: **Internet Only**, **Corporate or Workgroup**, or **No E-mail**. Making the proper choice here is a crucial decision.

If you upgraded over a previous version, Outlook offers to make this choice for you. The first time you start Outlook 2000, if the program finds details of a previous configuration of Outlook 97 or Outlook 98, you see a dialog box asking you whether you want to use the same configuration as the previously installed version.

- If you click **Yes**, Outlook selects a configuration type for you and automatically picks up your previous settings, such as the mail server you use and your username and password. You see a series of dialog boxes that let you confirm (and, if necessary, change) each of these settings.
- If you click **No**, Outlook searches for other email programs that you might be using. If you currently use Outlook Express, Eudora, or Netscape Mail, and you want to switch to Outlook 2000, pick the program name from the dialog box you see here. Outlook then configures itself to use Internet Mail Only mode and imports the settings from the program you selected.

If Outlook does not find a previous version, you see the dialog box shown in Figure 28.1. Which of these three options should you choose? Although the basic Outlook interface looks the same regardless of which choice you make, many of your setup options and some key features are dramatically different.

Fax users, look carefully

If your previous Outlook configuration included the Microsoft Fax program, Outlook 2000 may set up in Corporate/Workgroup mode. If you don't use this fax program anymore, and your only email account is with an Internet service provider, click **No** when asked whether you want to upgrade; then choose the **Internet Mail Only** option.

Choose carefully

In general, Outlook does a good job of configuring your system automatically, but it's not foolproof. If you make the wrong configuration decision, you might discover that some email features on your corporate network aren't available, or that some third-party programs don't work the way they used to. If that's the case, you can easily change the configuration type; see the instructions later in this section.

Sorry, no AOL support

AOL users can't read or compose mail using Outlook 2000—at least, not using version 4.0 or earlier of the AOL software. It's possible that AOL will make this capability available sometime in the future. Check `http://www.aol.com` for more details.

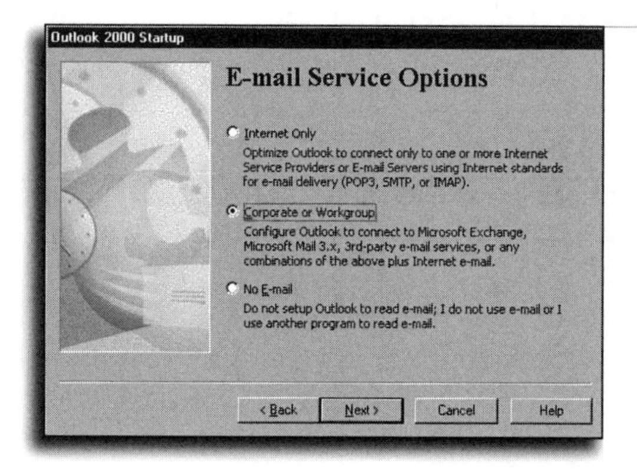

FIGURE 28.1
Outlook actually behaves like three separate programs; the choice you make here determines what types of email you can send and receive.

- Choose **Internet Only** if your only email account is with an Internet service provider (including The Microsoft Network or CompuServe) that uses standard *SMTP* servers.
- Choose the **Corporate or Workgroup** option if you get your email from a corporate network that uses *Microsoft Exchange Server*, Microsoft Mail, or another mail program that uses *MAPI drivers*. This mode also allows you to connect to an Internet-standard SMTP mail server, although you may encounter setup hassles and performance problems.
- Choose **No E-mail** if you want to continue using your previous mail program (such as Eudora, Netscape Mail, or Lotus Notes) or if you do not want to send or receive email at all.

SEE ALSO

➤ *For step-by-step instructions on how to set up your Internet mail account, see page 572*

How do you know which configuration type you're currently using? Pull down the **Help** menu and choose **About Microsoft Outlook**; then look at the line just below the Outlook version number.

Don't panic if you make the wrong configuration choice! You can switch between IMO and CD modes with just a few mouse clicks. Pull down the **Tools** menu and choose **Options**. If you're currently using Corporate/Workgroup mode, click the **Mail Services** tab; from Internet Mail Only mode, click the **Mail Delivery** tab. Then click the **Reconfigure Mail Support**

Acronym alert! IMO and CW

If you need help with Outlook, memorize these acronyms: IMO, for Internet Mail Only mode; and CW, for Corporate/Workgroup mode. As I mentioned at the beginning of this chapter, the procedures for working with Outlook are different depending on the mode you select. If you search for help on Microsoft's Web site, the IMO and CW acronyms will help you tell which set of instructions is right for your Outlook setup.

button. Outlook swaps a few files and then lets you run through the initial setup all over again and choose another mode.

Using and Customizing the Outlook Interface

Outlook 97, 98, 2000?

Many users criticized Microsoft for releasing Outlook 97, which was slow, difficult to set up, and not especially good for Internet mail users. In early 1998, Microsoft released a significant upgrade called Outlook 98. If you installed this upgrade, you've already seen the Outlook Today page and several other enhancements in Outlook 2000. If you upgraded to Outlook 2000 from Outlook 97, however, many of these improvements will be welcome.

If you're willing to trust the details of your life to software, Outlook can help you keep your days organized just as effectively as any paper-based system. For some people, in fact, Outlook will be the Office program they use most often. Regardless of which configuration you choose, the basic Outlook interface is the same. Each piece of information is stored in an *Outlook item*: electronic mail messages, contact records, appointments in your personal calendar, and so on. Built-in folders organize related items into views so that you can sort, find, and print the information you're looking for.

When you start Outlook and click the top icon on the *Outlook Bar* at the left, you see a window like the one shown in Figure 28.2. The Outlook Bar is made up of a stack of seven icons that let you quickly switch among folders displaying different types of information. To the right is the *Outlook Today* page, which summarizes current tasks, appointments, and messages.

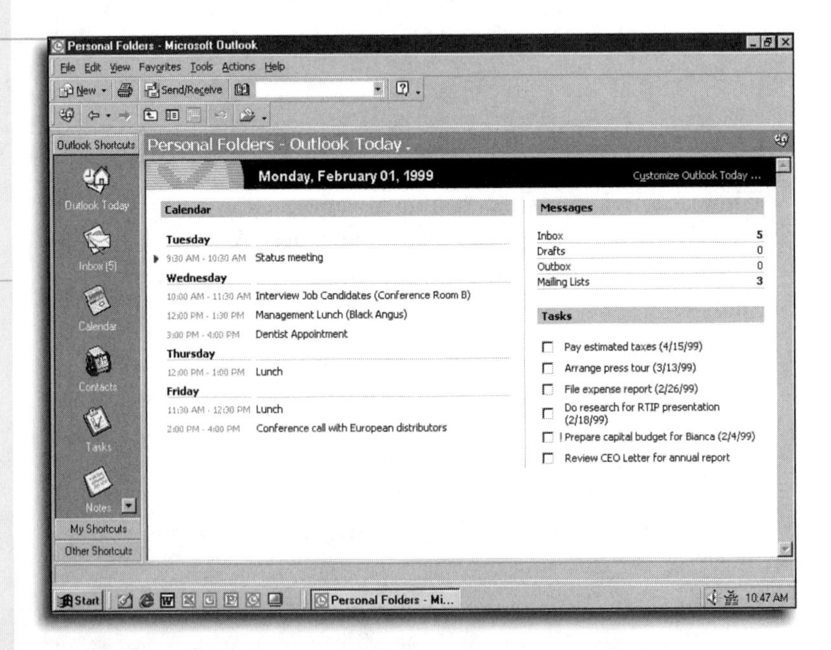

FIGURE 28.2

Click any icon in the Outlook Bar (left) to display that folder's contents. The Web-style Outlook Today page gives you a quick overview of upcoming appointments and tasks.

Customizing the Outlook Today Page

Click the Outlook Today icon at the top of the Outlook Bar to see your schedule at a glance. Other icons in the Outlook Bar display a single folder's contents when clicked; Outlook Today is different because it gathers items from several folders and organizes them into a compact page. By default, this view shows upcoming appointments, current tasks, and unread messages, as in Figure 28.2.

The Outlook Today page includes three basic types of items: appointments, tasks, and a counter that tells you how many new messages you've received. To fine-tune the display to your preferences, click the **Outlook Today** icon in the Outlook Bar; then click the **Customize Outlook Today** link on the page itself (the exact location of this link varies, depending on the style you've selected). Figure 28.3 shows some of the options available to you.

Start with Outlook Today

If you like Outlook Today's "day at a glance" style, make it your default view. Click the **Customize Outlook Today** option on the Outlook Today page; then check the box that reads **When starting, go directly to Outlook Today**.

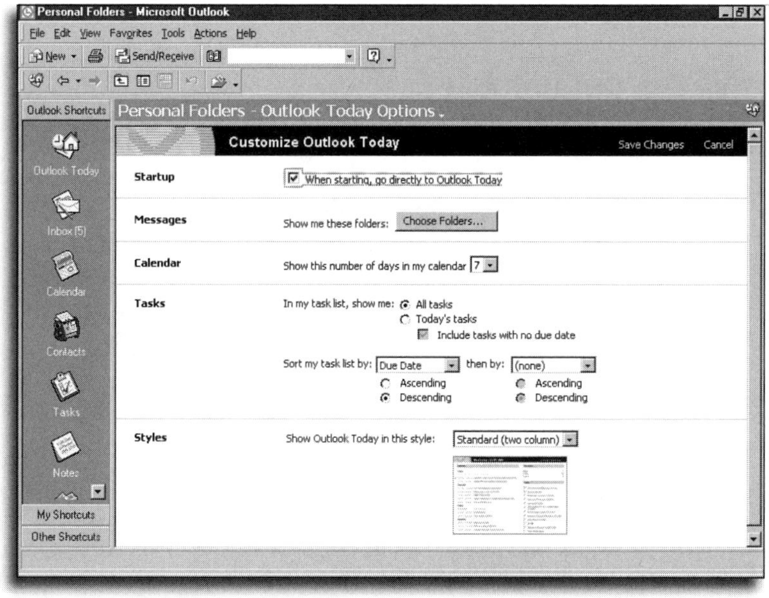

FIGURE 28.3

Customize the Outlook Today page to see a different view of upcoming appointments, tasks, and unread email.

- By default, Outlook Today shows how many new messages are in the Inbox, Outbox, and Drafts folders. Click the **Choose Folders** button in the **Messages** section to keep track of other folders as well. I use this option for several additional folders because I've defined rules that automatically move new messages into alternate folders as they arrive, based on who they're from.
- In the **Calendar** section, you can choose how many days' worth of appointments, meetings, and events you want to see at a time. If your calendar is full and you check it every day, choose **1** to see only today's items; pick a number up to 7 if you want Outlook Today to warn you of appointments up to a week in advance.
- Use the **Tasks** section to select whether you want to see all tasks or only those due today; you can also define how you want to sort your Tasks list.

SEE ALSO

➤ *To learn how to set up rules that process incoming mail automatically, see page 596*

Using the Outlook Bar

The Outlook Bar is unlike other Office toolbars. For starters, it's vertical, running from top to bottom along the left edge of the Outlook window. The icons are also much bigger than those you see on other toolbars. Each icon opens one of Outlook's built-in folders; Table 28.1 describes what you find when you click each one.

The Outlook Bar is fully customizable

Outlook Bar icons are simply shortcuts, and as with any Windows object, you can right-click to see a full range of options available. Rename a shortcut, delete its icon, or drag and drop icons to rearrange them in the Outlook Bar. Want to see more icons in the same space? Right-click in any empty space in the Outlook Bar and choose **Small Icons** to show more than twice as many icons in the same space.

TABLE 28.1 Outlook's Standard Folders

Outlook Bar Icon	What It Does
Outlook Today	Provides a Web-style overview of your current appointments, tasks, and messages; by default, it shows how many unread messages are in your Inbox and lists items due within the next five days.
Inbox	Exchanges electronic mail with other people, using a corporate email system or accounts with an Internet service provider.

Outlook Bar Icon	What It Does
Calendar	Keeps track of scheduled appointments and events, including recurring items such as weekly meetings and your wedding anniversary.
Contacts	Stores names, addresses, phone numbers, email addresses, and other details about people and companies.
Tasks	Basically provides a to-do list; arrange your commitments by category and by priority, and delegate the tasks you can't handle to someone else who can.
Notes	Acts like an electronic version of the sticky yellow squares that have taken over offices. (I always have at least three pasted along the edge of my monitor; now they can have company right on the display.)
Deleted Items	Stores items you delete from any Outlook folder; by default, you can undelete items if you discover you made a mistake in tossing them. In some cases, Outlook trashes the contents of the Deleted Items folder whenever you close Outlook. To enable or disable this option, click the **Tools** menu and select **Options**. Click the Other tab and then add or remove the check mark from the **Empty the Deleted Items folder upon exiting** option.

Actually, three different groups of shortcuts are included on the default Outlook Bar. The Outlook Shortcuts group includes shortcuts for the standard folders—one for each type of Outlook item. The group labeled My Shortcuts includes all mail folders except the Inbox (Drafts, Sent Items, and Outbox); when you create a new folder, Outlook asks whether you want to create a shortcut here. The last group, Other Shortcuts, lets you browse files on your hard drive, including Internet shortcuts in your Favorites folder, much like you can do with the Windows Explorer; files appear directly in the Outlook window, where you can manage them just as you would in an Explorer window.

To switch to a different Outlook Bar, click its title. The title slides to the top of the bar, displaying all the icons stored there.

What about the Journal?

If you upgrade over Outlook 97 or 98, your Outlook Bar may include a Journal icon as well. Although this folder still exists in Outlook 2000, it's essentially useless except in rare circumstances. See Chapter 30, "Managing Personal Information with Outlook," for details on the preferred way to track things you do using Outlook.

Open more than one Outlook window

Want to keep your email messages in one window, your Calendar in another, and your Contacts list in still another? You can open each Outlook folder in a new window, if you prefer. To do so, right-click its icon in the Outlook Bar and choose **Open in New Window**. The second and subsequent windows don't include the Outlook Bar.

Add new items and groups

You're not limited to the default icons and groups on the Outlook Bar. To add a new item, right-click any empty space in the Outlook Bar and choose **Outlook Bar Shortcut**; then pick the folder you want to add. To create a new group, right-click and choose **Add New Group**. You can create up to 12 groups on the Outlook Bar.

As you'll see shortly, icons on the Outlook Bar serve one other important function. You can drag any item out of the main Outlook window and drop it onto one of the Outlook Bar icons to create a brand-new item, using the original item as a starting point.

Navigation shortcuts

After you've clicked several different Outlook Bar icons, notice that the **Previous Folder** and **Next Folder** buttons change color. This change is your signal that you can switch between views more quickly than using the Outlook Bar shortcuts. If you've used the equivalents to these buttons on the Internet Explorer toolbar, you already know exactly how they work. Click the drop-down arrows to the right of either button to see a list of folders to which you can switch immediately.

Using the Folder List

If you've organized your Outlook items into many folders, you may find working with Outlook's Explorer-style *Folder List* easier than working with the Outlook Bar. Click the **Folder List** button on the Advanced toolbar, or pull down the **View** menu and choose **Folder List** to open the complete list in its own pane, as shown in Figure 28.4.

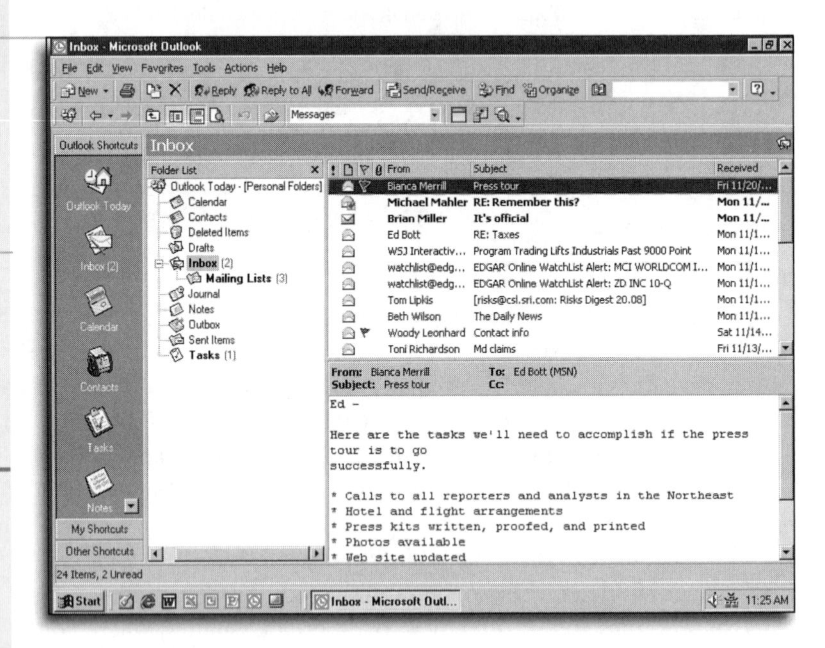

FIGURE 28.4

Use this Folder List along with the Outlook Bar or hide the Outlook Bar completely. Drag-and-drop operations work the same in either place.

Open the Folder List for temporary use

To display the Folder List quickly without locking it into place, click the folder name just above the contents window. As the arrow to the right of the folder name suggests, this action displays the drop-down version of the list. Click the pushpin icon to lock the pane in place, or click anywhere outside the pane to hide it after switching folders or dropping an item on a folder.

If you prefer to use only the Folder List, you can hide the Outlook Bar by clearing the check mark from its entry on the **View** menu. Click **x** to close the Folder List.

Viewing Personal Information in Outlook

Although each Outlook item and folder gets its own icon, Outlook doesn't actually store these items separately. Instead, it gathers items into larger files and stores them there. In essence, each of these larger files functions as a database holding many types of Outlook items. The exact format and location of these files depends on how you've configured Outlook: It might be a file on your local hard drive, for example, or it could be a set of folders on a Microsoft Exchange Server.

- If you've configured your system using Internet Mail Only (IMO) mode, your data is stored in a *Personal Folders file* with the extension .pst. If you set up Outlook 2000 in Internet Mail Only mode without upgrading over a previous version, your data is in a file called Outlook.pst. If you upgraded over Outlook 97 or Windows Messaging, your data may be in a file called Mailbox.pst or Exchange.pst. In this configuration, your Personal Folders file is the place where all new email messages are delivered, and it's also the place where items in other folders (Calendar, Contacts, and so on) are located.
- If your company uses a Microsoft Exchange Server, you can create one (and only one) *Offline Store file* and save it on your computer. This file type, which uses the extension .ost, closely resembles a Personal Folders file. This type of configuration is most appropriate if you use a notebook computer or you connect to your office network from home through a dial-up connection. Unlike an Internet configuration, where you actually move mail from the server to your computer, in this configuration all your mail stays on the server, and you download copies of messages to your computer by choosing **Synchronize** from the **File** menu. Most of the time, you work with the data in the Offline Store file, and you connect to the server only when you want to pick up new mail or send messages you composed offline.

Where is your data stored?

Tracking down the file in which your primary Outlook data is stored is a job that would challenge Sherlock Holmes. The exact location depends on whether you've upgraded over Outlook 97 or Outlook 98, your Windows version, and whether you've enabled user profiles on your system. To see the location of your default Personal Folders file, right-click the **Outlook Today** shortcut in the Outlook Bar, select the **Properties** command, click the **Advanced** button, and then look in the box labeled **Path**.

Opening a new Personal Folders file

You can store additional information in other Personal Folders files. This technique can be useful for managing the size of your Outlook file. To create a new Personal Folders file, pull down the **File** menu, choose **New**, and select the **Personal Folders File (.pst)** option from the bottom of the cascading menu. To open a Personal Folders file, pull down Outlook's **File** menu and select **Open**. Use the Folder List (described earlier in this chapter) to move between multiple Personal Folders files.

Back it up!

If you store your Outlook data in a Personal Folders file, don't take it for granted; if anything happens to this file, you lose your email messages and every name and address in your Contacts Folder. Make a backup copy of this important file and store it in a safe place. You must shut down Outlook before you can copy a Personal Folders file, or export your data to another Personal Folders file on a hard drive or a removable storage device such as a Zip drive.

- If you use Outlook at work to connect to a Microsoft Exchange Server, you can skip all local storage and simply open items directly from Mailbox folders on the server. If you lose the network connection, you lose all access to your email messages and items in other folders (Calendar and Contacts, for example). For that reason, you would be wise to keep a backup copy of your Outlook data in an Offline Store file.

Using Views to Display, Sort, and Filter Items

When you click an Outlook Bar icon, the data in that folder shows up in the main window to the right, arranged in the same *view* you used the last time you opened that folder. For example, the default Calendar view shows today's appointments, meetings, and events alongside a list of tasks; if you click the Contacts icon, names and phone numbers in that folder appear as small address cards. You can arrange your data using a different built-in view—with all the names in your Contacts Folder in a table, for example, with one record per row—or create a custom view of your own.

To change the way data appears in the current folder, click the **Organize** button and choose the option labeled **Using Views**. Figure 28.5 shows the choices available for the Calendar folder.

Outlook offers an extensive choice of built-in views for each folder. Your exact choices vary, depending on which folder is open, but in general a view starts with one of the following arrangements:

Table The default view for the Tasks Folder and mail folders like the Inbox, but you can use it with any folder. Your data lines up in neat rows and columns, like an Excel worksheet.

Card Most useful for the Contacts Folder, this view type displays names in bold, with selected details underneath.

Day/Week/Month These options determine how much of your Calendar folder you can see at once;

	the more days you select, the less detail you see for each entry.
Icon	Large or small icons, similar to those in an Explorer window. This is the default for the Notes folder.
Timeline	A bar along the top of the window displays days or hours; tiny icons underneath show all the items in the folder according to when they were created or received.

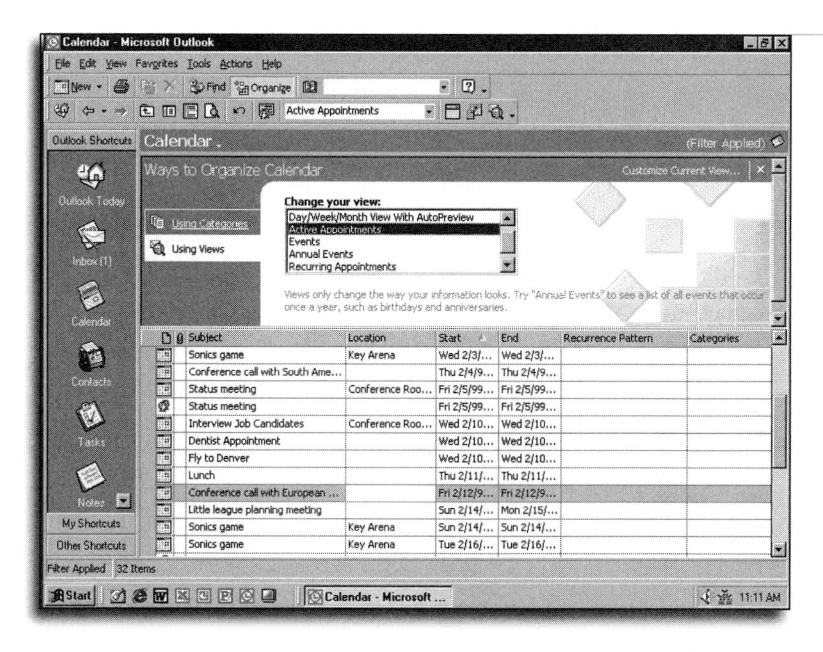

FIGURE 28.5

Click the **Organize** button and pick a new view of your data. This selection, for example, shows active appointments in a table view.

In addition to the basic arrangement, views can include these special characteristics:

- **Filters** show a subset of the items in the folder, based on defined criteria. The Overdue Tasks view in the Tasks Folder, for example, displays only those tasks that you should have completed by now, and the Annual Events view of the Calendar folder shows all the birthdays and anniversaries you've defined.
- **Sorting** arranges your data in a specific order—by due date, for example, or by last name.

Click a heading to sort

You can sort any view, any time, using one of two techniques. In table views, click the heading to sort by that field; click again to sort in reverse order. In all other views, open the **View** menu, choose **Current View**, and then select **Customize Current View**. Click the **Sort** button and choose up to three fields for sorting.

AutoPreview on-the-fly

You don't need to customize a view to show or hide the quick AutoPreview summaries. Just make sure the Advanced toolbar is visible; to do so, right-click any visible toolbar or the main menu bar and then choose **Advanced** from the list of toolbars. Click the **AutoPreview** button to hide and show this information in any mail folder, the Contacts Folder, or the Tasks Folder.

- **Grouping** lets you arrange the contents of a folder by sorting on any of several different fields. For example, you can group your Contacts Folder in a list by company so that you can see at a glance who works for whom.
- **AutoPreview** is one of the most useful viewing options. In your Inbox Folder, it shows the first three lines of each message so that you can tell at a glance what's inside without having to open and read each message. You can also use it to see notes about each person in your Contacts Folder or to see the beginning of an appointment's description.

Customizing a View

If none of the built-in views offer the arrangement of data you're looking for, you can customize the current view or create a completely new view from scratch.

To see all your customization options, pull down the **View** menu, choose **Current View**, and then select **Customize Current View**. The View Summary dialog box appears, as shown in Figure 28.6.

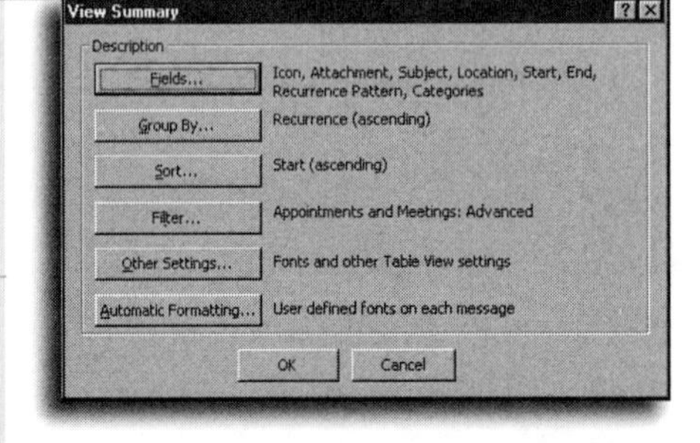

FIGURE 28.6

Use this dialog box to customize all available options for the current view. Not every option is available for every type of view.

Preview versus AutoPreview

Don't confuse AutoPreview with the Preview pane. When the Preview pane is visible, you can read an entire mail message in a window just below the message list; by contrast, the AutoPreview feature shows only the first three lines of a message, and it disappears after you've opened and read the message.

Click the **Fields** button to add fields to the current view. If many of your contacts have cellular phones, for example, you might want to add that field in the Address Cards view of the Contacts Folder rather than switch to Detailed Address Cards view, which shows too much information. Use the Show Fields dialog box, shown in Figure 28.7, to add, remove, or rearrange fields in the current view.

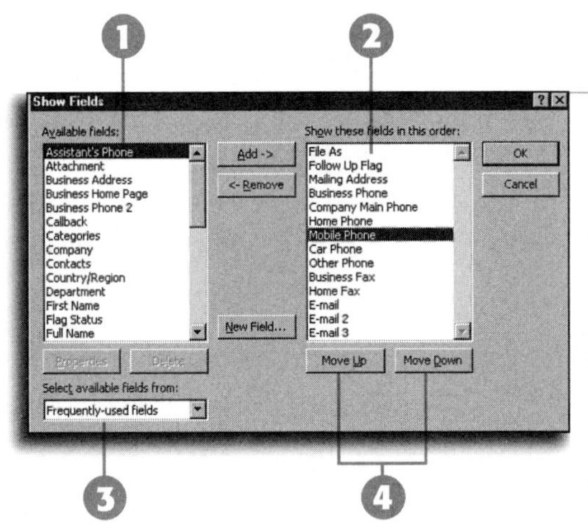

FIGURE 28.7

Use this dialog box to add or remove fields from a view.

1. Choose a field from this list and click **Add** to add it to the view.
2. Choose a field from this list and click **Remove** to eliminate it from the view.
3. By default, Outlook shows only a short list of fields; if the field you want is not visible, choose a different selection from this list.
4. Use these buttons to change the order of fields in the view.

Click the **Group By** and **Sort** buttons in the View Summary dialog box to change the order in which your data is displayed. You can group and sort by multiple fields; for example, if your Contacts Folder includes the names of many people from your own company, you might want to customize the built-in By Company view so that it sorts by Last Name and then by First Name. (You don't need to sort by company in this view because the settings in the Group By box take care of this task for you.)

Click the **Filter** button to show a subset of the items in any folder, based on criteria you define. The dialog box Outlook displays here is the same one you use for an Advanced Find.

SEE ALSO

➤ *For instructions on how to use this dialog box to create a filter, see page 566*

Use filters with new views

In general, applying a *filter* to one of Outlook's built-in views is a bad idea. Instead, use the instructions in the next section to create a new filtered view based on the existing view. For example, if your Contacts Folder includes the names of several dozen people from your own company, create a copy of the Address Cards view and then filter it so that only items with your company's name are in the view. Save the new view under a new name so that you can quickly see just the names and numbers of your coworkers.

Creating a New Custom View

One easy way to create a custom view is to make a copy of an existing view and then modify it to meet your needs. For example, I've created a custom view based on the Address Cards view that shows the name, home address, and home phone number of my friends and family.

Defining a New Custom View

1. Switch to the folder that contains the view you want to modify—in this case, the Address Cards view of the Contacts Folder.
2. Pull down the **View** menu, choose **Current View**, and then choose **Define Views**. Outlook displays the Define Views dialog box shown in Figure 28.8.

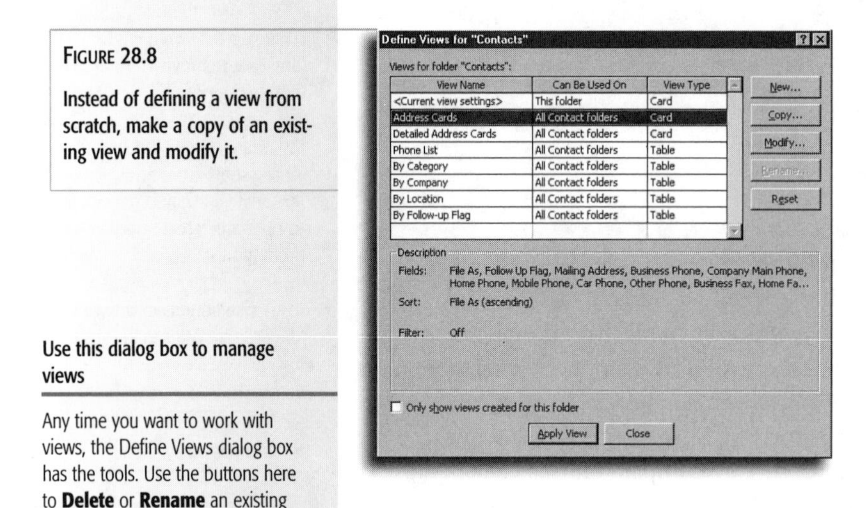

FIGURE 28.8

Instead of defining a view from scratch, make a copy of an existing view and modify it.

Use this dialog box to manage views

Any time you want to work with views, the Define Views dialog box has the tools. Use the buttons here to **Delete** or **Rename** an existing view, for example. Click **Modify** to adjust any settings for the selected view or click **New** to start from scratch.

3. Click the **Copy** button to display the Copy View dialog box shown in Figure 28.9. Give the view a name (`Friends and family` in this example) and click **OK**.

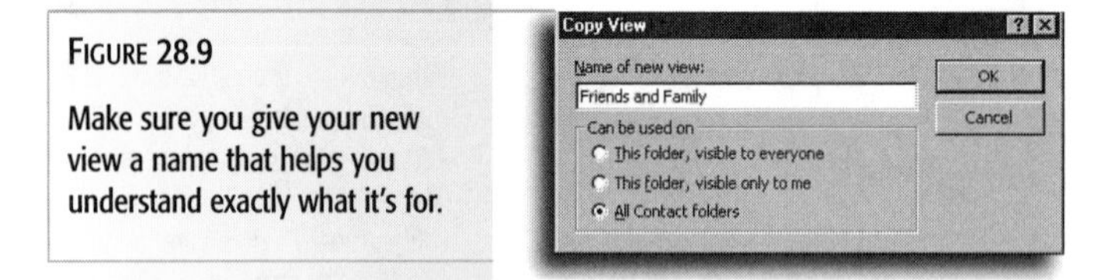

FIGURE 28.9

Make sure you give your new view a name that helps you understand exactly what it's for.

4. When the View Summary dialog box appears, you can modify any of the view's settings. In this case, click the **Filter** button and define the records you want Outlook to display. In this example, I defined a filter that includes all records where the last name is Bott or where I have assigned the Contact item to the Friends category.

5. Click the **Fields** button. Remove the **Mailing Address** field from the view and replace it with the **Home Address** field.
6. Click **OK** to save the changes; then click **Apply View** to see the filtered view showing only the records you want.

SEE ALSO

➤ *For details on how to use categories, see page 561*

Opening Items

Double-click to open any item and see or edit its full details. Outlook uses a variety of custom forms to make sure that when you open each type of item you can view, edit, and store the data it contains.

Each form includes its own customizable toolbars. Use the **Previous Item** and **Next Item** buttons to move through the contents of the current folder one record at a time in the current sort order, using any filters you may have applied. Clicking either of these buttons replaces the contents of the current form with the next or previous item, respectively. Using these buttons is an excellent way to quickly scroll through your Contacts Folder and see all details, for example.

SEE ALSO

➤ *To learn how to add or remove toolbar buttons, see page 92*

Creating and Managing Outlook Items

When you install a fresh copy of Outlook 2000, the only data you see is a brief Welcome message in your Inbox and a sample item in each folder. If you upgraded from a previous version of Outlook or from another email program, the Setup program offered to import your messages and address information, if at all possible. If you skipped this step initially, you can ask Outlook to search for and import those messages at any time by pulling down the **File** menu, choosing **Import and Export**, and selecting **Import Internet Mail and Addresses** from the Import and Export Wizard.

Want to reuse that view?

If you want the custom view type to be available for all folders containing the same types of items as the current folder, choose **All *<item type>* folders** instead of the default shown in this dialog box. In general, this is your best choice when working with mail folders.

Oops! Undoing a custom view

What do you do if you discover you accidentally customized one of Outlook's built-in views so that it doesn't work properly? Open the Define Views dialog box, select the view name, and click **Reset** to remove all customizations and restore it to its default settings. You might need to switch to another view and then switch back to reapply the view. This option is not available for custom views you define.

Import help is available

Do you have some messages and contact details stored in another program? Ask the Office Assistant to help you import the data into Outlook. Click the **Office Assistant** button on the Standard toolbar, type `Import information` into the text box, and click **Search**. Read the Help topic "About Importing Information into Outlook" for detailed instructions.

To add one item at a time into an Outlook folder, start with a blank form. Alternatively, you can drag an item out of another folder to let Outlook begin filling in information for you.

Creating a New Item from Scratch

When you click the **New** button on Outlook's Standard toolbar, it pops up a form that you fill in to create a new item in the current folder—name and address information, for example, if the Contacts Folder is open. The exact layout of the form is different, depending on the type of data appropriate for that folder.

Use the **New** button to create any kind of new item, regardless of which folder is showing in the Outlook window. When you click the drop-down arrow to the right of the **New** button, Outlook displays a list of all the items you can create (see Figure 28.10).

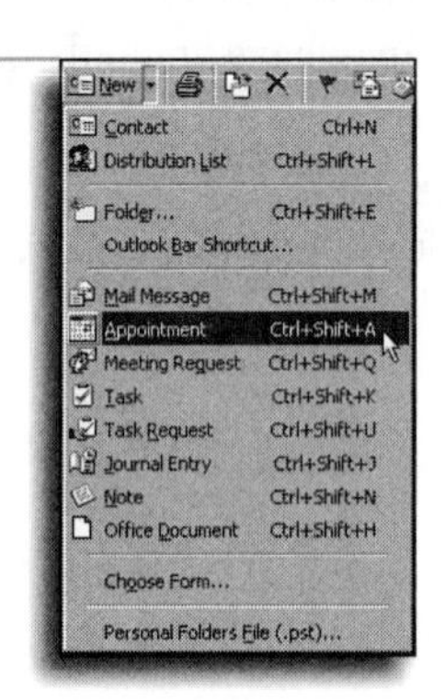

FIGURE 28.10

Pick a new item, any new item. Use this drop-down list to create a new item in any folder, regardless of which folder's contents are currently on display.

Use the keyboard shortcuts

Each of the options on the **New** menu has its own keyboard shortcut, Ctrl+Shift+*letter*. Expert typists can work faster by memorizing the most common ones. Ctrl+Shift+A, for example, creates a new Appointment item, and Ctrl+Shift+N opens a new Contact item. All the keyboard shortcuts are listed alongside the menu choices when you open the **File** menu and choose **New**, or when you click the drop-down list of New items at the left of the Standard toolbar.

Creating a New Item by Dragging and Dropping

Filling in all the blanks on an Outlook form can be a tedious process. So why not ask Outlook to do some of the work? When you drag an item from the main window and drop it on an icon in the Outlook Bar, Outlook creates a new item and automatically fills in some information from the item you dragged and dropped.

It should come as no surprise that Outlook calls this feature *AutoCreate*. You can AutoCreate nearly any type of item by dragging one type of item and dropping it onto a shortcut for another type of item. For example,

- Drag a task onto the Calendar icon to turn the task into an appointment.
- Drag an email message onto the Contacts icon to create a new Contact record automatically, using the name and email address of the person who sent the message.
- Select an address card from the Contacts Folder and drag it onto the Notes icon to create a yellow sticky note with that person's name and address; then add your own notes.

Most of the default drag-and-drop actions assume you work in an office where other people use Outlook as well. When you drag an Address Card out of the Contacts Folder and drop it on the Calendar icon, for example, Outlook assumes you want to send an invitation to a meeting. Dropping the Contact record opens a meeting invitation form; when the person you selected receives the mail message, he or she can accept or decline the invitation simply by replying to your message.

SEE ALSO

For more details on how to use Outlook to schedule meetings, see page 628

If you don't use Outlook for group scheduling but instead simply use it to read your own email and track your personal schedule, you probably want AutoCreate to work differently. For example, you might use a Contact record to find a phone number and make a call; then, after you hang up, you can drag that Contact item onto the Tasks icon to create a reminder for yourself to follow up on commitments you made during the phone call. If the new Task item includes the Contact information, you don't need to jump back to the Contacts Folder to look up the phone number.

As is true elsewhere in Office, the secret is to hold down the right mouse button as you drag any item and drop it on any Outlook Bar shortcut. When you do, you see one of five menu choices (in each of the following examples, replace the word *item* with the name of the default item type for the target folder):

Experiment with different techniques

You can't damage Outlook data by dragging and dropping, so feel free to experiment with drag-and-drop techniques to create new items automatically. (Just don't drag items into the Deleted Items Folder unless you really want to delete them.) To see the full range of AutoCreate options, select a folder and pull down the **Actions** menu. If the Contacts Folder is visible, for example, this menu includes a **New Letter to Contact** choice, which starts Word's Letter Wizard and inserts the name and address of the currently selected contact.

- **Address New *item*** adds the email address from any Contact item to a meeting request, task request, or mail message.
- **Copy Here as *item* with Text** creates a new item and inserts the message text, contact information, or other data as text in the details box.
- **Copy Here as *item* with Shortcut** creates a new item and adds a shortcut in the details box; the item you dragged and dropped remains in its original folder.
- **Copy Here as *item* with Attachment** creates a new item and attaches a copy of the item you dragged and dropped; double-click the icon in the details box to view the attachment.
- **Move Here as *item* with Attachment** creates a new item and attaches the item you dragged and dropped; this choice deletes the original item.

Which option should you choose?

When you drag one item onto another and add text or an attachment, you create a new item with absolutely no link to the original. If you're simply creating a follow-up item for next week, text is a good choice because you can read it with no extra effort. But if there's any chance the original information will change, create a shortcut instead; that way, when you open the linked item, you'll be certain to see the most up-to-date information.

In the example in Figure 28.11, I've used the right mouse button to drag Liz's record from the Contacts Folder; when I dropped it on the Tasks icon, I chose **Copy Here as Task with Text**. Outlook created a new task, filling in the contact information in the details box at the bottom of the record, and then positioned the insertion point at the beginning of the **Subject** line. I added details to the task, including a due date.

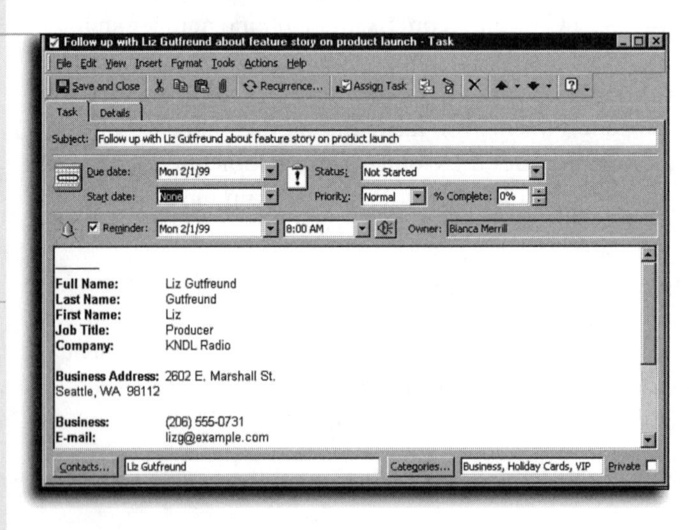

FIGURE 28.11

Outlook adds the name and address to this new item when you drag a record from the Contacts Folder and drop it on the Tasks icon. Fill in the subject and due date, as I've done here, to finish.

After you add details to the new Task item, click the **Save and Close** button to store the new item in the Tasks folder.

Moving and Copying Items

To move or copy items between Outlook folders, use some of the same techniques you would use with files in an Explorer window. Drag an item out of one folder and drop it into another to move the item; hold down the Ctrl key while dragging to make a copy. Alternatively, use shortcut keys to cut (Ctrl+X) or copy (Ctrl+C) and then paste (Ctrl+V) the item into the destination folder. Curiously, although Outlook's pull-down **Edit** menu includes all three choices, the right-click shortcut menus don't allow you to cut, copy, or paste.

Moving Items to a New Folder

1. Select the items you want to move. Hold down the **Ctrl** key and click to select multiple items.
2. Right-click the selection and choose **Move to Folder** from the shortcut menu. The dialog box shown in Figure 28.12 appears.

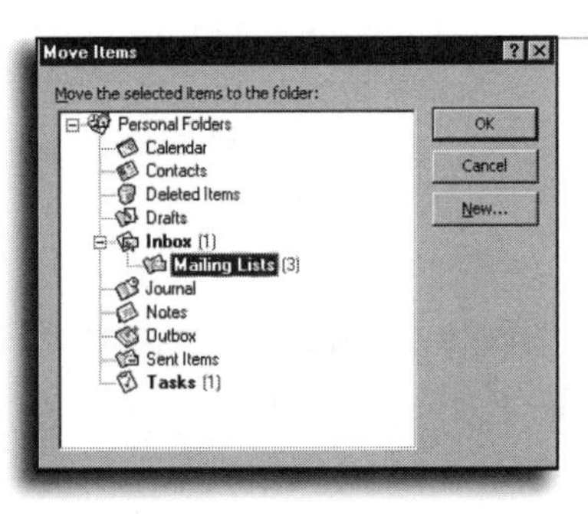

FIGURE 28.12
Use this dialog box to move items between folders.

3. Select the folder to which you want to move the selected items. Click the plus sign next to any folder to see its subfolders.
4. Click the **New** button to create a new folder in any open Personal Folders file.
5. Click **OK** to move the selected items and close the dialog box.

Choose the right destination folder

You can move items only to folders that are capable of storing that type of item. If you use the techniques detailed here to move one type of item to a folder intended for different items, Outlook tries to create a new item, just as if you had dropped the original icon on the folder's shortcut in the Outlook Bar.

Move items to the desktop

You can drag any item onto the desktop to create a copy of that item. This capability is a good way to keep a contact's personal information handy or to save a copy of a mail message where you can find it easily.

Flagging Items for Follow-Up

When you enter the details of an appointment or a task, Outlook also gives you an opportunity to set a reminder to pop up far enough in advance that you don't miss a meeting or deadline. You can create pop-up reminders for email messages and contacts, too. Instead of filling in a Reminder box, however, you attach a *follow-up flag* to the item.

You can choose the exact time you want Outlook to pop up a follow-up message. With these messages, unlike reminders, which simply display the Subject line of the item, you can specify custom text that appears in the pop-up window.

SEE ALSO

➤ *To learn how to create reminders for appointments and events, see page 613*

Flagging an Item for Follow-Up

1. Open the email message or Contact record you want to flag and click the **Flag for Follow Up** button. To flag several items at once, select them in the appropriate folder window, right-click, and choose **Flag for Follow Up** from the shortcut menu.
2. In the Flag for Follow Up dialog box (see Figure 28.13), choose a text message from the **Flag to** box. You can use any of the default messages or enter text of your own, such as `Send press release`.

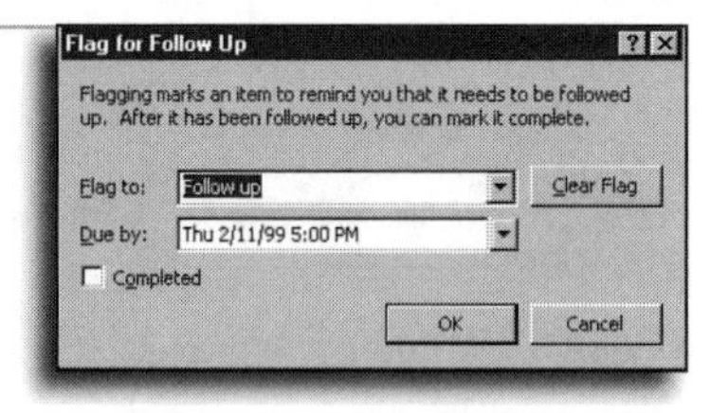

FIGURE 28.13

Choose one of these ready-made messages or enter a text message of your own.

3. Although it's not required, you can also enter a date and time in the **Due by** box. You can enter a full date and time; if you enter only a date, Outlook sets a reminder for the end of your workday—by default, 5 p.m.—on that date. If you've mastered the AutoDate tricks that work so well with

appointments, use them here, too. For example, enter `tomorrow 9 am` if you want to see a follow-up reminder first thing tomorrow morning.

4. Click **OK** to save the flag.

SEE ALSO

➤ *To learn how Outlook can enter dates and times for you, see page 611*

How do you know an item is flagged? Outlook adds a red flag icon in table views (such as the Inbox or the Phone List view of your Contacts Folder). When you open a flagged message or Contact item, you see the follow-up message text and date in the information bar at the top of the item, as in Figure 28.14.

Why flag without a reminder date?

Sometimes a follow-up date isn't necessary. If you routinely get requests for information from potential customers, for example, you might want to enter their names in Outlook and then flag them with text that says `Sent brochure`. Then, once a month, send a follow-up letter to everyone in this category and change the flag to `Sent follow-up letter`.

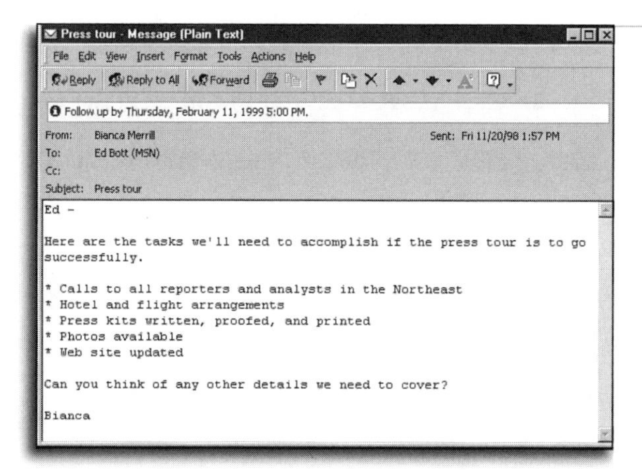

FIGURE 28.14

When you flag a mail message or contact, your follow-up information appears in the bar at the top of the item.

To see all the items you've flagged for follow-up, switch to the Inbox or the Contacts Folder and then switch to the built-in By Follow-up Flag view. To remove a flag from an item, right-click and choose **Flag Complete** (if you want to keep the flag information) or **Clear Flag** (to remove the flag completely). Both of these options are also available in the Flag for Follow Up dialog box.

Follow-up flags work for others, too

You can use follow-up flags in mail you send to other people, as well. While you're composing a message, click the **Flag for Follow Up** button and choose **For Your Information** or **No Reply Necessary**, for example. Or add your own text and a date. If your recipients use Outlook, they'll see the text and date you entered when they open the message.

Assigning Items to Categories

One effective way to divide big groups of Outlook items into manageable groups is to use *categories*. Outlook gets you started with a *Master Category List*, which gives you 20 mostly useful entries, such as Key Customer, Business, Personal, VIP, Waiting,

Several categories for one item

You can assign more than one category to a single item. This capability is useful for contacts that fall into several groups; you might want to put your most valuable clients in the Key Customer and Holiday Cards categories, for example.

No Categories button? No problem

The Organize pane doesn't let you assign categories to email messages or appointments; in either of these cases, you must click the **Categories** button at the bottom of the form, or you can select the item, right-click, and choose **Categories** from the shortcut menu.

and Holiday Cards. You can also add your own categories if the built-in list doesn't include the ones you want.

You can assign categories to email messages, contacts, appointments, meetings, and tasks. In general, this feature is most useful with items in the Contacts and Tasks Folders; in these folders, the **Organize** button lets you quickly and easily assign categories.

Assigning Categories to an Item

1. Open the Contacts or Tasks Folder and select the items you want to categorize. Then click the **Organize** button.
2. In the Organize pane, click the **Using Categories** option (see Figure 28.15); then choose the category to which you want to assign the items you selected.
3. Click the **Add** button to complete the assignment.

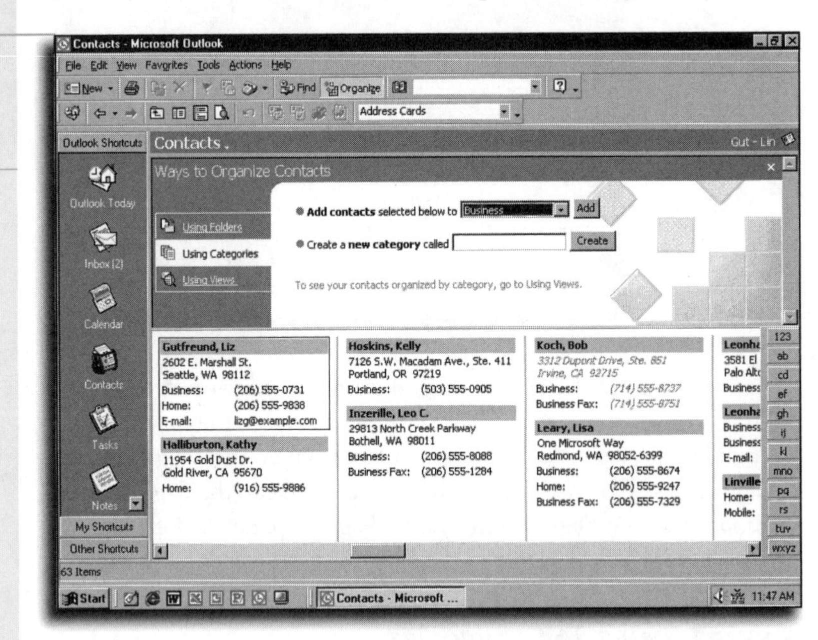

FIGURE 28.15

To assign Outlook items to categories, use this list.

4. Repeat steps 2 and 3 for other categories. To add a new category and make it available to all items, enter the category name in the box labeled **Create a new category called** and then click the **Create** button.

5. Click the **X** in the upper-right corner to close the Organize pane.

The Calendar, Contacts, and Tasks Folders include built-in By Category views. To see all the items that you've assigned to categories, use the Organize pane or the Views list on the Advanced toolbar to switch to this view.

Always use the Master List

Although you can enter category names directly in the Categories box (on a Contact form, for example), I don't recommend doing so. Use the Master List to make sure the category you use will be consistent with other items.

Deleting and Archiving Outlook Information

When you no longer need an item stored in Outlook, you can easily delete it. First, select the item or items you want to delete. Then click the **Delete** button on the Standard toolbar, use the keyboard shortcut Ctrl+D, or drag the item and drop it on the **Deleted Items** icon in the Outlook Bar.

By default, Outlook saves the contents of the Deleted Items folder. (You'll appreciate this feature if you accidentally toss the contact information for your best customer, or you clean out your Inbox and discover you threw out a crucial piece of email.) To empty this folder, right-click its shortcut in the Outlook Bar and choose **Empty "Deleted Items" Folder**. If you prefer to empty the trash automatically, you can tell Outlook to tidy up every time you exit. Pull down the **Tools** menu, choose **Options**, click the **Other** tab, and check the box labeled **Empty the Deleted Items folder upon exiting**.

Using yet another one of its Auto features, Outlook automatically moves items out of your Personal Folders file after a specified amount of time has passed. Using this *AutoArchive* feature can be confusing because it's actually a two-step process. Outlook performs its AutoArchive check every two weeks, scanning every folder in search of items that are older than the specified settings for that folder. When it finds appointments, tasks, and email messages that are more than six months old, for example, it flags them for archiving; items in the Deleted Items folder that are more than two months old are scheduled for permanent deletion. In the second part of the operation, AutoArchive goes through and moves or deletes items, but only after you give your approval. By using this feature, you can keep your Personal Folders file a bit more manageable.

Use rules to keep mail organized

Cleaning up your mail folders is easier if junk mail and other nonessential messages never get there in the first place. Use Outlook's Rules Wizard to move all but the most important messages directly into folders, where you can AutoArchive more frequently and keep your data file from bulging at the seams. See Chapter 29, "Sending and Receiving Email," for an explanation of how to use the Rules Wizard.

Checking through all those records can take time and slow down your system, so you might want to have Outlook check for outdated items less often—say, once a month. If you're a neat freak, you might want to clean out your Personal Folders file once a week. (To run the AutoArchive process anytime you want, pull down the **File** menu and choose **Archive**.) To specify how often you want Outlook to check for items to be AutoArchived, pull down the **Tools** menu, choose **Options**, click the **Other** tab, and click the **AutoArchive** button. You then see a dialog box like the one in Figure 28.16.

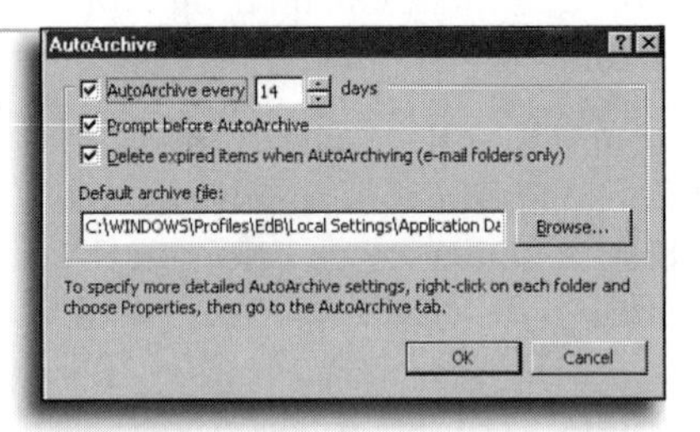

FIGURE 28.16

Outlook automatically checks for old items every two weeks and moves them to an archive file based on the settings for each folder.

Old items don't die

When AutoArchive runs, it doesn't delete email messages, tasks, or appointments. Instead, it moves them to a Personal Folders file called Archive.pst. If you want to look through your archived items, pull down the **File** menu, choose **Open**, and choose **Personal Folder File (.pst)**. If you're not sure where the archive file is stored, check the settings in the AutoArchive dialog box.

Outlook performs its AutoArchive scan every 14 days. You can enter any interval (in days) from 1 to 60. If you want this process to happen automatically, once a week, without requiring your approval, use the setting **AutoArchive every 7 days** and clear the box marked **Prompt before AutoArchive**. On the other hand, if you prefer to clean out old items yourself, you can skip AutoArchive completely; just clear the check mark from in front of the **AutoArchive every *n* days** box.

Next, you need to set your preferences for how you want Outlook to handle each folder. I prefer to clear out old tasks and appointments that are more than a month old, but I like to keep a full year's worth of mail in my Personal Folders file. To adjust the AutoArchive options for individual folders, right-click each Outlook Bar icon, choose **Properties**, and check boxes on the **AutoArchive** tab, as I've done with the Calendar folder in

Figure 28.17. Using options within each folder's AutoArchive dialog box, you can specify the name of a different Personal Folders file in which you want to store old items, or you can choose to automatically delete items that are no longer current.

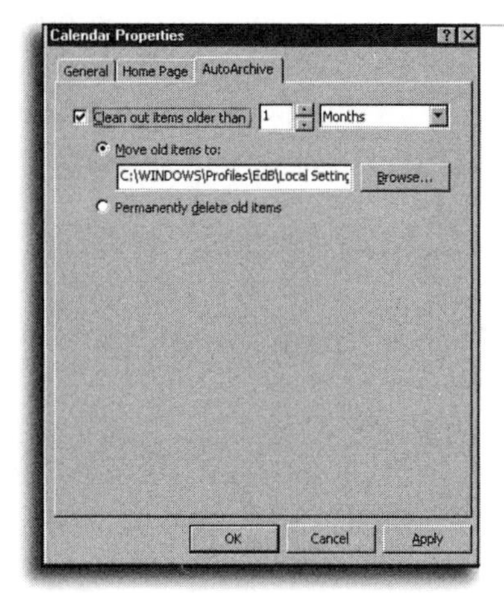

FIGURE 28.17
Right-click each icon in the Outlook Bar to set different AutoArchive options for each folder.

Reducing the Size of Your Outlook Data Files

Whenever you add a new Outlook item, your Personal Folders file gets a little bigger; when you receive a bulky email attachment, it can get a lot bigger. If you and your coworkers regularly send and receive email *attachments*, your Personal Folders file can easily hit 100MB or more, making it difficult to copy or back up. Deleting items doesn't help shrink that file, either; Outlook tosses the items, including the attachments, but it doesn't automatically recover the space the deleted items used. Squeezing this wasted space out of your files is possible, however.

Compressing an Outlook Data File

1. Right-click the **Outlook Today** icon at the top of the Outlook Bar and choose **Properties** from the shortcut menu.
2. Click the button labeled **Advanced**. You then see a dialog box like the one in Figure 28.18.

3. Click the **Compact Now** button. Depending on the size of the file, recompressing the space in the Personal Folders file may take awhile.
4. Click **OK** to close the Personal Folders dialog box and click **OK** to close the Properties dialog box.
5. To compress other open Personal Folders files, display the folder list, right-click the main icon for each file, select **Properties for *filename*** from the shortcut menu, and repeat steps 2 through 4.

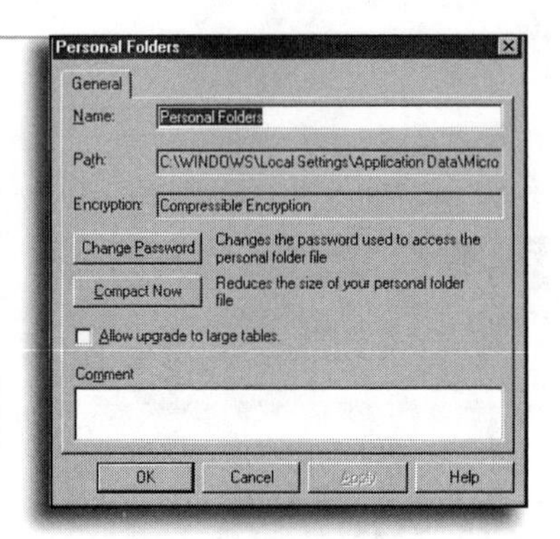

FIGURE 28.18

Click the **Compact Now** button to squeeze space out of a Personal Folders file after deleting items.

Finding Outlook Items

If you use Outlook regularly, your collection of personal data will eventually become so large that you won't be able to find key information simply by browsing through items. Instead, you can click Outlook's **Find** button to search for words and phrases in common fields in the current folder. The Find pane slides open just above the right-hand contents pane, as shown in Figure 28.19.

Searching with the Find pane is a simple, four-step process, and because it uses indexed fields, it's also amazingly fast.

FIGURE 28.19

Use this simple search tool to find items in the current Outlook folder.

Finding an Outlook Item

1. Check the text at the left of the Find pane to see which fields Outlook will search; then enter the word or phrase in the text box labeled **Look for**. In mail folders, for example, you can enter the name of a person who sent you a message or a word from the **Subject** line.
2. To search through all text in the folder, check the box labeled **Search all text in the *item***. Clear this box to speed up searches when you're certain the text you entered is in one of the fields at the left of the dialog box.
3. Click the **Find Now** button to begin searching. The search results then replace the contents below the Find pane.
4. To start over with a new search, click the **Clear Search** button and enter new text in the **Look for** box.

Looking for a contact?

The fastest way to pull up information about a contact, from any folder, is with the help of the unlabeled **Find a Contact** button on the Standard toolbar. It's just a fill-in box, with no icon or text to identify it (the ScreenTip gives it away). After you enter a first or last name and press Enter, Outlook immediately searches for matching names in your Contact Folder. If it finds only one, it opens the record instantly. If it finds more than one matching item, it presents a list and lets you choose which one you want to see.

Careful with that check box!

Checking the **Search all text** box is fine in your Calendar or Contacts Folder, where the number of items is unlikely to be large. Avoid this option, however, in mail folders that contain thousands of items. You can't stop the Find operation after it starts, and searching through all those items can take five minutes or more, during which time you can't do anything else. The Advanced Find dialog box is a better choice for searching through text because it allows you to see the search results as they pop up and hit the **Stop** button at any time.

If a simple search doesn't turn up the information you're looking for, click the **Advanced Find** link in the upper-right corner of the find pane. (To skip the Find pane completely, pull down the **Tools** menu and then choose **Advanced Find**.) This option opens the more sophisticated (and much more complicated) dialog box shown in Figure 28.20.

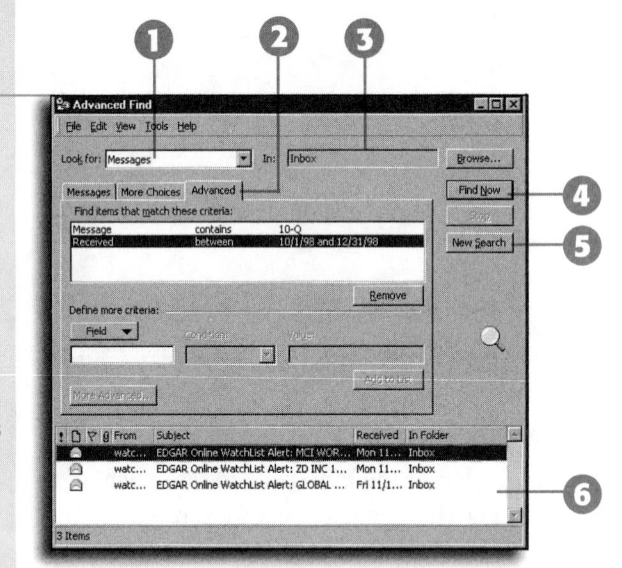

FIGURE 28.20

Use this dialog box to search for Outlook items using a combination of criteria.

1. Specify the type of items to look for—messages or appointments, for example.
2. Fill out the boxes on these three tabs to tell Outlook what to search for. (The exact options vary slightly, depending on the type of item you're looking for.)
3. Pick one or more folders from the same Personal Folders file.
4. Tell Outlook to begin searching based on what you've entered.
5. Click here to clear every entry and start all over again.
6. The results of the search appear here. Double-click to open the item, or click and drag to move, copy, or edit items.

The Advanced Find dialog box lets you search for combinations of criteria, which you can't do using the Find pane. For example, when filling out an expense report, you might search for appointments that include the word *Dinner* in the description and that occurred in the current month. Or if you know you received an important email message containing budget figures sometime in the month of January, you can search your Inbox for items that were received between January 1 and January 31 and included the word *budget* in the message body. In some cases, you can pick from drop-down lists or check boxes; for the most complex searches, you need to define the field you want to search (such as the `Received` date for an email message) and the criteria you want it to match (such as `between 1/1/99 and 1/31/99`).

If you've performed a complex search, you can save the parameters and reuse them later. For example, if business takes you to a certain region regularly, you can create and save a search that finds all your friends and business associates in that region; then you can save the search to display the most up-to-date version of the list later.

To save a search, first select its settings in the Advanced Find dialog box. Then click the **File** menu and choose **Save Search**. Outlook saves searches as files, which you can store in a folder or on the Windows desktop. To reuse that saved search, open the icon, or open the Advanced Find dialog box, click the **File** menu, and choose **Open Search**.

CHAPTER

29

Sending and Receiving Email

- Set up Internet email accounts
- Configure Outlook to dial the Internet automatically
- Choose between HTML and plain text message formats
- Use Outlook's Address Book
- Create and send a message
- Check your email
- File and flag messages
- Use the Rules Wizard to manage email automatically

What about other Microsoft mail programs?

Microsoft Exchange Inbox and Windows Messaging are nearly identical versions of the same all-in-one email client that comes free with Windows 95 and Windows NT. It looks somewhat similar to Outlook, although it handles only email (no contacts or appointments), and it doesn't have the Outlook Bar. Outlook Express more closely resembles Outlook 2000 (in fact, some features are absolutely identical), but it too handles only email; it includes an Address Book but doesn't let you track tasks or appointments. When you upgrade to Outlook 2000, you can import messages, addresses, and settings from any of these programs.

Want help with corporate email?

In this section, I assume you want to establish a connection to an Internet-standard mail server–generally for retrieving your personal or small business mail (although some larger companies do use SMTP mail servers). If you need to connect Outlook 2000 to a Microsoft Exchange server, a Microsoft Mail post office, or another supported mail system at a corporate workplace, your setup procedures are different. In some cases, the administrator might need to set up or reconfigure your account before you can successfully send and receive mail. For best results, ask your mail administrator for help; someone may have already prepared a set of step-by-step instructions you can use.

Setting Up Internet Email Accounts

Outlook 2000 helps you quickly and easily communicate with anyone in your company or in the outside world—as long as those people have access to electronic mail, too. You can send and receive mail, exchange documents and other files, and even use electronic mail to invite other people to meetings or request that they take over a task for you.

Before you can use Outlook to send and receive email, you must supply basic configuration information, including the name and type of the mail server that stores and forwards your messages, along with the username, password, and email address for your mail account. If you receive Internet mail from multiple sources—from a corporate server and via a personal account with an Internet service provider, for example—you need to establish separate mail accounts for each one.

The procedures for setting up an Internet mail account are different, depending on the mode you selected when you set up Outlook—**Internet Only**, **Corporate or Workgroup**, or **No E-mail**.

SEE ALSO

➤ *For a detailed description of each of Outlook's setup modes, see page 542*

Using Internet Mail Only (IMO) Mode

When you install Outlook in Internet Mail Only (IMO) mode, the Internet Connection Wizard walks you through the process of configuring a default mail account. You can rerun this wizard at any time to set up a new mail account.

Setting Up an Email Account in IMO Mode

1. Pull down the **Tools** menu and choose **Accounts**. You then see a dialog box like the one shown in Figure 29.1.
2. Click the **Add** button and choose **Mail** from the cascading menu. Outlook displays the opening dialog box of the Internet Connection Wizard.
3. Follow the wizard's prompts to enter the following information:

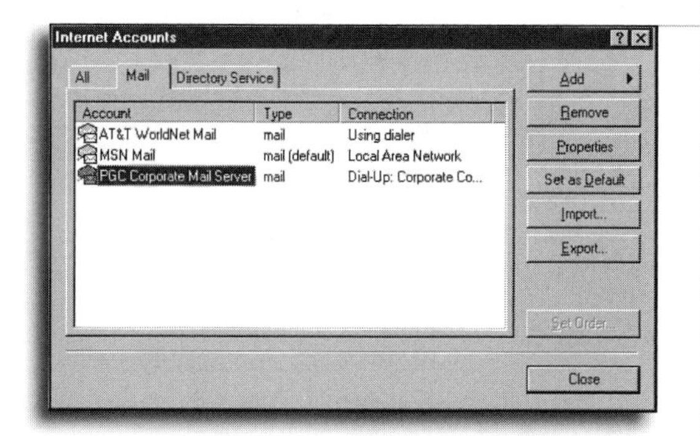

FIGURE 29.1
This dialog box lists all mail accounts you've set up. Open this dialog box again to add or remove accounts, or to change any mail account information.

- Your name—This display name will appear in the **From** field when you send a message. Most people enter their real names; you might want to add a company affiliation or other information to help mail recipients identify you more readily.
- Your Internet email address—When recipients reply to messages you send, their mail software will use this address.
- Mail server information—Fill in addresses for incoming and outgoing mail servers, even if the same server does both jobs. Be sure to specify the mail protocol your incoming server uses: POP3 (the default setting) or IMAP.
- Logon information—Check **Log on using** and enter the account name you use to log on to the mail server. If you enter a password in this dialog box, Outlook will store the password and use it each time you check mail. If you share your computer with other people, and you don't want them to be able to send email from your account (accidentally or deliberately), leave the password box blank. In this configuration, Outlook will ask you to enter your password each time you send or receive mail. Choose **Log on using Secure Password Authentication** if you connect to the Microsoft Network (`msn.com`) for email. CompuServe (`csi.com`) users also have the option to use this feature, which displays a different password dialog box. Do not use this option with any other Internet service provider unless specifically instructed to do so.

SMTP versus POP3 versus IMAP

Outlook 2000 supports three widely used mail standards. When you send email, most Internet service providers transfer it using servers that run *Simple Mail Transfer Protocol (SMTP)*. To download messages from Internet-standard mail servers, you typically use version 3 of *Post Office Protocol (POP3)*. A newer standard, *Internet Message Access Protocol (IMAP)*, is less widely used. Your Internet service provider or network administrator can provide you with details of your mail system's configuration.

- A friendly name for the account—This label will appear in the Accounts list and on the Send and Receive menu. If you don't specify a name here, Outlook will enter the name you specified for the incoming mail server. Take the time to enter a name here: `MSN Mail` takes much less space on the menu than `pop3.email.msn.com`—and it's much easier to remember.
- Connection type—Tell Outlook whether you access the Internet through a network or over a dial-up connection. If you choose the latter option, you can enter details for a new dial-up connection as part of this step.

4. After you've entered all information, click the **Finish** button to add the new account.
5. If you want to send all outgoing mail using this account, select the new entry in the accounts list and click the **Set as Default** button.
6. Click the **Close** button to close the dialog box and return to Outlook.

Cable modem?

If you have a cable modem or another type of high-speed Internet connection, such as *Digital Subscriber Line (DSL)* technology, choose the network option. If you connect to an Internet server by dialing up over an analog modem, choose the dial-up option.

Using Corporate/Workgroup (CW) Mode

In Corporate/Workgroup (CW) mode, you don't set up Internet email accounts directly. Instead, you add an *information service* to your Outlook *profile* and enter configuration details in the Properties dialog box for that service.

If you upgraded over an existing version of Outlook or another email program (such as Netscape Mail or Eudora), Outlook automatically migrates your configuration settings as part of the Setup process. You can add an Internet mail account at any time.

Setting Up an Email Account in CW Mode

1. Pull down the **Tools** menu and choose **Services**. You then see a dialog box like the one shown in Figure 29.2.

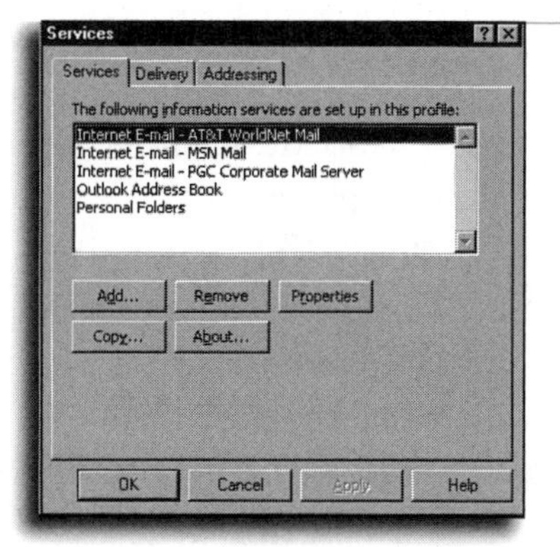

FIGURE 29.2

In Corporate/Workgroup mode, you set up accounts by adding services to a profile.

2. Click the **Add** button, choose **Internet E-mail** from the Add Service to Profile dialog box, and click **OK**. Outlook displays the Mail Properties dialog box.
3. Click the **General** tab and enter a descriptive name for the account, plus your username and email address, as shown in Figure 29.3.

Look familiar? It should...

The Mail Account Properties dialog box is almost exactly the same in both IMO and CW modes. In IMO mode, however, you can use the wizard to fill in its settings, whereas in CW mode you have to fill out each tab without prompting.

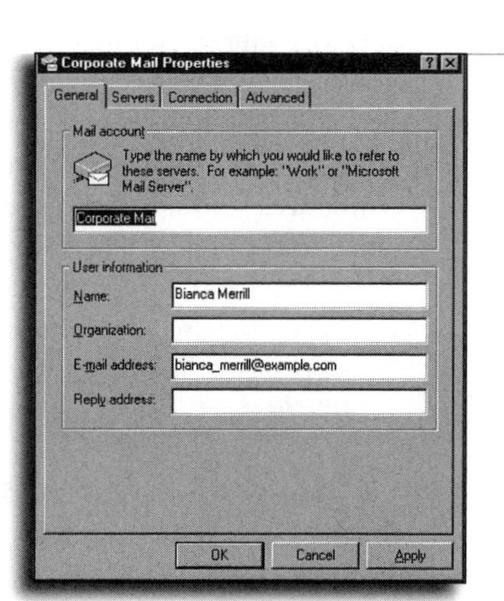

FIGURE 29.3

In CW mode, you have to fill out this dialog box without a wizard's help.

4. Click the **Servers** tab and enter the name of your incoming and outgoing mail servers. Then enter your username and password. If you leave the password box blank, Outlook will ask you to enter your password each time you send or receive mail.

Don't forget to restart Outlook

In CW mode, whenever you add or change a service, you must restart Outlook. From the **File** menu, choose **Exit and Log Off**. Wait for Outlook to close all open windows and then restart the program. You don't need to restart your computer.

Notebook users, take note

Do you use Outlook on a notebook computer that's sometimes connected to the network and sometimes connected via modem? Choose the option to connect via the network; then check the box that reads **Connect via modem if the LAN is not available**. In this configuration, Outlook attempts to send and receive your mail over the office network but uses the Dial-Up Networking connection when you're working in a hotel room.

5. Click the **Connection** tab and specify whether you use a network or a dial-up modem to connect to the mail server. (See the following section for more information on your options here.)
6. Click **OK** to save the account information. The new account appears in your Services list. Click **OK** to close the Services dialog box.

Selecting Connection Options

For each account, you an specify how you prefer to connect to the Internet—over a local area network (LAN), manually, or by using a modem. If your computer is permanently connected to a network with Internet access, set all accounts for LAN access; you don't need to fiddle with other options. However, when you use a dial-up connection to access the Internet, you should pay close attention to these settings.

Each time you create a new account, you have a chance to specify connection properties. To adjust these settings after you've created an account in Internet Mail Only mode, pull down the **Tools** menu, choose **Accounts**, select the account name, click **Properties**, and click the **Connection** tab. If you've configured Outlook in Corporate/Workgroup mode, pull down the **Tools** menu, choose **Services**, and click the **Services** tab. Select the Internet Email account whose configuration you want to check or change, and click the **Properties** button. In either case, you see a dialog box like the one in Figure 29.4.

What's the difference between the three connection options?

- **Connect using my local area network (LAN)**—The LAN option assumes you have a full-time connection to the Internet through a local area network. Unless you choose to work offline, Outlook checks for mail every 10 minutes by default. (I'll explain how to change this setting later in this chapter.)

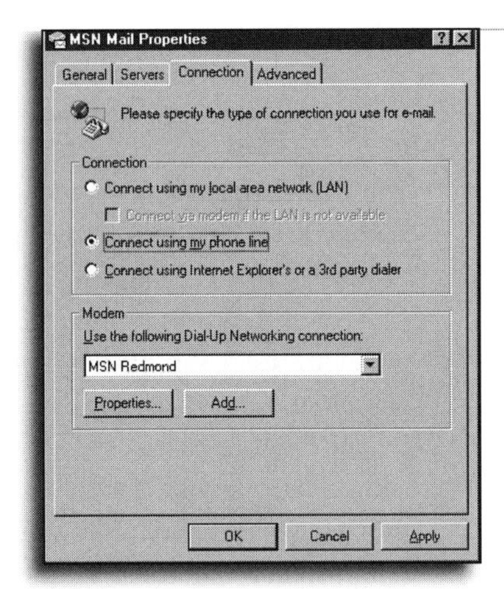

FIGURE 29.4
The choice shown in this dialog box allows Outlook to dial your Internet service provider automatically every time you access a mail server.

- **Connect using my phone line**—Choose a Dial-Up Networking connection from the list at the bottom of this dialog box or click the **Add** button to create a new one. Outlook dials this connection whenever you attempt to send or receive mail. Use this option if you want Outlook to dial your Internet connection automatically when sending or receiving email.
- **Connect using a 3rd party or Internet Explorer's dialer**—You choose when and how to connect to the Internet; Outlook does not dial automatically. This option is your best choice if you use the same phone line for voice calls and Internet access.

Adjusting Properties for an Existing Mail Account

To change settings for a mail account after you've set it up using the Internet Connection Wizard, click the **Tools** menu, choose **Accounts**, select the account you want to change, and click the **Properties** button.

For both types of accounts, use the **General** tab (see Figure 29.5) to change the friendly name for the account or to edit personal information. This dialog box lets you add the name of your organization and specify a different reply-to address. For example, if you send a message using your corporate mail account but prefer to receive replies via your personal Internet mail account, enter the personal address in the **Reply address** box.

You can also use this option when you want replies to come to a special mailbox that other people in your department can check. Figure 29.5, for example, shows the settings you can use if you're sending out a bulletin to your customers about a support problem. Let's say that five people take turns covering your customer support desk during the week. Each of the people on that list will have a personal email account, of course, but you can also set up one account that each of them can access when they're on duty. When recipients reply to your message, their mail software should automatically insert the address you specify here.

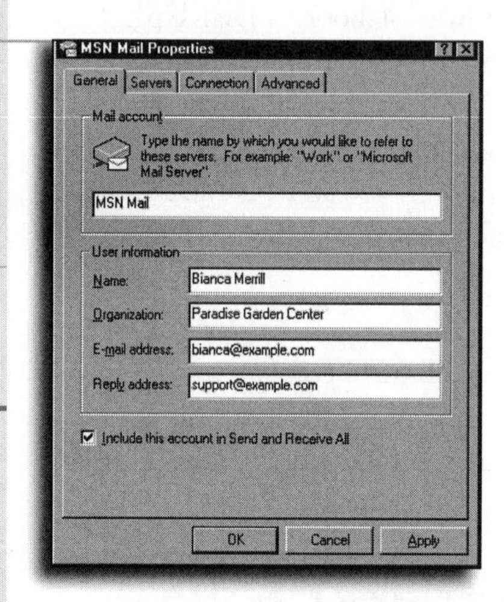

FIGURE 29.5

Edit the reply-to address shown here if you want replies to go to an address other than the one from which you send messages.

You can leave messages on the server

An option on the **Advanced** tab of the Mail Properties dialog box lets you specify that you want messages to remain on the server. Use this option when you're checking your mail from a PC where you don't normally check mail. Outlook then downloads messages but does not delete them from the server as it usually does. When you return to your normal working PC and connect to the server, you can retrieve all the messages so that you have a complete mail file. This option is great for those who need to occasionally check their personal email accounts from work, or work accounts from home, without mixing messages.

Click the **Servers** tab to change the name or logon settings for mail and news servers. On the **Advanced** tab, you can adjust timeout settings (sometimes necessary over very slow connections) and break apart lengthy messages (required by some mail servers running older software). Do not adjust these settings unless specifically instructed to do so by the server's administrator.

Choosing a Message Format

Each time you compose message using Outlook, you have a choice: you can use plain text, or you can add graphics, colors, and rich text formatting, including fonts and attributes. Outlook lets you select a default format for new messages you create, although you can choose another format for any given message.

Your three choices are as follows:

- **HTML** produces messages that look and behave like Web pages. As the example in Figure 29.6 shows, HTML mail messages can include background graphics, pictures, hyperlinks, bullets, rules, different fonts and font sizes, and even colors (although you'll have to take my word on that one, because this book shows only shades of gray).

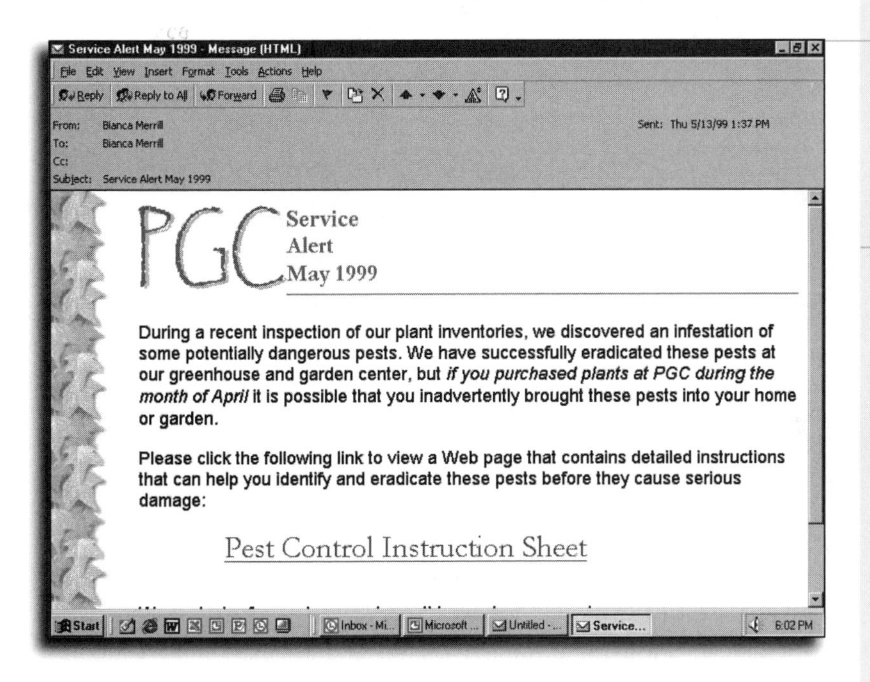

FIGURE 29.6
Email messages created using HTML format look a lot like Web pages, with graphics, colors, font formatting, and other designer touches.

- **Microsoft Outlook Rich Text** is an old format used in early Exchange client programs before HTML was a widely accepted standard. This format allows you to send and receive formatted text (fonts, colors, and so on) with users of older Exchange client programs, such as the Exchange Inbox from early versions of Windows 95. Using this format will invariably cause problems with people who use other email software. I strongly recommend that you avoid setting this as your default message format.
- **Plain Text**, as the name implies, sends your message with absolutely no formatting or graphics. Figure 29.7 shows what the message in the preceding figure looks like if you receive it as plain text and open it in Outlook. This is the best all-around option, especially if you don't know whether your email recipients use HTML-compatible email clients.

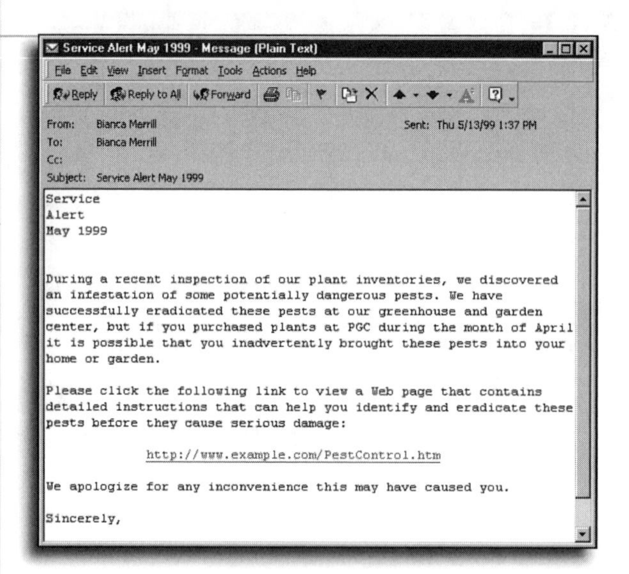

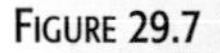
FIGURE 29.7

This message, in plain text format, contains the same information as the preceding example, without any formatting.

HTML formatting can make your messages more interesting. If most of your messages go to people who use Outlook, Outlook Express, or recent versions of Netscape Mail and Eudora, your recipients should have no trouble opening messages you send in this format. For recipients who use an email program that can't interpret your formatting, the message appears as plain text only, with an attached file that opens in a Web browser.

Unless you're certain that the overwhelming majority of your email recipients can handle HTML attachments, your best bet is to choose plain text as the default setting for mail messages. In fact, many people prefer text mail, even when they can read HTML-formatted messages, because text messages take less time to download.

Which mail programs read HTML?

Anyone using Netscape mail software can send and receive HTML-formatted mail, as can users of Outlook 98 or Outlook Express, the free email program included with Windows 98 and Internet Explorer 4.0 and later. Outlook 97, Microsoft Mail, Microsoft Exchange Inbox, older versions of Eudora, Lotus Notes, and cc:Mail do not recognize HTML-formatted messages.

Setting a Default Message Format

1. Pull down the **Tools** menu, choose **Options**, and click the **Mail Format** tab. You then see the dialog box shown in Figure 29.8.

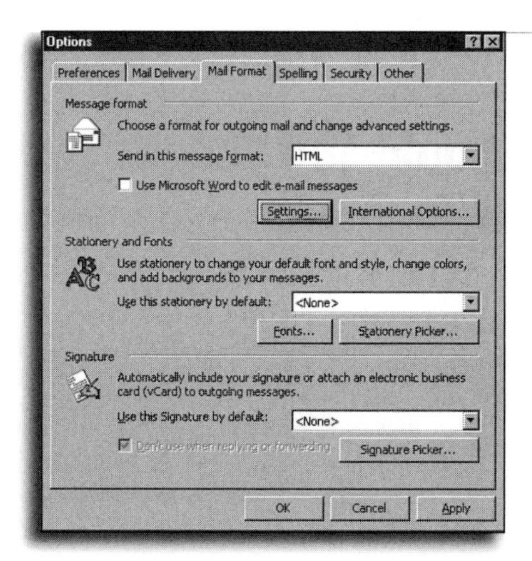

FIGURE 29.8

When you use these settings, all your mail messages will go out in HTML format. You can choose plain text for individual messages.

2. From the list labeled **Send in this message format**, select a default format for mail messages. Other options in the **Mail Format** tab change, depending on the mail format you select. Only options that are appropriate for the selected format are available here.

3. If you choose the HTML format, select a default stationery type from the **Stationery and Fonts** section. These options define the background image, colors, and fonts your messages will use. If you choose Microsoft Word as your editor, select these options in Word.

Leave MIME settings at their defaults

If you choose **HTML** or **Plain Text**, you can click the **Settings** button to view MIME and text-wrapping options and adjust them if necessary. *MIME*, which stands for *Multi-Purpose Internet Mail Extensions*, controls how Outlook translates special characters (such as symbols or accented letters) and file attachments so that other mail client software can interpret them correctly. The default MIME settings work correctly under most settings. Don't adjust them unless you're certain you know what the effect will be.

4. Click the **Fonts** button to select the default fonts that Outlook will use to display plain text messages you compose or receive. If you've chosen **HTML** format, you can specify separate fonts for messages you compose and messages to which you reply. If you choose **Plain Text** format, the fonts you select here apply to your message windows only; when you send a plain text message, it includes no formatting information at all.
5. Click **Apply** to save your changes and adjust other mail options. Click **OK** to save changes and close the dialog box.

Change fonts for incoming text messages

By default, Outlook displays all incoming text messages using an ugly standard font, 10 point Courier. I routinely change these settings to use the Tahoma font (which I find more readable and easier on the eye), and I increase the font size to 12 points so that I don't have to squint at the screen.

SEE ALSO

➤ *To read more about options for composing individual messages, see page 589*

Should You Choose Word As Your Email Editor?

The **Mail Format** tab of the Options dialog box includes a seemingly innocuous check box: **Use Microsoft Word to edit e-mail messages**. When you check this box, you make a dramatic change to Outlook. Whenever you begin composing a message, Outlook opens your new message in Word. As Figure 29.9 shows, this window includes all the Word menus and toolbars, plus an extra set of toolbars that match the address boxes and the Standard toolbar on an Outlook message window.

The option to use Word as an email editor has been available since the first version of Outlook; in previous versions, this feature even had it own name, WordMail. Unfortunately, the first incarnations of WordMail also included so many bugs that it was practically unusable. In Outlook 2000, Word works surprisingly well when pressed into service as an email editor. Its chief advantage is that it gives you Word's full set of editing tools—including AutoText, styles, and multilevel undo—when working with email messages. Its chief disadvantage is that it slows down your system and uses extra memory.

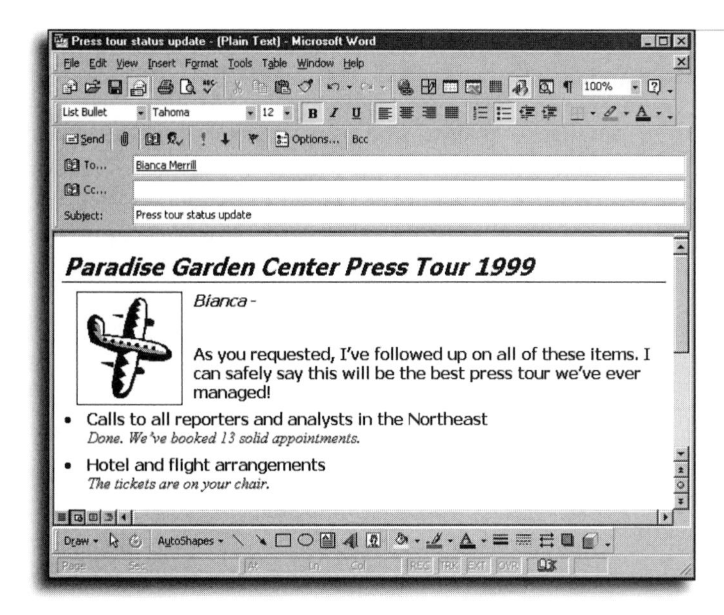

FIGURE 29.9

When you use Word as your email editor, you can use its full set of editing tools to compose a message.

If you tried this feature in previous versions and gave up because it was slow and crashed your system, give it another try. If you don't like the results, you can change back to the Outlook mail editor by removing the check mark from the **Mail Format** tab of the Options dialog box.

Use Word for any email message

If you don't want to use Word as your default email editor, you can still use it to compose any email message. Just open a new blank document in Word and click the **E-mail** button. Using this option adds the Outlook-style toolbars to your document window, so you can send it when you're ready.

Creating, Managing, and Using Email Addresses

Just as your post office needs a complete address to deliver your letters properly, your mail server requires you to enter a valid address before it can deliver your message. Outlook lets you choose one of several options to store email addresses, although the preferred location is in your Contacts Folder. You can add individual addresses to a message in several different ways.

How Email Addresses Work

Using Outlook 2000 and an Internet-standard email account, you can send a message to just about anyone who also has an email account. The details vary, but here are some general guidelines:

- To send mail to someone using a corporate email system like Exchange Server, you can usually just pick that person's name from a public Address Book. Your network administrator can provide instructions on how to use the public Address Book on your system.
- To send mail to someone on the Internet, use the standard Internet addressing scheme: `username@domain`. For example, the development editor on this book was `rkughen@mcp.com`; email him if you have questions or comments about this book!
- To send mail to someone using an online service, translate that person's name into its Internet equivalent. For example, to reach an address on America Online from the Internet, enter the address in this format: `username@aol.com`.

Connect the dots

Although the most popular *domain names* include `.com` at the end, other suffixes are acceptable as well. To send email to a student at Stanford University, for example, you might address the message to `username@stanford.edu`. The `.org` extension is for organizations such as the American Cancer Society (`acs.org`), `.net` is for Internet service providers, and `.gov` is the extension for government agencies (to make your voice heard, send email to `president@whitehouse.gov`). Outside the United States, two-letter suffixes denote countries: `.uk` for the United Kingdom, for example, or `.ca` for Canada.

Using the Outlook Address Book

By default, Outlook stores email addresses along with other address and contact information in items in your Contacts Folder. In a number of Outlook windows—including the Inbox and the form for composing a new message—you can find an **Address Book** button on the Standard toolbar. If you click this button while composing a new message, you open a Select Names dialog box like the one in Figure 29.10.

If you've installed Outlook using IMO mode, using the Outlook Address Book is simply a different way to view the data in your Contacts Folder. Select a name from the list and click **Properties** to see details about that person, as in the example in Figure 29.11. Clicking the **Home** or **Business** tab of a record in the Address Book, for example, displays the address and telephone information from that item in the Contacts Folder. The view from the Outlook Address Book is designed to make it easy for you to select email addresses for use in new messages. If the contact has multiple email addresses, you can choose which one you want to use for each message.

Use the To button

When you compose a message in Outlook, the label in front of each address field (**To**, **Cc**, or **Bcc**) is actually a button. Click to open the Outlook Address Book and begin filling in that box with addresses.

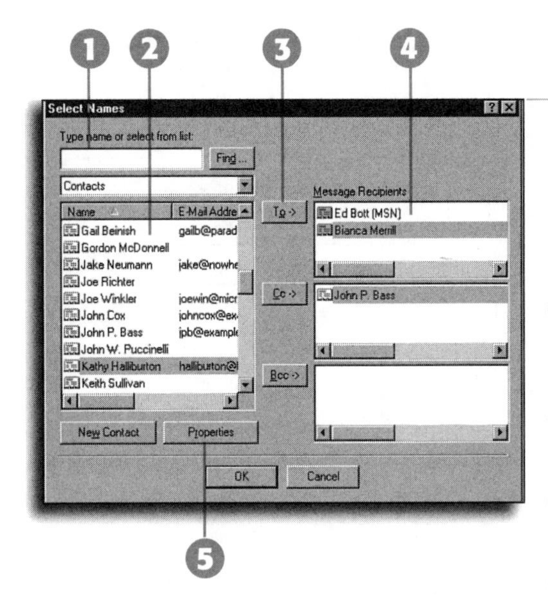

FIGURE 29.10

When you type in email addresses, you run the risk of making an error that could cause your message to get lost. Use the Address Book for foolproof results.

1. Enter part of a name here to find matching entries in the address list.
2. Select one or more names to add to your message.
3. Click here to add the selected addresses to the message.
4. If you make a mistake, right-click any name from the three boxes on the right and choose **Remove**.
5. Click this button to see details about the selected name.

Anyone who used Outlook 97 knows how thoroughly confusing working with email addresses can be. Outlook 97 used both the Contacts Folder and a file called the *Personal Address Book* to store addresses. These two files are mostly incompatible and hard to reconcile. In IMO mode, Outlook 2000 eliminates the Personal Address Book file completely. In CW mode, you can continue to use the Personal Address Book, but I recommend that you import this file into your Contacts Folder instead. When you upgrade to Outlook 2000 from a previous version, regardless of which configuration option you choose, Outlook offers to import this information. Just say yes!

If you're using CW mode, and you want to use the Outlook Address Book to access the Contacts Folder, you must first install the Outlook Address Book service. Pull down the **Tools** menu, choose **Services**, click the **Add** button, and choose **Outlook Address Book** from the list. Then, on the **Addressing** tab, make sure you specify that you want to check the Outlook Address Book first.

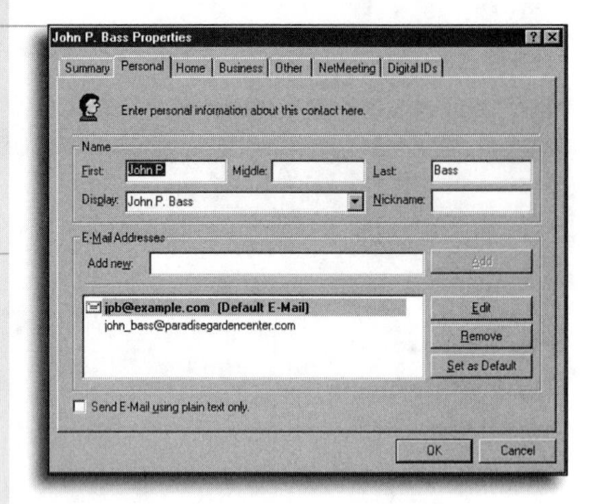

FIGURE 29.11

Your email Address Book displays details from your Contacts Folder in a different form. If you change information here, it changes in the Contacts Folder as well.

Addressing a Message

The most tedious way to add an address to a mail message is to type it in yourself. Click in the **To** box and enter the exact address of the person to whom you want to send a message. To add multiple addresses, separate each entry with a comma or semicolon. (Outlook adds these separator characters automatically when you pick names from the Address Book.) Click in the **Cc** box to enter names of anyone to whom you want to send a courtesy copy.

When you reply to a mail message you've received, you don't need to worry about entering the address. Just select the message in the message list (or open it in its own message window) and click the **Reply** or **Reply to All** buttons. Outlook picks up the exact address from that message, even if the person's name isn't in your Address Book.

To add an address from your Contacts Folder to a new message, open the Address Book, select one or more names, and click the **New Message to Contact** button. Outlook opens a blank message form, with the addresses you selected already filled in for you.

Information, please

What's the best way to find someone's email address? Outlook 2000 includes pointers to several email directory services on the World Wide Web, including 411, Bigfoot, and InfoSpace. To search for a name using these tools, open the Address Book, click the **Find** button, choose a directory service from the drop-down list, and follow the instructions. You also can enter or update your contact information with these directory services, making it easier for long-lost high school or college friends to locate you via email.

Letting Outlook Complete Addresses Automatically

You don't have to use the Address Book to enter email addresses. When you enter a name in the address box, Outlook tries to match it with an entry in your Address Book, if possible; partial addresses or names work also, although Outlook may require you to step in and make a selection if it can't find the exact address you're looking for.

To put this feature to work, begin entering an address in the **To** box; then type a comma or semicolon and space to begin another address, or press Tab to move to the next field. Outlook searches for a matching name and fills it in for you. For example, if only one *Bill* appears in your Address Book—the entry for *Bill Gates*—you can type `Bill` in the address field, and Outlook automatically fills in the rest of the name.

When you enter a fully qualified email address, such as `billg@microsoft.com`, Outlook adds a black underline to the entry. If you enter a partial address, and only one entry in the Address Book matches the entry, Outlook completes the address and you see the same indicator.

When more than one name in your Address Book matches a partial name you entered, Outlook adds a wavy red line beneath the name—the same indicator. A green dotted line means you've used this name before, and Outlook will use the name you picked last time unless you right-click to pick a different one. When you click the **Check Names** button or try to send the message, Outlook pops up a dialog box like the one in Figure 29.12, suggesting a list of possible addressees.

Force Outlook to look up names

When you enter a partial name in the address box, Outlook waits to check the entry in the Address Book. If you want to speed up the process, click the **Check Names** button. Outlook steps through every address you've listed, changing it to a confirmed mail address or letting you pick the correct entry from a list of suggestions.

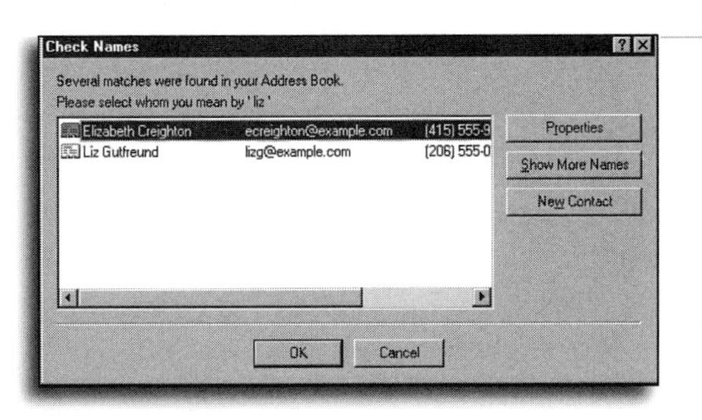

FIGURE 29.12

When you try to send a message with an incomplete address, Outlook lets you choose the matching name from your Address Book or create a new entry if necessary.

Right-click any name to see all options

When you see a line—black, red, or green—under a full or partial email address, right-click to see a full range of options. If multiple matching entries appear in the Address Book, you see a menu choice for each match. If the contact has more than one email address, right-clicking lets you choose a different email address instead of the default. You can also choose **Properties** from the shortcut menu to view and edit details in that contact's record.

Using Distribution Lists

Sometimes you find yourself addressing email messages to the same group of names, time after time. For example, you might send a weekly sales report to the managers of each regional office in your company. At home, you might send news about your family to parents, grandparents, sisters, and brothers with email accounts. Outlook lets you create personal distribution lists in your Contacts Folder. You give the group a name—such as `Steering Committee` or `My Family`—and then add names from your Address Book to the list.

After creating a personal distribution list, you can address a message to everyone on the list by simply entering the name of the list. If you create a personal distribution list called `Steering Committee`, for example, you can simply type `Steering` in the **To** box of a new message. Outlook automatically fills in the rest of the name, and when you send the message, it substitutes the names from your list.

To begin creating a new distribution list, open the Contacts Folder, pull down the **File** menu, choose **New**, and then choose **Distribution List**. You see the dialog box shown in Figure 29.13.

Personal distribution lists appear in your Contacts Folder as boldfaced names with no details and a special icon.

Or use the Address Book

You can also create distribution lists using the Outlook Address Book. Select one or more names, right-click and choose **New**, and then choose **New Group**. The form is slightly different from the one you use in the Contacts Folder, but the principle is the same. You can create or open a list using either form, and Outlook stores it in the same location.

Sending a Blind Copy

Want to send a copy of a message without the knowledge of other recipients? As you're composing a message, open the **View** menu, select **Bcc Field**, and then enter the email address for the blind courtesy copy (BCC) here. Only the two of you will know that you've sent this copy of the message.

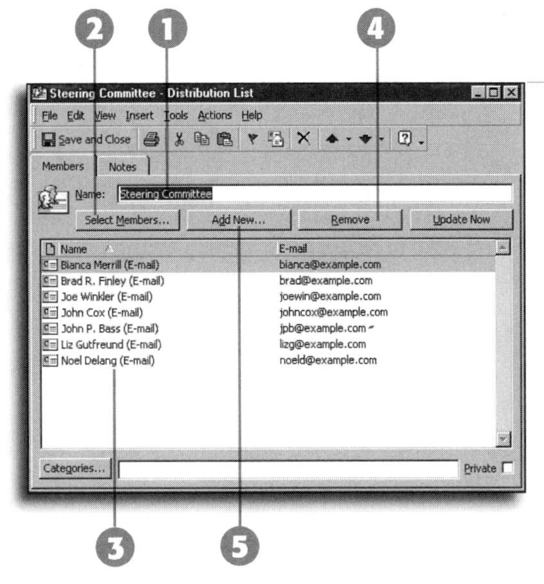

FIGURE 29.13

Use personal distribution lists to send mail to a group of people without having to enter each individual address.

1. Enter a name for the list here. Keep it short but descriptive.
2. Click this button to begin picking names from the Address book.
3. Double-click any name to edit its record in the Contacts Folder.
4. Select a name and click here to remove it from the distribution list.
5. Click here to add a new item in your Contacts Folder and then add it to the list.

This technique is also useful when you want to send a message (such as a press release or a promotional mailing) to a large list of recipients. If you add every name in the **To** box, you'll broadcast the entire list of addressees to everyone, and some recipients will have to scroll through several screens of address information before they can read your message. The solution? Address the message to yourself and add the remainder of the recipients to the **Bcc** list. Each recipient will see your name as the sender, without seeing any other addresses.

Composing and Sending a Message

After you've properly addressed your message, you're ready to complete the message itself.

Creating and Sending a Mail Message

1. Press the Tab key to move to the **Subject** box and enter the text you want the recipient to see before opening the message.

Get to the point quickly

Unless you're sending email to your mother or sweetheart, keep messages short and straightforward. Include a meaningful subject line and make your point in the first few lines. Your message is more likely to get read if the receiver can see at a glance that it's important.

HTML to Plain Text, and vice versa

You can switch between message formats anytime. Create a new message, pull down the **Format** menu, and choose **Plain Text** or **Rich Text (HTML)**. If you have already begun entering formatted text, you lose all formatting when you switch to the Plain Text option.

Outlook chooses the format for replies

Even if your default message format is Plain Text, Outlook switches to HTML format whenever you reply to a message that contains HTML codes. Likewise, if you reply to a Plain Text message, Outlook uses that format regardless of your default settings. Pull down the **Format** menu to switch formats, if necessary.

Delayed delivery

What do you do when you've completed a message, but you don't want to send it yet? If you think you might want to work on it later, open the **File** menu and choose **Save** or **Close**. Outlook saves the message in your Drafts folder. You can open, edit, and send it later. If you want Outlook to send your message at a specific time in the future, click the **Options** button and check the box labeled **Do not deliver before**. Edit the date and time in the box to the right and click **OK**. When you click **Send**, the message moves to your Outbox, but Outlook does not deliver it until the time you specified. Make sure that Outlook is running at that time. Saving messages to your Drafts folder also is a good option if you are angry when composing email. This gives you a chance to review the email and tone it down, if necessary—after you've cooled off a bit.

2. Press the **Tab** key again to position the insertion point in the message window. If your default message format is HTML or Microsoft Outlook Rich Text, the Formatting toolbar is visible. If you've chosen Microsoft Word as your email editor, the message editing window includes all Word menus and formatting options.
3. Enter the message text. If you've chosen HTML format, you can adjust fonts, attributes, colors, alignment, and other formatting options.
4. Click the **Insert File** button if you want to attach files (such as a Word document or Excel workbook) to the message. Select one or more files from the Insert File dialog box and click **OK**. Attachments appear at the bottom of the message window.
5. Use the **Message Flag**, **Importance High**, and **Importance Low** buttons if you want the recipient to see special icons on the left of the Subject line and in the information banner. For most routine messages, you don't need to touch these buttons.
6. To select from additional message options, click the **Options** button Options... . For example, you can choose which mail account you want to use for a specific message or specify that you want replies to this message sent to a different email address.
7. Click the **Send** button Send . Your message goes into the Outbox. If you've configured Outlook to send messages immediately, this message goes out right away; otherwise, Outlook transfers the message to the SMTP server the next time you check for mail.

Would you like to add a signature automatically to the end of every email message you create? Outlook lets you create multiple signatures; every time you send a message, you can choose which one to include in your message. Using signatures is an excellent way to make sure that mail recipients have important information about you, including your address, phone number, job title, and company affiliation, for example.

Creating a Signature to Add to Mail Messages

1. Open the Inbox folder, pull down the **Tools** menu, choose **Options**, and click the **Mail Format** tab.
2. Click the button labeled **Signature Picker** to open the Signature Picker dialog box.
3. Click the **New** button to create a signature file. (If you've already created a signature, you can choose it from the list and click **Edit** instead.)
4. In the next dialog box, choose a name and tell Outlook whether you want to create a signature from scratch or base the new signature on an existing signature or text file. Click **Next** to continue.
5. In the Edit Signature dialog box (see Figure 29.14), enter the text you want to include with your signature. Note that formatting buttons are available only if the default message format is HTML or Microsoft Outlook Rich Text.
6. Click **Finish** to save the signature and return to the Signature Picker dialog box.
7. Select the signature and make sure that the preview appears correctly; then click **OK** to return to the **Mail Format** tab of the Options dialog box.
8. If necessary, adjust the option labeled **Don't use when replying or forwarding**. By default, this option is checked, meaning you add signatures only to new messages you create.
9. Click **OK** to return to Outlook.

When you create a new message, Outlook automatically adds the default signature to the end of the blank message, leaving a line at the top for you to begin entering text.

Choose your server

When you click the **Send** button, Outlook sends messages using the mail account you've set as your default. To choose another account in IMO mode, don't use this button; instead, pull down the **File** menu, click **Send Using**, and choose the account from the cascading menu.

Check the address list before you send!

Be extra careful when you use the **Reply To All** button. One infamous email writer at a large computer company accidentally sent a steamy love letter intended for his sweetheart to all 5,000 employees at his company. And never send a message when you're angry. Remember: Email is forever–especially when it's embarrassing, ill considered, or possible evidence in a court case.

Add a disclaimer to your signature

At some companies, it's common practice to add boilerplate text at the end of every message, reminding the recipient that any opinions expressed are your personal opinions and don't necessarily represent those of your company. You can add this text to one or more signatures to make sure that you never forget.

Move over, Emily Post

An unwritten rule of netiquette says you should keep your signature to no more than five lines. That's good advice; if your signature runs longer, try cutting out any information that isn't essential.

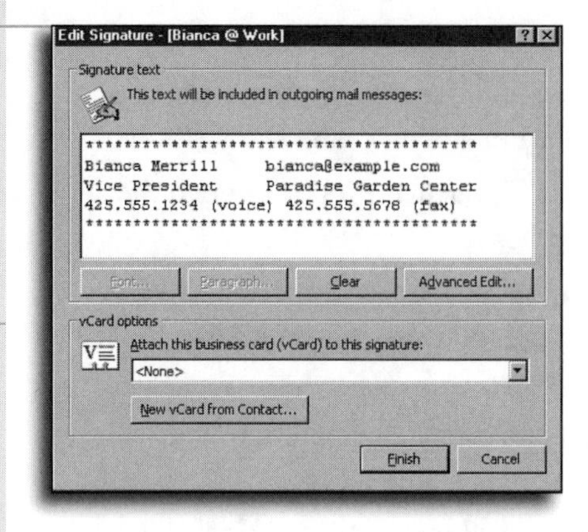

FIGURE 29.14

This signature will be tacked onto the end of every message you create. An unwritten rule of email etiquette says to keep your signature to no more than five lines.

Choose your own signature

If you prefer to select a signature for each message rather than let Outlook add it automatically, set the default signature to **<None>**. Then, when you create a new message, position the insertion point within the message, pull down the **Insert** menu, choose **Signature**, and select your preferred signature from the cascading menu.

Select which accounts you want to check

When you click the **Send/Receive** button, Outlook checks all mail accounts you've set up. If one or more of your accounts is on a server where you don't need to check mail regularly, remove the account from this list. In Internet Mail Only mode, open the **Tools** menu, choose **Accounts**, and click the **Mail** tab. Select the account name from the **Internet Accounts** list, click the **Properties** button, click the **General** tab, and clear the check mark next to the box labeled **Include this account when doing a full Send and Receive**. In Corporate/Workgroup mode, pull down the **Tools** menu, choose **Services**, and clear the check mark in front of the account name on the **Mail Services** tab.

Checking Your Mail and Reading New Messages

Outlook delivers messages to your Inbox automatically, at regular intervals. If you have a permanent Internet connection through your company network, you can use Outlook's default settings, which check for new messages every 10 minutes. If you collect your mail by connecting to a dial-up Internet service provider, you might choose to work offline and check for mail only when you're connected.

To check messages manually, click the **Send/Receive** button, or pull down the **Tools** menu and choose **Send/Receive**. Choose **All Accounts** or pick a specific account from the cascading menu.

Setting Automatic Mail-Delivery Options (IMO Mode)

1. Pull down the **Tools** menu and choose **Options**.
2. Click the **Mail Delivery** tab and set the following automatic delivery options using the check boxes labeled **Send messages immediately** and **Check for new messages every *xx* minutes**.
    - If you have a full-time Internet connection, check both boxes and choose the default interval.

- If you have a dial-up Internet account, and you want Outlook to make a connection automatically, check both boxes and choose a default message-checking interval.
- If you want to send and receive mail only when you choose to connect to the Internet, clear both check boxes.

3. If you connect to the Internet through a modem, adjust the four dial-up options to suit your preferences.
4. Click **OK** to close the dialog box and save your preferences.

Regardless of how you check your mail, Outlook can let you know when you've received new email. To set any or all of these three options, pull down the **Tools** menu, choose **Options**, click the **Preferences** tab, and click the **E-mail Options** button.

- To see a dialog box every time new messages appear in your Inbox, check the box labeled **Display a notification message when new mail arrives**. This option is off by default, and for good reason: The pop-up message can be annoying and distracting if you check mail automatically and receive a lot of mail during the workday.
- To hear a sound file when new messages arrive, click the **Advanced E-mail Options** button and check the **Play a sound** option. (You cannot customize this sound.)
- To see a visual signal that doesn't interfere with your work, click the **Advanced E-mail Options** button and check the box labeled **Briefly change the mouse cursor**. With this option enabled, the mouse pointer changes to an envelope shape briefly when mail arrives.

When new messages arrive, you also see a message icon in the *notification area* (sometimes called the *system tray*) at the right of the Windows taskbar. Double-click this icon to jump to your Inbox and begin reading messages. This icon disappears after you've read the new messages.

Email, special delivery

The default settings for dial-up connections automatically call your Internet service provider but don't hang up the line after retrieving your mail. If you want Outlook to be able to retrieve mail throughout the day and night, even when you're not there, check the **Automatically dial when checking for new messages** and **Hang up when finished sending, receiving, or updating** boxes. Together, these options handle the entire connection with maximum efficiency.

How many new messages do you have?

The number of new messages appears in parentheses to the right of the Inbox icon on the Outlook Bar and in the Folder List. It also appears in the Mail section of the Outlook Today page.

Picking out unread messages

Right-click any message and choose **Mark as Unread** or **Mark as Read**. This action toggles unread status or displays the first three lines if AutoPreview is turned on. Switch to the predefined Unread Messages view to show only new messages.

You can easily spot new messages in the message list. The icon to the left of the Author and Subject column shows an unopened envelope (after you read a message, the icon changes to an opened envelope). The sender's name and the subject appear in bold text; if you've enabled the **AutoPreview** option, the first three lines of the message appear in blue.

If the Preview pane is open, you can read an entire message by scrolling through the pane below the message list. When you double-click a message in your Inbox folder, it pops up in its own window. After you've finished reading it, use the toolbar buttons to file it, reply to the sender, forward the message to another person, or leave it in the message list without further action.

Organizing Your Email

Outlook includes several tools especially designed to help you keep important messages from getting lost in a busy Inbox. In the preceding chapter, I explained how you can move related messages to folders, add a *follow-up flag* to messages, and sort messages into lists or groups.

How can you spot a flagged message in your message list? Whether you added the flag yourself or received it from someone else, you see a bright-red flag icon just to its left. To sort through all your flagged messages and act on them, switch to the Inbox folder and choose one of the two predefined views: By Follow Up Flag or Flagged for Next Seven Days.

To clear a message flag, open the Flag for Follow Up dialog box and click the **Clear Flag** button. To leave the message flag in place but change the flag icon from red to clear, check the box labeled **Completed**.

SEE ALSO

- *To find detailed instructions on how to create a new Outlook folder and move items from one folder to another, see page 559*
- *For a description of how to use follow-up flags, see page 560*
- *To find step-by-step instructions on how to change views, see page 550*

Sorting Your Mail

One way to get a grip on an overflowing Inbox folder is to sort it, either alphabetically by subject or sender, or by date received. You can also sort messages into groups, letting you quickly file, delete, or categorize the messages.

Sorting is easy. Open the Inbox folder and make sure that you've selected a table view, such as Messages or Messages with AutoPreview. Click any heading to sort by that heading; for example, click the **From** heading to organize all your messages by sender. Click again to sort the messages in reverse order.

After sorting a mail folder, you can quickly jump to all the messages that start with a particular sequence of letters in the sorted field. For example, if you've sorted your Inbox folder by sender, you can jump to the messages from Jill by quickly typing the letters `JI`. Don't hesitate when typing; after a second or two, Outlook assumes you want to start over. If you type `J`, then pause and type the `I`, Outlook will jump to the first message whose sender's name begins with `J` and then jump to messages from senders whose names begin with `I`.

Outlook is smart about sorts

When sorting by subject, Outlook ignores certain phrases that are typically used at the beginning of the subject line. If the Subject is `Re: Sales forecast`, for example, Outlook files it under `S`, right beneath the original message that kicked off the conversation. When you sort by subject, you see the entire thread in one place, just as if the `Re:` weren't there.

Filtering Messages by Sender or Subject

All the techniques you can use to find items elsewhere in Outlook work just as well in folders containing mail. But two especially useful shortcuts are always just a right-click away in message folders.

When you display the contents of the Inbox (or any mail folder) and right-click a message, the shortcut menu includes a **Find All** choice. Click here and a cascading menu offers two additional menu options: Click **Messages from Sender** to pop up a list of all other messages from that person; choose **Related Messages** to see all messages with the same subject as the one you've selected.

Handling Junk Email

How much spam do you receive in a typical week? I get dozens of unwanted mail messages promising to make me rich if I just send $5 to each of 10 names at the bottom of the list, or offering to sell me a surefire get-rich-quick scheme. Occasionally, I get a piece of mail from a triple-X-rated site offering unspeakably obscene images in exchange for my credit card number. Usually, these messages are from senders with forged email addresses, so I can't even complain to the administrator of their mail system.

Outlook 2000 includes Junk Mail and Adult Mail filters designed to trap this sort of garbage and keep it from ever landing in your Inbox. To turn it on, click the **Organize** button and choose **Junk E-Mail** from the list on the left. Choose whether you want to move or simply color-code suspected Junk or Adult messages; then click the **Turn On** button.

How does junk e-mail filtering work?

Want more details on how junk e-mail filtering works? Click the Office Assistant icon and ask it to find Help topics that include the term *junk e-mail.*

After you enable junk e-mail filtering, you can add any sender to the junk e-mail list; just right-click and choose either of the options on the **Junk E-mail** menu. Every so often, you'll need to go through your Junk E-mail folder and clean up the mess. But at least you don't have to see these messages in your Inbox.

Does this option work perfectly? No. In fact, there's a good chance some messages you want to read will end up in the Junk E-mail folder, generally because it was addressed to another person and you were on a blind copy. When you find a message that gets into the Junk E-mail folder by accident, fine-tune the list so Outlook knows not to discard those messages in the future. Pull down the **Tools** menu and choose **Rules Wizard**. In the box labeled **Apply rules in the following order**, choose **Exception List**. In the **Rule description** list at the bottom of the dialog box, click the underlined phrase **Exception List**. In the Edit Exception List dialog box, click the **Add** button and enter the email address of the sender you want to remove from the list of suspected junk e-mail senders. Click **OK** to close the dialog box and return to Outlook.

Letting the Rules Wizard Manage Your Mail

One of Outlook 2000's most valuable features is the Rules Wizard. If you receive only a few messages a day, you don't need it. However, anyone who works for a company that's driven by email will find it indispensable. I know managers who receive more than 200 messages on a slow day. Many of them are simply courtesy copies of routine messages that don't require special attention. Others require prompt handling, before the issues they deal with turn into crises. How do the managers discard the trivial messages and spotlight the important ones? By defining *rules* and then letting Outlook use those rules to delete useless messages, move low-priority messages to other folders, and add color coding that makes the most important messages stand out in the list.

Let's say you've just received a message from one of your favorite Web shopping sites. You're happy to read about the latest special offers, but you would rather move the message to another folder so that it doesn't clutter up your Inbox. On the other hand, you might want to see I-need-it-yesterday messages from your boss or your best customer in bright red so that those messages stand out from others in the list.

Creating Simple Mail-Handling Rules

1. Click the **Organize** button. The message list slides down to make way for the Organize Inbox pane shown in Figure 29.15.

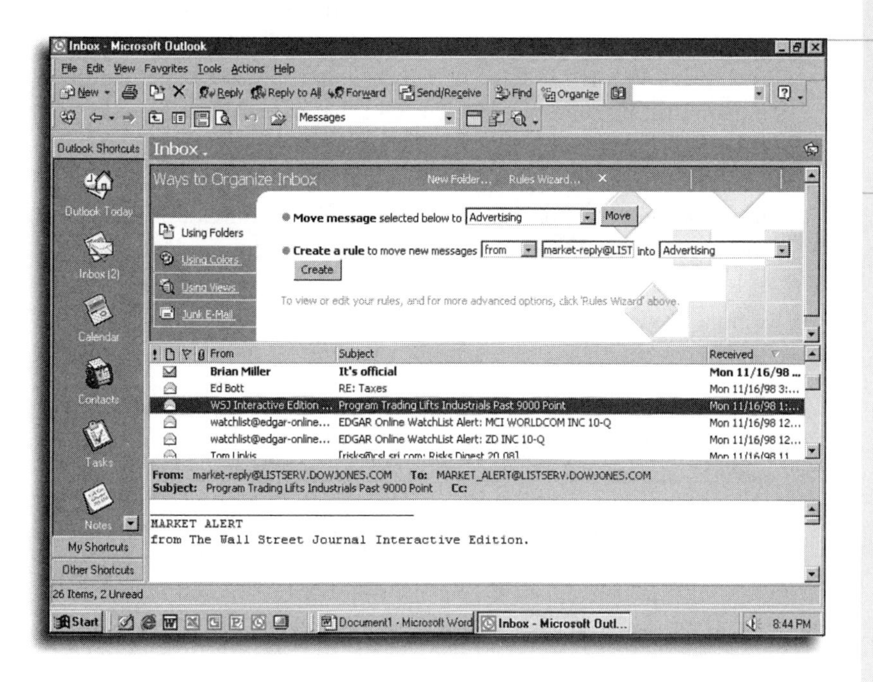

FIGURE 29.15
Use this collection of check boxes and lists to define simple rules for handling messages.

Some colors are unreadable

Although Outlook lets you choose from a list of 16 available colors, your practical choices are far more limited because only a handful of colors actually allow you to read message text. Choose purple, teal, gray, red, blue, or fuchsia for best results.

2. Choose the action you want the rule to perform:
   - To move messages automatically to another folder, select the message you want to use as the basis for your rule and then click **Using Folders**.
   - To highlight certain messages using colors, select the message you want to use as the basis for your rule and then click **Using Colors**.
3. Adjust the options in the line that begins **Create a rule**. You can choose to file messages based on the sender's name or the recipient's name; the latter option is useful if you receive mailing lists that are addressed to the name of a group rather than to you personally. Depending on the option you selected in step 2, choose a folder where you want to move messages that match the specified criteria and then click the **Create** button, or choose a color from the drop-down list and then click the **Apply Color** button.
4. Click the **Close** (**x**) button at the top right of the Organize Inbox pane to close the pane and restore the message list to its normal size.

What if these simple rules don't offer the options you need? To create more complex rules, select **Using Folders** and click the **Rules Wizard** button, or select **Using Colors** and click the **Automatic Formatting** button. Use the Rules Wizard to create rules that can handle virtually any set of options. For example, you can search the message text or the header for certain words, look for messages to or from a specific email address, or find messages that include attachments. Based on the results of the rule, you can move or delete messages, flag them for follow-up, send a reply, play a sound, or perform any combination of these and other actions.

The Rules Wizard's capabilities are nearly endless, and covering all its permutations could fill a book of its own. The following several examples should help you understand its possibilities.

Let's say you occasionally get email notifications of serious problems at one of your regional offices. Through long and painful experience, you know that the words *crisis* and *urgent* usually mean trouble. Use this set of procedures to make sure you never miss a message addressed to you that contains these words.

Highlighting Urgent Mail with the Rules Wizard

1. Pull down the **Tools** menu and choose **Rules Wizard**. Click the **New** button, and the Rules Wizard begins walking you through the process of defining a rule using the dialog box shown in Figure 29.16.

FIGURE 29.16
Create a rule by checking boxes and clicking links at each step of the Rules Wizard. The conditions and actions you define appear in the bottom of this dialog box.

2. Although the Rules Wizard contains a number of predefined conditions, none matches the conditions we want to set, so choose the generic option **Check messages when they arrive** and click **Next**.
3. In the box labeled **Which condition(s) do you want to check**, place a check mark in the boxes for **where my name is in the To box** and **with specific words in the subject or body**.
4. Notice the underlined text (`specific words`) in the **Rule description** box below the list of conditions. That's a signal that the Rules Wizard needs additional information. Click the underlined text to pop up the Search Text dialog box.
5. Enter the word `crisis` and click the **Add** button; then enter the word `urgent` and click the **Add** button. Click **OK** to return to the Rules Wizard dialog box.

6. Click **Next** and specify how you want to handle messages that match the criteria. In this case, choose **notify me using a specific message**. Click the underlined text `a specific message` in the **Rule description** box and enter a suitable warning message: `URGENT EMAIL!` Click **OK** to continue.
7. Click **Next** to add any exceptions to this list. If one of your coworkers attaches the word *urgent* to every message, for example, you might want to tell Outlook to ignore messages from that sender. Click **Next** to continue.
8. The last step of the Rules Wizard lets you give the rule a name, review its conditions, and turn it on. When you're finished, the rule should look like the one shown in Figure 29.17. Click **Finish** to put the rule to work for you.

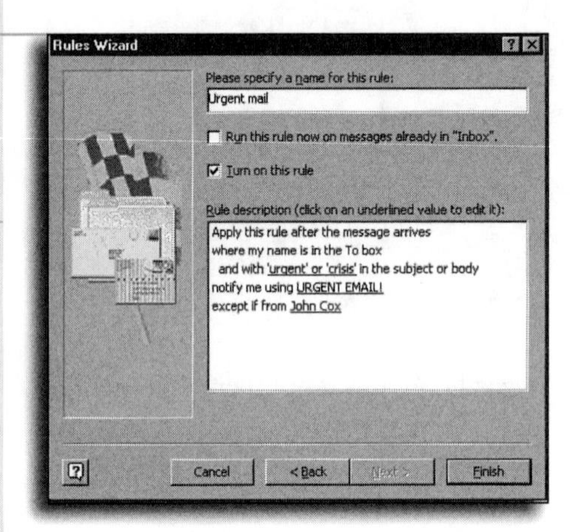

FIGURE 29.17

Use this rule to make sure urgent messages literally jump out of your Inbox.

Now, whenever any message arrives in your Inbox containing the words *urgent* or *crisis*, Outlook will notify you with the pop-up message shown in Figure 29.18. And you don't have to worry about losing an important message again.

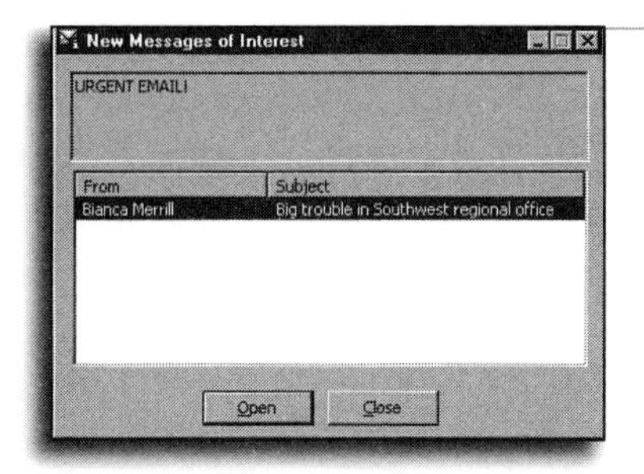

FIGURE 29.18
Outlook can pop up this impossible-to-miss warning message based on a rule you specify.

You can use rules to accomplish all sorts of tasks. For example, you can filter out all messages that contain the words *for sale* and aren't addressed specifically to you. Of course, that could be embarrassing if you're on the cc list of a message from your boss announcing that your company is for sale. Fortunately, there's a solution. You can assign priorities to individual rules so that one always takes precedence over another.

If you've assigned a "for sale" rule, just move it down the list of rules below the one that says all messages from your boss get a high-priority flag in your Inbox. In the "messages from boss" rule, find the dialog box labeled **What do you want to do with the message** and add the options **Mark it as high importance** and **stop processing more rules**. That last choice means no matter what your boss puts in an email, you'll see it.

Sending and Receiving Files As Email Attachments

You can send one or more files to another person (or to multiple recipients) as *attachments* to an email message. To share a Word document or an Excel workbook, for example, you can send it along with an email message explaining its purpose; all the recipient has to do is double-click its icon to see (and edit) the file.

Attachments aren't foolproof

Almost all mail systems can exchange attachments with each other these days, thanks to standards used by leading mail server software. However, that compatibility doesn't mean your attachments will get through every time. If the person on the other end of the mail connection receives mail through a corporate *gateway* that uses an older mail program, the standard attachment-handling formats might not work properly, and the attached file may be lost or damaged in transit. If you plan to exchange an important attachment with someone, your best bet is to first try a test with a small data file to make sure both mail systems can handle the attachment properly.

Open any attachment without opening the message

Click the large paper-clip icon in the message header of the Preview pane to display a list that shows the name and size of all attachments in the selected message, along with icons that tell you the file type. Click any item on the list to open it. If you plan to edit the file, be sure to save it under a new name.

To insert a file into an email message, click the **Insert File** button or pull down the **Insert** menu and choose **File**. You can also drag a file from the Windows desktop or a folder window and drop it into the body of any Outlook item.

If a message you receive includes one or more attached files, you see a small paper-clip icon to the left of the subject line in the message list. If the Preview pane is open, you see a larger paper-clip icon at the top right of the message header just below the message list.

To work with an attached file, open the message that includes the attachment and right-click the file icon in the bottom of the message window. Use the choices on the shortcut menu to open, save, copy, print, view, or remove the attachment.

Using Email to Share Office Documents

When you want to send a file out for comments and changes, you can simply attach it to an email message, or you can add a routing slip that helps ensure you get the file back with comments. You can attach a routing slip to any Word document, Excel workbook, or PowerPoint presentation. This option is not available for Publisher files, however.

Routing a File

1. Open the file you want to route for comments.
2. Pull down the **File** menu, choose **Send To**, and click **Routing Recipient**. The Routing Slip dialog box appears, as shown in Figure 29.19.
3. Click the **Address** button to add names from your Outlook Address Book; click **OK** after adding all names.
4. Edit the **Subject** line, if you want, and add a brief message in the **Message text** box.

5. In the **Route to recipients** section, choose how you want the message to travel: Use **One after another** if you want each recipient to see the previous recipient's comments. Use the **Move** buttons to adjust the order in which the document is routed. Choose **All at once** if you want all recipients to receive the message simultaneously and return changes directly to you.
6. Click **Add Slip** to save the routing slip without sending it. Click **Route** to send the file and its routing instructions immediately.

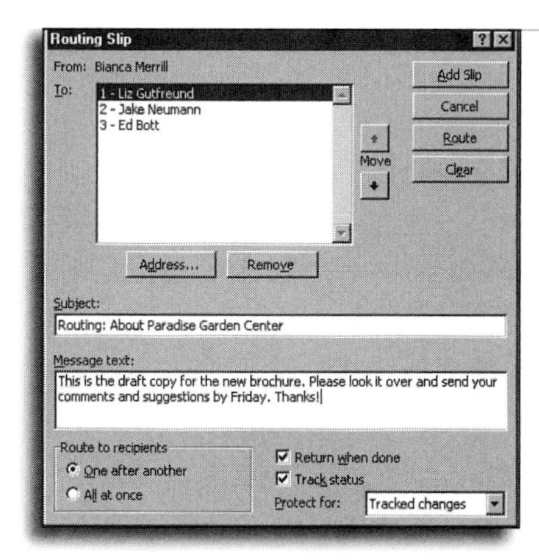

FIGURE 29.19

To ensure that other people get their comments back to you on time, click the **Track status** box.

The routing slip causes the file and its accompanying email message to land in the recipient's Inbox in a special format. As a note in the message explains, all the recipient has to do is double-click to open the file and then choose a simple menu command to send it to the next stop in the routing process. When the document has made it through the entire list, it comes back to you automatically.

Keep a watchful eye

Wondering why it's taking so long for that urgent file to get back to you? You wouldn't wonder if you had checked the **Track status** box on the routing slip. This option sends an email message every time the package moves to the next name on the routing slip.

CHAPTER

30

Managing Personal Information with Outlook

Manage events and appointments in your Calendar

Let Outlook remind you of important meetings

Share schedules and plan meetings

Track names and numbers in the Contacts Folder

Keep track of tasks and to-do items

Create yellow sticky notes

Print your schedule and phone list

Managing Your Personal Calendar

Outlook's Calendar folder lets you keep track of three similar types of items. *Appointments* have starting and ending times blocked out in your schedule; *events*, such as vacations or business trips, last 24 hours or more; and *meetings* are appointments to which you invite other people.

SEE ALSO

➤ *For details on how to use Outlook to create and manage meetings, see page 628*

Scheduling a New Appointment or Event

To begin creating a new appointment in the Calendar folder, click the **New Appointment** button to open a blank form (a filled-in version is shown in Figure 30.1). Start in the field labeled **Subject**. Use the Tab key to move from field to field, and then click the **Save and Close** button when you're finished.

SEE ALSO

➤ *For a more detailed discussion of the many forms and fields used in Outlook, see Chapter 27, "Outlook Essentials," in* Special Edition Using Microsoft Office 2000.

You can also create a new appointment by dragging an item (such as a mail message) from another folder and dropping it on the Calendar icon in the Outlook Bar.

If you know the time you want to schedule the meeting, you can double-click that time slot in any Calendar view to begin creating a new appointment. Or you can drag the mouse pointer to select an interval, right-click the selection, and then choose **New Appointment** or **New All Day Event**.

SEE ALSO

➤ *To learn about the many ways you can drag and drop to create Outlook items, see page 556*

Using the Date Navigator to Jump to a Specific Date

When you first click the Calendar icon in the Outlook Bar, you see today's schedule in Day/Week/Month View. The *Date Navigator* is the small calendar that appears on the right side of the Calendar window, just above the list of tasks. Like similar controls elsewhere in Office, the Date Navigator lets you quickly jump to any date to see the appointments and events scheduled for that date.

FIGURE 30.1

Filling in a new appointment is a simple matter of filling in the blanks. Use the Tab key to move from field to field.

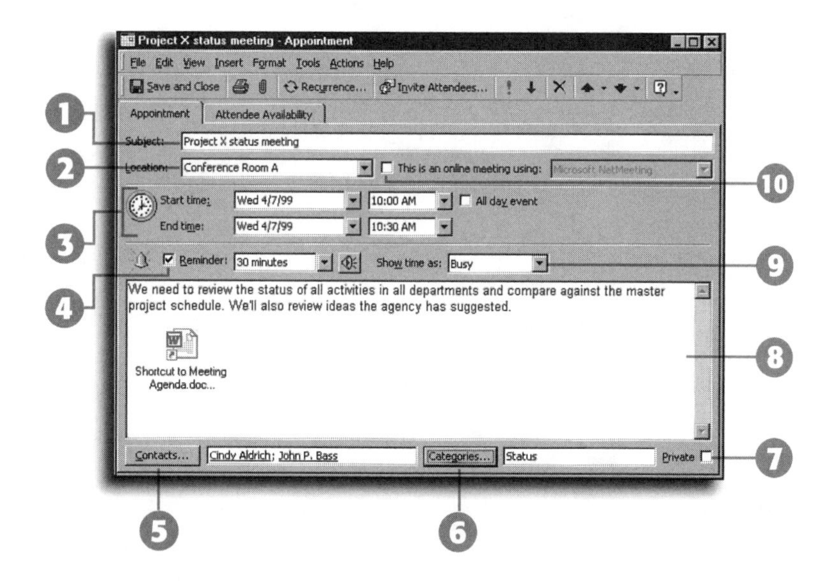

1. Enter the text you want to see in Calendar view.
2. Enter a location. To choose a location you've entered in other appointments, use the drop-down list.
3. Enter starting and ending times and dates. These boxes are unavailable for all-day events.
4. Appointments can pop up reminders at times you define. Click the **Sound** button to play a sound file when your reminder pops up.
5. Click this button to link the appointment to one or more items in your Contacts Folder.
6. Assign appointments to categories, just as you do contacts and tasks.
7. Check to designate an appointment as private so that no one who looks at your shared schedule will know that you've gone to the ball game.
8. Add detailed notes here. You can also attach shortcuts to other Outlook items or attach files or copies of Outlook items here.
9. Specify how others view your calendar by designating the time an appointment takes as Busy, Free, Tentative, or Out of Office.
10. Check this box to create a link to NetMeeting or other online conferencing software.

By default, the Date Navigator displays the current month and the following month when you switch to any Calendar view. To change the number of months in the Date Navigator, drag the left border, the bottom border, or both. Figure 30.2, for example, shows two months at a time in the Calendar view, but you could easily change this to one month or four.

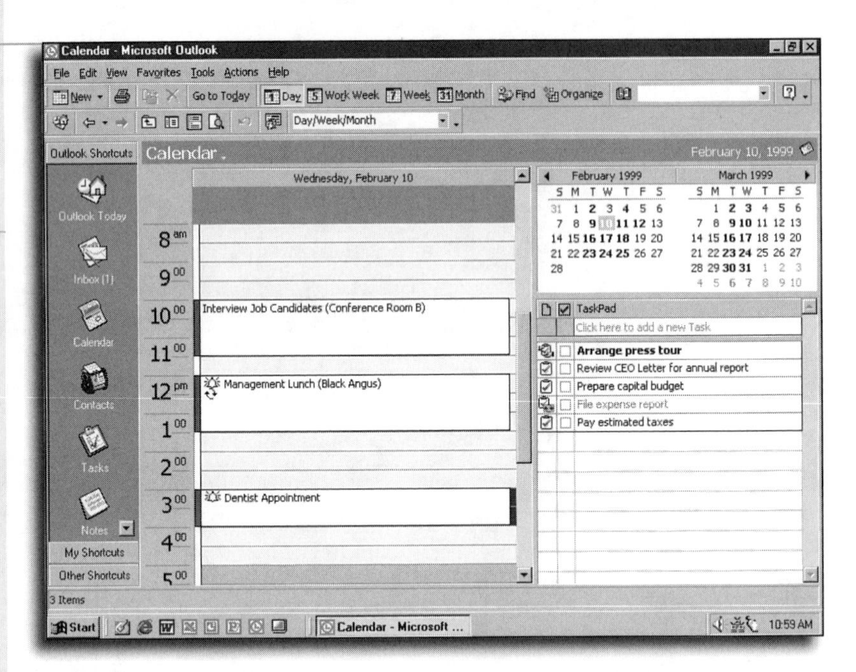

FIGURE 30.2

Bold numbers in the Date Navigator tell you that appointments or events are scheduled on those days.

Viewing a Daily, Weekly, or Monthly Calendar

The default view of your appointments shows just one day at a time, but you can expand the view to cover appointments that span a week or a month at a time. Use buttons on the Calendar folder's Standard toolbar to switch between four views:

Day	Shows one day's events; use the Date Navigator to show another day's schedule, or click the **Go to Today** button to display today's appointments.

Work Week	Shows a side-by-side view of five days at a time, excluding weekends.
Week	Shows a full week at a time, with each day's appointments in a box; Saturday and Sunday listings are half the size of other days.
Month	Shows a "month at a glance" calendar, with event descriptions truncated to fit; the Date Navigator and Taskpad are normally hidden in this view, although you can drag the right border of the calendar to make them visible.

Figure 30.3 shows a typical monthly view. Events that span multiple days appear in banners in this view.

Outlook includes a variety of Calendar options, stored in two different locations. To adjust the basic look and feel of this folder, pull down the **Tools** menu, choose **Options**, click the **Preferences** tab, and then click the **Calendar Options** button. Options available in this dialog box (Figure 30.4) let you tell Outlook which days make up your work week and a typical working day. If you regularly travel on business or work with a division in another part of the world, you can also specify a second time zone to display in daily views of the Calendar folder.

To change options for Outlook's built-in Day, Week, and Month views, right-click any unused space in the calendar display and choose **Other Settings**. The dialog box shown in Figure 30.5 appears. The most useful option here lets you adjust the **Time scale** from its default setting of 30 minutes. Professionals who bill in 15-minute increments may want to set this value lower; set this value to one hour if you want to see your entire schedule without scrolling.

Create a custom view of your schedule

Use the Date Navigator to create a custom view of your calendar that's different from the standard day, week, and month views. Hold down the Ctrl key while you click two or more dates (they don't have to be adjacent), and the display changes to show you a side-by-side view of the schedules for the selected days. This technique is especially useful if you're checking several days on your schedule to see which one works best for a meeting or business trip.

Change your work week

Does your job have a different work week than the conventional Monday through Friday grind? To adjust your working days, pull down the **Tools** menu, choose **Options**, and click the **Calendar Options** button on the **Preferences** tab. Check the boxes that correspond to the days in your work week, and tell Outlook which day your week starts with, as well.

View today's appointments

Go ahead and use the Calendar to look through future days, weeks, or months. You can always click the **Go To Today** button to return instantly to today's schedule.

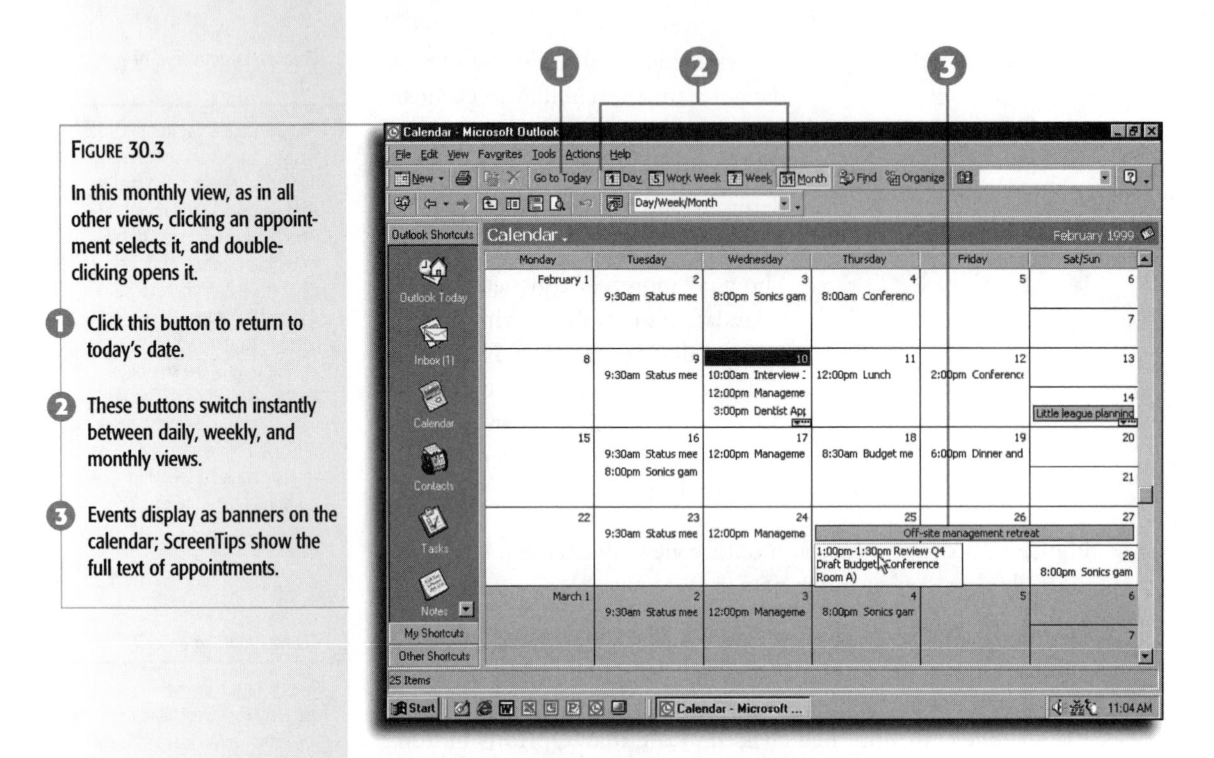

FIGURE 30.3

In this monthly view, as in all other views, clicking an appointment selects it, and double-clicking opens it.

1. Click this button to return to today's date.
2. These buttons switch instantly between daily, weekly, and monthly views.
3. Events display as banners on the calendar; ScreenTips show the full text of appointments.

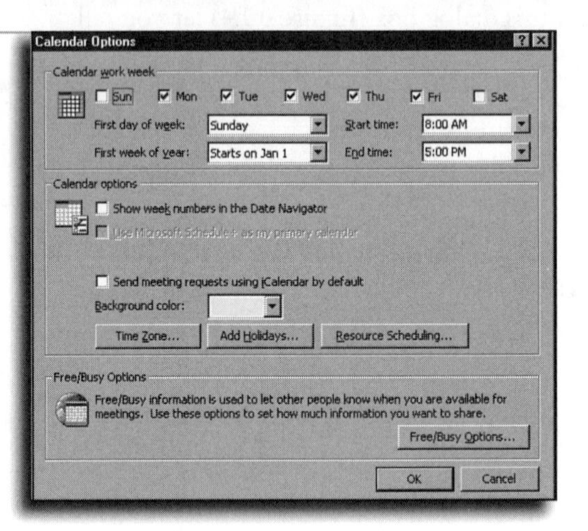

FIGURE 30.4

Frequent flyers can click the **Time Zone** button to add a second clock to the display of daily Calendar events.

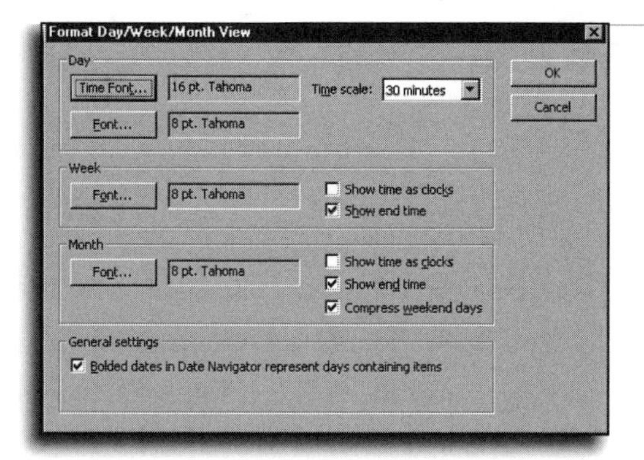

FIGURE 30.5
Adjust these options to change the way Outlook's default Day/Week/Month views display your schedule.

Letting Outlook Enter Dates and Times for You

To enter a date in any date field, you can type the date in a format that Outlook recognizes, such as `3/1` or `Mar 15`. If you'd rather pick from a calendar, click the drop-down arrow to the right of the date field to display the current month. Use the arrows to scroll backward or forward, and then click the date you want.

When you enter dates and times for appointments, you don't have to be precise. One of my favorite Outlook features is *AutoDate*, which can recognize text such as `next Thursday`, `one week from today`, or `tomorrow`, substituting the correct date for you. To schedule a doctor's appointment for next Tuesday at 2:00 p.m., for example, just click in the **Start time** box, enter `next tue`, press Tab, and type `2` (Outlook assumes that times are during the workday unless you specify otherwise).

AutoDate understands dates and times that you spell out or abbreviate, such as `4p` (for 4:00 p.m.) or `first of jan`. It recognizes holidays that fall on the same day every year, like New Year's Eve and Christmas. It can also correctly interpret dozens of words you might use to define a date or an interval of time, including `yesterday`, `today`, `tomorrow`, `next`, `following`, `through`, and `until`.

What else can you type for a date and time?

For a detailed list of words and phrases AutoDate can recognize, type `AutoDate` in the Office Assistant's search box and read the Help topic, "What you can type in date and time fields."

Entering a Recurring Appointment

You can easily enter a *recurring appointment*—one that happens on a regular basis, such as a weekly status report, a monthly sales meeting, or a regular deadline that falls on the second Tuesday of each month.

Setting Up a Recurring Appointment or Event

1. Click the **New Appointment** button.
2. Enter the **Subject**, **Location**, and other details of the appointment.
3. Enter the starting and ending time for the appointment or check the **All day event** box.
4. Click the **Recurrence** button to display the Appointment Recurrence dialog box (see Figure 30.6).
5. Adjust the options as needed to match the schedule of your event. Enter an ending date or a fixed number of occurrences, if appropriate.
6. Click **OK** to close the Appointment Recurrence dialog box; the Appointment tab changes to display the recurrence details.
7. Click **Save and Close** to add the recurring appointment or event to your Calendar folder. Outlook adds a recurrence icon to the left of the event description.

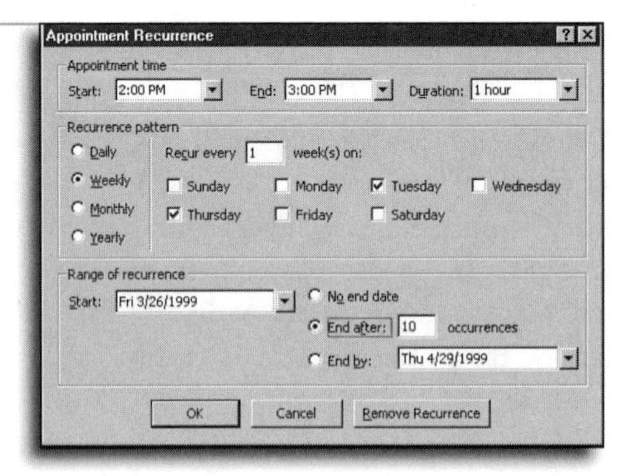

FIGURE 30.6

Use this dialog box to schedule even complicated recurring appointments, like this one every Tuesday and Thursday at 2:00 p.m. for the next five weeks (or 10 occurrences).

To change a single instance of a recurring appointment or event (if a regularly scheduled meeting is canceled or postponed, for example), open the item. A dialog box lets you specify whether you want to change the entire series or just the selected instance.

See all your recurring events

To see a list of all recurring appointments and events (and edit one or more of them, if necessary), switch to Outlook's predefined Recurring Appointments view. Note that this list includes birthdays and anniversaries, which Outlook treats as recurring annual events.

Editing an Appointment or Event

As with any Outlook item, you can edit every part of an event or appointment by opening it and adjusting information in individual fields. However, you can use several time-saving shortcuts if you simply want to change the time, date, or description of an appointment or event:

- To edit the description of an event or appointment, click its listing in any calendar view and add or edit text.
- To change the scheduled starting time for an appointment, point to the left border of the item until you see a four-headed arrow, and then drag the item to its new time.
- To move an item to a different day, point to the left border of the item until you see a four-headed arrow, and then drag the item and drop it on the selected day in the Date Navigator or in the Week or Month view. (If the date you want is not visible in the Date Navigator, click the arrows to display that month before you drag the item.)
- To copy an item, hold down the Ctrl key and drag it to the new date using the Week or Month view or the Date Navigator.

You can't edit everything

In Outlook's Day view, every item shows a time, a description, and the location in parentheses. When you click on the item to begin editing it, the time and location disappear, leaving you only the description to edit.

Letting Outlook Remind You of Appointments and Events

When you set a *reminder* for an appointment or event, Outlook adds a reminder icon in the Day, Week, and Month calendar views. When the reminder time rolls around, Outlook plays a sound (if you selected that option) and pops up a reminder message similar to the one in Figure 30.7.

Leave Outlook running

Do you depend on reminders to keep you on schedule? Then leave Outlook running at all times. Outlook displays past-due reminders the next time you start the program, but these reminders don't do you much good if you've already missed an important business meeting or a dentist appointment. To make sure Outlook starts up every time you turn on your PC, add a shortcut to the StartUp group on the Programs menu.

FIGURE 30.7

If the Outlook Assistant is visible, it displays reminder messages like this one.

When you see a reminder, you have three choices:

- Choose **Dismiss this reminder** if you don't need to see the message again.
- The middle option works like the snooze button on an alarm clock. **Remind me again in 5 minutes** is the default choice. Use the drop-down list to select a new reminder time as much as one week later, and then click the entry to reset the reminder.
- Click **Open this item** to display the appointment or event that includes the reminder. This option is useful when the appointment includes notes that you want to review.

Change the default reminder time

By default, Outlook adds a reminder to all appointments, set for 15 minutes before the scheduled time. To change this setting, pull down the **Tools** menu, choose **Options**, and click the **Preferences** tab. Set the preferred interval by using the pull-down list (or typing an entry) in the box labeled **Default reminder**. If you want new appointments to include reminders only when you specifically set them, clear the check box to the left of the box labeled **Default reminder**.

Managing Your List of Contacts

Outlook's *Contacts Folder* is a useful place to store names, addresses, phone numbers, and other important information about friends, family, and business associates. Use these records to address new email messages, start personalized letters in Word, or create follow-up reminders.

For a complete list of what you can do when you select an item in the Contacts Folder, pull down the **Actions** menu. Right-click any item to see an abbreviated list that includes only the most popular choices.

Entering Personal Information for a New Contact

Switch to the Contacts Folder and click the **New Contact** button to open a blank form. Figure 30.8 shows a filled-in Contact form. Start in the field labeled **Full Name** and use the Tab key to jump from field to field. After you've entered all the information, click the **Save and Close** button to store the new item.

Outlook's form for creating a new item in the Contacts Folder includes a number of smart features that help you enter properly formatted information quickly and accurately. For example, you can enter phone numbers any way you like, with or without hyphens and parentheses; Outlook reformats the numbers using standard punctuation when you exit the field. If you omit the area code, Outlook assumes the number is local and adds your area code to the entry.

When you enter a name or address, Outlook checks to make sure that all information is there. If you omit a key bit of information, such as city, state, or postal/zip code, the dialog box shown in Figure 30.9 pops up, asking whether you're sure you want to enter the incomplete record.

Base one contact on another

To begin a new contact item by copying key information from another, right-click the first item in Address Card or Phone List view, and then choose **New Contact from Same Company**. If the item is already open, click the **Actions** menu to choose this option. Outlook creates a new item, entering the company name, address, and phone number, but clearing all other fields.

Entering telephone extensions

Does your contact's phone number include an extension? Add this information at the end of the phone number, preceded by a space and the letters `x` or `ext`. Outlook ignores this information when formatting the phone number or using the AutoDial feature.

Using Address Cards to View Essential Contact Information

When you click the Contacts Folder icon in the Outlook Bar, you see the default *Address Cards view*, shown in Figure 30.10. This view includes the contact's name (as defined in the **File as** field) plus the mailing address and all phone numbers defined for the contact. This view lets you see a fairly large number of records at one time, but it doesn't display company or job title information for every contact.

To see more information about each contact, switch to the Detailed Address Cards view, which displays virtually all fields in each contact record.

SEE ALSO

➤ *For full instructions on switching to another view of the current folder, see page 550*

Entering one contact after another

To create several new Contact items in a row, enter the information for the first item, pull down the **File** menu, and then choose **Save and New** to save the current record and clear the form so that you can begin a new contact.

FIGURE 30.8
Outlook automatically fills in some of the blanks when you create a new item in the Contacts Folder, and it checks the rest to make sure that you left nothing out.

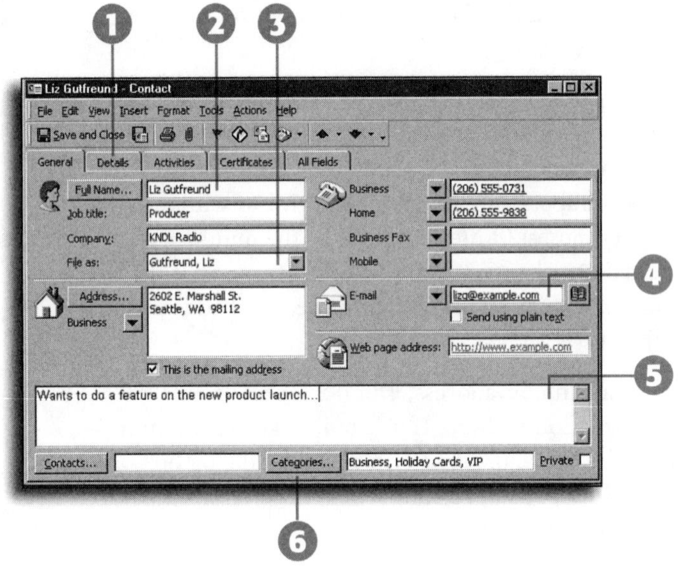

1. Click here to enter extra details, such as the contact's birthday or assistant's name.
2. Enter the full name here, in any order; Outlook breaks it into first and last name for you.
3. Outlook guesses how you want the entry filed. Use the drop-down list to pick another alternative or type your own entry, such as `Travel Agent`.
4. Enter up to three email addresses in this box.
5. Enter free-form notes in this box. You can also drag icons for files or shortcuts and drop them here.
6. Assign the new entry to categories, and then filter to create holiday card lists and other special views.

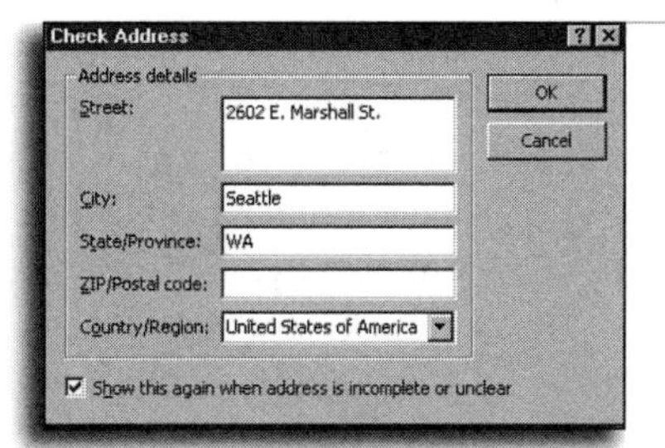

FIGURE 30.9
If you leave out information in an address, you get a chance to correct it in this dialog box.

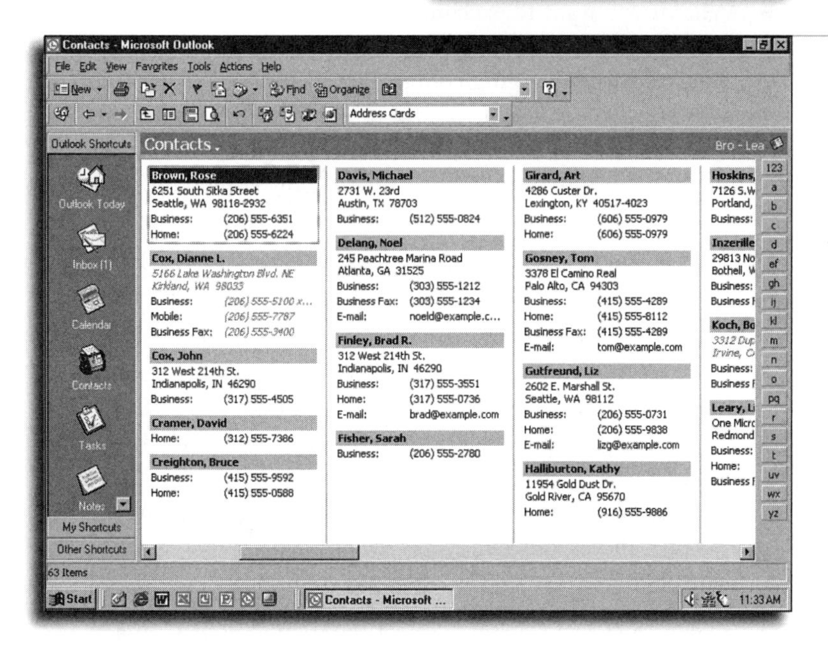

FIGURE 30.10
The default Address Cards view packs the maximum number of records onto the screen by displaying only essential address and phone information.

Editing a Contact Record

If you simply want to change an address or phone number or edit a misspelled name, you don't need to open a Contact item. You can edit information directly in Address Cards view. Click the letter along the right side of the window that matches the first letter of the item you're looking for. Use the scrollbars, if necessary, to find the name you're looking for, and then just click and start typing.

Exchanging Contact Records with Other People

If you've asked a coworker to follow up with a customer on your behalf, you can make the job easier by sending along your

Contact item for that person. If you're certain the other person uses Outlook, the procedure is easy: Create a new email message and address it to your coworker, and then drag the item from the Contacts Folder and drop it in the message window. Add some comments, if you wish, and click the **Send** button. After your coworker opens the message, he or she can drag the icon into the Contacts Folder to add the item.

What if you want to exchange information with someone who doesn't use Outlook? Outlook fully supports an emerging standard for exchanging contact information over the Internet. This standard, called the *vCard* format (short for "virtual business card"), packs standard name, business, address, and phone fields into a simple text file that any compatible program can import.

When you send your vCard to another person via email, that person can easily import your address information into Outlook, Lotus Organizer, or any compatible contact management program. You can also attach a vCard for another person to an email message. Of course, before you can send a vCard containing your personal or work information, you have to create it. Make sure the card doesn't include any sensitive information, such as your home address and phone number or notes about your family, before you send it to a casual acquaintance!

Not sure? Use vCard format

Unless you're absolutely certain the person to whom you're sending a mail message uses Outlook, you'll have better luck sending contact information in vCard format. In fact, because this card uses plain text, you can even open a vCard in a text editor such as Notepad!

To send a vCard via email, select the item in your Contacts Folder, pull down the **Actions** menu, and then choose **Forward as vCard**. Outlook saves the contact information as a file, opens a blank email form, and attaches the vCard file. Address the message, add explanatory text if you wish, and send it just as you would any email message.

Changing the Way a Contact Item Is Filed

In both Address Cards views, the field used for sorting and displaying information is the **File as** field. By default, this field uses the information you type in the **Full Name** field, displaying it last name first. If you don't enter a name, Outlook assumes the record refers to a business and uses the information from the **Company** field. You can accept the default, or you can change the information displayed here.

Changing the Way an Address Card Is Filed

1. Open the item you want to change and position the insertion point in the **File as** field.
2. Click the drop-down arrow to choose from the list of available default choices. If the **Full Name** and **Company** fields contain data, Outlook offers the following choices:
   - Full name, first name first
   - Full name, last name first
   - Company name
   - Full name, last name first, followed by company name in parentheses
   - Company name, followed by full name, last name first, in parentheses
3. If you want to enter a label other than these default choices, replace the contents of the **File as** field with an entry of your own choosing. Whatever you type will appear in alphabetical order in all views of your Contacts Folder.
4. Click **Save and Close** to store the change and update your Contacts Folder immediately.

A new feature in Outlook 2000 lets you define the order of names in the Full Name and File As fields for new Contact items. Pull down the **Tools** menu, choose **Options**, and click the **Contact Options** button on the **Preferences** tab. If you prefer to enter all your new contacts last name first, with the company name in parentheses, you can select that format in the **Default "File As" Order** box.

Tracking Activities for Each Contact

Simply having a contact's name, address, and phone number in your Contacts Folder is only a start. Over time, you'll exchange email messages and phone calls with business associates, and you'll also schedule meetings or appointments that involve other people. Outlook lets you maintain links between contacts and *activities*. You can use those links to see, at a glance, all the interactions you've had with an individual.

Don't send vCards indiscriminately

Outlook's signature feature offers an option to send your vCard as an attachment with every message you send. Resist the urge to turn on this option. Although vCards are relatively compact, they do take up space, and many correspondents may find it annoying if even a two-line message from you includes a 1KB attachment. Send vCards only when you're certain that the recipients will welcome it.

Mix and match filing systems

Although organizing a phone book by last name is traditional, you might choose to mix different filing orders within the Contacts Folder. For example, when you enter a record for a person who serves as your main contact with a company, file the record under the company name with the person's name in parentheses. No matter how you file it, though, you can always use Outlook's **Find** button to look for information.

Do you need more than Outlook?

If your job depends on closely tracking activities with contacts and keeping that information available at a moment's notice, Outlook probably isn't powerful enough for you. Many salespeople, for example, use Symantec's Act! or similar software to maintain detailed information about customers, prospects, sales calls, and follow-up strategies.

What types of activities can you link to a contact? In theory, you can link any Outlook item or file to a contact, but these are the most common:

- Email messages—Outlook automatically creates links based on the address fields.
- Meetings and appointments—Outlook automatically creates links to meetings when you send an invitation. You must manually create a link for appointments.

SEE ALSO

To learn how to use meeting invitations, see page 628

- Tasks—Outlook automatically creates links when you assign a task to another person. You must manually create links for items that exist only in your own Tasks Folder.
- Documents—You can manually create a link between a contact and a Word document, Excel worksheet, PowerPoint presentation, or any other file.

You don't need to do anything to create a link to a mail message or meeting. Use any of the following three techniques to manually link a contact to a file or another item:

- Open the item, click the **Contacts** button, and select one or more names from the list that pops up. Click **OK** to add a link to another person's record. This trick is useful if one person is your main contact at a company, but you want to be able to display the name, address, and phone number for a backup contact when that person is away on business or vacation.
- Open the Contacts Folder and select an item. Pull down the **Actions** menu and choose any of the options that begin with New. For example, **New Task for Contact** creates a Task item and adds the contact's name as a link. These menu choices are also available if you open the Contact item.

You can't just type a name

The Contacts field at the bottom of an appointment or task item doesn't work the same as the address field in an email message, where you can simply type a name and look it up in your address book. To create a link here, you must click the **Contacts** button and use the dialog box to select a name. Links appear in the item with an underline.

SEE ALSO

For instructions on how to use Word's Letter Wizard, see page 300

- To manually create links between a contact and one or more items or documents, start by selecting the contact item. Then pull down the **Actions** menu, choose **Link**, and then select **Items** or **File**. If you select the latter option, choose one or more documents from the Open dialog box; to link other Outlook items, select the items you want to link from the dialog box shown in Figure 30.11.

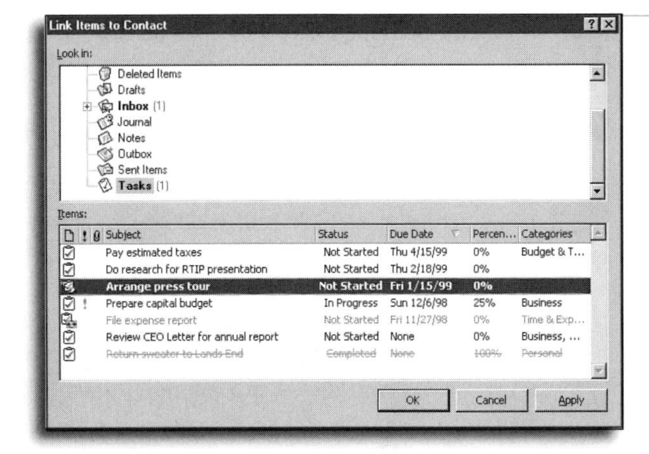

FIGURE 30.11

Choose one or more items from this list to link them to a Contact item; in this example, I've linked a task to a specific contact.

How do you see the activities that are linked to a contact? Open the Contact item and click the Activities tab to see a full list similar to the one in Figure 30.12. Click the **Show** drop-down list to restrict the search to only email messages, documents, upcoming activities such as meetings or appointments, or other specific categories.

Document Links use the Journal folder

When you create a link between a document and a contact item, Outlook creates a *Journal item* with all the correct links, adding a shortcut to the document in that item. If you use the phone dialer to make a call based on a Contact item, you also have the option to create a Journal item. These are the only situations in which activity links use the Journal folder.

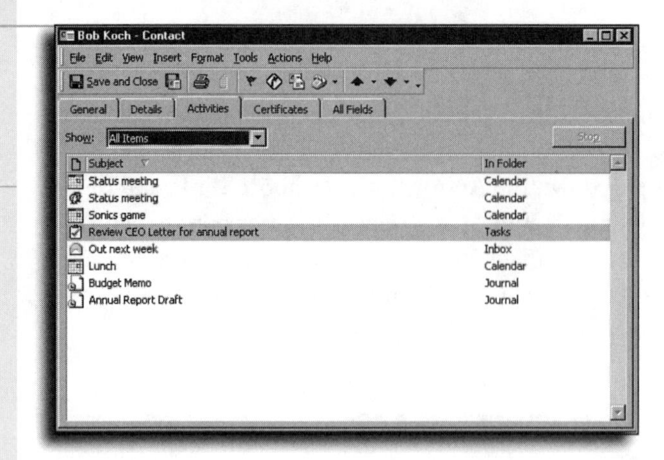

FIGURE 30.12

Use this list to see activities that you've linked to an individual contact.

Tracking Tasks and To-Do Items

The *Tasks* Folder offers a convenient place to keep track of items on your to-do list. You can move tasks around, sort, categorize, prioritize, and assign due dates, so you can do first things first, as shown in Figure 30.13. Items in the Tasks Folder resemble appointments or events in some respects, with the crucial addition of deadlines and status fields. If you expect that completing a task will take awhile, you can include a start date and due date, and you can keep track of your progress by recording how much of the task you've completed.

A selected list of tasks appears in the *TaskPad* at the right of the default Calendar view. Changes that you make in this view appear in the Tasks Folder as well. By default, the TaskPad shows today's tasks, but you can change this view to display tasks for the days visible in the calendar, all tasks, or only overdue tasks. To change the view, right-click any empty space in the TaskPad, and choose **TaskPad View** from the shortcut menu.

You can also get a quick overview of your tasks by looking at the Outlook Today page. This view, too, is customizable.

SEE ALSO

➤ *For details on how to customize the Outlook Today page, see page 545*

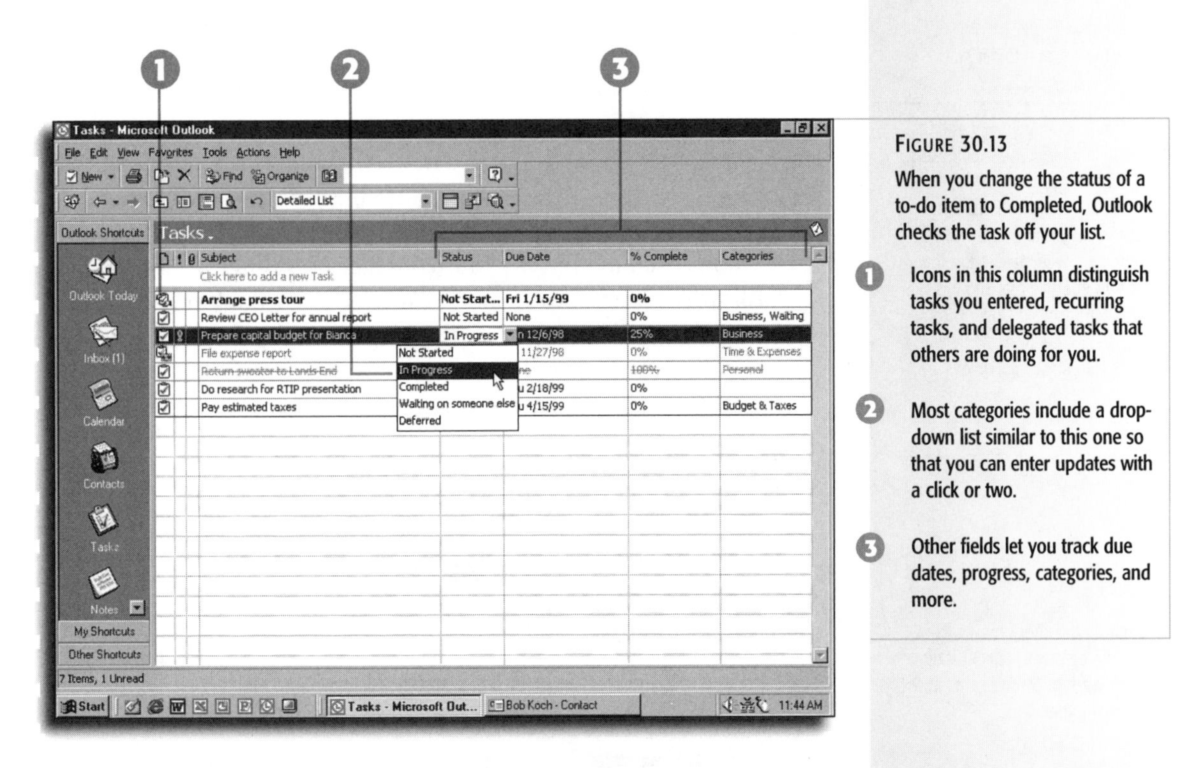

FIGURE 30.13

When you change the status of a to-do item to Completed, Outlook checks the task off your list.

1. Icons in this column distinguish tasks you entered, recurring tasks, and delegated tasks that others are doing for you.
2. Most categories include a drop-down list similar to this one so that you can enter updates with a click or two.
3. Other fields let you track due dates, progress, categories, and more.

Using the Journal to Track Activities

In theory, Outlook's Journal acts as an electronic diary that automatically tracks items as you work. Each time you do one of the things on a long list of items—send or receive an email message, open or print a file, receive an assigned task or meeting request—Outlook can make an entry in the *Journal folder*. Later, you can switch to the Journal folder's timeline view to see what you did on a given day (or week or month). You can also filter the Journal to see a list of activities you performed on behalf of a certain client or in connection with a project.

In practice, Outlook's Journal is an example of a good idea that doesn't work. Microsoft introduced the Journal feature in the original version of Outlook, but users found it confusing and nearly useless. As a result, Microsoft no longer recommends that you keep track of events this way. Instead, they suggest you use Outlook's activity-tracking features to link events with contacts.

Use the right mouse button!

No matter which Outlook folder you work with, use the right mouse button often, and be sure to watch the buttons on the toolbar carefully. As you switch between different types of items, you'll discover that the options available to you change as well. When you right-click an item in the Tasks Folder, for example, you can assign it to someone else, mark it complete, or send a status report, all using shortcut menus.

Why is the Journal folder still here?

If Microsoft no longer recommends the Journal folder for Outlook users, why is it still in Outlook 2000? For compatibility reasons. Some long-time users of Outlook, especially in corporations, were able to put the Journal to effective use, and this capability remains in Outlook 2000 so that those users will still be able to work with these applications.

SEE ALSO

➤ *For details on how you can track phone calls, mail messages, and other activities, see page 619*

If you install Office 2000 on a new PC, the Journal keeps track of files you open. If you install over an existing copy of Office 97, the Setup program will use the settings from your previous version. Each item in the Journal folder uses roughly 5KB of disk space. That doesn't sound like much, but the Journal folder can quickly swell to several megabytes if you don't monitor it carefully. I recommend that you check your Journal settings and adjust them if necessary to make sure the program isn't needlessly filling this folder with entries. Pull down the **Tools** menu, choose **Options**, click the **Journal Options** button, and inspect the list shown in Figure 30.14.

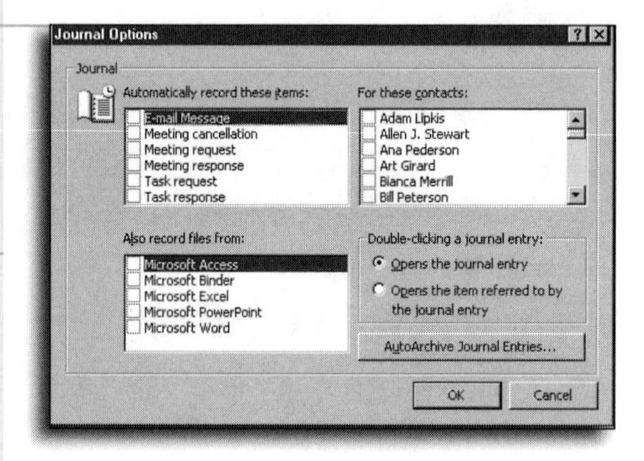

FIGURE 30.14

Clear all the check marks from this dialog box to tell Outlook you don't want to track actions in the Journal folder.

Working with Notes

Imagining how the average office survived before the invention of yellow sticky notes is difficult. Outlook 2000 includes a computer version of these indispensable little reminders. To add a new note, click the **Notes** button in the Outlook Bar. Then click the **New Note** button and begin typing, as I've done in Figure 30.15.

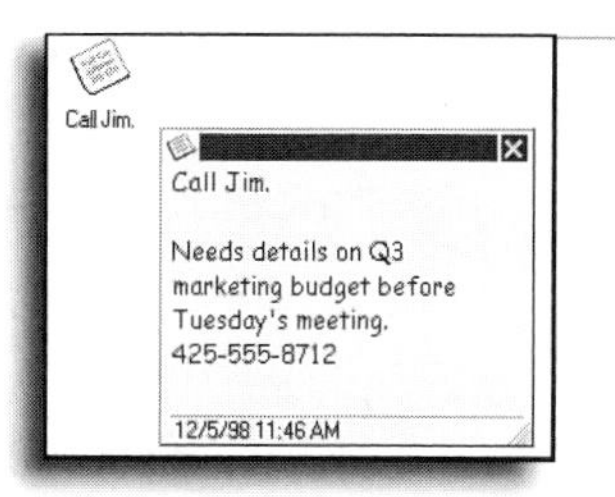

FIGURE 30.15
Just start typing, and this little note sticks to your Outlook screen. Right-click to switch colors from yellow to pink or green.

Enter a short title for the note and press Enter. This is the text that will appear underneath the icon in your Notes folder. Then type the rest of your note. In theory, you can enter up to 30,000 characters in a single note, although short notes are most effective.

Put a sticky note on the desktop

Outlook's sticky notes are useful, and they work outside Outlook just as well. Try dragging a note directly onto your Windows desktop so that you don't forget it. Right-drag the note from the Outlook window onto the desktop, and you can choose whether to move the note or create a copy.

Printing Calendars and Phone Lists

Even the most confirmed desk jockey has to get away from the computer sooner or later. If you trust all your important schedule details and your phone list to Outlook, what do you do? Put it on paper.

You can print calendars and contact lists in a variety of styles and formats. Before printing, you can select a subset of the records in either folder. This feature can be useful when you're heading off on a business trip, for example, and you want to print your schedule plus the addresses and phone numbers of contacts in that area.

To print your schedule for one day or for multiple days, weeks, or months, first switch to the Calendar folder.

Printing Your Calendar

1. If you plan to print one day, week, or month, select the corresponding view for the period.
2. Click the **Print** button. Outlook displays the dialog box shown in Figure 30.16.
3. Choose one of the five page formats from the **Print style** list.
4. In the **Print range** box, adjust the **Start** and **End** dates, if necessary.

Only one view offers full details

If you've added detailed notes to items on your schedule, only one view allows you to print those details so that you can see them on paper. Choose **Calendar Details Style** to format the pages so that they include all details, not just the description, time, and location.

5. Click the **Preview** button to see what your page will look like when printed. Use the Page Up and Page Down keys (or the corresponding toolbar buttons) to see additional pages.
6. Click the **Page Setup** button to adjust layout options, paper sizes, fonts, headers, footers, and other settings.
7. Click **Print** to send the schedule to the printer.

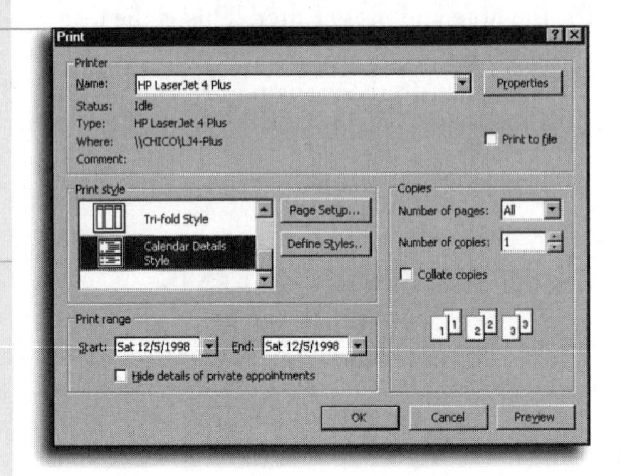

FIGURE 30.16

Choose the **Calendar Details Style** option to print all the notes you've added for individual appointments and events on your calendar.

Try printing on both sides of the paper

If your printer supports two-sided printing, you can print the contents of your Contacts Folder in booklet form using both sides of the paper. When you choose either of the pre-built booklet styles, a dialog box will remind you to set your printer's double-sided printing options.

The procedures for printing items from your Contacts Folder are nearly identical. Before printing, select individual items or use the **Find** button to filter the list, and then click the **Print** button. Choose **Memo Style** if you want to see detailed notes for one or several contacts. Choose **Phone Directory Style** for a simple list that includes only names and phone numbers.

CHAPTER

31

Managing Meetings and Tasks

Plan and request a meeting using Outlook's meeting organizer

Send and process meeting invitations

Check meeting and attendee status

Reschedule or cancel a meeting

Assign tasks to other people

Accept or decline assigned tasks

Planning a Meeting

To Outlook, a *meeting* is different from an *appointment*. An appointment is a block of time on your own personal calendar. If the appointment involves other people, they're completely unaware of the details on your calendar, and they're responsible for maintaining their own calendars. A meeting, on the other hand, uses email to send identical items to the Calendar folders of two or more people. As part of the planning process, the *meeting organizer* can reserve a conference room or other resources, such as overhead projectors. If possible, Outlook checks for free and busy time on everyone's calendar before confirming the meeting details. And confusion never occurs over the agreed-upon time, because Outlook lets the meeting organizer send invitations and automatically track who has accepted or declined an invitation.

Publishing your schedule

If you want to share details of your schedule with other people, you need to publish your free and busy time. If your office includes a *Microsoft Exchange* email server, your network administrator can show you how to make your Calendar available for other users to see free and busy time. You can also publish your Free/Busy information (but not schedule details) to a Web server for sharing over the Internet or a company intranet. To specify the name of the Web server, pull down the **Tools** menu, choose **Options**, click the **Calendar Options** button, and click the **Free/Busy Options** button.

Creating a New Meeting Request

To get started creating a new meeting request, switch to the Calendar folder, pull down the **File** menu, click **New**, and choose **Meeting Request**. (If you already know the meeting time, you can select the date and time in any Calendar view and then right-click and choose **New Meeting Request** from the shortcut menu.) The **Appointment** tab of this dialog box (shown in Figure 31.1) looks exactly like any other item in your Calendar folder, with the crucial addition of the **To** field. If your meeting request is simple, fill in the details on this tab, add one or more names to the **To** list, and send the request via email.

Send attachments with meeting invitations

To help attendees prepare for a meeting, you might want to send an agenda or a background memo or worksheet with the invitation. Click in the message body window at the bottom of the **Appointment** tab, open the **Insert** menu, choose **File**, and pick the file from the folder in which it's stored.

What if you want to avoid a lengthy exchange of email messages over schedules and details? If all the people in your office have shared their calendars over the network, Outlook can help you find a time when everyone is free and can automatically add the meeting to their calendars. To get started, click the **Attendee Availability** tab, and then fill in the details in the dialog box, as shown in Figure 31.2. Don't forget to include the details in the window at the bottom of the **Appointment** tab, which serves as the text of the emailed invitation.

You can't change the meeting organizer

When you plan a meeting, your name always appears at the top of the Attendee Availability list; your Attendance status is listed as meeting organizer. You cannot change this status, although you can delete your name from the list.

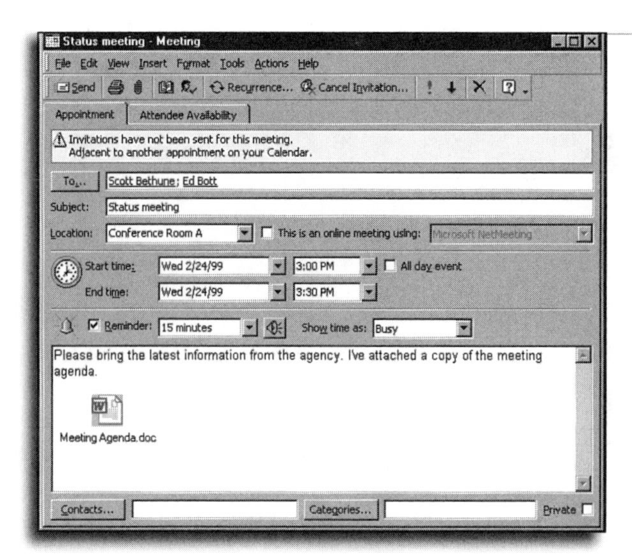

FIGURE 31.1

A meeting request looks like a cross between an appointment and an email message. Enter the names of other attendees; Outlook will look up their addresses from your address book.

This tab also lets you designate some attendees as Required and others as Optional. By default, anyone you invite to a meeting is Required. To change the status to Optional, click the **Show attendee status** option on the **Attendee Availability** tab. Use the drop-down arrow in the Attendee column for each name to adjust an invitee's status.

Outlook adds addresses automatically

When you enter names on the **Attendee Availability** tab, Outlook checks the names automatically and adds the addresses in the **To** field on the **Appointment** tab.

Processing Meeting Invitations

After you've finished entering all the details in your Meeting Request, click the **Send** button. Outlook delivers the requests via email to all the prospective attendees.

A *meeting invitation* looks a bit different from an ordinary mail message. A Meeting Request icon appears to the left of the invitation in the message list, for example, and the default toolbar contains a few extra buttons, as shown in Figure 31.3.

Click one of the three buttons along the top of the message window to **Accept** the invitation or **Decline** to attend. Click the **Tentative** button when you think you can make it, but you're not ready to commit. The status bar at the top of the message changes to remind you what you did, and if you accept the invitation, Outlook adds the item to your calendar. You can add a note to the response or just send it back to the meeting organizer.

Start with the Contacts Folder

If the names of all your meeting attendees are in the Contacts Folder, use it as your starting point. Select one or more contact records, click the **Actions** menu, and then choose **New Meeting with Contact**. Outlook opens a new Meeting Request form already addressed to the persons whose records are selected. Use the **Attendee Availability** tab to pick common free times for everyone.

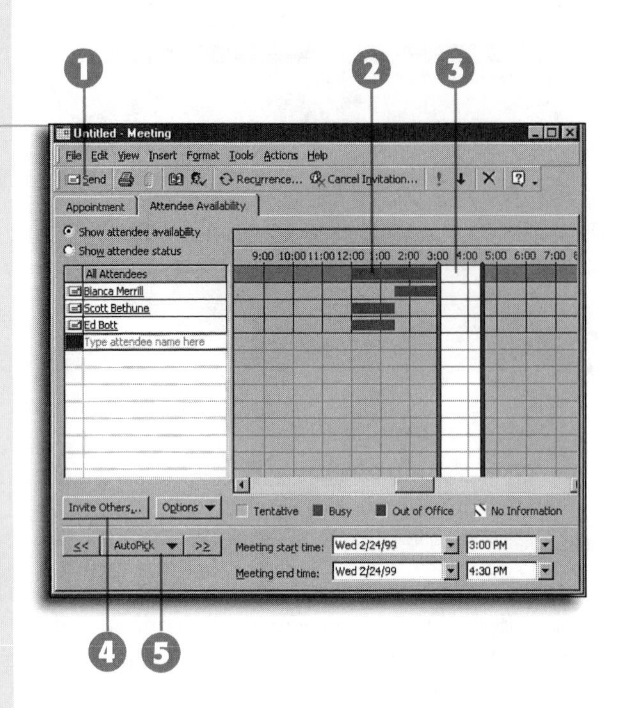

FIGURE 31.2

Outlook lets you compare schedules to pick the right meeting time, but the process works only if people keep their calendars up-to-date.

1. Click here to add the meeting request to your calendar and send invitations.
2. Color-coded blocks show free and busy times on the schedule.
3. The white zone is the block of time set aside for your meeting; click a new time if you want and then drag the left and right borders to make the meeting longer or shorter.
4. Click here to invite additional people to the meeting; you can choose whether their attendance is required or optional.
5. Click here to have Outlook automatically pick the next free time in other people's calendars; click the left or right arrows to pick an earlier or later time.

Checking the Status of a Meeting You've Arranged

By default, meeting invitations include the equivalent of an RSVP option. As people accept or decline the invitation, Outlook sends the responses to you and keeps track of who said yes and no. As the meeting organizer, you can open the meeting item on your calendar at any time to check its status. The status bar at the top of the **Appointment** tab keeps a running tally of the number of prospective attendees who have accepted, declined, or failed to respond.

Click the **Attendee Availability** tab to see a detailed list of responses to your invitation. Select the **Show attendee status** option to switch from a view of free and busy time to the list of responses.

Be careful when rescheduling a meeting

Don't simply change the time on a meeting invitation you receive. Unless you're the meeting organizer, your change is not sent to other attendees, and you might end up in a conference room by yourself. To ask for a different date or time, decline the meeting and send a message to the organizer with your suggestion.

Rescheduling or Canceling a Meeting

After you've arranged a meeting, communication of any changes is crucial. Each attendee who accepts the meeting invitation has an item on his or her calendar, but only the meeting organizer can reschedule or cancel a meeting.

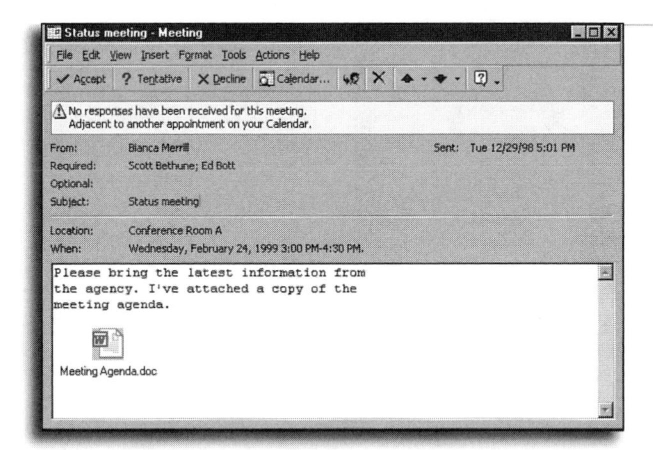

FIGURE 31.3

When you receive a meeting invitation, you can accept, tentatively accept, or decline.

If you're the organizer, and you want to change the date or time of a meeting, open the item in your Calendar folder, click the **Appointment** tab, and change the meeting details; then click the **Send Update** button. When you change the date or time this way, Outlook sends a special Update message to everyone on the list.

An Update message looks and acts exactly like the original request. Everyone who receives it will see the **Accept**, **Decline**, and **Tentative** buttons, just as if it were an original meeting request.

If you're not the meeting organizer, how should you suggest that the meeting be rescheduled? Don't just change the date or time on your calendar; when you do that, the original meeting item on the meeting organizer's calendar will remain the same, and you'll find yourself all alone when the meeting time rolls around.

- If you can attend the meeting, but you would prefer that it be at a different time, open the item and click the **Tentative** button. Outlook displays the dialog box shown in Figure 31.4. Choose the default option, **Edit the response before sending**, and click **OK**. Enter a message to the meeting organizer to suggest a new date or time, but don't change those details on your calendar.

Keep your schedule up-to-date

Group scheduling works only when everyone actively participates. In particular, you need to make sure that every appointment you make is entered in your Calendar folder; if you don't, Outlook constantly reports to other people that you have free time, even when you're booked solid. Make sure that you check the **Show time as** box for every appointment. You can select any of four options: **Free**, **Tentative**, **Busy**, or **Out of Office**. Check the **Private** box if you've published your Calendar folder on an Exchange server and you want others to see only that you're busy, without being able to view details.

FIGURE 31.4

Use this default option if you want to suggest a new date or time for a meeting organized by someone else.

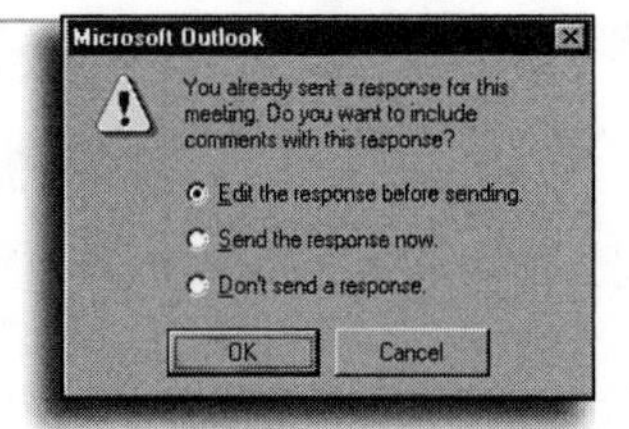

- If you originally accepted the meeting but now discover you can't attend, open the item and click the **Decline** button; then send a message to the organizer explaining that your schedule has changed.

If you're the meeting organizer, you can cancel a meeting at any time simply by deleting it from your calendar. Outlook offers to send a cancellation message on your behalf to all the attendees you previously invited.

Assigning Tasks to Other People

Assigning tasks to multiple people

You can assign the same task to two or more persons at once, but you lose the ability to keep an updated copy in your task list. If you want to assign work to several people and receive updates on their progress, break the task into multiple items and send each one individually.

If your coworkers or employees also use Outlook, you can transform your task list into a management tool. Instead of creating an item for your personal to-do list, create a *task request* and assign the job to another person. You send and receive task requests by email; when you keep a copy of the task on your own list, Outlook updates its status automatically based on reports you get back from coworkers via email.

You can turn an existing task into a task request or create a new one from scratch. Fill in the task details as you would to create a personal task, and then click the **Assign Task** button. In the Task Request form (see Figure 31.5), enter the email address of the person to whom you want to assign the task. Add a message or more details about the task, if you want, and click **Send** to move the task request to your Outbox.

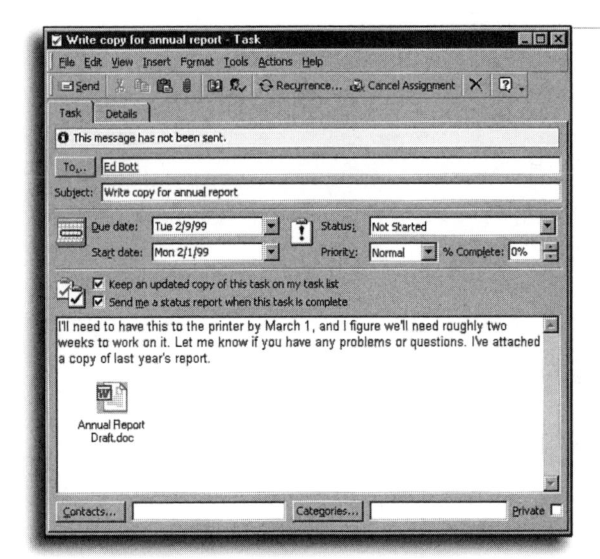

FIGURE 31.5

This task request form looks exactly like a task but includes space for an email address. After you send a task request, you're no longer able to edit its details.

Accepting or Declining Assigned Tasks

If you are the task recipient, you see a form that looks much like the one in Figure 31.6 in your Inbox. Unlike an ordinary mail message, a task request includes three buttons:

- Click the **Accept** button to add the item to your task list. If the person who sent you the task checked the option to keep an updated copy of the task, this action prepares an email message saying you've accepted the task.
- Click the **Decline** button to pop up a mail message so that you can explain why you've chosen not to accept; this action returns the task to the person who sent it.
- Click the **Assign Task** button to assign the task to another person.

FIGURE 31.6

If you accept a task request, Outlook adds it to your task list; if you decline the task, return it to the sender with an explanation.

When you accept an assigned task, you can update its details, change its due date, and file status reports at any time. To send a mail message to the person who assigned you the task, right-click the task item and choose **Send Status Report** from the shortcut menu. This action opens a mail message that contains details about the task. Update details, add a message, and click **Send**.

It's all automatic

When you send a status report that includes a new due date or new information in the **Status** or **% Complete** fields, Outlook automatically updates this information in the task item on the other person's task list.

PART

VI

Using Publisher 2000

CHAPTER

32

Getting Started with Publisher

- Learn what Publisher is and how you should use it
- Learn when to use Publisher instead of another Office 2000 tool
- Use wizards—the easiest way to get started
- Identify parts of a Publisher document
- Change your document using a wizard
- View your document
- Create a wizard-driven document
- Create publications from scratch

What Is Publisher and How Should You Use It?

If you're intimidated by the very thought of desktop publishing, you'll probably welcome Microsoft Publisher with open arms. Publisher includes a broad array of ready-to-use design templates—from small-business-oriented essentials like newsletters and brochures, to slightly less serious projects like paper airplanes. These templates are predesigned documents that give you a serious kick start: You just add text and graphics to the canned layout and print the finished document. It's undeniably fast and easy, but you'll probably find that Publisher's templates have limited use for professional documents unless you're willing to modify the templates heavily.

If you occasionally want to create a simple newsletter, memo, or brochure, Publisher should fit the bill. Although creating more complicated documents with Publisher is possible, you might find Publisher's set of features to be too limiting. In these cases, you'll most likely turn to Word, Excel, and PowerPoint to create truly dazzling documents.

For high-impact professional documents, where your entire business plan is on the line, you may have to go beyond Office to a full-strength desktop publishing application, such as Adobe PageMaker.

If you're curious as to just how many types of documents you can create and what they look like, start Publisher and take a look at the list displayed in the Catalog dialog box. You can find wizards grouped by type on the **Publications by Wizard** tab, as shown in Figure 32.1. Each entry preceded by an arrow-shaped bullet (such as Invitation Cards) has a drop-down list displaying more specific document types (such as Birthday Party, Housewarming, or Fund-raiser invitations). The right side of the dialog box lets you preview the document design.

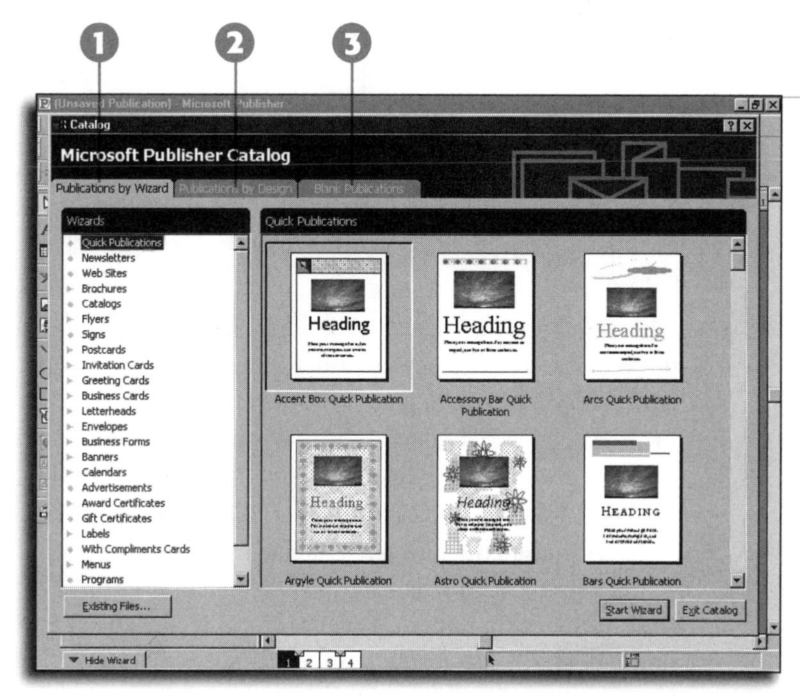

FIGURE 32.1

Publisher's "Catalog" is your starting place for creating a document.

1. **Click here to see wizards organized by publication type.**
2. **Click here to choose from coordinated sets of documents, forms, and other items.**
3. **Click here to create a publication from scratch.**

Now take a look at the choices on the **Publications by Design** tab. Here, you can find coordinated sets of documents, forms, and other items. Businesses and organizations typically use many types of documents—letterhead, envelopes, shipping labels, business cards, invoices, and purchase orders, for example—and these items are most effective when they have a consistent design and color scheme. On this tab, you can also find special-purpose coordinated sets for fund raisers, holidays, programs, and so on.

Want to use a specialized paper?

PaperDirect is a company that produces special stylized paper. The paper looks similar to some of the design themes found in Publisher, usually with a colorful header, header and footer, or border on all edges of the paper. Publisher 2000 lets you choose from a selection of these paper styles; the design details of the paper appear on screen but not in your Publisher document. You format the text and other objects in your document and then load the PaperDirect paper into your printer to put it all together. You can preview some of these papers by clicking the **Publications by Design** tab in the Catalog dialog box and then choosing the **Special Paper** option at the bottom of the list.

When to Use Publisher Instead of Another Office 2000 Tool

Office offers so many ways to do the same thing that determining which tool is the best to use for your particular task is sometimes difficult. When should you use Publisher for a newsletter or letterhead instead of Word? Is PowerPoint a better choice than Publisher for a Web page?

In truth, sometimes it doesn't matter which tool you use. If your letterhead has a simple logo with few graphical elements, you can probably create it just as easily in Word as you can in Publisher, and if you're more comfortable with Word, why not use that program? The more detailed or stylized the document, however, the more likely you'll need to make your choice based on the capabilities of each program. Here are several guidelines to help you:

- The most important question to ask is, how do you want the document to look? Does Publisher offer a design theme that conveys the tone and image you want to project in the document? Do you prefer one of the design themes available in Word or PowerPoint? If the look you're seeking is already available in one of those programs, your choice is easier.
- If you're considering using a template from Word or PowerPoint, does the template accommodate the *content* of the document appropriately? Can you easily include a headline, clip art or scanned pictures, page numbers, or other elements that are required for your publication? If so, use the tool you're comfortable with. If not, look through Publisher templates to see if one fits your needs.
- Do you want the freedom to design and create the document exactly as you envision it? If so, you probably won't use a wizard or template offered by *any* of the Office tools. In this case, use the tool that best accommodates the content of the document, such as Excel for a table or chart, or Word for a text document.
- Does the document (or the majority of the content for the document) already exist in another Office program? If so, using that program might be easier and quicker than re-creating the document in Publisher.
- Will the document be part of a coordinated set of documents? If you want a consistent look and feel across several types of documents, Publisher is probably your best choice. If you're leaning toward using another Office program, make sure it includes templates for all the types of documents you want in your coordinated set.

- Will you want to mail your document to a large list of people (as in a newsletter)? If so, use Publisher or Word, which both offer mail merge functions. Word's mail merge features give you significantly more options, however; if you want to sort your list, for example, Word is probably a better bet.

Using Wizards–The Easiest Way to Get Started

Each of Publisher's *wizards* helps you create a specific kind of publication. When you use a wizard, Publisher lays out the framework for your document and then lets you "fill in the blanks" with your information. And, of course, you can modify the layout if necessary.

To use a wizard, start Publisher and choose a wizard from the **Publications by Wizard** tab in the Catalog dialog box. Wizards preceded by a diamond-shaped bullet include a wide variety of layout options. When you click a wizard preceded by an arrow-shaped bullet, a drop-down list lets you choose a more specific wizard. After you've made your choice, click the **Start Wizard** button.

Publisher wizards work by asking you a series of questions about the design, layout, and type of information you want to include in your document. For instance, if you're creating a brochure, the wizard asks about color scheme, paper size, and whether to include an order form and an address block for mailing. The number and type of questions vary, depending on the type of document you're creating. After each response, click the **Next** button, and the wizard asks another question. You can change your response at any time by clicking the **Back** button. After the last question, click **Finish**, and Publisher displays your document onscreen.

Identifying Parts of a Publisher Document

Figure 32.2 shows a document created using the Blends Newsletter Wizard. Many of the screen elements—toolbars, menus, status bar—are similar to those found in other Office programs. Other elements in the document itself are described next. You'll learn more about how to use each one later in this chapter and in Chapter 33, "Expanding Your Publisher Skills."

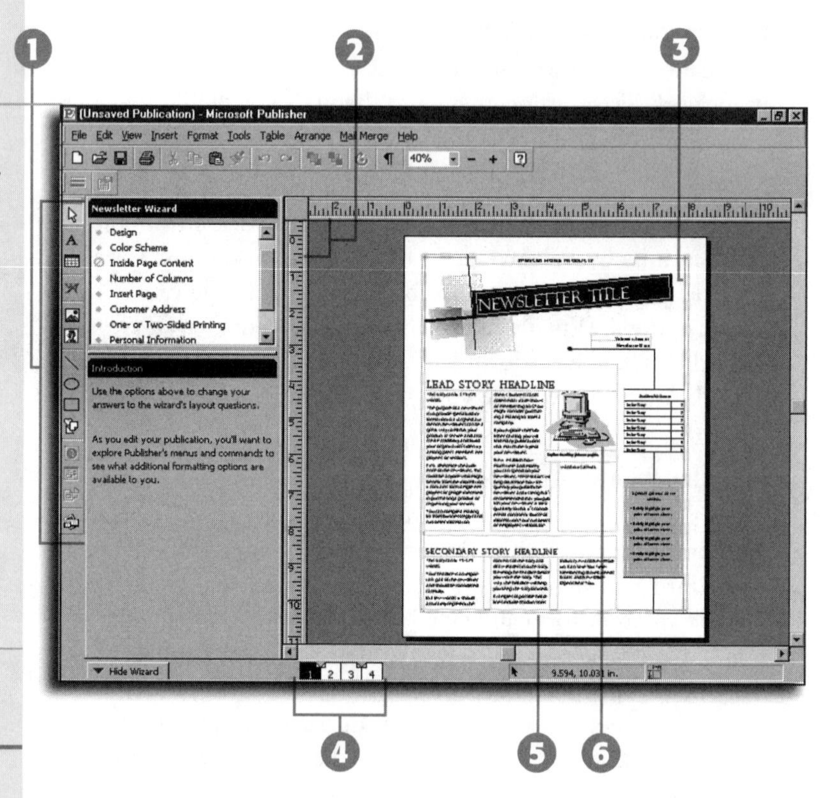

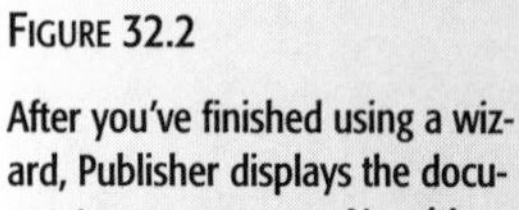

FIGURE 32.2

After you've finished using a wizard, Publisher displays the document on your screen. Now it's ready for you to enter your unique information.

1. Objects toolbar
2. Document rulers
3. Grid guides
4. Page navigators
5. Margin guides
6. Frame

Is it a frame, or is it an object?

The distinction between a *frame* and an *object* in Publisher can be subtle, especially if you're not a computer expert. The term *object* usually refers to external data, such as a drawing, a scanned image, or a piece of clip art within a publication. A *frame* generally refers to the "box" that surrounds an object. In a Publisher publication, every piece of text and every object must be contained in a frame.

Following are descriptions of some basic items you'll see in Publisher documents:

- Frames—Notice the highlighted text in Figure 32.2. This text is enclosed in a box, or *frame*, with handles that appear at each corner and on each side when the frame is selected. In Publisher, every element, whether textual or graphical, must be enclosed in a frame. As you've just seen, wizards put frames in the document for you. You can also create new frames to add to or modify a document, as you'll learn in Chapter 33.

- Text—Whenever you use a wizard to create a document, the document contains sample text. The text is intended to be a *placeholder*, so you can see what text in the frame should look like. To complete your document, you replace the sample text. In some publication templates, such as a newsletter, the text placeholder tells you approximately how many words the frame can hold.
- Pictures or clip art—Like text, pictures are often included in a wizard-created document as placeholders. They indicate the locations where you can insert your own pictures or clip art.
- Layout guides—Publisher uses *margin guides* and *grid guides* to help you position objects accurately in a document. (Virtually all wizard-created documents include both.) The faint pink lines on the screen are margin guides, which define the top, bottom, right, and left page margins. The faint blue lines are grid guides, which let you divide up the page vertically and horizontally in as many "rows" and "columns" as necessary. Margin and grid guides don't actually print; they are displayed on the screen simply to make it easier for you to place objects in the document.

SEE ALSO

➤ *Layout guides help you position objects in your Publisher documents; see page 654*

Changing Your Document Using a Wizard

After you've created your document by answering the wizard's questions, you might want to alter the content of your document. But after you click the **Finish** button, the **Back** button is no longer available. Notice, however, that even after you've finished using a wizard, the wizard menu remains open as long as you have your document open (refer to Figure 32.2). Also, take a look at the topics shown in the wizard menu; you'll see that the topics correspond to the questions you answered while creating your document with the wizard. To change a particular feature of your document, click on the corresponding topic in this list. The question is displayed on the lower-left side of the screen. Choose a response, and the wizard immediately makes the change in your document.

Viewing Your Document

If you've used a wizard to create your document, you'll notice that the wizard window takes up about one-third of the space on the screen. When you're finished using the wizard, you can reclaim some of that screen space by hiding the wizard. Just click the **Hide Wizard** button [Hide Wizard] in the lower-left corner. Clicking this button gives you a full-screen view of your document. Notice the button now says **Show Wizard** [Show Wizard], so you can bring the wizard back whenever you want.

Viewing Pages

Near the bottom of the screen, the status bar displays page icons. The number of icons displayed depends on the type of document you've created. A newsletter typically has four pages, for example, while a catalog includes eight pages. Switch from one page to another quickly just by clicking the page icon you want.

As you're clicking page icons, you might notice that two pages—for instance, pages 2 and 3 of a four-page document—are displayed together (see Figure 32.3). When this happens, it's an indication that the **Two-Page Spread** option on your **View** menu is selected. This format is helpful when you're working on larger documents, such as a newsletter, so that you can see how your layout looks across two facing pages. If you want to display pages individually, just remove the check mark from the **Two-Page Spread** option on the **View** menu.

Setting Zoom Options

The **+** and – buttons on the Standard toolbar are zoom buttons. Using them, you can quickly enlarge (+) or contract (–) your view of a document. When you click either button, the current zoom percentage is displayed just to the left of the buttons. If you want to select a specific zoom percentage, click the arrow next to the number percentage and choose a specific percentage from the drop-down list that appears.

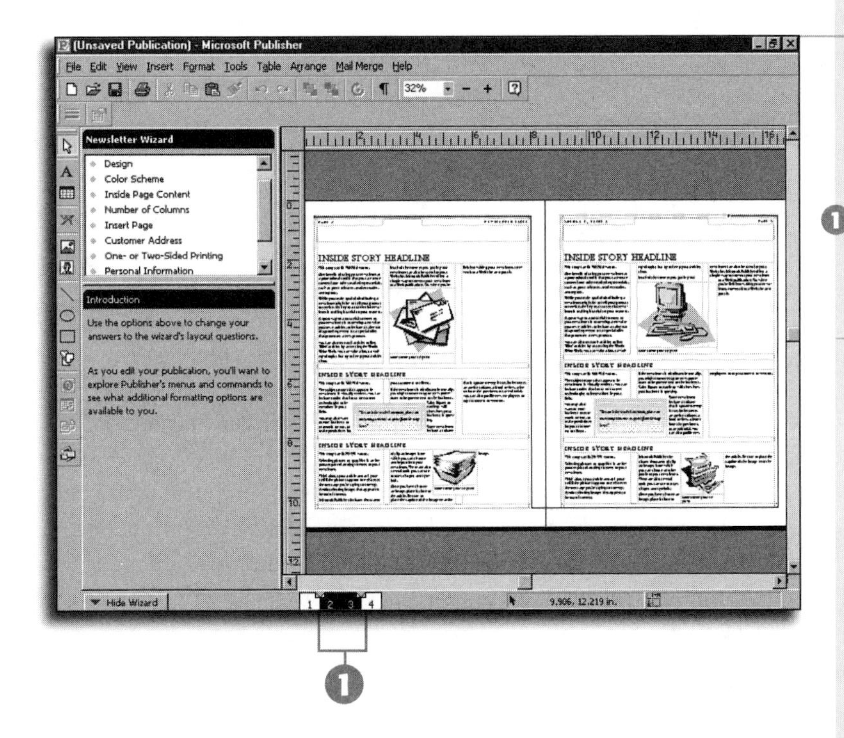

FIGURE 32.3

By using the **Two-Page Spread** option on the **View** menu, you can view the layout of two facing pages.

1. When two pages are highlighted here, the **Two-Page Spread** option on the **View** menu is selected.

Displaying Pictures

Have you ever tried to view a Web page that seems to take forever to display on the screen? The most likely reason is that the page contains many highly detailed pictures. The larger the picture or the more detail it contains, the longer it takes to display. A similar effect can occur when you edit a Publisher publication, especially if your video hardware is less than state-of-the-art. If your document takes too long to redisplay on the screen when you move from page to page or change zoom percentages, consider changing the way Publisher displays pictures on the screen while you work.

As you work on a publication, especially when you're adding and editing text, seeing all the details of a picture is not necessary;

the important thing is that they print accurately when the time comes. Publisher lets you display pictures at maximum detail or reduced detail, or you can choose not to display pictures at all while you're working. To choose one of these options, click the **View** menu and then choose **Picture Display**. In the Picture Display dialog box, choose **Detailed display**, **Fast resize and zoom**, or **Hide pictures**; then click **OK**.

Hiding Guides

Earlier in this chapter, you learned that the faint pink and blue lines displayed on your document are margin and grid guides. These guides are used only to help you position objects in your document; they don't print when you print your document. Depending on the number of guides you are using, your document can become cluttered with guides, text, pictures, and other graphical objects. If you find the guides distracting as you're working, hide them by choosing the **Hide Boundaries and Guides** option on the **View** menu. Hiding guides is also useful when you want to preview your document exactly as it will print. Often, when the guides are hidden, you can see clearly where frames are out of place or misaligned. To redisplay the guides, simply open the **View** menu and choose **Show Boundaries and Guides**.

SEE ALSO

➤ *For information on using layout guides to help you position objects, see page 654*

Creating a Wizard-Driven Document

As you've already seen, when you use a wizard to create a document, the format and framework for your document are laid out for you. Publisher does this by inserting frames in your document that are used as *placeholders* for text and other objects. Now it's time to "fill in the blanks" of your document with your unique information.

Before you can make changes in a document, you must select the frame you want to change by clicking on it. The frame handles are visible when a frame is selected. To select all the text in a text frame, click the frame and then press Ctrl+A. Publisher highlights all the text.

Replacing Text

You have two options for replacing sample text in your document: You can type new text, or you can paste text from another location. To replace existing text, first select the text frame and then press Ctrl+A to select all text. When you begin typing, Publisher automatically replaces the existing text.

If you want to include in your newsletter an article that someone sent you by email, you certainly don't need to retype it; just copy it to the Clipboard and paste it into your publication.

Reformatting pasted text

Unlike other Office applications, Publisher doesn't have a Paste Special command that lets you choose how you want to paste text, so formatting is copied whether you want it or not. To reformat the text, set the attributes by selecting the **Format** menu and choosing **Font**, or copy the attributes from other text using the Format Painter.

SEE ALSO

For instructions on how to use the Windows Clipboard, see page 134

Using Connected Frames

Sometimes the text of one frame overflows into another text frame. A good example of this is with a newsletter. Often a story starts on page 1 and is continued on page 4. When you use a wizard to create a document, the wizard often connects frames for you automatically. When you type beyond the limits of the first frame, the remaining text is automatically placed in its connected frame.

SEE ALSO

To learn more about flowing text from frame to frame, see page 667

Inserting Clip Art and Pictures

Nearly every wizard-created document includes picture frames with sample pictures or clip art. These frames are logically placed in the document. For example, in a newsletter, a picture frame accompanies each article. In a business card, a frame is placed where your company logo might go. Replacing sample pictures or clip art is as simple as selecting the frame and then specifying a new file.

Office 2000 stores clip art in a shared folder so that all clip art files are available in each Office application. You therefore can choose from literally hundreds of clip art files.

SEE ALSO

➤ *For more details on how you can add clip art to publications, see page 131*

Inserting a Piece of Clip Art into Your Publisher Document

1. Click the frame where you want to insert clip art. Open the **Insert** menu, choose **Picture**, and then choose **Clip Art**. Publisher displays the Insert Clip Art dialog box shown in Figure 32.4. In this dialog box, you see several examples of available clip art matching a similar style to the sample clip art in your document.
2. If you don't see a file you like, click in the **Search for clips** box and type a subject or description of what you're looking for.
3. When you find a file you like, click it. A drop-down list showing four buttons appears—the first of which is the **Insert Clip** button.
4. Click the **Insert Clip** button, and the clip art automatically replaces the sample file in the frame.

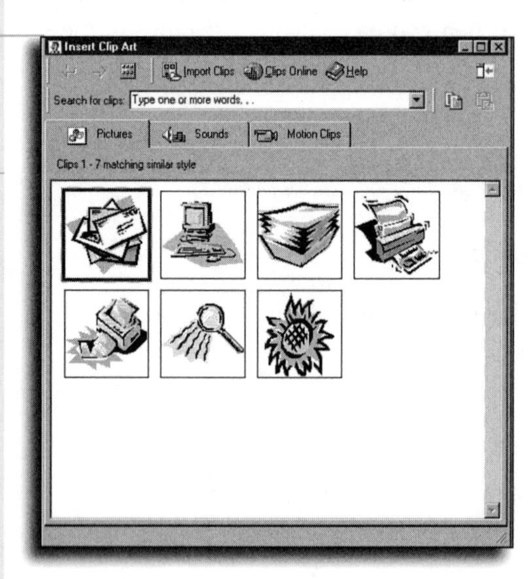

FIGURE 32.4

Choose a picture from the Insert Clip Art dialog box.

You can also insert pictures in a document. (A picture is loosely defined as a digitized image of a photograph or painting, whereas clip art is defined as a drawing.) The procedure is similar to inserting clip art; however, Publisher doesn't display a dialog box directing you to a central folder of picture images. Instead, Publisher displays a folder called c:\My Documents\My Pictures, which Windows creates for you. When you first use Publisher, this folder is empty. If you have pictures stored in other folders on your system, you might want to move them to this folder and use it as a central location for all pictures. Until then, you must know the name of the folder in which your picture file is located.

Inserting a Picture in Your Document

1. Click the frame where you want to insert a picture. Open the **Insert** menu, choose **Picture**, and then choose **From File**. Publisher displays the Insert Picture dialog box shown in Figure 32.5.
2. In the **Look in** box, click the down arrow to choose a directory and folder.
3. Highlight the filename and then click **Insert**. Publisher replaces the sample picture or clip art in the selected frame with the file you specify.

FIGURE 32.5
Choose a picture from the Insert Picture dialog box.

SEE ALSO

➤ *For information about adding clip art and other graphics to your publications, see page 130*

Are picture frames different from clip art frames?

No. Publisher uses the same type of frame for pictures and clip art. In other words, if the wizard inserts a picture in a document, you can replace it with clip art if you choose. Conversely, if a wizard inserts clip art in a document, you can replace it with a picture.

Give up finding a wizard?

Don't give up too easily. Often, if you search for an appropriate wizard by name, you might not find it, but you might find one that works under an entirely different name. For example, if you want to create a half-fold product brochure on 8 1/2 by 11-inch paper, Publisher doesn't offer a *Brochure* Wizard with those specifications. However, Publisher does offer a *Catalog* Wizard with those specifications. So, don't get hung up on a name; keep searching!

Creating Publications from Scratch

There's no question that wizards can save you a great deal of time laying out a publication. But that assumes you can find an appropriate wizard. When you can't find a wizard to suit your needs, you can create your publication from a blank document.

Creating a document from scratch needn't be intimidating. You select a general page type (flat or folded), page size, and orientation. After you've done that, Publisher displays the Quick Publication Wizard—a "generic" sort of wizard to help you add a color scheme, graphical elements, and selected frames to your publication.

Creating a Publication from Scratch

1. Start Publisher and click the **Blank Publications** tab in the Catalog dialog box. The Catalog dialog box now looks like the one shown in Figure 32.6.
2. From the dialog box, choose a blank publication style that most closely matches the type of document you want to create; then click the **Create** button. Note that labels and envelopes are not included in the catalog of blank publications, but you can create them using the Custom Page button as described in step 3.
3. If you don't find what you're looking for in step 2, you can create a customized document (page size or fold) by clicking the **Custom Page** button. In the dialog box that appears, specify a custom fold or size, or choose labels or envelopes. Be sure also to check either **Portrait** or **Landscape** for print orientation and then click **OK**.

   To customize a Web page, click the **Custom Web Page** button. In the dialog box that appears, specify a page size and then click **OK**.
4. Publisher creates your blank document and displays it on the screen along with the Quick Publication Wizard (unless you create a custom page, in which case, just the document is displayed). Now use the wizard to add design elements, specify a color scheme, or change your page size, page layout, or personal information.

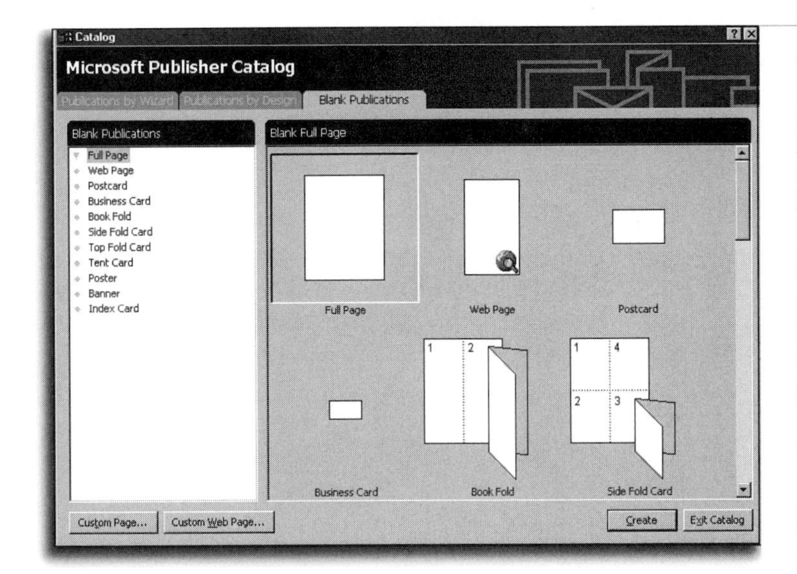

FIGURE 32.6
Choose a publication style from the blank document choices.

Figure 32.7 shows an example of a business card created from scratch. Design elements, a color scheme, and personal information were added using the Quick Publication Wizard.

Chapter 33 includes details for editing a Publisher document.

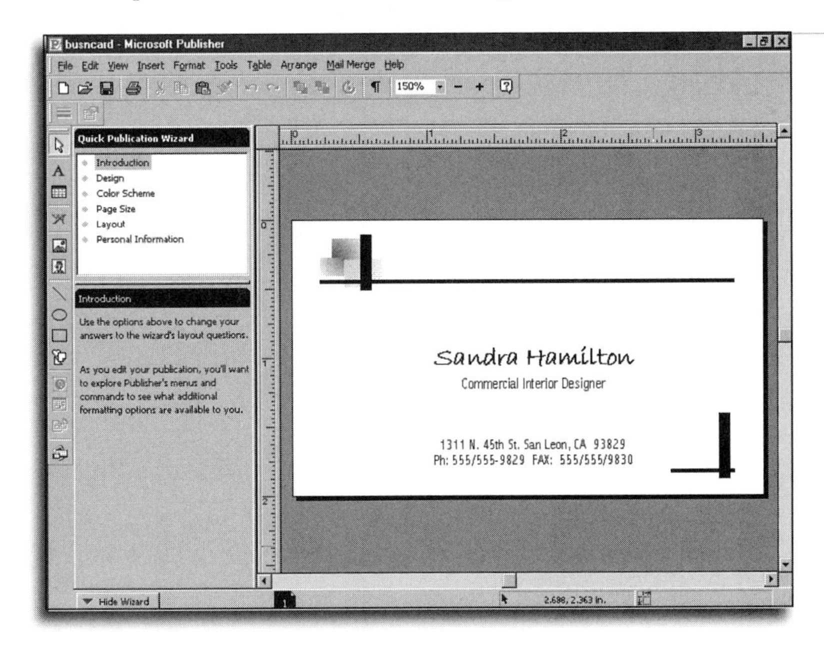

FIGURE 32.7
Created from scratch, this business card has so much design detail that it looks almost like one created with a specialized wizard.

CHAPTER

33

Expanding Your Publisher Skills

- Use layout and ruler guides
- Create and delete frames
- Size, crop, scale, connect, and position frames
- Copy, group, and layer frames
- Change picture and object characteristics
- Copyfit in text frames
- Change text attributes and formatting
- Wrap text around pictures
- Print your document

Using Layout Guides

If you're going to create Publisher documents from scratch, it's essential to understand how Publisher's layout guides work. Layout guides are nonprinting lines that represent margins and gridlines on a page. When you create a blank document, Publisher automatically inserts margin guides and grid guides on a background layer of the document. Margin guides appear in pink; blue grid guides are placed just inside the margin guides. Both types of guides apply to the entire document and help you lay out your document so that one page is consistent with the next.

Publisher determines margin width based on the size of paper you choose for your blank document. For instance, Publisher uses 1-inch margins for documents intended for printing on 8 1/2 by 11-inch paper, but 1/4-inch margins for postcards. Of course, you can change margin width any time by choosing the **Arrange** menu and selecting **Layout Guides**. Just be sure to set the margin width within the printable area for your printer.

Publisher uses the blue gridlines to divide your page horizontally and vertically into rows and columns. When you create a blank document (full page, 8 1/2 by 11 inches), Publisher assumes you don't want to divide your page; it therefore defines just one row and one column, which places the grid guides just inside the margin guides (about 3/16 inch). If you divide your page into three columns and two rows, for example, the grid guides would look like those shown in Figure 33.1.

In Figure 33.1, notice that whenever you define grid guides, Publisher automatically adds margin guides for each column and row. This consistent margin width becomes important when you start adding text and pictures to the document. The margins remind you to line up objects consistently and leave space between columns.

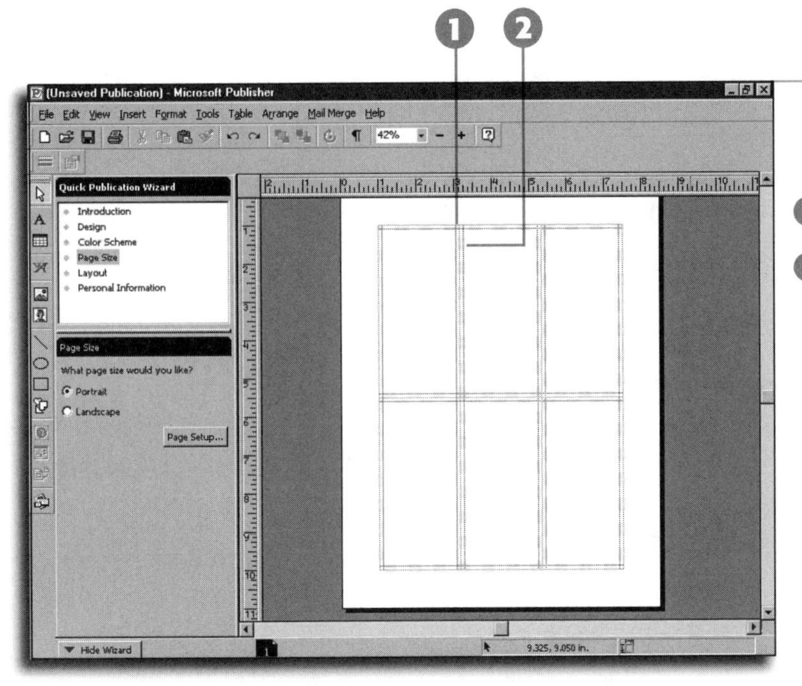

FIGURE 33.1
Layout guides help you lay out the space in a document.

1. Grid guides
2. Margin guides

Defining Special Margin or Grid Guides

1. Choose the **Arrange** menu and then select **Layout Guides**. The dialog box shown in Figure 33.2 then appears.
2. To redefine margins, click the up or down arrows in the **Left**, **Right**, **Top**, or **Bottom** boxes, or click the box and type a new number.
3. To set grid guides, click the up or down arrows in the **Columns** and **Rows** boxes.
4. Click **OK**.

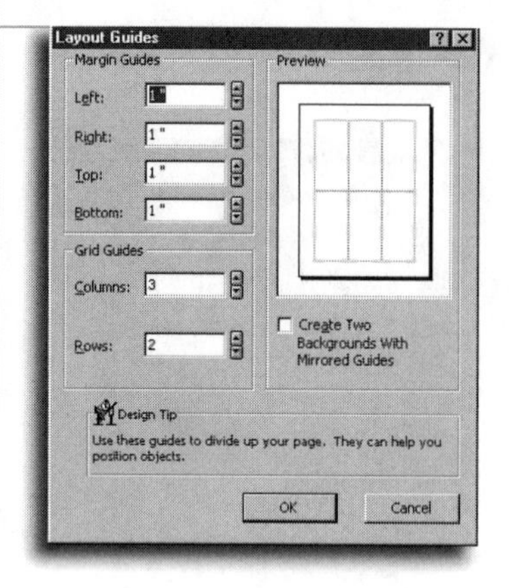

FIGURE 33.2

Change margin settings above, grid settings below. The outer margins and grid are shown in the Preview window.

A quick way to adjust margin and grid guides is to drag them.

Adjusting Margin and Grid Guides

1. Choose the **View** menu and select **Go to Background**.
2. Press and hold the **Shift** key.
3. Move the mouse pointer over the guide you want to move. The mouse pointer changes to an Adjust pointer.
4. Drag the guide until it's positioned where you want it. Notice that you can't move a grid guide and its corresponding margin guide independently; they automatically move together.
5. Release the **Shift** key and the mouse button when the guide is positioned where you want it.
6. Choose the **View** menu and select **Go to Foreground**.

Creating Ruler Guides

In addition to margin and grid guides, you can also create *ruler guides*. Unlike margin and grid guides, ruler guides apply to a single page in a document. Create ruler guides when you want to place an object at a specific location, such as three inches from the top edge of the paper and four inches from the left edge of the paper. Ruler guides appear in green on your screen.

Creating Ruler Guides

1. Press and hold the Shift key.
2. Move the mouse pointer over the horizontal or vertical ruler until you see the Adjust pointer.
3. Drag the pointer onto the page until the green ruler guide appears. Use the rulers to position the guide exactly where you want it.
4. Release the Shift key and the mouse button.

Creating and Deleting Frames

Every element in a Publisher document—text, pictures and clip art, graphics, and other objects—must be enclosed in a frame. When you use a Publisher wizard to create a document, it automatically creates frames for you, but you can create your own frames as well. The vertical toolbar in the Publisher window is the *Objects toolbar*. It contains the tools you use to create frames and other objects (see Figure 33.3).

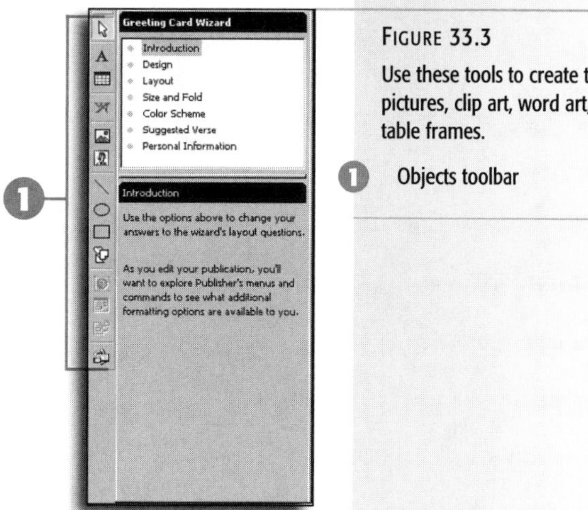

FIGURE 33.3
Use these tools to create text, pictures, clip art, word art, and table frames.

1 Objects toolbar

A frame is only faintly visible in a document until you select it. To select a frame, just click on the content (text, graphic, or picture). When the frame is selected, you can see its *handles*, which are small boxes at each corner and along each side of the frame (see Figure 33.4). The frame handles are used for resizing the frame, as you learn later in this chapter.

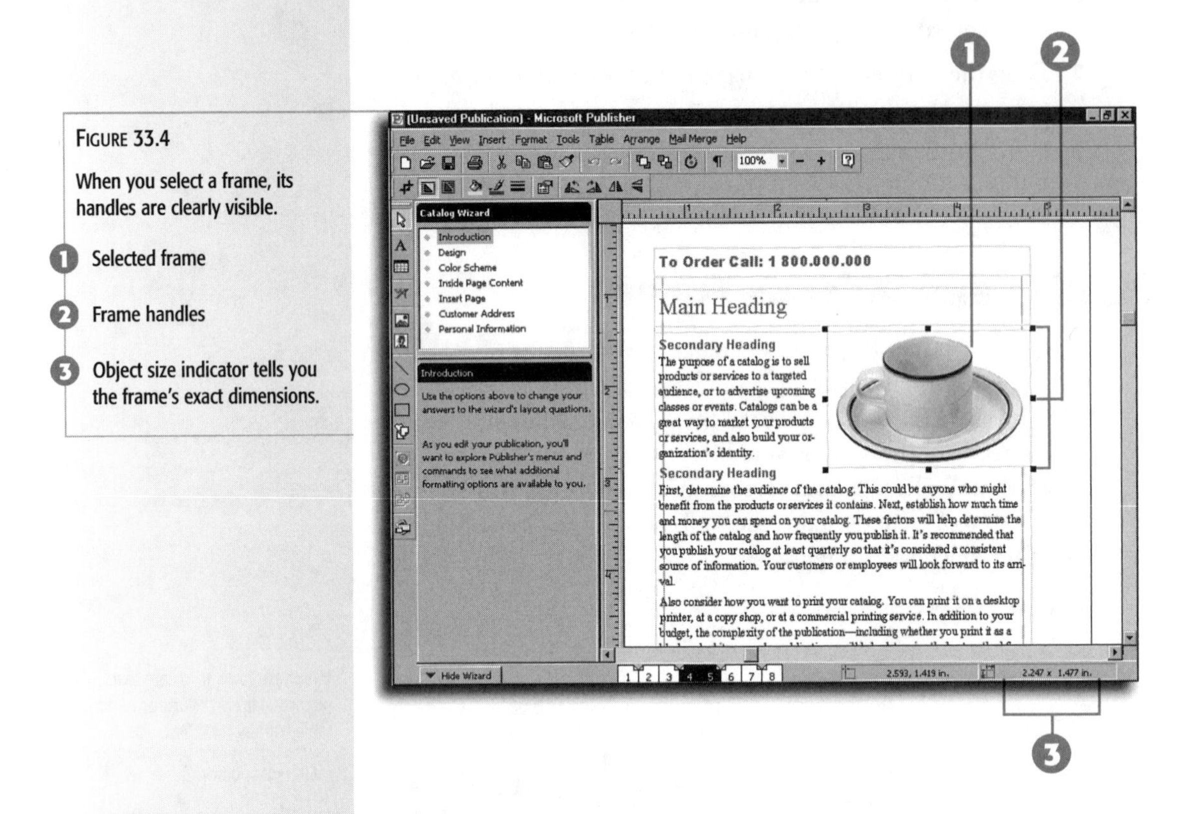

FIGURE 33.4

When you select a frame, its handles are clearly visible.

1. Selected frame
2. Frame handles
3. Object size indicator tells you the frame's exact dimensions.

Want a specific size?

If you want your frame to be a specific size, such as 3.5 inches wide by 4.6 inches high, keep an eye on the object size indicator at the right end of the status bar as you draw your frame. As you move the mouse, the first number indicates the frame's width; the second, its height.

Regardless of the type of frame you want, you use the same basic steps for creating all frames.

Creating a Frame

1. Click the frame tool you want to use.
2. Move your mouse pointer into the document area. The pointer changes to a crosshair.
3. Place the crosshair approximately where you want one corner of the frame to begin. Then, while you're holding down the left mouse button, drag the mouse to create the frame.
4. Release the mouse button when the frame is about the size you want.

What happens next depends on the type of frame you create. Each of the different types of frames is explained here:

- Text frame—As soon as you release the mouse button, you see a blinking insertion point in the text frame. The frame is ready for you to enter text. If you don't want to enter text right now, just click anywhere else in the document to deselect the frame.
- ClipArt frame—When you release the mouse button, the Insert ClipArt dialog box shown in Figure 33.5 appears. Choose a clip art file by clicking on it. When the pop-up toolbar appears, click the **Insert** button and then close the Insert ClipArt dialog box.

FIGURE 33.5
Choose a clip art file from the Insert ClipArt dialog box.

- Picture frame—After you create a picture frame, the frame is still selected. You then can open the **Insert** menu, choose **Picture**, and then choose **From File** to insert a picture file. In the Insert Picture dialog box that appears, select the file to insert.
- WordArt frame—When you create a WordArt frame, the WordArt applet opens, displaying the WordArt dialog box and toolbar. Enter your text in the box and then use the tools on the WordArt toolbar to stylize your text.

- Table frame—After you create a table frame, you see a table with rows and columns in your document. The dark gray bars represent the row and column headings; cells are delineated by faint gray nonprinting lines. Fill in each cell by clicking on it and then typing.

SEE ALSO
- *To learn how to insert clip art in a publication, see page 131*
- *To find out more about adding pictures to a publication, see page 130*
- *To find details about using WordArt, see page 128*

Frames are as easy to delete as they are to create. Just select the frame and click the **Cut** button on the toolbar, or select **Edit** and then choose **Cut**.

If you change your mind and want to restore the frame, remember that the frame stays on the Clipboard until you cut something else from the document. To bring it back, just click the **Paste** button or select **Edit** and then choose **Paste** before you cut anything else. If you forget and cut other objects or make other editing changes, you can bring back the frame by continuing to click the **Undo** button until the frame is restored.

Want to include a worksheet?

Don't confuse tables with Excel worksheet files. If you want to include an existing Excel worksheet, you insert it as an object instead of creating a table. This approach embeds the worksheet in your Publisher document, so whenever the worksheet is updated, it's updated in your Publisher document as well. To embed a worksheet, open the **Insert** menu and choose **Object**. When the Insert Object dialog box appears, choose the **Create from File** option. Then enter the filename in the File box and click **OK**.

Creating Special Shapes

You can add special interest and emphasis to a document by including other shapes in it. For instance, draw attention to a special offer in a flyer by adding a bright red arrow. Or highlight a sale price by tagging it with a bright yellow sunburst. You can find both of these shapes on the Frames toolbar under the **Custom Shapes** button . Click the **Custom Shapes** button to reveal the menu of special shapes shown in Figure 33.6.

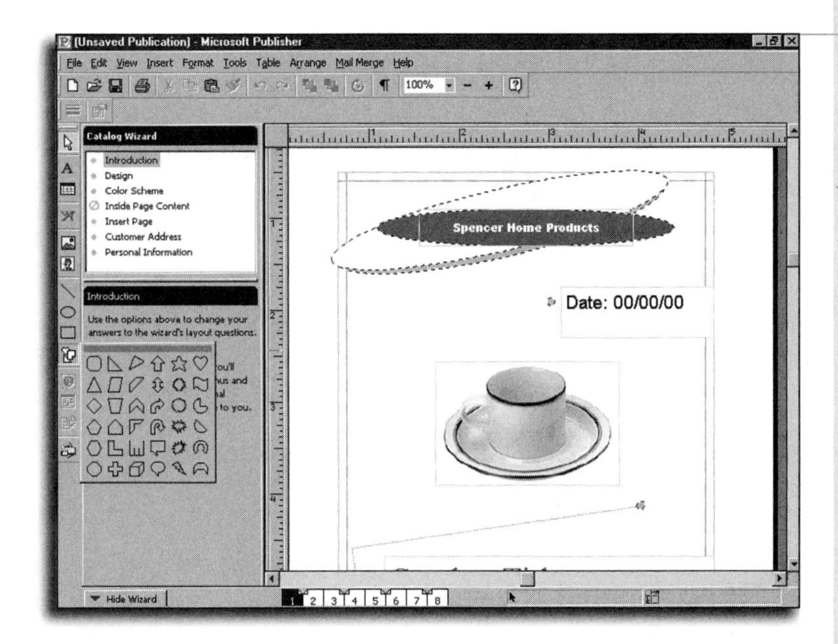

FIGURE 33.6
Click the **Custom Shapes** button to reveal a menu of 36 special shapes.

To use one of these custom shapes, click its icon, move your mouse pointer into the document area, and then draw the shape just as you would draw a frame. For emphasis, these shapes can be filled with color or patterns and outlined in a contrasting color, as you learn later in this chapter.

The Frames toolbar also includes three basic drawing tools: Line, Oval, and Rectangle. The Line tool is useful for creating a *rule*, a line that separates one part of a document from another. You can also create circles, ovals, squares, or rectangles and add text to them, or use these shapes as borders or "mattes" for a picture.

Creating a Line, Oval, or Rectangle

1. Select the tool you want to use.
2. Move the mouse pointer into the drawing area. The mouse pointer changes to a crosshair.
3. Press and hold the left mouse button as you drag the mouse in any direction. The object begins at the point where you clicked the mouse button.

To draw the object in any direction around a center point, hold the Ctrl key as you draw a line. To draw a perfectly horizontal, vertical, or 45-degree line, or a perfect circle or square, press and hold the Shift key as you draw.

4. Release the mouse button when the object is the size you want.

Figure 33.7 shows examples of custom shapes, a heavy rule, and a rectangle used as a border for a clip art picture.

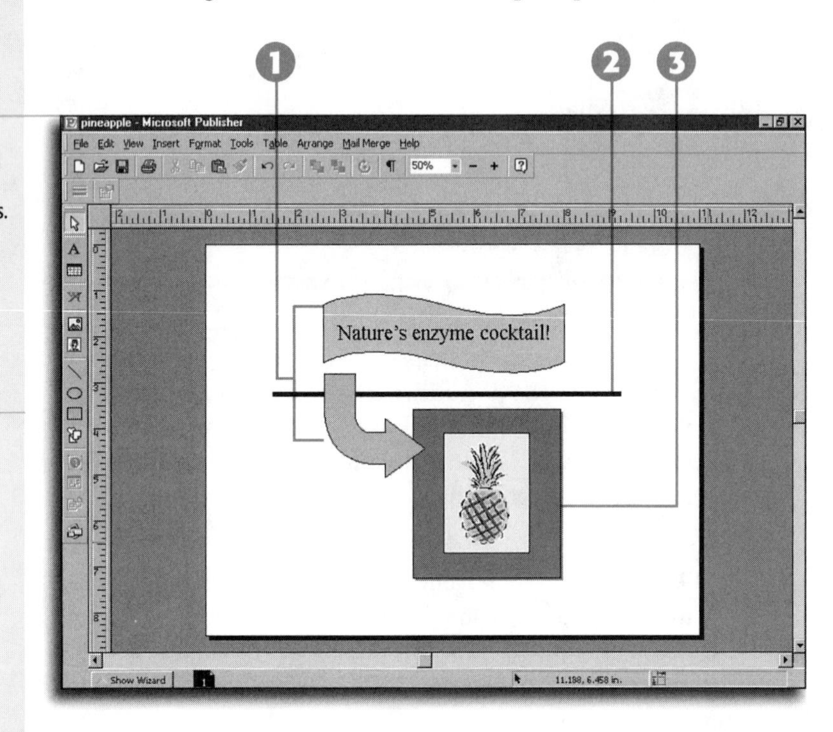

FIGURE 33.7

Use the wide variety of drawing tools to enhance your documents.

1 Custom shapes

2 Rule made with the Line tool

3 Rectangle used as a border

Sizing, Cropping, and Scaling Frames

Luckily, a frame's size is never permanent. You can easily resize a frame in a document and will probably need to do so in most documents. Closely related to sizing are *cropping* (only for pictures) and *scaling* (only for pictures or clip art). When you crop, you actually "cut away" part of a picture. Scaling allows you to change the size of a picture or clip art by a specific percentage.

Sizing Frames

Generally, you change the size of a frame either for aesthetic reasons or to make it fit into the layout of a document alongside other frames.

Resizing a Frame

1. Click the frame to select it. Its handles are then visible.
2. Move your mouse pointer over one of the handles and drag it to resize the frame. Handles on the sides of a frame allow you to resize in one direction only; corner handles allow you to resize in two directions at a time.
3. When the frame is the size you want, release the mouse button.

When should you resize a frame?

Remember that resizing a frame is not the only way to make the content of a document fit on the page. You have other options as well, such as choosing a different font or size for text, altering margins, cropping pictures, altering whitespace on the page, or using AutoFit Text, described later in this chapter. Whatever choices you make, always avoid overcrowding a page. Few people are willing to read, much less comprehend, a cluttered page crammed with too much information.

Cropping Pictures

Sometimes you might include a picture that is "larger in content" than necessary. For instance, suppose you include a photograph of a boat in the water. The picture is perfect for your document, but there's too much water in the picture. You can zero in on the boat by cropping out some of the water.

Cropping a Picture

1. Select the picture frame you want to crop.
2. From the Formatting toolbar, click the **Crop** button, or right-click the picture, choose **Change Picture**, and then **Crop Picture**. When you move the mouse pointer over one of the frame handles, it changes to the Crop icon (see Figure 33.8).
3. Drag one of the frame handles until you've cut away as much of the picture as you want. To crop in two directions at once, drag one of the corner handles.
4. Release the mouse button when the picture is cropped the way you want it.

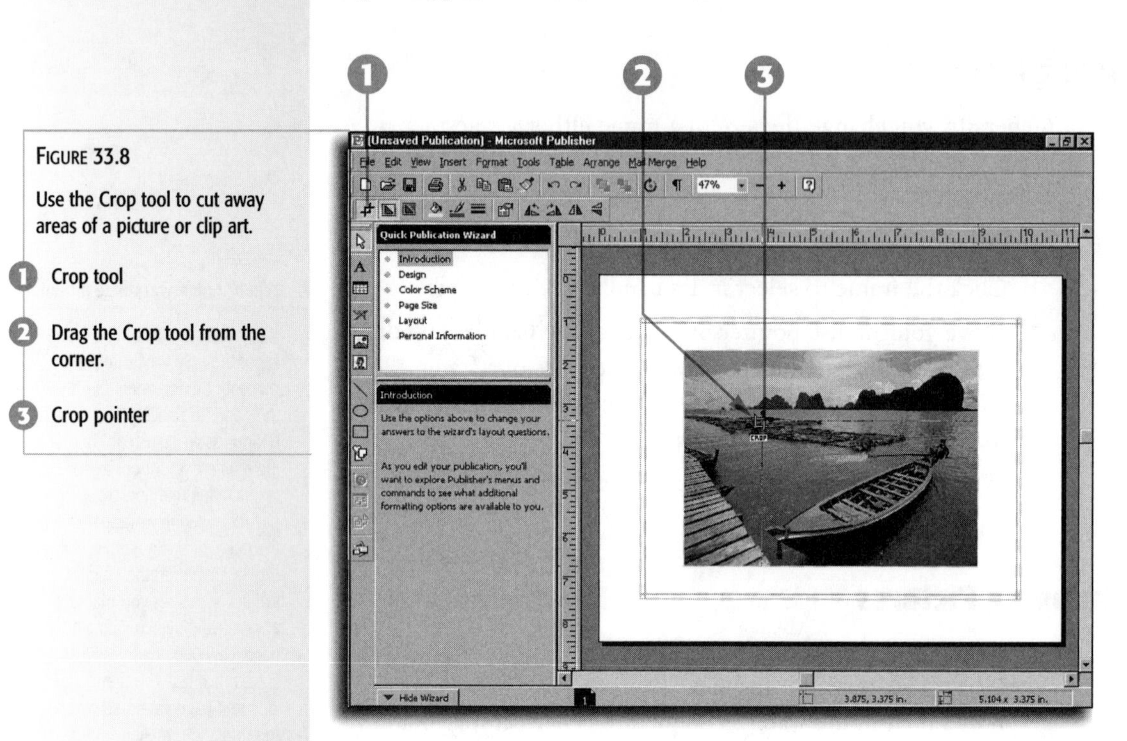

FIGURE 33.8

Use the Crop tool to cut away areas of a picture or clip art.

1. Crop tool
2. Drag the Crop tool from the corner.
3. Crop pointer

Remember, if you ever cut away too much of a picture, you can restore it by clicking the **Undo** button or choosing **Edit** and then selecting **Undo**.

Scaling Pictures

Pictures you insert might be too large or too small for your publication. You can *scale*—that is, reduce or enlarge—a picture by a percentage you specify.

Scaling a Picture

1. Click the picture you want to scale.
2. Choose **Format** and then select **Scale Picture**. The Scale Picture dialog box then appears.
3. To see the picture at 100 percent (that is, the size at which it was created), click the **Original size** box. When you see the picture full size, you'll have an idea what percentage to use to scale it.

4. In the **Scale height** box, type a percentage.
5. In the **Scale width** box, type a percentage.
6. Click **OK**.

When you return to your publication, the picture is scaled. If you want to maintain the picture's correct proportions (height-to-width ratio), be sure to enter the same number for **Scale height** and **Scale width** in steps 4 and 5.

Positioning Frames

Eventually, you'll want to move a frame in a document. This task is one of the easiest you can perform: Just click somewhere in the center of the frame to see the frame's handles. The mouse pointer changes to a moving truck. Now drag the frame in any direction and release the mouse button when the frame is positioned where you want it. If you view two pages at once (by opening the **View** menu and choosing **Two-Page Spread**), you can drag a frame from one page to the other.

Moving a Frame to a Different Page in the Document

1. Select the frame.
2. Choose the **Cut** button or choose **Edit** and then select **Cut**.
3. Use the page navigation tools on the status bar to go to the new page.
4. Choose the **Paste** button or choose **Edit** and then select **Paste**.

Nudging Frames

Sometimes placing a frame exactly where you want it using the mouse can be difficult. To place a frame more precisely, you can *nudge* it into place. Nudging moves the frame a very small increment (several hundredths of an inch) at a time in the direction you choose. To nudge a frame, select the frame and then press and hold the Alt key as you use the arrow keys on your keyboard to nudge the frame right, left, up, or down. Release the keys when the frame is positioned where you want it.

If you want to nudge an object by a precise measurement, such as .23 inch, you can do so using the Nudge dialog box.

Nudging an Object by a Precise Measurement

1. Click the **Arrange** menu and choose **Nudge**.
2. In the Nudge dialog box that appears (see Figure 33.9), click the **Nudge by** option.
3. Enter a value.
4. Click the arrow in the dialog box for the direction you want to move the frame. Publisher automatically adjusts the position of the frame.
5. Click **Close**.

FIGURE 33.9

Use the Nudge dialog box to move a frame by a precise measurement.

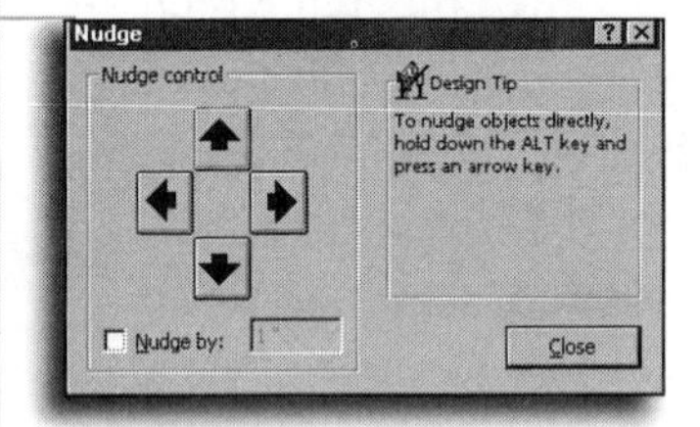

Snapping Frames in Place

Earlier in this chapter you learned about adjusting the position of layout guides and ruler guides, lines that define page boundaries and help you position objects in a document. Guides are not just visual tools. You can *snap* objects to guides so that they align perfectly. Snap works like an invisible magnet to pull an object to the nearest guide line and hold it in place. You can also snap objects to other objects or snap them to measurement marks on the rulers.

To use snap, you must turn on the feature you want to use. From the **Tools** menu, you can choose any of the three snap options. A check mark appears next to the options when you select it.

Your snap options are as follows:

- The **Snap to Ruler Marks** option allows you to align a frame at any of the 1/8-inch increments on the vertical or horizontal ruler.
- The **Snap to Guides** option works with margin guides, grid guides, and ruler guides.
- The **Snap to Objects** option pulls the selected frame into alignment with the edge of another object on the page.

To use the snap feature, select one of the snap options and move a frame close to a guide or object. As you get close to it, you see the frame jump to position itself right on the guide or the edge of the object you choose.

How does snap affect nudge?

You can still use the nudge feature described earlier without having to turn off any of the snap features. Nudge overrides all snap features and lets you move an object in increments as small as several hundredths of an inch.

Connecting Text Frames

In almost every newspaper, you'll find that a front-page article is seldom complete on that page. The article starts on page 1 but might end, for example, on page 10. One of the reasons publishers arrange articles this way is so they can include as many eye-catching headlines or titles on one page as possible; they want to capture your attention before you move on to something else. It's a good strategy for keeping a reader interested. You'll want to use the same strategy if you're using Publisher to create a newsletter, for example. You can designate a frame on the first page for a particular article and then continue it on another page.

But how exactly do you accomplish this feat? Begin by entering all the text in the first frame. When the frame is full, a "Text in Overflow" indicator appears at the bottom-right corner of the frame (see Figure 33.10). This indicator is a reminder to you that there is more text in the frame that isn't visible.

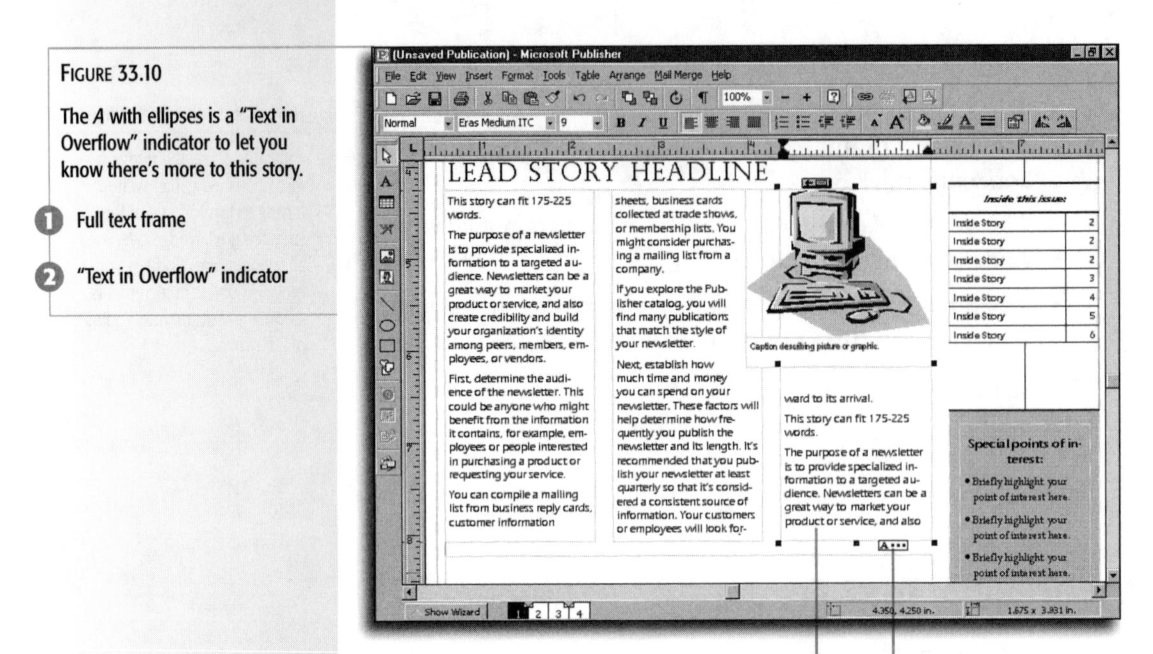

FIGURE 33.10

The *A* with ellipses is a "Text in Overflow" indicator to let you know there's more to this story.

1. Full text frame
2. "Text in Overflow" indicator

To continue the text on another page, decide in which frame you want the remainder of the text to be placed. Then connect one frame to another.

Connected or not?

You can tell immediately whether a text frame is connected to another by checking the toolbar. If the **Disconnect Text Frames** button is highlighted, you know that the selected frame is connected to another. If the **Connect Text Frames** button is highlighted, you know that the selected frame is not connected to another.

Connecting Text Frames

1. Select the frame that contains too much text.
2. Click the **Connect Text Frames** button on the Standard toolbar, or choose the **Connect Text Frame** option from the **Tools** menu. Your mouse pointer changes to an overflowing pitcher.
3. Move your mouse pointer to the frame where you want the text to continue. The mouse pointer changes to a tipped pitcher, as if pouring out the overflow.
4. Click in this frame. Publisher inserts the remaining text. If you have too much text to fit in this frame, you see the "Text in Overflow" indicator again. Repeat steps 2 through 4 until all text is positioned.

Typically, when an article is continued on another page, the text is preceded by a reference such as "Continued from page 1." To add this type of pointer to an article, right-click in the continuation frame. From the shortcut menu, select **Change Frame** and then choose **Text Frame Properties**. In the dialog box that appears, click the **Include "Continued from page..."** option and then click **OK**. Use these same steps in the original text frame to add a pointer at the bottom of the frame saying **"Continued on page..."**. Don't try to enter a page number; Publisher automatically enters the correct page number for you (see Figure 33.11).

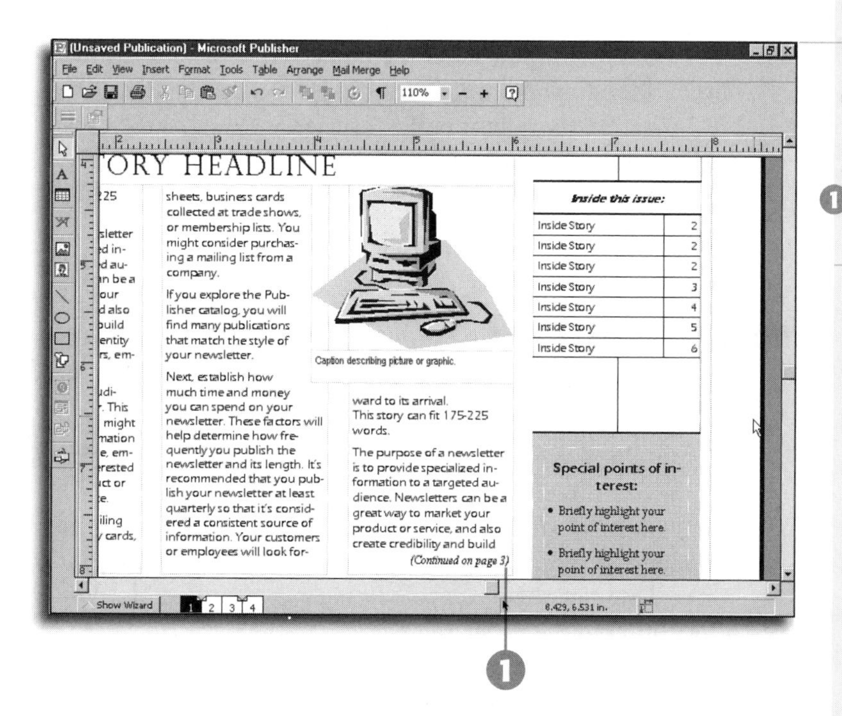

FIGURE 33.11

The same article shown in Figure 33.10 now includes the note "Continued on page 3."

1 Publisher enters the correct page number automatically.

SEE ALSO

➤ *For complete instructions on using the Office Assistant, see page 72*

Copying Frames

Copying a frame in a document can often be useful. You may or may not want to duplicate the content of the frame, such as a picture or the text of a paragraph. Often it's only the size and special attributes of the frame you want to copy. For example, suppose your frame is exactly 1 3/4 inches by 2 3/8 inches, has a blue fill color, an artwork border, and is set to display text in the Colonna font, size 14. You want another frame just like it, even though you're going to fill it with different text. With all these special attributes, copying the frame is easier than re-creating it.

Copying a frame is probably one of the easiest tasks you can perform in Publisher. Just select the frame and then click the **Copy** button on the toolbar, or choose **Edit** and then select **Copy**. Now click the **Paste** button, or choose **Edit** and then select **Paste**. Publisher copies the frame and pastes the new frame on top of the old one, slightly offset, so that you can move it to a new location.

Grouping Frames

Grouping allows you to designate two or more frames and treat them as a single unit. Why would you want to work with frames this way? Well, suppose you're creating an expense report form like the one shown in Figure 33.12. In the lower-left corner are your company logo in its own frame, address in a second frame, and phone numbers and email address in a third frame. As you're designing the form, you decide you want to move this information to the upper-right corner of the form. You want all this information to stay together and aligned, so you group these frames. Now you can move the three frames as a single unit. Grouping also lets you resize or rotate the frames as a single unit.

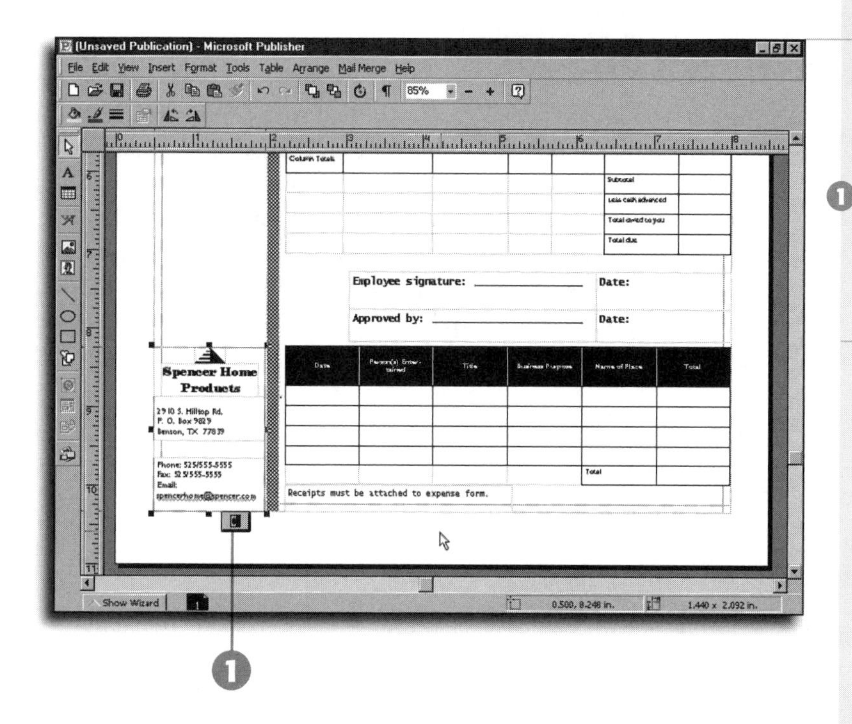

FIGURE 33.12

When frames are grouped, you can move, resize, or rotate them as a unit.

1. The Group button looks like two connected pieces of a jigsaw puzzle. When you ungroup the frames, the puzzle pieces are separated.

Grouping Frames Together

1. Press and hold the **Shift** key.
2. Click all the frames you want to group.
3. Choose **Arrange** and then select **Group Objects**, or press Ctrl+Shift+G.

OR

1. Click the **Selection** tool on the Frames toolbar.
2. Draw a selection box around all objects you want to include in the group and then release the mouse button. The Group button appears in the lower-right corner of the selection box with the two puzzle pieces separated.
3. Click the **Group** button. The two puzzle pieces are connected.

To ungroup frames, select the group and then click the **Group** button at the bottom of the frame, or choose **Arrange** and then select **Ungroup Objects**.

Layering Frames

When you create new objects in a Publisher document, the most recently created object appears on top of existing objects. Think of these objects as a stack of papers on your desk. When you drop a new paper on your desk, it falls on top of the stack and hides what's already there. Take a look at Figure 33.13. The vertical box was drawn first, the horizontal border next, and the square box third. You can tell by the way the boxes overlap one another.

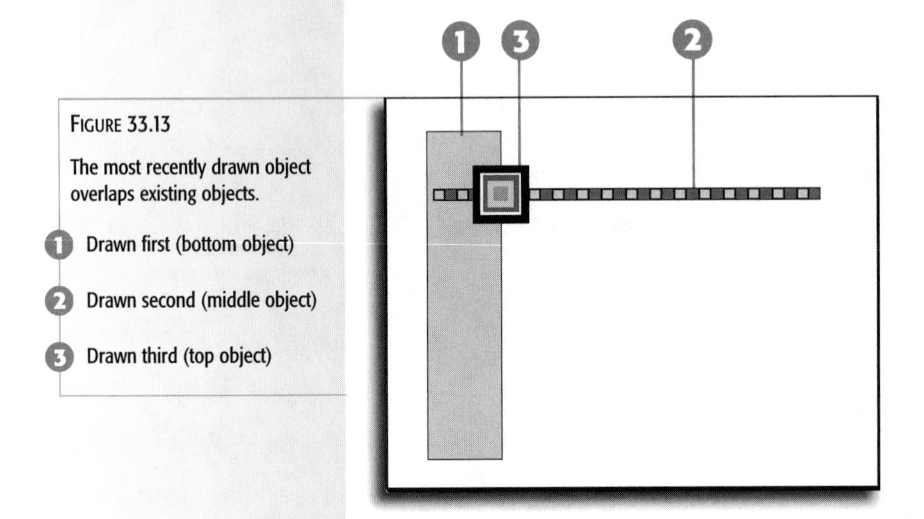

FIGURE 33.13

The most recently drawn object overlaps existing objects.

1. Drawn first (bottom object)
2. Drawn second (middle object)
3. Drawn third (top object)

Sometimes you might want to rearrange the stacking order of objects. Suppose, for example, that you want the horizontal box in Figure 33.13 to move to the bottom now (see Figure 33.14). Publisher provides four commands for rearranging the order of objects. Click the frame you want to rearrange, choose the **Arrange** menu, and then select one of the following commands:

- **Bring to Front**—Brings the object you select to the top of the stack
- **Send to Back**—Sends the object you select to the bottom of the stack

- **Bring Forward**—Brings the selected object up just one layer
- **Send Backward**—Sends the selected object down just one layer

In addition, the toolbar contains **Bring to Front** and **Send to Back** buttons.

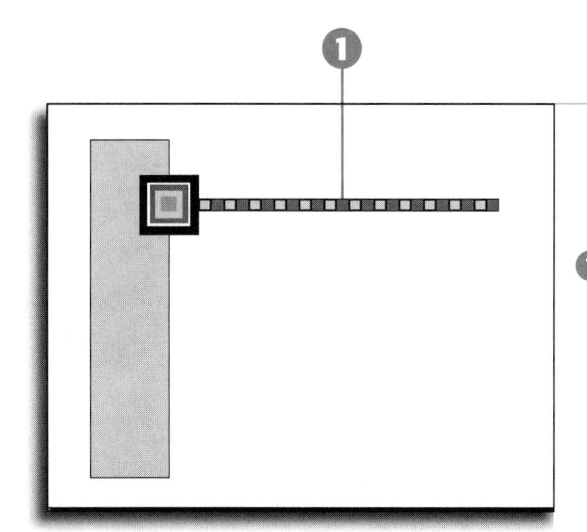

FIGURE 33.14
The horizontal box was moved to the bottom of the stack by using the **Send to Back** toolbar button.

1 This object is now on the bottom of the stack.

Changing Picture and Object Characteristics

For all objects (pictures, clip art, drawn objects, and text frames), you can change the following:

- The color and style that fills the frame
- The frame's line color (that is, its border color)
- The style of the frame's border
- Shadowing

Picture or object?

For this section, *picture* is defined as a photograph or clip art image, and an *object* refers to any other type of frame, such as a text frame or special shape.

Fill Options

Objects are either filled with a color and pattern or not filled. When an object is filled with a color, the color is usually obvious, unless it's filled with white, which is typically the background color for a document. A white-filled object on a white background appears to be transparent, but it's not. Layer a white-filled object on top of a colored one, and the white fill color becomes obvious. When an object is not filled, it is transparent. Layer an unfilled object on top of another object, and the lower object shows through.

Changing an Object's Fill Color and Pattern

1. Select the object you want to change.
2. Right-click to reveal the shortcut menu.
3. Depending on the type of object selected, choose **Change Frame** and then select **Change Rectangle** or **Change Shape**.
4. From the shortcut menu, choose **Fill Color**. Another shortcut menu like the one in Figure 33.15 then appears.

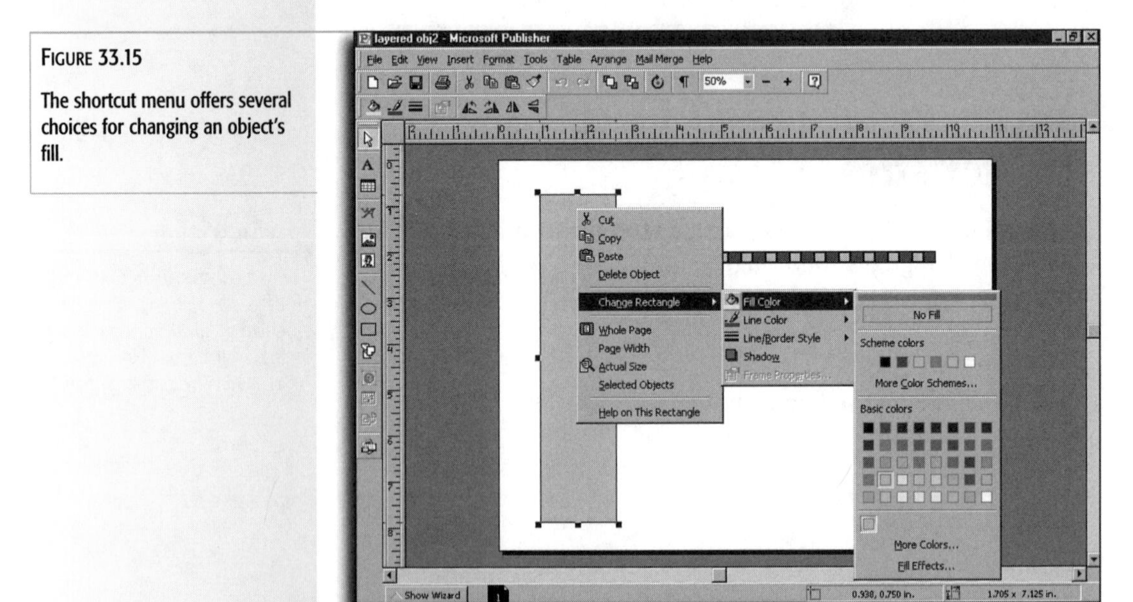

FIGURE 33.15

The shortcut menu offers several choices for changing an object's fill.

From the shortcut menu in Figure 33.15, you have several choices. Experiment with each of them until you achieve the effects you want.

- Click **No Fill** to leave your object transparent.
- Click one of the **Scheme colors** shown.
- Click **More Color Schemes** to reveal another dialog box from which you can choose a coordinated set of colors. Because all wizards define a color scheme, be aware that choosing a new color scheme changes the colors of other objects placed in your document by a wizard.
- Click **More Colors** to reveal a dialog box from which you can create new colors. A particularly useful option in this dialog box is **Show basic colors in color palette**. When you choose this option, a set of basic colors is always displayed in the shortcut menu shown in Figure 33.15.
- Click **Fill Effects** to display a dialog box from which you can specify a color tint, a fill pattern, or a color gradient. **Fill effects** is also a handy option to experiment with until you achieve the effects you want.

Line Color

Similar to **Fill Color**, **Line Color** lets you change the color of the outline of an object. Just select the object and then right-click. From the shortcut menu that appears, choose **Change Frame**, **Change Rectangle**, or **Change Shape**; then choose **Line Color**. The shortcut menu that appears is similar to the one shown in Figure 33.15. Choose a color from the current color scheme, a basic color, another color scheme, or look at more colors.

Line/Border Style

Line/Border Style refers to the design and thickness of the outline of an object. Many objects have no line or just a hairline outline in black. However, you can change the outline to any color and any thickness (point size) you define. In the case of a rectangle, *outline* doesn't necessarily mean all four sides. You can specify which sides of the rectangle you want to have a border: top, bottom, right, left, or any combination.

To change an object's line or border, select the object and then right-click. From the shortcut menu that appears, choose **Change Frame**, **Change Rectangle**, or **Change Shape**; then choose **Line/Border Style**. Now choose **More Styles**. When the Border Style dialog box, shown in Figure 33.16, appears, make your selections and then click **OK**.

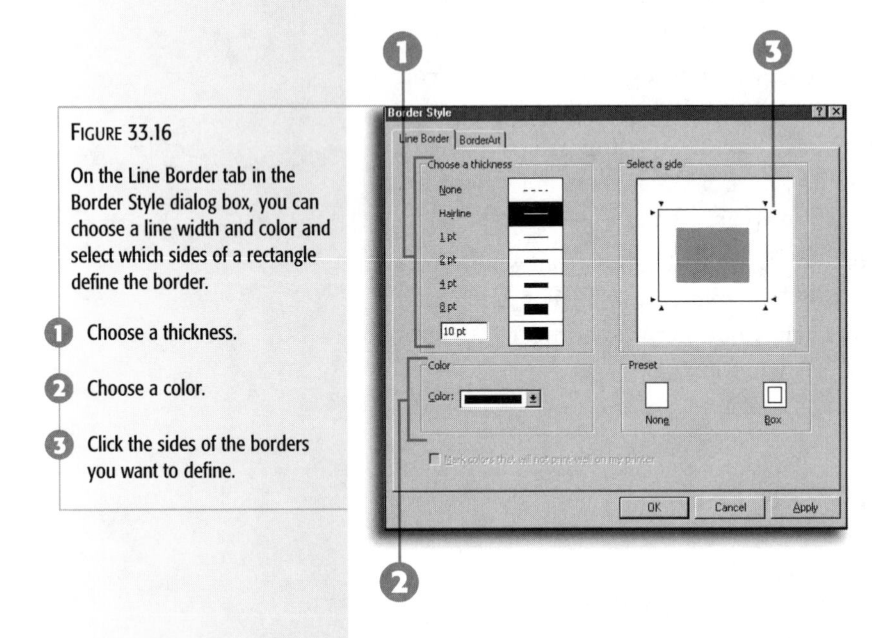

FIGURE 33.16

On the Line Border tab in the Border Style dialog box, you can choose a line width and color and select which sides of a rectangle define the border.

1. Choose a thickness.
2. Choose a color.
3. Click the sides of the borders you want to define.

If you want a decorative border, click the **BorderArt** tab in the Border Style dialog box (see Figure 33.17).

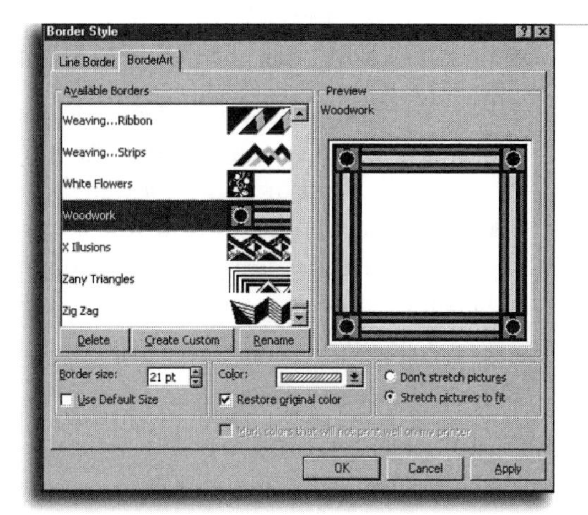

FIGURE 33.17
Using the BorderArt tab of the Border Style dialog box, you can decorate an object with a stylish border.

In this dialog box, scroll through the available borders. Be sure to use the **Border size** option to determine the best size border for your object.

Shadowing

Shadowing adds depth to an object, and it's easy to apply. Just select the object and then right-click. From the shortcut menu that appears, choose **Change Frame**, **Change Rectangle**, or **Change Shape**; then choose **Shadow**. Publisher automatically adds shadow to the bottom and right sides of your object. The color of the object is determined by the current color scheme.

Want a different kind of shadow?

If Publisher's "automatic" shadows are not what you want, you can create your own by copying the object you want to shadow. Fill the new object with a shadow color; then choose **Arrange** and select **Send Backward** to place the shadow below its original object. Adjust the position of the objects until you're pleased with the placement.

Copying Text

In Publisher, you copy text the same way you do Word. In the text frame you want to copy from, select the text to copy. To select all the text in the frame, press **Ctrl+A**. Click the **Copy** button on the toolbar, or choose **Edit** and then select **Copy**. Next, move to the location where you want to place the text and then click the **Paste** button on the toolbar, or choose **Edit** and then select **Paste**.

Copy Fitting in Text Frames

One of Publisher's slickest features is automatic copy fitting. It is especially useful for newsletter titles or in other documents where text must fit in the allotted space. Copy fitting automatically adjusts the size of your font to fit the existing text in the frame. The more text you add to a frame, the smaller the font becomes. Likewise, when you delete text, the overall font size is larger to "fill up" the frame.

Turning On Copy Fitting

1. Select the text frame you want to copy fit.
2. Right-click and choose **Change Text**. Then select **AutoFit Text** from the shortcut menu. Alternatively, choose **Format** and then select **AutoFit Text**.
3. From the submenu, choose one of the following options (Publisher automatically adjusts the text based on the option you choose):
   - **Best Fit** to shrink or expand text to fit the current frame
   - **Shrink Text On Overflow** to automatically shrink overflow text until it all fits in the selected frame
   - **None** to turn off the AutoFit feature

Changing Text Attributes

One of the most common changes you make in a document is to the text attributes. They include font, size, color, alignment, and so on. For the most part, the methods you use to change these attributes in Publisher are similar to those in other Office programs.

Font, Style, Size, Color, and Effects

Settings for font, style, size, color, and text effects are all located in the Font dialog box shown in Figure 33.18. To display this dialog box, select the text you want to change, choose **Format**, and then select **Font**.

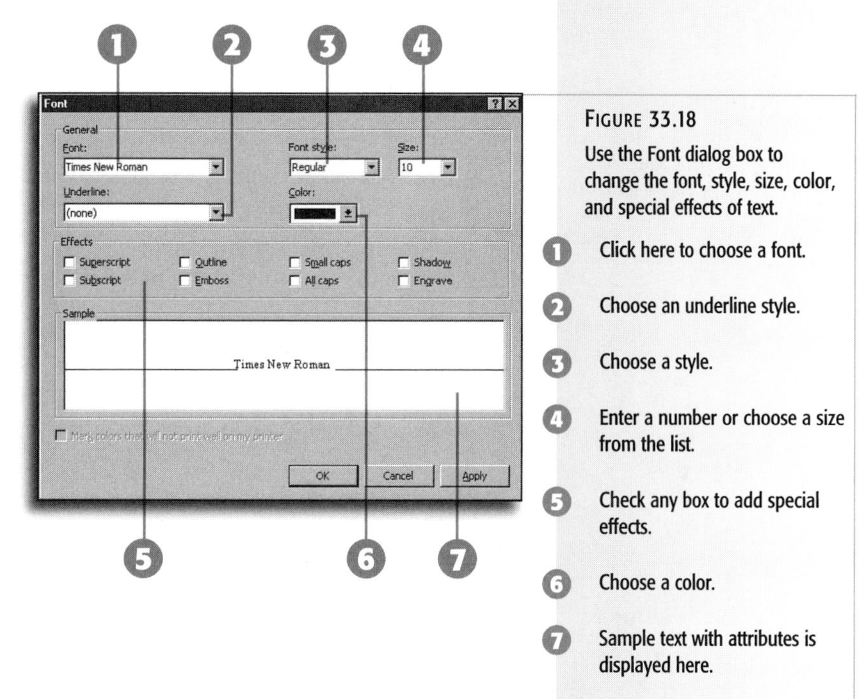

FIGURE 33.18

Use the Font dialog box to change the font, style, size, color, and special effects of text.

1. Click here to choose a font.
2. Choose an underline style.
3. Choose a style.
4. Enter a number or choose a size from the list.
5. Check any box to add special effects.
6. Choose a color.
7. Sample text with attributes is displayed here.

Using Drop Caps

Drop caps are a stylistic effect that adds to the professional appearance of your document (see Figure 33.19). Until recently, they were not easy to create in an average word processing program. Publisher makes creating them as easy as possible and also offers style by using special fonts.

Applying Drop Caps to Text

1. Select the text you want to change to a drop cap (usually the first letter in the first paragraph of a story, although you can experiment with drop caps on other characters as well).
2. Choose **Format** and then select **Drop Cap**.
3. In the Drop Cap dialog box, choose a style from the **Available drop caps** box.
4. Click the **Custom Drop Cap** tab in the dialog box.
5. Choose a letter position and size. Keep your eye on the Preview window as you try different options.
6. If you want, choose a font, style, and color in the lower half of the dialog box.
7. Click **OK**.

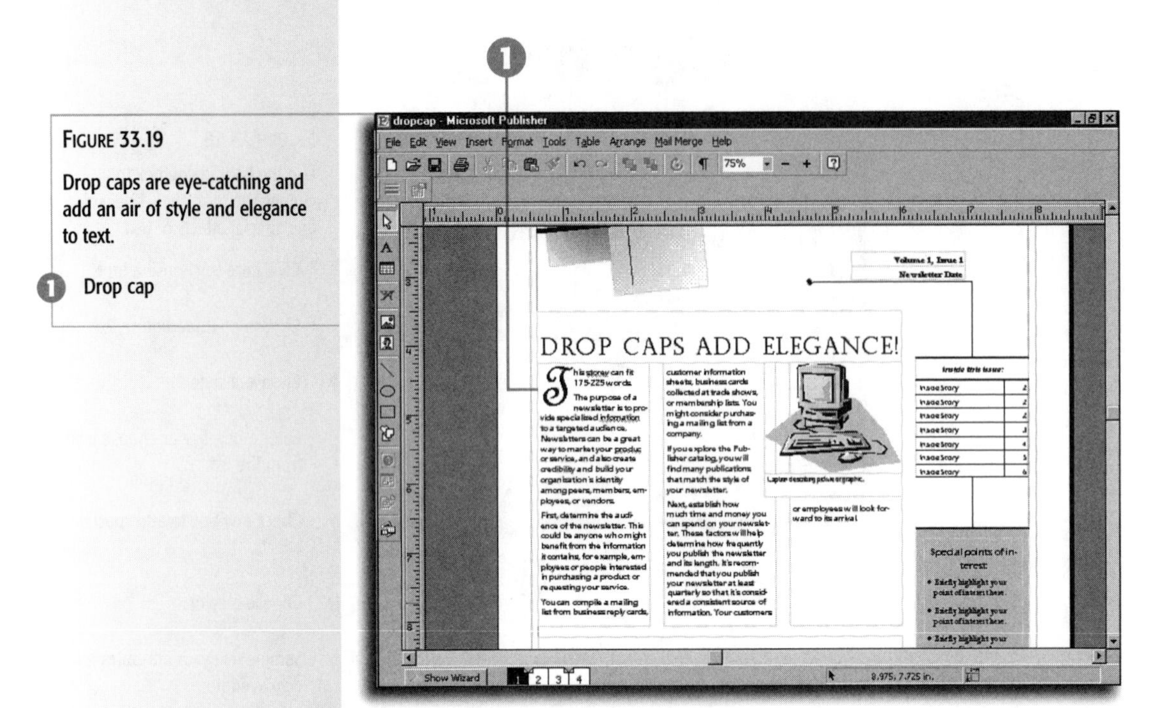

FIGURE 33.19

Drop caps are eye-catching and add an air of style and elegance to text.

1 Drop cap

To change a drop cap back to regular text, select the drop cap in the text, choose **Format**, and then select **Change Drop Cap**. In the resulting dialog box, click the **Remove** button.

Setting Text Alignment

Text alignment refers to the horizontal position of text in a frame. Characters can be aligned left, aligned right, or centered in the frame between the left and right borders. Justified alignment stretches characters on each line between the left and right borders so that the text has no ragged edges on either side. Alignment applies to *paragraphs* of text. You can apply different alignments to different paragraphs in the same frame.

Changing alignment is as simple as selecting the text to align and then clicking any of the alignment buttons on the toolbar. Each button illustrates the alignment of the text. It's as simple as that. When you click one of the alignment buttons—**Left**, **Center**, **Right**, or **Justify**—Publisher instantly adjusts the alignment.

Picking Up and Applying Text Formatting

Suppose you have a text frame that's set up with the Marigold font, bold, all caps, size 18, red, shadowed, right alignment, and double underlining. This text has no less than eight nonstandard attributes. You want another text frame to have these same attributes. Rather than set each attribute individually, you can save yourself some time by *picking up* the attributes and then *applying* them to the new text.

Picking Up and Applying Attributes

1. Select the text whose attributes you want to copy.
2. Pull down the **Format** menu and then select **Pick Up Formatting**.
3. Select the text to which you want to apply the formatting.
4. Pull down the **Format** menu again and choose **Apply Formatting**.

Publisher automatically applies all the formatting to the selected text. Note that if Publisher's **AutoFit Text** feature is turned on in the frame to which you're applying formatting, Publisher adjusts the font size automatically, if necessary. To avoid this automatic adjustment, disable AutoFit by opening the **Format** menu, choosing **AutoFit Text**, and then selecting **None**.

Of course, if you want to save even more time, you can use the Format Painter tool on the Standard toolbar to accomplish the same thing. Select the text whose attributes you want to copy, click the **Format Painter** button, and then select the text you want to copy the attributes to. The attributes are automatically copied to the text you select.

Wrapping Text Around Pictures

When you insert a picture in the middle of text, it's up to you to choose how the text will wrap around the picture. Figure 33.19 shows two examples. In the first, text wraps around the *frame* of the object. In the second, the text wraps to fit the *contour* of the object. Either of these styles is easy to achieve because Publisher provides a toolbar button for each.

Wrapping Text Around Pictures

1. Select the text frame where the picture will be located.
2. Choose **Format** and then select **Text Frame Properties**.
3. Be sure the **Wrap text around objects** setting is checked.
4. Click **OK**.
5. Select the picture frame.
6. Click the **Wrap Text to Frame** button or the **Wrap Text to Picture** button on the Formatting toolbar.

In the preceding steps, you define text wrap options for the text frame (steps 1 through 4) as well as the picture frame (steps 5 and 6). When the **Wrap text around objects** option is turned off, text does not wrap at all.

Checking Your Spelling

Publisher offers several options for checking your spelling. You can choose to check as you type, flag repeated words, and ignore all words in uppercase. Publisher underlines suspect words with a wavy red line. When you install Publisher, these options are automatically selected. To turn off any of them, open the **Tools** menu, choose **Spelling**, and then select **Spelling Options** and uncheck the options you don't want to use.

To check spelling in a document, select the text frame you want to check, choose **Tools**, and then select **Check Spelling**. Publisher displays the dialog box shown in Figure 33.20.

FIGURE 33.20

The Check Spelling dialog box gives you several options for suspect words.

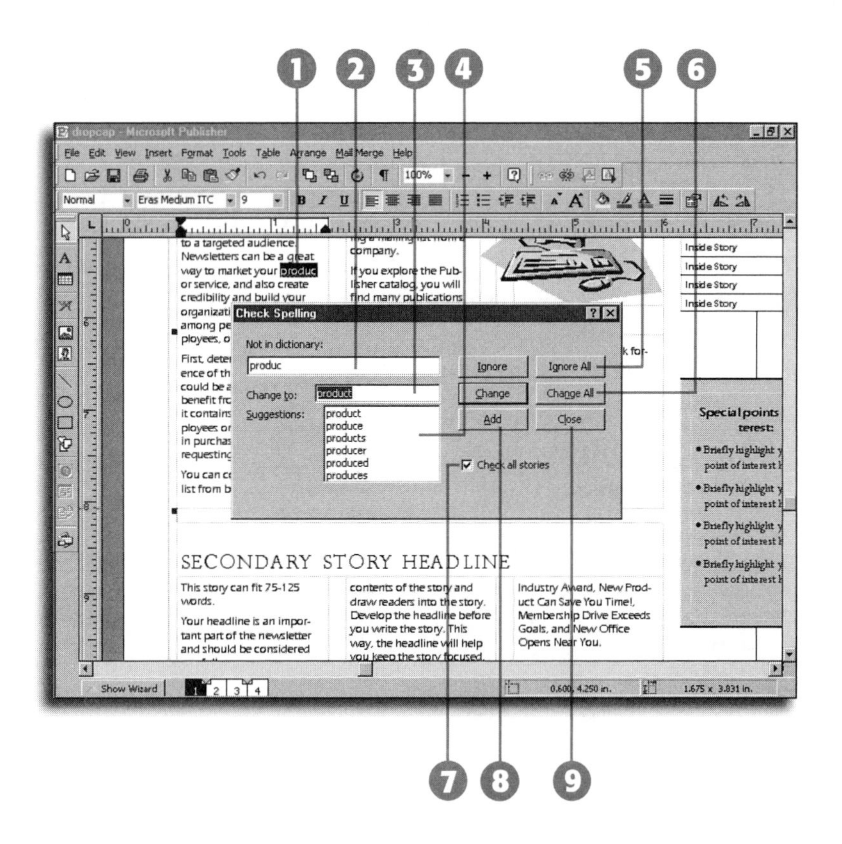

1. Publisher highlights the suspected word in the document.

2. You can edit the word directly here.

3. The preferred replacement word appears here.

4. Suggested replacement words appear here.

5. Click **Ignore** to leave the word as is. To ignore all occurrences, click **Ignore All**.

6. Click **Change** to replace the word with the suggested word. To change all occurrences, click **Change All**.

7. Check this box if you want to check all text in your publication (not just the selected text frame).

8. Click **Add** to have the spell checker recognize the word and add it to the dictionary.

9. Click **Close** to exit the spell checker.

Checking Your Design

In addition to the spell checker, Publisher also provides a tool for checking your design to see that you haven't made any common design errors. This is a nifty tool that I highly recommend you use. It checks to see that your document doesn't have any empty frames, hidden objects, objects off the page, overflow text that's unaccounted for, and so on. When you install Publisher, all the design check options are selected. To pick and choose your options, choose **Tools**, select **Design Checker**, and then click the **Options** button in the Design Checker dialog box. When the Options dialog box appears, you can select features you want Publisher to check.

To use the design checker, choose **Tools** and then select **Design Checker**. The dialog box shown in Figure 33.21 then appears.

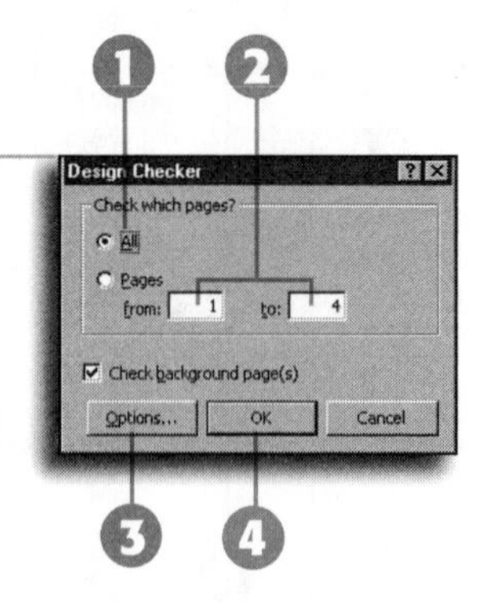

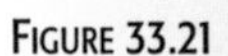

FIGURE 33.21

The design checker checks your document for design errors you might not catch on your own.

1. Click here to check the entire document.
2. Enter page numbers here to check specific pages.
3. Click here to select design checker options.
4. Click **OK** to begin.

Printing Your Document

When it comes to printing, Publisher is incredibly well designed. It makes your job of printing as easy as it can possibly be. When you use a wizard to create a Publisher document, you need to do very little, if any, adjusting and setting up for printing. The wizard sets up everything for you automatically. For instance, if you've used a wizard to create shipping labels, the wizard automatically chooses Avery 5164 shipping labels for your paper.

When you create a document such as an eight-page brochure on half-fold 8 1/2 by 11-inch paper, you don't have to think about which pages need to print next to each other to make them appear consecutively when folded. You create the content consecutively (pages 1 through 8 with 1 being the front cover and 8 being the back cover). When you're ready to print, Publisher saves you a lot of work. It knows that page 1 and page 8 must print on the same sheet, page 2 and page 7 on the same sheet, page 3 and page 6 on the same sheet, and page 4 and page 5 on the same sheet. It prints the pages this way for you automatically so that your content comes out correctly. If you add pages to the publication, Publisher handles them and prints them correctly. Publisher does so for any type of document you create using a wizard.

Changing Your Page Setup

Page setup refers to the page size, orientation (portrait or landscape), height, width, and layout for a document. When you create a publication using a wizard, you never need to change these settings. Even when you create a document from scratch, you need to adjust these settings only if you create a custom paper size, fold, or orientation.

If you do need to change these settings, open the **File** menu, choose **Page Setup**, and then follow the steps shown in Figure 33.22.

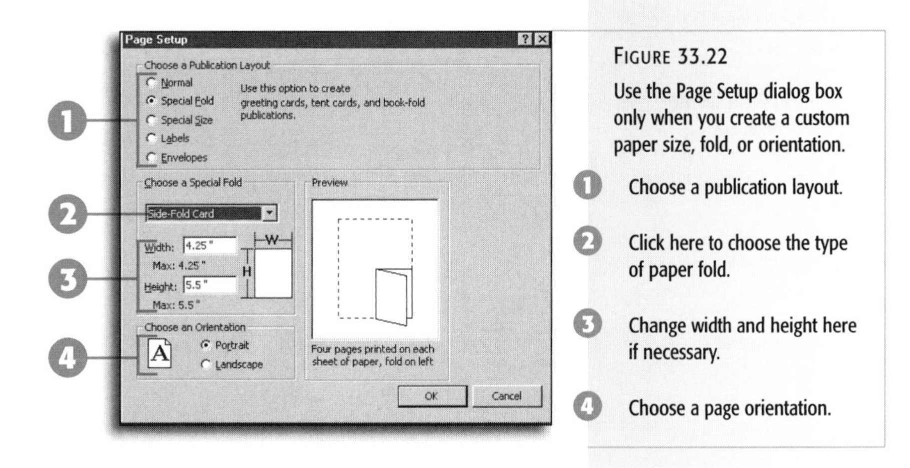

FIGURE 33.22
Use the Page Setup dialog box only when you create a custom paper size, fold, or orientation.

1. Choose a publication layout.
2. Click here to choose the type of paper fold.
3. Change width and height here if necessary.
4. Choose a page orientation.

Adjusting Printer Settings

Every printer's settings are slightly different, based on what it's capable of doing; for example, a color laser printer with three paper trays has significantly more options than a tiny inkjet printer that holds 50 sheets of paper. However, some settings are universal: All printers need to know what size paper you're printing on, what the orientation is, which pages you want to print, the number of copies you want to print, and so on.

Most of the information you need for printer settings you can get from your printer manual. For printing Publisher documents, one of the most important settings is paper orientation. Make sure the orientation for your printer matches the paper orientation set for your document. If your document is set for landscape, and your printer is set for portrait, your document will not print correctly.

To set printer options, open the **File** menu and choose **Print Setup**. You then see the dialog box shown in Figure 33.23.

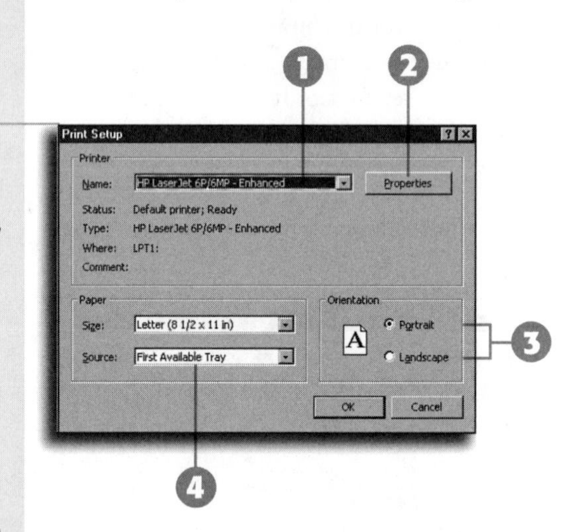

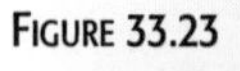

FIGURE 33.23

Use the Print Setup dialog box to set orientation, number of copies, and specific pages to print.

1. If you have more than one printer, click here.
2. Click here to set advanced printing features.
3. Choose print orientation here.
4. Specify a paper size and source here.

Using Special Paper

PaperDirect is a company that produces special stylized paper. The paper looks similar to some of the design themes found in Publisher, usually with a colorful header, header and footer, or border on all edges of the paper. Publisher contains several wizards that allow you to use PaperDirect's special paper. When you create a document specifying a PaperDirect paper, you need to load your printer with this paper before printing; no other settings need to be changed. In the Properties dialog box shown in Figure 33.24, make sure you specify the correct location of the paper (upper tray, lower tray, manual feed, and so on) before you print.

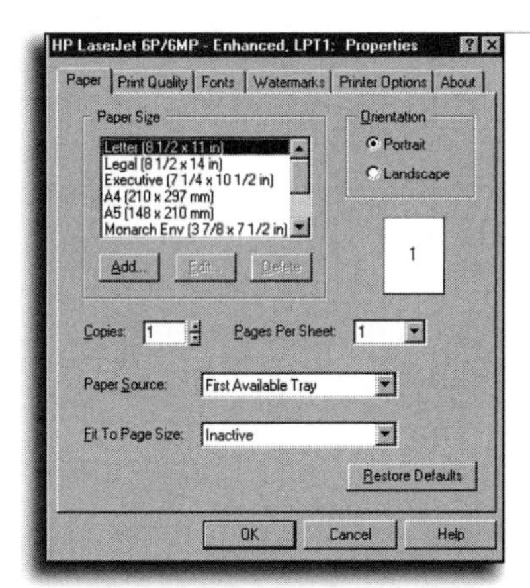

FIGURE 33.24

Use the Properties dialog box to specify the correct paper source, size, and orientation.

PART VII

Appendixes

APPENDIX

Adding, Removing, and Updating Office Components

Set up Office 2000 for the first time

Add and remove Office options with ease

Find other Office patches and updates

Fix Setup problems

How the Office Setup Program Works

No more Acme

Although it sounds like the gag from a *Roadrunner* cartoon, the old Office Setup program was called Acme Setup.

Just as in previous versions, Office 2000 uses a program called Setup.exe to install and configure programs and options. If you've used the Setup program from Office 97 or Office 95, though, you'll notice some dramatic differences when you set up Office 2000. In fact, this new version of Setup actually runs a brand-new program called the *Windows Installer*.

You use the Office 2000 Setup program to handle both a first-time installation (including upgrades over older versions of Office) and maintenance tasks, such as adding and removing individual Office programs and optional components.

Want more details on network setup?

If you have administrative access to a network, you can create a shared folder on any network PC (workstation or server) and install a shared distribution point that other network users can connect to when they need to install Office. This process is considerably easier than handing out a CD to each user. For full details, see Appendix A, "Advanced Setup Options," in *Special Edition Using Microsoft Office 2000,* also published by Que.

If you're setting up Office 2000 at home or in a small office, you'll use a CD-ROM to handle most Setup chores. In a corporate setting, you'll most likely be able to skip the CD and install Office from a location on a network server. Network administrators can use a utility in the Office 2000 Resource Kit to create custom installation scripts that bypass ordinary setup options and user prompts. If you encounter problems when installing Office 2000 from a network, call your corporate help desk or ask your network administrator for assistance.

One advantage of the Windows Installer is that it keeps track of your actions and lets you "roll back" the Setup program if necessary. For example, if you click the **Cancel** button while Setup is copying files, the Windows Installer undoes everything it did earlier and restores your system to its previous condition. If your system crashes or the power fails in the middle of Setup, you can normally restart your computer and resume setting up at the place where the Windows Installer stopped previously.

Setting Up Office 2000 for the First Time

The first time you install Office 2000 on a given computer, the most important preliminary step is to verify that the system meets the minimum system requirements, especially in terms of the amount of free disk space required. A full installation of

Office uses several hundred megabytes of hard disk storage. Of course, you must have a computer with Windows 95, Windows 98, Windows NT, or Windows 2000 installed.

Minimum System Requirements

Officially, Microsoft recommends that you install Office on a computer that meets these minimum requirements:

System Component	Requirement
Processor	Pentium or compatible processor
Memory	32MB or more
Free disk space	At least 200MB for a typical installation

NT requirements

To install Office 2000 on a machine running Windows NT, you might need to upgrade the operating system with the latest service pack. To set up Office on a machine running Windows NT 4.0, you must first upgrade with Service Pack 3 or later.

In practice, a system that meets only these minimum standards may have trouble running multiple Office programs at the same time, and performance in some situations may be unacceptably slow, especially when you're working with documents that contain many graphics files. I recommend that you install Office 2000 only on a computer with a processor running at 150MHz or faster (preferably a Pentium or compatible). If you can afford to upgrade the amount of memory to 64MB or better, you'll notice a dramatic increase in speed. Finally, even though it's possible to do so, don't install Office 2000 on any system where doing so will result in less than 200MB of free disk space *after* installation. Office 2000 needs gobs of extra space for options and data files.

Performing a Standard Installation

The simplest way to install Office 2000 on an individual PC is to simply insert the first CD from the Office package into the system's CD-ROM drive. On most PCs running Windows, doing so starts the Setup program automatically. (Depending on the version of Office you're installing, some programs may be on a second or third CD.)

Setup doesn't start automatically?

If Setup doesn't run automatically when you insert the CD, the AutoPlay feature is probably disabled on your computer. To run Setup in this case, open the My Computer window or Windows Explorer and display the contents of the Office CD. Then double-click the **Setup** icon in this folder window to begin the installation process.

Don't lose the key!

As part of the installation process, Office 2000 demands that you enter a 25-digit alphanumeric *CD key*. Don't lose this number because it's required if you want to reinstall Office, as you might have to do in the event of a disk crash or other catastrophe. You can find the serial number on a sticker attached to the CD's jewel case.

When you install Office for the first time, the Setup program prompts you for some basic information, including your name, company name, and a product identification code. If you're installing an upgrade version of Office on a new PC, you might have to insert a disk or CD from the previous version of the program to prove that you qualify for the upgrade.

After these preliminaries, you see the dialog box shown in Figure A.1, which allows you to choose a standard or custom installation. If you're upgrading over an existing version of Office, the top button reads **Upgrade Now**; if Setup does not find an existing version of Office, the button reads **Install Now**. (Additional options might be available if your network administrator has created a custom setup script.)

Click **Install Now** (or **Upgrade Now**, if you're setting up on a system that includes a previous version) to install Office with the most common program options. This option represents the quickest way to get to work, and adding or removing components later is relatively simple.

When you use this installation option, Setup uses the following default settings:

- Program files go in a default location on the same drive as your Windows files, or in the same folder as your previous Office installation, and you do not have an opportunity to specify a different location.
- Setup removes your previous Office installation and replaces all installed programs, migrating your personal settings and preferences to Office 2000.
- Your current default browser is replaced with Internet Explorer 5.0. This option eliminates previous versions of Internet Explorer; however, it does not remove Netscape Navigator or other non-Microsoft browsers.
- Setup installs a standard set of features. In the case of an upgrade, it automatically replaces all previously installed components with new versions, even if they're not part of the standard installation.

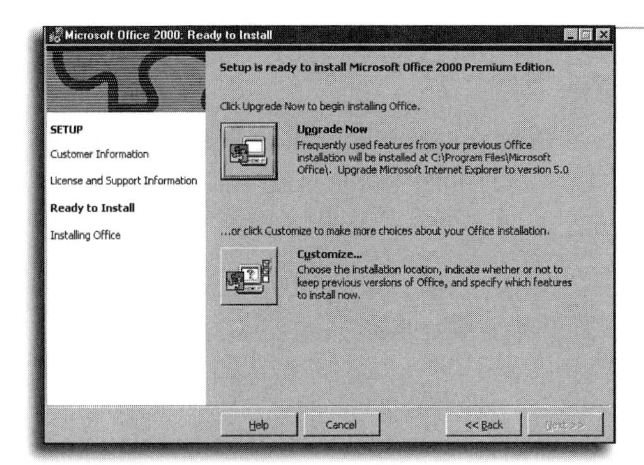

FIGURE A.1
Use the top button in this dialog box to begin setting up Office 2000 using default options.

Using Custom Setup Options

Click **Customize** to choose exactly which Office programs and optional components you want to install. This option is most appropriate for advanced users who want to avoid having to run the maintenance setup program later.

When you choose the **Customize** option, the Office Setup program displays a series of dialog boxes in which you can select exactly which Office options you want to install.

When in doubt, pick Custom

If you're not sure which option is right for you, click the **Customize** option. When you do so, Setup lets you review all your options, and if you accept the default settings at every opportunity, the effect is the same as if you had performed a standard installation.

Changing the Installation Location

The first dialog box in the custom installation sequence lets you select which folder Setup will use to store the Office program files. Normally, this is a folder in the Program Files folder on the same drive as Windows. I strongly recommend that you use the default location unless one of the following conditions is true:

- You do not have sufficient free space on the default drive. In this case, choose another drive that does have enough space for Office and its program files. Note, however, that Office will still insist on putting some files on the same drive as Windows.
- You want to continue to use your previous version of Office. In that case, as I explain in the following section, you must specify a different location.

Most people don't need previous versions

Office 2000 uses file formats that are almost exactly the same as those in Office 97, and you can save and open files using formats from Office 95 and Office 4. (The lone exception is Access 2000, included in the Professional and Premium versions of Office, which uses a new file format that isn't compatible with older versions.) If coworkers are still using earlier Office versions, you can continue to share files with them even after you upgrade to Office 2000.

Option grayed out? Go back and try again...

If the option to save your previous Office programs is grayed out, you forgot to enter an alternate location for program files. Click the **Back** button to return to the previous step; after specifying this location, click **Next**.

To choose a new location, click the **Browse** button and then click **Next** to continue.

Upgrading or Retaining Previous Office Versions

Although Microsoft doesn't recommend doing so, you can install Office 2000 and continue to use a previous version of Office. Choose this option only if you absolutely must retain previous versions of individual Office programs. Make sure you have sufficient free disk space as well.

As noted in the preceding section, if you want to preserve the capability to run previous versions of Office programs, you must specify an alternate location where you want Setup to install Office program files. In this case, I recommend that you specify a new folder on your system drive, such as C:\Program Files\Microsoft Office\Office2K.

When you see the dialog box that asks whether you want to remove previously installed applications, as in Figure A.2, inspect the list of available programs and check the **Keep these programs** box.

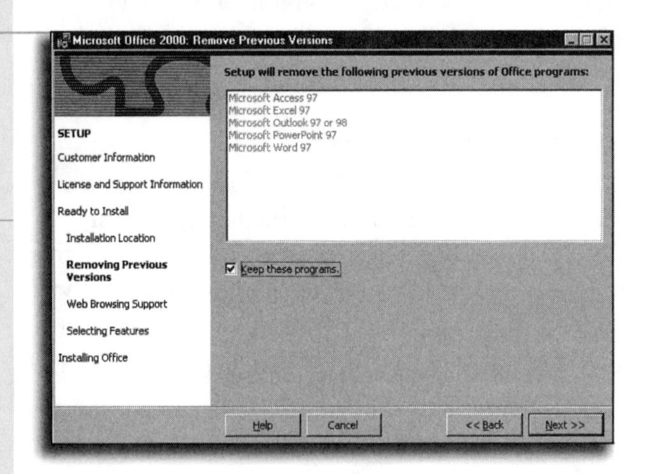

FIGURE A.2

If you want to continue to use one or more programs from a previous version of Office, use this custom option.

Choosing a Browser Upgrade

As I noted earlier, choosing the standard installation automatically installs Internet Explorer 5.0 and configures your system so that it is your default browser. If you choose the **Customize** installation option, however, you can choose exactly what you want to do with Internet Explorer:

- Choose the standard option to install the IE5 browser, Outlook Express, various Office 2000 enhancements, the Windows Media Player, and a handful of multimedia enhancements.
- Choose the minimal installation to add only the IE5 browser, Outlook Express, and the Office 2000 enhancements.
- Choose **Do Not Upgrade Microsoft Internet Explorer** if you do not want to install IE5 at all. This option is your best choice if you want to continue to use your previous Microsoft browser. You do not need to upgrade to IE5 to use Office 2000 with any version of Internet Explorer or Netscape Navigator, although you will lose some features by not upgrading to IE5.

SEE ALSO

For a list of problems you're likely to encounter if you use a browser other than Internet Explorer 5.0, see page 46

Save your old shortcuts

If you install Office 2000 on the same computer as Office 97, the new version wipes out all the program shortcuts on the Start menu. To make sure you can still start your old programs, try this trick: Before you run the Office 2000 Setup program, right-click the **Start** button and choose **Explore**. Create a new folder called Office 97 in the Programs menu and then drag all your existing Office shortcuts (Word, Excel, and so on) into this folder. Close the Explorer window and begin Setup.

Selecting Programs and Optional Features

When you choose a custom setup, the final dialog box lets you change which pieces of Office are installed. Unlike previous versions, Office 2000 also lets you decide how to install each program and option: You can copy the files to the hard disk, run from the CD, or configure some features so that they're installed automatically as needed.

In the Select Features dialog box shown in Figure A.3, look at the icon to the left of each feature. A white box means all options will be installed using the method you've specified, whereas a gray box with a drive icon means that some of the options available in that feature will not be installed. Click the plus sign to the left of each feature to expand the full list of options and adjust each one as needed.

Not certain? It's okay to skip IE5

If you're uncertain whether you want or need to upgrade to IE5, you can safely defer your decision by choosing the **Do Not Upgrade** option. You can install IE5 at any time after installing Office 2000 by rerunning setup.

FIGURE A.3

When you choose a custom installation, you select the exact installation method for each Office feature.

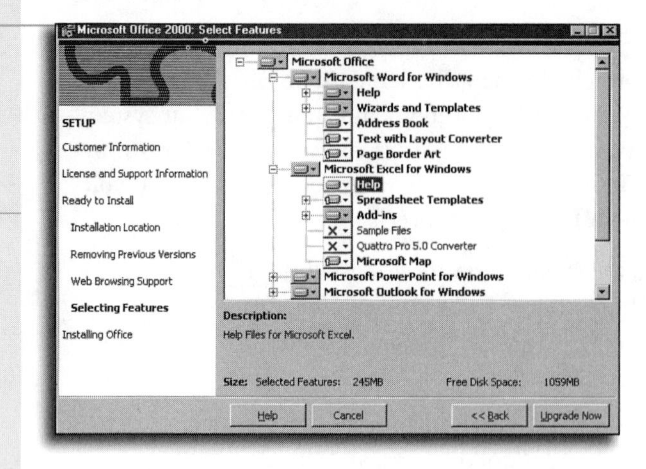

This dialog box is brand-new in Office 2000

If you have experience setting up custom options in Office 2000, you might find this new dialog box discomfiting at first. Read the instructions here carefully, and you should have no problems.

In previous versions of Office, your setup options were relatively limited. In Office 2000, you can configure each Office feature separately, allowing you to save considerable disk space; for example, if you use Word and Excel regularly, but you rarely use PowerPoint or Publisher, you can set up Word and Excel to run from your local computer but run PowerPoint and Publisher from the CD or from the network server.

Four settings are available for most features and options. Click the drop-down arrow to the left of any feature to see the full list of available settings, as in Figure A.4.

FIGURE A.4

When setting up Office, you can choose whether and how to run each feature.

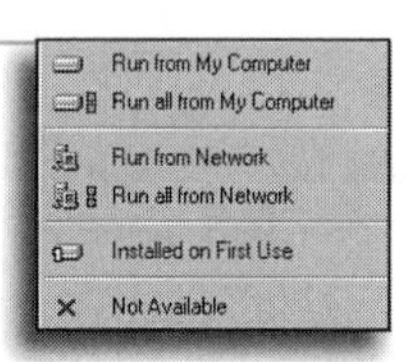

- When you choose **Run from My Computer**, Setup copies all the program files for that program or feature to your hard disk. This option results in the best performance and should be your choice in most cases.

- Depending on how you install, you can choose either **Run from CD** or **Run from Network** for some features. In this configuration, Setup doesn't copy program files to your PC but does add menu choices and program shortcuts. This option minimizes the amount of disk space used on your PC, but it also decreases performance. Use this option only for features that you rarely use, and then only when you're certain you'll have ready access to the Office CD or network connection so you can load the program files.
- When you specify **Installed on First Use** for a program or optional feature, the Setup program creates a menu item or shortcut on your system, but it doesn't actually install the files used by that feature. The first time you click that menu choice or shortcut, the Windows Installer starts up and copies the necessary files to the local hard disk just as if you had chosen the **Run from My Computer** option.
- Choose **Not Available** when you do not want to install a feature or create shortcuts that refer to it. In some cases, built-in menus include options that refer to features you've chosen not to install; if you select one of these menus, you see an error message that instructs you to rerun Setup.

Note that the standard Office installation includes a mix of all these installation options. For example, most Office Assistant characters are configured using the **Installed on First Use** option. The first few weeks after installing Office 2000 can be downright annoying as you discover all the little pieces that Setup didn't install. Keep the CD handy for those first few weeks because you'll need it frequently.

The display at the bottom of the Select Features dialog box shows how much space the options you've selected will require. Be sure you have enough space available before continuing. After you select all options, click the **Upgrade Now** (or **Install Now**) button to start copying files.

All for one...

If you want to install an entire group of features using the same settings without having to expand the list and set each one individually, choose **Run all from My Computer**, **Run all from Network**, or **Run all from CD**. The setting you choose applies to all options under the selected feature.

Portable users, beware!

Be extremely careful when using the **Installed on First Use** option on portable computers. When the Windows Installer runs, it must be able to access the Office CD-ROM or the network installation point to complete the installation. If you're on an airplane or in a hotel room, and the CD is on your desk back at the office, you cannot use the feature until you can get your hands on the CD again.

The kitchen sink...

Want to install every single option in Office? In the Select Features dialog box, click the icon to the left of the **Microsoft Office** option at the top of the list and choose **Run all from My Computer**. The effect is the same as if you had chosen that option for every item in the entire list. But think before you make this choice! Indiscriminately installing every Office option uses a frightening amount of disk space—well over 300MB for the Professional edition, for example.

Adding and Removing Office Components

After you set up Office 2000 for the first time, running the Setup program again gives you a different set of choices. When Setup detects that Office 2000 is already installed, it runs in *Maintenance mode*, displaying the dialog box shown in Figure A.5.

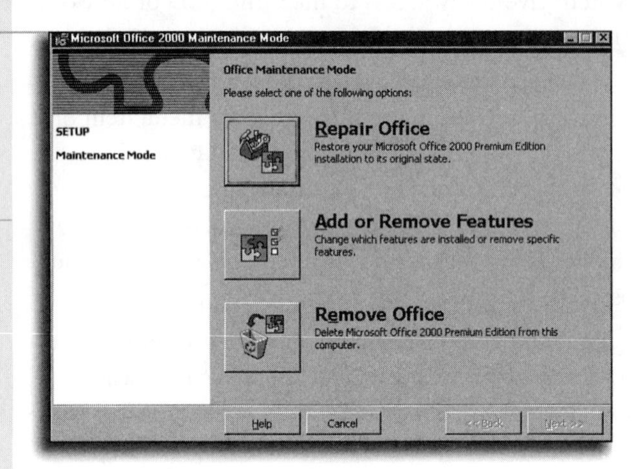

FIGURE A.5

After you install Office 2000, running Setup displays the Maintenance Mode dialog box shown here.

All roads lead to Setup

If you open the Windows Control Panel, start the **Add/Remove Programs** option, and choose **Office 2000** from the list of installed applications, the effect is the same as if you had run Setup from the Office 2000 CD-ROM. In either case, you need to insert the CD or have access to the network installation point to continue.

Available options in the maintenance version of Setup include the following:

- Click the **Repair Office** button to repeat the previous installation with all the settings you selected at that time. This option is useful if you know that some Office files have been damaged or corrupted.
- Click the **Add or Remove Features** button to install or remove options or entire programs.
- Click the **Remove Office** button to completely uninstall Office 2000.

Adding and Removing Office Components

1. Insert the Office 2000 CD-ROM and run the Office Setup program.

2. Click the **Add or Remove Features** button to display the full list of Office programs and optional features. (This list is exactly the same as the one you see if you choose the **Customize** option when first setting up Office 2000.) If necessary, click the plus sign to the left of an item to see additional options for that item.
3. To install an option, click the box to its left and choose **Run from My Computer**, **Run from CD**, or **Run from Network**.
4. To remove an option, click the box to its left and choose **Not Available**. Note that if you choose this option for an item that contains a list of additional options, you remove all those options as well.
5. To change the configuration of a feature—for example, to change a feature so that it runs from your computer instead of from the CD—click the icon to the left of the feature and choose the appropriate option.
6. Click the **Continue** button to start copying new files or deleting existing files.

Installing Patches and Updates

From time to time, Microsoft releases bug fixes and patches for Office and Office programs. In previous versions, for instance, Microsoft provided separate *patches* that fixed recalculation bugs in Excel and security problems in Outlook. After a large program like Office has been out for a year or more, it's not surprising to see a service release that consolidates previous patches and adds some new features.

To check for updates and patches, connect to Microsoft's Office Update Web site. The easy way to get there is from the **Help** menu of any Office program: Choose **Office on the Web** to start your browser and connect to that site; then search for updates.

Detecting and Repairing Damaged Files

When things really go wrong

What should you do if you're unable to start a particular Office program, or if you suspect that several programs are damaged? Rerun Setup in Maintenance mode and choose **Repair Office**. This option lets you completely reinstall Office using all the settings you originally specified. You can also ask the Windows Installer to simply look for missing or corrupted files and Registry settings and repair them as needed.

The Windows Installer maintains a complete record of all Office components you've installed. If you accidentally delete a file, or if an entry in the Windows Registry becomes corrupted after installation, the Windows Installer can automatically reinstall the damaged component the next time you try to use it. In most cases, these repairs are automatic: The Installer starts automatically when it detects a problem. You might need to supply the Office CD to continue, but the rest of the process happens quickly and painlessly.

If you find that some other features of an Office program, such as fonts or templates, are missing or damaged, you can force Setup to inspect your configuration and reinstall the missing pieces. To use this option for a single program, pull down the **Help** menu and choose **Detect and Repair**; then follow the prompts.

APPENDIX

Using Macros to Automate Tasks

- Record a macro
- Edit a macro
- Run a macro
- Attach a macro to a toolbar button or menu command

How Office Macros Work

Is there an Office task you absolutely dread? The workdays I least look forward to are the ones when I have to step through a series of mindless, repetitive tasks before I can even think about getting any real work done. If you have a chore that involves repetitive tasks, why not automate it? Office *macros* are sets of commands and instructions—essentially small programs—that you can use to automate Office tasks. By creating a macro to perform the steps of a repetitive task, you save yourself time and avoid possible errors.

What can you do with a macro? The following are just a few ideas (see the "Editing a Macro" section later in this appendix for more details on several of these macros):

- Perform routine editing or formatting. For example, I've created a set of nearly identical Word macros to apply specific font and highlight colors to selected text. Normally, I have to click the drop-down arrow to the right of the Highlight or Font Color tools, then click the color I want; with this macro, I have separate buttons to turn the selected text blue or green, or to highlight the selection in yellow or green, or to remove highlighting. I save one mouse click every time I use each of these macros (hey, eventually those clicks add up).
- Combine several commands into one keyboard shortcut. I use Excel lists for countless tasks. For the ones I use most often, I've created keyboard shortcuts that sort and filter the list exactly the way I want to see it.
- Use an option without having to go through dialog boxes. In Excel, I have a love-hate relationship with the Auto-Complete feature. When I'm entering data in a list, it's sometimes useful, but most of the time I want to leave it turned off. To reach this option, I have to pull down the **Tools** menu, choose **Options**, click the **Edit** tab, set or clear the check mark from the **Enable AutoComplete for cell values** box, and then click **OK**. That's five clicks, versus one for the macro I created that toggles this setting on or off.

- Automate a complicated set of tasks. For example, you might import and consolidate sales information every Monday morning, then format and subtotal the new table the same way every time. Rather than perform the same formatting and subtotaling tasks over and over again, create a macro that does the entire job for you.

Word, Excel, and PowerPoint let you choose two methods for creating macros: the *macro recorder* or the *Visual Basic Editor*. The recorder acts something like a tape recorder, noting each command and instruction you use when performing a task, then translating those instructions into a programming language called *Visual Basic for Applications* (*VBA*) and repeating them at your command. All the programming happens behind the scenes, totally hidden from you unless you decide to peek at the code comprising the macro.

You can use the Visual Basic Editor to modify recorded macros; if you're willing to learn some programming skills, you can create powerful macros by entering VBA commands directly in the Visual Basic Editor.

Writing VBA code goes far beyond the scope of this appendix. I'll stick to stepping you through the macro recorder and some basic macro editing skills. If you want to learn more about writing your own VBA code, I suggest that you pick up a copy of *Special Edition Using Microsoft Office 2000*, also published by Que.

Of course, just because you can write a macro doesn't mean you should. In many cases, you can find a better way to tackle the problem you're trying to solve. Let me give you some examples:

- If you want to apply a set of styles to words or paragraphs in a Word document, or to cells in a Worksheet, consider using styles instead. In Word, you can assign all sorts of formatting to a style, then assign that style to a keyboard shortcut or toolbar button so that you can apply it instantly. No programming required.

Publisher doesn't do macros

As I've pointed out several times in this book, Publisher is unlike other Office programs in many ways, and this is no exception. Publisher doesn't support macros of any kind.

SEE ALSO

- *For more information on what you can do with Word styles, see page 250*
- *To learn about applying formatting with Excel's styles, see page 399*
- *For instructions on how to customize menus and toolbar buttons, see page 92*

- Do you want to insert *boilerplate* text or graphics into a Word document? Use the AutoCorrect or AutoText features instead of messing with macros.

SEE ALSO

➤ *For examples of how you can use these features to automatically insert text and graphics, see page 202*

- Don't underestimate the Find and Replace features in all three of the main Office programs. Word, in particular, has a huge bag of tricks, including the capability to replace one style with another.

Of course, before you begin working with macros, you need to remember that macros created by other people can contain viruses. Office 2000 contains extensive protection against macro viruses, and in some cases these protections can make it difficult for you to run macros other people create.

SEE ALSO

➤ *For details on how to configure antivirus options, see page 112*

Recording Keystrokes and Mouse Clicks As Macros

The easiest way to create a macro is to record it. Word, Excel, and PowerPoint all enable you to record a macro instead of having to write a program in the Visual Basic Editor.

As the name implies, recording a macro is similar to making a tape recording of all the steps you take to perform a particular task. You turn on the recorder, and it writes the macro instructions for you, based on your actions. Sounds great, doesn't it? Unfortunately, I have to tell you that most recorded macros don't work properly right away. Why? Because the macro recorder captures the *effect of* your actions, not the actions themselves. Understanding this principle is essential if you expect to record a macro and have it work the way you want it to work. The macro recorder is still tremendously useful, but most of the time you need to edit a recorded macro before you use it.

Outlook macros? Fuggedaboutit!

I can think of hundreds of macros I want to create for Outlook, but I don't even bother. Outlook 2000 doesn't allow you to record macros; instead, you have to type in commands from scratch in the Visual Basic Editor. Maybe someday Outlook will get its own macro recorder. Until then, don't even think about trying to create Outlook macros–it's not worth the hassle.

Here are some things you should know about how the macro recorder works:

- The macro recorder "watches" what you do, but it ignores most of the steps you go through. For example, if you pull down Word's **File** menu, choose **Open**, type in the name of a file (`Summer Sales Letter.doc`), and then click **OK**, the recorder simply notes that you opened Summer Sales Letter.doc—not that you went through all the clicking.
- The macro recorder sometimes records more than you expect. If you select a range of cells in an Excel worksheet, for example, then open the Format Cells dialog box and change the font to Garamond, the macro recorder makes a note of that change. It also includes all the other formatting settings you didn't change, including the font size, style, color, underlining, and so on.
- The macro recorder doesn't record mouse movements. If you want to record the fact that you've moved to the top of a Word document or the first cell in an Excel worksheet, you have to use the keyboard (Ctrl+Home) instead.

Keep these tips in mind when working with macros:

- Always plan the steps you want to include in the macro before you start recording. You might even want to run through the task once to be sure what commands you use; write them down if the task is complicated. Although you can correct a mistake as you're recording, the error and the correction become part of the macro. You have to go back later and edit the macro to remove any unnecessary steps.
- Think ahead to avoid unnecessary steps in the macro. A different order or different method might be cleaner and faster, or prevent having to set up conditions or open an additional dialog box. For example, using the **Find** command is a great way to position your insertion point at a particular phrase but the Find dialog box retains its last entries. If the last setting was to search up or down, the macro may stop when it reaches the beginning or end of the document. Instead, you should include in the macro a step to change the Search setting to All.

A little extra code isn't always bad

As I mention in this section, recorded macros often capture more than you intended. That's not necessarily bad, however. In some cases, the extra macro instructions are completely harmless. Test the macro, and if it needs editing, follow the instructions I've outlined here. But if the macro does what you want, leave well enough alone.

- If you plan to use the macro with other types of documents, workbooks, or presentations, don't include anything that is specific to the file you have open when you create the macro. For instance, if you record an Excel macro that assumes you have exactly eight column headings in a list, you may have trouble using that same macro in a list with only five columns.
- Whenever you create a macro it's a good idea to assign it to a toolbar button, a menu, or a shortcut key so that you don't have to open the Macro dialog box every time you want to use the macro. Word lets you create a custom toolbar button or a keyboard shortcut at the same time you start recording the macro; Excel lets you create a keyboard shortcut at this point.

The following steps work with Word, Excel, or PowerPoint.

Recording a Macro

1. Pull down the **Tools** menu, choose **Macro**, and then select **Record New Macro**. The Record Macro dialog box appears (see Figure B.1). This dialog box is slightly different for each of the three main Office programs.

FIGURE B.1

Word lets you enter a name for your new macro and then assign it to a toolbar or keyboard shortcut; Excel and PowerPoint offer fewer options.

Is the OK button grayed out?

If you enter a macro name that isn't valid, the recorder will not let you continue. The most common cause of this stumbling block is a space character. The solution? Instead of calling your macro `Format Company Name`, take out the spaces and run your words together: `FormatCompanyName`.

2. In the **Macro name** box, type a name for the macro you're about to record. The name must begin with a letter. It can contain as many as 80 letters and numbers, but it cannot include spaces or symbols. Be careful not to give the macro the same name as an existing, built-in command such as FileOpen because the new macro actions will replace the existing actions for the built-in command.

3. Use the **Store macro in** drop-down list to tell the recorder where you want to store the macro you're about to create. Each program offers a different range of choices:
   - In Word, the default setting is **All Documents (Normal.dot)**. If you store a macro in this global template, it is always available, regardless of which document is open. If another template is open, you can store the macro in that template, or you can simply store it in the document you're working with right now.
   - Excel's default setting is **This workbook**. If you want your macro to be available for all workbooks, choose **Personal Macro Workbook**. (You can also select **New Workbook** if you want to create a new file just to hold the macro, but this option is only for advanced macro developers.)
   - PowerPoint lets you choose the current presentation or any other open presentation. Unfortunately, PowerPoint doesn't include any way to save macros so that they're available to all presentations.
4. To assign a Word macro to a toolbar or menu, click the **Toolbars** button; click the **Keyboard** button to create a keyboard shortcut that activates the macro. In Excel, click **Keyboard** (see the "Change an Excel keyboard shortcut" margin note for instructions). To assign a keyboard shortcut to an Excel macro, click in the **Shortcut key** box, shown in Figure B.2, then press the *hotkey* you want to use to run the macro. Be careful that you don't assign a common Office keyboard shortcut, such as Ctrl+C to copy or Ctrl+V to paste.

SEE ALSO

➤ *For more details on how to create custom toolbar buttons, menus, and keyboard shortcuts, see page 92*

Where's the best place for a macro?

Most of the time, you'll want to store a Word or Excel macro in a location where you can reuse it with other documents or workbooks. The exceptions? Any file you update constantly, such as a budget workbook whose numbers change every week or month, or a sales summary memo you revise each Monday morning. In that case, storing your macro in the document or workbook itself makes perfect sense.

What's the Personal Macro Workbook?

The *Personal Macro Workbook* is a hidden file that Microsoft Excel creates when you select the Personal Macro Workbook option; it opens automatically whenever you start Microsoft Excel, but you don't see it because it's hidden.

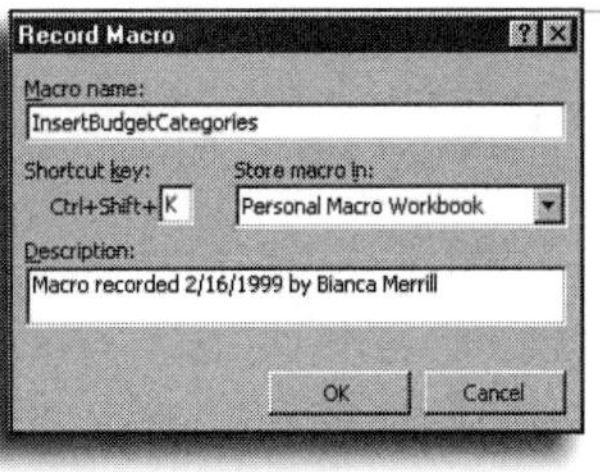

FIGURE B.2

Before you record an Excel macro, assign a keyboard shortcut here.

Use the Shift key, too

Excel's Record Macro dialog box might lead you to think you have to choose a letter plus the Ctrl key. Not so. You can also use numbers and symbols. If you press the Shift key when you enter a letter, as I've done in Figure B.2, your shortcut key is Ctrl+Shift+*letter*. To run a macro using this shortcut, press all three keys at the same time.

Move the toolbar, if you need to

You can move the Stop Recording toolbar out of the way while you record the actions for your macro, if necessary; the macro recorder pays no attention when you move this toolbar.

5. If you want, type a description for the macro in the **Description** box. Word automatically enters the date the macro was recorded and who recorded it. This step is optional, but taking a few seconds to enter a simple description here might save you some puzzlement later, when you try to figure out why you recorded this macro in the first place.
6. Click **OK** to begin recording the macro. The Stop Recording toolbar appears, and your mouse pointer changes to resemble a tape cassette with a pointer.
7. Begin performing the actions and choosing the commands that make up the task you're automating with the new macro. Use the buttons on the Stop Recording toolbar as follows:
   - In Word, click the **Pause Recording** button to temporarily stop recording while you perform an action; click this button again to resume recording. The pause is not recorded as part of your macro.
   - In Excel, click the **Relative Reference** button to switch between recording *relative references* and *absolute references*.

SEE ALSO

➤ *For an explanation of the difference between relative and absolute references, see page 376*

8. Click the **Stop Recording** button when you want to quit recording your actions and save the macro.

Running a Saved Macro

To run a macro after you've created it, click the **Tools** menu, select **Macro**, and then select **Macros** from the submenu. The Macros dialog box appears (see Figure B.3). Select the name of the macro you want to use and then choose **Run**.

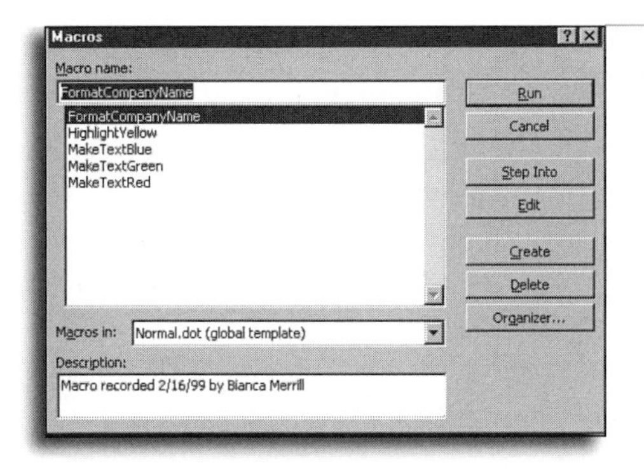

FIGURE B.3
This dialog box shows all the macros available in the specified location; choose a different entry from the **Macros in** list, if necessary.

Of course, if your goal is to save keystrokes and reduce repetitive steps, that cumbersome procedure doesn't exactly help, does it? That technique is just fine for macros that you use on rare occasions to do a big job. But for everyday macros, those you use to cut a 10-step job down to one or two clicks, use any of the following techniques instead:

- Assign it to a toolbar button and click that button.
- Assign it to a menu and choose that menu option.
- In Excel or Word, press the key combination you created as the keyboard shortcut.
- Press Alt+F8 to bypass the menus and pop up the Macros dialog box. Select the name of the macro you want to use, and then choose **Run**.

Missing a macro?

What do you do if the macro you recorded isn't in the list in the Macros dialog box? Chances are you're just not looking in the right place. Click the drop-down **Macros in** list to specify the location where you saved the macro; in Excel, for example, you might need to choose **Personal Macro Workbook** instead of **This Workbook**.

You can add macros to toolbar buttons and menus in any of the big three Office programs, and you can create keyboard shortcuts in Word and Excel. But my absolute favorite way to store a list of macros is to put them on a custom drop-down menu. I've added a single menu item called My Macros to Word and Excel, the two programs I use most often, and I've added each of my macros to that menu. Most of the time, the macros are out of sight, but it takes just one click to drop down the menu and let me choose from the entire list.

Creating a Custom Menu for Macros

1. Pull down the **Tools** menu and choose **Customize**; the Customize dialog box appears.

Change an Excel keyboard shortcut

If you forgot to assign a keyboard shortcut to an Excel macro, you can do so after the fact. Press Alt+F8 to open the Macros dialog box (I love this shortcut). Select the name of the macro you want to change, and click the **Options** button. Click in the **Shortcut key** box and type the hotkey you want to use (with or without the Shift key); then click **OK** to save your change. Unfortunately, almost all the Ctrl+*letter* combinations are already used by Excel. Only the letters E, J, L, M, Q, and T are available. If you discover you've assigned a combination by mistake (such as Ctrl+S, which normally is the shortcut for Save), repeat the process and delete the letter in the hotkey box.

Menus, toolbars—they're all the same

Remember, you can mix menus and buttons on any toolbar, so if you prefer to put the new menu on the Standard toolbar (say, just to the left of the Office Assistant button), go right ahead.

2. Click the **Commands** tab. Scroll to the bottom of the **Categories** list and select **New Menu**.
3. The **Commands** list in the right pane includes only one entry: **New Menu**. Click to select this entry; then drag it onto the main menu bar or any toolbar and drop it into position. (You see a thick black bar to indicate where the menu will appear.)
4. Leave the Customize dialog box open and right-click on the new menu you just created. Select the text in the **Name** box on the shortcut menu and replace it with the title `My Macros`.
5. Return to the Customize dialog box. Scroll up through the **Categories** list and select **Macros**.
6. From the list of macros on the right, select each one and drag it onto the new menu you just created. When you hover the item over the menu bar, a blank gray square drops down. Drop the macro there to add the first item, and repeat the process for all other macros you want to include.
7. Follow the instructions in step 4 to rename each macro with a name that's easy to understand. It's okay to use spaces on this menu.
8. Choose **Close** to close the Customize dialog box and return to your editing window. Click the My Macros menu to see a drop-down list of all your macros.

Troubleshooting Macros

After you've recorded a macro, it's always a good idea to test it and iron out any little glitches before you use it on an important file or pass it along to someone else. Test it a few times, under a variety of circumstances, to make sure it works in all conditions. If you have problems, you might be able to re-record the macro using a slightly different technique, or you might have to edit the macro to fix it.

Use these tips when testing your macro:

- Copy a group of files and use those copies as your guinea pigs. Don't risk destroying important data because your macro doesn't work correctly.
- If you assigned the macro to more than one method—keyboard shortcut, toolbar, or menu—test all the methods to make sure it works equally well in all situations.
- Open a new Word document or Excel workbook and test the macro to be sure it works.
- Make sure your macro works when you change the situation. For example, if your macro applies a font attribute, try it on selections with a wide variety of formatting, especially unusual formatting types.

Troubleshooting Excel macros adds an extra dimension, depending on whether you used absolute or relative references when you recorded the macro. If the first step in your macro is to select a cell, and you record the macro using relative references, the macro selects a cell relative to the cell that is active when you run the macro. In other words, if you turn on the macro recorder with the active cell in A1 and then go down four rows and right 10 columns to cell K5, Excel records the number of cells you move as part of the macro instructions. When you play back the macro, the active cell moves four rows down and 10 columns to the right from your starting point. If you have problems with your macro beginning in an unexpected cell, this could be the source of your trouble. If you really want to go to cell K5 when you run the macro, regardless of where you start, either re-record the macro with the Relative Reference button turned off (not highlighted or depressed), or edit the macro to replace the relative reference with an absolute reference.

SEE ALSO

➤ *For an explanation of how relative and absolute references work, see page 376*

If you didn't intend for the macro to begin by selecting a cell, but instead to begin carrying out procedures in whatever cell you select before running the macro, either re-record your macro and don't select a starting cell after you turn on the recorder, or edit the macro to remove the cell selection at the start of the macro.

Editing a Macro

Want more information on VBA?

For programming details on using Visual Basic for Applications, press Alt+F11 to open the Visual Basic Editor, then click the Office Assistant button. (This reference may not have been installed with the rest of Office, so you may have to supply the primary Office CD-ROM or point the Installer program to the location of your setup files.) For an absolutely first-rate introduction to the essentials of programming in VBA, run to your nearest bookstore and pick up a copy of *Special Edition Using Microsoft Office 2000*, also published by Que. While you're at it, pick up another copy of this book, too, and give it to a friend who uses Office.

The Visual Basic Editor window can be intimidating, but it needn't be so. Unless you plan to write your own programs, you can safely ignore most of the parts of this window and just concentrate on the code in macros you recorded. It's helpful to have a working knowledge of the Visual Basic programming language and how it works (especially if you want to add steps and conditional statements), but that's not a prerequisite. Even a nonprogrammer can fix common macro problems in a hurry using this tool.

At the beginning of this appendix, I mentioned a Word macro that I use to change the color of selected text to blue. If I record this macro using the Font Color tool on the Formatting toolbar, my macro works perfectly; in fact, if I look at it in the Visual Basic Editor, I see that it consists of exactly one line of code:

```
Selection.Font.Color = WdColorBlue
```

But what happens if I record this macro using dialog boxes? I pull down the **Format** menu, choose **Font**, change the **Font color** to Blue, and then click **OK**. Although it seems as if I've done exactly the same thing, the effect on my macro is very different. I end up with 23 lines of code between the With and End With lines, as you can see from Figure B.4. If I reuse this macro as is, I'll change the color of the text to blue, but I'll also change the font to New Times Roman and the font size to 12 points, and if my selection has bold or italic formatting, this macro will remove it. That's not what I want to do, so I need to edit this macro to make it do only what I want it to do.

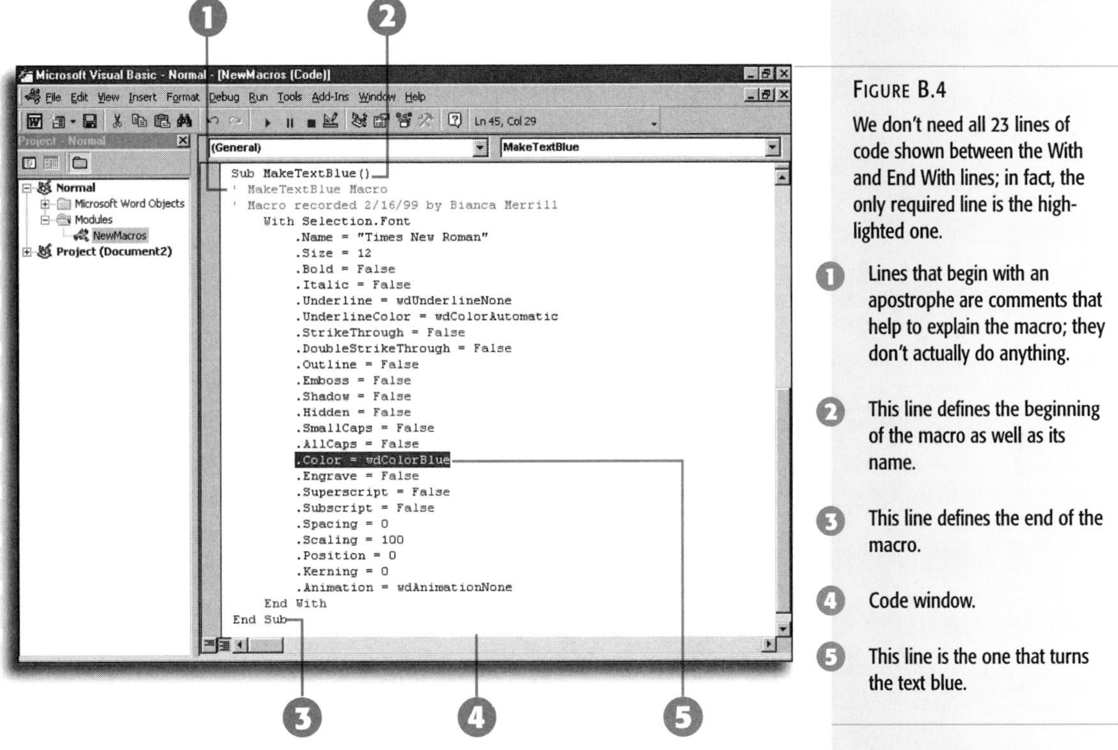

FIGURE B.4

We don't need all 23 lines of code shown between the With and End With lines; in fact, the only required line is the highlighted one.

1. Lines that begin with an apostrophe are comments that help to explain the macro; they don't actually do anything.
2. This line defines the beginning of the macro as well as its name.
3. This line defines the end of the macro.
4. Code window.
5. This line is the one that turns the text blue.

Editing a Macro

1. Open the **Tools** menu, select **Macro**, and then select **Macros** from the submenu. The Macros dialog box appears.
2. From the **Macro name** box, select the name of the macro you want to edit.
3. Click the **Edit** button. The Microsoft Visual Basic window opens (refer to Figure B.4).
4. Make the necessary changes in the code window (some suggestions follow these steps). In this case, delete all the lines between the With and End With lines except the one that reads `.Color = wdColorBlue`. You can scroll through all your macros in this window, so be sure you are in the correct macro before making changes.

Know the color code

In the Visual Basic Editor code window, some text is displayed in green, some in blue, and some in black. Green text indicates a *comment* that has no effect when you run the macro. (Comments are always preceded by an apostrophe.) Blue text indicates *keywords* that the Visual Basic Editor recognizes (`Sub` and `With`, for example); these represent important steps of the macro. Black text indicates macro steps that are not keywords.

5. Pull down the **File** menu and choose **Close and Return to Microsoft Word** after you complete your modifications.
6. Test the macro to make sure that your changes worked.

As long as the Visual Basic Editor is open, why not make some other changes? For example, you can copy the newly edited macro to create versions that change text to green or red. Just select everything from the `Sub` line to the `End Sub` line, and press Ctrl+C to copy it to the Clipboard. Now position the insertion point at the beginning of the line after this macro and press Ctrl+V to paste the copied macro. Change the text on the Sub line to read `Sub MakeTextGreen ()` and change the value in the macro itself from wdBlue to wdGreen. Easy, isn't it?

How do you know which values you can type after the equal sign? Position the insertion point after the equal sign and pull down the **Edit** menu, and then choose **List Constants** to pick from a list of options.

Creating a Toggle Macro

One of the most useful types of macros you can create is a *toggle macro*, in which clicking a single button turns on an option if it's off, or off if it's on. (The Bold, Italic, and Underline buttons on the Formatting toolbar are toggles.)

In fact, you can reduce some toggle macro commands to a single line by creating a macro and then editing its code to turn it into a toggle macro. Earlier, I mentioned that I like to toggle AutoComplete on and off in Excel; here's how you can create a macro that does the same.

Creating a Toggle Macro

1. Open Excel and use the procedures defined earlier in this chapter to record and save a macro called ToggleAutoComplete. Record the following actions: Pull down the **Tools** menu, choose **Options**, click the Edit tab, set or clear the check mark from the **Enable AutoComplete for cell values** box, and then click **OK**. Specify that you want to save the macro in your Personal Macro Workbook.

2. Your new macro is stored in the Personal Macro Workbook, which is a hidden workbook. Before you can edit the macro, you first have to unhide this workbook. Pull down the **Window** menu, click **Unhide**, choose **Personal** from the list of workbooks, and click **OK**.
3. The Personal Macro Workbook looks like an empty workbook; don't type anything in it. You're only going to edit the macro stored there. Pull down the **Tools** menu, choose **Macro**, then click **Macros**.
4. Select ToggleAutoComplete from the list of available macros and click the **Edit** button.
5. The Visual Basic Editor opens, and you should see code that looks something like this (your version may say True instead of False, depending on how this option was set when you began recording):

```
Sub ToggleAutoComplete()
'
' ToggleAutoComplete Macro
' Macro recorded 2/16/1999 by Ed Bott
'
    Application.EnableAutoComplete = False
End Sub
```

6. Right now, this macro tells Excel to turn AutoComplete off. Select the first part of the line (before the equal sign) and copy it to the Clipboard; then select the second half of the line, type the word `Not`, followed by a space, and paste the contents of the Clipboard. The results should read as follows:

```
Application.EnableAutoComplete = Not
      Application.EnableAutoComplete
```

The `Not` after the equal sign tells Excel that running this macro should change the AutoComplete setting to the opposite of its current setting: on to off, or off to on.

7. Pull down the **File** menu and choose **Close and return to Microsoft Excel**.

On or off? It doesn't matter

For the purposes of this macro, it doesn't matter whether you check or uncheck the **Enable AutoComplete for cell values** box. The trick is to make this setting the opposite of whatever it is when you open the dialog box; that's the only way Excel's macro recorder can make a note of your change.

More about the Personal Macro Workbook

The Personal Macro Workbook doesn't exist until you store a macro in it; Excel creates it to hold the macro, keeps it hidden (unless you unhide it), and opens it every time you start Excel–which is why your macro is available to every workbook you open. To keep it out of your way, make sure it stays hidden except when you need to edit a macro that's stored in it.

Hiding the Personal workbook is important

If you don't hide the Personal workbook, it will open every time you start Excel; to get it out of your way, you must remember to hide it.

The Visual Basic Editor closes, but the Personal Macro Workbook remains open. Test the macro to make sure it works as you expect, then assign the macro to a button or menu command. Finally, hide the Personal Macro Workbook before you exit Excel; when you exit the program, Excel asks whether you want to save Personal.

Copying, Renaming, and Deleting Macros

You can delete any macro by using commands in the Macros dialog box. However, if you've assigned the macro to a menu command or toolbar button, you need to remove those separately—they remain behind, although they don't do anything after you delete the macro.

Deleting a Macro

1. Open the **Tools** menu, choose **Macro**, and then select **Macros** to open the Macros dialog box.
2. From the **Macro name** box, select the name of the macro you want to delete.
3. Choose **Delete**.
4. When Word asks for a confirmation that you want to delete that macro, choose **Yes**.
5. Choose **Close** to close the Macros dialog box.
6. To remove the toolbar buttons and menu commands you assigned to the macro, open the **View** menu, choose **Toolbars**, and then select **Customize** from the submenu. When the Customize dialog box appears, drag the button for the macro from the toolbar on the screen or the macro menu command from the menu.

SEE ALSO

➤ *To learn more about customizing toolbars and menus, see page 92*

Word lets you copy a macro to another document or template, rename a macro, or delete a macro using the Organizer. To open the Organizer, use the Macros dialog box.

Copying, Renaming, or Deleting a Word Macro

1. Open the **Tools** menu, choose **Macro**, and then select **Macros** to open the Macros dialog box.
2. Choose **Organizer**. The Organizer dialog box appears with the **Macro Project Items** tab selected (see Figure B.5).

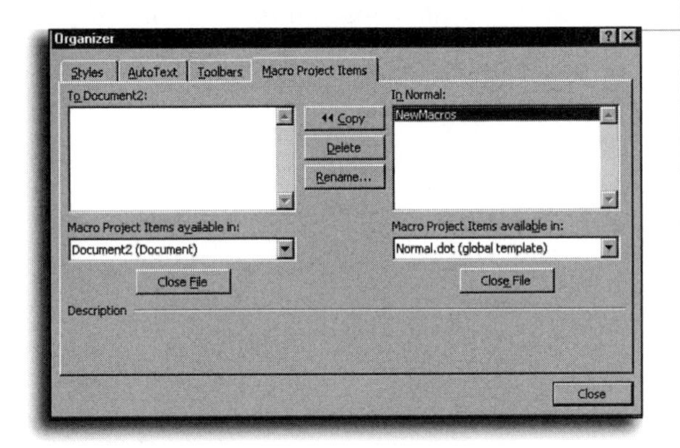

FIGURE B.5
Use Word's Organizer to copy, delete, or rename macros.

3. The two boxes in the dialog box are the **In Normal** box on the right, which displays the macros in the Normal document template, and the **To Document** ***x*** box on the left, which displays the macros used in the document you have open. From either list, select the macro you want to copy, rename, or delete.
   - If the macro is in another template that's attached to the current document, select that template from the **Macro Project Items available in** drop-down list on the right.
   - If the document you want isn't listed, choose **Close File**, and then choose **Open File**. Select the file you want to use and then click **Open**. The file's macros will appear in that box.
4. Click the appropriate button for the action you want to perform:
   - **Copy** copies the macro from one box to the other, thus copying it from the Normal template to the current document or vice versa, depending on where the macro was stored.

- **Delete** deletes the selected macro (to delete more than one macro, hold down the Ctrl key and click each one you want to delete before choosing **Delete**).
- **Rename** opens the Rename dialog box. Enter the **New name** for the macro and choose **OK**.

5. Click the **Close** button.

Glossary

absolute address In Excel worksheets, use these cell references when you want to copy a formula to a different cell without changing its address. To create an absolute address, begin with a dollar sign (A1, for example). Also known as *absolute reference*. See also *relative address*.

absolute addressing A way of specifying the location of an electronic document so that a hyperlink to it will open a document in a fixed location, such as a page on a different Web site. See also *relative addressing*.

Action Buttons Special-purpose hyperlinks, used only in PowerPoint presentations, that allow users to navigate from slide to slide and perform other functions by clicking buttons.

active cell In an Excel worksheet, the cell that is currently available for editing.

activities Outlook items that are linked to a record in the Contacts Folder, including email messages, meetings, and tasks.

Address Cards view One of two built-in views of the Outlook Contacts Folder, showing name, address, and other details for each contact.

adjustment handle The diamond-shaped handle used to adjust the appearance (but not the size) of many AutoShapes. See also *sizing handle*.

alignment The arrangement of text and objects on a page, on a slide, or in a worksheet cell. Common alignment options include left, right, and centered.

animated GIF A graphic, commonly used in Web pages, that appears to move.

animation In PowerPoint, visual and sound effects that allow you to reveal parts of a slide (such as bullet points or bars on a chart) individually.

anonymous FTP The act of transferring files using the Internet's File Transfer Protocol (FTP) without logging on to a server with a user account.

appointment An Outlook Calendar item that includes a starting and ending time. See also *event*.

argument Numbers, text, or logical values used in an Excel function to perform a predefined calculation.

arithmetic operator In Excel, a sign or symbol that specifies mathematical operations within elements of a formula;

the plus sign (+), for example, is the operator for addition.

ascending A sort order that organizes text or numbers from lowest to highest values (A to Z, 1 to 9).

attach In Word, to create an association between a template and a document. Attaching a template allows you to use macros, styles, and AutoText entries stored in that template.

attachment A file included as part of an email message; the message recipient sees an icon for the attached file, and can open or save it.

AutoArchive Outlook's feature that automatically moves items out of your main data file after a predetermined interval has passed.

AutoContent Wizard This PowerPoint option lets you start with a canned presentation, complete with content, and replace the generic content with your own words and ideas.

AutoCreate To automatically create a new Outlook item by dragging an item from one Outlook folder into another.

AutoDate Outlook's capability to recognize natural-language text, such as `two weeks from tomorrow`, and convert it into a date.

AutoFill An Excel feature that automatically extends a series of data—numbers or dates, for example—to fill the cells you select. See also *fill handle*.

AutoFilter An Excel data-management feature that automatically adds drop-down boxes for each field in a list. When you select unique values from an AutoFilter list, Excel displays only matching rows.

AutoFormat In Word and Excel, a feature that analyzes the current document, worksheet, or selection and automatically applies fonts, alignment, styles, and other formatting options.

automatic hyphenation Word's capability to break words at the end of a line, automatically adding a hyphen at the correct point so that a document doesn't have lines that are too short.

automatic word selection A Word and PowerPoint feature that selects an entire word when you drag the mouse over it, even if you start by clicking in the middle of the word.

AutoRecover A Word feature that, when enabled, automatically saves your document at regular intervals as you work. When your computer crashes, Word may be able to recover some or all of your document the next time you start the program.

AutoScroll When you install a Microsoft IntelliMouse, use the wheel between the buttons to scroll automatically through Office documents.

AutoShape A group of ready-made shapes—circles, lines, arrows, and banners, for example—available from the Drawing toolbar in all Office programs.

base style In Word, the underlying style on which one or more other styles are based. When you change an attribute of the base style, you change all styles that are based on that style.

binder An Office file format that lets you combine multiple files, including Word documents, Excel worksheets, and PowerPoint presentations, into a single file. Creating a binder lets you more easily control styles, page numbering, headers and footers, and other common elements in a big project.

binder pane The vertical region on the left of the Binder window that contains icons for each of the files that make up sections of the binder.

boilerplate Standard text, graphics, and other objects, such as a legal disclaimer or a company logo and address; Office templates and the shared AutoText feature let you easily add boilerplate material without retyping.

bookmark A named location or text selection in a Word document.

border The line around a cell, range, or chart in an Excel worksheet, a Word table or text box, or a drawing object.

browser A software program that lets you view documents on the World Wide Web, typically documents created in the HTML format.

build The outdated term for a PowerPoint *animation*.

bullet character In Word and PowerPoint, the character that introduces a bulleted list. Both programs allow you to use graphics as well as characters from any font.

bulleted list A collection of generally short items in Word documents and PowerPoint presentations, each of which is introduced by a distinctive character, called a bullet.

calculated fields In an Excel list, these fields contain formulas that calculate a result based on the contents of other fields in the same row.

callout Cartoon-style text labels, usually with an attached line, used to label items. The Office Drawing toolbar includes a wide selection of callouts.

cascading style sheets The portion of a Web page that defines fonts, colors, margins, and other advanced formatting.

categories A way to organize Outlook items; Outlook includes a built-in list of categories, such as Business, Personal, and Customer, or you can define your own.

category axis In a chart, the axis (usually horizontal) that arranges your data by category, such as by time or by region.

CD key A serial number, found on the case or sleeve of the program's CD-ROM, that Office requires you to enter during setup.

cell In Excel, the rectangular area in which you enter data. The intersection of a row and column defines a cell.

cell address The name used to refer to an Excel worksheet cell within a formula; default cell addresses combine the letter of the column heading with the number of the row heading so that the top-left cell in a worksheet is always A1.

change history The detailed list of changes to an Excel workbook; available only when you turn on the Track Changes option.

changing cells In an Excel worksheet, the cells whose values will change to define different scenarios. Changing cells usually contain formulas or values used in formulas.

character formatting A Word formatting option that defines the font, color, and other attributes of individual characters, without affecting alignment, borders, and other paragraph options. See also *paragraph formatting*.

character style In Word, a saved group of options from the character formats in the Font dialog box. A bold, underlined letter *a* appears to the right of character styles in the Style list. See also *paragraph style*.

chart A graphic representation of numeric data that helps display patterns, trends, and relationships between data in a worksheet. In Excel, common chart types include bar, pie, and line charts.

Click and Type A Word 2000 feature that automatically adds paragraph marks, tabs, and alignment formatting when you click in specific places on the document.

clip art Line drawings that can be inserted into any Microsoft Office document. Clip art pictures add interest to documents and help illustrate main points.

Clipboard toolbar An Office 2000 feature that allows you to cut or copy up to 12 items and paste them, individually or all at once, into an Office document.

Collapse Dialog button The button in an Excel dialog box that allows you to temporarily hide most of the dialog box so you can select a cell or range.

collate To arrange printed pages in order, so that all the pages in each copy come out of the printer in a perfect set; collating pages in the printer usually takes longer than printing all copies of each page at once.

color scheme In PowerPoint, a predefined set of eight complementary colors designed for use in presentations.

column The vertical part of an Excel worksheet grid. Each worksheet contains 256 rows, each with an alphabetic label at the top.

column field In a PivotTable, the fields that make up each column. See also *row field*.

column heading The letters that identify each column in an Excel worksheet.

combination charts Excel charts that represent data in two ways in the same space. A stock chart, for example, might use bars to show trading volume and a line to show price trends.

Command Bar A descriptive name for Office toolbars, which can contain buttons, menu commands, or both.

comment An Office feature that lets you add a question or suggestion without changing the document text or worksheet values.

comment indicator The tiny red triangle in a worksheet cell that contains a comment.

comment marker An indicator that begins each comment in the comments pane of a Word document, usually with the initials of the author of the comment.

comment reference mark The marker in a Word document that indicates the location of a comment.

comments pane The window that appears below a Word document when you view or edit comments.

comparison operators In Excel formulas, symbols that indicate a comparison between values. Common comparison operators include greater than (>), less than (<), and equal to (=). See also *logical operators*.

concatenate To combine two or more pieces of text into a single value in a worksheet cell, using an ampersand (&).

conditional formatting A format that Excel applies to selected cells only when the contents match a condition you specify. You might use conditional formatting to highlight numbers below a defined level in bold red, for example.

connectors Lines that snap into position automatically between AutoShapes. Available in all Office programs except Word.

constant A value (such as a number, date, or text) typed directly into a worksheet cell. See also *formula*.

Contacts Folder The Outlook folder that holds information about people and companies.

context sensitive Used to define help, shortcut menus, and other program features that change to match the activity you're currently performing.

contiguous range A group of cells on an Excel worksheet that form a rectangle. Select this type of range by clicking and dragging; to select a noncontiguous range, hold down the Ctrl key while selecting cells. See also *range*.

copyfitting A Publisher feature that automatically adjusts the font size of text within a frame so it fits inside the text frame boundaries.

criteria When you're working with Excel data management tools, a value or range of values that a record must meet in order to be selected.

cross-reference An automatic link between locations in a Word document; clicking a cross-reference takes you directly to the referenced text or object.

curly quotes Single and double quotation marks in matched pairs, to mark the opening and close of a block of text. See also *smart quotes*.

current region In an Excel worksheet, the block of filled-in cells that includes the current cell and extends in all directions to the first empty row or column.

custom chart type Detailed chart options, including formatting, that you can save and reuse in Excel.

custom dictionary Text files that hold words that you want to flag as correct when using the Office spell-checker, even though they're not in the built-in dictionaries.

data forms An alternative way of displaying and entering data in an Excel list. Forms simplify data entry by arranging one row of data at a time in a dialog box format.

data labels Text markers that identify values, percentages, or items in a data series on an Excel chart.

data marker The colored dot or geometric shape in the legend of an Excel chart that identifies each data series.

data point One piece of data plotted on a chart.

data series A group of data points that are related to a specific topic.

data source The location (cell or range address) on an Excel worksheet that is plotted in a chart.

Date Navigator In Outlook, the control at the right of the Calendar window that displays dates for the current month. Select a date to jump to that day's appointments, or drag an item onto a date to reschedule it.

default chart In Excel, the chart options used if you select a range of data and press F11. Normally this is a column chart, although you can redefine the default chart to any settings.

dependent Cells that contain formulas that reference other cells. For instance, if cell A10 contains a formula adding cells A8 and A9, cell A10 is a dependent of both A8 and A9.

descending A sort order that organizes text or numbers from their highest to their lowest values (Z to A, 9 to 1).

design template A saved PowerPoint presentation that includes backgrounds, master slides, color schemes, and other consistent formatting elements for reuse with any presentation.

destination The location where you want to paste the copied data when you're cutting and copying information using the Windows Clipboard.

Digital Subscriber Line A high-speed Internet access technology that uses standard phone lines.

direct formatting In Word, formatting that you apply to selected text without using styles.

document template A Word file that holds styles, macros, AutoText entries, and boilerplate text; it can be used to create a new document or change the appearance of an existing document.

drawing layer The portion of an Office file that holds AutoShapes and other drawing objects; typically, you can move or edit objects here without affecting text in the document itself.

drop cap A large initial cap at the beginning of a paragraph in a Word document or Publisher publication; so named because it "drops" into lines of text below the first one.

dynamic HTML An advanced Web authoring technique that allows you to use special effects in Web pages, such as text that changes color or pops up when clicked.

effects Special character formatting in a Word document, such as shadows, outlining, and strikethrough lines.

embed To insert an object, such as a chart, drawing, or even a complete document, within another file. When you activate an embedded object, you can edit it using tools from the program that originally created it. See also *link*.

End mode In Excel, a set of navigation shortcuts that let you move and scroll through a worksheet by pressing the End key followed by Home, Enter, or an arrow key.

Enhanced Metafile A Windows-standard graphics format, used for many objects in the Clip Gallery, for example.

event An Outlook appointment that spans more than one day, such as a vacation or business trip. See also *appointment*.

Extend Selection mode In Word, a set of keyboard shortcuts that let you select text without using the mouse; press the F8 key to turn on this mode, and then use the arrow keys or the F8 key to extend the selection.

Extensible Markup Language (XML) Code that allows Office programs to save documents as a Web page and reopen them with all features intact.

field In an Excel database, a column of data. Each complete collection of fields in a row equals one record.

field code In Word, programming instructions that tell Word to display a calculated value, such as today's date, or to prompt for input in a form letter. When you display field codes, they appear between curly brackets, or braces.

file extension The characters that follow the final period in a filename. Most extensions are three letters; Windows uses extensions to identify the program you should use to edit a file.

file type A file attribute that tells Windows which program to use when viewing or editing that file. File types are identified by extensions and are registered with Windows.

fill handle The small black square in the lower-right corner of an Excel cell or range. When you point to the fill handle, the pointer changes to a black cross; drag to copy the cell's contents or fill in a series of numbers or dates. See also *AutoFill*.

filter In Word mail merge file, Excel lists, and Outlook views, filters restrict the display of information based on criteria you enter.

Find A feature that lets you search for specific values or formatting within any Office application.

Find Fast Poorly documented Office utility that automatically indexes files to speed up searches; to set options, open the Windows Control Panel and look for the Find Fast icon.

first line indent Word formatting that begins the first line of a paragraph at a different location than the default margin for that paragraph. A control on the

Horizontal Ruler lets you adjust this setting visually.

Folder List In Outlook, an Explorer-style list that shows all folders in all open data files. See also *Outlook Bar.*

follow-up flag Reminders that you attach to contact items and email messages in Outlook; flags include a message and a date or time.

followed hyperlinks Links from one electronic document to another that have been accessed at least once.

font A complete description of text formatting that includes typeface, font size, style, and other attributes. See also *typeface*.

footer Information (such as the date or page number) that appears at the bottom of every printed page. See also *header*.

form A type of Word document that includes fill-in-the-blank spaces (called fields) in which users enter information.

Formatting toolbar One of two common toolbars found in all Office applications. This collection of buttons lets you change fonts, text attributes, alignment, and other formatting with a click. See also *Standard toolbar*, *toolbar*.

formula An equation that analyzes worksheet data. Formulas can do simple arithmetic or complex mathematical operation; they can also perform logical comparisons and manipulate text. See also *function.*

Formula bar In Excel, the bar just above the worksheet grid in which you enter or edit data in cells or charts.

frame A container for text and graphics in a Word document; text boxes are the preferred way of working with most document objects. In Web pages, frames are independent panes typically at the top or left edge of the page that scroll independently of other parts of the browser window. In Publisher, a frame refers to a box that encloses all text, pictures, or other objects.

free and busy time An Outlook 2000 feature you use to share details of your schedule with other users over the Internet.

freeze In Excel, to lock one or more rows or columns into position so that labels remain visible as you scroll. See also *split box*, *pane*.

FTP server An Internet server that allows users to upload and download files using File Transfer Protocol (FTP). See also *anonymous FTP*.

function A built-in Excel formula that performs a calculation using one or more values. Excel includes a variety of statistical and financial functions. See also *formula*.

gateway A mail server that processes messages intended for foreign servers running different mail software; typically used in corporate networks to communicate with Internet-standard mail servers.

GIF Graphic Interchange Format, a widely used format for storing and retrieving image files over the Internet.

global template A Word template whose contents are available to all documents, even those based on another template. See also *Normal document template*, *template*.

Goal Seek An Excel feature that lets you start with a formula and work backward to find the value or values that produce the desired result.

gradient fill Sophisticated graphic technique that uses two colors to add shading to a PowerPoint slide or the background of a chart or graphic object.

grammar checker Word's built-in tool that analyzes your writing and suggests changes; the grammar checker in Word 2000 is greatly improved over the one found in previous versions.

graphics Pictures, drawings, and other nontext data in an Office document.

graphics filter Software that converts images between different graphics formats, such as GIF, JPEG, and Windows Bitmaps. Office includes a wide variety of filters, although not all of them are installed in a Typical setup.

Graphics Interchange Format See *GIF*.

gridline In a Word table or Excel spreadsheet, the nonprinting lines that separate rows, columns, and cells. See also *border*.

gutter Extra space in the margins of Word documents you intend to bind. If you choose mirror margins, the gutter is on the right of left-hand pages and the left of right-hand pages.

handles In Publisher, the small boxes at the corners and sides of a frame used for resizing. Handles are visible when you click on an object.

handout A specially formatted version of a PowerPoint presentation designed to be printed and distributed to members of the audience.

Handout Master The PowerPoint master slide that contains text and formatting for handouts.

hanging indent In Word, a format that defines a paragraph in which the first line hangs to the left of the second and following lines.

header Information (such as the title or date) that appears at the top of every printed page. See also *footer*.

header row The optional first row of an Excel list, which contains names for the fields in each column.

heading In Word, the first row of a table; in Excel, the letters and numbers that identify row and column addresses.

Help engine The Windows-standard program that displays information contained in Help files.

help topic A single entry in a Help file; use the Contents, Index, or Find tabs to locate the topic you need.

hidden slides Slides that are part of a PowerPoint presentation but are not intended to be shown; generally, hidden slides are used for details that you want to have available if asked.

hidden text A Word formatting attribute that prevents text from being seen when viewed onscreen, in printouts, or both.

home page The first page you see when you visit a Web site. The term also is used to describe the default page you see when you start your Web browser.

horizontal scrollbar A scrollbar that appears at the bottom of a document window and allows you to move from left to right when there's too much data to fit on the screen.

hotkey The keyboard shortcut assigned to a macro in Word or Excel.

HTML Hypertext Markup Language, a standard set of formatting codes used to create documents that can be posted to a Web server and accessed through a browser.

hyperlink A "hot spot" within a document that includes instructions to open a file or Web page when clicked. All Office programs allow you to create hyperlinks, which appear as colored and underlined text or graphics.

hyphenate In Word, to add hyphens within a word that are used only when the Word appears at the end of a line; used to make documents look better by reducing the number of lines that are unnecessarily short.

indent To adjust the distance of a paragraph from the margins (in Word or PowerPoint) or from the left edge of the active cell (in Excel). See also *first line indent*, *hanging indent*, *negative indent*.

information service Elements you add to an Outlook configuration when using Corporate/Workgroup mode.

inline video A video clip that automatically plays when a user opens a Web page, or when the mouse pointer rests on top of the clip.

Insert mode Word's default editing mode, in which text you enter pushes existing text to the right rather than replacing it. See also *Overtype mode*.

insertion point A vertical blinking bar that shows your location in any editing window. Click to move the insertion point and enter text or graphics in a new location.

IntelliMouse A Microsoft mouse that includes a thumbwheel between the two buttons; use the thumbwheel to scroll through documents and Web pages. See also *AutoScroll*.

Internet A global computer network composed of many other networks linking millions of computers in homes, offices, schools, libraries, and government agencies.

Internet Message Access Protocol (IMAP) An alternative mail server and client standard, used by recent versions of Microsoft Exchange. See also *Simple Mail Transfer Protocol*, *POP3*.

intersection operator In Excel, a single space. If you enter a space between two addresses, Excel finds the cell or cells that are common to both ranges. This operator is also used to name a cell automatically using row and column labels: `=Jan 'Sales Results'` identifies a cell in the column labeled `Jan` and the row labeled `Sales Results`.

intranet A computer network used within an organization such as a corporation. Intranets work much like the World Wide Web, although addressing formats may differ slightly.

invitation When you schedule a meeting in Outlook, each participant receives an invitation via email; recipients can accept, decline, or accept tentatively.

item The basic unit of data storage in Outlook; item types includes mail messages, contacts, appointments, and more.

Journal folder A built-in Outlook folder that stores details about activities, such as email messages you create or files you open.

Journal item An item in Outlook's Journal folder containing links between two items.

JPEG Joint Photographic Experts Group, a standard format used for image files, especially over the Internet. Some JPEG files use the .JPG extension.

Jump button In a Help topic, a "hot spot" that opens a related topic when clicked.

justified text An alignment option in Word and Publisher that distributes extra space between words so that each line begins and ends at the same place on the right and left.

keyboard shortcut A keystroke (such as a Function key) or combination of keys (such as Ctrl+Alt+A) that performs a command.

keywords In the Visual Basic Editor, these are words that represent program instructions for a macro.

kiosk A self-running presentation created in PowerPoint. Kiosks are often used as marketing and sales tools to play presentations continuously for potential customers walking past a product display or counter.

label In Excel charts, the text that identifies items along an axis.

landscape mode Print option that rotates the page 90 degrees so it prints sideways. See also *portrait mode*.

layout The arrangement of words, graphics, and other objects on a PowerPoint slide.

layout guides In Publisher, faint blue or pink lines that represent margins and gridlines, used to help you place objects in a publication.

leader Dots or other characters that fill the space used by a tab character in a Word document. See also *tab*.

legend In an Excel chart, the text box that helps identify each data series, using colors or geometric shapes.

Letter Wizard A Word feature that lets you fill in the blanks in a template to quickly create a properly formatted letter.

line spacing The amount of space between lines or paragraphs in a Word document.

link To insert a copy of an object within a file while maintaining the link to the source document that contains the original object. When you change the source document, the linked object changes as well. See also *embed*, *object linking and embedding*.

list An Excel worksheet made up of continuous columns and rows of data.

lock To protect individual cells in a worksheet so that users can view but not change their contents.

logical function Worksheet formulas that allow you to compare values and define actions based on the results of the comparison.

logical operators Symbols used in Excel formulas to perform comparisons and test true-false conditions—equals (=) and greater than (>), for example.

macro A program that performs a series of commands and instructions to perform a task automatically. Use the Visual Basic Editor to create and edit macros for all Office programs.

macro recorder In Word, Excel, and PowerPoint, a utility that automatically writes Visual Basic code based on your actions.

macro virus Unwanted program code that can cause side effects ranging from annoying to disastrous. Office 2000 includes features that can detect and disable macro viruses automatically.

Magnifier A button in Word's Print Preview screen that lets you zoom in for a closer look at text and objects. See also *zoom*.

Mail Merge In Microsoft Word, a feature that combines a form letter (Main Document) and a list of personalized data (Data Source) to create custom letters, labels, or forms.

main document A document that stores the text that will appear in all copies of the merged document when you're using Word's Mail Merge feature.

maintenance mode Options that appear when you run the Office Setup program after initially installing the program for the first time—to add new features, for example.

MAPI drivers Software used in Outlook's Corporate/Workgroup mode to add support for other mail programs using the Mail Application Programming Interface. See also *information service*.

margin Blank (nonprinting) space on the sides, top, and bottom of a document, worksheet, or presentation. Use the Page Setup dialog box to define margins.

margin boundary On Word's horizontal ruler, the line that defines the left and right margins; click and drag to reset margins for the current section.

Master Category List The list of 20 built-in Outlook categories to which you can assign items.

Master Document view A special Word view that shows the structure of long documents. See also *subdocument*.

master slide Four locations in a PowerPoint presentation that store all formatting details for every type of slide.

meeting An Outlook Calendar item that includes two or more people. See also *appointment*.

meeting invitation A cross between an Outlook appointment and an email message; sending a meeting invitation allows you to add a single item and all its details to the calendars of other Outlook users.

meeting organizer In Outlook, the person who plans a meeting, schedules resources, and invites other attendees. See also *resource*, *invitation*.

menu bar The main pull-down menu for all Office programs.

menu handle The vertical line at the edge of a toolbar that allows you to drag the toolbar to a new location.

merge criteria When performing a mail merge in Word, use these options to choose a subset of the records in your data source. See also *filter*.

message flag A red flag icon added by Outlook when you flag an email message for later follow-up; the message flag can include reminders that pop up at a date and time you define. See also *follow-up flag*.

Microsoft Exchange Confusingly, refers to older email client software and to Microsoft's most popular email server software.

Microsoft Exchange Server Microsoft's corporate email program; used with Outlook, it allows users to share information and post messages in threaded conversations in public folders.

Microsoft Knowledge Base An online repository of known bugs, workarounds, and tips for Windows, Office, and other Microsoft products. To search the Knowledge Base, go to `http://support.microsoft.com`.

MIME See *Multi-Purpose Internet Mail Extensions*.

Multi-Purpose Internet Mail Extensions A standard that defines how email software should exchange attachments, including multimedia.

multimedia Any graphic, sound, video, or audio file, such as those found in a PowerPoint presentation.

Name box The box at the left end of Excel's formula bar; it displays the address of the selected cell or the name of a chart item or range.

named range A convenient way to refer to Excel ranges using descriptive names rather than cell addresses.

narration A synchronized soundtrack for a PowerPoint presentation.

negative indent In Word, a paragraph indent that extends to the outside of the existing margin.

nest To include one function as an argument for another function.

nonmodal A description of a dialog box that remains on the screen as you work. When you use Word's Find and Replace feature, for example, you can edit text in your document without closing the dialog box.

Normal document template Word's default template for new documents; AutoText entries, toolbars, custom menu settings, shortcut keys, and macros stored here are available for all documents.

Normal view In Word, this default view shows text formatting but simplifies page layout for quicker formatting and editing. See also *Print Layout view*.

notes Also known as speaker notes, these are text intended for the presenter, but not the audience, to see in a PowerPoint presentation. In Outlook, notes are items that resemble yellow sticky notes.

Notes Master One of four master slides in PowerPoint, these define the look of printed pages that include speaker notes.

notes pages The printed version of speaker notes, which typically includes a thumbnail of the slide and its accompanying notes.

notification area Sometimes also called the "tray," the region at the far right of the Windows taskbar, where informational icons appear.

numbered list Like a bulleted list in Word and PowerPoint, except that instead of a bullet character the program automatically numbers each item using the correct format. As you add or move items in a numbered list, the numbering changes automatically.

object A self-contained collection of data, complete with instructions for viewing and editing it; typical objects include drawings, charts, and document files. In Publisher, the word *object* also refers to frames. See also *object linking and embedding*.

Object Browser In Word, a set of controls at the bottom of the vertical scrollbar that lets you quickly jump to another page, bookmark, table, or other location.

object linking and embedding (OLE) Technology that allows a program to work with types of data created with other programs. All Office programs support OLE. See also *link*, *embed*.

Office Assistant An animated character that offers onscreen help with Office applications; use the Office Assistant to search Help files using questions in natural language.

Office Shortcut Bar A customizable toolbar that appears on the Windows desktop; it lets you open Office programs, create new files, and edit existing files.

offline folders If you use Outlook with Microsoft Exchange Server, messages are stored on the server; create copies in offline folders for access when you are not connected to the server. See also *Personal Folders file*.

Offline Store file An Outlook data file used with Microsoft Exchange Server; you can synchronize items in this file with those on the server so that you always have access to information, even if the network is not available.

Online Layout view Word setting that makes it easier to read documents on the screen. In this view, characters are larger than their specified formatting, and paragraphs wrap to fit the window.

operator A sign or symbol that specifies a calculation (such as addition or multiplication) or a logical operation to perform on the elements of an Excel formula.

orientation A specification that determines how documents are positioned on a printed page. Typical choices are Portrait (vertical) and Landscape (rotated 90 degrees clockwise).

Outline view In Word, a view that shows document headings indented by level; in PowerPoint, a view that shows slide titles, bullet headings, and other text indented similarly. Outline view makes it easier to move through a document and to move large blocks of text.

Outlook Bar The vertical bar at the left of the Outlook window, containing shortcuts to the Outlook Today page and the most commonly used folders. This bar is divided into groups, all of which are fully customizable.

Outlook item The basic unit of storage in Outlook. Items can contain almost any kind of information, from name and address details, to email messages, to appointments.

Outlook Today The optional opening screen for Outlook, which shows unread messages and upcoming tasks and appointments in a view that resembles a Web page.

Overtype mode A Word editing feature that replaces existing text as you enter new text. See also *Insert mode*.

page break In Word or Excel, the point at which one page ends and another begins. Both programs insert automatic page breaks where needed. To force a page break at a specific location, you can insert a manual page break.

page break preview A special view of an Excel worksheet that shows exactly how the worksheet will appear when printed.

pane The separate viewing region that appears when you split a window for an Excel worksheet or a Word document. See also *split box*.

paragraph formatting Word formatting options that apply to the entire paragraph, including fonts, line spacing, and alignment. See also *character formatting*.

paragraph mark The ¶ symbol, which marks the end of each paragraph in a Word document and holds all paragraph formatting and styles.

paragraph style A collection of character and paragraph formats that Word stores under a style name. When you apply a paragraph style to an entire paragraph, you change all formats for that paragraph. If you select part of a paragraph and then apply a paragraph style, only the character formats of the selection change. Paragraph styles are identified by a paragraph mark (¶) to the right of the style name in the Style list. See also *character style*.

patch An update to a program, usually small and designed to fix a specific, serious problem.

paths The routes between the addresses of electronic documents. You determine paths when you create hyperlinks. See also *absolute addressing*, *relative addressing*.

Personal Address Book One data format for storing addresses in Outlook. This file was required in Outlook 97 but is usually unnecessary in Outlook 2000.

Personal Folders file The default file format (with the .PST extension) used by Outlook 2000 in an Internet Only setup. See also *offline folders*.

personal information manager (PIM) Software that manages names, addresses, schedules, and other personal information. Outlook is a PIM that includes email capabilities.

Personal Macro Workbook A hidden Excel file that stores macros for use in all open workbooks.

personalized menus Office 2000's feature that hides some menu options and shows others, based on the ones you use most often.

PivotChart Charts based on a *PivotTable*; you can rearrange the chart by dragging field buttons on the screen.

PivotTable Summary or cross-tabulated reports generated from an Excel worksheet using row headings from one or more fields, column headings from other fields, and calculated results (sum, average, or count, for example) from other fields for the body of the table.

placeholders In PowerPoint, the text boxes on a slide layout where you enter your text. In Publisher, a frame inserted by a template in a publication.

Places Bar The five icons to the left of the list of files in the Open and Save As dialog boxes, which give you one-click access to the locations you use most often.

point A unit of measurement for fonts; 72 points equals one inch.

POP3 Version 3 of the Post Office Protocol, an Internet standard that mail clients like Outlook use to retrieve mail from an SMTP server.

portrait mode Print option that positions text and objects on the page with the narrow edge at the top, as in a letter.

Post Office Protocol See *POP3*.

POSTNET bar code Standard bar codes that make it easier for the post office to deliver mail; Word can add these to envelopes automatically.

PowerPoint Viewer A utility program that allows you to deliver a PowerPoint presentation even if PowerPoint is not installed on the computer you want to use.

precedent Cells that are referred to by a formula in another cell. For instance, if cell A10 contains a formula adding cells A8 and A9, cells A8 and A9 are precedents for A10.

presentation The basic file type for PowerPoint. Each presentation consists of one or more pages or slides, which can contain text, bulleted lists, graphics, charts, and other data types.

preview A view that shows how a document, worksheet, or presentation will look when you print it.

print area In Excel, the group of cells that will go to the printer; if you don't define a specific print area, Excel will print the entire worksheet.

print job An item in the print queue; a document sent to the printer.

Print Layout view A Word view that displays a document as it will appear when printed; headers, columns, and objects appear in their actual positions. You can edit and format text in this view.

Print Preview In all Office programs, a special view that lets you see what printed pages will look like.

print queue A group of documents waiting to be printed; use the Windows Printers folder to view and change the status of waiting documents.

printer driver Windows system software that translates output from Office and other programs into a format that a selected printer can use.

printer font A font (such as a PostScript font) installed on the printer. If Windows can't find a matching screen font, it will substitute a similar-looking TrueType font when displaying text formatted with this type of font.

profile For Outlook users who configure their systems using Corporate/Workgroup mode, a profile contains all the information services required to send, receive, and store mail and other items.

protected A description of a document or worksheet that is locked so users can view but not change the file; may be used with passwords to control access.

protection An Excel feature that allows you to lock individual cells or an entire workbook, with or without a password, to prevent accidental or unauthorized changes.

pull-down menu Standard Windows and Office menus, located just below the title bar of a program window. These menus typically give you access to all program functions, sometimes by way of submenus and dialog boxes.

Quick Launch bar The region just to the right of the Start button on the Windows taskbar that holds shortcuts to programs and data files.

range Two or more cells on an Excel worksheet. A range can be contiguous, with all cells in a rectangular pattern, or noncontiguous, including cells that are not adjacent to one another.

record In an Excel database, a single row of data. See also *field*.

recurring Meetings, appointments, tasks, and other Outlook items that occur more than once, in a specified pattern.

relative address In Excel formulas, a cell reference that describes how to find another cell by counting from the cell that contains the formula—for example, "one cell to the right and two cells down." When you're moving or copying formulas with relative cell references, Excel changes the address to match the relative position as measured from the new location. Also known as *relative reference*. See also *absolute address.*

relative addressing A way of specifying the location of an electronic document so that a hyperlink to it will still work when you move the page to another location, such as a Web server. See also *absolute addressing*.

relative link In a Web page, a hyperlink that contains a link to a subfolder name rather than a full address, so that the links will work properly when you move the entire folder and all its subfolders.

relative reference See *relative address*.

Replace A feature used with the Find feature to locate all occurrences of one value and change them to another value in any Office program.

resolution The number of screen pixels used in the current display; available resolutions are defined by your video hardware. Higher settings let you see more data onscreen.

resource In Outlook 2000, a meeting room, overhead projector, or other physical object you might want to reserve for a meeting.

result The value that Excel calculates when you enter a formula or function.

Rich Text Format (RTF) A standard file type used for preserving formatting when exchanging Word documents with users of other word processing programs.

row The horizontal part of an Excel worksheet grid. Each worksheet contains 65,536 rows, each with a numeric label at the left.

row field In a PivotTable, the fields that make up each row. See also *column field.*

row headings The letters that identify each row in an Excel worksheet.

rule In Outlook 2000, conditions that you can define to specify how the program should handle mail when it arrives.

ruler In Word and PowerPoint, guides that let you position objects precisely on the printed page.

ruler guides In Publisher, lines you drag out from the horizontal or vertical rulers into the drawing area to use as guides for placing pictures, frames, or other objects.

sample documents In all Office applications, a large selection of documents that demonstrate how features and formats work; in some cases, they can serve as the basis for new documents you create.

sans serif A font that uses simple lines without decorative elements. Arial is the default Windows font in this category.

scalable A description of TrueType fonts, which are stored as outlines that Windows can resize (or scale) as needed.

scale A percentage of a document, worksheet, or presentation. You can change the scale of a worksheet to print more rows and columns in a selected space.

scenario A What-if analysis tool that saves different values in specific cells. Useful when changing the same group of data repeatedly to achieve a specific result.

screen font Also known as a raster font, it is designed for use only on the screen and typically comes in fixed sizes only. If Windows can't find a matching printer font, it will substitute a TrueType font when printing text formatted with this type of font.

ScreenTip Pop-up description of an onscreen object such as a toolbar button or part of the Word ruler; a ScreenTip appears automatically when you let the mouse pointer hover over the object.

script Advanced Web-page code that automates the actions that occur when a user opens the page or clicks a link, for example.

secondary axis An additional axis in an Excel chart (to the right of the chart, for example), used when you want to plot two data series that use different scales.

secondary mouse button By default, the right mouse button, which you use to display shortcut menus. Left-handers may want to use the Windows Control Panel to redefine the secondary mouse button.

section In Word documents, a break between sections to change formatting elements, such as margins, page orientation, and headers and footers. In Normal view, a section break appears as a double dotted line that contains the words `Section Break`.

select To mark an item, usually by clicking it with a mouse, dragging the mouse pointer, or pressing a key. After selecting an item, you choose the action that you want to perform on the item.

separator character Tabs, commas, and other characters that identify the end of each item or each row when converting a table to text in Word, or converting worksheet data to or from text files.

serial date format In Excel, the standard format for storing dates as a value that represents the number of days since January 1, 1900. This system makes date calculations possible; use formats to control the display of dates.

serif Decorative part of a typeface design, usually at the edges and corners. Also, the category of fonts that contain these elements; the Windows default serif font is New Times Roman. See also *sans serif*.

service pack or **service release** A collection of bug fixes and updated components for a program, such as Windows NT or Office 2000.

shortcut A pointer to a file, folder, or other object stored elsewhere. Opening the shortcut (by clicking or double-clicking) has the same effect as opening the object to which the shortcut refers.

Simple Mail Transfer Protocol (SMTP) The Internet standard for sending mail between servers; when you send mail using an Outlook account with an Internet service provider, it uses this format.

size A way of defining fonts; font size is typically measured in points, with 72 points equal to 1 inch.

sizing handle A square you drag to change the size of a selected drawing object or AutoShape; sizing handles normally appear at each corner and along the sides of the object. See also *adjustment handle*.

slide The basic unit of a PowerPoint presentation. Each slide typically includes a title and one or more objects, such as charts, pictures, and bullet points.

Slide Master The template used by a PowerPoint presentation for all the slides in the presentation. Changes to the Slide Master automatically change all corresponding slides in the presentation.

slide show The end result of a PowerPoint presentation. When delivering a slide show, PowerPoint hides menus and other items, showing only the slides.

Smart Cut and Paste A Word and PowerPoint feature that automatically adjusts spaces and punctuation around text or objects when you move or copy it to a new location.

smart quotes In Word and PowerPoint, a feature that automatically replaces straight quotation marks with the open or close quotation marks used by professional printers and typographers. See also *curly quotes*.

SMTP See *Simple Mail Transfer Protocol*.

snap When you add any object on the drawing layer or in a Publisher publication, it naturally attaches to the grid or to ruler or layout guides for easy positioning.

sort To reorder data, usually in a worksheet list or Word table. See also *ascending*, *descending*.

source When copying or moving data from one location to another, the source is the original location.

speaker notes See *notes*.

special characters In Word, tabs, spaces, paragraph marks, and other items that are not normally visible.

special effects In a PowerPoint presentation, a way to add animation or movement to text and objects.

split To divide a Word or Excel window so that you can see and edit two portions of the same file side by side.

split bar The dividing line in an Excel worksheet or Word document window after you split it into multiple panes; double-click to close the second pane.

split box A small box at the top of the vertical scrollbar or the right of the horizontal scrollbar. You click this box to view two parts of a Word document or Excel worksheet simultaneously, and then drag to create a second pane. See also *pane*.

spreadsheet Another name for an Excel worksheet; more commonly used to describe the data files of competing programs such as Lotus 1-2-3.

Standard toolbar One of two common toolbars in all Office applications; it contains buttons that let you perform basic actions such as opening or saving a file. See also *Formatting toolbar*, *toolbar*.

startup switch Information that follows the name of a program in a shortcut or at a command line; you use startup switches to open documents automatically or control which parts of the program load automatically.

status bar The area along the bottom of the main window for all Office programs, typically used to display information about the current selection, such as the number of the current page in a Word document.

style In Word and Excel, a collection of formats, such as font size, paragraph spacing, and alignment, that you can define and save as a named group. See also *character style*, *paragraph style*.

subdocument One of several separate Word files saved as part of a master document.

subtotal In an Excel list or database, calculations (sum, count, or average) that automatically appear at each change in value of a specific field or column of information. You can add these subtotals.

summary action In a *PivotTable*, the operation you want Excel to perform on data fields—sum, count, or average, for example.

Summary information Details about the author, subject, and countless other attributes of an Office document; to view and edit this information, open the **File** menu and choose **Properties**.

symbol A special character that is different from standard alphabetic and numeric characters; most fonts include some symbols, whereas other fonts include only symbols and special characters.

syntax In Excel formulas and functions, the correct structure, order, and format of elements such as the function name, operators, and arguments.

system tray The area at the right of the Windows taskbar that contains the system clock and status icons for programs. See also *notification area*.

tab In a Word document, tabs define the alignment of columns and indents in paragraphs.

Tab key A key used to navigate between cells in a worksheet or a Word table, or to move to the next item in a dialog box.

tab stop Markers on Word's ruler that define the location of tabs. In documents based on the Normal document template, default tab stops are located every half inch.

table In Word or PowerPoint, an arrangement of rows and columns that resembles an Excel worksheet.

target The intended destination of the copied data when you're cutting, copying, and pasting information using the Windows Clipboard.

task request Similar to a meeting invitation in Outlook, this item type allows you to assign a task to another person and track its progress via status reports.

TaskPad The selected list of tasks that appears at the right of the Calendar view in Outlook.

TCP/IP Transmission Control Protocol/Internet Protocol, the standard protocol, or data-transfer format, of the Internet.

template In Word, a document that stores boilerplate text, custom toolbars, macros, shortcut keys, styles, and AutoText entries. Excel uses templates to store formatting, styles, text, and other standard information. See also *Normal document template*.

text box Special AutoShapes designed to hold text. Because they sit in the drawing layer and not within a document, it's easy to move a text box anywhere on the page.

theme A collection of backgrounds, bullets, and font formatting, primarily for use with Web pages.

thesaurus A Word utility that allows you to look up synonyms for words.

thumbnails Small versions of images that can serve as both previews for and hyperlinks to larger versions. Thumbnails take up less space and therefore decrease the amount of time needed to access a page through a browser. In PowerPoint, they are small pictures of PowerPoint slides that allow several slides to show at once in the Slide Sorter view.

TIFF Tagged Image File Format, a standard format used for image files. If you're creating a Web page in Word and you insert a TIFF image, it will be converted to GIF format when you save. Some TIFF files use the .TIF extension.

timings When rehearsing a PowerPoint presentation, the program tracks the amount of time you spend on each slide. You can also define these intervals manually to control the pace of a slide show.

Title Master The template used for all titles in a PowerPoint presentation. Changes to this slide automatically appear on all slides in the presentation.

title slide The default opening slide of a PowerPoint presentation, which includes the title of the presentation, the speaker's name, and other introductory details.

toggle macro A special macro that turns a feature or option on or off, depending on its current state.

toolbar A collection of buttons and/or menus that organize frequently used commands. Office toolbars are fully customizable, and you can move them to any part of the screen.

tracking A feature available in Word and Excel that displays revisions and changes to a document or worksheet.

transitions In a PowerPoint presentation, movie-style special effects (dissolves, wipes, and fades, for example) that appear when you move between slides.

TrueType font The Windows standard for displaying and printing fonts. TrueType fonts are stored as outlines and can be scaled and rotated.

typeface The graphic design of a collection of alphabetic characters, numbers, and symbols. The definition of a font includes a typeface, plus size, spacing, and other attributes. See also *font*.

Unicode An international standard for encoding characters from any language. Unicode supports characters, punctuation, technical symbols, dingbats, and other characters from virtually every language on Earth.

Universal Naming Convention (UNC) A standard system for specifying locations of shared network resources—for example, in dialog boxes. UNC names use the syntax *servername**sharename**path*.

unprintable area Minimum margins at the top, bottom, and sides of a page; Windows printer drivers do not allow you to print data in these regions.

URL Uniform Resource Locator, the address of a Web page or other Internet resource. See also *hyperlink*.

value In Excel, text or numbers entered in a cell.

value axis Typically the vertical axis in a chart, which displays the values of the charted data.

vCard A standard format for exchanging contact information in a "virtual business card" file. Outlook 2000 lets you share contact information using vCards.

version number A way of identifying upgrades to software. All Office 2000 programs are version 9; numbers to the right of the decimal point identify minor upgrades (9.1) and bug fixes (9.01).

vertical ruler In Word, PowerPoint, and Publisher, a ruler that lets you position objects such as headers and footers.

vertical scrollbar The scrollbar that appears at the right of the editing window.

view In all Office programs, these are different ways to display data for different tasks. Word includes four basic views, for example, used for editing Web pages, working with outlines, seeing what printed output will look like, and quick editing without graphics.

Visual Basic Editor A specialized editor that allows you to write and edit macros, including those created by the macro recorder.

Visual Basic for Applications The built-in programming language used for macros in all Office programs except Publisher.

voice-over track A recorded narrative synchronized with slides in a PowerPoint presentation. Voice-over tracks are useful with self-running presentations. See also *kiosk*.

Web component One of several Office 2000 features that allow you to create interactive Web pages from worksheets, charts, or PivotTables.

Web Folders Special shortcuts that allow you to save and open files directly on a Web server.

Web page A single document on the Web. Created in the HTML format, a page can include text, images, audio, and video.

Web publishing The process of creating electronic documents and making them available to a global audience via the World Wide Web.

Web Publishing Wizard A utility from Office 97 that allows you to post groups of Web pages to a Web server. Largely unnecessary in Office 2000, except for a handful of specialized tasks.

Web server A computer program that provides ("serves") stored documents to other computers via the World Wide Web.

Web site A collection of related Web pages, usually maintained by an organization or individual. Most Web sites include a primary, or home, page that serves as a guide to other pages in the collection.

weight The thickness of a font—bold or demibold, for example. Windows programs include weight and other attributes in the font style. See also font.

"what-if" analysis The collective name for a group of Excel features that allow you to enter different data to analyze scenarios.

"What's This?" help Pop-up definitions of onscreen tools and of choices in Office dialog boxes; when the What's This? pointer is visible, click on any object to see a helpful description.

Windows Bitmap A standard graphics format used in Windows; in general, not as useful as GIF or JPEG formats, because Bitmap files tend to be larger than those formats.

Windows Clipboard Temporary storage in Windows memory. You can use the Cut and Copy commands to add text, graphics, or other objects to this area; choose Paste to transfer the copied material to a new location.

Windows Desktop Update An optional component of Internet Explorer 4.0 that upgrades Windows 95 and Windows NT 4.0, replacing the Windows Explorer with a new program that lets you browse files, folders, and Web pages.

Windows Installer The utility that installs and configures Office programs and their individual components.

Windows Metafile A standard graphics format, used with many files in the Clip Gallery.

wizard A series of step-by-step dialog boxes that help you complete a complex process by filling in the blanks.

word list An index of words (and, optionally, phrases) used by the Windows Help program to help you find information in Help files.

workbook Excel's basic document type. Every workbook must contain at least one visible worksheet.

worksheet In Excel, the place where data is stored. Also known as spreadsheets, worksheets consist of cells organized into columns and rows. A worksheet is always part of a workbook.

World Wide Web (WWW) The most popular part of the Internet; Web pages are written in HTML and can include text, graphics, and multimedia.

WYSIWYG What You See Is What You Get, a description of a program whose onscreen text and graphics look exactly like the results you can expect when printing.

zoom To increase or decrease the apparent size of text, graphics, and other objects on the screen. Zooming does not affect printed output.

Index

Symbols

A

B

C

D

E

G

H

J

K

M

N

O

P

Q

R

T

U

V

W

X-Y

Z